IDEOLOGY, STRATEGY AND PARTY CHANGE: SPATIAL ANALYSES OF POST-WAR ELECTION PROGRAMMES IN 19 DEMOCRACIES

The relevance of this book to central concerns of Political and Social Science hardly needs emphasizing. Parties are the organizing force of democratic governments, giving coherence and direction to their policies and relating them to popular preferences. Election programmes are crucial to this role, providing electors with some insight into the policies they are voting for, and parties themselves with a starting point for their activity in government.

Discussion begins with a comparative assessment of the impact of election pledges on government action. The book goes on to describe systematically the place of the programmes in the political process of 19 democracies. It subjects them to detailed qualitative, quantitative and spatial analyses to answer such questions as: Who prepares election programmes and how? What is the nature of modern party divisions? Do they differ across countries? Is there indeed an 'end of ideology' or an intensification? Does the need to attract votes weaken old partisan attachments?

Combining individual studies of each country with comparative analyses on a scale never previously undertaken, the book will interest country specialists and comparativists and prove indispensable to research on voting and party behaviour, coalition formation, ideology, and rational choice.

IDEOLOGY, STRATEGY AND PARTY CHANGE: SPATIAL ANALYSES OF POST-WAR ELECTION PROGRAMMES IN 19 DEMOCRACIES

———— ∽ ————

Edited by

IAN BUDGE, DAVID ROBERTSON
DEREK HEARL

Department of Government, University of Essex
and St Hugh's College, University of Oxford

The right of the
University of Cambridge
to print and sell
all manner of books
was granted by
Henry VIII in 1534.
The University has printed
and published continuously
since 1584.

CAMBRIDGE UNIVERSITY PRESS

Cambridge
London   New York   New Rochelle
Melbourne   Sydney

Published by the Press Syndicate of the University of Cambridge
The Pitt Building, Trumpington Street, Cambridge CB2 1RP
32 East 57th Street, New York, NY 10022, USA
10 Stamford Road, Oakleigh, Melbourne 3166, Australia

First published 1987

Printed in Great Britain at the University Press, Cambridge

British Library cataloguing in publication data

Ideology, strategy and party change: spatial analyses of
post-war election programmes in 19 democracies.
1. Political parties – Manifestos – History – 20th century
I. Budge, Ian   II. Robertson, David, 1946–   III. Hearl, Derek
324.2'3   JF2112.M3

Library of Congress cataloguing in publication data

Ideology, strategy, and party change.
Bibliography.
1. Political parties. 2. Electioneering. 3. Elections.
I. Budge, Ian. II. Robertson, David, 1946–   . III. Hearl, Derek.
JF2011.I34 1986   324.7   86–9612
ISBN 0 521 30648 5

CE

CONTENTS

——— ∿ ———

LIST OF TABLES

———— ❧ ————

LIST OF FIGURES

———— ∿ ————

PREFACE

——— ❧ ———

Since we were constituted as a research group of the European Consortium for Political Research, and participated in its second Joint Research Sessions in the autumn of 1979, we have amassed many debts to individuals and institutions. It is hard for any cross-national group to keep together, even in receipt of unified and generous foundation funding. Cross-European research does not receive that kind of support, but what we have lacked in the way of funds has been balanced by the prompt aid given to us from a variety of sources.

The Consortium is responsible both for the creation of the group and for its continuing existence. Its support is part of a long term strategy for the encouragement of inter-European research, which has covered the work of groups like ours, and is still expanding. But nobody could have been more personally concerned to make our group a success than the successive Chairmen of its Research Board, Jean Blondel and Ken Newton; and its Chairman Rudolf Wildenmann.

The grant which gave us our initial impetus came (without bureaucratic delays or conditions) under the enlightened Small Grants Scheme of the Nuffield Foundation (Soc./205/125): the sympathetic Administrator was Pat Thomas. Later we received help, like the other ECPR Research Groups, from a general grant from the Tercentenary Fund of the Bank of Sweden, which Professor Leif Lewin, of the University of Uppsala, was particularly instrumental in obtaining for the ECPR programme. The mainstay of our effort for two years was a grant to the Editors from the British Social Science Research Council (E/00/23/0020/1). The then Chairman of the then Political Science and International Relations Committee, Prof. Peter Naylor, was notably sympathetic to the idea of bringing together younger political scientists on a cross-European basis, and even secured a small extension of the grant when we had unexpected extra work. After its expiry, research was supported by the European University

Institute, under its Future of Party Government project. Currently, extensions to our work are the subject of a generous grant from the *Stiftung Volkswagenwerk* (II/38850) which Dr. Helga Junkers has administered with understanding.

Individuals in the group have received help from a variety of institutions: the British Academy, the Social Sciences and Humanities Research Council of Canada, the U.S. National Endowment for the Humanities, and many others which are acknowledged in the individual chapters.

In addition facilities and financial support for special group meetings have been provided by the University of Limburg, Maastricht; the European University Institute, Florence; and the University of Essex, Colchester. All members have drawn heavily upon the facilities and research funds of their own Departments and Institutes, especially in periods when no other money has been forthcoming.

As must be evident from the number of sources we have tapped, financing the group has been a major effort. Our research has not been expensive (about £25,000 over four years) and most of the work of data-collection, preparation and analysis has been borne by our universities. But a cross-European group needs to meet sometimes, and a central facility is necessary if one wishes to make data like ours comparable and to store it systematically. A major reason for the effort which has had to go into quite small problems of finance is the absence of any West-European foundation operating like national Research Councils to assess cross-national projects on a genuinely competitive basis and to award grants without tying them to a particular national contribution. In spite of the existence of several self-styled 'European' foundations, it is actually only the Swedish Tercentenary Fund and the *Stiftung Volkswagenwerk* which approximate this role – in a truly enlightened way, but one which (as they themselves would stress) does not make up for the absence of a genuine European body to match the achievement of social scientists in forming the Consortium. It is amazing that this most practical contribution to the growth of a European consciousness should have been neglected so long, given the plethora of other, peripheral, bodies.

Besides its necessarily modest financial assistance the ECPR has helped administratively through the particular efforts of Valerie Stewart and Georgina Sheppard. Elizabeth Webb at the European University Institute has been our indefatigable Research Secretary throughout the latter stages of this book which was piloted to final press by Clare Gardiner. For collection of documents in particular countries we acknowledge especially Audrey Shouksmith in New Zealand and Nicola Sabbadini in Australia. Our thanks also go to Aroldo Marinai who produced the graphics. We hope the book repays their efforts. For errors we must take the blame .

It is important to note that our vast collection of documents, along with subsidiary analyses, data-sets in various forms, and other relevant material, are not simply deposited in the leading European Archives. They are also available in microfiche from Sauer-Verlag, Munich, Germany.

Our group hopes that this major new source of comparative data will be utilized in ways we have not envisaged. The present volume however constitutes an essential first step in the exploration and exploitation of these key strategic documents.

CHAPTER 1

THE INFLUENCE OF ELECTION
PROGRAMMES: BRITAIN AND
CANADA 1956–1979

1.1 PURPOSES OF THE ANALYSIS

Most of this book is concerned with the 'internal' analysis of election programmes – the examination, that is, of the concerns and emphases which parties write into their text and which distinguish them from other parties. In Chapter 2 we discuss the background and design of this type of research; Chapters 3–17 apply it to individual countries; and Chapter 18 extends it in a truly comparative, cross-national direction.

The first question people ask in this regard is not, however, what do election programmes tell you about parties, but how far do they get implemented in government? It is the essence of theories of representative democracy that parties gain power on the basis of election pledges which they then have a 'mandate' to put into effect (Kavanagh, 1980). If they do not do this, the usual justifications of the system of government would not apply; electors are being defrauded; the system is not functioning as a sensitive way of translating popular preferences into action.

A full investigation of the relationship between programmatic commitments and government reactions is possible only on the basis of an extended examination of what the commitments are and how they are expressed. The bulk of our book describes this preliminary, but essential, investigation. On its basis we are currently examining relationships with (single-party) government policy (Rallings, Budge and Hearl (eds.), 1987) and with coalition government programmes (Laver, Budge and Hearl (eds.), 1987).

Textual analysis is essential to research on the impact of the programmes, but we, like most people, would feel that large investment here is only worthwhile if the programmes have some external impact.

Such a chicken and egg situation is quite typical of political research. To some extent we have to proceed to textual analysis on faith. Some

1

indication of external impact however can be given through a study of two countries – Britain and Canada – where it is more reasonable than elsewhere, given the nature of their party systems, to assume that a winning party will be able to do what it has said it wants to do. To make the check more clear-cut, we have confined the study to definite 'pledges' committing parties to some sort of action, rather than extending it to the more general 'emphases' examined elsewhere in the book. If these do not produce action there is little likelihood that other, less binding, statements will.

This chapter, therefore, constitutes a 'strongest-case' analysis, designed to allay some but not all doubts about the governmental impact of election programmes. If none were discernible under these very favourable conditions we should obviously have to think again. If some are found, this says nothing about a less favourable situation (under a strong federal structure for example or perpetual government coalitions). But it does provide a stimulus for more intensive, extended investigation of the type we are now undertaking. Hence the importance of this comparative 'pilot study' to the rest of our analysis.

1.2 RESEARCH DESIGN

In examining implementation in Britain and Canada we shall concentrate on the period 1945–1979. In 1945 the post-war elections held in each country produced majority party governments; 1979 marked the electoral rejection of two administrations with only a tenuous majority. In the interim, ten elections were held in Britain – nine producing a Government with an overall majority in the House of Commons, and seven resulting in a Parliament whose life exceeded three and a half years. Parties understandably assert that election pledges can only be fulfilled 'over the lifetime of a Parliament'. In Canada in the same period there were eleven elections – though here only six Parliaments lasted longer than three years. Moreover, governments in Canada face two other constraints on their ability to carry out their platform promises. In four out of eleven cases they lacked an overall parliamentary majority, and the federal nature of the Canadian constitution means that many potential policy changes have to be the subject of prior negotiation and often compromise with the Provincial authorities. However, on matters clearly within federal jurisdiction and when a parliamentary majority does exist, Canadian governments are well able to legislate.

Differences between their unitary and federal structures notwithstanding, British and Canadian parliamentary systems produce both 'party manifestos' and annual statements of governmental legislative intentions. These 'speeches from the throne' – read in Britain by the monarch and in

Canada by the Governor-General – can be used as a check on whether manifesto commitments actually reach the Government's putative legislative programme. The inclusion of a particular commitment in the Queen's Speech may simply be cosmetic, but Burton and Drewry argue that 'it would seem fair to regard the Queen's Speech as the Government's shop window where its major policy aspirations are displayed. It follows that the "success" or "failure" of a government's . . . programme can be accurately gauged by analysing the products of the Queen's Speech' (Burton and Drewry, 1970 p. 310). Thus we can trace policies from their initial appearance in party platforms to their formal articulation in the speech from the throne, and beyond this to their eventual enactment. We can then see how far they survive or fall at each stage.

Thus we shall analyse the manifestos of the winning parties at each relevant election in Britain and Canada and calculate – through an examination of throne speeches, Acts of Parliament, economic statistics and executive action – the number of pledges they fulfill during their period of office. Actually determining what is and what is not a 'pledge', and whether or not it is met, presents problems. In the first place we shall be interested only in specific commitments to act, and thus will exclude from consideration rather vague general policy statements such as 'we will continue to support the Atlantic alliance' and such regular and formalistic announcements as 'estimates will be laid before you'. However, even particular commitments can be of different kinds and weight. It is difficult to justify a mode of analysis which ranks any given pledge as of higher priority or as more important or controversial than any other. But nonetheless an intention to introduce an annual Wealth Tax, has different implications from a promise to raise old age pensions. Manifesto commitments also differ in the extent to which they can be effected. A 'promise' to reduce the level of unemployment is a firm pledge and of a different order from the pious intent to pursue 'an economy based on more jobs' (Conservative Manifesto, Britain 1970). But it is also something about which the government may simply be unable to take effective action. It seems likely that manifestos which contain a high proportion of 'large' policy intentions will be less fully implemented than those which concentrate on smaller, but more readily achievable, aims.

We also need to define the 'implementation' of a pledge. Often a Government legislates a manifesto commitment and then finds enforcing it easier said than done. In Britain, for example, the Equal Pay Act of 1970 had not been fully adhered to in every sector of industry by 1982. In this preliminary study, it is impossible to deal adequately with the complications raised by such differences between 'outputs' and 'outcomes'. It seems reasonable to say that appropriate legislation or action equals the effective fulfillment of a pledge and that that is the limit to which a

TABLE 1.1

NUMBER OF SPECIFIC PLEDGES IN BRITISH MANIFESTOS
AND CANADIAN PLATFORMS 1945-1974

BRITAIN			CANADA		
1945	LAB	18	1945	LIB	7
1950	LAB	15	1949	LIB	19
1951	CONS	15	1953	LIB	7
1955	CONS	20	1957	CONS	16
1959	CONS	33	1958	CONS	5
1964	LAB	50	1962	CONS	8
1966	LAB	47	1963	LIB	33
1970	CONS	52	1965	LIB	14
1974 FEB.	LAB	43	1968	LIB	39
1974 OCT.	LAB	57	1972	LIB	1[x]
			1974	LIB	20
	AVERAGE	35		AVERAGE	15.3
	LABOUR	38.3		LIBERAL	17.5
	CONSERVATIVE	30		CONSERVATIVE	9.7

[x] ONLY ONE FIRM PLEDGE IDENTIFIABLE IN A SMALL BROADSHEET REVIEWING THE LIBERAL GOVERNMENT'S ACHIEVEMENTS FROM 1968.

SOURCES: FOR BRITAIN, F.W.S. CRAIG 1975a
　　　　　FOR CANADA, D. CARRIGAN 1968 AND LEAFLETS SUPPLIED BY W. IRVINE.

Government's (or party's) responsibility can run. Similarly one cannot really count as a pledge those instances where a party manifesto asserts a desire to 'try to do '*x*' or to achieve '*y*' as soon as practicable', for in neither case is failure to deliver reneging on a firm commitment. Difficulties of interpretation also surround those rare, but significant occasions where a government fulfills a pledge only to undo it later. Here we simply use the situation at the end of a government as a bench-mark against which to measure success or failure in implementing its manifesto.

Our rather tight definitions produce fewer 'pledges' in each manifesto than other scholars have discovered (Rose 1980), p.62; Finer 1975). Although certain stated aims are ignored as too vague, virtually all manifestos contain a large number of clear pledges whose implementation through executive or parliamentary action is both possible and analysable.

1.3 INITIAL ANALYSIS

The actual number of pledges has risen fairly consistently in Britain from 18 in 1945 to 57 in October 1974, and in Canada reached a peak of 39 iin 1968 as compared with 7 in 1945. Obviously the growth in the scope of governmental activity since the Second World War has played an important part. Edward Heath may also have been correct in commenting that 'people today are so cynical and sceptical about the whole machinery of government that detail is needed to convince them that you really intend to carry out your promise', (quoted in King, 1972). Formal party platforms in Canada have not increased in either size or number of firm commitments so consistently as their British counterparts, and it is clear from the description of formatting in Chapter 4 that their type and origin has varied considerably over this period. However, although the Liberal leader was moved to comment in 1949 that each and every plank in his party's manifesto could only be implemented 'when and if feasible' (Carrigan 1968), p. 167), there is a surprising similarity in the degree to which the pledges made in these documents are fulfilled, in both countries (see Tables 1.6 and 1.7).

If manifestos are increasing in length, what effect has this had on the kind of topic with which they concern themselves? In Britain the economy has unsurprisingly remained as the issue attracting most attention in the programmes of both parties of government (see Table 1.2). Individual topics within this broad area – inflation, unemployment, industrial relations or whatever – have all at one time or another since 1945 been a consuming interest of both government and public opinion and thus obvious candidates for pledges. The changing nature of government involvement in society is reflected in the increasing attention given to environmental and health and social security issues.

The economy, as can be seen from Table 1.3, is an important area of concern to Canadian political parties too, but the actual number of pledges varies considerably – perhaps because of a lower level of direct government involvement. This, together with the responsibility taken for many such matters by Provincial governments, also explains the lesser emphasis on 'Welfare State' issues. Agriculture, on the other hand, attracts more specific attention in Canada than in Britain, and the prominence of Internal Affairs in the 1968 Liberal manifesto is a reflection of the topicality of constitutional issues at that time. It is interesting that the distribution of pledges by subject is roughly equivalent to the overall distribution of themes and emphases measured in Chapters 3 and 4 by coding all statements in the programmes. Parties clearly feel under some obligation to make promises of action on those matters to which they have given general prominence in their election manifestos.

TABLE 1.2

PLEDGES BY SUBJECT MATTER – BRITAIN 1945 – 1974

	1945	1950	1951	1955	1959	1964	1966	1970	FEB. 1974	OCT. 1974
ECONOMY/TRADE/INDUSTRY/ EMPLOYMENT	7	10	8	5	8	16	13	14	20	21
ENVIRONMENT/HOUSING/ LOCAL GOVERNMENT	3	3	2	5	8	11	12	8	7	8
HOME OFFICE	0	2	2	4	4	5	9	11	0	9
HEALTH AND SOCIAL SECURITY	4	0	0	2	3	5	3	8	8	11
EDUCATION	2	0	0	4	6	9	7	6	3	4
FOREIGN/DEFENCE	2	0	1	0	1	4	2	3	4	2
AGRICULTURE	0	0	2	0	3	0	1	2	1	2

SOURCE: AS FOR TABLE 1.1

6

TABLE 1.3

PLEDGES BY SUBJECT MATTER - CANADA 1945 - 1974

	1945	1949	1953	1957	1958	1962	1963	1965	1968	1972	1974
ECONOMY/TRADE INDUSTRY/EMPLOYMENT	3	4	0	10	0	3	11	0	4	1	7
ENVIRONMENT/HOUSING	1	5	1	0	1	3	2	1	6	0	4
INTERNAL AFFAIRS - AND FED. - PROVINCIAL RELATIONS	0	4	3	3	1	0	3	2	13	0	0
HEALTH AND SOCIAL SECURITY	3	1	1	3	1	1	8	3	0	0	3
EDUCATION	0	0	0	0	0	0	3	2	1	0	0
AGRICULTURE	0	4	2	0	2	1	4	6	3	0	6
FOREIGN/DEFENCE	0	0	0	0	0	0	2	0	5	0	0

SOURCES: AS FOR TABLE 1.1

Colin Rallings

TABLE 1.4

IMPLEMENTATION OF THRONE SPEECH 'PLEDGES' - BRITAIN

	NUMBER OF INTENTIONS MENTIONED	NUMBER OF INTENTIONS PASSED	%
1945-6	10	9.5	95
1946-7	15	15	100
1947-8	16	14	87.5
1948-9	21	18.5	88
1950	8	7	87.5
1950-1	12	11	91.7
1951-2	7	6	85.7
1952-3	10	9	90
1953-4	18	16	88.9
1954-5	11	6	54.5
1955-6	15	13.5	90
1956-7	13	10.5	80.7
1957-8	15	15	100
1958-9	14	14	100
1959-60	16	13	81.3
1960-61	19	17.5	92.1
1961-62	20	18	90
1962-63	15	15	100
1963-64	24	20	83.3
1964-65	22	17	77.3
1965-66	20	14	70
1966-67	23	22	95.6
1967-68	25	21	84
1968-69	25	22	88
1969-70	32	16	50

Continued...

TABLE 1.4 Continued

1970-71	16	15.5	96.9
1971-72	21	20	95.2
1972-73	18	17	94.4
1973-74	20	10	50
1974	18	8	44.4
1974-75	26	21.5	82.7
1975-76	29	22	75.9
1976-77	19	14.5	76.3
1977-78	22	6	27.3
1978-79	28	14	50

NOTE: AN INTENTION MENTIONED AND PASSED IN THE SAME PARLIAMENTARY
SESSION SCORES 1; AN INTENTION MENTIONED IN ONE SPEECH AND
PASSED IN A SUBSEQUENT SESSION OF THE SAME PARLIAMENT SCORES .5.

SOURCE: F.W.S. CRAIG, 1975b.

The manifesto pledges, whose number and type we have just analysed, are 'on the table' as soon as their sponsoring party assumes office. Most of them will, in the course of a full Parliament, find their way into the speech from the throne – in other words the Government will serve formal notice of its intention to act. Throne speeches usually contain a fairly heavy legislative programme and many of the Bills outlined are of a technical or highly topical nature, but those pledges that make it this far have a good chance of reaching the Statute book. There is certainly no evidence of governments in either Canada or Britain stating their intentions as a mere cosmetic measure and then letting them drop. Indeed, as Herman (1974) has shown, and as our more extensive and comparative figures confirm, governments in both countries have a general record of success in implementing their legislation – especially when they have a secure Parliamentary majority and a full session at their disposal.

As can be seen from Tables 1.4 and 1.5, British governments have been successful in passing at least 70 per cent of their proposed legislation in four out of every five parliamentary sessions and their Canadian counterparts have achieved the same rate in two out of three. On those occasions in mid-Parliament when this figure is seriously undercut it is usually possible to explain the shortfall by reference to the political situation. In 1977–8 the British Labour Government was seriously constrained by its lack of an

Colin Rallings

TABLE 1.5

IMPLEMENTATION OF THRONE SPEECH 'PLEDGES' - CANADA

	NUMBER OF INTENTIONS MENTIONED	NUMBER OF INTENTIONS PASSED	%
1945	9	7	77.8
1946	5	4.5	90
1947	7	6.5	92.8
1948	11	9	81.8
1949	21	10	47.6
1949	17	15.5	91.2
1950	23	19	82.6
1950	2	2	100
1951	16	14	87.5
1952	22	19.5	88.6
1952	36	34	94.4
1953	21	20.5	97.6
1955	27	24.5	90.7
1956	20	17	85
1956	2	2	100
1957	11	8	72.7
1957	8	6	75
1958	28	23.5	83.9
1959	31	27	87.1
1960	21	19.5	92.8
1960	19	15.5	81.6
1962	24	13	54.2
1962	30	10	33.3
1963	14	12	85.7
1964	16	10.5	65.6
1965	35	8	22.8

Continued ...

TABLE 1.5 Continued

1966	48	38	79.2
1967	17	8	47
1968	47	40.5	86.2
1969	71	48.5	68.3
1970	68	38	55.9
1972	29	6	20.7
1973	34	19	55.9
1974	46	7	15.2
1974	68	48.5	71.3
1976	21	14.5	69.0
1977	11	4	36.4
1978	15	7	46.7

NOTE: DEFINITIONS AS IN TABLE 1.4

SOURCE: PARLIAMENTARY DEBATES (HANSARD), CANADIAN HOUSE OF COMMONS.

overall majority and the need to enter into a pact with the Liberals; and in Canada the same 1977–8 session, for example, was characterized by Liberal failure to get support for certain controversial constitutional and economic proposals in the Commons.

1.4 GENERAL CONSIDERATIONS AND CONCLUSIONS

It is not of course appropriate for all manifesto pledges to be implemented by specific legislation. Promises to raise social security benefits or to cut taxes, are usually met through action under the auspices of the annual Finance Bill; pledges to initiate a particular project or to alter spending priorities in a particular policy area can be executed through direct government instruction. Yet other types of pledges – to reduce the rate of unemployment or to build a certain number of houses per year – can be effected only through taking measures which it is *hoped* will have the desired outcome.

In such cases we are forced by the difficulty of measuring success, to regard the pledge as unfulfilled. Notwithstanding this very conservative assumption in the analysis, an impressive percentage of pledges are met through the government legislative programme. The British show an average implementation of 63.7 per cent – a figure which rises to 72.7 per cent if the three Parliaments which lasted less than two years are excluded (Table 1.6). Canadian parties in government have been similarly successful

TABLE 1.6

MANIFESTO PLEDGES IMPLEMENTED - BRITAIN

	NUMBER OF PLEDGES	NUMBER IMPLEMENTED	%
1945–50	18	15	83.3
1950–51	15	4	26.7
1951–55	15	12	80
1955–59	20	16	80
1959–64	33	27	81.8
1964–66	50	29	58
1966–70	47	32	68
1970–74	52	34	65.4
1974–74	43	14	32.6
1974–79	57	40	70.2

AVERAGE: 63.7

TABLE 1.7

MANIFESTO PLEDGES IMPLEMENTED - CANADA

	NUMBER OF PLEDGES	NUMBER IMPLEMENTED	%
1945–49	7	6	85.7
1949–53	20	17	85
1953–57	7	7	100
1957–58	17	9	53
1958–62	5	4	80
1962–63	8	5	62.5
1963–65	33	25	75.7
1965–68	14	10	71.4
1968–72	40	27	67.5
1972–74	1	1	100
1974–79	20	12	60

AVERAGE: 71.5

in keeping their promises – Table 1.7 shows an average 71.5 per cent of pledges kept. This is surprising since governments in Canada have been shorter with less secure majorities than their British counterparts. But it may reflect the fact that Canadian manifestos have remained more modest and proposed fewer specific measures. This prior recognition of the limitations likely to be imposed by both parliamentary and Federal constraints means that there is little difference in the end, in the degree to which parties in Britain and Canada have fulfilled their commitments to the electorate.

On closer examination though, these broad figures disguise differences in the type of pledge most likely to be carried out. Clear promises to increase pensions and other benefits (often by a named amount) and to repeal ideologically unacceptable legislation passed by a previous admin-istration, are almost invariably kept. Easily-effected pledges, such as appointing a new Minister with particular responsibilities, and minor legislative changes clearly in keeping with a party's general philosophy (e.g. the British Conservatives' promise in 1970 to encourage the sale of council houses), are generally adhered to. A government with an overall parliamentary majority can also hope to legislate on one or perhaps two major and controversial proposals in any given session, but if its manifesto contains too many items of this kind some may well fall by the wayside. For example, the 1974–9 British Labour Government's programme was held up not only by its fragile parliamentary position, but also by the inordinate time required for the Scotland and Wales Act.

The pledges least likely to be fulfilled are the small minority where the government cannot ensure their passage or which involve the expenditure of large amounts of public money on electorally unappealing and/or low priority projects. On a number of occasions Canadian parties have included in their platform a promise to increase overseas aid to a specified level, but this target has never been reached. There will always be manifesto proposals for which sufficient resources can simply not be found during the lifetime of a Parliament – no government has recently been able to avoid financial constraints on its programme as the result of internal or world recession. Finally, governments will sometimes need to go against one of their pledges because of unforeseen and urgent political develop-ments. The 1970–4 Conservative Government's nationalization of Upper Clyde Shipbuilders and Rolls Royce, and its agreement to the large-scale immigration of Ugandan Asians, fall into this category.

Although the overall record of political parties in Britain and Canada is good, the electorates take a less rosy view. Why? The explanation starts with media concentration on economic policy and the 'U-turns' which have been associated with it. It was all very well for Conservative Central Office to claim in 1974 that the Heath Government had implemented 97 of its 105 manifesto pledges (Rose 1980, p. 66). However, what impinged more heavily on public consciousness was the introduction of a compulsory incomes policy and the failure to reduce price rises 'at a stroke'. Statements like this, however much politicians claim that they are taken out of context, are seized upon by the press and elevated to the status of campaign promises. Inevitably couched in less careful and considered terms than is usual in manifestos themselves, they thus, almost accidentally, become the hostage of a party's fortunes. In fact, clear pledges to act in particular areas of macro-economic policy are rare, and certainly a declaration in favour of the 'maintenance of a high level of employment and national income' does not meet our criteria for a 'pledge'. Nonetheless, such statements leave a general impression of a party's intentions and then it scarcely matters what the manifesto itself actually says (see Watkins 1981). Governments have in recent years failed to meet expectations. Hence they are blamed more for their ineffectiveness in achieving large, vaguely stated, economic and social goals than credited for what is – in objective terms – a solid record of publishing and then implementing a fairly coherent and wide-ranging policy programme.

Some commentators actually argue that 'manifestosis' has gone too far. There is a feeling that programmes are devised to 'bribe' voters and to assuage party activists, and that 'mandates for shopping lists of 60 to 80 specific items are without meaning' (Finer 1975). If what is meant is that voters cannot possibly know, or even care about, each specific pledge, then of course Finer has a point. As we have said electors do judge in terms of general gap between promise and performance rather than against an 'objective' check-list of what has actually been achieved.

Despite this, manifestos are essential to the operationalization of representative democracy. They are 'the only direct and clear statements of party policy available to the electorate and directly attributable to the party as such' (Robertson 1976, p. 72). 'Many citizens (may) vote without knowing what is in the manifesto' (Lord Denning 1981), but the fact that the major political parties have become increasingly 'programmatic' cannot be an accident. They interpret their role as encouraging electoral support not only through their image but also through the articulation of concrete policy proposals. Far better than seeking a blank cheque 'party manifestoes provide voters with a clear-cut choice between teams of politicians with differing intentions about what government should do' (Rose 1974, p. 316). They may on occasion give the impression that governments are omnipotent. However, as long as it is realized that they are important guides to action which must be taken seriously, but which will necessarily also be partial and incomplete, then they surely aid rather than hinder the process of representative government.

CHAPTER 2

THE INTERNAL ANALYSIS OF
ELECTION PROGRAMMES

———— ∾ ————

2.1 INTRODUCTION

The cautionary but moderately encouraging conclusions from Britain and Canada are also likely to hold for other countries – certainly for those (like Australia and New Zealand) with similar governmental and party arrangements – but probably for others too.

The country studies reported in Chapters 3–17 all assess the place of the manifesto or its programmatic equivalent in national political processes. The qualitative evidence produced there suggests (even within the context of coalition negotiations) that they form genuine statements of preference rather than mere bargaining counters. The elaborate negotiations of joint programmes *before* an election, as in Ireland and France in 1973, is an indication of the importance accorded them by parties as well as by the electorate.

These bits of evidence require more systematic investigation to tie them conclusively together. Even so, they allow us to proceed to our 'internal' analysis with further reassurance that the texts have an effect on the external world.

Of course election programmes are interesting not only for their bearing on government action, but also for their contribution to the electoral success of the party, to the formation of like-minded coalitions, and to the study of policy-spaces constraining the choices rational actors will make. All these lines of investigation are followed up below and in the parallel analyses currently underway.

2.2 THE COMPARATIVE FRAMEWORK

Regardless of the particular interest one has, campaign appeals are studied to best advantage on a comparative rather than on a single-country or single-party basis. This is because the grounds of judgement must inevitably be relative rather than absolute. To take simple examples, it is difficult to estimate for one party in isolation what its position is, or whether it has exploited the full range of appeals open to it. We have no final and absolute list of what appeals are available, to compare with those actually made. Even comparisons with other parties in the same country may not be illuminating, since they are likely to have different ideologies, rendering different appeals accessible to them (Budge and Farlie, 1983, Chapter 2). What is needed is a comparison with other parties of the same kind in other countries, so that we may see what position the party under consideration has and whether it has made use of all the appeals used elsewhere, or left some out in its campaigning. Most single-party or single-country investigations use comparisons of this kind implicitly. The advantage of an explicitly comparative investigation is that it enables such judgements to be based on firm evidence .

Our investigation is not simply comparative but also very extensive. Few investigations of any political phenomenon, let alone of elections, have included 19 democracies with parties encompassing such cultural, socio-economic and institutional variations. This enables us to judge whether, in spite of radical socio-cultural differences, similar party systems generate similar appeals on the part of individual parties. On the other hand the inevitable inclusion of a large bloc of Western European democracies enables us to see whether institutional differences produce a divergence of appeals in otherwise similar countries. At the level of parties rather than countries, we can also enquire whether parties within a common ideological tradition, such as the Socialist parties, show more resemblances to each other across national boundaries than they do to rival parties operating within the same system.

Any study of democratic parties is bound to cover as many as possible of the established systems of Australasia, North America and Western Europe. Within these areas, our choice of countries was constrained by the availability of a specialist willing and able to analyse party strategies according to our common framework. In most cases we found such a specialist, and have thus ended up with a reasonable representation. Because of the analytic advantages of wide cross-cultural comparisons we have included other party systems often neglected in comparative analyses (Israel, Japan and Sri Lanka; India has been excluded because of its variety of languages, and the absence of uniform party documents across these). On the other hand we have not wished to cover countries where party competition has been interrupted by coups or takeovers or where it has not had long enough since independence to stabilize itself. One old-established party system, that of Northern Ireland (Chapter 8), is anomalous in not belonging to a sovereign state, but on the other hand functions quite independently of any other.

Little need be said to justify the post-war basis of the study. The disruption and change which occurred in all party systems (with the possible exception of the United States) as a result of war and occupation provide a natural starting point. With the possible exceptions of France (where we study only the Fifth Republic), and Japan (where we begin in 1960), no fundamental political changes seem to have occurred which would *a priori*, force a split into two or more sub-periods. Naturally we are alert to this possibility. What our analyses seem to show, however, is interesting variation and change within the parameters of existing party systems. The Lipset and Rokkan thesis on the freezing of party dimensions from 1920 indicate that a more extended period could possibly be regarded as appropriate (Lipset and Rokkan, 1967). But at any rate it seems safe to take the whole post-war period as being so.

Our object then is to investigate the ideology and strategy of post-war parties across countries within a common framework, so as to facilitate comparisons and ultimately to support generalizations about the way parties shape their appeals. Given the wide range of conditions (political, social and economic) in our countries it is of course open as to whether or not generalization is possible – whether party behaviour differs so radically across national boundaries that extensive comparisons cannot be made. We cannot therefore leap directly into a general quantitative analysis without first reviewing party appeals and their place in elections within each country in turn.

Such country chapters (3–17) constitute the bulk of our book. It is on the basis of the separate and partly qualitative assessments made there that we move to the largely quantitative and general Chapter 18. The country chapters are not simply prolegomena to a comparative spatial analysis. They contain substantive descriptions of the way appeals are designed by each party, their place in the national political process, influence on subsequent government actions, etc. The comparable information given on these points should provide a useful basis for cumulative future research. At the same time idiosyncratic variants are picked out and commented upon. This ensures an overall balance between the general and the individual in our discussion, and renders it of use to country specialists as well as to comparativists.

2.3 MANIFESTOS AND PLATFORMS: THE ELECTION PROGRAMME

So many statements, broadcasts, documents, films and reports, emanate from parties in the course of an election, that under practical constraints one has to make a choice. Either all the output can be studied for a few elections, or some representative portion can be analysed over many. Which choice is made depends on the purposes of the investigation. As our intention was to trace the broad development of party appeals over the post-war period, we chose to focus on a set of key central statements of party positions through which we could map the movements of the parties over time.

These key statements were the party manifestos or platforms, or, in their absence, the nearest equivalent, ranging from the specially authoritative and comprehensive statements made by party leaders at the outset of the campaign in Australia, to the summary of individual commitments published by the Party Groups of French Deputies after the election. The choice of these equivalents is justified in the individual country chapters where they are described in detail. In all, ten of the countries studied do not produce a manifesto as such. Some countries on the other hand (for example, the Netherlands, Austria, and Germany) produce several different types of documents which each perform different functions of the Anglo-Saxon manifestos. Such variations in the way of organizing electoral appeals are themselves interesting, and therefore detailed in each country chapter. Decisions about which to take as the equivalent of the manifestos are also justified in terms of their political role. In every country there is a recognizable statement of policy, which has the backing of the leadership as the authoritative definition of party policy for that election. Usually the manifesto (the British term) or party platform (the American usage) and their equivalents are the only statement of their kind made by the whole party during an election: many others are of course initiated by party spokesmen of various kinds, including the leader, but it is unclear how far the party as a whole is officially committed to them. Such partial statements are subject to the prior orthodoxy enunciated through the manifesto or its equivalent and cannot stray far from it without provoking reactions (Robertson 1976, Chapters 3 and 5).

Manifestos and their equivalents are read by relatively few electors in most countries. As the British and Canadian evidence suggests, and as our qualitative analyses confirm, they do nevertheless constitute the major indirect influence on what parties are seen as standing for. This is because they form the basis for comment in the mass media and provide the cues for questions raised with party candidates at all levels, as well as staple issues for their campaigns. Not only does the manifesto-equivalent determine the main campaign themes and lines of discussion, it has usually been the subject of extensive prior debate and negotiation inside the party. So it can be singled out as a uniquely representative and authoritative characterization of party policy at a given point in time.

Focusing on the manifesto also allows us to use a distinct, specifically dated pamphlet available for a plurality of countries in archives or published collections: where not physically available it is at least reported or summarized in the press. This 'ideal-type' provides a guide even where such documents are not issued, since we can then seek for the nearest equivalent in the form of an authoritative and guiding statement on behalf of the whole party. Findings show we were correct to follow this course, since we thereby obtain a plausible picture of party similarities and differences across the various countries.

2.4 PREVIOUS STUDIES

Justification for concentrating on manifestos can also be found in most previous research on party strategies. They have always been used as a major source by historians. A comparative study utilizing historical material (coded into ten broad 'issue dimensions') has traced a 'decline of ideology' among parties in 12 countries from 1900–65 (Thomas 1975). However this based itself on party statements in government as well as election programmes, so it is not strictly comparable with our investigation. Platforms and manifestos provided the source for other counts of specific election pledges made by parties (Pomper 1980; Page 1978), which can be compared with government actions to see how many were honoured.

A more extended analysis related American policy *emphases*, rather than specific pledges, to subsequent action by parties in government (Ginsberg 1976). Democratic and Republican platforms from 1844–1968 were analysed in terms of seven broad categories: capitalism, internal sovereignty (Federal *vs*. State Power); redistribution; international cooperation; universalism (equality of rights); labour; and ruralism (farms and rural way of life). Each paragraph of the text was scored according to whether it contained positive or negative references to each of the categories. To determine whether major differences in election commitments were followed by changes in government policy, all United States statutes between 1789 and 1968 were scored as favouring or opposing policy objectives within the same broad categories. A broad correspondence between platform emphases and the bases of subsequent government policy was found – further confirmation of the conclusions of Chapter 1.

Ginsberg's research is of interest not only substantively but also methodologically. His characterization of party policy through the use of broad categories rather than counts of specific pledges is more or less dictated by the long time span over which he works. Specific pledges will change so much over 30 or 40 years, let alone a century and a quarter, that any analysis of trends has to group these into invariant categories. Otherwise there is nothing similar between the beginning of the period and the end. A second aspect of his analysis is the importance given to the number of times a topic is mentioned in a platform. Saliency in this sense is given equal weight with polarity – the difference in positive and negative mentions of a category between party platforms – in measuring policy contrasts between Democrats and Republicans. This is logical as the tendency by one party to harp on a particular topic being studiously ignored by the other is surely as important a party difference as direct opposition of policies. Indeed, we shall argue below that it is the most common form of party difference.

Analyses of party platforms over such an extended period are rare. The only other example known to us is one in which Namenwirth and Lasswell (1970) coded a selection of U.S. party platforms from the mid-nineteenth and twentieth centuries into eight value categories, and noted variations in their relative salience between parties and over time. Temporal differences were most marked, bringing Democrats and Republicans closer to each other in the later period. Again it is interesting that change over time can be measured only within invariant general categories.

A similar point emerges from the pioneering study by Olavi Borg (1966), where he analysed the basic ideological values of post-war Finnish party manifestos by counting words or statements (whichever seemed most relevant in a given context) into a set of 24 categories. These bear a remarkable similarity to the ones used here (see Appendix B) and in other contexts (Robertson 1976, 73–6; Budge and Farlie, 1977) which were conceived totally independently. Borg's method gives primacy to the relative saliency of categories – the degree of emphasis and repeated references made by a party to a particular topic – rather than to the particular policies advocated or the degree of policy oppositon between the parties.

Using methods which further anticipated those of our comparative investigation, Borg measured the degree to which emphases on the categories went up and down together – which through factor analysis (Section 2.8 below) can be interpreted as evidence for the existence of common underlying 'factors' or 'dimensions'.

He identified:

Opposition between capitalist and socialist organization of the economy.
Contrast between group norms and individual values.
National independence and democracy.
Social justice.
Support of the legal political system.

Another Scandinavian study of manifestos over the post-war period (Kuhnle and Solheim, 1981) has focused specifically on Norwegian parties' commitment to social welfare, and uses emphases and pledges to measure this. Most work in Scandinavia has been concentrated however on an intensive study of all material (including radio and television transcripts and films) emanating from the parties during a single, or 2–3 continuous, election campaigns (Isberg, Wettengren, Wibble and Wittrock, 1974); Siune 1982; Pettersen 1973, 1979). The existence of studies which take the opposite tack from ours, of intensive explorations of all party appeals and messages within one specific campaign, is extremely useful as a check on some of our assumptions (see Section 2.5 below) and as a reassurance that manifesto (or equivalent) emphases do not diverge too much from other, more specific, party utterances.

Studies of particular campaigns, inevitably affected by the particular circumstances of the moment, do not however provide much of a basis for generalizing widely about the way parties handle their appeals, even within one country. There is a place for a broader cross-time and cross-temporal investigation which is capable of placing studies of particular campaigns in context. Given the proliferation of specific studies, there is indeed some urgency in providing a broader comparative analysis to complement them.

2.5 CODING FRAME AND CODING PROCEDURES

Our own investigation took its start from studies of British manifestos and American party platforms of the mid-seventies. These originated in a coding and factor analysis of Conservative and Labour manifestos from 1924–66, the purpose of which was to refine the standard 'rational choice' model of party competition (Robertson 1976). The analysis was replicated within a different spatial framework, extended to the General Elections of 1970 and 1974, and to Republican and Democratic platforms from 1920–72 (Budge and Farlie, 1977, Chapter 11).

This work was completed in ignorance of the earlier studies described in Section 2.4, so its methods and theoretical assumptions evolved independently. It is interesting that common problems of investigation provoked the same methodological responses. This was particularly evident in the use of invariant coding categories within which to group policy references. Specific pledges and promises change so rapidly that they offer no stable basis of comparison between non-consecutive elections (besides constituting only a small minority of all sentences in the documents). Even references to broader 'issues' are too time-bound and specific to provide the necessary framework. Eventually Robertson conducted his analysis within a framework of 21 broader 'topics' or 'issue-types'. These had to be modified to some extent for the extension of U.S. party platforms, but in essence remained the same. The names of the 21 original categories are: 1 – Foreign Special Relationships, 2 – Regionalism, 3 – Freedom, 4 – Enterprise, 5 – Democracy, 6 – Controlled Economy, 7 – Economic Planning, 8 – Special Groups, 9 – Culture, 10 – Decolonization, 11 – Economic Stability, 12 – Productivity, 13 – National Effort, 14 – Social Justice, 15 – Technology, 16 – Military, 17 – Economic Orthodoxy, 18 – Incentives, 19 – Peace, 20 – Social Services, 21 – Internationalism.

For the American study categories were added as follows: 3A – Defence of American Way, 3B – Support of Morality, 3C – Law and Order, 5A – Constitutionalism, 7A – Regulation, 8A – Labour Groups, 8B – Agriculture, 8C – Veterans, 8D – Underprivileged Minority Groups, 8E – Non-Economic Demographic, 11B – Protectionism, 15A – Conservation, 17A – Economic Orthodoxy, 17B – Government Efficiency, 17C – Government Corruption 22 – Isolationism.

There is a substantial resemblance to Borg's independently-derived groupings (very similar in number and content) – and to Ginsberg's seven categories. In all cases they derived from a) the need to code *all* the content of the election programme on the assumption that references and emphases can be as informative as specific pledges; and, given this, b) the need to discover politically relevant but substantively permanent concerns of the election programmes over an extended time-period.

In Robertson's case the creation of categories summarizing such concerns involved repeated readings through the documents and groupings of related concerns, until a set was achieved with substantial mutual independence, and which attracted reasonable, though inevitably varying, numbers of responses over the inter-war and post-war periods (Robertson 1976).

For the extension to the United States Robertson's original categories were used as a guide but were tested informally through a pre-reading of all the documents and grouping of responses in the manner originally used with British data. They stood up as reasonable categorizations in the sense of being both relevant and invariant. The additions and amendments were for specifically American concerns which had at one time or another assumed central importance but which were not part of the British experience – such as isolationism or opposition to (other countries') colonialism.

The same process of extension based on pre-readings of the different country documents, and debate at the level of the full research group, was applied to the original set of categories at the very beginning of the present investigation. Pre-tests using the modified U.S. codings had been made in each country and performed well – to the surprise of many who had felt the special conditions of their country ruled out use of a common coding frame. Obviously, however, each country investigator also felt that there were some points where essential detail was lost – a worry which led to substantial splitting of original groupings, particularly in the areas of economics and of social groups, to the extent of doubling their number (27 became 54). Only one entirely new category was added: this was communalism, in the sense of the continuing existence of separate, often culturally or religiously differentiated, groups. This might be approved (as in the case of the 'pillars' of traditional Dutch society) or deplored as an incitement to violence and civil disorder. But it obviously constituted a different order of concern from references to interest groups in British and American politics. Otherwise the original broad range of groupings sub-divided in the manner described, seemed adequate to encompass most variations of emphasis in the new documentation. The 'standard categories' as we refer to them in the country chapters, are listed and specified in detail in Appendix B.

The uniqueness and particularity of national politics were allowed for in the freedom given to the individual country investigators who performed the coding to subdivide even the new, more detailed comparative categories in different ways on condition that they could be recombined into the general category for the comparative analysis. Some investigators used this facility more than others: and in certain cases sub-categories derived for particular national cases attracted so few references that they had to be recombined even for the country analysis. What was done is described in the relevant chapter and in Appendix B. In all cases however, coding was based on the general set of 54 standard categories in the Appendix B, which are consequently only mentioned in passing at the outset of each chapter.

The obvious danger from sub-differentiation to accommodate particular country conditions, is that the frame loses its generalizing and summarizing capacity to become simply an assemblage of different codes applying to different countries and not used much in common, even though nominally available. The ability to recombine into the 54 general categories is one guarantee against this danger. However, for certain purposes 54 separate categories might themselves be too diffuse. Therefore from the start of production coding a grouping of the 54 into seven general 'domains' characterized by their subject area was also agreed. The domains were: 1 – Foreign Affairs, 2 – Freedom and Democracy, 3 – Government, 4 – Economy, 5 – Welfare, 6 – Fabric of Society, 7 – Social Groups. Most of these distinctions are self-evident and refer to normally differentiated areas of social life. 'Government' refers to government structure and operations covering both the actual government and the State in a more extended sense. 'Fabric of Society' covers morality, and social links and activities generally. For tracing the broad changes in party concerns over time, as well as picking out related groups of categories to analyse together, such general divisions are invaluable and structure discussion in all the individual country chapters.

Country coding using this general framework was normally done by or under the direct supervision of each country investigator. Technical and other problems caused the British data to be recorded as a methods class exercise under the supervision of Laver at the University of Liverpool, and the American, Australian, New Zealand and Austrian data to be coded by research assistants under the supervision of Hearl at Essex (besides the Belgian and Luxembourg data for which he was the investigator). In such 'centralized' coding the emphasis was put on central supervision and reliability of the procedure rather than on specific coding checks. Tests of reliability and validity varied between countries and are detailed in individual chapters.

The basic object of all coding with the exception of West Germany (where paragraphs were used) was to place each sentence in each of the manifestos/platforms or their equivalents under one (and no more than one) of the categories. Sentences were coded since they form the natural grammatical unit in most languages. However, very long grammatical periods were composed into 'quasi-sentences' where the sense changed between colons or commas. This is essentially the counting procedure followed by Isberg and his associates in their Swedish study. A count was also kept of uncoded (quasi-) sentences whose numbers were acceptably low in most cases. Again details are given in country chapters. A more detailed and technical description of coding procedures along with the general coding frame itself, is given in Appendix B.

2.6 THE SALIENCY THEORY OF POLITICAL CAMPAIGNS

Underlying most technical decisions about methods is some theory of the process being studied. This is true even for the seemingly straightforward procedure of counting all sentences in the manifesto/platform within broad categories, without separating out specific pledges from other references to a topic, and without generally discriminating between positive and negative references. For this implies that the most important aspect of the documents is the degree of emphasis placed on certain broad policy areas, rather than each party's support for, or opposition to, a specific policy within these areas. The picture of party competition in other words changes from the classical 'great debate', or direct argument over a common range of problems, to one where parties talk past each other, glossing over areas which might favour their rivals while emphasizing those on which they feel they have an advantage. Coding sentences into broad categories rests in other words on a saliency theory of party competition, as opposed to a confrontation theory (Robertson 1976; Daalder and Mair (eds.) 1983; Budge 1982; Budge and Farlie 1983, Chapter 2).

What is implied by saliency theory, and why should it be considered more generally applicable to party competition than direct confrontation? The implication is that different parties are associated in the different policy areas with generally desirable goals. In Britain for example it is hard for Labour to argue that it will do better on law enforcement than the

Conservatives, the traditional party of order. Even mentioning the topic runs the danger of bringing it into prominence and thus benefiting their rivals. Rather than arguing about it, the best strategy is not to mention it at all – or if some reference must be made in view of public concern, to deal with it cursorily. If party leaders feel that they and their rivals 'own' various issues in this way, differential emphases in their treatment of them are entirely logical. A coding scheme designed to separate areas of differential advantage and to group references into them is best designed to catch this aspect of competition.

The arguments in favour of changing from a confrontationist to a saliency point of view are plausible, but since the step involves radical re-thinking it needs to be justified. One finding which is relevant is the limited number of direct references made in each party's manifesto either to the other main parties, or to their policies, or both. If the parties did argue directly, we should expect to find the bulk of the manifestos and platforms filled with such references. In fact in the original British and American studies, at most a quarter, and on average only around seven per cent of the sentences, refer even broadly to other parties or their policies. It was this finding which prompted a coding based on emphasis in the first place since it was the only approach which covered all sentences in the manifesto and not just some of them. In the event the studies presented below also find that references to parties are limited, and direct contrasts between policies even more so.

On this there is independent confirmation from Sweden for elections of the sixties. In spite of including direct television confrontations between politicians of different parties among the material coded, a study (Isberg, Wettengren, Wibble and Wittrock, 1974) found that less than half the quasi-sentences incorporated any kind of reference to parties (43 per cent). These were of course not necessarily references to party policy. So this investigation too followed the practice of counting sentences into policy-areas as the only practical way of proceeding.

Support also comes from the data produced by this investigation, in the shape of contrasts from a simple count of sentences within each broad issue area over the post-war elections. This is a standard procedure carried out in the original studies and in all the country analyses reported below. It will be seen that parties differ markedly in their emphases as anticipated by the saliency theory. Moreover the differences make good practical sense – conservative and liberal parties stressing their 'proprietal topics' like enterprise, traditional morality and freedom, while radical and reformist parties emphasize redistribution and welfare.

A coding based on saliency assumptions does therefore get a known difference between the parties and usefully specifies them. More extended investigations and hence a severer check are provided by spatial analyses, the leading ideas of which are described in the next section.

2.7 SALIENCY THEORY WITHIN A SPATIAL CONTEXT

It is important to be able to plot manifestos, platforms, and equivalents as points in some kind of space, for two reasons:

(a) The documents, for the reasons we have given, represent an authoritative summation of the party view at a particular point in time – the equilibrium attained by conflicting forces within the party. If we are able to talk about the way parties are developing and whether they are moving together or distancing themselves from each other, as commentators and politicians frequently do, we need to have some measure of the positions which parties take up over time. Present positions can be compared with past positions to estimate the degree and direction of ideological movement, and the current distance between them compared with former distances to see whether it is wider or smaller. The manifestos/platforms/equivalents, as authoritative summaries of policy, represent overall party positions better than anything else.

(b) However, to consider party positions, the distances separating them, tendencies to the centre or extremes, and direction of change, is to imply the existence of some kind of space within which locations can be specified and movement charted. Since phenomena of this kind form a staple of everyday political discussion, a spatial context is assumed by almost everyone when they talk about politics. The usual practice is to characterize parties as left, centre and right, which only makes sense in terms of a single line continuum on which parties can locate themselves and along which they can change from an extreme position on the ends of the line to a more moderate position nearer the centre.

It was on this everyday postulate that Hotelling (1929) and Downs (1957) worked out the best known rational choice theory of party competition. They assumed: (i) a uniform or single-peaked distribution of electors over such a line between the most left-wing and the most right-wing positions; (ii) that electors always vote for the party whose position is nearest their own on the line; (iii) that the party leaders have no fixed commitments but simply adjust their policy position so as to attract the largest number of votes and so gain office. From these it follows that party policies will 'converge' on the position of the middle (median) elector (not necessarily of course on moderate policies: this depends where the middle elector is). It is less clear what will happen if electors are spread unevenly over such a continuum (a multi-peaked distribution) or if issues additional to left–right policies are involved, thus necessitating a multi-dimensional rather than a unidimensional space within which to locate the parties. The outcome then may well depend on particular circumstances which render theoretical prediction impossible (for a review and critique see Budge and Farlie, 1977, Chaps. 4 and 5; Budge and Farlie, 1978).

To counter such unpredictability, the very elaborate mathematical models dealing with party movement have been forced to make restrictive assumptions which have little bearing on the real world. The basic ideas behind Hotelling and Downs' speculations can, however, be modified to come closer to our everyday view of politics, and then be checked against the data derived from our documentary analysis. Two major changes are necessary. First one must recognize that parties are under considerable constraints. As noted above, a Socialist or Reformist party is not going to be believed if it suddenly says that Law and Order or Defence are more important than Social Welfare. Nor can its rivals promise to do better than the Socialists in expanding and consolidating welfare (for example). No matter how many electors support a particular policy, therefore, only in some areas can a party move closer to them. Where it has a clear record it has by and large to stick with it. In spatial terms this implies that certain areas (or segments, in the case of a single line) are open only to one party – certain policy areas 'belong' to it, as do the votes of electors found there. In other words we are dealing with a 'party-reserved' space, with some areas open to only one party, rather than a pure policy space of unlimited free movement for parties, such as that postulated by Downs and Hotelling.

For a more realistic model we must also recognize that office is not a goal for most politicians if they cannot pursue their policies at least to some extent. Therefore they will not substantially alter their main commitments. They will however modify their *emphases* somewhat if winning votes will secure victory. Typically this involves de-emphasizing the usual policy areas and stressing non-partisan areas (such as technology) – but marginally. Normal policy will always be reiterated to some extent so we are never going to be in danger of mistaking one party's manifesto or platform for the other.

In terms of a spatial analysis based on a saliency coding, a toning-down of partisan emphases will appear as a move towards the centre. The modified office-seeking hypothesis for two-party competitive systems like the British and American (leaders emphasize general appeals when they anticipate competitive elections (Robertson 1976)) was tested through comparative analyses of the British and American material cited earlier (Budge and Farlie, 1977, Chapter 11).

This showed that:

1 Each party's manifesto/platform for each election was sharply distinguished from the other party's, though less so in the less ideological United States than in Britain. This country contrast fits common sense notions.
2 Movement though limited, conformed to historical patterns, e.g. British Labour was most 'characteristic' and hence most extreme in the two elections of the thirties and least in 1964 when Wilson concentrated on the 'white heat of technology' and other pragmatic, non-class-based

appeals. In the U.S. positions were furthest apart in the Goldwater
election of 1964 and closest in the 'issue-less' fifties (the series only went
up to 1972).

3   Relative party movements upheld the modified office-seeking hypo-
    thesis. Leaders did stress purely partisan appeals when they were very
    likely either to win or lose the election (and hence extra votes did not
    count) and inserted 'across-the-board' appeals when they were in a
    competitive situation.

The important modification to conventional choice ideas implied by the
hypothesis of modified office seeking, and of competition as relative
saliency rather than direct confrontation, is thus supported by previous
analyses. The clear-cut and plausible results tell in favour of using relative
emphases in coding rather than contrasting policies. We cannot just
assume *a priori* that what applies to Britain and the U.S. necessarily works
elsewhere but it is more likely to do so than otherwise untested schemes,
and its general relevance has been confirmed by the successful comparative
analysis reported below.

2.8 FACTOR ANALYSIS

Spatial analyses are not of course the only way in which our data can be
analysed. Much can be learned simply by reading the documents, particularly when reading is focused through the attempt to devise suitable
categories for the quantitative analysis. More can be inferred from the
distributions of sentences over domains or leading categories of the coding
frame. Party movements can be studied by directly comparing sentence
totals in each area for each of the individual election programmes.

Fruitful though they are, each of these approaches involves visual
examination of masses of words or figures. They can be usefully supplemented – indeed it is essential to supplement them – with precis and
summaries. In the case of the sentence counts, these take the form of the
averages or condensed distributions reported in each country chapter.
Their advantage lies in emphasizing the strong central tendencies and
trends which may exist in the data, where we might otherwise be inclined
to take striking individual deviations as the norm. Clarity is of course
achieved by suppressing other elements in the data – no summary measure
can report everything, otherwise it could not summarize.

Spatial analyses, at least in our use of them, are also summary measures
which enable us to identify major tendencies over time, as well as the
structure of the post-war situation in which they take place. They have the
additional advantage of showing whether some of the theoretical ideas
discussed above actually work out in relation to the data. Like other

summary measures, however, they will only express certain aspects of the data. The important point is to be aware of this and to ensure that the aspects expressed are the ones we want expressed (see Budge, Crewe and Farlie (eds.), 1976, Chapter 21, Budge and Farlie, 1977, Chapter 7; Budge and Farlie, 1978)

As we are interested both in movement and the structure of the underlying situation (i.e. the way the space is made up) the best technique from our point of view is factor analysis. This will be known to many readers already and there are excellent technical descriptions available (Harmon 1974) so we simply summarize its major principles here before considering specific problems of its application to our data.

Assume we have a score for each document on each of a number of broad policy areas – the score consisting of the percentage of sentences which refer to that area out of the total number of sentences in the programme. Each score can be checked to see how far high percentage references to each topic occur in the same documents, and how far low percentage references also occur together. If two topics go up together and down together systematically in terms of their scores (i.e. if they 'covary' with each other) there are grounds for saying that they are systematically linked and that both, with others which share the linkage, reflect the same underlying party conflict.

Another form of relationship is when references to a particular area are consistently low, where references to the other area are high; and *vice versa*. In such a case we would be justified in inferring that the policy areas belonged to opposite ends of the same underlying 'continuum' or 'dimension' of conflict which can be represented by a straight line (other names for this are 'factor', 'component' and 'cluster' – terms which give their name to alternative techniques of dimensional analyses).

On the basis of such positive and negative associations between percentage scores, we can identify sets of related policy areas. In most cases these will appear in several sets. Each can be represented spatially by a line, as we have said, thus becoming a 'dimension' of some space. The lines formed by other 'dimensions' will cross this at right angles in an 'unrotated' analysis and also in the kinds of 'rotated' analyses which we use. Of course if there are more than three clusters or dimensions, we cannot represent the multi-dimensional space directly but we can calculate relative distances between points lying within the space from the numeric locations they have on each dimension.

The ability to calculate distance is important, because each manifesto can be represented by a point in space. It is located on each dimension by the percentage of references made to the issue-areas associated with it, multiplied by the 'loading' of these areas on the dimension. (Areas are more or less strongly associated with each dimension, and the degree of association is expressed by a decimal figure for its 'loading'.)[1]

The interesting points which arise from a factor analysis are:

1 The nature of the dimensions, which give the underlying structure of the space and hence the nature of the party conflict from which it emerges. This is inferred from the set of policy areas particularly associated with each dimension.

2 The relative location of the various election programmes within the multi-dimensional space, from which we can infer the movement of party positions over time and estimate convergence, divergence, etc.

As explained above, we use factor analysis as a simplifying and focusing device to bring out certain trends present in the data. To simplify, we have to discard much information originally contained there. We want to be sure however that we have not discarded too much – that the dimensions and movements produced by the analysis are not marginal. In part this possibility can be checked through our substantive knowledge of the politics of the country – unexpected findings are interesting but only if they do not flatly contradict what we otherwise know. Factor analysis is after all only one way of summarizing information among others and is far from a final criterion of the validity of our knowledge.

'Internal' criteria of how useful the summary is are also available however from the 'percentage of explained variance' and the 'Eigenvalues', quoted in each chapter for first- and second-stage factor analyses. The first is simply the proportion of all variance in the original data associated with the underlying dimensions or factors produced by the analysis. Obviously the higher this percentage, the more strongly are the differences in the original scores reflected in the emergent dimensions.

The Eigenvalue is a special measure computed in the process of deriving a factor. It is a measure of the relative importance of the factor. The sum of the Eigenvalues is a measure of the total variance existing in the factor solution.

2.9 CHARACTERISTICS OF OUR DATA

As we have stressed, all the relationships and movements revealed by factor analysis are present in our original data, though perhaps hard to see there. The spaces are simply presentational techniques (though very important ones) for emphasizing what is there already. Our data consists of all (or almost all) significant party programmes in our countries over the post-war period. In the factor analyses we are not therefore concerned with making inferences to relationships and movements in some hypothetical wider 'universe' of programmes – only with clarifying relationships internal to our data.

Naturally the nature of those data is crucial. So before going into the actual application of the technique we should comment on some of their characteristics which influence results:

(*a*) We have coded all the programmes of 'significant' parties, but how are these selected? In general, we have followed the criteria suggested by Sartori (1976, 121–5). A party is taken as 'significant' if it obtained at least 5 per cent of the national vote in any one post-war election; or if, failing this, it still managed to influence the formation of governments ('coalition' and 'blackmail' potential). However, these are general guidelines rather than iron rules to be applied mechanically. They are to be modified in light of specialists' knowledge of national conditions or of special difficulties (where for example small parties lack a stable identity and hence shift so much from one election to another as to totally confuse the underlying relations between major parties). Of course difficulties occur only in marginal cases: we exclude few parties that would be accepted on other reasonable criteria.

(*b*) The numbers which go into the factor analysis are percentages – of the number of sentences referring to each policy area out of the total number of sentences in the programme. Sentences were counted rather than single words or phrases because we want to catch the stress laid on certain ideas and concerns rather than on slogans (the meaning of which may in any case vary across languages: 'ordre publique' has for example quite different connotations from the common law notion of 'public order'). Percentages were used rather than raw frequencies because we did not think that the constantly increasing length of election programmes – an almost mechanical tendency – should affect analyses of their internal concerns.

(*c*) Parties share different preoccupations across countries. Naturally a coding scheme which aims to capture such a wide variation has to cover all possibilities and thus to include categories which receive much attention in some places and none at all – or very little – in others. In the actual analysis, the inclusion of diminutive scores for categories which had no substantive importance for that country's politics would only add to the complexity of interpretation when the whole object was to simplify. Again therefore we adopted a general guideline that where a category received less than one per cent of mentions, on average, over the post-war period it should be dropped, unless its importance to one party (measured by having an average of 3 per cent of its references) justified retention. These are the 'exclusion/inclusion' rules referred to in the country chapters but obviously not described for each in detail. Again there are a few cases where country specialists argue for retention of a category in spite of this (e.g. importance in one particular election). Such cases are specifically made, where appropriate, in the chapters and allowed because we are more concerned with substantive significance than with mechanical generality. Category scores actually used for the factor analyses are referred to as 'qualifying variables' in subsequent chapters.

(*d*) As noted in Section 2.5, the standard categories fall fairly naturally into seven domains, within which tendencies and emphases can also be analysed. This feature of the coding also affects the factor analyses in that a first concern is to examine the cleavages and movements of parties within the substantive domains. We are more likely to get meaningful correlations and to uncover important attitudes structures by concentrating on 8–10 aspects of foreign affairs or 14 economic variables than by lumping together all 54 categories of domestic and foreign politics.

Each country chapter therefore presents a 'first-stage' factor analysis within each of the domains before going on to the general 'second-stage' analysis of the whole set of data.

(*e*) The division into domains has further effects on this second-stage factor analysis, in conjunction with another feature of the data – the limited number of cases for many countries. As this problem is central to our whole analytic strategy we devote a whole section to it below.

2.10 TWO-STAGE FACTOR ANALYSES

The limited number of cases available for analysis in some countries is not of course a limitation of our procedures but of objective reality. In the United States for example there *are* only two significant parties and nine Presidential elections from 1948 to 1980 giving 18 programmes as cases.

The problem this presents is that in any second-stage factor analyses using all 54 categories (or even excluding some of these), the number of variables will far exceed the number of cases. This disparity gives rise to dimensions which are highly unstable, grossly affected by the addition or removal of individual programmes. Because of this it is misleading to perform factor analyses where variables outnumber cases.

Of course such instability does not constitute a problem for the domain analyses, where even the most populous domain, economics, with 14 internal categories, still has less than the least number of cases available for analysis.

Given the other advantages of factor analysis as a data-summarizing technique, and its use in the domains analysis, we still wish to apply it to the second order analysis so as to get an overall 'picture' of party differences and movements. There are in fact a number of potential means to reduce the number of variables below the number of cases. Categories could be combined or collapsed in some way. The problem here, given the varying relevance of different categories for countries and parties, is that this would be carried out in individual and idiosyncratic ways, undermining the comparability of the data-set and hence of the analyses.

Given the internal homogeneity of the domains and the decision to carry out prior factor analyses, within them the obvious method of reducing the number of variables for second-stage analysis – while preserving comparability and still giving weight to country investigators' judgement – is to use dimensions from the separate domain analyses as variables for second-stage analysis. While the strategy is associated with the limited number of cases in some countries, it is a simplifying device which we might well have adopted in any case. A 'first-off' analysis of 54 categories of very different types would produce blurred results, very difficult to interpret.

Psychologists for this very reason have adopted an identical approach in their studies of attitudes and of intelligence. In Eysenck's (1971) work on personality, several batteries of tests were applied in questionnaires, each covering a particular area of attitudes. These were factor-analysed separately to examine the structure and reduce the complexity of the data. At the second stage, the factor scores from these primary analyses were used as a set of variables in their own right, and factor-analysed again. Thus the pursuit of a 'higher-order' or over-arching structure to personality, or to intelligence, is carried out on a much smaller and simpler set of variables than existed in the original data-set.

Following this technique, the leading two factors in each of our domains have been used to produce new variables fed into the second-stage factor analysis to get a simple description of the over-arching structure of party competition.

Normally 14 such constructed variables have been used; two from each domain. Exceptions occur in two cases:

(*a*) Where the internal structure of the domain is so simple as to generate only one dimension – which naturally is the only one we can use.

(*b*) Where owing to the operation of the exclusion rules, only one or two original categories remain in the domain. In that case the original percentage scores on these categories are fed into the second-stage analysis.

Though the second modification occurs frequently, our normal procedure is to use the two leading dimensions, ignoring others. Like all procedures, this has substantive implications. It means we ignore possible variations in importance between domains, and the possibility also that these occur also between countries. In the Netherlands and Belgium for example, the domain dealing with social structure is unusually important and in Ireland foreign policy is unusually unimportant.

A possible complication is therefore that by allowing each domain to contribute equally without taking country differences into account, we distort the final combined policy space. This assumes, however, that there *is* some kind of objective policy representation in terms of which ours can be judged to be distorted. On the contrary, no such representation exists: there are only differing representations with different kinds of bias built into them through their procedures and assumptions. As an example, consider an alternative solution using all dimensions produced by the domains analysis for the second-stage analysis. This gives most weight to domains which produce more dimensions. The fact that a domain has a more complex multi-dimensional structure does not, however, prove its objective importance: indeed it might be argued that its complexities have not been hammered smooth through discussion, so complexity indicates marginality. Obviously both arguments can be made. The point to emphasize is that no way exists of avoiding bias. The only possible reaction is to choose a representation – in full consciousness of its biases and of those of the alternatives – as best adapted for the overall analysis in hand.

As our purpose is above all to compare, there is an overwhelming case for following reasonably standard procedures. If we want for example to ask about the nature of basic cleavages in two or more countries, and foreign policy is important in one, we need to see how a dimension which includes it looks in the other. Only equal weighting of each domain allows that. This is also in line with our earlier decision to give equal treatment to each domain.

2.11 INTERPRETATION OF FACTOR-ANALYTIC RESULTS

Having discussed detailed applications, we should add some consider-ations about how we generally interpret factor analyses of this kind of data. To recapitulate, factor analysis is one among a number of techniques of interpretation which we apply, though obviously a central one. It gives us a highly abstracted simplification of underlying relationships as shown by the correlations amongst our set of variables. There is no 'objective', 'true' or 'correct' simplification, because any consistent set of linear additive equations can be fitted to a covariance matrix. Factor analysis is replete with 'options', with alternative computing procedures, with restrictions placed on the models and assumptions made. It is imperative to be clearly aware of these assumptions, but no set gives a uniquely 'true' account.

It is here that a substantive knowledge of each country's politics and the application of the analysis by a specialist is important. For the choice of the various options and assumptions has to be guided by a concern for what is relevant in the particular case; and even more importantly, the results thrown up by the factor analysis have to be interpreted in light of the substantive context. If the Belgian second-stage analysis did not produce a dimension of ethnic conflict for example we would be more inclined to question the technique rather than the fact that such a dimension exists. The substantive discussion which opens each of the country chapters is therefore an integral part of our investigation, not just a preface to the quantitative analysis.

The purpose of the factor analyses is thus to simplify usefully and relevantly. In doing so it inevitably ignores some aspects and conflates others. The most important distinction which it ignores is that between two different forms of variance in the data. The correlations on which our analysis is based can arise between a pair of variables in two basic ways. As a result one can think of the factors we derive as abstracting over 'time' and 'ideological space' simultaneously. Time can produce a correlation thus: suppose all parties in a system begin by ignoring both of two categories, and as time goes by, political pressure forces all the parties to increase the attention they give to both. The result will be a correlation between the two, because as the scores on one goes up, so do the scores on the other. The two variables go together because they are both a product of change in the society. Many of our chapters present factors like this, with dimensions that contrast 'new issues' with 'old issues'. It is a feature of recent politics that parties appear whose ideologies hang together because of their determined focus on concerns that have nothing to do with each other except that they have not previously been presented to the electorate, and are still ignored or rejected by larger established parties. Of course this is substantively important.

In saying our analyses also abstract over 'space' we mean one can treat a single variable (references to controlling the economy, for example) as a one-dimensional distance measure. The different scores on this variable by a Conservative and a Socialist party (high attention and therefore scores for the latter, low for the former) represent distancing on a sort of spatial dimension. A second variable may be logically, ideologically, or psychologically linked; for example welfare issues. This too represents a 'space' or 'distance measure' between the two parties. If a party gives a high score to one issue, it will give a high score to the other, and *vice versa*. Consequently the scores obtained by different parties will covary on the two variables, and the variables will be correlated.

Our model treats both these sources of variation as equivalent.

Usually *both* sources of correlation will be present simultaneously. Parties will alter their emphases in a similar way because of common reactions to social developments over time, *and* alter them differently as they compete with each other. The result is a model, often presented spatially, which averages over the whole time span, and over the election-specific changes due to synchronic competition.

This abstracting, or averaging, is deliberate (though it is unclear how it could be avoided anyway). We are indeed stipulating that, in some senses, the space of party competition is the same at the beginning, middle and end of our time period, though issue saliency will have changed. Purists may object to this, arguing for example that the presence of the Social Democrats and free-enterprise economics in the Britain of the eighties make it a different system from the simple two-party fight over the mixed economy and welfare state in 1945. Perhaps they are right, but that position is one that would ultimately prevent any over-time comparisons, not just factor-analytic ones. In fact people *do* see it as an intelligible question to ask 'Is the Labour party today further left than it was in 1945?' The response that this question cannot be asked is inadequate. Moreover, the results indicate that it *does* make sense to proceed this way.

One potential difficulty is that this approach may result in plotting into the factor space a set of parties of which some, as it were, never knew each other. In the Danish case, for example, parties that died by the mid-sixties, and those that were not born until 1973, are combined in analysis with those that continued to be important throughout the time period. The resulting 'map' of party positions can be shown to be highly stable and reliable, despite this curious abstraction. When we re-run the analysis using only the parties that existed throughout the time span, they turn out to be located in exactly the same positions in a space the substantive meaning of which is unchanged. The new and the old parties are located, with reference to the 'permanent' areas, where informed observers would put them when asked to think how they would be positioned had all thirteen parties competed in the same election.

Such confidence is not always possible, of course. The changes between the Fourth and the Fifth Republic in France were judged too great to allow an analysis of the whole 1945–1981 period, and only the Fifth Republic is covered. In Japan analysis starts from 1960. On the other hand in Northern Ireland an overriding concentration on the very existence of the State justified extending the analysis from 1922–73. In the vast majority of countries however the whole post-war era formed a natural and stable period both in the comparative context and in the judgement of country investigators.

Like all non-coding decisions, this initial judgement did not constitute a once-and-for all imperative for the rest of the investigation. It could be judged against results and brought up at continuing group meetings for comparative assessment. Where particular elections appeared as turning points (e.g. 1958 in Belgium or 1973 in Denmark), trends were examined before and afterwards for signs of differentiation. The fact that none appeared renders the choice of time period – at least in part – an inductive decision.

This is true also for the choice of factor-analytic methods. Besides the standard analyses many country authors tried out a variety of alternative approaches to their own data. Some of these are briefly mentioned in individual chapters, but lack of space precludes detailed description. The ones cited however are only the tip of the iceberg. For Northern Ireland (Chapter 8) practically every type of approach was tried because of the anomaly that a religious division never explicitly mentioned in the programmes appeared as a dominant feature of the spatial representation.

For West Germany (Chapter 14) time was controlled as a reaction to the overwhelming emergence of a new *vs.* old issue dimension. For the United States (Chapter 3) the analysis was run with and without programmes for the 1980 election.

The main point about the many alternative analyses was that none of them made any substantial difference to the results. As a result of this they are not generally reported and may be undervalued. In particular, because our report takes the form of a standard type of analysis replicated in each country, it may be thought that no adaptability to specific circumstances was allowed. The situation is entirely the opposite. In fact we have overwhelming validation for the comparative analysis through the coincidence of findings from other methods. All the evidence points to our results being robust and stable enough to survive most changes in the mode of factor-analytic representation.

2.12 PLAN OF DISCUSSION

These two introductory chapters of the book are followed by individual country reports, in rough progression from Anglo-Saxon democracies and countries directly influenced by them, through Scandinavia, the Low Countries, Germany and Austria, to France, Italy and Japan – large democracies with certain features of a dominant multi-party system in common. The juxtaposition of countries is to some extent arbitrary and not very important.

The first half of the final Chapter 18 reviews country findings (notably the unexpected emergence of a left–right dimension almost everywhere). The second half extends our comparative analysis to the integrated cross-national data-set and general features of party ideology.

While the general practice is to deal with each country in one chapter, there are two exceptions, owing to constraints of space and time. We go on immediately, in Chapter 3, to a parallel analysis of the United States, Britain, Australia and New Zealand. And in Chapter 9 we deal with our two Scandinavian countries, Denmark and Sweden, together. Practical considerations made it necessary to have multi-country chapters. The actual groupings are justifiable in that the countries analysed together share many elements of political culture and constitutional practice. The four Anglo-Saxon countries are all dominated by two major political parties. Sweden and Denmark have a similar type of multi-party system with a dominant Social Democratic party (certainly in a weaker position in Denmark). The analyses of each country's electoral programmes are carried on separately with unpooled data, so they are directly comparable with results reported in the single-country chapters.

Both multi-country and single-country chapters follow a fairly uniform

38 *Ian Budge*

internal plan. First they give a general description of politics with particular reference to the role of parties. Then they discuss the preparation and role of election programmes, go into sources and methods of collection, and describe physical format and coding. Quantitative analysis begins with the average percentage of sentences in the leading categories and domains and some discussion of trends since the war. First-stage factor analyses of each domain follow – usually summarized in a comprehensive table at the end of the section. A second-stage analysis of all the documentary material is then presented: emergent general dimensions are discussed in terms of correlations with the original categories used in the analysis as well as loadings of leading domain dimensions. Chapters close with a spatial representation of party movement over time on the main general dimensions, and assessments of this.

While each chapter also introduces its own material, their common format and unified treatment of general points should help readers find their way through the various national analyses, the backbone of the book, to which we now turn.

Notes

1 In terms of the actual 'factor-loadings' of categories on dimensions in the country analyses which follow, we have adopted .30 as the general level below which policy areas are not regarded as 'particularly associated'. However, this is a guideline to country analysis, not a hard and fast rule. Loadings somewhat below this point are considered, if they fit with the general pattern or reflect substantively important aspects of politics. In such cases, however, country analysts have to argue for the importance of the policy area.

CHAPTER 3

BRITAIN, AUSTRALIA, NEW ZEALAND AND THE UNITED STATES, 1946–1981: AN INITIAL COMPARATIVE ANALYSIS

——————— ∽ ———————

The bulk of this book presents separate analyses of fifteen democratic party systems, using a common methodology. We begin however, with a more compact study of four nations, sharing an 'Anglo-Saxon' political culture and a system of two dominant parties. Two (Britain and the United States) have already been analysed in detail using similar methodologies (Robertson 1976; Budge and Farlie, 1977, Chapter 11). So it has been established that the structure of party competition in Britain and the United States can usefully be examined through a saliency coding of party programmes subjected to Factor Analysis. The other two are frequently associated with an Anglo-Saxon political culture (Alford 1962) or treated as examples of the export of the 'Westminster Model' (Butler 1963), thus they permit a natural extension of the technique and approach.

3.1 POLITICAL PARTIES

Britain and the United States have so often been discussed as prototypes of the two-party competitive system or used as the starting point for a discussion of other systems that the leading features of their party politics need only be summarized here.

(i) American parties

The United States, though so familiar, has perhaps the most atypical parties and elections of all. Its parties have the oldest continuous history, dating in something like their present form to the 1860s. However, they have nothing like the developed ideology, centering around class, common to most other parties considered below: over the years the Democrats have emerged (with many exceptions) as defenders of peripheral regions, particularly the South, and of underprivileged groups – particularly recent

39

immigrants, and in a broader and vaguer sense, of the working class. The Republican Party, the only other contender for power, is most easily defined as *not* possessing these vague attributes.

There are, however, many inconsistencies and exceptions owing in part to the complexity of American society; but above all to the existence of a very strong Federal structure (Democrats and Republicans form a coalition of 50 state parties rather than unified national groups); and to the separation of powers at Federal level.

The separation of the Executive from Congress also implies the existence of separate Presidential and Congressional elections and parties, and considerable ambiguity about the relationships between them. Parties often seem to find their strongest expression in the psychological attachments of the electorate rather than in a particular institutional structure.

This is not to say, however, that leaders are indistinguishable in policy terms. The Budge and Farlie study showed that Democratic and Republican national platforms could never be easily confused. Democratic Presidents and Presidential candidates have usually been more liberal in their economic and welfare stances than their Republican counterparts – a difference which continued through to Reagan and Mondale in 1984, surviving the shift in campaign tactics from whipping up enthusiasm through party organizations (now heavily eroded) to more general television advertisements and appearances.

Periods of one party's dominance have alternated with those of its rival over the whole of the modern period. The radical coalition built by Roosevelt and centred around the New and Fair Deals (1932–52) slowly crumbled with the impact of booming prosperity under the Republican Eisenhower (1952–60). Kennedy and Johnson (1960–8) pushed welfare programmes even further and to some extent took up new issues such as environmentalism and technological progress. United States involvement in the Vietnam war thrust these concerns into the shade and aided Nixon's victory over the old New Dealer Humphrey in 1968 and the younger and radical McGovern in 1972. The lingering shadow of the Watergate scandal which forced Nixon's resignation in 1974 produced the conservative Democrat Carter's victory in 1976. A revival of neo-conservatism (economic orthodoxy, traditional morality and national strength) brought the Republicans back to power with Reagan in 1980 and 1984. Over the whole of this period Democrats have however tended to dominate the separate Congressional elections and most of the individual states.

(ii) British parties

In Britain strongly centralized national parties, aided by a unitary system in which the Executive is drawn from and depends on the party majority in the Lower House of the Legislature, and an absence of significant Federalism, have focused political attention on General Elections, called by the Prime Minister at irregular dates on the basis of party-strategic considerations. The Conservatives have a long history in various forms, but as a modern mass party they date back to the 1870s and 1880s. From then to the 1930s they were strengthened by the accession of various groups of Liberals, who thus added a new set of individualist and orthodox economic values, to a traditional rather paternalist ideology.

The other major party is Labour, founded in 1902 as a result of Trade Union initiatives and forming, at least in constructional theory, the political wing of a unified Labour movement. Organizationally, however, it is autonomous, with a well developed structure of branches in each constituency (like the Conservatives). Trade Unions have however continued to finance the party in large part, and play an important role in its annual Conference.

There is then a much more marked ideological difference between the parties than in the American case. Politically, the modern period starts with the massive nationalization and welfare measures initiated by the 1945–51 Labour governments. Conservative governments from 1951–64 accepted these, by and large, and towards the end of the period even began cautious experiments with State economic planning. A further feature of the whole period was the successful withdrawal from colonial and military commitments overseas and increasing concentration on the alliances covering Western Europe. The Labour leader Wilson won the 1964 election on the basis of new issues and expansionary appeals, but the government was then pressured into cuts and restrictive policies by a declining economic situation. The Conservative Heath began his period of office (after an unexpected election victory in 1970) as an advocate of private enterprise and Government disengagement from the economy. He was, however, forced into extensive economic intervention through the threat of massive industrial closures. Government regulation of incomes and prices in turn provoked miners' strikes in 1974 which resulted in election defeat. In the face of this, Britain's accession to the European Community seemed almost a side issue.

Growing economic difficulties again constrained Labour under Wilson and Callaghan to reverse their policies and turn to orthodox financing and massive cuts in Government expenditure (1974–9). This marked a decisive rupture in the acceptance of Keynesianism as the framework for the economic policies of both parties. No longer could it be maintained that Government could, and indeed, should, spend their way out of a recession and thus avoid massive unemployment. The tactic no longer seemed to work. The Conservatives under Mrs Thatcher, who won the elections of 1979 and 1983, therefore embraced financial orthodoxy.

Unusually, this produced well defined Conservative factions in the early years of the government. Divisions between out-and-out Socialism and Social Democracy (in the sense of a commitment to the Welfare State and positive economic planning) are much more a feature of the Labour Party, which has at times been immobilized by its internal struggles during periods of opposition.

Britain also differs from the United States in having substantial and recently growing third parties. Apart from strongly organized regional parties in Wales, Scotland and Northern Ireland, the Liberal party gained about 15 per cent of the vote in the 1970s. In alliance with the Social Democratic Party, it gained 26.4 per cent of the vote in the General Election of 1983, though the single member simple plurality constituency system limited the return in seats to about 4 per cent. These electoral successes are fragile however because they depend almost entirely upon the unattractiveness of the two leading contenders. Should Labour in particular regain its appeal it would once again attract most of the protest votes against the Government and reduce the Alliance to practical impotence. Only when the latter has actually penetrated Government can it hope to establish a positive image of its own.

(iii) New Zealand

The same holds true for the minor Australian parties (the Country Party of course is a different proposition) and for New Zealand Social Credit. The latter is a populist party with a somewhat hazy economic policy but strong on new issues such as environmentalism. It grew strongly in the seventies and eighties – again in response to the negative image of both main parties.

The origins of New Zealand parties are similar to those of the British parties, their development having in any case been decisively affected by the attachments and practices carried over by immigrants (almost exclusively British until the middle of the post-war period). The framework has been different, however, as New Zealand developed an advanced Welfare State at a much earlier stage. As a primary food producer it has also been dependent on international trading conditions rather than being able to shape them. There is less to nationalize and Labour has never encouraged serious interference with the medium-sized family farms which constitute the backbone of the economy.

All this has resulted in a blurring of differences between the National Party (conservative) and the Labour Party, with greater concentration on the personality of the Prime Ministerial candidate. During the prosperous 1950s and 1960s the National Party under Holyoake generally won the three-year fixed elections, held under a British type of system. Labour, however, won in 1957 and 1972. By that time the effects of the first world oil crisis and British entry to the EEC, with restrictions on New Zealand exports, weighed heavily on the government. The National Party, under the abrasive and eccentric leadership of Muldoon, won heavily in 1975, and scraped in even with high unemployment, in 1978 and 1981. Labour at last pulled themselves together and ousted their rivals in 1984, again inheriting an economic recession with a consequent need for measures of austerity.

(iv) Australia

The modern Australian party system took shape only at the start of our period, when the Liberal Party reformed itself (1944). It has, however, predecessors stretching well back into the nineteenth century, who generally represented the interests of the various constituent States. The Australian Labor Party was also formed in the States during the 1890s. As in New Zealand the parties were heavily influenced by the ideas and activities of British immigrants and share most structural features of British parties.

Major differences appear however in the moderately strong Federal structure: in the sustained prosperity of a country rich in the most basic and almost most rare materials, especially minerals; and in the existence of an agrarian party, the Country Party, formed in 1922 as the political vehicle of primary producers and rural residents. For the post-war period the Country Party has been in permanent alliance with the Liberals.

The period opened with the reforming Labor government of Chifley. This was succeeded for the whole of the fifties and early sixties by the Liberal-Country coalition headed by Menzies. In most areas of life this had very much a *laissez-faire* attitude, but shared a consensus on the need for fairly advanced welfare measures. The government very astutely exploited cold war fears with tales of Communism in the docks and in essential industries, aided by the Labor leader Evatt's sympathy with Radicals and with China.

As a result the growing Southern European immigrant community split from the Labor Party to form the Democratic Labor Party under the influence of Conservative Catholic Bishops. By encouraging its supporters to give their second votes to the government under the complicated preferential voting system, Labor was effectively kept out. Menzies' successors did not manage the system so well, Labor reformed itself under Whitlam, Democratic Labor practically disappeared and Australian involvement in Vietnam was unpopular. Whitlam came to power in 1972 and won again in 1974. His inept handling of government and the ruthless blocking tactics employed by the new Liberal leader Fraser forced a new election which the latter won along with two subsequent ones until he lost to the new Labor leader in 1983.

(v) Two-party dominance

While some tendencies such as recent neo-conservatism are common to the politics of all four countries, there are obvious structural and cultural differences. One underlying common feature however is the dominance of the two leading parties, whatever the distribution of votes. Major parties set the tone and issues of political debate, to which minor parties react. While they may effectively aid a major party – like the Democratic Labor Party – or gather protest votes against it, they are unable to develop a sustained general appeal of their own. This point assumes importance in Section 3.3. For the moment, however, we turn to a consideration of the election documents produced within the context we have described.

3.2 ELECTION PROGRAMMES AND THEIR PREPARATION

(i) United States

Historically, U.S. party platforms were the first general appeals to the electorate to be drafted on behalf of the organized group seeking political power. They thus constitute almost a prototype of the way mass parties set about preparing and propagating them. Platforms are written for each presidential election campaign, normally by the Resolutions Committee of the National Convention of party delegates assembled primarily to elect, or at least to ratify, the party's Presidential nominee. The Committee hears testimony from interested groups many of which have a traditional affiliation with the party. The positions of the latter will be incorporated into the platform, plus those of any non-partisan tendency which might enhance the document's general appeal. On occasions, such as 1972, interest groups may be allowed to transmit appeals in their own words, though few platforms go so far as the Democratic programme of that year and include whole transcripts of committee hearings. The platform also, of course, includes references to traditional party positions and to currently fashionable topics of concern (such as conservation). Pledges of specific action are rare compared to emphases on the importance of an area and on the past party's record with references to such an area.

The platform is the authoritative statement of party policies for the current election. Delegates value it highly enough to fight provisions to a direct vote in the Convention, when satisfactory compromises cannot be obtained; and even on occasions to leave the party when defeated (as Southern delegates did over the Civil Rights plank in the Democratic platform of 1948). Where a presidential nominee has fully established his position prior to the Convention he is likely to control proceedings in the

Resolutions Committee through his nominees, or even to present a substantially final draft to the Committee for approval. (Roosevelt's draft of 1936 is said to have had only one sentence altered!) The realities of the drafting process are therefore, that it is less open than a formal description might imply. In terms of content, tighter central control may not make a great difference: delegates and candidate both wish to secure party victory, so they will both seek to consolidate interest group support, gloss over controversial issues and renew traditional popular emphases.

After approval by the full Convention, post-war platforms are issued as a substantial booklet in a glossy cover. There has been a steady secular increase in length to the platforms of the seventies and eighties which consist of 80–100 quite closely printed pages of good quality approaching a thin paperback. Recent plaforms are widely available commercially, and through party sources, though with a document of such length it would be difficult (and even counterproductive) to arrange for household circulation. They reach ordinary electors mainly through press and television coverage.

(ii) Britain

In contrast to United States platforms, British national manifestos – although intended to fulfill essentially the same purposes, have never been the product of a representative meeting of party members. With the stronger permanent organization of the British parties, their annual delegate conferences and the uncertainty of the election date, they have rarely had the time or opportunity to hold a special pre-election conference. In the Conservative and Liberal parties, manifestos developed out of the Party Leader's election address to his own constituency, which he fights like any other M.P. As late as 1950 Churchill seems to have written the Conservative party manifesto largely by himself. Most usually the Conservative manifesto is drafted by a small nominated committee of senior political figures under the Party Chairman, on the basis of specialized reports in various areas prepared by the Research Department. This then goes to the Leader and the Cabinet or Shadow Cabinet for approval. Very often the actual manifesto has been anticipated by strategy programmes published up to two or three years previously. While the theoretical control exercised by the Conservative leader markedly differentiates the drafting process from that of American platforms, its connection with earlier programmes (widely discussed and debated), the necessity of appealing to clear interests, not to mention the frequent control of a presidential nominee over the drafting process, all serve to make them resemble each other more closely.

In theory Labour's manifesto is prepared more democratically, by the

National Executive Committee of the Party Conference in conjunction with the leaders of the Labour legislators. Since the two have been increasingly at loggerheads over the last 20 years, the Party Leader has largely imposed his own version on the Joint Drafting Committee – by holding the formal meeting in the month before the election when pressures for unity and quick acceptance of his draft are at their maximum. In this way the specifically Socialist programmes of the National Executive Committee have been watered down, sometimes to invisibility. As a result the question of control of the manifesto was one of the questions dividing the Labour Party in the early eighties. While Conference has re-asserted the authoritative position of the National Executive Committee, it remains an open question as to who will actually take control under the pressures of a campaign. Although Labour manifestos have up to now been almost totally drafted by the Prime Minister's personal associates, they do of course, like the more widely based Conservative and American documents, reflect the imperatives of attracting electoral support – and hence reassure Labour's traditional supporters, by referring to suitable issues, and glossing over internal disputes, just like the others.

Physically British manifestos are shorter than United States platforms – some 20–30 printed pages – although they too have increased substantially in length over time. Baldwin's 1931 manifesto is a mere page. There has been an accompanying progression from badly printed, paper covered pamphlets to glossy covered booklets with good quality reproduction. Manifestos are printed only in the month before the election. They are available from bookshops and even newspaper shops at a price, circulate widely to party activists and opinion-makers and can readily be obtained – often free – from party sources. They are not, however, handed to ordinary electors when they are canvassed for support (a function performed in Britain by the individual Parliamentary candidates' election address, a one or two page sheet which selectively reproduces bits of the manifesto, along with messages tailored to local conditions; see Robertson (1976, pp. 134–56) for a detailed analysis of these for two elections). The manifesto also reaches electors through the press conferences held to launch it, and through its influence over media discussion.

(iii) New Zealand

The general resemblance of New Zealand party documents to the British conceals detailed differences, often reflecting Australian and American influences. The generally fixed dates for elections (effectively every three years) gives time for fuller consultation of party representative bodies and for a very full working out of policy, which is in fact detailed in supporting, specialized booklets often directed to specific groups such as the young;

and available on demand. The layout of the document is unique. Until the 1970s manifestos were in a reference-type format enabling one to look up policy on particular points. These 'planks' began first with a broad statement of policy in the area concerned (one or two sentences) and were then followed by the 'details' – intended to flesh out and to specify the broad policy contained in the first part. This is of interest, as in the absence of original documents we had to use newspaper reports of the manifesto in some cases (see Appendix A). It is clear that these gave the basic policy planks without the details – which accounts for their shorter length.

The manifestos themselves are long (typically about 1,000 quasi-sentences) and getting longer. The quality of production has improved from cyclostyled, loose-leaved documents to attractive glossy booklets. Print runs averaged about 650,000 in the early 1960s which would imply that they were intended for distribution to every family. Newspapers carry extensive reports and summaries of the policy content, and these and television are probably the means through which party messages reach most members of the general public. Manifestos are 'announced' and summarized by the party leader at a major rally at the outset of each election campaign in the manner analogous to the leader's 'Policy speech' in Australia (see below).

The exact documentary sources for our study are listed in Appendix A, so readers can see what type of document forms a basis for the analysis in particular elections. Comparisons between actual manifestos, and news-paper reports for elections where both were available, show that the distribution of sentences is similar, though necessarily shorter, in the latter case (for the reasons explained above). We have no reason to think therefore that the use of (extensive) newspaper summaries causes undue distortion, either in the case of New Zealand or of the two Irelands (Chapters 7 and 8 below), where similar problems are confronted.

(iv) Australia

Australia shows stronger divergences from the British model, reflected in the nature and presentation of the election programmes. There are problems even with the notion of a manifesto in the Australian case. Party platforms are long and detailed documents, e.g. the Liberal platform of 1974 had 240 pages and 140,000 words. They are usually attempts to clarify the 'philosophy' of the party, drawn up by a committee and, in the case of the A.L.P. ratified by a full convention (held federally every two years, and annually in the States). The problem is that the Liberals have written only two platforms since World War II – in 1946 and 1974 – and hence these are useless for studying variations in policy. On the other hand there is a superfluity of (often personal) policy statements at election time.

The really authoritative statement is made in the election policy speech of the Party Leader. This is prepared and written by a small committee of M.P.s and normally delivered in person to the party faithful (accompanied by a handful of robust and defiantly Australian hecklers), who are also presented with an abridged version. A general failure to obtain full copies of leaders' policy statements – in many cases the party officers could not lay hands on one – has necessitated using newspaper reports or the parties' own abridged versions. The Australian data then, consists of these reports – one from each of the opening of thirteen electoral campaigns from 1946–80.

(v) Coding

The (quasi-) sentences of all the source documents described were counted into the 54 standard categories summarized in Section 2.5 above and listed in Appendix B. Coding for Australia, New Zealand and the United States was sub-contracted and checked in detail by Hearl. The U.S. codes were also checked personally by the latter against the earlier coding by Budge of platforms from 1922–76. Extensive agreement was found. All British manifestos were independently coded twice and often three times by different individuals and compared statistically. The results were satisfactory but are too complex to be presented here. A full report is given in the associated microfiche (Appendix C).

3.3 DATA-ANALYSIS

A preliminary point relates to the presentation and form of the analysis below, which is already very complex from attempting (through publishing necessities) a parallel exposition of results for four countries. It is obviously clearer where, as in the United States, we have to deal only with two parties.

Presentational convenience would not justify leaving out British Liberals, Australian Democratic Labor and New Zealand Credit. But there are substantive grounds for doing so, modifying the general criterion for the selection of parties (Section 3.1 above), and so producing a clearer presentation:

(*a*) The New Zealand Social Credit Party has an ideological approach so far from the accepted terms of political argument in that country that its inclusion would produce what in a broader sense is a distortion of results (cf. Chap. 11 where a similar point is made about Belgian Nationalists in their earlier days). Inclusion would make New Zealand seem radically different from the others when, in its basis, it is actually similar. Of course this is not an *a priori* judgement. Analyses with and without the party have been compared. Here, however, for the reasons given, only the analysis involving the two major parties is reported.

(*b*) Exactly the opposite holds for British Liberals and Australian Democratic Labor. Their inclusion and exclusion make no difference to the analyses except for fudging the results a little. Again the judgement is based on a comparison of the actual results from parallel data-analyses. The 'fudging' comes from the fact that these smaller parties have greater latitude to make idiosyncratic policy variations.

These are points which would hold in the absence of presentational considerations. However they do reinforce them. The underlying conclusion from comparing analyses is that the minor parties are irrelevant to the mainstream debate. They do not influence it because they either place themselves quite outside or, if they are inside, have to follow the lead of the major parties. Our data-analyses therefore reinforce the conclusion from Section 3.1 that these countries have basically two-party competition and that our discussion should focus on it. (We do, however, include the Country Party in Australia as, in effect, now the agricultural faction of the Liberals. Were it to be excluded from actual politics, the Liberals themselves would have to voice established rural interests in their manifestos.)

Our presentation therefore covers two parties in the United States, Britain and New Zealand; and three in Australia. Although we compare these countries, each is analysed separately. We have not pooled the scores on each variable, because we do not wish to foreclose the question of whether these are so dissimilar as not to have a sufficiently close identity of meaning across countries to permit an aggregate approach. This point is assessed in Chapter 18 on the basis of the various national analyses.

For all analyses we use the standardized exclusion rules mentioned in Section 2.9, by which a variable (i.e. any category of the overall coding frame) is entered only if it has an overtime average percentage of mentions of at least 1 per cent for the whole country. This is qualified in that a variable can stay in if it is unusually important for a particular party. Party importance is operationalized, arbitrarily, at an average of 3 per cent over time for that party. These rules were applied separately to each of the countries in this chapter, so that in this respect too the analyses are specific and individual.

The essential similarity of these 'Anglo-Saxon' political cultures is shown by the overlap in variables qualifying for analysis. Only seven variables are included for one country and not for the others. One of these, (references to the European Community) is not applicable to the non-European nations. The others are accounted for by peculiarities of the U.K. and the U.S. In the former case, the British Labour Party's concentration on government control of the economy, or outright nationalization, leads to the related variables entering the British analysis. America's inevitably stronger focus on foreign affairs leads to both decolonization and opposition to military expenditure attaining significance. In addition appeals to 'Traditional Morality' as a route to social cohesion attain significance in the United States but not elsewhere.

TABLE 3.1

SUMMARY OF MAJOR ISSUES IN FOUR COUNTRIES

(MEAN PERCENTAGES OVER ALL MANIFESTOS FOR EACH COUNTRY AND PARTY OF LEADING TEN TOPICS)

ISSUE	U.K.			U.S.			AUS.				N.Z.		
	COMBINED	CON	LAB	COMBINED	REP	DEM	COMBINED	LIB	CP	ALP	COMBINED	NAT	NZLP
FOREIGN SPECIAL RELATIONS													
MILITARY	2.5			4.1	4.7		3.6	6.2					
PEACE	3.5	3.2	3.8	5.5	8.2								
INTERNATIONALISM		3.0		6.2	6.0	6.3			3.6				2.8
GOVERNMENT EFFICIENCY				3.5		3.8							
GOVERNMENT AUTHORITY							4.8	5.9	3.6	4.9			
FREE ENTERPRISE		3.0			3.7			4.8	2.5			3.8	
INCENTIVES	2.3	3.5								5.6	5.3	5.4	5.1
REGULATION OF CAPITALISM			3.4			3.8				3.5	4.5		7.0
ECONOMIC PLANNING													
PROTECTIONISM									3.5				
SPECIFIC ECONOMIC GOALS	3.5	4.0	3.1			3.8	4.3		2.1	7.4	6.3	5.2	6.9
PRODUCTIVITY	2.8	2.9							1.8		8.9	10.0	7.7
TECHNOLOGY				5.5	4.3	6.6	4.2	4.3	6.2	3.8			
CONTROLLED ECONOMY			3.0										
NATIONALIZATION	2.5		3.8										
ECONOMIC ORTHODOXY		2.9		4.0	4.5						2.4		2.4
ENVIRONMENTAL PROTECTION						4.6							
ART, SPORT, LEISURE, MEDIA	3.9		5.2								2.6	3.6	
SOCIAL JUSTICE	6.1	5.0	7.3										
SOCIAL SERVICES	3.3	3.4				4.2	4.0	3.8		7.4	10.4	7.8	13.0
EDUCATION		2.9	3.2							4.5	6.1	5.2	6.9
LAW AND ORDER												3.0	
NATIONAL EFFORT						4.6	4.6	4.6	5.6	3.7			
LABOUR GROUPS			3.0	4.8	5.1	4.6	8.5	9.4	2.0	13.6			
AGRICULTURE & FARMERS	2.4			5.1	5.5	4.7	13.5	6.1	29.2	6.2	9.2	7.2	11.1
UNDERPRIVILEGED MINORITIES				3.4									
NON-ECONOMIC GROUPS				7.8	6.9	8.7	3.8	4.9		5.0	9.6	11.4	7.7

Table 3.1 suggests from a different perspective that this impression of inter- and intra-national consensus may be overdone. It forms the standard report, repeated in all the country chapters, of the ten most important categories for each party. This is a rough but powerful way of considering the salience of issues in party competition. There are 28 categories that get into at least one party's 'top ten', and they overlap relatively little. Omitting the Australian Country Party to avoid an element of double counting, we find that out of a possible maximum of eight mentions, only seven categories are of sufficient inter- and intra-national salience to get into more than four party lists. Even this over-emphasizes the degree of consensus if that is to have any theoretically important meaning. One of the seven, Internationalism, comes from the foreign affairs domain where the categories are somewhat 'blunt' ideologically, and may have different implications in different contexts. Three more categories come from the social groups domain and do no more than confirm that in these four pluralist societies many feel the need to say something or other about protecting farmers, Labour and Non-economic Social Groups. It may be more interesting that Britain, almost certainly the least pluralist of the countries, does not make either category a priority for any political party. The other three common references are indeed to basic policies – Social Services and Education, and the (uncontroversial) need to develop the technological and infrastructural elements of the economy. Apart from these, selective and rather exclusive emphases dominate the table. Such a finding does of course accord nicely with our underlying saliency theory of competition.

3.4 FIRST-STAGE FACTOR ANALYSIS OF DOMAINS

(i) External relations

We turn now to compare, as far as possible, the structure of party ideology inside each of the broad subject domains identified in our work. The first such domain, External Relations, is a good test for the existence of common concerns. On the one hand the four countries concerned are all 'developed' Western societies, and part of the same broad international alliance. However they differ enormously in power, and their geopolitical context.

The Australian structure for Foreign Affairs is remarkably simple. Only three variables qualify; those covering mentions of Foreign Special Relations (in these cases, with Britain and the United States), Military Expenditure and Internationalism, they load respectively at .92, .56 and .47, and produce a single factor which accounts for 60 per cent of the overall variance. The factor refers to the general question of whether Australia should have a world politics role at all. It is unipolar with its character at one end set by a stress on the need for Australia to have an internationalist rather than isolationist perspective, to have the military force to back such a role, and especially a need to keep up its membership in the Western alliance. Highly supportive of this as a real result and no artefact is its mirroring in New Zealand. Here the same three variables qualify. The structure is slightly more complex, because their intercorrelations produce two significant factors, (though the second, with an Eigenvalue of 1.06, is only marginally significant). Together the two factors account for 86 per cent of the variance. The first is more or less identical to Australia's one dimension – all three variables load positively, though it is the Military category that has the highest loading (.84) with the other two roughly equal (Internationalism, .49; Foreign Special Relations, .43). Again the obvious question of whether small South Pacific nations ought to have a conventional, Western oriented role in world politics appear as a unipolar factor. The second factor in New Zealand's case indeed raises the question explicitly. Should their role be confined to support for the traditional allies (Britain and NATO), or should it be more oriented to the United Nations? The factor reflects this with a zero loading on the Military variable, and opposed equal loadings of .54 and −.51 for, respectively, Foreign Special Relations and Internationalism. The resemblance to Australia is comforting for the validity of this comparative analysis, and the actual results are plausible because of their close relationship to the real problems confronting these countries.

The results in the U.S. and U.K. understandably reflect a more complex underlying structure, and, in the U.S. considerably greater importance for Foreign Affairs in general. The American results are so important and relatively complex that they are summarized in Table 3.2

One could not expect these domains to be easily comparable between the U.S. and the U.K., partly because of Britain's inevitable interest in the EEC, and partly because of the centrality of the U.S. in world affairs. Structurally, however, the two analyses are not dissimilar, with five qualifying variables for the U.K. and six for the U.S., producing solutions in three factors and two respectively. These account for just over 60 per cent of the variance in both cases. Though in neither case are interpretations easy, a little reflection on their political context puts flesh on the abstractions of the variable labels and gives meaning to the structures.

In the British case the first (varimax-rotated) factor (1) is heavily loaded by the EEC category (.83), and is probably unipolar. To the extent that it does have an opposite pole with loadings of −.46 and −.37 for Peace and Foreign Special Relations, it becomes a contrast between an American-oriented Special Relationship with involvement in world problems of peace, and the more inward looking European identity recently emphasized by British politicians. The second factor seems clearly to be a

TABLE 3.2

THE FOREIGN POLICY DOMAIN: U.S.A.

TWO FACTORS:
FACTOR 1 EIGENVALUE = 2.13   % OF VARIANCE = 36%
FACTOR 2 EIGENVALUE = 1.41   % OF VARIANCE = 24%

VARIABLE	FACTOR 1.1	FACTOR 1.2
FOREIGN SPECIAL RELATIONS	-.311	-.628
DECOLONIZATION	.556	.376
MILITARY (POSITIVE)	.780	-.522
MILITARY (NEGATIVE)	-.470	.638
PEACE	-.803	-.110
INTERNATIONALISM	.499	.430

'NATO' dimension, giving high loadings (.73 and .67) to 'Military' and again to Foreign Special Relations.

There is a third factor, not used in the rest of the analysis, best described as 'Peaceful Internationalism' from its two loadings, on Peace and Internationalism, of .46 and .67.

Both American dimensions oppose positive and negative attitudes to military expenditure and strength. Associated with support for the military on the first factor are Internationalism (i.e. involvement overseas as opposed to isolationism) and Decolonization (which in the post-war situation has incorporated many references, in the United States, to Soviet Imperialism in Eastern Europe). Associated with negative attitudes to the military are support for peace and Foreign Special Relationships. Apart from this last loading the dimension interprets easily as support for a strong international role based on military strength, against a de-emphasis of the military as the best way of reducing international tensions. Foreign Special Relations come in because a more pacific international role is also commended as improving relations with Latin America.

The second dimension reverses the clusterings to a considerable extent, associating foreign special relationships with support for the military in opposition to military de-emphases, internationalism and decolonization. The change in variables associated with different attitudes to the military is explained by the fact that each also picks up a set of rather different emphases from those highlighted in the first dimension. Thus decolonization also reflects American opposition to West European colonialism and to direct U.S. intervention in Latin America. Once this is seen the dimension becomes the familiar contrast between Hawks and Doves, i.e. full military support for allies opposed to a de-emphasis for the military role overseas, support for the international bodies dedicated to peaceful solutions, and a renunciation of dominance relations between one country and another. This second dimension is not in essence so very different from the first. The fact that both centre around a contrast between forceful as opposed to peaceful international strategies, reflects the centrality of the issue for the leader of the Western alliance. Had the coding scheme allowed for finer distinctions inside non-military categories this might well have become clearer.

(ii) Freedom and democracy

There is no domain two (covering concern for Democracy, Freedom, Rights, etc.) in any of the countries. However much argument about such matters may concern commentators and theorists, they are not of great partisan salience. Only one or two variables at most qualify by our exclusion rules (in New Zealand none), and those that do can enter directly into the later stages of analysis.

(iii) Government

Nor does domain three, dealing with questions of the nature of government, require factoring to produce a simple structure in the two unitary countries. Only the two federal societies whose governmental structure is inevitably more complicated, have enough qualifying variables. In Australia there are three, covering the needs for Decentralization, concern for Government Efficiency and Government Effectiveness and Authority. To these is added for the U.S., a variable dealing with Corruption in Government, a long term American concern and not purely a 'Watergate variable'.

In Australia the Efficiency and Authority variables are counterposed, loading at respectively .43 and $-.41$ on the first factor, and representing an apparent contrast between Efficiency and Authority. Changing emphases by Australian parties at the time of the sacking of the Whitlam government by the Governor-General highlight the general question of the legitimacy of forceful government action at the federal level which is not actually a question of 'states rights' in the usual sense. There appear to be contrasting orientations to the nature of central government power. However, a contrast between Federal and State levels comes up as the second factor, loading at .35 on Decentralization, with a slight negative loading of $-.25$ for Government Authority. The two factors between them account for 73 per cent of the variance.

America, with the one extra variable, nonetheless has a simpler, one dimensional structure explaining 41.2 per cent of the variance, which combines the contrast between Federation and States with that between efficiency and authority.

TABLE 3.3

SUMMARY OF FACTOR ANALYSES IN ECONOMIC DOMAIN

COUNTRY:	U.S.		U.K.		N.Z.		AUSTRALIA	
FACTOR:	1	2	1	2	1	2	1	2
EIGENVALUE	2.98		3.48	1.58	2.68	2.21	1.95	1.35
% OF VARIANCE EXPLAINED	50%		35%	16%	25%	25%	22%	15%
VARIABLE:								
401 FREE ENTERPRISE	-.900	-	.871	.160	-.174	-.643	-.319	.395
402 INCENTIVES	-	-	.690	.423	-.848	.338	.358	.091
403 REGULATION OF CAPITALISM	.648	-	-.568	-.047	.356	.514	.351	-.283
404 ECONOMIC PLANNING	-	-	-.494	.098	.549	.652	.295	-.061
406 PROTECTIONISM	-	-	-	-	.273	.274	-.012	.098
408 SPECIFIC ECONOMIC GOALS	.724	-	.078	-.709	-.345	-.092	.476	-.104
410 PRODUCTIVITY	-	-	.038	.342	.283	-.132	.182	.840
411 TECHNOLOGY AND INFRASTRUCTURE	.671	-	.175	-.328	.505	-.509	-.019	.039
412 CONTROLLED ECONOMY	-	-	-.518	-.178	-	-	-	-
413 NATIONALIZATION	-	-	-.644	.461	-	-	-.8?(	-
414 ECONOMIC ORTHODOXY	-.884	-	.753	-.139	-.420	.426	-	-.125

(iv) Economy

Economic Policy is the most complex domain in all four countries. Though we only discuss the first two factors in each solution, rather more are in fact present. The Australian case requires four factors to explain 61 per cent of the variance and the U.K. needs four for 73 per cent. New Zealand, with only two, and the U.S. where only one factor is required show a much simpler structure. The details of the one or two most important are given in Table 3.3. A simple picture emerges of conflict among classic Left/Right terms, once one takes account of the constitutional and political cultures.

The American political parties compete, in economic policy terms, along a single bipolar dimension, measured by five variables, which accounts for almost 60 per cent of the variance. It is a pure *laisser-faire* dimension, with Free Enterprise and Economic Orthodoxy (which means, in the U.S. context, mainly balanced budgets) opposed to Regulation of Capitalism (i.e. the creation of semi-autonomous regulatory commissions like the C.A.B. or the F.C.C.), Technology and Infrastructure, and Specific Economic Goals. This latter can mean many things, but the point is that deliberate pursuit of *any* economic target by the Federal Government is opposed to *laisser-faire*.

The solution given in the table for the U.K. is the unrotated one, (from which the resulting factor scores are, deliberately, derived!). It is a beautifully clear picture of British economic policy debate. The first factor, accounting for 35 per cent of the overall variance and almost half of the explained variance, is a classic Left/Right clash, with Free Enterprise, Incentives and Economic Orthodoxy *vs.* Regulation of Capitalism, Planning, Economic Controls, and Nationalization. Within the second factor a stress on Economic Goal Attainment and on 'neutral' mechanisms (specific economic goals and technology and infrastructure) is contrasted to Economic Ideology *per se*, with both Incentives and Nationalization equally weighted at the negative end. This is a prime example of where a rotated solution, by separating out this opposition, actually hides a true result – much British economic debate has indeed been a striving after goal attainment and a 'plague on both your houses' approach to economic ideology. These are the two factors to be used in the second-stage analysis. The remaining two not shown in the table are simple loadings with single variables, repeating familiar themes – factor three is about productivity, factor four about the need to redevelop the economy, with its stress again on technology.

For New Zealand analysis produces two roughly equal factors explaining 61 per cent of the variance. The first factor contrasts two classic 'right-wing' economic symbols, Incentives and Economic Orthodoxy with Technology and Infrastructure and, less important, Productivity. Thus one pole clearly represents a Conservative position of relying on rational pursuit of interests and strict orthodox economic policies, as opposed to government intervention to increase productivity and modernize the economy. Direct opposition between conservative and socialist economic theory comes rather in the second factor, which opposes Free Enterprise directly to Economic Planning and Regulation of Capitalism.

The first Australian dimension is again a straightforward Left/Right clash, especially as it is dominated by one very powerful loading of $-.88$ for Economic Orthodoxy. This is the only variable loading above 0.5 and hence dominates the dimension. It is associated with a much weaker emphasis on free enterprise and contrasted with pursuit of Specific Economic Goals and Regulation of Capitalism, presumably because they involve intervention of a kind. With allowance made for the dominance of economic orthodoxy in Australia, this result is very similar to that from the United States.

It must be remembered that the Federal structure of both polities makes a much wider range of central government intervention politically significant than would be the case in Europe. Indeed in Australia, there is a High Court ruling that Nationalization by the Commonwealth Government is unconstitutional. One should see the inclusion of Incentives, normally a conservative ideological category, in this light, along with Regulation of Capitalism in opposition to Orthodoxy. To the extent that Incentives involve tax reductions, they can indeed offend against Orthodoxy, the prime element of which is a strict insistence on balanced budgets. The second Australian dimension is really a unipolar and single category stress on Productivity (buttressed by free enterprise) reminiscent of the second factor in the U.K. solution.

Overall, the emergence of clear left–right dimensions even in the United States and across all four countries foreshadows their strong emergence in the second-stage solutions and in the whole comparative context.

(v) Welfare

Welfare policies in the later, if not immediate, post-war world tend to be noncontroversial in terms of content, but vitally important in terms of relative stress and salience. Very similar findings emerge in all our countries which can be briefly summarized as involving an emphasis on expenditure in this area generally, and an opposition between expenditure on old areas of concern like the social services, and new ones like culture, respectively, education comes somewhere between. This opposition could be interpreted as one between industrial and post-industrial values, using terms drawn from the popular thesis of the seventies.

The details of the analyses are as follows:

In New Zealand, three factors collectively account for 76 per cent of the variance. The first has a very strong positive loading for Art, Sport, Leisure, Media at .93, with a low one for Environment (.35), contrasted with −.50 for Social Services. The second factor is unipolar and univariate (Education .78).

In Australia the first factor in a two factor solution (accounting together for 65 per cent of the variance) is unipolar – Education at .78, and Social Services at .67. The second factor contrasts Environmental Protection at .46 (with a mild loading for Education again) with a negative (−.31) loading for the 'traditional' welfare value of Social Service Expansion.

For the U.K. there is a two dimensional solution which accounts for 57 per cent of the variance. The first factor is a general one with Education dominating (.69) supported by Art, Sport, Leisure and Media (.49) and Social Service Expansion (.38). The second factor has only the single variable Environmental Protection (.73).

America has a similar first dimension dominated by support for Social Services and Education, but adds to that combination, not Arts, Sport, Leisure and Media, which is of particular constitutional complexity, but Environmental Protection. The second dimension, accounting in the unrotated version for about half as much variance as the first, contrasts Arts, Sports, Leisure and Media with Social Justice. In both rotated and unrotated solutions the dominance of the Social Justice variable is so great as to render the dimension essentially unipolar. In line with general patterns elsewhere we can see a conflict existing over the resources needed to establish some degree of Social Justice for the badly-off, and a general improvement of quality of life for whole populations.

(vi) Social Fabric

Social Fabric is, to some extent, a rag-bag for policy concerns roughly linked to Social Stability. In fact it does not exist as problematic at all in New Zealand (only Law and Order, unproblematic in itself, reaches the inclusion level), nor in Australia, where only the occasional appeal is heard for National Effort and Social Harmony.

The domain does exist in both the older countries, and it is perhaps surprising that multi-ethnic and Federal Australia, like the U.S. a country of European immigrants, does not have it.

By the very nature of the amorphous but culturally important subjective meanings we attempt to capture in the coding categories here, interpretation becomes more a matter of *verstehen* than elsewhere. In fact perfectly sensible structures emerge for both countries, but it is harder than usual to compare them or to know whether essentially similar or rather different factors emerge as characterizing party competition. However, satisfactory and structurally similar solutions occur in both countries, with two-dimensional structures accounting for 70 per cent of the variance. In the U.K. however only three variables appear in the analysis: National Way of Life, Law and Order, and Social Harmony. The first factor, which explains 51 per cent of all the variance by itself, is a very straightforward Social Discipline dimension, with roughly equal loadings on Law and Order (.75) and National Effort–Social Harmony (.71). The second is loaded only by National Way of Life at .37.

The American two-factor solution (with 74 per cent explained variance and Eigenvalues of 1.69 and 1.28 respectively) has an additional variable – an appeal to the virtues of Traditional Morality. Even if the Moral Majority as a movement has only recently become noticeable it represents a long-standing tradition especially in the Bible-belt.

The American factors in their rotated form are easy to interpret. The first, contrasts National Way of Life (−.57) with Law and Order (.78) and National Effort and Harmony (.76). It probably represents a conflict of ideas in this immigrant society about how to maintain order and internal peace. So we have a contrast between Americanization in the sense of assimilating all people, but especially blacks (and in the past, European immigrants), and a more hard line Law and Order approach, associated with effort and advancement within this externally imposed framework. The second dimension has echoes of the Social Discipline dimension in the U.K., with its formula for containing social strain through adherence to a traditional (and highly puritan) Morality (.79) which buttresses the National Way of Life (.68) and encourages National Effort (.33).

(vii) Social groups

The final domain covers the social groups to which political parties offer help and support. It is, of course, one of great political importance, especially in pluralistic societies. But it is not of great theoretical interest. The particular correlations between group emphases reflect the political sociology of voting in the countries, itself often a matter of historical tradition.

Australia fits perfectly into these expectations. Three variables, reflecting concern for labour groups, agriculture and farmers, and non-economic demographic groups qualify. The correlations between them produce a single dimension (reflecting, of course, relative emphases rather than outright opposition to any group) which contrasts labour and the other demographic groups (.54, .56) with concern for agriculture and farmers (−.72). This single factor accounts for 57 per cent of the variance in group concerns. In New Zealand the same three variables are unpacked in a slightly different way, which does not change the basic similarity of group interest representation. In this case a first factor loads simply on Non-Economic Groups (−.61), whilst the second represents Labour (.49) *vs.* Agriculture (−.33). The two factors collectively account for 78 per cent of the variance.

As befits the greater complexity of their societies, the U.S. and British parties emphasize a wider range of groups. In both, five variables qualify, although this means little. Only negative references to Farmers are omitted, and it is almost axiomatic in the political cultures that no party will ever actually *attack* any group. In the United States the first dimension contrasts support for Labour groups and underprivileged minorities with emphases on Non-Economic Groups (the 'new minorities' like women, for example, and the traditional recipients of government aid like war veterans). Supporting one group has little implication for stress on others – support is clearly unconstrained, and hence the two dimensions can easily appear as orthogonal.

In Britain the first dimension is dominated by other economic groups (.75), followed by specific groups with supporting loadings, agriculture and farmers (.56), and labour groups (.42). It seems to consist of a general pluralist recognition of group demands. The second factor produces the expected conflict between labour and other economic groups (.54 and .58), and the agricultural lobby (−.41). These two factors, the only ones to be used subsequently, account respectively for 30 per cent and 28 per cent of the total variance.

3.4 SECOND-STAGE ANALYSIS

A major aim of this research is to derive data based ways of summarizing the complexity of party competition as economically as possible. Though the blow by blow account of parties in each subject domain is both interesting and necessary, it is not particularly economical. Consequently we have used the technique of taking the one or two factors that appear in each domain *themselves* as variables, and using them directly for a second-order factor analysis. The factor scores on each first-stage variable are added to original variables for those domains where no factoring could be undertaken. They are fed into a second factor analysis, and the first two dimensions emerging from this are used as summary indicators of the ideological space in which parties compete. Apart from discussing the interpretations of these second-stage factors, we can also plot the party positions in the two dimensional space through their factor scores on each of the two leading second-stage factors. Elsewhere in this book and in subsequent publications, we use this form of dimensional representation on a reduced space to develop and test theories of party movement. At this stage, especially with four countries to deal with, we only describe the

American analysis in technical detail, and are more concerned with the substantive results for the other countries.

For the U.S. only one domain, Freedom and Democracy, did not produce factors and this is replaced with two original variables, the categories coding references to Freedom and domestic Human Rights, and Democracy. Thus there are 12 input variables, these two plus the factors from the other six domains. As these have already been discussed in the domains analysis, we refer to them here only by a summary name. To aid interpretation, it is worth looking back to the discussion under each of the separate domains to see in detail what they represent.

It is characteristic of the factors extracted at a second level, that their nature is determined by differentiating between parties, and that the actual variables do not always form clusters that are meaningful *in themselves* but because they are in practice found in clusters. Thus the meaning of the factors can only be found at a level above the primary meaning of the original variables. The typical use of two-stage factoring, for example, has been in psychology. A battery of variables intended to measure introversion will be analysed, along with another battery measuring perhaps neuroticism, and a third measuring paranoid tendencies. The factors from these separate areas are then refactored to find dimensions that separate individuals with scores on these separate areas of mental behaviour into overarching types. Our domains are very like the separate psychic areas, and our second-stage factors have this same sense of abstraction. Introversion and neurosis have nothing in common except that the same people tend to score highly on the factors that measure both characteristics, and low on the factors that describe paranoia. With this caveat we can proceed to our country analyses.

The American case produces four significant second-stage factors, of which the first two are much more important than others. The first factor contrasts a peaceful and forceful international role, Freedom and Human Rights, Americanism and Law and Order, and Regulation of Capitalism, as positively loaded variables, with Clean and Good Government, Traditional Morality, and support for Economic Groups rather than Non-Economic Groups. In general it is a straightforward Democrat *vs.* Republican dimension – those who believe in military strength, free enterprise and traditional morality, will all get low scores; those who seek to regulate the economy and put a high value on civil liberties and take a more 'doveish' international line will get high scores.

The second factor deals more directly with economic and social matters. The high scores in this case are those who emphasize Welfare and Environment and the Regulation of Capitalism: the negative loading for Containment also pushes those 'soft on Communism' towards the high end. There is a certain anomaly in that supporters of internal Law and

TABLE 3.4

SECOND STAGE ANALYSIS FOR U.S.A.
FACTORS AND VARIABLES INPUT TO ANALYSIS

NUMERIC IDENTIFICATION FROM DOMAIN ANALYSIS	INTERPRETATION OF FIRST ORDER FACTORS/VARIABLES	FACTOR 1 DEMOCRATIC ISSUES VS. REPUBLICAN ISSUES	FACTOR 2 WELFARE AND ECONOMIC REGULATION
F11	ANTI-ISOLATIONISM	.768	.300
F12	CONTAINMENT	.358	-.508
CATEGORY 201	FREEDOM	.754	-.384
CATEGORY 202	DEMOCRACY	.168	-.385
F31	CLEAN AND GOOD GOVERNMENT	-.572	-.212
F41	REGULATED CAPITALISM VS. CAPITALISTIC ORTHODOXY	.410	.765
F51	WELFARE AND ENVIRONMENT	-.146	.926
F52	SOCIAL JUSTICE	-.358	-.164
F61	LAW AND ORDER VS. AMERICANISM	.484	.568
F62	TRADITIONALISM AND SOCIAL HARMONY	-.700	.112
F71	LABOUR AND UNDERPRIVILEGED VS. NON-ECONOMIC GROUPS	-.505	.300
F72	FARMERS AND OTHER ECONOMIC GROUPS	-.383	.253
	EIGENVALUE	3.37	2.85
	% OF VARIANCE EXPLAINED	28%	24%

TABLE 3.5

SECOND STAGE ANALYSIS FOR AUSTRALIA
FACTORS AND VARIABLES INPUT TO ANALYSIS

NUMERIC IDENTIFI- CATION FROM DOMAINS ANALYSIS	INTERPRETATION OF FIRST-ORDER FACTORS/VARIABLES	FACTOR 1 LEFT-RIGHT	FACTOR 2 DISCIPLINE VS.FREE PURSUIT OF GOALS
F11	INTERNATIONALISM VS.ISOLATIONISM	.360	-.137
F31	EFFICIENCY VS.AUTHORITY	.252	.195
F32	FEDERAL VS. STATES POWER	-.212	-.161
F41	ECONOMIC ORTHODOXY VS. GOALS AND REGULATIONS	.645	-.242
F42	PRODUCTIVITY	-.015	.028
F51	EDUCATION AND SOCIAL SERVICES	.829	.023
F52	ENVIRONMENTAL PROTECTION VS.SOCIAL SERVICES EXPANSION	.059	-.757
F71	LABOUR GROUPS VS.AGRICULTURE AND FARMERS	.429	.205
CATEGORY 201	FREEDOM	.115	-.018
CATEGORY 202	DEMOCRACY	-.155	-.052
CATEGORY 606	NATIONAL EFFORT AND SOCIAL HARMONY	-.251	.558
	EIGENVALUE	2.35	1.95
	% OF VARIANCE EXPLAINED	18%	15%

Order also occur here. The paradox is resolved, at least empirically, if we interpret this dimension too as reflecting on underlying opposition between Republicans and Democrats. The latter's working-class and ethnic supporters are likely to suffer more directly from a breakdown of Law and Order than Republicans and are hence more concerned about it – as their attraction to the 'tough minded' Independent Democrat Wallace in the 1968 Presidential election campaign demonstrated.

Apart from the Law and Order question, this second dimension appears a fairly conventional Right–Left contrast between Democrats and Republicans, as opposed to the more philosophical contrasts caught by the first dimension.

The real difficulty lies in distinguishing between two very similar dimensions, but the second factor in a two party system is bound to make distinctions that are usually submerged in a simplified overall contrast. We suggest therefore that American party competition is best viewed along a dimension of international toughness and Economic Orthodoxy *vs.* Economic Regulation and a less 'hawklike' stance. Differential emphases on direct intervention are also involved, particularly on welfare and the economy.

Australia produces a clear traditional, Left/Right dimension as the first of the second-order factors extracted. In all there are five significant second-stage factors, but the first two, which are all we are concerned with here, account for one third of all the variance over the input variables. Table 3.5 reports this analysis.

The first general dimension is loaded by the factor (F41) that represents a Left/Right clash in economics, by the welfare dimension (F51) and the Labour Groups *vs.* Agriculture dimension from the Social Groups domain. It clearly represents wide-ranging differences between left and right. It also loads, though less heavily, with the Foreign Policy dimension, in such a way that Internationalism rather than Isolationism is correlated with 'left' positions on the other factors. In fact Isolationism in the Australian context is a more conservative position, largely because of an 'Australia first' orientation on the part of the Country Party.

The second factor requires more interpretation. In terms of first-stage factors, it loads mainly on F52, giving a high score for those who oppose a Welfare Orientation to environmentalism and related issues. This groups them with those who put a high value on National Effort–Social Harmony. To some extent we have here a contrast between traditional and new social concerns, already touched upon in the domain analysis for welfare. (The only marginally less significant third dimension is one that our alternative analyses, using a larger set of Australian parties, pick up as second in importance. This is a factor repeating on a high level the first-stage factor that emerged in domain three (Fabric of Government) concentrating on

Government Efficiency and States Rights. At some periods in Australian post-war politics this opposition must have been important.)

The first two New Zealand factors account together for over 40 per cent of the variance, though another three are significant as in Australia. The first second-stage dimension in the second stage is clearly an orthodox Left/Right split. It loads on F42, the straightforward Left/Right Economic Policy factor, has a loading on F51, the Bourgeois *vs.* Traditional Welfare factor, loads on the group variables in such a way as to indicate support for farmers rather than demographic groups, and loads on both Law and Order and Government Efficiency (often a conservative code for cutting expenditure). It is a simple middle-class interest, capitalist economics, authoritarian dimension of a classic Left/Right nature.

The second factor, though, contains a strong element of foreign policy; Anti-isolationism is the more 'left' position, along with the Interventionism of the first economic factor. Thus to be keen on a world role for New Zealand, to wish to intervene to make the economy grow, and for that matter, to wish to decentralize government, are all versions of a different sort of left-wing position from that endorsed by Labour Party scores on the first dimension. As has to be the case with orthogonal factors, this is a form of Left/Right split on which one can take a position largely independent of the one adopted on the more usual economic and welfare style issues of the first dimension. Alternatively it might be thought of as a Modernization dimension.

For all its richness, the British case is easiest to interpret. The first dimension of the five that have significant Eigenvalues is the most important. The first two dimensions together account for 41 per cent of the variance.

The first dimension combines Foreign Policy, Economic Policy and other issue-emphases to form a good one-dimensional summary of what can only be called national and international capitalism. The EEC Foreign Policy dimension, and the NATO orientation load on this as does the original variable of Government Efficiency (often a code for expenditure cutting). There are also strong connections with the two economic policy dimensions, and the social fabric stress on National Way of Life. This combination of three or more forms of conservative politics in Britain is intuitively pleasing, especially when it emerges at a rather abstract level of analysis.

The second dimension which cross-cuts this represents an alternative Left/Right conception, concerned almost entirely with the 'soft' side of political conflict. It loads on to the original variables of Democracy and Decentralization, and on both factors from the Welfare domain. In addition there is a very strong loading on the first of the 'groups' factors, Pluralism or Group Concern. The loading is strong and negative ($-.77$),

TABLE 3.6

SECOND STAGE ANALYSIS FOR NEW ZEALAND
FACTORS AND VARIABLES INPUT TO ANALYSIS

NUMERIC IDENTIFICATION FROM DOMAIN ANALYSIS	INTERPRETATION OF FIRST-ORDER FACTORS/VARIABLES	FACTOR 1 LEFT-RIGHT	FACTOR 2 INTERNATIONALISM AND WELFARE V. ISOLATIONISM
F11	INTERNATIONALISM VS. ISOLATIONISM	.195	.807
F12	TRADITIONAL ALLIES VS. GENERAL INTERNATIONALIST ALIGNMENT	-.111	-.251
F41	ECONOMIC ORTHODOXY VS. GOVERENMENT INTERVENTIONISM	.130	-.608
F42	FREE ENTERPRISE VS. PLANNING	.755	.246
F51	"OLD" and "NEW" WELFARE CONCERNS	-.553	.373
F52	CONCERN FOR EDUCATION	.237	.221
F71	NON-ECONOMIC GROUPS	.640	.169
F72	LABOUR GROUPS VS. AGRICULTURE AND FARMERS	.315	.277
CATEGORY 301	GOVERNMENT EFFICIENCEY	-.308	.523
CATEGORY 303		-.708	-.070
CATEGORY 605	LAW AND ORDER	-.546	.422
	EIGENVALUE	2.81	2.11
	% OF VARIANCE EXPLAINED	24%	18%

TABLE 3.7

SECOND STAGE ANALYSIS FOR BRITAIN
FACTORS AND VARIABLES INPUT TO ANALYSIS

NUMERIC IDENTIFI- CATION FROM DOMAIN ANALYSIS	INTERPRETATION OF FIRST-ORDER FACTORS/VARIABLES	FACTOR 1 NATIONAL AND INTERNATIONAL CAPITALISM	FACTOR 2 "COMMON GOOD" WELFARE AND LIBERALISM vs. SPECIAL GROUP INTEREST.
F11	EUROPEAN DIMENSION (E.C.)	.603	-.027
F12	NATO	.524	-.137
CATEGORY 201	FREEDOM	.266	-.164
CATEGORY 202	DEMOCRACY	-.119	.640
CATEGORY 301	DECENTRALIZATION POSITIVE	.073	.488
CATEGORY 303	GOVERNMENT EFFICIENCY	.667	-.067
F41	FREE ENTERPRISE VS. REGULATION	.793	-.131
F42	ECONOMIC EXPANSION VS. IDEOLOGY	.405	.069
F51	EDUCATION, ARTS AND SOCIAL SERVICE EXPANSION	-.135	.480
F52	ENVIRONMENTAL PROTECTION	.373	-.679
F61	SOCIAL DISCIPLINE	.415	.215
F62	NATIONAL WAY OF LIFE	.664	.091
F71		-.045	-.767
F72		-.453	.171
	EIGENVALUE	3.??	2.50
	% OF VARIANCE EXPLAINED	?%	18%

suggesting that there is a 'common good' Welfare-and-Liberalization position opposed to any sort of group orientation. Members of both major parties could take up a variety of stands on this dimension.

The second-stage dimensions are represented pictorially in Figures 3.1–3.4. In each case party scores on the two dimensions for each election have been averaged over a sub-period, to give a summary overall party position for the whole time-span. Lines connecting each point are arrowed to show progress through time, and the sub-periods broadly coincide with political epochs. Thus for the U.S. we show the Republican and Democrat average position for the Truman/Eisenhower years immediately after the war, for the Kennedy/Johnson 'New Frontier/Great Society', the Nixon victories of 1968 and 1972, and the regimes of Carter and Reagan. The graphs confirm the utility of the approach. Not only are the parties neatly and economically depicted in ideological spaces clearly derived from their concerns, but movements over time correspond to general historical judgements. In Australia, for example, all three parties are arrayed along the major Left–Right dimension (second-stage factor one) in the order one would expect, with no overlap of 'party areas'. All the parties can be seen to swing towards the right in the last period (1974 to 1980), just as the conservative Liberal and Country parties can be seen flirting with a more moderate position (as indeed does the ALP, by moving away from the left) during the middle of the post-war periods.

Exactly the same reaction is seen with the movement of the British parties rightwards during the third and fourth periods, on the first dimension (reflecting changes in economic policy). It is often forgotten, in the perspective of the Thatcherite regime, that Heath's policies in 1970 were seen as a distinct shift to the right from the Butskellism still practised by the Macmillan–Home governments. Figure 3.3 catches this very clearly.

In America the basic liberalism of Nixon's domestic and economic policies, as well as his pressure for *détente*, are normally also overlooked because of Watergate. This also appeared in his campaign of 1960, which in this respect outweighs Goldwater in 1964. Yet the graphs distinctly show how much the Ford and Reagan period is a right-wing shift, on both dimensions, after Nixon, a return to a Republican position much like that of Eisenhower. Similarly, for the Democrats, the general leftward shift inaugurated by McGovern appears to have been continued by Carter. One can also see how Johnson's massive support for Welfarism on the second dimension, was *not* extended even by McGovern, and how the pressure of the economic recession has again caused a slight movement away from luxuries.

The New Zealand graph is perhaps most notable for the absence of much movement on the main dimension by either party, especially if one

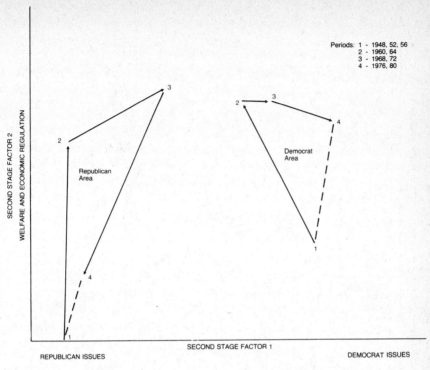

3.1 U.S. party positions, 1948–1980

discounts the once and for all shift away from left-wing economic policies by New Zealand Labour after the immediate post-war period. It is generally accepted that party competition in New Zealand has been remarkable *immobiliste*. The two parties are, indeed, some distance apart, and largely static. It appears that what convergence has been attempted by the right is almost entirely on the second dimension, one that in many ways reflects the 'New Issues', the 'soft' leftness of the whole democratic world in the sixties, and which has been abandoned almost everywhere else as well as by New Zealand Labour.

We lack space here for further development of these important points. But they will be taken up subsequently. To a large extent discussion and analysis in this book is cumulative, each later country chapter assessing results against those produced earlier. Chapter 18 attempts a comparative assessment of all the individual results, (Table 18.1), as well as presenting an aggregate dimensional analysis. Besides its substantive findings this chapter has also provided a methodological introduction to the techniques used later – perhaps made clearer through their application to countries

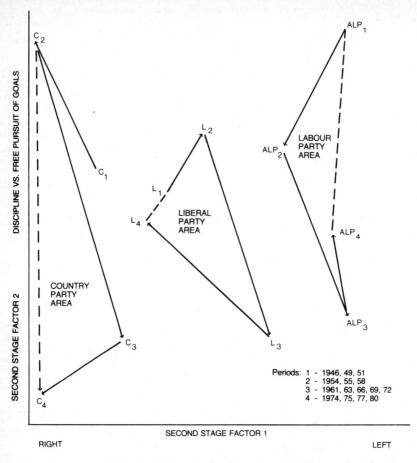

3.2 Australian party positions, 1946–1980

already discussed extensively in the literature of political science. The easy interpretability of results at the domain and second-stage level, across all four countries, shows the utility of the techniques for comparative analysis, and forms a background against which to assess the findings produced in individual country chapters, which – starting with Canada and other states influenced by the British connection – now follow.

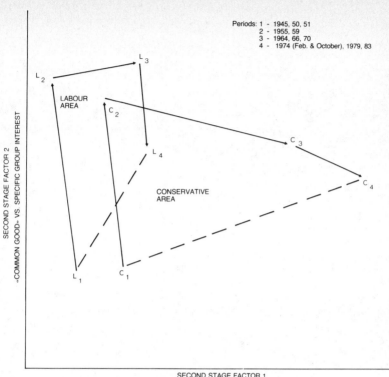

3.3 U.K. party positions 1945–1983

Notes

1 Factor analysis first produces dimensions at right angles (orthogonal) to each other which are therefore independent. This solution is preferable, other things being equal, because it comes directly out of the application of the technique without further analytic decisions being involved. However, since there is no constraint on the extent to which variables may load on all dimensions it is often difficult to interpret them.

'Rotation' is a procedure in which dimensions are rotated round the space in order to find clusters of variables which load heavily on one factor and not on others. Analytic decisions are then required on when to stop this process. There is also a question of whether orthogonality should be maintained (varimax rotation) or whether the dimensions should be allowed to be at angles less than 90 per cent to each other in the interests of better fit to the clusters of variables (oblique rotation of various kinds). In the book we have used only varimax rotations, as we often wish to examine movements within the two dimensional spaces, which could not be done of course if the dimensions were not orthogonal. In all cases of first- and second-stage analyses we have carried through rotated

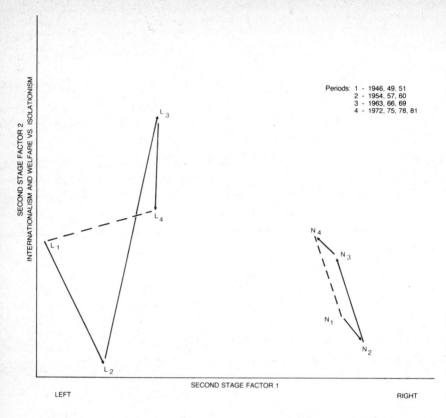

3.4 New Zealand party positions, 1946–1981

and unrotated analyses and compared results. If the unrotated solution interprets easily it is preferred and used as the basis of discussion. If not, the various
rotated solutions which make best sense are presented.

Again many alternative analyses are done which are not explicitly referred to
in the text. Our interpretation and comparison of solutions is very much guided
by the substantive context of politics in the country, which is presented at the
outset of each chapter. The comparison of rotated and unrotated solutions, as in
Table 3.3, is a comparison of like to like in the sense that each has emerged as the
best solution for the particular country within this substantive context.

CHAPTER 4

CANADA 1945–1980:
PARTY PLATFORMS AND
CAMPAIGN STRATEGIES[1]

———————— ◇ ————————

Nowhere more than in Canada has printed election material been influenced by the electronic bias that increasingly dominates party campaign strategies. Long and relatively complex manifestos have been replaced by shorter pamphlets – themselves dominated by photographs and headlines. Though the responsibilities of government have become broader and more complex (indeed, partly *because* of this), the short-term stances of parties have been increasingly simplified and focused. The evolution in the style and format of party election documents in Canada is as striking as changes in their content and indeed, the two are related. In this chapter we shall examine both developments.

4.1 PARTIES AND DOCUMENTS

Our analysis covers the thirteen elections from 1945 to 1980. The dominant federal party during this period was the Liberal Party of Canada (Whitaker 1977). It held office from 1945 to 1957, winning paraliamentary majorities in three successive elections. After a narrow electoral defeat in 1957, it resigned and was in opposition until 1963. Thereafter, it governed, confidently or precariously, until 1979. In 1963, 1965 and 1972 it could manage only a minority government. In 1968 and 1974, the party won parliamentary majorities. Its defeat in 1979 led to nine months in opposition, after which it returned to power. The fortunes of the Progressive Conservative Party, the main opposition party, are naturally the mirror image of this.

The supporting cast ('supporting' in a literal sense during periods of minority government) was made up of the CCF/NDP and the Social Credit parties. From the 1930s, the Cooperative Commonwealth Federation was a democratic socialist party with a Western agrarian base and an agrarian leadership. Virtually decimated in the Diefenbaker sweep of 1958, the party began a slow transformation, seeking closer cooperation with the Canadian trade union movement. Reborn in a meeting in 1961, it took the name of New Democratic Party and turned to Ontario for its leadership: a labour lawyer being followed by a former university professor (Young 1969).

The Social Credit Party was originally a conservative populist party, appealing to farmers in the West by criticizing Eastern-based economic power, the banks, and the Canadian Pacific Railroad. It lost all its Western parliamentary seats in 1958. It made especially dramatic gains in Quebec in 1962, and thereafter became spokesman for rural small business from that province. It ceased to be a national party after the 1968 election, and its programmes for the last four Canadian elections are unavailable for analysis. It gained no parliamentary representation in the 1980 federal election (Stein 1973).

What is a party's position? Clearly the most useful source is the platform document, published by political parties at each election and intended for public distribution. These are used here, whenever possible, (but for the Liberal Party position in 1965 and 1969 the handbooks prepared for use by candidates had to be used). Platforms are more and more difficult to find in Canadian elections. Even when put together, as by the NDP, their format has become one of presenting a single issue area on each page, with the candidate encouraged to reprint and use locally one or more pages as he thinks appropriate. Occasionally, no single platform document is released at all and in these cases we have relied on collections of pamphlets issued at each election. Often, some themes will show up on every pamphlet while others will be restricted to a single pamphlet which may be aimed at a particular audience. However, a collection of centrally produced pamphlets is a reasonable surrogate for the public electoral strategy we are seeking to analyse.[2] The balance between normal plaforms and pamphlets in the data base is reported in Appendix A.

For this analysis therefore a party's position is taken as the range of themes touched upon in centrally produced party documents, with only the most broadly comprehensive document being coded if one exists. If no such broad document exists, all more narrowly focused documents are coded. Conceptually, this does seem a good source for determining where a party *wishes* to stand *at the time of planning* the campaign. It is not always an accurate indicator of where the party *does* stand as a campaign progresses – with the best laid plans often marred by the intrusion of themes beyond the party's control.

4.2 PLANNING CAMPAIGN THEMES

All parties hold policy conventions, though not so regularly as do British or continental European parties. Moreover, it is always clear, (sometimes brutally so) that these conventions are only advisory to the leader. The campaign documents studied here are largely the work of the parliamentary party – sometimes narrowed to just the leader and trusted advisors (in the case of the Liberal party), sometimes broadened to include representatives of party organizations (in the case of the NDP).

The Liberal Party, in power for most of this century, has tended to de-emphasize the policy role of the national headquarters and of national conventions (Winn and McMemeny, 1976), in favour of the civil service (Meisel 1962; Wearing 1981; Penniman (ed.), 1981) – or more recently, of the mixture of political and professional staff that now makes up the Prime Minister's office. All their advice is vetted (at least since 1960) by a campaign committee composed largely of professionals in public relations.

Out of power, the Liberals have had to be more innovative. After the debacle of 1957–8, leading figures within the party organized a conference drawn selectively from Liberals and outside academics and professionals, which provided a new vision of the welfare state and a broad outline of possible accommodations with the new French-Canadian nationalism. Subsequent Liberal governments lived off the intellectual capital of this conference.

The Progressive Conservative Party is most typically a party of opposition. Members of the (publicly funded) caucus research office have thus played important roles in initiating policy proposals or in co-ordinating the work of sympathizers from academic life. The typical pattern is for the office or the outside expert to draft a position paper for the party leader. When the document meets with his approval, it is presented to the parliamentary caucus for modification and approval, and subsequently again filtered by a campaign committee.

The New Democratic Party differs, but only in degree, from the Liberals and Progressive Conservatives. Like them it also has a caucus research office attached to the leader, but its campaign committee is drawn from professionals in the federal or provincial party headquarters, and the federal council, elected by party activists in convention, plays a more important role in the preparation of the campaign platform.

4.3 FORMATS AND DISTRIBUTION

What kinds of documents are produced through these processes? It is difficult to be precise, especially for very early elections, due to haphazard record-keeping by the political parties and to the incompleteness of public and University archive collections.

It is for the Liberal Party that the collection seems weakest. Only one fully-fledged manifesto could be found for an election which the Liberals contested as a governmnent. In 1949, extensive use was made of

TABLE 4.1

CAMPAIGN PAMPHLETS AND PRINT-RUNS, 1979 CANADA

TITLE	FORMAT	ENGLISH	FRENCH	OTHER
LIBERAL				
"A LOOK AT THE FACTS"	41 CM X 21 CM HEAVY PAPER PRINTED ON BOTH SIDES AND FOLDED IN FOUR	90,000	40,000	0
"OUR ECONOMY SECOND TO NONE"		50,000	30,000	0
"FORWARD WITH TRUDEAU"				76,000[x]
PROGRESSIVE CONSERVATIVE				
"LET'S GET CANADA WORKING AGAIN"	28 CM X 21 CM GLOSSY PAPER PRINTED ON BOTH SIDES AND TRIPLE-FOLDED			0
"THE RIGHT CHOICE"	AS ABOVE			0
"NEW LEADERSHIP FOR CANADA"	23 CM X 21 CM GLOSSY PAPER PRINTED ON BOTH SIDES AND DOUBLE-FOLDED			0
"IF IT'S JUST A JOB YOU WANT, MY HEART DOES NOT BLEED FOR YOU"... TRUDEAU	28 CM X 42 CM HEAVY PAPER PRINTED ON BOTH SIDES AND DOUBLE-FOLDED			0
"HOMEOWNERS AND BUYERS DESERVE A BREAK"	AS ABOVE			0
NDP				
NEW DEMOCRATIC IDEAS FOR CANADA'S FUTURE	20 PAGE BOOKLET PRINTED ON MEDIUM-WEIGHT PAPER; EACH PAGE 28 CM X 21 CM	50,000	8,000	0
"A POSITIVE OPTION FOR CANADA"	35 CM BY 21 CM ON CHEAP PAPER, PRINTED ON ONE SIDE AND DOUBLE-FOLDED	10,000	5,000	0
"FIVE WOMEN"		50,000	0	0

[x] N.B.   THE LIBERALS ISSUED 50,000 ITALIAN, 12,000 PORTUGUESE AND 14,000 GREEK PAMPHLETS.   NO OTHER PARTY PRINTED IN MINORITY LANGUAGES.

resolutions passed at the leadership convention of 1948. Otherwise we have relied on pamphlets from election campaigns.[3]

In opposition, however, three election manifestos were issued in 1958, 1962 and 1963. After 1963, the form of documents was influenced by changing strategies of campaigning. Under the influence of the Kennedy strategy of 1960 in the United States, an even larger share of the campaign budget was devoted to television. Printed material was heavily laden with pictures and slogans and was exclusively in the form of short pamphlets.

The 'technological imperative' does not seem to have affected the Conservative Party until 1972 (though pamphlets are all we have left from the 1953 and 1963 elections). The Progressive Conservative victory of 1957 was preceded by a very long analysis of the weaknesses of the country and a statement of redirection. Similar long booklets were used in 1965 and in 1968.

The minor parties have always had campaign plaforms giving very broad policy statements. In 1945, the CCF distributed a long book of resolutions from the 1944 party convention seeking a new post-war reorientation of Canadian policy. For the 1962 election, there was the Founding Programme of the New Democratic Party, adopted at the convention of the previous year. For other elections, the national party executive distilled a programme from resolutions of earlier conventions. Their most recent manifestos have devoted between one-third and one-half of each page to photographs and line drawings. The Social Credit Party always issued a formal statement of the party programme at each election, though it may not have been extensively used as a campaign document.

The flavour of current campaign documents is given in Table 4.1. References are to centrally produce documents only. As can be seen from the numbers printed (unavailable for the Progressive Conservative Party) these are not distributed to all households in Canada. Local candidates can order copies of these brochures. The ones in the mother tongues of various immigrant groups may be used extensively in particular constituencies or sections of constituencies. The others may be more usefully distributed to members of local organizations or kept on hand for voters sufficiently interested to come to the candidates' election headquarters or to candidates' meetings. If my own constituency is at all typical, candidate biographies with brief statements of policy, locally conceived, designed and printed, are the documents most usually finding their way into the hands of the voters.

The Progressive Conservative Party had five centrally produced documents in 1979. One highlighted the mortgage deductibility plan which was one of the major and (from party polls) one of the most attractive policy innovations of the party. 'New Leadership for Canada' was a statement on defence policy and external affairs, while the other three were virtually

evenly divided between criticism of the Liberals' economic performance
and promises of change.

The New Democratic Party was the only one to produce a pamphlet
specifically aimed at women voters. It was also the only party to issue even
an approximation of the traditional campaign manifesto.

Under the current election Expenses Act, political parties are unable to
subsidize local candidates by providing free or low-cost promotional
material. The party is not barred from supplying the material, but the
candidate must pay full value for it, (or report the difference as a
contribution) and include the cost as one of his allowable expenses. This
has reduced the importance of central campaign documents relative to
constituency-produced brochures.

4.4 CAMPAIGN THEMES 1945–1980

In spite of the various difficulties mentioned above, 48 programmes were
collected for the series of elections starting in 1945 and ending in 1980.
These documents can be studied in various ways. Here we follow the
standard analysis described in section 2.12 – first grouping sentences
within one of the 54 categories of the general coding scheme (Appendix B),
secondly looking at certain aspects of the distribution of references over
such categories, and last applying the kind of factor analysis which has
already been used for the other countries of the Anglo-American connection in Chapter 3. No particular problems arose with the Canadian coding.
It was mainly carried out by a Research Assistant, but some documents
were coded independently by the principal investigator: and a comparison
of the (quasi-) sentences assigned to the various categories showed
agreement at a high level.

Our five categories are generalized into seven domains: external relations, freedom and democracy, government structure and performance,
economic policy, social policy, the preferred view of society, and the set of
social groups to which a party could choose to make reference. Generally
issues of economic policy are the most dominant – by a large margin. Only
in 1965, when Canada's government medical care plan was about to be
introduced, did social policy (the next most common) approach the
intensity of discussion of economic policy. Up to 1962 approximately 35
per cent of the mentions in the typical platform were devoted to the
economy. Attention fell somewhat in 1963 and subsequently but recovered
to 36 per cent in 1972. Since then, between 40 and 50 per cent of the
discussion has dealt with economic matters.

The decline in the sixties related to the emergence of new types of issues.
Although the Liberals put the completion of the welfare state in Canada
high on the agenda, there was also the place of Quebec and of French-

Canadians within the Confederation. Consequently, the domains of 'governmental structure' and 'nature of society' began to bulk larger than they had earlier. Indeed, since 1968, these together equal or surpass social policy in number of mentions.

Overall, however, social policy has been the second most important focus of attention in the period. The immediate post-war saw the beginnings of pension, unemployment and family allowance policy. From the mid-fifties to the mid-sixties, attention turned to hospital (and later, to physician) care and to comprehend welfare policy. Only in 1980 did social policy take a distinct backseat to other issues.

As befits a non-ideological party system, the third (occasionally the second) most common type of reference is simply to named groups as beneficiaries of particular policies. Group references clustered in two broad categories defined by major economic role or by social need. No other domain is very prominent.

With a few exceptions, political parties have not varied greatly, in the aggregate at least, in the attention they have devoted to domains since the Second World War. The Progressive Conservative and Social Credit parties give more stress to economic policy than do the Liberal or New Democratic parties. Not surprisingly, the NDP pays much the most attention to social policy. It is also the most internationally minded of the parties. Its average attention to international relations is almost twice that of any competitor. The major parties are more likely to talk in terms of specific group beneficiaries than are the minor parties. Liberals and Social Credit, with their stronger bases in Quebec, give more prominence to the 'nature of society' than do the others. 'Freedom' was particularly the preserve of the Social Credit Party, which gave it an anti-government, freedom for enterprise twist.

Positive and negative references to each party and party leader were also noted separately, in order to check the point made in Chapter 2 about the tendency of the parties to ignore each other. On average such references occur in 10 per cent of Liberal sentences, 5 per cent of the NDP and 4 per cent of Social Credit. They emerged with inordinate frequency in the 1980 campaign, and seemed to be increasingly prominent in the elections of the seventies. This tendency coincides with the virtual abandonment of the platform document which we noted at the outset. Similarly it is the Liberal Party in particular whose documents have the highest proportion of party-related references. The Liberals are perhaps the most expert in the image campaign.

The proportion of categories left uncoded was reassuringly limited overall, coming to 8.7 per cent of all (quasi-) sentences in the documents with a range from 11 per cent (Liberals) to 5 per cent (Social Credit). Categories were excluded from the factor analysis if they received less than

TABLE 4.2

MAJOR ISSUE THEMES IN CANADA, BY PARTY, 1945–80
(MEAN/STANDARD DEVIATION, DECIMALS OMITTED)

	LIBERAL	P.C.	NDP	SOCIAL CREDIT	TOTAL
1. SOCIAL SERVICES+	12/06	06/04	16/09	09/06	11/07
2. DEMOG. MIN.	06/03	08/05	05/02	03/03	06/04
3. INCENTIVES	06/06	07/04	04/02	07/03	06/04
4. ECONOMIC GOALS	06/06	07/06	06/04	10/06	06/05
5. TECHNOLOGY/INF.	07/06	07/05	03/02	02/02	05/05
6. PRIMARY PRODUCERS	06/06	05/08	04/01	02/02	05/05
7. ENTERPRISE	04/06	04/04	0/0	06/06	03/05
8. REGULATION OF CAPITALISM	0/0	0/0	04/02	02/01	02/02
9. INTERNATIONALISM+	01/01	01/01	05/03	03/02	02/02
10. FREEDOM	01/02	01/02	01/01	04/03	02/02

1 per cent of references overall and less than 3 per cent from any party.
They are not numerous, and do not show any systematic patterning.

Coming to the presentation common to all our country analyses, of the
attention devoted by particular parties to the leading categories of the
coding frame, strong contrasts emerge between the parties of the left and
centre-left, (the New Democratic Party and the Liberal Party), and the
right (Social Credit) and centre-right parties (Progressive Conservative).
As can be seen from Table 4.2, the overall most popular theme was the
provision of social services, but this was only the second most frequent for
Social Credit and only the fifth most frequent for the Progressive Conservatives.

The differences between left and right parties are less but still evident
across the range of other issues. The NDP makes no reference to the need to
encourage enterprise. Similarly, the Liberals and the Progressive Conservatives make no reference to the regulation of capitalism. Combining
the categories of 'technology and infrastructure', 'incentives' and 'enterprise' shows quite strikingly the contrast between the NDP and all the
other parties. Only 7 per cent of NDP campaign references dealt with one
of these themes. The other parties gave them more than twice that
attention: 15 per cent for Social Credit, 17 per cent for the Liberals and 18
per cent for the Progressive Conservatives. By way of contrast, were we
to add to the 'regulation of capitalism' category one other that does not
appear in Table 4.2 ('nationalization'), we would have captured over 6 per
cent of the NDP's campaign references but not more than 1 per cent of
Liberal or Social Credit references and only 0.3 per cent of those of the
Progressive Conservative Party. Although differences are smaller, it also
seems true to conclude that the older Canadian parties, the Liberals and
Progressive Conservatives, are the most likely to make group based appeals

– the general pluralistic appeal normally associated with North American parties. Their preference for concrete appeals does not carry over to 'labour' or 'business'. The NDP is noteworthy for its positive references to internationalism. It is the third or fourth most common NDP theme in the post-1945 period. When combined with mentions of 'peace' it would include 7 per cent of all NDP campaign references, while the two categories make up no more than 4 per cent of the campaign themes of the Social Credit Party and less than 2 per cent of the themes of any of the major parties.

Although these are the leading themes, it is worth noting for most of them, that the standard deviation of the rate of mentions over time is as large as the average rate of mention. What this implies is that the parties could, in any election, easily either be ignoring the dimension entirely or giving it twice the weight it tends to have on average. Conversely, where we find the mean proportion of mentions to be substantially larger than its standard deviation, we have identified issues whose discussion is virtually obligatory for the party. On this test, discussion of social policy has been obligatory for all parties, but most particularly for Liberals and NDP. The same is true of concern for particular demographic (usually age or regionally-defined) groups. Such references arise commonly for all parties but Social Credit, while calls for particular incentives for particular producers seem to be a standard appeal for all parties but the Liberal Party.

4.5 FACTOR ANALYSES BY DOMAIN

Though illuminating, combining categories in the way we have just done is clearly *ad hoc*. Factor analyses of the discrete coded themes provides another way of reducing the data to meaningful dimensions, as they show which individual issues are systematically grouped together.

(i) Economy

Table 4.3 illustrates this type of first-stage factor analysis applied inside the economic domain and is particularly important given the prominence of economic issues in the party debates. It suggests that Canadian parties' references to thirteen economic policy themes can be collapsed to three dimensions which seem to correspond to the dominant thrust of economic discussion, to a stress on economic production, and to a stress on direction of the economy. The first dimension unites three themes in particular – the articulation of economic goals, the stress on Keynesian techniques of economic management, and the stress on economic orthodoxy. The latter is clearly an incongruous member of this dimension, but one must recall

TABLE 4.3

THE ECONOMIC POLICY DOMAIN

VARIMAX ROTATED FACTOR MATRIX	FACTOR 1 DOMINANT POLITICAL ECONOMY	FACTOR 2 PRODUCTION	FACTOR 3 DIRECTION
401 ENTERPRISE	10	-08	-69
402 INCENTIVES	21	56	04
403 REGULATION OF CAPITALISM	-26	-63	53
404 ECONOMIC PLANNING	-26	-46	12
405 QUASI - CORPORATISM	-34	-10	-02
406 PROTECTIONISM+	14	31	32
408 ECONOMIC GOALS	84	-09	12
409 KEYNESIAN DEMAND MANAGEMENT	77	03	-14
410 PRODUCTIVITY	-30	62	19
411 TECHNOLOGY + INFRASTRUCTURE	-30	57	-01
412 CONTROLLED ECONOMY	26	08	65
413 NATIONALIZATION	-22	-30	60
414 ECONOMIC ORTHODOXY	71	04	04

FROM UNROTATED FACTOR SOLUTION			
EIGENVALUE	2.58	1.91	1.52
% OF VARIANCE	20	15	12

NOTE:　AN UNCONSTRAINED FACTOR ANALYSIS YIELDED 7 FACTORS WITH EIGENVALUES GREATER THAN 1.0 TOGETHER EXPLAINING 78 PERCENT OF TOTAL VARIANCE. HOWEVER ALL FACTORS BEYOND THE THIRD GENERATED HEAVY LOADINGS FROM ONLY A SINGLE VARIABLE.

the political economy of the period. By far the greatest number of elections were fought during periods of economic growth when there was no incongruity between stressing a reduced government debt or the value of the currency (orthodox objectives) and speaking of government macro-economic management as a way of realizing those objectives. We have already observed that the economic goals were quite uncontroversial. The Social Credit Party were especially adept at combining the articulation of uncontroversial economic varieties with a quite interventionist, if not radical, monetary and credit policy for farmers and small businessmen. Economic orthodoxy was also uncontroversial simply because Keynesianism 'worked' and there was no apparent need to persuade voters to abandon the analogies of the household budget. Thus the first dimension seems one of *Dominant Political Economy* since its articulation involved a fight for position among the parties to occupy an uncontroversial 'space' (Robertson 1976; Budge and Farlie, 1977). Not all could occupy it, so some parties left the field and sought to reserve other spaces for themselves (at least in particular elections) thus providing the varying emphases necessary for factor analysis in the first place.

The other two dimensions in the economic domain are clearly more substantive. Factor 2 deals with production or economic growth. The dominant theme is that of encouraging productivity. Clearly, government was expected to help with this. Those scoring high on this dimension wanted incentives for various types of activity, and the provision of technological and physical infrastructures for production. Parties loading high on this dimension apparently did *not* want the federal government to plan the objectives of that production, nor to own the industry that carried it out. Factor 3 includes such items as 'controlled economy', 'nationalization', and 'regulation of capitalism' and a negative loading for 'enterprise'. There are traces of a left/right contrast in the two leading dimensions but it is most strongly expressed in this third one. Consistent left-right differences do not underlie policy differences to the extent they did in the other Anglo-Saxon countries however, as a relatively low proportion of total variance is explained by our three factor solution – less than 50 per cent. This is the least for any factor solution for the policy domains to be considered below.

(ii) Welfare

The next most frequently addressed domain in Canadian elections is that of social policy or, more accurately, 'social policy and quality of life' since the domain also includes reference to the environment and to leisure activities. Though Canadian parties only addressed with any frequency five themes from this domain, three factors were required to summarize the discussion. The first factor related to state responsibility for social services and for education and advanced training. Unlike the first dimension in the economic policy domain, this one dealt with controversial items. Both types of activity raise questions of the proper role and responsibility of the state and, in Canada, of the role of the federal government. On the whole parties do not strongly dissent from the desirability of supporting these activities but some parties do choose to ignore the particular issue. Factor 2 seems to be a 'social goals' factor stressing both care for fellow citizens and care for environment. Factor 3 has a high loading from the 'cultural' variable of Art, Media, Leisure and Sport.

(iii) Groups

Five separate themes could be used to classify the 'group appeals' and factor analysis collapsed these into two quite meaningful dimensions. The first factor could be labelled a 'pluralist' factor since it typically involved

TABLE 4.4

GOVERNMENT STRUCTURE DOMAIN

VARIMAX ROTATED FACTOR MATRIX	FACTOR 1 EFFECTIVENESS	FACTOR 2 EFFICIENCY
301 DECENTRALIZATION+	70	-02
302 DECENTRALIZATION-	73	-15
303 EFFICIENCY	-03	96
305 EFFECTIVENESS	71	36

FROM UNROTATED FACTOR MATRIX

EIGENVALUE	1.54	1.04
% OF VARIANCE	38	26

addressing a number of discrete groups (farmers, fishermen, loggers, old people, youth, westerners, etc.) in a way that suggested that all groups could be served and that there was no incongruity in addressing them together. The second dimension is another left/right contrast – the opposition of business and labour in an industrialized society. Again, 'opposition' refers to the pattern of emphasis given by the parties. The different loadings on Factor 2 simply indicate that those parties making reference to the one tend not to refer to the other. It does not imply an overt opposition to one or the other and no such opposition is typically manifested in Canadian elections. As with social policy, the solution is quite neat with high loadings or low loadings on each dimension.

(iv) Government

Table 4.4 examines the 'government structure' dimension which, in Canada, combines two substantively different aspects (1) how well organized government as such is, and (2) centralization of power in the federal government or its decentralization to the provinces. The latter has been a leading problem in Canadian politics since the 1960s and difficult for all parties to handle. In general, both Quebec and the West have sought more power from the central government – the West since the 1970s, Quebec since 1960. In addition, Ontario has the greatest interest in, and shows the greatest support for, strengthening the central government. That is to say that the core areas for both the Liberal and the Progressive Conservative parties – Quebec and the West respectively – favour decentralization but the most electorally volatile and competitive region, Ontario, favours just the opposite. Parties have sought to manage their dilemma by resorting to ambiguity, which generates the interesting structure we highlight in Table 4.4 – formally incongruous but politically very rational. Both positive *and* negative references to decentralization load on the same dimension; the same one, indeed, on which references to government effectiveness are also loaded. As with the other 'first dimensions' so far discovered, the one in this domain seems to group the consensual themes even though, in this case, the consensus among the parties is to blur the issue of centralization as much as possible. The second dimension is uniquely an 'efficiency' dimension, with the opposition parties making, and the government party seeking to refute, charges of inefficient administration. Such themes are quite independent of the general debate over the most effective way for government to provide services.

(v) Other domains

The four domains so far analysed exhaust the major themes of Canadian elections. The others emerge only episodically in campaigns. The fifth most frequently addressed is foreign and defence policy. Only four specific themes occur with sufficient frequency to be retained for the factor analysis. These do, however, fall into a neat structure. The first factor is an 'internationalism' factor including both internationalism and themes of world peace and disarmament. This emerges because the NDP, almost alone, chooses to raise it in Canadian campaigns. Both military preparedness and reference to traditional foreign links (with the United States, with NATO, and with the Commonwealth) emerge on the second 'security' factor and are more properly the themes of the dominant Canadian parties.

In the remaining issue domains, that of 'freedom and democracy' and 'fabric of society', only two themes in each domain received over 1 per cent of post-war references or 3 per cent from any one party. As a result, factor analysis was unnecessary. 'Freedom' and 'Democracy' are the surviving variables in their domain. Interestingly, they are virtually orthogonal in any case (Pearson Correlation .07).

'Fabric of society' is represented by two themes that recur with some frequency, as one might expect. These deal with the legitimacy of subgroups, particularly French Canadian communalism and identity. While one might expect these to be treated either positively or negatively by individual parties, such an expectation implies more forthrightness on a potentially explosive topic than is politically rational. Over the set of platforms, positive and negative mentions of communalism are virtually independent of each other. They reflect a resort to ambiguity to skirt a divisive issue. In this case it is both an issue on which parties are divided and an issue on which the country could be fractured.

(vi) Conclusions

The factors emerging from our analyses of references in the seven broad issue domains (or the original variables where no factor analysis was done)

TABLE 4.5

MEANS AND STANDARD DEVIATIONS OF FACTOR SCORES BY PARTIES

	LIB X̄	LIB SD	P.C. X̄	P.C. SD	N.D.P X̄	N.D.P SD	S.C. X̄	S.C. SD
EXTERNAL RELATIONS								
1.1 INTERNATIONALISM	-.49	.45	-.43	.90	.83	1.13	.13	.78
1.2 SECURITY	.40	1.45	.03	.92	-.41	.60	-.01	.64
FREEDOM AND DEMOCRACY								
2.1 FREEDOM	-.16	.96	-.30	.63	-.23	.52	1.00	1.46
2.2 DEMOCRACY	-.33	.43	.43	1.25	-.39	.33	.29	1.46
GOVERNMENT STRUCTURE								
3.1 EFFECTIVENESS	.28	1.25	.10	.95	-.16	.82	-.31	.92
3.2 EFFICIENCY	.20	.97	.39	1.11	-.72	.35	.19	1.13
ECONOMY								
4.1 DOMINANT POLITICAL ECONOMY	.12	.47	-.15	1.11	-.44	.47	1.02	1.38
4.2 PRODUCTION	.35	.81	.82	.91	-.99	.63	-.27	.26
4.3 DIRECTION	-.27	.99	-.35	.84	.87	.84	-.35	.74
SOCIAL POLICY AND QUALITY OF LIFE								
5.1 SERVICES	-.30	.59	-.44	1.00	.68	1.20	.10	.70
5.2 SOCIAL GOALS	-.34	.76	-.02	1.11	.63	1.02	-.37	.77
5.3 CULTURE	-.39	.42	-.33	.56	.05	1.01	.96	1.45
FABRIC OF SOCIETY								
6.1 PRO-COMMUNALISM	.05	1.09	-.40	.98	.48	1.03	-.18	.61
6.2 ANTI-COMMUNALISM	.65	1.19	-.20	.80	-.30	.79	-.23	.93
GROUPS								
7.1 PLURALIST	.21	.90	.39	1.56	-.23	.38	-.53	.29
7.2 INDUSTRIAL	-.13	.41	.20	.74	.13	1.01	-.29	1.75

were used to calculate standardized scores (with zero mean and standard deviation taken as the unit in each case). These locate the parties on the dimensions emerging from the analysis. They are reported in Table 4.5 and, on the whole, fit quite readily with conventional conclusions about the spatial configuration of the Canadian party system. On factors in the four dominant domains, the Liberal Party is rarely in an extreme position and it is almost always closer to the position of its main competitor, the Progressive Conservative Party, than to the position of its competitor on the left, the New Democratic Party. On the dimension of culture, the differences between the Liberals (at $-.39$) and the Progressive Conservatives (at $-.33$) are very small and the two might be said to share the extreme negative position on this dimension. The 'effectiveness' dimension was one treated ambiguously as noted above, and the fact that the Liberals and the Progressive Conservatives both score positively suggests that they were the two parties most adept at straddling the issues and thus most vocal on the component themes.

The image of the Canadian party system as consisting of the NDP on the left and Social Credit or Progressive Conservative parties on the right with the Liberal Party dominating the middle ground is discernible on some dimensions, particularly in the area of economic policy, but admits of more exceptions than confirmations. It is particularly evident in the articulation of economic policy themes which, of course, predominate in electoral campaigns. Both the Liberal and the Progressive Conservative parties have managed to remain dead centre on the uncontroversial themes of political economy, but the NDP is much below the zero mean on the 'production' dimension and almost as much above on the 'direction' dimension. On 'production', the Progressive Conservatives are almost in a mirror image position. Though not extremely opposed to economic direction by the state, they share with Social Credit a position below the mean on that dimension. The same ordering holds for the 'services' dimension of domain five, though none of the parties are as extreme as they are on the second and third dimensions of the economic domain. On the second and third social policy dimensions, the Progressive Conservatives move closer to the centre than the Liberals. The difference is small on the 'culture' dimension. While more substantial on the 'social goals' dimensions, it may be a case of an opposition being freer to espouse large objectives than is the habitual governing party.

The most incongruous ordering is that for the industrial, business *vs.* labour dimension in the social groups domain. Recalling that business loaded positively and labour negatively, we might have expected the NDP to score extremely negatively on this dimension. Rather, we observe that the NDP scores moderately positively, and the Liberals score moderately negatively. The NDP, when naming particular groups as beneficiaries, is

William P. Irvine

TABLE 4.6

SECOND STAGE FACTOR ANALYSIS

CORRELATION OF FIRST STAGE FACTORS AND SELECTED[1]
ORIGINAL VARIABLE WITH SECOND STAGE FACTORS

FACTOR:		1	2	3	4	5
VARIMAX ROTATED FACTORS		NEW LEFT	OLD LEFT	SMALL BUSINESS	DEMOCRACY	FREEDOM AND ANTI-COMMUNALISM
1.1	SECURITY	-23	-14	-66	17	-06
1.2	PEACE	65	34	-46	15	-17
CATEGORY 101	SPECIAL FOREIGN RELATIONS	-19	-09	-56	23	-05
CATEGORY 104	MILITARY	-22	-21	-54	01	-06
CATEGORY 106	PEACE	52	-17	-35	08	-30
CATEGORY 107	INTERNATIONALISM	56	44	-33	19	04
2.1	FREEDOM	-01	08	-13	31	80
2.2	DEMOCRACY	-15	-18	-19	71	-07
3.1	EFFECTIVENESS	-09	-02	11	06	01
3.2	EFFICIENCY	-12	-72	25	28	-10
CATEGORY 303	EFFICIENCY	-10	-68	24	31	-07
4.1	CONSENSUAL ECONOMIC POLICY	-09	-41	54	29	-04
4.2	INTERVENTION	47	57	16	02	-03
CATEGORY 403	REGULATION	42	80	21	15	-09
CATEGORY 413	NATIONALIZATION	41	51	18	-07	-00
5.1	SOCIAL SERVICES	-11	80	22	12	-09
5.2	POST MATERIALISM	78	04	11	03	15
CATEGORY 501	ENVIRONMENT	61	00	06	-02	-02
CATEGORY 503	SOCIAL JUSTICE	57	14	13	12	-14
CATEGORY 504	SOCIAL SERVICE	-04	64	26	07	-17
CATEGORY 506	EDUCATION	-11	68	14	15	09
6.1	COMMUNALISM+	67	-14	09	-02	29
6.2	COMMUNALISM-	-07	-09	02	-27	73
7.1	NON-INDUSTRIAL	-30	-13	-11	-84	-10
7.2	INDUSTRIAL	-06	05	83	03	-16
CATEGORY 701	LABOUR	-02	08	-52	19	06
703	AGRICULTURE	-31	-10	-27	-75	-09
704	BUSINESS	-11	17	75	18	-18
706	DEMOGRAPHIC/NON-ECONOMIC	-28	-15	09	-67	-16
FROM UNROTATED SOLUTIONS						
EIGENVALUE		2.49	2.03	1.72	1.40	1.18
% OF VARIANCE EXPLAINED		18	15	12	10	8

NOTES TO TABLE:

1. A VARIABLE WAS SELECTED FOR INCLUSION IF IT LOADED AT AT LEAST 0.5 ON
   AT LEAST ONE OF THE SECOND STAGE FACTORS.

2. NOT PRECISELY THE SAME FACTORS REPORTED IN TABLE 3.3. THESE WERE
   CALCULATED FROM A SOLUTION CONSTRAINED TO TWO FACTORS.

3. NOT PRECISELY THE SAME FIVE FACTORS REPORTED FOR THE SOCIAL POLICY
   DOMAIN. THESE WERE CALCULATED FROM A SOLUTION CONSTRAINED TO TWO
   FACTORS.

more likely to name small businessmen than it is to name trade unions – obviously taking more care not to scare potential supporters than to reassure committed ones. It is important not to over-interpret the differences, however. References to labour and to business had a combined average of about 2.5 per cent of all platform themes, compared to over 4.5 per cent devoted to primary producers and almost 6 per cent to one or more demographic groups.

The Liberal and New Democratic parties are at opposite ends of the two foreign policy dimensions. As we have seen, the NDP is the most internationalist and the Liberals the most security minded. For the freedom and democracy domain, the first dimension is exclusively a Social Credit preserve, while the second theme is monopolized by the Progressive Conservative and Social Credit parties. Both freedom and democracy tend to be images to which appeal is made in denigration of the bureaucratic state which these two parties associate with the Liberal and New Democratic parties. In the 'fabric of society' domain, the NDP is the only party with a formally consistent position on the two issues. It is well above average in statements supporting communalism and well below average in statements opposing it. The Liberals are almost as clearly at the opposite poll – well above average in statements opposing communalism and about average in statements supporting it. The Progressive Conservative and Social Credit parties have sought to avoid either dimension.

4.6 GENERAL DIMENSIONS AND PARTY MOVEMENT

What links exist among these 'within domain' factors? To answer this question, fourteen variables (first-order factors and original categories from each domain) (4) are again factor-analysed to determine if any overarching structure exists. The results are presented in Table 4.6.

To aid interpretation, the table presents both loadings of each first-order factor on the five emergent second-order dimensions (5), and major correlations between selected original categories and the second-order factors. (The position is slightly complicated by the fact that certain original categories were entered in the analysis where no first-order factors could be extracted. Their loadings on the second order factors are shown.)

The first three second-stage factors emerge clearly and have simple interpretations as appeals to the 'New Left', 'Old Left' and 'Small Business' respectively. The first factor is labelled 'New Left' because it correlates strongly with themes of 'peace', 'internationalism', 'social justice', the 'environment' and with support for communal organization of social life – all themes which Inglehart has identified as themes appropriate to a party wishing to appeal to a 'post-material' culture (Inglehart 1977). The 'Old Left' factor calls for government regulation and nationalization in the economy, government support for social welfare and education and underplays discussion of 'government efficiency' – often a mask for budget-cutting. The third factor is dominated by references to consensual economic policy (though no theme within the economic domain correlates with second-order Factor 3 at .5 or better), above average references to business and avoidance of references to labour. High scores on this third factor tend to shun all aspects of foreign policy – avoiding in particular Canada's traditional commitments but also avoiding any redefinition of those commitments in a more pacifist direction. It is for this reason that the domain seems to tap small business themes.

The fourth and fifth second-order factors are less easily labelled and seem to tap themes and strategies of appeal most characteristic of the Social Credit Party. The fourth factor appeals to the symbol of 'democracy' and avoids reference to the main groups in pluralistic politics – primary sector producers and demographic groups. The fifth factor touches the theme of 'freedom' and 'anti-communalism'.

Table 4.7 shows the positions of the parties on the five second-order dimensions, as Table 4.5 did for the first-order dimensions. On the first three, the New Democratic Party always occupies one pole, and the Progressive Conservative Party the other, though the central positions are more variable. Indeed, in two of the first three dimensions, the Social Credit Party is closer to the NDP than is the Liberal Party, suggesting a 'major party/minor party' ordering as well as a 'left/right' one. (Note that the table columns are arranged according to a conventional 'left/right' characterization of the party system). The left–right ordering comes in because the NDP always emerges to the (directional) left of the Social Credit Party, and the Liberals to the left of the Progressive Conservatives. The table confirms that the fourth and fifth dimensions, particularly the fourth, 'belong' to Social Credit.

Note that the factor spanning the widest range is the second or 'Old Left' factor. The ordering puts the Social Credit Party to the left of the Liberal Party. Party positioning here seems to be an admixture of the party's normal ideology and the needs of its social base. The Social Credit Party, though right-wing populist, had even more of a working class base than the NDP, particularly after 1962. Though Liberal electors are as well-off, on average, as Conservative, its more urban electoral strategy pulls it slightly to the left of their rivals on this dimension.

These inconsistencies of positioning indicate a certain lack of ideological differentiation on the part of the Canadian parties. Another striking feature is the very high standard deviations of party positions over time. Of the 20 mean scores reported in Table 4.7, the standard deviation exceeds the mean in some sixteen cases, and virtually equals it in another two. The only cases where the mean substantially exceeds its standard deviation are for

TABLE 4.7

MEANS AND STANDARD DEVIATIONS OF SECOND STAGE FACTORS BY PARTY

FACTOR		NDP		LIB		S.C.		P.C.	
		X	S.D.	X	S.D.	X	S.D.	X	S.D.
1	NEW LEFT	1.08	1.07	-.32	0.81	-.36	0.32	-.51	0.98
2	OLD LEFT	1.28	1.01	-.44	0.54	-.18	0.96	-.71	0.84
3	SMALL BUSINESS	.32	1.01	-.16	0.86	.01	1.47	-.17	0.86
4	DEMOCRACY	-.09	0.43	-.50	0.90	1.05	0.70	-.14	1.50
5	FREEDOM, ANTI-COMMUNALISM	-.23	0.60	.28	1.07	.54	1.46	-.43	0.66
N		13		13		9		13	

the Social Credit Party on the fourth factor – the factor most clearly identifiable as 'its' preserve – and for the NDP on the 'Old Left' factor, on which the NDP likes to regard itself as the sole propellent if not as the sole committed legislator.

The same information is presented visually in Figure 4.1 which plots the parties' average post-war position in two-dimensional spaces defined by the first three second-order factors. Each of the plots show the NDP by itself in one quadrant of the graph and the other three parties virtually indistinguishably located in, or very near to, the opposite quadrant. The Liberal Party's success in moving closer to the origin (i.e. the centre of the space) than its major rival emerges quite clearly, though the differences are not large.

Does this clustering on the right confirm the oft-heard charge, levelled mainly by NDP partisans, that they are the only party to offer some choice to the electorate? An answer comes from the distribution across time of party positions on the 'Old Left' factor, the factor which produced the widest inter-party divergences. What emerges is a surprising amount of choice from election to election, even between the two major parties, but also a quite inordinate amount of leap-frogging among the parties, and between the Liberals and the Progressive Conservatives in particular. In four elections since the war, the Progressive Conservative Party has proclaimed a more interventionist social policy than the Liberal Party. Still, one should not overemphasize the confusion that this could cause. The Liberal Party has the stronger 'social welfare' image in the post-1945 period. Of the thirteen elections in this period, the two parties have been separated by more than .5 (more, that is, than one-half of a standard deviation) on nine occasions on the 'Old Left' factor.

This positioning is probably important to many Liberal activists and voters. On two occasions, 1958 and 1979, the two parties were within 0.2 of a standard deviation of each other. The first saw a massive defeat of the

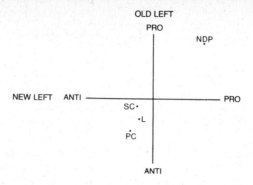

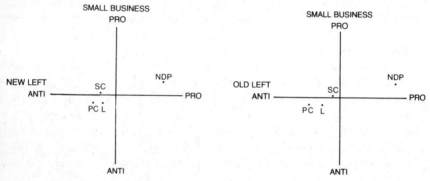

4.1 Average Canadian party positions on three second-stage factors

Liberal Party; the second a close and ultimately impermanent defeat. Interestingly, although the Liberal Party gave a good deal of thought to social policy, and made it a part of their rebuilding from the electoral defeat of 1958, it did not become especially prominent. The party also devoted much attention to the place of Quebec within the Confederation. After 1958, the Liberals gave less prominence than the Progresive Conservative Party to 'Old Left' themes right up to 1968. It is perhaps noteworthy that the Liberals failed to score a decisive victory until the 1968 election. There is some evidence that the lesson was learned. Before the 1979 election, the Liberal government moved sharply to accommodate the neo-conservative movement prominent in Canada and elsewhere. This brought them very close to the Progressive Conservative position which had not changed substantially since 1972, and also brought them to defeat. Although the Liberal Party sought to avoid promises in the 1980 campaign, the few it did make were in the area of social policy. Because so few other promises were being made, the Liberals' relative emphasis on social policy was the

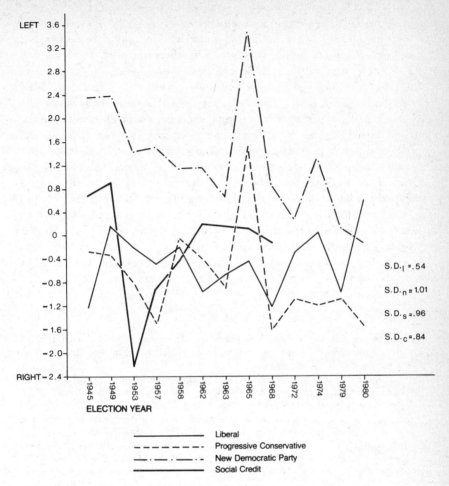

4.2 Old Left factor by party and year for Canada

sharpest it had been in the post war period. It certainly responded to the 'return to the left', sought by some activists in the aftermath to 1979.

Of those elections that have offered a substantial choice between the parties the Liberals were farthest toward the positive pole in seven. The CCF/NDP has been clearly distinct from the two older parties, only straying into the Liberals' territory in the 1980 election and never once crossing the path of the Progressive Conservatives. Social Credit has traced the most erratic path. Reflecting its Depression origins, it was second only to the CCF in calling for state social programmes in the post-war period. By the time of the 1953 election, however, its Western populist base was pulling it to the most conservative social position, and this was not reversed until it made its breakthrough in Quebec in 1962

The party time-paths on other second-order dimensions are similar, but more closely bunched, and cross into each others' territory. In Figure 4.2, for example, we find five instances of cross-over between the Liberal and the Progressive Conservative parties, one crossing of the Liberal and New Democratic parties and none of Progressive Conservatives and New Democrats. By contrast, there are nine exchanges of position between the major parties on the 'New Left' dimension, four between Liberals and NDP, and four between Progressive Conservatives and New Democrats.

Our conclusion must take account both of these results and of changes in the format of platforms. There is a diminution of consistent policy-competition between the parties. The recent search for the striking slogan has led them to pick and discard themes like a beggar going through a trash heap. This produces inconsistency both in the positioning of the parties *vis-à-vis* each other, and in the changes of their policy position over time. Nonetheless our factor analyses do suggest that Canadian parties can be scored on a left-right ideology of some vintage – new or old.

Notes

1 Thanks are due to the Social Sciences and Humanities Research Council of Canada for support of this research and Geoff Gomery for his excellent work as primary coder of the Canadian party platforms.

2 The General source for Canadian party platforms between 1945 and 1968 is D. Owen Carrigan, *Canadian Party Platforms, 1867–1968*, (Toronto: Copp Clark 1968). Later election platforms were taken from collections in the Public Archives of Canada and the Documentation Service of the Douglas Library at Queen's University. For a more complete listing, see Appendix A.

3 This could be an artifact of poor data collection, but is consistent with two more specific studies as well: Whitaker 1977, pp. 192–4, 206–8, 216–51; and John Meisel 1962.

4 Since we had initially settled for three-factor solutions for domains four and five, these were reanalysed subject to a constraint that only two factors were to be extracted. The two factors are similar to, but not the same as, those discussed and have been renamed to help avoid confusion.

5 In the second-order factor analysis, six factors obtained an Eigenvalue greater than 1.0 but the sixth was at 1.10 and seemed to tap only one of the original factors – that of government effectiveness.

CHAPTER 5

SRI LANKA 1947–1977
ELITE PROGRAMMES AND
MASS POLITICS[1]

——————— ∿ ———————

5.1 INTRODUCTION

Sri Lanka is an island nation lying twenty-five miles off the southern tip of India. It is densely populated, with about fifteen million people residing within its 25,332 square miles. The population consists of roughly 71 per cent Sinhalese (largely Buddhist), 21.6 per cent Tamil (largely Hindu), and smaller racial groups. Each is a self-conscious and well-defined community. Much of the island was dominated from the late sixteenth century by European powers – first the Portuguese, then the Dutch and finally the British who displaced the Dutch in the 1790s. In February, 1948, Ceylon became a self-governing state within the Commonwealth, and in 1972, a republic retaining Commonwealth membership, under the name of Sri Lanka.

The British shared power more generously with the Ceylonese[2] than with other non-Western peoples. As a result, the island has had a longer experience of elections on the basis of universal suffrage than any country in Afro-Asia with the exception of Japan and the Philippines. Nonetheless, the first two Ceylonese elections under universal suffrage in 1931 and 1936 are omitted from this discussion because the Donoughmore Constitution, under which they were conducted, intentionally prevented the formation of political parties by fragmenting power among seven discrete committees in the State Council (the island's legislature) and among the Ministers which each committee elected.

Our study begins with the general election of 1947 which was held under a new constitutional structure based on the Westminster model which continued in use until 1972. Under this bicameral system, sovereign powers rested with the lower house called the House of Representatives, members of which were directly elected from territorial constituencies on a first-past-the-post basis.[3] The leader of the largest party in the House was called upon to form a government which operated on the principle of collective responsibility, and could be dismissed by a vote of no confidence. The republican constitution of 1972, under which the last election studied was held in 1977, abolished the upper house and replaced the Governor-General with a non-executive President. But all other elements were maintained. In 1978, a second republican constitution was broadly modelled on the Fifth French Republic. It created a powerful executive President and introduced the principle of proportional representation into parliamentary elections (Manor 1979).

This chapter deals with eight general elections in Sri Lanka: in 1947, 1952, 1956, two in 1960, and one each in 1965, 1970 and 1977. We will examine seven sets of manifestos since parties presented the same policies at the two 1960 elections, held at an interval of only four months. Sri Lanka is almost unique among the less developed countries in having evolved something akin to a two-party system. At the six general elections from 1956–77, voters rejected the ruling party and brought in the major opposition alternative (sometimes in coalition with minor parties). This has meant that one of two parties has always held a dominant position in government in Sri Lanka: the centre-right United National Party (UNP) or the centre-left Sri Lanka Freedom Party (SLFP).

In this study we will only deal with the manifestos of these two major parties. This means that we have excluded the manifestos of various minor parties, among which are those of the Communist Party and the so-called Trotskyists who appear in various factional forms at all elections. We exclude them for two reasons. First, although these parties often possess potential as coalition partners, the factionalism, petty quarrels, vendettas, purges and defections that have marked the behaviour of leftist politicians has meant that many of the persons who fight under one banner at one election may appear under another at the next. As a result a party label on one occasion may be affixed to a group of people different from those to which it applied on the previous or succeeding occasion. Second, these parties have never succeeded in penetrating much beyond urban workers (a small minority in predominantly rural Sri Lanka).

We also exclude the various parties of the substantial Tamil linguistic minority, since they have changed their labels, leaders, personnel and character so often as to make comparisons from election to election misleading. Furthermore they do not compete much outside the Northern Province and even there have not had great success in attracting strong and lasting support. Their transitory existence and marginality to the mainstream of politics means that documents are in any case hard to come by and manifestos in some cases do not seem to have been produced.

5.2 THE PARTY SYSTEM

The party system of Sri Lanka is not easily categorized, but if we take Sartori's typology (Sartori 1976, 131–45 and 173–85), we find that Sri Lanka falls broadly (if somewhat imperfectly) under the heading of 'moderate pluralism'. There have been phases in the island's political history in which the two main parties achieved such prominence that the system took on, for a time, the appearance of something close to a two-party system.

But the other parties have never been sufficiently eclipsed to warrant the use of that term. At first glance, the sheer number of minor parties at some elections might also suggest the existence of 'polarized pluralism'. More importantly, there are very few examples of *genuine* anti-system parties. The Tamil parties have at most times accepted the legitimacy of the political system. The main left parties – the Communist Party and the various Lanka Sama Samaja Parties (who claim to be Trotskyists) – have also accepted elections, Parliament and other liberal institutions, not only in practice but in explicit statements as well. They have been strongly oriented towards participation in coalitions with the centre-left SLFP, both in government and (less formally) in opposition. This has inclined them towards compromises to allay the fears of potential voters at the centre of the political spectrum. The only major example of an anti-system party was the Janatha Vimukthi Peramuna which developed during the late 1960s and mounted an abortive insurrection in 1971. But even they, since 1977, have functioned as a marginal force that tacitly accepts the rules of the existing political order.

The other reason for the use of the term 'moderate pluralism' is the tendency of both major parties (and, as we have seen, many minor parties) to seek the political centre. One of the interesting findings to emerge from this study is the considerable similarity between the UNP and the SLFP in the thematic content of their manifestos. The dominant tendency in politics has been *centripetal*. Even the Tamil parties have essentially sought a greater share within the existing framework (e.g. devolved power to regional councils): the nascent guerrilla war in the Tamil areas from 1984–5 is too recent and its outcome too uncertain to affect this characterization.

Power in the two major parties in Sri Lanka has always been highly centralized, partly because of the personalized rule which two families have exercised. In the UNP, D. S. Senanayake – the most prominent pre-independence leader, to whom the British transferred power – was succeeded by his son Dudley who was in turn succeeded by his first cousin, Sir John Kotelawala. (Hence the oft-made comment that 'UNP' stands for 'Uncle Nephew Party'). Sir John was succeeded by his predecessor who retained the leadership despite more than one electoral disaster until his death in 1973. He was succeeded by a slightly more distant and deserving relative, J. R. Jayewardene, who had to fight off a challenger from another Senanayake to become leader. The SLFP was dominated by its founder, S. W. R. D. Bandaranaike, until his assassination in 1959 and he was succeeded – after a year of confusion – by his widow. Mrs Bandaranaike has kept control ever since and has relied heavily upon her son, daughters, erstwhile son-in-law and assorted uncles, cousins, etc.

One by-product of this has been the near-total control which the leader of each party has exercised over the process of manifesto-making at each election. S. W. R. D. Bandaranaike personally drafted the manifestos of the SLFP in 1951 and 1956. In every other case except one[4] the aides to the party leaders drew up early drafts (usually on close instructions from the leaders) and then the party's supreme leader revised them. Power within the parties was sufficiently centralized that leaders seldom felt the need to placate intra-party pressure groups. On three occasions (1956, 1965 and 1970), the SLFP has stood for elections in alliances with left parties. In 1956 and 1970, they issued common manifestos. But the SLFP was so powerful that it had to make few substantive concessions to its allies.

We have obtained manifestos for both major parties at every general election except those of 1952 and 1956. In those years, the full texts were not published in the press or in books on the election, and the original documents have not been traced. We are thus left with somewhat imperfect press summaries of the UNP manifestos and no summaries at all of the SLFP manifestos since the press was generally hostile. We have been forced to rely (for 1952) upon newspaper summaries of the statement of policies and purpose which the SLFP issued in 1951, at its establishment, and (for 1956) upon reports of statements of policy by the SLFP leader. (Interviews with former party officials indicate that the final election manifesto of 1952 differed little from 1951 statement and that the reports for 1956 conform broadly to the final manifesto.)

There is little evidence that voters read or hear of manifestos, despite high literacy and great popular interest in politics (turnout was 86.3 per cent in 1970). This is partly the fault of the two main parties. With their consistently poor organization, they do not make as much of their manifestos as they might. Other, wider appeals are made to voters – who have more in common with other populations of the Third World than the Westernized facade would suggest (Smith 1974). During election times excitement, and expectations from politics, soar to wildly unrealistic heights. As their heady visions of political transformation lead people naturally to support the opposition, elections in Sri Lanka have normally been lost by the government. But this period of intoxication is only the first state in a cycle which leads on to disillusionment, cynicism and sometimes violence.

5.3 CODING THE MANIFESTOS

The general scheme fitted the documents of the UNP and SDLP surprisingly well.[5] But two of the original categories required expansion in order to reflect more accurately certain characteristics of the political culture. The category of 'Communalism Positive' was divided into three sub-categories pertaining to religion, language and culture, all of which reflect ethnicity and have played a dominant role in the island's political history and development. We felt that these elements should be investigated separately at least in the first instance, in order to determine whether they were dominant in terms of frequency of manifesto references for either or both parties. The sub-categories were not divided up in terms of the different ethnic groups since specific references to the Sinhalese and Tamils were rare, and in any case were reflected by other characteristics, such as religion.

Similarly the category of 'Non-economic Demographic Groups' was divided into four specific and one residual sub-category. This enabled the ethnic dimension of politics to be further tapped, and the importance of other groups to be examined. The four specific subcategories were Ayurvedic Physicians (practitioners of traditional, non-Western medicine closely linked to Buddhist-Sinhalese culture), Indigenous Language Teachers, Clergy and Local Government Personnel. The residual subcategory included a variety of groups such as students, school-leavers, tenants and house owners (which reflect status relationships), villagers (of special importance to an agriculturally-based economy), Indian immigrants (most of whom are disenfranchised and represent a special issue in Sri Lanka) and women.

Three general categories also require clarification. 'Internationalism Positive' was largely used to account for references to Sri Lanka's status as a non-aligned nation, which was of particular importance to SLFP Banderanaike governments. 'Underprivileged minorities' mainly accounts for references to the Moorish minority, and 'Other economic groups' covers a wide range of references.

With these clarifications the scheme applied surprisingly well. The average percentage of sentences left uncoded (usually because of excessive vagueness) was 14.45 per cent (a range from 0.00 per cent to 39.34 per cent). Direct references to the other party or to its policies constituted an average 4.83 per cent, with a range from 0.00 per cent to 27.32 per cent. In the case of Sri Lanka therefore, the saliency approach to coding is thoroughly justified.

TABLE 5.1

LEADING CATEGORIES FOR UNP AND SLFP MANIFESTOS 1947 – 1977

CATEGORY	UNP		SLFP		BOTH PARTIES	
	X̄	S.D.	X̄	S.D.	X̄	S.D.
AGRICULTURE	9.18	0.17	8.25	0.10	8.72	0.01
COMMUNALISM+	7.74	4.11	7.64	1.20	7.69	3.52
SOCIAL SERVICES+	6.04	0.01	5.29	3.30	5.67	2.19
FREEDOM	3.46	0.28	7.70	0.06	5.58	0.61
DEMOGRAPHIC GROUPS	4.82	1.60	5.57	0.00	5.20	0.17
PRODUCTIVITY	6.74	0.99	3.67	0.11	5.20	0.27
DEMOCRACY	3.35	0.01	5.90	0.00	4.63	0.38
LABOUR GROUPS+	2.69	0.97	5.68	1.34	4.19	1.14

5.4 LEADING THEMES

Turning now to the more substantive aspects of the analysis, we can see from Table 5.1 above that although there are important issues common to both parties there are also some significant differences.

In both cases the category mentioned with greatest frequency is Agriculture, which is hadly surprising given the basis of the Ceylonese economy and the nature of the political elite. Positive references to 'Communalism', i.e. religion, language and culture also rank highly for both parties. The main difference between the UNP and SLFP is that in the case of the former, only four categories manage to achieve a mean percentage score which is greater than five per cent, whereas in the case of the latter there are seven. Three of the UNP's categories are also meaningful to the SLFP, whereas the fourth, Productivity, only attains 3.67 per cent in the case of the SLFP. The additional SLFP categories similarly have low mean percentage scores in UNP manifestos – 3.46 per cent for Freedom, 3.35 per cent for Democracy and 2.69 per cent for Labour Groups Positive.

All the categories which scored mean percentages above five per cent for the individual parties also achieve this level taking all manifestos together, apart from Democracy and Labour Groups Positive. Thus it would seem that six of the categories appear to reflect major manifesto issues, and that the SLFP generally regards a greater number of issues as being of major importance than the UNP, throughout the time period under consideration. We now consider each topic briefly:

(i) Agriculture

The difference here between the SLFP and the UNP is quite marked. The UNP's references to agriculture vary greatly. Its high mean percentage is mainly due to the fact that on two occasions – 1957 and 1970 – it represented a very high proportion of manifesto content (19.8 per cent in the latter case). However, in 1952, 1960 and 1965 it did not even manage to reach the five per cent threshold. The SLFP on the other hand has consistently increased its emphasis on agriculture, apart from a slight fall in 1960 as compared with 1956.

(ii) Communalism positive

This was also an interesting category in terms of differences between the two parties, as it reflects the issue of Tamil status, especially with regard to language. It appears that until 1970 each party emphasized the issue whilst the other de-emphasized it in turn. It also seems that use of communalism as an issue began to decline after 1960 in the UNP, and after 1965 in the SLFP. Since then both parties seem to have moved closer in their emphases.

(iii) Social Services – pro-expansion

Like the two issues discussed above, the UNP is more volatile in its emphases. There is also the 'pendulum' effect of each party stressing it when the other does not. This trend becomes more marked after 1960.

(iv) Freedom

Freedom is an issue that is of greater importance in SLFP than in UNP manifestos. Indeed only in 1947 and 1965 did it account for more than five per cent of UNP references, whereas it passes five per cent in half those of the SLFP and never falls below 3.4 per cent in the rest. Again, we have the phenomenon, at least until 1970, that when the issue is stressed by one party, it is of apparently little concern to the other. This general pattern again confirms the relevance of a saliency approach. In 1977 it seems to change, with a decided decline in the importance of the issue for both parties. It is also the only category where the SLFP behaves more erratically than the UNP.

(v) Demographic groups

This category is particularly weighted, in the Sri Lankan context, by references to youth and women. It shows similar variations for both parties from 1956 onwards, although variations are less for the SLFP than for the UNP. From 1947 to 1965 the UNP placed increasing emphasis on the area; culminating in the latter year with 15 per cent of references compared to just under five per cent in 1960. It then fell even more dramatically in 1970 to just over two per cent, and rose again in 1977, to over 8 per cent. Although SLFP emphases have also varied largely, fluctuations are less marked, ranging from 1.5 per cent to 9.5 per cent. The interesting feature of this category is that the 'pendulum' effect apparent in the others is absent, and with one exception both parties either emphasize or de-emphasize it at the same election.

(vi) Productivity

This is of greater importance to the UNP, where it accounts for well over five per cent of references in the manifestos of 1947, 1956, 1960 and 1970. With the SLFP it only passes the 5 per cent threshold in 1965.

5.5 THE SEVEN DOMAINS

When the individual categories are collapsed into the standard seven domains, the most salient (when both parties are taken together) is the Economy, followed by Social Groups. This reflects the results of the original content analysis in that Agriculture and Demographic Groups, the most salient categories, are included in the Social Groups domain. Individual economic categories were not, however, particularly evident apart from productivity, and that mainly for the UNP.

5.6 THE FIRST-ORDER FACTOR ANALYSIS

(i) Social Groups Domain

Negative references to Labour Groups and references to Underprivileged Minorities were omitted from the analysis due to zero references and very low use respectively. The solution to this factor analysis – a factor with heavy loadings of positive references to Labour Groups and positive references to Agriculture – is representative of one of the basic socio-economic factors of this society, the division between agriculture and non-agricultural sectors, and totally unsurprising.

(ii) Fabric of Society

Again, the emergence of a single factor with heavy positive loadings from National Way of Life and Communalism, and negative loadings $(-.35)$ from National Effort, is a straightforward solution, reflecting the communal nature of Ceylonese society and political culture. It catches the reluctance of both main parties to be seen to urge the Sinhalese to take account of Tamil demands.

(iii) The Economy

The analysis actually produced a four-factor solution, but the third and fourth factors are not considered further. They added only a further 27.80 per cent to explained variation, compared to 50 per cent for the first two factors.

These are difficult to interpret. The first seems to consist of support for planned production, but also embraces a negative attitude towards Incentives, accompanied by a negative attitude towards Nationalization. Perhaps the factor reflects a 'middle of the road' approach to economic policy, which would support a mixed economy and a degree of government intervention rather than extremes based on a leftist or rightist approach. The second factor is more straightforward in that it seems to posit a belief in the Regulation of Capitalism and Economic Goals as opposed to Enterprise (which loads at $-.32$). Collectively the two factors suggest a centre-left approach to Sri Lanka's economic problems, and so may not be particularly useful in differentiating between the two main parties.

(iv) Welfare

The single factor solution with a heavy loading (.88) in both cases for Education and Art, Sport, Leisure, Media suggests an essentially positive attitude towards these areas. Although not a unipolar solution, the positive aspects of this factor appear much stronger than the negative (a $-.36$ loading for Social Justice). There may be some opposition between spending priorities in this area.

(v) Government

The first factor, which is unipolar, may be identified as government efficiency. It has heavy loadings from Government Efficiency (.87); positive references to Decentralization (.52) and Government Corruption (.50). The second seems largely concerned with government corruption (.67), but has a high negative loading ($-.74$) for positive references to Decentralization.

(vi) Freedom

Since only two of the original categories included in this domain remained after application of the one per cent threshold test, these are used as inputs

TABLE 5.2

FIRST ORDER FACTOR ANALYSIS: MEANS AND STANDARD DEVIATIONS
OF FACTOR SCORES BY PARTY AND DOMAIN   (%)

DOMAIN AND FIRST-ORDER FACTOR SCORE FOREIGN RELATIONS:^{x}	UNP		SLFP	
	$\bar{x}$	S.D.	$\bar{x}$	S.D.
DECOLONIZATION	1.21	0.45	2.72	0.09
INTERNATIONALISM	2.38	0.00	1.52	0.01
FREEDOM: ^{x}				
FREEDOM	3.46	0.28	7.70	0.06
DEMOCRACY	3.35	0.01	5.90	0.00
GOVERNMENT:				
EFFICIENCY	−0.06	0.83	0.07	1.25
CORRUPTION	−0.18	1.12	0.21	0.89
ECONOMY:				
PLANNED PRODUCTION	0.21	1.25	−0.24	0.62
REGULATION OF CAPITALISM	−0.36	0.50	0.42	1.31
WELFARE:				
EDUCATION AND CULTURE	−0.17	0.62	0.27	1.36
FABRIC OF SOCIETY:				
COMMUNALISM	0.10	1.31	−0.11	0.55
SOCIAL GROUPS:				
NON-AGRICULTURAL	−0.26	0.99	0.30	1.01
AGRICULTURAL	−0.17	1.09	0.20	0.93

x − ORIGINAL VARIABLES WERE USED SINCE NO FIRST-ORDER FACTOR ANALYSIS WAS DONE

directly into the second-order factor analysis and hence no first-order
factor analysis was carried out. The two categories are those of Freedom
and Democracy.

(vii) Foreign Relations

Once again, only two original categories − Decolonization and Internationalism Positive − remained after application of the one per cent
threshold test.

Table 5.2 summarizes the results of the first-order factor analysis, giving

TABLE 5.3

RESULTS OF SECOND-ORDER FACTOR ANALYSIS

| | SECOND ORDER FACTORS | |
	FACTOR 1	FACTOR 2
FOREIGN RELATIONS ORIGINAL CATEGORIES:		
DECOLONIZATION	-.16	.01
INTERNATIONALISM	-.68	-.27
FREEDOM:		
ORIGINAL CATEGORIES:		
FREEDOM	-.03	-.01
DEMOCRACY	.00	-.01
GOVERNMENT:		
F1 EFFICIENCY	.08	.11
F2 CORRUPTION	.68	.31
ORIGINAL CATEGORY CORRELATIONS:		
DECENTRALIZATION +	-.37	-.19
GOVERNMENT EFFICIENCY	-.03	.11
GOVERNMENT CORRUPTION	.68	.27
ECONOMY:		
F1 PLANNED PRODUCTION	-.48	.38
F2 REGULATION OF CAPITALISM	.52	.75
ORIGINAL CATEGORY CORRELATIONS:		
ENTERPRISE	-.31	.03
INCENTIVES	.30	.18
REGULATIONS OF CAPITALISM	.59	.33
ECONOMIC PLANNING	-.50	.30
PROTECTIONSISM+	-.12	.58
ECONOMIC GOALS	.31	.65
PRODUCTIVITY	-.53	.29
TECHNOLOGY	.11	.33
NATIONALIZATION	.11	.31

continued...

TABLE 5.3 continued

	FACTOR 1	FACTOR 2
WELFARE		
F1 EDUCATION AND CULTURE	.35	.80
ORIGINAL CATEGORY CORRELATIONS:		
ART, SPORT, LEISURE, MEDIA	.32	.52
SOCIAL JUSTICE	-.34	-.12
SOCIAL SERVICES+	.06	.12
EDUCATION+	.27	.74
FABRIC OF SOCIETY		
F1 COMMUNALISM	-.59	-.42
ORIGINAL CATEGORY CORRELATIONS:		
NATIONAL WAY OF LIFE+	-.30	-.52
NATIONAL EFFORT	.36	.05
COMMUNALISM+	-.51	-.06
SOCIAL GROUPS		
F1 NON-AGRICULTURAL GROUPS	.92	.24
F2 AGRICULTURE	.02	.77
ORIGINAL CATEGORY CORRELATIONS:		
LABOUR GROUPS+	.41	.66
AGRICULTURE	-.17	.22
OTHER ECONOMIC GROUPS	.84	.08
DEMOGRAPHIC GROUPS	.71	-.05

the names of the factors or variables within each domain and the mean scores and standard deviations of the parties in regard to each. The parties are clearly distinguished in terms of their average position on the different factors, which can also be interpreted as showing the moderately conservative position taken by the UNP and the moderately radical position of the SLFP. This is, however, with the already made proviso that these positions may shift drastically from one election to another.

5.7 THE SECOND-ORDER FACTOR ANALYSIS

Twelve inputs were introduced into the second-stage factor analysis. These consisted of the 'four original' categories which represented two inputs each for the Freedom and Foreign Relations domains, and the first-order factor solutions discussed previously. A four-factor solution was obtained as the result of this second-stage operation, but only the first two of these factors, which account for 52.2 per cent of the variation are discussed below after the overall summary of results in tabular form.

At first sight it appears that these factors may not offer much clarification either of the nature of the major underlying dimensions of Ceylonese

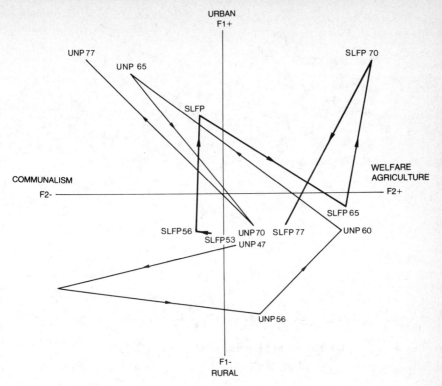

5.1 Spatial analysis of UNP and SLFP in terms of manifesto content, 1947–1977

politics or of the differences between the two main parties. The first factor combines positive attitudes to non-agricultural groups and negative attitudes to internationalism. The latter is anomalous since foreign policy issues are not a major concern of either party, nor are they particularly important in Sri Lanka. However, if we investigate this factor further, we find there is also a respectable positive score for Government Corruption, and negative scores for Communalism. If we then apply a wider interpretation, it could be said that the factor essentially reflects social structure; and, particularly, an emphasis on urban concerns as against rural groups.

Communalism also represents the major negative focus of the second factor, as opposed to a positive component relating to welfare (education and culture) and reinforced by Agricultural Groups and Regulation of Capitalism. This factor is easier to interpret and reflects major elements of political culture. Welfare issues are indeed central to politics and persistent cleavages are related to communalism, and divisions between agriculture and non-agricultural groups.

Thus it appears that the two principal factors reflect some of the major

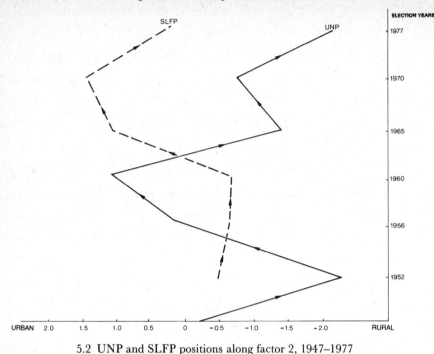

5.2 UNP and SLFP positions along factor 2, 1947–1977

underlying elements of Ceylonese politics – social structure, welfare considerations and moderate economic philosophies.

5.8 SPATIAL ANALYSIS

Another use of factor analysis is in identifying characteristics which enable distinctions to be made between parties. This can be done by plotting scores for each party along one factor, against its scores along the other. The picture emerging in the case of Sri Lanka is unfortunately less clear than one would like. Of course in certain respects there *is* a lack of difference between the parties. They emerge from the same roots and tend to occupy similar areas of ideological space. Figure 5.1 illustrates these tendencies.

We find that indeed no portion of the graph may be said to represent the exclusive territory of one party or the other. Both parties behave erratically, although the SLFP's positions do not seem to shift as dramatically as those of the UNP. On the other hand, the SLFP manages at one time or another to occupy a position in all four quadrants, whereas the UNP is only to be found in three. It is also interesting that the specific positions of each party at each given election are not close to each other. In this sense we can say that the factors help us to distinguish party positions, although this distinction seems to be a reflection of party strategy at given elections. There also seems to be tendency for the parties to differentiate themselves more consistently towards the end of the period, which may indicate a consolidation of both ideology and strategy with greater maturity. All these phenomena appear more clearly when we compare the plots of each party's position along each factor individually, as in Figure 5.2. Using the second, more clearly interpretable of the factors, gives a simpler picture of the tendencies emerging in Figure 5.1.

5.9 MAJOR ISSUES AND ELECTORAL SUCCESS

As a final exercise we decided to identify the categories of importance in the manifestos of each party relative to elections won by that party. The 1947 UNP manifesto is excluded since there was little meaningful alternative to the party and the election was therefore not truly competitive.

The UNP won the elections of 1952, 1965 and 1977. In 1952 the only major issue (i.e. accounting for over five per cent of sentences) was positive references to Communalism. In 1965 there were five: positive references to Communalism, Social Services, Freedom, Demographic Groups and Productivity. In 1977 there were only two, Agriculture and Demographic Groups.

The SLFP won the elections of 1956, July 1960 and 1970. In all three elections the manifestos stressed Agriculture and expansion of the Social Services as major issues. Additionally Freedom appeared as a major issue in 1956 and 1970, positive aspects of Communalism were stressed in 1956; and Demographic Groups in 1960.

It would appear that the SLFP is slightly more consistent than the UNP in terms of what it considers to be issues which are basic to its ideological position. The UNP did not have a single issue of major importance in all three manifestos pertaining to elections which it won. Although conditions at each election may well be different, this result does indicate a link between issues stressed in the manifestos, and issues which the electorate feels are important in terms of choosing a government. The five issues appearing in years of SLFP victories all fall within the six categories that the parties stress collectively with greater frequency. They are Agriculture and positive references to Communalism for elections in the 1950s and 1960s; and Freedom, Expansion of the Social Services and Demographic Groups for elections in the 1960s and 1970s.

5.10 Conclusions

At first sight it might appear that these internationally derived coding categories were unsuitable for Sri Lanka since no dramatic ideological difference appears between the parties. On the other hand, it may be said that the analysis has been successful and that the coding scheme was appropriate, because there *are* no clearly identifiable differences.

The keys to understanding the results are firstly, that the two parties are both controlled by an elite from the same social stratum; and secondly that neither is clearly identifiable as being to the left or the right of the party spectrum. At the same time there are differences between the parties in terms of their positions on specific issues, but these are generally differences of degree rather than of substance. A further complicating factor is that both parties have shifted the emphasis given to issues and their positions on these issues from one election to the next. Finally we must reiterate that in spite of high literacy rates and apparently high rates of electoral participation, the manifestos are not generally available to a wide readership, nor are they necessarily regarded as binding commitments to a programme of action by the party elites.

Given these limits, analysis does seem reasonably successful. The coding scheme has identified an issue-based tradition within each of the parties over time. The absence of sharply conflicting ideologies is in itself a reasonable and illuminating finding, while the results highlight certain specific similarities and differences between what the UNP and the SLFP have regarded as important in terms of their party image.

Notes

1 Thanks are due to the European Consortium for Political Research, the British Academy, the Nuffield Foundation, the U.S. National Endowment for the Humanities and Ealing College of Higher Education, London, for grants and encouragement in support of research for this essay. A. Jeyaratnam Wilson gave indispensable assistance in obtaining copies of manifestos.
2 Despite the change of names, the word 'Ceylonese' has continued to be used to describe the whole population of the island and it will be so used in this essay.
3 There were a small number of multi member constituencies returning two, and in one case, three representatives.
4 This was the odd case of the UNP manifesto of 1947, when the party leader Senanayake delegated the drafting of the manifesto to Bandaranaike the man who shortly after founded the major opposition party, the SLFP. As a result the UNP manifesto for 1947 sounds less conservative, more Sinhalese-chauvinist and indeed far more coherent in its views than was the party itself.
5 In order to check coder reliability, the authors each coded samples of the manifestos and compared coding techniques, which were then standardized. All manifesto coding was equally divided, but checked again at the end of this phase of the study to ensure complete homogeneity.

CHAPTER 6

ISRAEL: 1949–1981[1]

———— ᘐ ————

6.1 INTRODUCTION

Israel forms a self-contained case in terms of post-war elections, since the first national election to take place after independence was held in 1949. The party system however predated Israel's existence as an independent state. Earlier events also helped shape the constitution, which is unwritten, and derives its legitimacy from statute, precedent, custom and ideology. The most important statutes are the Transition Law of 1949, which provided the legal basis of government; the Law of Return of 1950, which affords any Jew the right of settlement in Israel; and the Basic Law, which is a series of enactments dating from 1948 which set out the fundamental rules of government. The British Mandate (1920–48) is of particular relevance for the way in which the party system developed.

Government is based on the principle of representative parliamentary democracy. Parliament, the supreme legislative organ, consists of a single chamber, the Knesset, composed of 120 members. The Executive consists of a cabinet which is formed on the basis of consultation between the State President and representatives of the political parties, and which has to submit to a vote of confidence by the Knesset. The Opposition can challenge the Executive at any time by calling for a motion of confidence. All governments in Israel have been coalitions, often involving a lengthy process of inter-party bargaining, which is controlled by the central committees of the parties involved.

The basis of the electoral system is enshrined in the Election Law of 1955 and its subsequent amendments. It is a straightforward proportional list system with the whole country acting as a single constituency. Seats are allocated according to the d'Hondt principle as presently set down by the Bader-Ofer Amendment of 1973. Elections are supervised by a 34-member Central Elections Committee headed by a Supreme Court judge, and

membership of the committee is proportional to party strength in the
outgoing Knesset. Parties are allowed one member for every four seats, and
all those with less than four seats are allowed one representative. This
committee is responsible, *inter alia*, for the validation of lists of candidates,
the publication of results, and the allocation of broadcasting time per party
in the final month of the campaign. From 1969 parties submitting lists at
both national and local elections have been able to receive funds from the
Treasury towards election expenses.

6.2 THE PARTY SYSTEM

Although Israel only became independent in 1948, the party system at that
time was already well developed. Almost all present day parties have their
roots in the Mandatory period and indeed some can trace their origins back
to the Zionist movements of late nineteenth-century Poland and Czarist
Russia (Lucas 1974). However, contemporary parties really date from the
1920s. The League of Nations had recognized the existence of two distinct
communities in Palestine, and provided for the development of separate
Arab and Jewish community organizations. In the case of the Jews these
formed a quasi-state within a state known as the Yishuv (Horowitz and
Lissak, 1978). This network included an influential trade union organization (the Histadrut), health insurance schemes, educational and defence
organizations, newspapers, a form of parliament and a representative
executive.

Most aspects of social, economic and political life within the Yishuv were
organized, some having their own network of subsidiary organizations,
such as schools, agricultural settlements, housing schemes and para-
military organizations. Parties evolved from the factions that had developed on the basis of different conceptions of Zionism within the framework
of the World Zionist Organization from the end of the nineteenth century.
At Independence therefore, a politically experienced provisional government, used to administration and diplomatic manoeuvering, was able to
fulfil the essential tasks of government immediately the British left
Palestine. They were also able to conduct a war, cease-fire negotiations, the
consolidation and training of an army and a general election within one
year of independent statehood.

The Israeli party system has long been characterized by multi-partism,
factionalization and unstable alliances between parties. Indeed, Sartori
found the system difficult to classify according to his scheme and regarded
it as 'a case by itself to be understood as such' (Sartori 1976). If anything,
in the years since Sartori wrote, the situation has become even more
confused! As he pointed out, the system has certain characteristics of
extreme pluralism but is not polarized. In addition, several parties have

changed their names more than once since 1948, which makes the system appear even more complicated than it is in reality, and much of the fragmentation is personality-inspired rather than ideological.

Overall, the party spectrum is characterized by five tendencies each of which may well be represented by more than one party or alignment. Even where alignments do exist, the individual components tend to retain their separate organizations within the larger entity and indeed some put forward their own lists at local elections. The tendencies are Communist, Labour, Right, Centre and Religious. The present discussion focuses on only three of the tendencies, Labour, Right and Religious. Labour and Right are the only potential electoral victors, but with insufficient support to form governments without help from elsewhere. The Religious parties, although small in terms of votes and seats, are important in terms of both blackmail and coalition potential.

After eight of the ten elections considered in this study, labour parties formed the nuclei of coalitions and dominated governments from 1949 to 1977. Coalitions formed after the elections of 1977 and 1981 have been led by the Likud.

(i) Labour parties

The mainstay of the centre-left MAPAI (Israel Workers Party) was formed in 1929 and derived its power base from a dominant position within the Histadrut. It was the party of the veteran pioneers of the Yishuv, such as David Ben-Gurion and Golda Meir. Its ideals were based on the 'Labour Zionism' of Be'er Borochov and A. D. Gordon which developed in Eastern Europe. (Lucas 1974; Vital 1975). MAPAI came to be regarded as both the architect of independence and the party of the establishment, and developed a dominant position within the party system (Sartori 1976). Ideologically, the party claimed to have a social democratic interpretation of Zionism, although the precise definition of this varies over time and between individuals and factions. From 1949 MAPAI became identified as the party of government and developed the characteristics of a catch-all party. In 1965 MAPAI entered an electoral alignment with Achudut Ha'Avoda, a minor party with policies geared towards foreign affairs, stressing the need for peace and non-alignment whilst at the same time maintaining a state of military preparedness.

MAPAM (United Workers Party) founded in 1948 was an authoritative voice within the trade union and kibbutz movements, and the only non-Communist party to fight for the rights of Israeli Arabs. It called for the nationalization of land and the means of production and was originally pro-Moscow. However, in the early 1950s, the party began to disintegrate, largely over foreign policy. It split and the more militant members joined the communist camp, leaving the decimated remains to act mainly as a spokesman for left-wing kibbutzniks. Its electoral support waned and in 1968 it effected a rapprochement with Achudut Ha'Avoda and MAPAI within the Ma'arach (Labour Alignment), although it continues to offer a separate list at local elections.

It might appear that by the late 1960s the Labour tendency was becoming more consolidated, and although this is true to a certain extent, the mergers between MAPAI and the other groups themselves exacerbated tensions within the MAPAI nucleus. In 1965, a splinter group broke away to form RAFI (Israel Workers List) headed by Ben-Gurion, Moshe Dayan and Shimon Peres. Many factors were involved, especially the personal animosity between Ben-Gurion and Prime Minister Levi Eshkol, the party's abandoning its policy of electoral reform, and the dispute between veteran and younger members. Although RAFI fared remarkably well in the 1965 election, it was too weak to offer a significant challenge to the Alignment, and in 1968, many of its members joined the reconstituted Ma'arach. There has been no major split since then, although prominent individuals have defected. In addition to the factions mentioned, the Labour camp has also included a number of minority groups composed of Arabs and Druze, such as the Israel Druze List, Progress and Unity, and Cooperation and Brotherhood, which traditionally support the Ma'arach in the Knesset.

(ii) The right

The nucleus of the right is the Herut. This is the successor to the Revisionist movement founded in 1925 by Vladimir Jabotinsky as an organized opposition within the World Zionist Organization, and which also developed its own para-military wing, the Irgun Zvei Leumi in opposition to the MAPAI-dominated Haganah. After the dissolution of the Irgun in 1948, its members regrouped to form the Herut in order to fight the MAPAI establishment within the constitutional framework of the new state. Herut subscribed to fundamental Revisionist ideals such as the 'ingathering of the exiles' and the 'reconquest' and settlement of what some consider to be traditional Jewish land in Judea and Samaria (i.e. the West Bank territories). In addition government intervention in the economy and the Histadrut's hegemonic position within health insurance schemes and certain industrial and commercial enterprises have been vehemently opposed. It is always dangerous to exaggerate the importance of personalities to party images and relationships, but in the case of Herut (and later, Likud) the leadership of Menahem Begin has undoubtedly been crucial, especially during the years of Ben Gurion's leadership of MAPAI. Although the latter's withdrawal from mainstream party politics dissipated much of the animosity, Begin remained central to the Herut/Likud image.

In 1965 a pact was forged between Herut and the General Zionist faction of the Liberal Party, which led to the formation of GAHAL (Herut-Liberal Bloc). The General Zionists had contested elections in the 1940s and 1950s as spokesmen of the upper-middle-class, especially businessmen, and were staunch supporters of free enterprise, opposed to state intervention in or control of the economy and the influence of the Histadrut. GAHAL formed the basis of the Likud (Union) which was established in 1973 in the hope of providing a viable alternative government to the Ma'arach. Likud also encompassed other elements at different times; the State List (the RAFI faction that did not re-enter the Ma'arach in 1968); the Free Centre, a dissident Herut faction; Ariel Sharon's Shlomzion (Realization of Zion) faction; the ultra-nationalist Tehiya (Resurrection) groups which presented a separate list in the 1981 election and won three seats; and the extremist organization, Kach, which failed to win any Knesset representation.

(iii) Religious parties

The main force within the religious tendency is the MAFDAL (National Religious Party) which represents a merger between the Mizrahi and the Poalei Mizrahi groups. Both are theocratic in essence, with the Mizrahi presenting a liberal orientation on social and economic issues, and the Poalei Mizrahi, a social democratic orientation. In addition, there are the two 'Agudah' (Association of Israel) parties, the Agudat Israel asnd Poalei Agudat Israel. These are similar in outlook to Mizrahi and Poalei Mizrahi respectively, but are much more orthodox and uncompromising on matters pertaining to religion.

In 1949, all four groups contested the election under one banner, but split immediately afterwards. Mizrahi and Poalei Mizrahi retained their close relationship and in 1956 formally entered a permanent electoral alliance, which has been maintained. They generally poll the third highest percentage of votes. The Poalei Mizrahi has generally been regarded as the stronger element and hence MAFDAL's economic policies have often reflected a social democratic stand, not dissimilar to that of the Ma'arach. MAFDAL has served as a coalition partner in almost every government, bartering their support in parliament for a recognition that they have authority to pronounce on questions concerning religion. Since religious law intrudes in a host of areas that are generally considered as secular elsewhere, such as education, health, personal status and hotel management, MAFDAL's influence has been considerable, and they have generally held the portfolios of the Interior, Education, and Religious Affairs.

Just prior to the 1981 general election, a splinter group led by the out-going Minister for Religious Affairs, Aharon Abuhatzeira, broke away from the MAFDAL to present an independent list known as TAMI (Movement for Israeli Tradition). Although this split was partly due to personal disagreements, Abuhatzeira argued that his main purpose was to allow religious Sephardic Jews (originating mainly in Arab countries) a vehicle for the expression of their political preferences. TAMI joined the new Likud-led coalition after the election.

The influence of the two Agudah parties far outweighs their numerical strength. On occasion, the two parties contest on the basis of one list (the Torah front) but this makes very little difference to their vote. It has been suggested that their influence lies in 'their very intransigence' (Fein 1967) for no government can afford to ignore them totally. If they sense that this is happening, they have an uncanny ability to marshall their supporters to join effective demonstrations, and governments feel that it is bad for both their domestic and international images if the political elite of the only Jewish state is seen to be ignoring the demands of the faithful. From 1977 Agudat Israel was a partner in the Likud-based coalition.

6.3 POLITICAL CULTURE

It is usually assumed that the basic social cleavage in Israeli society is that of confessionalism–secularism (Zelniker and Kahan, 1976) especially since religion is a major legitimating factor for the state. However, if one also takes acount of the electoral performance of the religious parties (and judging by the traffic jams on the sabbath) it would appear that religion has little day to day significance for most Israelis. Both views over-simplify. It is clearly unrealistic to assess the role of religion by the share of the vote obtained by the religious parties. Nor is religion the sole preserve of MAFDAL and the Torah front, for many parties refer to the positive role of Judaism at some time, and religion acts as both a positive and negative influence in political and social terms. This influence is closely bound up with other aspects of Israeli political culture.

Although class, and more particularly status, is important, it is not easy to discuss the party system or voting behaviour in terms of a simple 'left–right' distinction. Some parties may be 'left' of their approach to some issues, but 'right' in the case of others. Similarly, one cannot say that any given party represents *the* middle class or *the* working class since they all derive support, in differing proportions, from both. Indeed, survey evidence shows that most of GAHAL's support came from people who live in 'crowded' conditions, whereas that of the Ma'arach is greater among the 'moderately well-to-do' (Arian 1973).

Class is in any case cross-cut by other social differences in this society of immigrants, notably education and ethnic origin. The early settlers who emigrated to Palestine during the late nineteenth and early twentieth centuries were of Central and East European origin, and came for ideological reasons, so it is hardly surprising that the political elite of the Yishuv and later the State was of Russian or Polish descent. This elite had absorbed European political and cultural values, which were consolidated by the immigrants arriving in the 1930s as a result of Nazi persecution, and in the 1940s by the survivors of the Holocaust. These values could be summed up as nationalism, secularization, modernization and politicization, and were implanted in the system through the development of the Histadrut and the political parties.

However, after the War of Independence, Jews from the Arab countries arrived in large numbers. In the main they had little experience of what Zionism meant and were unused to the modern political values which formed the basis of Israel's developing political culture. Their experience of politics was from a subject rather than participant role, and this made them prey to manipulation by party machines. They have consistently failed to develop effective parties or pressure groups of their own. They have however a higher birthrate and lack technological skills and education. They have lower incomes, cannot afford to see their children through high school or university, and live in poor overcrowded conditions. They also tend to retain a higher degree of religious orthodoxy. In the early years after their arrival many were excluded through lack of skill from benefitting from the MAPAI-Histadrut network and in political terms gravitated to the Herut. In spite of their orthodoxy, the religious parties were not a natural haven for this group, since they practise a ritual tradition based on Sephardi custom and the religious parties are largely products of European Ashkenazi tradition. Since Afro-Asians now represent the largest single group in the Jewish population, their reactions carry important implications for electoral politics.

6.4 THE DOCUMENTS

In the case of the major parties election platforms are largely determined by the party central committees and represent a compromise agreed by the main factions (Torgovnik 1972). These platforms are issued as discrete party documents, but do not normally circulate widely outside the party membership. Smaller parties, especially in the past, have not always issued formal platforms but simply make a statement through the press, either in the form of a specific document or a speech by a prominent leader. In any case, the parties advertise extensively in the press throughout the campaign and since this is the main source of party documentation which is widely available to the electorate, it forms our basic data. Much of this material, especially in the cases of the Ma'arach and Likud, represents a replica of the official party platform or a series of officially determined extracts from this. For other parties the documentation is generally of a similar nature. Where this was not available, campaign speeches or newspaper articles dealing with platforms are used.

The newspaper advertisements vary considerably in length, style and content. Sometimes they comprise virtually the entire platform, sometimes a verbatim extract which the party elite believes to represent the most important electoral issues. We ignore official platforms where the advertisements give a comprehensive precis. Of course advertisements are not the only way in which electors are addressed. Almost all parties supplement them with open letters to the voters; specific statements by the leadership, which often contain virulent attacks against opposing parties; and photographs. Since the election of 1969, television broadcasts by the parties have been introduced.

Most of the material comes from the *Jerusalem Post* (formerly *Palestine Post*) which is an independent daily newspaper published in English. This has been supplemented and corroborated by items drawn from the Hebrew press, notably *Ma'ariv* and *Ha'aretz*. The foreign policy aspects are also checked against platform material reprinted in the monthly *New Outlook*. Newspapers were examined from the date of the announcement of the election through to polling day itself. All elections are covered for the major tendencies.

The length of the documents varied considerably between both elections and parties. For the nine elections, the average length for Ma'arach documents was 183 quasi-sentences, 62 for Likud documents and 70 for MAFDAL documents. There is no clear pattern in terms of documents becoming longer or shorter over time, and the style of presentation changed quite radically between successive elections for all parties.

Given the changes of alliance which have occurred it is often not obvious which party platforms should be selected for analysis. It seemed most sensible to take the party or faction which most closely represented the nucleus of the alignment in question. This was not necessary for MAFDAL since the alliance between Mizrahi and Poalei Mizrahi has remained constant since 1949.

In the case of the Ma'arach, the actual platforms used to represent the 'party' viewpoint prior to 1969 (since when the alignment has remained constant in organizational terms at least), are as follows. For the elections of 1949, 1951, 1955, 1959 and 1961, the MAPAI platform is taken as the clearest indication of the alignment's stand as MAPAI is clearly the nucleus of the present Ma'arach. In 1965, the Israel Labour Party platform is used for the same reason.

Prior to 1973, Likud's development fell into two phases. In the first,

(1949 to 1961), Herut stood independently, and since this is clearly the nucleus of the Likud, Herut platforms are used in these cases. The second (1965 to 1969), begins with the merger between Herut and the Liberal Party in GAHAL, and thus the latter's platforms are used.

6.5 THE PLATFORMS

In some cases very careful contextual interpretation was necessary to identify exactly which category of the general coding scheme was most relevant. In many cases, the categories of Military Positive; Defence of National Way of Life Positive; and Peace, proved difficult to disentangle. Peace, security and Zionism are so closely bound up that it is hard to choose only one category for a given quasi-sentence. Where references specifically mentioned defence or the Israel Defence Forces as the basis for the survival of the state, they were assigned to Military Positive, and where peace was considered to be central for survival, they were coded as Peace. References to Zionism with vague allusions to defence or peace were coded as National Way of Life Positive.

There was a similar overlap between National Way of Life Positive; and Traditional Morality Positive. The distinction made here was whether or not religion or a religious precept was specifically mentioned. If it was, then the reference was coded as Traditional Morality Positive.

In order to ensure coding reliability certain checks were introduced throughout the early stages of the project. Since all coding of the party platforms was carried out by the author, this was regarded as a priority. In 1949 and 1951 data was coded in London at the start of the project. In a field trip to Israel to collect most of the remaining data, these documents were recorded along with the material covering the 1955 to 1977 period. Any differences (which proved to be minor) were standardized. Before the start of statistical analysis, a random set of 10 per cent of documents were again coded. Similarly, when the data pertaining to the 1981 election was collected, a similar amount of previously coded material was rechecked to ensure standardization.

The number of uncoded quasi-sentences varied between parties and elections, from 38 per cent for Likud in the election of 1981, to 0 per cent for the same party in the election of 1961. Ma'arach ranges between 2 per cent and 20 per cent and MAFDAL from 3 per cent to 31 per cent. This is not surprising given the extensive variation between the length and style of platform material, but there was no connection between the proportion of empty sentences and length of documentation, nor any trend in terms of this proportion increasing or decreasing over time. The vast majority of empty sentences represent material that was far too generalized to be coded meaningfully. Means are 9.6 per cent for Ma'arach; 12.2 per cent for

TABLE 6.1

LEADING ISSUES STRESSED BY ISRAELI PARTIES 1949-81

	CATEGORY	MA'ARACH X	S.D.	LIKUD X	S.D	MAFDAL X	S.D	ALL PARTIES X	S.D.
603	TRADITIONAL MORALITY+ (JUDAISM)	0.52	0.72	0.53	0.85	41.16	14.58	14.07	21.12
601	NATIONAL WAY OF LIFE+ (ZIONISM)	12.72	2.80	8.29	7.21	10.22	12.01	10.41	8.17
104	MILITARY+ (SECURITY)	9.31	4.51	14.18	18.97	1.65	1.67	8.38	12.10
106	PEACE	7.02	8.25	4.65	4.96	1.16	2.29	4.28	6.03
410	PRODUCTIVITY	6.65	3.21	3.54	3.04	1.28	2.78	3.82	3.67
706	DEMOGRAPHIC GROUPS	2.81	1.87	2.11	3.02	5.44	4.80	3.46	3.63
503	SOCIAL JUSTICE	4.26	2.20	2.51	2.29	2.91	4.52	3.22	3.17
201	FREEDOM	2.52	1.81	3.81	3.73	2.81	5.81	3.05	4.01

Likud; 12.8 per cent for MAFDAL. References to the party in question, one of its rivals, or leading politicians of the day, were recorded separately, and again show considerable variation (Ma'arach zero to 26.5 per cent: Likud zero to 42 per cent; MAFDAL zero – 28 per cent). Means are 5.4 per cent for Ma'arach, 9.03 per cent for Likud; 4.26 per cent for MAFDAL. On the whole such direct references to other parties or their policies constitute a small proportion of the text, although they do bulk larger in isolated cases.

6.6 IDENTIFYING MAJOR ELECTION ISSUES

All percentages discussed below are based on the total number of quasi-sentences within a plaform rather than the number of coded quasi-sentences. A threshold of 3 per cent was used as the cut-off point for indicating 'major issues'. A mean percentage of 1 per cent across all election platforms indicated a category worth pursuing in further statistical analysis. As a result, a number of categories appeared unimportant and were omitted.

Eight categories account for the major issues in the election platforms of Israeli parties. The mean percentage scores are ranked in Table 6.1

Party scores among the highest scoring categories vary considerably. We comment briefly below on each leading theme.

(i) Defence of Traditional Morality

The overall importance of this area is a distortion due to the over-whelming proportion of MAFDAL references. Indeed, it is only in MAFDAL platforms that the category consistently achieves over 5 per cent, sometimes indeed it accounts for over a third of platform content, and in two cases (1959 and 1965), it accounts for more than half! For Ma'arach and Likud it has virtually no significance at all, and indeed is only mentioned in four of the Ma'arach platforms and in four of the Likud.

(ii) National Way of Life Positive

This is the only category to obtain a score of 5 per cent or more in both the combined analysis and for the separate parties. It really reflects Zionist principles. Zionism is after all the fundmental legitimating factor in Israeli political culture. It is most consistently used in election platforms by the Ma'arach, accounting for at least 10 per cent of the content in eight of the ten cases. The Ma'arach, of course, regards itself as the spokesman of the state's founding fathers, responsible for establishing the framework upon which the present infrastructure is built. In a sense, the Ma'arach has itself almost become a symbol of Zionism in practice. The use of the category across elections is, however, cyclical, sequences of emphasis being followed by periods of de-emphasis. The category is stressed particularly in the platforms of 1949, 1955, 1965 and 1977.

Likud references are similarly cyclical but on the whole the emphasis appears when the Ma'arach de-emphasizes the category. The strongest Likud emphasis occurs between 1965 and 1977, reaching a peak in 1973. This is just after the Yom Kippur War when the Ma'arach score is at its lowest. The Likud actually omitted references to this category in 1949 and 1955, since when it has erratically climbed to a peak of 20 per cent of quasi-sentences. The behaviour of the category in MAFDAL plat-forms is even more erratic. In general terms it mirrors that of the Likud until 1973, when it scores almost 20 per cent, having had no references at all in 1965 and 1969. Its highest incidence is in 1977, when for virtually the first time, the documentation discussed the role that MAFDAL leaders had played in founding the state. This is indeed the highest score for any party on this category at almost 35 per cent and represents the same proportion devoted to religion in this platform by MAFDAL.

(iii) Military Positive

It is hardly surprising that this category should figure prominently in the Israeli data, especially in the cases of the two main contenders. For the Ma'arach and Likud, thirteen of a possible eighteen references score over 5 per cent, many of them significantly. Nevertheless, there are marked differences of emphasis, and cyclical patterns. However, in this case, party references vary together in response to outside threats, with one exception (1955). Ma'arach and Likud platforms emphasize the category in 1949, 1961, 1969 and 1973. Within the platforms differences in emphasis are much sharper for Likud than for the Ma'arach, ranging from 3.45 per cent of quasi-sentences to 64.29 per cent, as compared with a range of 2.61 per cent to 16.39 per cent. Again the Ma'arach is the more consistent. Here too it regards itself as the basis of the modern security organizations. Security issues are of little importance in MAFDAL platforms.

(iv) Peace

This is mainly of concern to the Ma'arach. Again it is more important in certain elections, i.e. 1949, 1969, 1973 and 1977, which were contested in the aftermath of wars. (For 1959, the first election after Suez, the category almost passes the 5 per cent threshold with 4.35 per cent.) Only in the 1949 and 1973 platforms of the Likud does the category achieve a score of more than 5 per cent, and for MAFDAL it is absent from all documents until 1961, and only passes the 5 per cent threshold in 1973. In the peace-security tangle, the Likud as a right-wing grouping with a strong nationalist streak tends to emphasize security rather than peace, especially in comparison with the Ma'arach.

(v) Other categories

For the Ma'arach, three other categories appear as significant. These are positive references to Internationalism, which is significant for four of the nine elections, mainly prior to the 1960s; Productivity, which is again significant in four (1951, 1959, 1965 and 1977); and support for expanding Social Services, which is important in five cases (1955, 1959, 1961, 1965 and 1977). For the Likud, Government Corruption is significant for the first five elections; and Government Efficiency for three (1951, 1969 and 1977). MAFDAL has only one other category of importance – Demographic Groups – which is particularly significant in the cases of 1949, 1955, 1969, 1973 and 1977.

6.7 IDENTIFYING UNDERLYING DIMENSIONS

In order to identify the ideological dimensions separating the Ma'arach, Likud and MAFDAL, a series of factor analyses were undertaken. In the first place, categories within the general domains identified in previous sections were used as inputs in a principal components analysis in order to identify two major components for each domain. The resulting component scores for each party election platform were then used as input variables in a second-stage factor analysis.

(i) Foreign Policy

The unipolar single factor resulting from this analysis – a single factor of 'peace and security' on which positive references to the Military, Internationalism and Peace have loadings from 1.38–1.49, is reflective of an important aspect of Israeli political life – the concern felt by all parties with the survival of the state. In terms of platform content, this is much more obvious in the cases of the Ma'arach and Likud than of the MAFDAL. In a sense, positive references to Internationalism also reflect the peace and security issues, since they stress good relations between Israel and her Arab neighbours, and between Israel and her allies, principally the U.S.

(ii) Freedom

Negative references to Constitutionalism are omitted since they accounted for a mean percentage of mentions of less than 1 per cent. From the three remaining variables (Freedom, Democracy and positive references to Constitutionalism) we again get one factor, on which they have loadings from 40–49. This is interpretable as an underlying dimension of 'democracy'. Democracy is a theme that is generally taken for granted in Israel. Many Israelis see their country as an island of democracy in a sea of Middle Eastern autocracies, and each party sees itself in some way as being the harbinger of democracy against the intrigues of its rivals to undermine the democratic process. The interpretation given to democracy differs between parties. For example, it is seen by the MAFDAL as the freedom for religious Jews to have their rights safeguarded, by the Ma'arach as working towards equality, and by the Likud as freedom for the individual to express his preferences.

(iii) Government

In terms of the emphasis given to individual categories, the domain is not of great importance. It is only really in the case of the Likud that any are related to perceived electoral gains. Here it is really the charge of Government Corruption which is levelled against former Ma'arach-dominated governments, generally in terms of their close relationship with the trade union movement. What we get from the analysis are two factors, interpretable as stability and corruption respectively. Government Effectiveness loads most heavily on the stability factor (.66), while the other two variables of Efficiency and Corruption load most (.61 and .76) on the 'Corruption' factor.

(iv) Economy

The first of the factors produced, which is unipolar, is of a rather general nature related to interventionism. The highest loadings are .39 for Regulation of Capitalism and Economic Goals. There is no strong indication of policy direction. The second factor reflects the two economic categories which seemed most prominent in the documents, Technology (.54) and Productivity (.43). Productivity was important to both secular parties, although the Likud stressed it more than the Ma'arach. None of the categories included in this domain were of any real significance in MAFDAL platforms.

(v) Welfare

The unipolar factor reflects the well-known concern which the parties claim to have for the development of a fully-fledged welfare state in Israel. Positive references to Social Services load at .56 and to Education at .48. This concern is not however always obvious in terms of being the most prominent issue in party platforms. Once again, the parties, and especially the Ma'arach and Likud, may put somewhat different interpretations on this issue. The Ma'arach sees the development of a health service as falling within the ambit of the trade union movement, which is at present responsible for running the most widespread health insurance scheme, whereas the Likud stresses the desirability of a state run health service as in Britain, using this issue as another means of attacking the perceived 'corruption' of the close relationship between the Ma'arach and the trade unions.

(vi) Fabric of Society

In many ways this is the most interesting domain, since it concerns the key values which justify and legitimize the existence of the State of Israel in the view of the majority of her Jewish citizens. The results of the analysis of this domain are reported in Table 6.2. Values here include the Zionist ideals of

TABLE 6.2

FACTORS EMERGING WITHIN THE FABRIC OF SOCIETY DOMAIN

		FACTOR 1 JEWISH SOLIDARITY
601 NATIONAL WAY OF LIFE+	(ZIONISM)	−.42
603 TRADITIONAL MORALITY+	(JUDAISM)	.52
606 NATIONAL EFFORT		.54

FROM UNROTATED SOLUTION:

EIGENVALUE	1.35
% OF VARIANCE	45.0

the 'return to The Land', 'the Ingathering of the Exiles' and, more recently, the 'Massada' spirit. In theory, this factor ought to be able to distinguish between religious and secular parties, since the Ma'arach and Likud base their central values on essentially socialist or nationalist interpretations and rely on modern Zionist rhetoric, whereas the MAFDAL stresses the religious aspects of Jewish solidarity to a far greater extent. One difficulty in differentiating the Likud from the MAFDAL, is that Begin has relied increasingly upon religious justifications for, e.g. the increase in the number of Jewish settlements in the occupied West Bank territories. Also, the voice of the religious element in Israeli politics has become more prominent, as secular governments have become dependent upon MAFDAL (and, more recently, Agudat Israel's) support for their survival.

(vii) Social Groups

In the case of the Social Groups domain, only two original categories remained after the application of the 1 per cent threshold. These were positive references to Labour Groups and Demographic Groups, which are therefore entered directly into the second-order analysis. A summary of results from the individual domain analyses is given in Table 6.3 below.

6.8 SECOND-ORDER FACTOR ANALYSIS: UNDERLYING DIMENSIONS

The analysis yielded three factors, with a cumulative variance of 84.9 per cent.

The first dimension, which has an Eigenvalue of 2.07 and covers 36.7 per cent of variation, is least satisfactory in terms of distinguishing between

TABLE 6.3

FIRST ORDER FACTOR ANALYSIS: MEANS AND STANDARD DEVIATIONS OF FACTOR SCORES

DOMAINS & FACTORS	MA'ARACH		LIKUD		MAFDAL	
	X	S.D.	X	S.D.	X	S.D.
FOREIGN POLICY:						
F1 PEACE AND SECURITY	.46	.87	.22	1.09	-.78	.26
FREEDOM:						
F1 DEMOCRACY	-.16	.64	.53	1.29	-.38	.82
GOVERNMENT:						
F1 STABILITY	.01	.47	.23	1.61	-.23	.55
F2 CORRUPTION	-.61	.20	1.03	.97	-.42	.68
ECONOMY:						
F1 INTERVENTION	.03	.43	.39	1.35	-.52	.81
F2 TECHNOLOGY	.68	1.16	-.25	1.00	-.43	.31
WELFARE:						
F1 WELFARE STATE	.45	1.13	-.21	1.00	-.24	.78
FABRIC OF SOCIETY:						
F1 JEWISH SOLIDARITY	-.40	.43	-.47	.46	.85	1.25
SOCIAL GROUPS:						
[x]F1 LABOUR GROUPS+	4.27	3.19	1.55	1.70	.88	1.38
[x]F2 DEMOGRAPHIC GROUPS	2.81	1.87	2.11	3.02	5.44	4.80

x ORIGINAL CATEGORY SCORES

parties. On the other hand, it does relate to a series of issues which are fundamental to the nature of Israeli politics. The dimension, which is essentially unipolar, is technically identifiable in terms of its high positive loadings for Jewish Solidarity, Labour Groups and Peace and Security, and its high negative loading on first-order factor 4.2 – Technology.

It is difficult to disentangle the party positions along this factor (although the three parties do differ in terms of their interpretations and symbols of nationalism), because most of their emphases are included in the positive inputs. For example, the secular parties both stress 'security'; and whilst MAFDAL stresses 'Judaism' as opposed to the 'Zionism' of the Ma'arach and Likud, both of these elements are combined in the input of 'Jewish Solidarity'. The difficulty of distinguishing exactly between notions concerning 'peace' and 'security' in positive references to the Military has been mentioned earlier in this chapter. Additionally, positive references to Labour Groups are made only by the Ma'arach and are strongly associated with that party's image of nationalism, being based on the movement of 'labour Zionism'. It is not an element which should,

TABLE 6.4

SECOND ORDER FACTOR ANALYSIS: SUMMARY TABLE OF RESULTS

DOMAINS, FIRST ORDER FACTORS AND ORIGINAL CATEGORIES	SECOND ORDER FACTORS		
	FACTOR 1 NATIONALISM <u>VS.</u> TECHNOLOGY	FACTOR 2 MODERNIZATION <u>VS.</u> DEMOCRACY	FACTOR 3 GOVT. STABILITY <u>VS.</u> DEMOGRAPHIC GROUPS
FOREIGN POLICY DOMAIN:			
F 1.1 PEACE AND SECURITY	.46	-.08	.05
ORIGINAL CATEGORIES (r)			
MILITARY+	-.17	.02	.78
PEACE	.02	-.13	.51
INTERNATIONALISM+	.15	-.15	.86
FREEDOM DOMAIN:			
F 2.1 DEMOCRACY	.08	-.49	-.32
ORIGINAL CATEGORIES (r)			
FREEDOM	-.07	.20	-.15
DEMOCRACY	.01	.26	-.13
CONSTITUTIONALISM POSITIVE	.02	.46	-.19
GOVERNMENT DOMAIN:			
F 3.1 STABILITY	-.02	-.12	.99
F 3.2 CORRUPTION	-.02	.37	-.21
ORIGINAL CATEGORIES (r)			
GOVERNMENT EFFICIENCEY	-.22	.60	-.15
GOVERNMENT CORRUPTION	-.29	.57	.24
GOVERNMENT EFFECTIVENESS	.10	.05	-.12
ECONOMY DOMAIN:			
F 4.1 INTERVENTION	.04	-.05	.08
F 4.2 TECHNOLOGY	-.39	.71	.09
ORIGINAL CATEGORIES (r)			
REGULATION OF CAPITALISM	-.23	.77	-.14
ECONOMIC GOALS	-.12	.75	-.08
PRODUCTIVITY	.59	.38	.08
TECHNOLOGY	.69	.17	.18
ECONOMIC ORTHODOXY	-.04	.48	.09

Continued...

TABLE 6.4 continued...

DOMAINS, FIRST ORDER FACTORS
AND ORIGINAL CATEGORIES

	FACTOR 1 NATIONALISM VS. TECHNOLOGY	FACTOR 2 MODERNIZATION VS. DEMOCRACY	FACTOR 3 GOVT. STABILITY VS. DEMOGRAPHIC GROUPS
WELFARE DOMAIN:			
F 5.1 WELFARE STATE	.05	.76	-.02
ORIGINAL CATEGORIES (r)			
SOCIAL JUSTICE	.48	.11	-.14
SOCIAL SERVICES+	.87	.11	.03
EDUCATION+	.65	-.09	-.20
FABRIC OF SOCIETY DOMAIN:			
F 6.1 JEWISH SOLIDARITY	.73	-.13	.21
ORIGINAL CATEGORIES (r)			
NATIONAL WAY OF LIFE+	.03	-.43	.20
TRADITIONAL MORALITY+	-.38	-.47	-.55
NATIONAL EFFORT	.06	-.28	-.17
SOCIAL GROUPS DOMAIN:			
F 7.1 LABOUR GROUPS+	.91	.04	-.12
F 7.2 DEMOGRAPHIC GROUPS	-.14	-.19	-.47

FIGURES RELATING TO FIRST ORDER FACTORS REPRESENT FACTOR LOADINGS AFTER
ROTATION BY MEANS OF THE "VARIMAX" METHOD. FIGURES RELATING TO ORIGINAL
CATEGORIES REPRESENT PEARSON CORRELATION COEFFICIENTS (r).

however, be regarded as particularly divisive in party terms, since neither
the Likud nor the MAFDAL is anti-trade union as such.

The loadings suggest that this factor is largely concerned with a
dimension which relates the internal character (or security) of Israeli
society to notions concerning her external security position. This would
certainly make sense given the strategic and defence problems faced by the
state. Israelis are primarily constrained to think of their physical survival
as a nation, but at the same time to have regard for the fundamental
structure of their society as a Jewish society and to guard against its
fragmentation in either way. It has often been suggested that if Israel were
at peace with her Arab neighbours, she would face increasing pressures
from within her own society which could have serious consequences for her
fundamental social institutions. The most damaging pressures would
emerge from a conflict between religious tradition and secularization on
the one hand and between European and Afro-Asian sub-cultures on the
other. With respect to the individual domains within this dimension, it is

interesting that Foreign Relations subsumes two of the four most frequently occurring categories within the individual platforms – peace and security – whilst Fabric of Society subsumes the other two – Zionism and religion. Hence it is best labelled as 'nationalism'.

The second factor, with an Eigenvalue of 1.47 and covering 26.2 per cent of variation represents a dimension based on 'Modernization *vs.* Democracy'. The positive loadings for Technology (.71) and Welfare State (.76) are stronger than the main negative one for Democracy (−.49). This dimension does not necessarily imply a choice between 'Modernization' *or* 'Democracy' but rather that certain parties may give considerably more emphasis to one element. Indeed the nature of the 'Modernization' involved seems to suggest support for a liberal-corporatist state in the future rather than for the more traditional liberal-democratic state. This dimension is the most successful of the three under discussion in terms of distinguishing between the Ma'arach and the Likud, with the former being associated with the element of 'Democracy', and the latter with that of 'Modernization'. It could therefore be considered as being related to 'New Issues', a dimension which appears in other country analyses in this book.

The third factor, with an Eigenvalue of 1.23 and a contribution of 22.0 per cent to variation, contrasts strong positive attitudes to government stability (.99) with negative values or an apparent lack of concern for Demographic Groups (−.47). This dimension is most successful in terms of distinguishing between religious and secular parties, and indeed it was really only the MAFDAL for which the original category of Demographic Groups represented a major concern. It thus represents a dimension concerned with traditional values and challenges to them.

6.9 THE SPATIAL LOCATION OF PARTY POSITIONS

An advantage of factor analysis is the ability to plot 'maps' of party positions over time in the form of scores relating to the data inputs along each factor. The first factor is of little use in distinguishing between the parties, as Figure 6.1 illustrates.

The main reason is that the first dimension, identifiable in simple terms as 'nationalism', reflects a series of issues basic to the surival of the State of Israel. Also, since one of the major components of this dimension concerns security, it reflects party unity when the state is threatened by attack from external forces. Even when 'normal' conditions prevail, this dimension is inadequate since it incorporates each party's varying interpretations of nationalism. It does however incorporate concerns fundamental to Israeli politics in general, and also highlights the fact that these politics operate at two distinct levels – the 'normal' conditions of party competition which operate in most liberal-democracies, and the 'special' conditions that

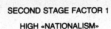

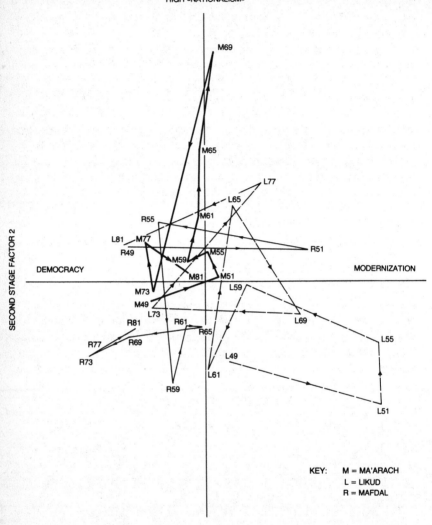

6.1 Spatial location of parties along factors 1 and 2: nationalism and modernization vs. democracy

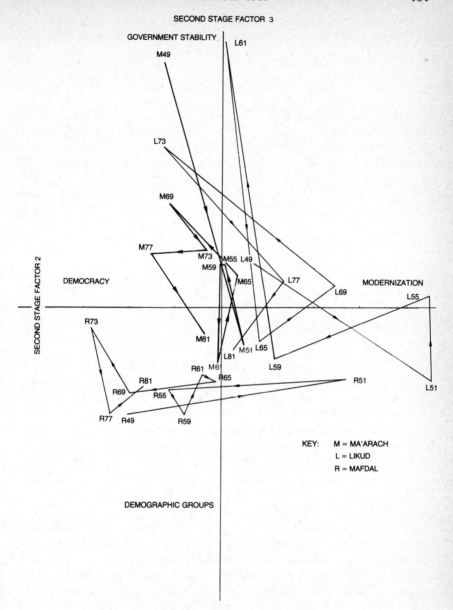

6.2 Spatial location of parties along factors 2 and 3

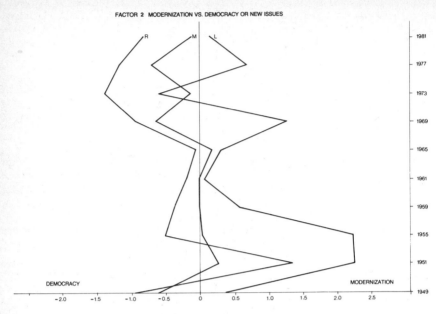

6.3 Factor scores plotted by party

operate when the survival of the Jewish state is threatened. For these reasons, Figure 6.2 and the discussion of spatial location is based on a combination of the second and third dimensions.

The second dimension of 'Modernization *vs.* Democracy' or of 'New Issues' is best in separating the two secular parties. Although there is at least one occasion where their paths cross (1973), it may be said in general terms, they occupy separate ideological spaces, both when this factor is related to the third dimension as shown in Figure 6.2, and when it is concerned independently (Figure 6.3).

Neither the Ma'arach nor the Likud however occupy extreme positions at either pole. Their positions suggest that they are essentially parties of the broad centre rather than of the left or right.

The third dimension (Government Stability *vs.* Demographic Groups) clearly distinguishes between secular and religious parties. The MAFDAL is the most compact party in terms of ideological space occupied, and this space is neither infiltrated by other parties' positions nor does MAFDAL encroach on the space of other parties. Also, with the exception of 1951, all MAFDAL positions are contained within one quadrant. The 1951 platform was in any case slightly 'deviant' in comparison to other elections, since the MAFDAL made a bid to become the main party of opposition to the Labour government, and its platform was far more varied than any other that it published.

6.10 CONCLUSIONS

The spatial locations of the three Israeli party groups along these two dimensions suggests firstly that there is a clearly religious grouping, a grouping of the centre-left and a grouping of the centre-right. Secondly, the distinction on the basis of religion is stronger than that based on secular values, and if anything, the secular parties have exhibited centripetal tendencies and come to occupy positions closer to both the centre of the ideological spectrum and to each other. Finally, the three main dimensions produced by the second-order factor analysis are valid in the context of Israeli politics, and may generally be identified as 'Nationalism', 'New Issues' and 'Government Stability' as against group concerns – all involving some element of conflict between traditional and new, secular values.

Note

1 Most of the data used in the analysis of the election platforms discussed in this chapter was collected in Israel during July and August 1980, with the help of a grant from the Nuffield Foundation, to which I am most grateful. I should also like to thank the Department of Political Science at Tel Aviv University for allowing me working facilities, the *Jerusalem Post* Archives and the British Library for help in obtaining data, and Ealing College of Higher Education for their administration of my grant and general encouragement.

CHAPTER 7[1]

IRELAND, 1948–1981:
ISSUES, PARTIES, STRATEGIES

———— ∾ ————

7.1 INTRODUCTION: ISSUE-DIMENSIONS AND PARTY SYSTEM

The primary purpose of this analysis is to identify the main issue-dimensions in the post-war politics of the Irish Republic and to locate the positions of the three major parties – Fianna Fáil, Fine Gael and Labour – along these dimensions. The data used for the analysis are the programmes, manifestos and major election speeches of the three parties in the ten general elections held between 1948 and 1981. These were coded according to the schemes described in Chapter 2 and Appendix B, the only modification in the Irish case being the definition of the category Foreign Special Relationships: Negative as including statements in favour of the unification of Northern Ireland and the Republic.

Although no systematic analysis of the programmes and policies of Irish parties has been carried out prior to this present study, the existing literature is reasonably consistent in identifying some version of the nationalist cleavage as the major dimension of party competition, along with various secondary cleavages, e.g. 'planned *vs.* market economy' (Cohan 1982, p. 269), or 'left *vs.* right' and 'town *vs.* country' (Chubb 1971, pp. 58–60). Elsewhere, in a study based on the attitudes of party activists in a Dublin constituency, the dominant dimension has been identified as 'pluralism *vs.* clericalism', with 'territorial nationalism' as a secondary, but still very important dimension (Garvin 1977b).

That varieties of the nationalist cleavage should figure prominently in the list of hypothetical issue dimensions is hardly surprising: Fianna Fáil and Fine Gael, the two largest parties in the post-war as well as the inter-war years, both owe their origins to Sinn Féin, the party which spearheaded the mobilization towards Irish independence in 1921. Fine Gael, or more properly its predecessor Cumann na nGaedheal, which

represented the more moderate wing of Sinn Féin, favoured initial acceptance of Britain's offer of dominion status for Ireland within the Commonwealth and thereafter the pursuit of a gradual and constitutional path
towards complete independence. Fianna Fáil grew from the nationalist
wing of Sinn Féin, favouring the immediate severance of all links with
Britain. Party competition in the inter-war years was dominated by these
two parties, Cumann na nGaedheal holding office until 1932 when it was
replaced by Fianna Fáil. The period of the late 1920s and early 1930s saw a
rapid polarization of the party system, as smaller parties such as Labour
and the Farmers Party lost votes to both Cumann na nGaedheal and
Fianna Fáil. From 1933 onwards Cumann na nGaedheal/Fine Gael itself
began to lose support, such that by 1948 – the beginning of our period – the
relative importance of the two larger parties had changed significantly.
From being (semi) equivalent opponents in the late 1920s and early 1930s,
by 1948 Fianna Fáil had established a clear electoral superiority over Fine
Gael. Significantly, when Fianna Fáil lost office in 1948 – for the first time
in sixteen years – the new government was an inter-party coalition. Not
since 1932 has another *single* party in Irish politics been in a position to
replace Fianna Fáil as the governing party. The 1948 election witnessed
the effective institutionalization of a new opposition setting Fianna Fáil
against all the other parties; in short, the institutional confirmation of the
emergence of a predominant party system (Mair 1979).

The Irish party system has remained relatively stable in the post-war
period. Two minor parties which had risen during the 1940s, Clann na
Talmhan and Clann na Poblachta, declined as quickly in the aftermath of
the first coalition, while the coalition experience proved sufficient to set
Fine Gael on the road to electoral recovery. In 1951 its vote rose to 26 per
cent, and to 32 per cent in 1954. Though declining to 27 per cent in 1957, it
increased again to 32 per cent in 1961 and to almost 37 per cent in 1981, the
last election dealt with in this analysis. The vote won by Labour – the third
party in the system – remained relatively stable in the period from 1948 to
1961, despite a brief decline in 1957. After 1961, however, the party
experienced a steady growth, particularly in the Dublin region, reaching 19
per cent nationally in 1969, and a record 28 per cent in Dublin. Since then,
the party has declined. A similar pattern of decline is shown by the minor
parties and Independents, the total vote for which has not exceeded 10 per
cent since 1957. Fianna Fáil has remained particularly stable during the
post-war period, with an average vote of 46 per cent.

Given this it is not surprising that the pattern of opposition has remained
essentially unchanged since 1948. At that election, Fianna Fáil was
replaced by a coalition government which received the support of all the
other parties in the Dáil,, and, on the three subsequent occasions when
Fianna Fáil was defeated – in 1954, 1973 and 1981 – it was again replaced

by coalitions receiving the support or tolerance of all other Dáil parties. The only variation in this pattern has been the changing composition and balance of the non-Fianna Fáil group, which now consists of only two parties – Fine Gael and Labour. (On the Irish party system generally see Carty 1981; Chubb 1969 and 1979; Gallagher 1976 and 1981; Garvin 1974, 1977a and 1981a; Mair 1979; Manning 1972; O'Leary 1979; Rumpf and Hepburn 1977; and Whyte 1974.)

Given such continuity in the major electoral alternatives, it is understandable that the nationalist cleavage should still be considered crucial to party competition. Despite this, our analysis of manifestos shows that nationalist rhetoric plays a minimal role in the programmes of the various parties. The category which included statements in favour of the unification of Northern Ireland and the Republic, Foreign Special Relationships, Negative, accounts for only 2 per cent of sentences in the post-war manifestos of all three parties. The case of Fianna Fáil is of particular interest, since it is the party generally reckoned to gain most from appeals to nationalist sentiment and yet, taking the post-war period as a whole, an average of only 2.1 per cent of sentences in the party programmes specify support of Irish unity, while the topic barely registers in programmes from the earlier part of the period (1948–1961). The category of Traditional Morality, which may express a facet of nationalist ideology, again counts for a negligible proportion of the party's statements, averaging only 0.1 per cent for the post-war period as a whole. The only category which does register reasonably highly within Fianna Fáil programmes, and which might be considered as part of some general appeal to nationalism, is National Effort and Social Harmony, which covers appeals to voters to act in the national interest in a way which reinforces national solidarity. But here the appeal is to Irish unity in social rather than territorial terms.

One explanation for the absence of nationalist appeals could be sought in the nature of the party programmes themselves: manifestos and surrogates such as party leaders' speeches, radio broadcasts and so on, can be seen as expressions of reasonably short-term policies. Nationalist appeals, on the other hand, are of a more long-term character, in that they express essentially timeless aspirations to 'eventual' national unity. Second, explicit nationalist appeals may play little part in party programmes simply because such appeals are almost inevitably devoid of policy content. There is little any of the parties can actually do to advance unity in any practical way. Though the recrudescence of violence in Northern Ireland at the end of the 1960s certainly increased the salience of the issue – hence the increased space devoted by Fianna Fáil to statements in favour of unity between 1969 and 1981 – the parties could not offer new concrete policies. Third, Northern Ireland has not been a major issue in the minds of the voters: despite the seriousness of the conflict, the post-1968 violence remained north of the border, and Irish voters have preferred to worry about inflation and unemployment (Rose et al. 1978, p. 36). Fourth, there is also the very consensual nature of the unity issue – at least until very recently. All three parties pledge themselves in favour of Irish unity as a basic political principle to the extent that this commitment is reflected even in the full titles of Fianna Fáil (*viz.* Fianna Fáil – the Republican Party) and Fine Gael (*viz.* Fine Gael – the United Ireland Party). The Republic's claim to territorial jurisdiction over Northern Ireland is also enshrined in Articles 2 and 3 of the Irish Constitution. The nationalist appeal is in this sense a given, as entrenched as the commitment to parliamentary democracy itself; it is something which the parties thus can take for granted. Fine Gael is perhaps an exception here: the 1921 Treaty with Britain and dominion status within the British Commonwealth; and as the party which contained a significant body of opinion hostile to Ireland's neutrality during World War II, Fine Gael has always been seen to be slightly suspect on the national question. Hence, the relative stress which the party has laid on statements supportive of Irish unity in its election programmes.

However, there may be a simpler explanation for the overall lack of emphasis on pro-unity statements, which is that *appeals to nationalism have played an insignificant role in electoral mobilization in post-war Ireland.* However important such appeals seem in light of historical differences between the parties, their absence from the election programmes suggests that they are no longer relevant to contemporary political alignments. In this sense, it is mistaken to assert that nationalism is still the basis of the major political opposition in Ireland.

The nationalist explanation is based on the view that the main division in post-war Ireland has been Fianna Fáil *vs.* Fine Gael, which inevitably generates an explanation emphasizing intra-nationalist divisions; there is little else which distinguishes these two essentially conservative parties. If the primary opposition is seen to be Fianna Fáil *vs. all* other parties, then the nationalist explanation makes less substantive sense. While Fianna Fáil may be in a position to play the green card when confronting Fine Gael on its own, it can do so with much less plausibility when confronting the combined, coalitional opposition of Fine Gael, Labour and other minor parties. And if this is taken as the primary opposition in post-war Ireland, then we must seek an alternative issue-basis for party competition.

The major issue-basis has in fact concerned 'ability to govern', rather than any persisting intra-nationalist conflict (Mair 1979). A secondary issue-dimension may well derive from the traditional left–right cleavage. The first of these dimensions divides Fianna Fáil from both Fine Gael and Labour, while the second divides Fine Gael and Labour themselves, with Fianna Fáil occupying a position roughly in the centre.

7.2 A NOTE ON THE GOVERNMENTAL SYSTEM

The governmental system is similar to that of the UK, and is characterized by cabinet government and a bicameral legislature in which most of the power rests with the lower house – the Dáil. The two systems differ in that Ireland has a written constitution; a proportional electoral system with multi-member constituencies; an upper house – the Senate – which is primarily elected (11 of the 60 seats are filled by appointees of the Taoiseach, i.e. prime minister) but which has a very restricted electorate organized in vocational and university panels; and an elective Head of State, the President, who in practice has very limited powers (Chubb 1971).

On a more informal basis, the most striking features of the Irish governmental system are the strength of the Cabinet (the executive) *vis-à-vis* the Dáil (the lower house of the legislature); a traditionally very limited committee system; and the tendency for individual TDs (i.e. MPs) to concern themselves with local constituency politics rather than national affairs. All this combines to create a situation in which the Cabinet has a virtual monopoly in the introduction and passage of legislation (Chubb 1974).

Irish elections are conducted with a type of proportional representation known as the Single Transferable Vote (STV), in which voters rank candidates nominated in multi-member constituencies on a 1, 2, 3...N basis (O'Leary 1979; Mair 1982a). Since the larger parties tend to nominate more candidates in each constituency than can hope to win seats, the most intense electoral competition often occurs between individual candidates of the same party. To the extent that such rivalry dominates elections at the local level, the manifesto or party programme is unimportant. Rather, individual candidates compete with their fellow party nominees on the basis of capacity to serve the constituency in a purely administrative sense. Thus the party programme, while perhaps determining to some extent the degree of national swing between it and its opponent(s), will in many cases be less influential in determining the fortunes of a particular candidate than ability to act as a broker of constituents' interest.

7.3 THE MANIFESTOS

The documents used for this analysis varied substantially from one party to another as well as from one election to another; the sources include formally defined manifestos, newspaper articles written by the party leaders, newspaper reports on programmes which were issued but are now unobtainable, speeches by party leaders, and short election addresses.

The sources for Labour are clearly the most authoritative. If we treat as formal programmes the articles prepared by all the parties for a series in the *Irish Independent* at the 1948 election, then the sources for Labour over the eight elections which it fought as a separate party include six authoritative statements of policy. In 1961 a 4,000 word election programme was certainly issued, but was unobtainable at the time of writing. It is not clear whether any programme was issued in 1954, and the source used here is an *Irish Press* report of a radio broadcast by Brendan Corish who later became party leader.

Manifestos for Fine Gael have been obtained for the years 1961 to 1981 (these include the Fine Gael-Labour joint programmes in 1973 and 1977), and the *Irish Independent* article for 1948. For 1951, 1954 and 1957, however, it is unclear whether a manifesto was issued. The source for 1951 is probably the least reliable, since it involves simply a four-page election leaflet issued in a particular Dublin constituency. The sources for 1954 and 1957 were newspaper reports of major speeches by the party leader.

Formal statements of policy for Fianna Fáil were issued and are available for only three of the ten elections – 1948 (the *Irish Independent* article), 1977 and 1981. For the bulk of the period, i.e. from 1951 to 1973, the sources used are reported speeches, radio broadcasts, and so on. It is unfortunate that these are exactly Fianna Fáil's most successful years. In general the sources for all parties appear to be comprehensive statements of policy which are arguably as authoritative as can now be found.

The format and circulation of manifestos or their equivalents are as varied as their sources, ranging from glossy pamphlets of 47–70 pages produced in the late 1970s, to simple cyclostyled three page documents. The programmes published in newspapers probably reached a wider audience. In years where both these sources are missing, messages must have reached electors – if at all – in a heavily edited and selective form.

In terms of mass impact, however, the manifesto *per se* is probably less important than are the election leaflets published by the parties and sent to every voter on the register. These leaflets normally include an address by the party leader, a brief summary of the party's policy, and information concerning the local candidates. The normal practice seems to be that party Headquarters prints the leaflets and then supplies them to the constituency organizers, who print in local details before distribution. These leaflets tend to be colourful, glossy and stylish, and the parties regularly distribute them in one free mailing to which they – or, more properly, the candidates – are entitled by law. Again, the normal practice seems to be that the policy proposals on the leaflets are drawn from the manifesto, and it is in this sense that the manifesto can be said to have its widest, albeit quite indirect, impact.

In terms of general circulation, the 1973 Fine Gael-Labour coalition programme was perhaps the most widely distributed manifesto, being printed in full by all three national dailies. But with this exception, it has proved impossible to get any reliable figures on the print-runs and distribution of any of the manifestos prior to 1981. In that election, Fianna Fáil printed 12,000 copies of its programme. These were then distributed on a geographical basis, with 200 going to each of the 41 constituencies, and the remainder going to individuals, journalists, etc. Fine Gael printed 10,000 copies of its programme, sending them to party members, journalists and interest groups. The party also published 10,000 summaries of the programme, though how these were distributed is unclear. Labour printed only 1,000 copies of its 1981 manifesto, and these were distributed to the media, as well as one copy to each branch of the party, each director of elections, and each candidate. Labour also published 2,000 summaries, distributing three or four to each of its branches.

In general the procedure by which manifestos are drawn up varies, as in Canada, according to whether or not the party is in government at the time of the election. If the party is incumbent, then the tendency seems to be to rely on the cabinet members and to produce a cautious set of proposals; if it is not in government, the officers of the party, and/or the Oireachtas Party tend to play a greater role. In any event, the procedure rarely – if ever – involves a wide range of party members (Mair 1982b, pp. 22–35).

7.4 WHAT IS SAID IN THE MANIFESTOS

(i) Coding procedures

The Irish manifestos were coded into the 54 standard categories (Appendix B), counting the quasi-sentence as the unit of analysis. 'Empty' sentences, that is statements with no particular reference and which could not be classified into any category, were not coded. The percentage of such sentences averaged 4.9 per cent for the post-war period (see Table 7.1), demonstrating a good fit between the coding scheme and Irish issues. Coding was carried out by the author in consultation with another experienced analyst of Irish politics. Certain themes were also selected and other experts asked how they might be coded; there was always agreement. It should also be noted as a preliminary to the full discussion that references to other parties were also coded and averaged only 1.3 per cent for the entire period.

(ii) What the parties emphasize

An initial count of the relative emphases on the different categories confirms the earlier hypothesis concerning the salience of 'governing-

TABLE 7.1

LEADING CATEGORIES, 1948-1981

CATEGORY	PARTY: FIANNA FAIL	FINE GAEL	LABOUR	COALITION (FG-LAB)	ALL PARTIES
1	GOVT. AUTHORITY AND EFFECTIVENESS	GOVT. AUTHORITY AND EFFECTIVENESS	PRODUCTIVITY	SOCIAL SERVICES- PRO-EXPANSION	GOVT. AUTHORITY AND EFFECTIVENESS
MEAN/SD	15.8/17.9	12.6/15.4	11.6/8.9	12.0/4.3	10.5/14.2
2	PRODUCTIVITY	INCENTIVES	AGRICULTURE/ FARMERS	SOCIAL JUSTICE	PRODUCTIVITY
MEAN/SD	11.9/9.3	7.9/8.0	9.0/5.6	7.0/9.1	9.7/8.3
3	AGRICULTURE/ FARMERS	ECCONOMIC ORTHODOXY	SOCIAL SERVICES PRO-EXPANSION	DEMOCRACY	AGRICULTURE/ FARMERS
MEAN/SD	8.3/6.1	7.6/4.8	8.1/5.9	7.0/6.0	7.4/5.2
4	SOCIAL SERVICES - PRO-EXPANSION	SOCIAL SERVICES - PRO-EXPANSION	SOCIAL JUSTICE	PRODUCTIVITY	SOCIAL SERVICES - PRO-EXPANSION
MEAN/SD	6.0/4.7	6.9/6.9	8.7/7.6	6.1/7.0	7.3/5.6
5	TECHNOLOGY/INFRA- STRUCTURE	GOVT. EFFICIENCY	LABOUR GROUPS	GOVT. EFFICIENCY	GOVT. EFFICIENCY
MEAN/SD	5.8/5.2	6.5/6.4	6.1/5.5	5.6/1.6	5.3/5.6
6	GOVT. EFFICIENCEY	PRODUCTIVITY	CONTROLLED ECONOMY	INCENTIVES	SOCIAL JUSTICE
MEAN/SD	4.3/6.9	6.1/5.9	5.7/5.7	5.5/3.1	4.8/5.5
7	EDUCATION: PRO-EXPANSION	AGRICULTURE/ FARMERS	GOVT. EFFICI- ENCY	AGRICULTURE/ FARMERS	INCENTIVES
MEAN/SD	3.9/3.9	5.3/4.0	5.1/3.6	5.3/0.5	4.1/5.2
8	NATIONAL EFFORT AND SOCIAL HARMONY	ENTERPRISE	TECHNOLOGY/ INFRASTRUCTURE	GOVT. AUTHORITY AND EFFECTIVENESS	TECHNOLOGY/ INFRASTRUCTURE
MEAN/SD	3.5/4.6	4.9/5.7	3.9/3.4	4.6/3.0	3.9/4.0
9	DEFENCE OF IRISH WAY OF LIFE	SOCIAL JUSTICE	NON-ECONOMIC DEMOGRAPHIC GROUPS	REGULATION OF CAPITALISM	NATIONAL EFFORT AND SOCIAL HARMONY
MEAN/SD	3.4/6.3	4.0/3.3	3.5/2.8	4.4/4.9	3.2/3.4
10*	LABOUR GROUPS	NATIONAL EFFORT AND SOCIAL HARMONY	GOVT. AUTHORITY AND EFFECTIVE- NESS	CONTROLLED ECONOMY	LABOUR GROUPS
MEAN/SD	2.7/2.7	3.9/3.5	3.3/3.9	3.3/1.7	3.0/3.9
NO. OF MANIFESTOS	10	8	8	2	28
NO. OF QUASI- SENTENCES	1482	1752	1382	414	5030
PERCENTAGE OF UNCODED SENTENCES					
MEAN/SD	8.5/8.6	2.7/3.2	1.8/1.7	8.2/1.1	4.9/6.2

related' issues in the party programmes. Table 7.1 reports the means and standard deviation of the ten categories receiving the highest average proportion of references in each of the parties' programmes, as well as in the two coalition programmes and when all parties are taken together, and it is from these preliminary results that we can finally begin to define the language of party competition in post-war Ireland.

Fianna Fáil

The ten leading categories in the case of Fianna Fáil reflect very closely those of all the parties taken together. As might be expected, Government Authority is far and away the most highly emphasized category, with Productivity second, Agriculture/Farmers third, and Social Services: Pro-Expansion fourth. All four suggest an appropriate image of Fianna Fáil in the post-war years as the dominant Irish political party, intent on maintaining its original rural base and, at the same time, setting out to modernize and expand the economy as well as to develop a welfare state which would be sufficiently strong to sustain the needs of the other major segment of its electorate, the urban working class. The high ranking of Technology/Infrastructure is perhaps more surprising, but in fact the category also easily fits into this image of a modernizing party, ranging from promises to develop 'rural electrification, arterial drainage, (and) Power Station construction' (FF48) to commitments that, in order 'to have a competitive advantage over foreigners, industry will be induced to have a structure which will more readily assimilate science and technology' (FF77). The relatively high ranking of National Effort and Social Harmony in Fianna Fáil manifestos further emphasizes the particularities of the party's appeal, in emphasizing the essence of Fianna Fáil's 'other' nationalism – an appeal to national unity which is expressed in social rather than territorial terms, and which stems from the party's self-image as the builder of a modern Ireland standing securely in the face of a hostile international environment.

Fine Gael

Though Fine Gael shows many leading categories in common with Fianna Fáil – in particular the emphasis on Government Authority – the few differences which do exist are very striking. The second ranking Fine Gael category, for instance, is Incentives, which does not figure at all in the ten leading Fianna Fáil categories, while the third category, Economic Orthodoxy is also absent from the Fianna Fáil list. Incentives is the category covering references to wage and tax policies which are designed to encourage enterprise, references to which abound in almost all Fine Gael's programmes. In the Just Society programmes in 1965, for instance, the party pledged itself to 'encourage the return from abroad of Irish nationals with managerial experience by moderating the incidence of taxation on earned incomes at certain levels' and to 'alter the present system of charging depreciation for tax purposes, so that adequate provision can be made for the replacement of fixed assets and thereby assist increased production'. This particular programme also specifies at great length 'the need for a rational determination of credit policy' and the need to strengthen the powers of the Central Bank, themes similar to those which again echo in other programmes of the party, and which contribute to the high ranking of the Economic Orthodoxy category. The party's emphasis on Enterprise is yet another example of this type of thinking and, indeed, ranks above Social Justice in the leading categories. In later programmes, however, Social Justice receives a greater emphasis by Fine Gael than does Enterprise.

Labour

Labour, the smallest of the three parties, is perhaps most striking for the relatively low emphasis which it places on Government Authority, which ranks tenth in the party's list of leading categories as against first for both Fianna Fáil and Fine Gael. The first ranking category for Labour is Productivity, a reflection of the party's persistent concern with the need to tackle unemployment and emigration. What is perhaps surprising to those not familiar with Labour's history is that Agriculture/Farmers ranks significantly higher than Labour Groups. Although orienting itself increasingly towards an urban electorate in the late 1960s, Labour has traditionally been a party of the rural and small town proletariat as well as a party which wins some support from small farmers. In many cases Labour's emphasis on agriculture appears to stem not so much from a desire to expand its rural base, but rather from the need to avoid alienating its traditional support. Moreover, while the emphasis on agriculture has declined over time, it remains relatively pronounced *vis-à-vis* the party's emphasis on Labour groups. Indeed, both categories evidence a decline over time, as does Labour emphasis on the 'other Groups' category in its leading ten issues. The decline in all three suggests that rather than attempting to change its base from one sector of the population to another, Labour has been seeking to generalize its appeal in a fashion similar to that of its larger opponents, but by using a more socialist rhetoric.

Party specific categories and valence issues

A recent analysis of election appeals by Budge and Farlie (1983) suggests that parties do not so much compete on the same issues but rather 'own' particular issues which they then stress at election time. In other words, parties talk past one another rather than engaging in direct confrontation, and individual parties succeed or fail according to the salience of, or electoral concern for their issues as against those of their opponents. To the extent that this is true, then in Ireland as elsewhere we should find evidence of such 'selective emphases' in the lists of the leading categories of the parties; that is, we could expect to find categories within one party's list which are not present in the other parties' lists, and each party could be expected to have its own set of exclusive issues. Conversely, to the extent that we find similarities across all the different lists of leading categories, these common categories could be seen to represent 'consensual' issues which all three parties find it necessary to emphasize.

Assessing the data in Table 7.1 in these terms suggests a rather intriguing picture whereby much of what Fianna Fáil emphasizes is not particular to it as a party, while much of what Fine Gael emphasizes is party-specific. Taking the Fianna Fáil case first, we see that its first four leading categories are shared by both Fine Gael and Labour (though the rankings differ), as is its sixth leading category. Of the remaining five categories, two (Technology/Infrastructure and Labour Groups) are shared by Labour, and one (National Effort/Social Harmony) by Fine Gael. Two categories alone are exclusive to Fianna Fáil – Education: Pro-Expansion, which is not of itself a very significant issue in Irish politics, and Defence of Irish Way of Life: Positive, which is rather appropriate in the case of a party which traditionally has seen itself as the repository of the national conscience. Neither category ranks particularly high in the Fianna Fáil list, however, the one being in seventh and the other in ninth position.

Fine Gael presents a quite different and in many senses more revealing picture. Though five of its leading categories are shared by both Fianna Fáil and Labour, a sixth (Social Justice) by Labour alone, and a seventh (National Effort) by Fianna Fáil alone, its three remaining exclusive categories rank relatively highly (second, third and eighth positions) and fit together in a wider, substantive sense. These categories are Incentives, Economic Orthodoxy and Enterprise, all three of which can be seen to represent a classic economic conservatism, and all three of which help to create the most clearly identifiable profile of any of the three Irish parties.

The profile presented by Labour is less distinctive. Five of its leading categories (including the first, second and fourth) are shared by both its opponents, one other by Fine Gael alone (Social Justice), and two by Fianna Fáil alone (Labour Groups and Technology/Infrastructure). There remain two exclusive issues, Controlled Economy and Non-Economic Demographic Groups, neither of which rank in the top five leading issues of the party.

The data further suggest the existence of five 'consensual' issues (those categories included in the leading categories of all three parties and of the two coalition manifestos); Government Authority, Productivity, Agriculture/Farmers, Social Services: Pro-Expansion, and Government Efficiency. Two come from the Government domain, and one each from Economy, Groups, and Welfare. That these are consensual is not in itself surprising; what is significant, however, is their relative rankings in the parties' lists. The five rank in the first four and the sixth positions in the Fianna Fáil programmes, in the first, fourth, fifth, sixth and seventh positions in the Fine Gael manifestos, and in the first, second, fourth, seventh and tenth positions in the Labour manifestos. If we score these rankings, giving 10 to the first position, 9 to the second position, and so on, then a maximum emphasis on the five consensual issues would be indicated by a score of 40 (10+9+8+7+6) and a minimum emphasis by a score of 15 (5+4+3+2+1). The closer a party's score on these categories approaches 40, then the closer that party comes to placing a maximum emphasis on consensual issues. The actual scores are revealing, with Fianna Fáil at 39, Fine Gael at 32, Labour at 31 and the coalition at 30.

Scoring exclusive issues, on the other hand (i.e. those categories which appear only in the list of one party – the coalition is excluded here), we find that Fianna Fáil scores 6 out of a possible maximum of 19, Fine Gael scores 20 out of a possible maximum of 27, and Labour scores 6 out of a possible maximum of 19. In other words, Fianna Fáil places the greatest emphasis on consensual issues, while Fine Gael places the greatest emphasis on party-specific issues. Here perhaps more than anywhere else we see the most concrete evidence to bolster Fianna Fáil's traditional claim to be the only 'national' party, as against the more 'sectional' appeal of its major opponent.

(iii) The domains

Irish manifestos are dominated by concerns in four of the domains into which the data can be grouped: Government, Economy, Welfare and Groups. There are also some very sharp changes between elections. In 1957, the Government and Social Fabric domains received more space in the manifestos at the cost of Economy and Welfare. The Groups domain received roughly equal prominence as Welfare in the earlier post-war elections, but then declined in relative terms before increasing again in the 1977 election

Domain percentages over time for each party show Labour as the most consistent of the three parties in the post-war period, with programmes generally dominated by Economy and Welfare, and with an increasing emphasis on Government and a decreasing emphasis on Groups during the

TABLE 7.2

FIRST-STAGE FACTOR ANALYSIS – GOVERNMENT

GOVERNMENT

VARIMAX ROTATED FACTOR MATRIX

		FACTOR 1 GOVERNMENT EFFICIENCY	FACTOR 2 GOVERNMENT AUTHORITY
CATEGORIES			
301	DECENTRALIZATION POSITIVE	.922	-.017
303	GOVERNMENT EFFICIENCY	.778	-.388
305	GOVERNMENT AUTHORITY AND EFFECTIVENESS	-.143	.971
	EIGENVALUE		
	PERCENT OF VARIANCE	.49	.36

CATEGORIES EXCLUDED DUE TO VERY LOW USE:

| 302 | DECENTRALIZATION, NEGATIVE |
| 304 | GOVERNMENT CORRUPTION |

1960s and 1970s. Fine Gael displays a more erratic pattern: there is no mention of Welfare in 1948 and 1957, while the latter programme also fails to refer to Groups, and devotes over 50 per cent of its content to questions of Government. Moreover, Fine Gael's attention to Welfare almost doubles in the early 1960s going from 10.3 per cent in the early period to 20.2 per cent during later elections.

Fianna Fáil is also erratic. The economy tends to dominate, with Government also being very prominent, while the other domains are squeezed. Welfare, for instance, received no mention in 1957, nor Social Fabric in either 1948 or 1957, nor Groups in 1961 or 1973. The omission of the two latter is particularly surprising since categories within them normally figure very prominently. In the case of Fianna Fáil, however, variations between elections are more understandable given that we are often not dealing with formal, structured manifestos, but rather with speeches given by the current leader or deputy leader of the party.

7.5 THE FIRST-STAGE FACTOR ANALYSIS

Following the general procedure, factor analyses were conducted in two stages. The first involves the data within each domain, and the second analyses the factor scores which result from the first. As the first-stage analysis normally includes only categories which receive at least 1 per cent of all quasi-sentences or at least 3 per cent of the manifestos of a particular party, only one category remains in the External domain and two in the Freedom and Democracy domain. These original categories are used directly in lieu of factor scores, as inputs into the second-stage analysis. The unusual character of the Fianna Fáil 'manifesto' of 1973 (a short statement by the party leader at the dissolution of the Dáil) necessitated its exclusion from the factor analysis.

Table 7.2 reports the results of the factor analysis in the Government domain, the first to be treated in this way. The loadings are quite straightforward and interpretable: Factor 1, which we call Government Efficiency, loads very heavily on Decentralization: Positive (.92) and slightly less heavily on Government Efficiency itself (.78). Factor 2 loads very heavily on Government Authority and Effectiveness (.97), and is called simply Government Authority.

In the Economy domain three factors were extracted. One factor loading positively on Enterprise (.71), Incentives (.49) and Economic Orthodoxy (.78), and negatively on Technology/Infrastructure (−.62) can be labelled Capitalist Economy. Another loads positively on Economic Planning (.80), Controlled Economy (.64) and Nationalization (.56), and this has been labelled Socialist Economy. The remaining factor is less readily interpreted, loading positively on Incentives (.60) and negatively on

TABLE 7.3

MEANS AND STANDARD DEVIATIONS OF FIRST-STAGE FACTOR SCORES BY PARTIES AND DOMAINS

PARTIES (N)	FIANNA FAIL (9)		FINE GAEL (8)		LABOUR (8)		COALITION (FG+LAB) (2)	
	X̄	SD	X̄	SD	X̄	SD	X̄	SD
DOMAINS AND FACTORS								
GOVERNMENT								
F 1 GOVT. EFFICIENCY	-0.109	1.053	0.191	1.068	-0.059	1.115	-0.034	0.120
F 2 GOVT. AUTHORITY	0.196	0.987	0.312	1.320	-0.443	0.652	-0.359	0.295
ECONOMY								
F 1 CAPITALIST ECONOMY	-0.385	0.589	1.116	0.984	-0.608	0.473	-0.300	0.663
F 2 SOCIALIST ECONOMY	-0.664	0.560	-0.123	1.004	0.744	1.027	0.508	0.164
WELFARE								
F 1 QUALITY OF LIFE	-0.056	0.396	-0.146	0.495	0.197	1.793	0.047	0.078
F 2 SOCIAL SERVICES VS. SOCIAL JUSTICE	0.409	1.014	-0.224	0.565	-0.275	1.170	0.150	1.849
SOCIAL FABRIC								
F 1 SOCIAL DISCIPLINE	0.057	0.758	0.320	1.638	-0.282	0.324	-0.409	0.256
F 2 DEFENCE OF IRISH WAY OF LIFE	0.360	1.501	-0.009	0.893	-0.315	0.177	-0.319	0.018
GROUPS								
F 1 NON-ECONOMIC GROUPS + LABOUR	-0.137	0.696	-0.169	1.037	0.398	1.327	-0.301	0.659
F 2 ECONOMIC GROUPS	0.243	1.019	-0.568	0.748	0.458	1.074	-0.653	0.261

Productivity (−.87). Since only the first two factors are used as inputs into the second-stage analysis, this third factor, labelled simply Incentives *vs.* Productivity, is not relevant to our concerns here.

In the Welfare domain, the first factor loads very heavily on to Environmental Protection (.93) and Art, Sport, Leisure, Media (.92), and has been called simply Quality of Life. The other factor loads positively on Social Services: Pro-Expansion (.605) and Education: Pro-Expansion (.85) and negatively on Social Justice (−.67). Perhaps this factor represents a tendency to make specific commitments to expand the welfare state as against purely rhetorical references to the general idea of social justice; in any case, it has been labelled Social Services *vs.* Social Justice.

In the Social Fabric domain, a first factor emerges which loads on Law and Order (.82) and National Effort and Social Harmony (.81). This could be seen to represent a view that all should work together in the national interest, and, if there is unwillingness to do so, then the forces of the state will be used to control dissidence. Both categories sit well together – the one representing the force of law, the other the force of persuasion – and the factor has been labelled Social Discipline. The other factor loads heavily only on Defence of the Irish Way of Life: Positive (.96), and has been labelled accordingly.

In the Groups domain, two factors emerge. One loads on to Labour Groups (.65) and Non-Economic Demographic Groups (.95), and suggests a concern for sections of the population which may be seen in some way to have little influence or to be discriminated against. It is labelled simply Non-Economic Groups and Labour. The other factor loads very heavily on to Agriculture/Farmers (.95) and slightly less heavily onto Labour Groups (.63), both of which represent economic sectoral interest. The factor is therefore called Economic Groups.

Finally, Table 7.3 reports the means and standard deviations, by party, of the factor scores derived from the first-stage analysis. These factor scores, plus scores for the remaining original categories in the External and the Freedom and Democracy domains have been used as the input data for the second-stage factor analysis.

The table itself needs little comment. The Government Efficiency factor tends to divide Fianna Fáil and Labour from Fine Gael, while Government Authority tends to divide the larger parties from Labour. Within the Economy domain, Labour scores positively on Socialist Economics and negatively on Capitalist Economics, with Fine Gael showing the completely reverse pattern, and Fianna Fáil scoring negatively on both. Fine Gael, in turn, scores negatively on both welfare factors, with Fianna Fáil scoring positively on Social Services *vs.* Social Justice and negatively on Quality of Life, while Labour shows the opposite pattern. Within the Social Fabric domain, Fianna Fáil is the only party with a positive score on

TABLE 7.4

DIMENSIONS EMERGING FROM SECOND-STAGE FACTOR ANALYSIS

ROTATED SOLUTION	1 PRINCIPLES GOVERNING THE ORGANIZATION OF SOCIETY: CONSERVATIVE (+) VS. LIBERAL (-)	2 EMPHASIS ON CAPITALIST ECONOMY AND IRISH UNITY	3 EMPHASIS ON RIGHTS OF THE INDIVIDUAL	4 EMPHASIS ON EDUCATION AND IRISH CULTURE	5 EMPHASIS ON SOCIALIST ECONOMY
DOMAIN : EXTERNAL					
1ST STAGE FACTOR 1:1	NA	NA	NA	NA	NA
1ST STAGE FACTOR 1:2	NA	NA	NA	NA	NA
ORIGINAL CATEGORIES					
102 RELATIONSHIP WITH BRITAIN NEGATIVE: PRO-IRISH UNITY	-.276	.672	.031	.319	-.298
DOMAIN: FREEDOM AND DEMOCRACY					
1ST STAGE FACTOR 2:1	NA	NA	NA	NA	NA
1ST STAGE FACTOR 2:2	NA	NA	NA	NA	NA
ORIGINAL CATEGORIES					
201 FREEDOM AND DOMESTIC HUMAN RIGHTS	-.148	.003	.643	.241	-.085
202 DEMOCRACY	-.138	.168	.670	-.272	.119
DOMAIN: GOVERNMENT					
1ST STAGE FACTOR 3:1 GOVERNMENT EFFICIENCY	-.082	.017	.135	-.143	.269
1ST STAGE FACTOR 3:2 GOVERNMENT AUTHORITY	.812	.091	-.032	-.198	-.108

Continued....

TABLE 7.4 continued

ORIGINAL CATEGORIES (r)	1	2	3	4
701 LABOUR GROUPS	-.443	-.400	-.504	-.136
702 AGRICULTURE AND FARMERS	-.227	-.749	.179	.226
705 NON-ECONOMIC DEMOGRAPHIC GROUPS	-.675	.192	-.590	-.133
EIGENVALUE	.15	.12	.11	.10

NO OF CASES : 27
NO OF ORIGINAL CATEGORIES : 27
NOTE ≫ .5 ARE UNDERLINED

151

TABLE 7.4 continued

	1	2	3	4	5
ORIGINAL CATEGORIES (r)					
501 ENVIRONMENTAL PROTECTION	-.098	.081	-.034	-.008	.520
502 ART, SPORT, LEISURE, MEDIA	-.111	-.060	-.113	.208	.384
503 SOCIAL JUSTICE	-.346	-.011	-.056	-.502	.203
504 SOCIAL SERVICES, PRO-EXPANSION	-.611	.128	-.230	.202	-.261
506 EDUCATION, PRO-EXPANSION	-.201	-.124	.003	.831	-.006
DOMAIN: FABRIC OF SOCIETY					
1ST STAGE FACTOR 6:1 SOCIAL DISCIPLINE	.844	.119	-.302	-.002	-.070
1ST STAGE FACTOR 6:2 DEFENCE OF IRISH WAY OF LIFE	.028	.192	.131	.691	-.021
ORIGINAL CATEGORIES (r)					
601 DEFENCE OF IRISH WAY OF LIFE, POSITIVE	-.011	.231	.114	.764	-.067
605 LAW AND ORDER	.669	.107	-.336	-.198	-.147
606 NATIONAL EFFORT AND SOCIAL HARMONY	.761	.114	-.186	.211	.016
DOMAIN: GROUPS					
1ST STAGE FACTOR 7:1 NON-ECONOMIC GROUPS AND LABOUR	-.622	.125	-.647	-.177	-.378
1ST STAGE FACTOR 7:2 ECONOMIC GROUPS	-.193	-.698	.066	.131	-.199

Continued...

TABLE 7.4 continued

	1	2	3	4	5
ORIGINAL CATEGORIES (r)					
301 DECENTRALIZATION, POSITIVE	-.201	.059	.196	-.226	.300
303 GOVERNMENT EFFICINECY	-.256	-.081	.045	.058	.280
305 GOVERNMENT AUTHORITY AND EFFECTIVENESS	.886	.074	-.085	-.161	-.171
DOMAIN: ECONOMY					
1ST STAGE FACTOR 4:1					
CAPITALIST ECONOMY	.103	.682	.134	.128	-.025
1ST STAGE FACTOR 4:2					
SOCIALIST ECONOMY	-.155	.047	-.028	-.295	.710
ORIGINAL CATEGORIES (r)					
401 ENTERPRISE	-.126	.517	.280	.421	-.386
402 INCENTIVES	-.348	.585	-.105	-.031	-.076
403 REGULATION OF CAPITALISM	-.201	-.169	.168	-.292	.290
404 ECONOMIC PLANNING	-.144	.072	.067	-.165	.743
406 PROTECTIONISM, POSITIVE	-.151	-.196	.356	-.104	-.051
410 PRODUCTIVITY	-.386	-.351	-.108	-.083	.100
411 TECHNOLOGY AND INFRASTPUCTURE	-.248	-.504	-.140	.005	-.381
412 CONTROLLED ECONOMY	-.277	.037	-.278	-.431	.433
413 NATIONALIZATION	-.104	-.228	.015	-.009	.511
414 ECONOMIC ORTHODOXY	.286	.456	.201	-.070	-.007
DOMAIN: WELFARE					
1ST STAGE FACTOR 5:1					
QUALITY OF LIFE	.062	-.024	-.004	.069	.422
1ST STAGE FACTOR 5:2					
SOCIAL SERVICES VS.SOCIAL JUSTICE	-.208	-.018	-.074	.647	-.165

Continued...

Defence of Irish Way of Life; Fine Gael scores quite highly on Social Discipline, while Labour records negative scores on both factors. Finally, in the Groups domain, Labour scores positively and Fine Gael negatively on both factors, with Fianna Fáil recording a positive score on Economic Groups and a negative score on Non-Economic Groups and Labour.

If any pattern is evident at this early stage, then it is one which suggests a division between Fine Gael and Labour, with Fianna Fáil somewhere in between: the two former parties show quite opposing scores in the Government, Economy, Social Fabric and Groups domains. Only in the second welfare factor do their mean scores look the same *vis-à-vis* a quite different Fianna Fáil mean score, although on the second factor in the Social Fabric domain Fine Gael's slightly negative mean score also tends to place it on the same side of the divide as Labour.

7.6 THE SECOND-STAGE FACTOR ANALYSIS

(i) The dimensions

The second-stage factor analysis reveals five principal issue dimensions in post-war Irish politics. Table 7.4 reports the loadings of these five dimensions on the factors derived from the first-stage analysis and on the three original categories used as input in the External and the Freedom and Democracy domains. Table 7.4 also shows the correlation coefficients between Dimensions 1–5 and the original categories used in the first-stage domain analysis. These provide a clearer picture of the substance of the five dimensions.

The first dimension (i.e. the first second-stage factor) has been defined as Principles Governing the Organization of Society, a bipolar factor with positive loadings (indicating conservative emphases) on the (first-stage) factors Government Authority and Social Discipline while it also correlates positively ($r > .5$) with Government Authority, National Effort and Law and Order. Dimension 1 also loads negatively (indicating Liberal emphases) on the factor Non-Economic Groups and Labour, and correlates negatively with Social Services pro-Expansion and Non-Economic Groups. Perhaps the closest approximation to this dimension – in terms of what has been identified as one of the major components in Irish political culture – is the phenomenon of authoritarianism (e.g. Schmitt 1973, pp. 43–54). But since the dimension relates so specifically to the original category and first-stage factor Government Authority, it can also be seen to reflect a variant of the hypothesized 'ability to govern' issue.

The second principal dimension has been identified as Emphasis on Capitalist Economics and Irish Unity. This dimension loads positively on the original variable pro-Irish unity (i.e. Foreign Special Relationships

Negative) and the factor Capitalist Economy, and correlates positively with the original categories of enterprise and incentives. Though less than 0.5, the relatively strong correlation with economic orthodoxy is also noteworthy. The negative loading of Dimension 2 is simply on the factor Economic Groups, while it also correlates negatively with the original categories Technology and Infrastructure and Agriculture and Farmers. The association in Dimension 2 of an otherwise straight 'capitalist economics' loading with Irish unity seems largely fortuitous. The Economy categories involved here are primarily the 'exclusive' issues of Fine Gael, while Fine Gael is also the party which has placed greater and more consistent emphasis on pro-Irish unity statements (not to be exaggerated however – an average of slightly less than 4 per cent). In this sense, Dimension 2 is party-specific, tapping the particular emphases of Fine Gael.

Dimension 3 is of less substantive importance. Identified here as Emphasis on Rights of the Individual, the only loadings of significance are on the original categories of Freedom and Domestic Human Rights and Democracy and the factor non-Economic Groups and Labour, on which it loads negatively. Dimension 3 also correlates negatively with two of the original Groups categories, Labour and Non-Economic Groups.

Dimension 4 is perhaps the closest to a purely 'Fianna Fáil dimension', correlating positively with Education and Irish Way of Life, both of which figure in the leading categories of Fianna Fáil but not of the other parties (cf. Table 7.1). Defined here as Emphasis on Education and Irish Culture, Dimension 4 loads positively on the factors Social Services *vs.* Social Justice and Defence of Irish Way of Life. It also shows a negative, but not very strong correlation with the original category of Social Justice.

Dimension 5 has been defined here as Emphasis on Socialist Economy, and may be considered the obverse of Dimension 2. It loads positively on to the factors Socialist Economy, and correlates positively with the original variables of Economic Planning, Nationalization, and Environmental Protection. Dimension 5 has no significant negative loadings, nor does it show any significant negative correlations with any of the original categories. In this sense it is a very unipolar dimension, appearing to tap specifically Labour emphases in the manifestos. It is interesting that in the Irish case 'party-specific' or 'party-owned' dimensions appear so clearly, thus focusing a phenomenon which also appears in other cases.

(ii) Plotting the parties

The definition of Dimensions 1–5 clearly represents one of the more important findings of this study. Further insights can be obtained by plotting the various parties' positions along combinations of the five

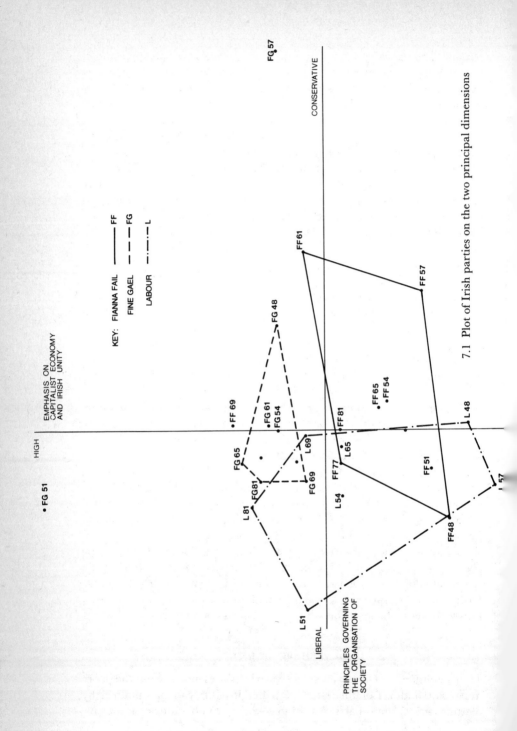

7.1 Plot of Irish parties on the two principal dimensions

156

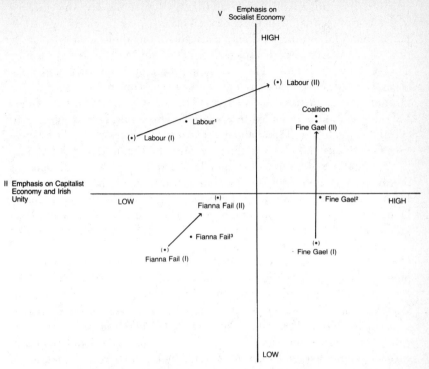

Notes: [1] Labour excludes 1951; Labour (I) includes 1948, 1954-1961; Labour (II) includes 1965, 1969 & 1931.
       [2] Fine Gael excludes 1951; Fine Gael (I) includes 1948, 1954-1961; Fine Gael (II) includes 1965, 1969 & 1981.
       [3] Fianna Fail excludes 1969; Fianna Fail (I) includes 1948-1961; Fianna Fail (II) includes 1965, 1977 & 1981.

7.2 Summary of Irish party positions along dimensions II and V

dimensions. For present purposes, however, only a limited selection will be discussed.

Figure 7.1 maps the parties' positions in the space created by the two principal dimensions. The first point to note here is the relatively consistent positioning of the two larger parties, Fianna Fáil and Fine Gael. If we ignore for a moment the clearly outlying FG51 and FG57, as well as FF69, we find that Fine Gael tends to lie in a relatively small area on the positive side of Dimension 2, while Fianna Fáil occupies a slightly larger area on the negative side of this dimension. Both parties straddle Dimension 1, Principles Governing the Organization of Society, while it is precisely this dimension (tapping a small *vs.* large party conflict?) which separates Labour from its two opponents. (There are parallels here with some of the Canadian findings in Chapter 4.) It is also interesting to note the marked conservative trend in Fianna Fáil programmes between 1948 and 1961 as shown by their increasing shift to the right along Dimension 1. Labour straddles the Capitalist Economy and Irish Unity dimension and, surprisingly, we can see that, with the exception of L51, all of the party's pre-1969 programmes fall on the 'low' emphasis side of this dimension. Moreover, none of the positions really suggests much of an issue-basis for the Fine Gael–Labour coalitions. The coalition programmes of 1973 and 1977 occupy a position very close to that of Fine Gael, while the average Labour position is quite distant. This suggests the only basis of the Fine Gael–Labour coalition is provided by the alignments along Dimension 1. Yet, even here, though both smaller parties lie on the 'Liberal' side, the average Fine Gael position is closer to that of Fianna Fáil than to that of Labour.

Combinations of the first or second dimension with the other dimensions reveal even greater complexity. Some indication of the issue basis of Labour – Fine Gael coalitions is however given by the parties' positions on Dimensions 2 and 5, the one emphasizing Capitalist Economics and Irish Unity, a largely Fine Gael dimension, and the other representing Socialist Economy, a largely Labour dimension.

Rather than showing each individual manifesto in the space, Figure 7.2 plots the average positions of the three parties in the space created by Dimensions 2 and 5, and further differentiates the party positions according to their locations in the periods 1948–61 and 1965–81. Over the period as a whole, Fianna Fáil lies in the lower left-hand quadrant, with a low emphasis on both dimensions; Labour lies in the upper left-hand quadrant, with a low emphasis on Dimension 2 and a high emphasis on Dimension 5, while Fine Gael lies (only marginally) in the lower right-hand quadrant, with a significantly high emphasis on Dimension 2 and a slightly low emphasis on Dimension 5. Finally, the coalition manifestos lie in the fourth upper right-hand quadrant, with a high emphasis on both dimensions. On the face of it, these data on average post-war positions do not suggest an issue basis for the Fine Gael–Labour coalitions.

By breaking the period into two, however, we get a very different picture: Fine Gael shifts position remarkably from Fine Gael (I), representing the position of the 1948, 1954, 1957 and 1961 manifestos, to Fine Gael (II) representing the later manifestos. Labour also moves into the upper-right-hand quadrant in the later years. *From 1965 onwards we find both parties in positions very close to one another, with the coalition manifestos in an intermediate location* – albeit slightly closer to Fine Gael. Thus by breaking the post-war period into two, we find a substantive issue-based basis for the anti-Fianna Fáil alliance in the 1970s. Tangentially, it is also interesting to note Fianna Fáil's slight shift towards the centre of the space in the latter part of the period.

This evidence for a coming together of the potential partners' issue positions and an actual trade-off in the joint coalition programmes, casts a suggestive light on the formation of Irish governments, which will be pursued in our current research on coalition bargaining. A more detailed analysis will appear in our Group's report in this area (Laver, Budge and Hearl (eds.)).

Note

1 Financial support from the Nuffield Foundation facilitated research on this paper.

CHAPTER 8

NORTHERN IRELAND 1921–1973
PARTY MANIFESTOS AND PLATFORMS

———— ∾ ————

8.1 GOVERNMENT AND THE PARTY SYSTEM

The same struggle for independence which produced the party system of
the Irish Republic also produced the Northern Irish State. In a situation of
diminishing British control the Government of Northern Ireland was
constituted in 1921 for the counties of Antrim, Armagh, Down, Ferma-
nagh, Londonderry and Tyrone, with its administrative centre in Belfast.
The rest of Ireland became a self-governing dominion. Thereafter the two
parts of Ireland moved apart, although the nationalists both within and
outside the North continued to demand unification of the island. In 1937
the new (Southern) Irish Constitution applied in theory everywhere. In
1949 the Irish Free State formally became the Republic of Ireland,
following the passing of the Republic of Ireland Act (1948). In response,
the Westminster Parliament in the Ireland Act (1949) gave a specific
guarantee that Northern Ireland would remain part of the United
Kingdom with legislative devolution over matters not of concern to the
U.K. as a whole.

The Parliament was not sovereign. However, its institutions were
modelled on those of Westminster. The legislature comprised the Crown,
represented by a Governor, a House of Commons and a Senate. From 1929
elections were held on a simple plurality system in single member districts.
The Senate consisted of 26 members and all but two ex-officio members
were elected, by proportional representation, by the Lower House.

The Governor appointed ministers to the various departments but this
was treated as a formal power, exercised on the advice of the local Prime
Minister who commanded a majority in the House of Commons. The local
Cabinet was the supreme executive and its members accepted the principle
of collective responsibility.

Having survived various attacks by nationalist groups based on the

160

Catholic third of the population, these arrangements broke down under communal strife from August 1969. Security was put in the hands of the army, policy was determined at Westminster and implemented at Stormont by British civil servants imported to key positions. The guiding principles of the U.K. Government were: first, no change in the constitutional position so long as the majority wished it; second, to ensure that the minority could play an active, permanent, and guaranteed role.

In an initiative in March 1972 the U.K. Government proposed periodic plebiscites on the border issue and the transfer of direct responsibility for law and order to Westminster. The Stormont Government accepted the first but could not accept the latter, an impasse which resulted in its abolition and direct rule from London. The British Government made various attempts to restore devolution on the basis of cooperation between elements of the Protestant, Unionist, majority and the Catholic, Nationalist, minority. The first stage was a poll (8 March 1973) on whether the Province should continue to be linked to Britain, or should be integrated with the Republic of Ireland. Fifty-eight per cent voted for the first alternative. This was followed by an attempt to set up an elected Assembly with a consociational Executive and limited local powers. It lasted, however, for only five months. In early 1974 direct action by the (Protestant) Ulster Workers Council brought the Executive down. Direct rule resumed and has continued to the present day.

Northern Ireland has a party system quite distinct from that of the United Kingdom. It can be described as a multi-party system, with one dominant party, based on disagreements over the constitutional link with Britain. The two major parties existing between 1921 and 1972, the Unionists and the Nationalists, reflected religious, cultural and national differences, and agreed upon the primacy of the constitutional issue. There were other parties, notably the Northern Irish Labour Party organized around other cleavages such as class, but they had to come to terms with the constitutional issue.

The party share of representation remained relatively constant over the period, with Unionists fluctuating around 60 per cent of the vote, and about 35 out of 51 seats, while opposition parties had about one third of votes and the rest of the seats. These results reflected underlying cleavages, although to an extent party stability was assisted by the electoral system. Between 1929 and 1969 the simple plurality system over-represented the two largest parties, Unionists and Nationalists, at the expense of all other groups, particularly Independent Unionists and Northern Ireland Labour. The stability of political attitudes, and the method of election combined to make seats safe for the one major party or the other, and produced a large percentage of unopposed returns.

In addition to party differences on the constitution, factions within each grouping also differed on policies and personalities. The result was a large number of small splinter parties, and between 1921 and 1969 parties with over 40 different labels contested general elections while candidates from 22 groups were successful. For example, in 1965 candidates from ten parties were nominated and candidates from six parties and one independent were elected. In the 1969 general election eight different parties, including five Unionist groups as well as a variety of independents, contested the election. Six parties and three independents were successful. After 1969, the established parties fragmented further and new parties emerged including the Alliance Party, Democratic Unionists, Vanguard Unionists, the Unionist Party of Northern Ireland, United Ulster Unionist Party, Republican Clubs, Unity, and the Irish Independence Party.

8.2 PARTIES AND MANIFESTOS

(i) Selection of parties

The case for the selection of two main parties, Unionist and Nationalist, is clear. The Northern Ireland Labour Party has been included because of its persistence as a third party of a different character. When all three parties are included they accounted for over 90 per cent of candidates nominated in 1925, and 58 per cent in 1969. Their share of the seats ranged from 90 per cent in three years 1929, 1933 and 1958, to 85 per cent in 1969. Their share of the vote ranged from 90 per cent in 1962 to 64 per cent in 1969.

(ii) Documentation

Ulster's problems have left their mark on the documentation of parties. The Nationalists were organized into a formal political party only towards the end of the period, and records are thus very scanty. The NILP is now more or less defunct although we have been able to acquire the full texts of the 1949–73 manifestos. The offices of the Unionist party were firebombed during the current troubles and most of their records destroyed.

We have therefore relied on newspaper reports of party policy in the *Irish News, Belfast Newsletter, Belfast Telegraph, Northern Whig, Irish Times* and *Irish Independent.* Here we are helped by the very partisan nature of the Belfast press. *The Newsletter,* with its almost exclusively Protestant readership, espoused a solid Unionist position, and usually reproduced the Unionist manifesto in its entirety. The *Northern Whig,* until its closure in 1963, was also a broadly Unionist paper, and very often reproduced the full text of the Unionist manifesto. When the versions reproduced in both papers are described as full texts, and when these corresponded exactly, we have assumed that they represent the whole of the manifesto. Sometimes, versions referred to as the text, or the full text, differ slightly between the two papers. This usually arises from slight differences in subediting, where minor sentences have been deleted in order to make the text fit the space available. In these cases we have put both reports together, in the hope that we then have a full text.

If the Nationalists had been organized as a political party, then our problems would have been over, since the *Irish News* was as firmly anti-partisan in its views as the *Newsletter* was Unionist. It does indeed report the full text in 1969, although it unfortunately let an editor loose in 1965 and 1962, and fuller versions appear elsewhere (with a complete text in the *Northern Whig* for 1962). Prior to that, we have taken the fullest report of the document which, in our judgement most closely fulfilled the function of a formal party platform. In 1921, 1929 and 1949, we are confident that we have the full text of the most appropriate document. In 1925, 1938 and 1956, we probably have the best that is likely to be available. That of 1945 is less satisfactory, being the election address of a single candidate, though published in full as an advertisement in the *Irish News*. So far we have been able to track nothing at all for 1933 or 1953.

The Northern Ireland Labour Party had no local newspaper which rallied to its cause. Reports of its manifestos are thus much more heavily edited, usually with a view to squeezing them into a relatively minor position on the inside pages. Fortunately we have obtained the actual manifestos for 1949–73. Otherwise we have taken the fullest version we can find. Our confidence in the completeness of the newspaper reports increased substantially when we acquired the actual text of manifestos for which we previously had only what appeared to be heavily edited versions in newspapers. Most Northern Ireland party manifestos were, in fact, until the late 1960s, prepared as press handouts in the hope that they would be reproduced in full in the newspapers.

(iii) Election manifestos and party policy formation

The outcome of most elections in Northern Ireland is determined by factors other than the contents of the rival manifestos. Only the Unionists were elected to office during the whole period and thus had the opportunity to put policies into practice. Nonetheless manifestos did have a role in party competition. The multiplicity of parties contesting elections and the umbrella nature of the Unionist Alliance (grouping working class and populist elements along with a middle class which provided the leadership) made it susceptible to appeals on social and economic issues. The fear of losing support forced the party to present comprehensive policy documents in years when electoral competition of this kind was prevalent. This can

clearly be seen in the response to Independent Unionists and NILP in 1938
and 1945 and to NILP in the 1960s.

For NILP comprehensive policy statements were essential to show the
electorate that other forms of politics could gain expression. This was
especially the case after 1949 when the party accepted the constitutional
position of Northern Ireland and was seeking votes essentially at the
expense of the Unionist Party. There was therefore effective electoral
competition between the policy platforms in the major urban centre of
Belfast.

Media coverage by radio and television in the 1960s gave a new
emphasis to party manifestos. Besides the extensive press coverage on
which we have already commented, the manifestos were also the basis for
the official election broadcasts on radio and television. Their main points
were therefore forced upon the attention of the public.

The Party Leaders, close colleagues at Stormont and the party officials
were responsible for the initial draft of the manifesto. While in government
(until 1972) the Party Leader, as Prime Minister, could draw upon
experience and the advice of the civil service as well as the party policy
research committees. The party officers and secretary could keep the
political leaders in touch with opinion if they were tempted to stray.
Further, the formal control by the Ulster Unionist Council, and after 1946
by the Standing Committee of over 300 members with a very strong
constituency representation, meant that the manifesto could be checked
against party policies and principles, and in terms of its impact across
Northern Ireland. When an election came suddenly, the whole process was
in the hands of the initial group of leaders.

After the organizational shake-up in 1949 NILP was almost identical in
organization to the British Labour Party. The Executive of seventeen
initiated a series of policy statements on social and economic issues such as,
local government, education, shipbuilding, housing, electricity, water
schemes and a development council. Party manifestos drew upon these
policy statements. By 1962 the party was so prepared that the manifesto
was called 'Ulster Labour and the Sixties' and intended as a comprehensive programme. With different emphases this programme was adapted to
meet the needs of 1965 and 1969.

The Nationalist Party had no formal policy making body. It was
essentially a collection of individuals with a personal following, the
minimum of organization and with whom the notion of a Party Leader
fitted uneasily. Constituency conventions, comprising local elected representatives, citizens and clergy, usually met close to an election to select
candidates and decide whether they should be pledged to abstain or
participate. In the period since 1921 a nascent central organization existed
on two occasions, the end of the 1920s and the end of the 1940s.

(iv) The format of manifestos

Most Unionist manifestos have been brief documents designed for press circulation. The length of the document was related to the nature of the political challenge in the election. Hence the documents were quite long in 1925, 1929, 1938, 1958, 1965, 1969 and 1973. With a sympathetic local press in the *Belfast Newsletter, Belfast Telegraph* and *Northern Whig* the manifesto was usually reproduced verbatim together with a message from the Party Leader. Hence most potential voters had access to the policy document.

Most NILP manifestos were short and directed towards the press, although Labour suffered from not having a directly sympathetic paper.

The Nationalist Party did not issue election manifestos until 1962. However, the Party Leader would usually make a keynote speech which could be used as a surrogate. The contents of such statements were often personal and reflected the interests of the leader. The manifestos of 1962, 1965 and 1969 were all brief statements. The Nationalist Party could rely on a sympathetic press coverage in the *Irish News* and a number of local weekly papers.

8.3 CODING PROCEDURES AND NORTHERN IRELAND

Despite the very special circumstances in Northern Ireland, the general coding scheme was usually flexible enough to incorporate most manifesto references, given some detailed interpretation, as follows:

Foreign Special Relationships

Since Stormont did not have responsibility for foreign policy, very few truly international references occur under this heading. Many references are, however, made to mainland Britain and the Republic of Ireland, and these have been listed in separate sub-categories.

Productivity

A significant aspect of each party's policy were statements proposing aid to specific sectors of the economy, such as agriculture, industry and tourism. Separate sub-categories were created for this information.

Democracy

Everywhere we have confined ourselves to what parties actually say, as opposed to what we think they really mean. We have, therefore, made no judgement on any reference to democracy, despite the fact that 'majority rule' has a very special meaning in Ulster, implying the maintenance of links with Britain and a denial of nationalist aspirations for a united Ireland. Direct references to the cleavage underlying this issue (between the Protestant majority for whom the province was created and the Catholic, nationalist minority) are never made, in spite of their underlying the whole of Northern Irish politics. There are certain parallels here with the absence of the unification and Nationalist issue from party debate in the Republic of Ireland, though that is far less central than in the North.

Constitutionalism

In 1973, the White Paper on Northern Ireland is taken as the constitutional status quo, since the elections were being held for the Assembly which was proposed in it. Hostile references to partition are coded as anti-constitutional in the pre-war period.

8.4 ANALYSIS OF MANIFESTO DATA

(i) Leading issues

Many of the issues covered by the general coding scheme made no appearance at all in the Northern Ireland party manifestos. A total of thirty-one categories were either completely ignored, or so little discussed that they were excluded under our rules. It is clear nevertheless from the overall average of uncoded sentences – just under 15 per cent – that the general coding scheme worked well even in this deviant case.

Those issues which figured prominently in the manifestos are listed in Table 8.1. This illustrates the heavy preponderance of non-sectarian issues. Overall, only one of the leading five issues (Ireland (positive)) was sectarian. The other four were matters of conventional socio-economic policy. Furthermore, these issues do not reflect the typical left–right polarization of such policy. This too is a product of special circumstances in Ulster. The principle of parity of services for parity of taxation in regard to the rest of the United Kingdom was highly esteemed by Unionists as a tangible expression of the benefits of the British connection: Unionist manifestos had a high proportion of favourable references to social service expenditure. Thus, while Unionists were allied to the British Conservative Party and could be regarded as being on the political right, they were not low spenders. This crucial element of the usual left–right dimension was conspicuous by its absence.

In contrast, the Nationalist Party, representing the Catholic minority and never in power during the fifty-year Stormont period, laid much more

TABLE 8.1

MEAN ORDER OF MENTIONS	ISSUE	MEAN REFS	S.D. REFS	ISSUE	MEAN REFS	S.D. REFS	ISSUE	MEAN REFS	S.D. REFS	ISSUE	MEAN REFS	S.D. REFS
1	IRELAND(+)	14.60	12.9	SOCIAL SERVICES(+)	15.0	11.0	PRODUCTIVITY	14.7	8.4	SOCIAL SERVICES	12.6	12.7
2	SOCIAL SERVICES(+)	10.4	18.6	ECONOMIC GOALS	11.8	8.5	SOCIAL SERVICES(+)	12.4	8.2	PRODUCTIVITY	9.2	9.0
3	GOVT. CORRUPTION	6.8	8.9	PRODUCTIVITY	8.9	9.1	ECONOMIC GOALS	7.0	9.8	ECONOMIC GOALS	7.4	8.4
4	CONSTITUTION(-)	6.8	17.4	EDUCATION (+)	4.7	4.5	TECHNOLOGY	5.8	6.8	IRELAND(+)	4.9	9.5
5	SOCIAL JUSTICE	4.9	4.8	DEMOCRACY	4.5	3.4	DEFENCE OF NATIONAL WAY OF LIFE	5.8	6.9	TECHNOLOGY	3.8	5.6
UNCODED		19.8	16.9		13.7	13.6		11.7	7.7		14.8	12.9
TOTAL QUASI SENTENCES		52.1	32.9		93.1	93.5		87.5	79.6		78.4	73.9

167

emphasis on political/sectarian issues. Only one of its leading five issues (Social Services Expansion) was socio-economic in character. Compared with Nationalist policy platforms, those of NILP and the Unionists look very similar. The two parties shared the same top three issues. NILP was rather more concerned with expanding the state sector (via education and other social services) while the Unionists were rather more concerned with Productivity and Technology, but the differences are small. Both NILP and the Unionist counted one political/sectarian issue in their top five. Of these, the Unionist concern of defending the national way was more conservative than NILP's concern for democracy.

(ii) Analysis by domain

Manifesto references are grouped into the seven domains used in all common analyses. The domains themselves are grouped into two clusters. These relate to political/sectarian, and to socio-economic issues. Over time within the political/sectarian cluster, there is a steadily increasing concern of all parties for issues concerned with government and freedom and a relatively decreasing concern for more 'overt' sectarian matters relating to external relations and the fabric of society. There is a moderate trend for all political/sectarian issues to become more prominent, distorted by an explosion of sectarian references in 1949. Within the socio-economic cluster, no particular time pattern is evident.

Turning to the differences between parties over the whole period, two striking features emerge. Firstly, the Nationalists are noticeably less concerned with socio-economic matters than the other two parties. The much smaller proportion of Nationalist references in these categories stems entirely from a relative lack of concern for *economic* policy. The level of discussion of social welfare matters and specific groups is very similar for all parties. Unsurprisingly, NILP has a noticeably higher proportion of references in the whole cluster than the other two parties. Within the political/sectarian cluster, concern for government and freedom is highest for the Nationalists. The proportion of 'overt' sectarian references is very similar for the two main parties.

The standard principal components analysis was performed on all of the non-excluded categories within each domain. The results of this can be found in Table 8.2. An attempt was made to extract two principal components from each domain. In fact, for three of the seven domains, only one principal component had an Eigenvalue greater than unity. For the remaining four domains, only two principal components had an Eigenvalue greater than unity.

Nearly all of the principal components were readily interpretable:

TABLE 8.2

FIRST STAGE DIMENSIONAL ANALYSIS (WITHIN DOMAIN) NORTHERN IRELAND

THEME/VARIABLES	FACTOR LOADINGS	
	COMPONENT A	COMPONENT B
1. EXTERNAL RELATIONS	(PRO BRITAIN/ANTI IRE.)	
101A RELATIONS WITH BRITAIN (+)	.93	(NO SECOND COMPONENT)
102B RELATIONS WITH IRELAND (−)	.89	
101B RELATIONS WITH IRELAND (+)	−.49	
EIGENVALUE	1.9	
% OF VARIANCE	6%	
2. FREEDOM AND DEMOCRACY	(FREEDOM AND DEMOCRACY)	(PRO CONTSTI-TUTION)
202 DEMOCRACY	.79	.12
201 FREEDOM AND DOMESTIC HUMAN RIGHTS	.79	−.13
204 CONSTITUTIONALISM (−)	−.39	−.70
203 CONSTITUTIONALISM (+)	−.36	+.73
EIGENVALUE	1.5	1.1
% OF VARIANCE	38%	26%
3. GOVERNMENT	(AUTHORITY)	(CORRUPTION)
305 GOVERNMENT EFFECTIVENESS AND AUTHORITY	−.82	.06
303 GOVERNMENT EFFICIENCY	.57	.04
307 DECENTRALIZATION (+)	.33	.75
304 GOVERNMENT CORRUPTION	.30	−.78
EIGENVALUE	1.2	1.2
% OF VARIANCE	30%	29%
4. ECONOMY	(ECONOMIC MODERNIZATION)	(REGULATION VS. MARKET FORCES)
410 PRODUCTIVITY	.88	.02
411 TECHNOLOGY & INFRASTRUCTURE	.85	.19
404 ECONOMIC PLANNING	.56	−.31
408 ECONOMIC GOALS	−.16	−.79
403 REGULATION OF CAPITALISM	.14	.65
EIGENVALUE	1.9	1.2
% OF VARIANCE	37%	23%

Continued...

TABLE 8.2 continued

THEME/VARIABLES	COMPONENT A	COMPONENT B
5. WELFARE AND QUALITY OF LIFE	(SOCIAL JUSTICE)	(NO SECOND COMPONENT)
504 SOCIAL SERVICES EXPANSION (+)	.69	
503 SOCIAL JUSTICE	-.67	
506 EDUCATION PRO EXPANSION	.63	
EIGENVALUE	1.3	
% OF VARIANCE	44%	
6. FABRIC OF SOCIETY	(SOCIAL CONSERVATISM)	(NO SECOND COMPONENT)
606 NATIONAL EFFORT	.86	
601 DEFENCE OF NATIONAL WAY OF LIFE (+)	.81	
605 LAW AND ORDER	.51	
EIGENVALUE	1.3	
% OF VARIANCE	44%	
7. SOCIAL GROUPS	(MINORITIES)	(LABOUR)
706 NON-ECONOMIC DEMOGRAPHIC GROUPS	.90	-.10
705 UNDERPRIVILEGED MINORITY GROUPS	.88	.15
701 LABOUR GROUPS	.03	.99
EIGENVALUE	1.6	1.0
% OF VARIANCE	53%	34%

External Relations

Within this domain, only one component was extracted. This linked favourable mentions of Britain with unfavourable mentions of Ireland, contrasting these with favourable mentions of Ireland. A high proportion of variance within the domain is explained by this pro-Britain/anti-Ireland dimension.

Freedom and Democracy

Two components were extracted. The most significant linked Freedom and Democracy, while the other contrasted positive and negative mentions of the constitution. On the first component, Freedom and Democracy are mildly contrasted to any form of mention of the constitution. This is also interesting. Northern Irish parties appeal to Freedom and Democracy when demanding either changes in, or a maintenance of, the constitution. To mention Freedom or Democracy is to imply nothing about your views on the constitution, and the principal components analysis picks this up quite clearly.

Government

The analysis of this domain is rather more obscure than that of the previous two. Two principal components were extracted. The first was strongly related to Government Authority, as opposed to Government Efficiency. The second contrasted Corruption with Decentralization. This is almost certainly a party-specific matter. Mentions of Corruption were almost exclusively the preserve of the Nationalists, while the Unionists were periodically concerned with the decentralization of power and consequent strengthening of Stormont. In terms of the parties' positions on this component, the striking feature is the polar position of the Nationalists. For this reason, the component has been labelled 'Corruption'.

Economy

The principal components analysis of the economic policy domain was straight forward. The first component linked productivity, technology and planning, and can be thought of as an economic modernisation. The second contrasted general statements of Economic Goals with mentions of the Regulation of Capitalism. In practice, many of these general statements referred to goals which would not be achieved by government regulation but more by manipulation of prevailing market conditions.

Welfare

The analysis of this domain is the most obscure of all, despite the fact that it accounted for many of the manifesto references. There are two clear reasons for this. In the first place, implementing social services was a matter for local concern, while raising *local* taxes to pay for them was not (they were covered by British subsidy). This meant that the Unionists were not low spenders, despite being allied with the British Conservatives. In the second place, the welfare domain is rather a hybrid in terms of Ulster politics. One issue, Social Justice, is very significant, but tends to be related to sectarian matters rather than to pure welfare.

The consequence of all this was that a single component was extracted, which related Social Service Expansion in general to the Expansion of State Education in particular, and contrasted these to Social Justice. This is in part an artefact of the sectarian overtones of 'social justice', though a contrast of this type also emerges in other country analyses where sectarianism is not necessarily an issue. It obviously fits uneasily with other 'purer' welfare concerns.

The dimension therefore contrasts emphases on immediate concrete expansion in specific social services with emphases on (social) justice – the first being linked with the Protestant parties and the other with the nationalists.

Fabric of Society

The single component illustrated a straightforward relationship between National Effort, Defence of the Way of Life and, to a lesser extent, Law and Order. This is clearly a dimension reflecting social conservatism.

Social Groups

The pattern within this domain was strongest of all. Demographic and minority groups were strongly linked, while mentions of Labour Groups were quite clearly separate. The two components reflected this, though it is worth remembering that the domain as a whole was mentioned much less by all parties than any other. Nearly ninety per cent of the variance within the domain was explained by a 'Minorities' and a 'Labour' component.

Each of the eleven principal components extracted in the first-stage analysis separated the three parties in an intuitively plausible manner (see Table 8.3). The 'pro-Britain/anti-Ireland' component placed Nationalists and Unionists at opposite ends of the scale, with NILP almost exactly half way between them. The 'freedom and democracy', 'pro-constitution', 'government authority', 'corruption', 'economic modernisation', 'social conservatism' and 'minorities' dimensions similarly discriminated very strongly between Unionists and Nationalists. The main differences between these components were where they located NILP in relation to the two main parties. NILP appears as being on the Unionist 'side' in terms of the constitution, corruption, modernization and minorities, while it is on the 'side' of Nationalists on freedom, government authority, and social conservatism. This accords with a view of NILP as constitutionalist opposition party, in favour of change, but accepting the legitimacy of the existing regime.

Exceptions to this pattern of party differentiation can be found in three of the eleven components. Two of these, the 'regulation of capitalism' and 'social justice *vs*. social welfare' placed NILP and the Nationalists at opposite ends of the scale. On the regulation of capitalism, the Unionists occupy a dead centre position. On social justice, they 'side' with NILP in favour of social welfare *as opposed* to social justice. This reflects the argument (see below) that this component is a surrogate for a dimension

TABLE 8.3

MEAN SCORES FOR EACH PARTY ON ROTATED PRINCIPAL COMPONENTS: FIRST-STAGE ANALYSIS

COMPONENT		NATIONALIST		NILP		UNIONIST	
		MEAN	SD	MEAN	SD	MEAN	SD
1.1	PRO BRITAIN/ANTI IRELAND	-0.74	0.35	-0.13	0.18	0.66	1.27
2.1	FREEDOM AND DEMOCRACY	0.47	1.33	0.24	0.76	-0.54	0.50
2.2	PRO CONSTITUTION	-0.66	1.08	0.19	0.62	0.36	0.98
3.1	AUTHORITY (- LOADING)	0.36	0.74	0.25	0.47	0.47	1.30
3.2	CORRUPTION (- LOADING)	-0.84	1.04	0.40	0.87	0.33	0.68
4.1	ECONOMIC MODERNIZATION	-0.62	0.48	0.17	1.23	0.35	0.95
4.2	REGULATION VS.MARKET FORCES	-0.56	0.65	0.57	1.19	0.00	0.87
5.1	SOCIAL JUSTICE (- LOADING)	-0.73	1.03	0.44	1.14	0.22	0.49
6.1	SOCIAL CONSERVATISM	-0.55	0.37	-0.21	0.84	0.59	1.17
7.1	MINORITIES	0.45	1.61	-0.16	0.64	-0.23	0.42
7.2	LABOUR	0.13	0.86	0.39	1.46	-0.40	0.46

contrasting those who want to work within the system with those who want to change it. The 'labour' component contrasted NILP with the Unionists, the Nationalists being rather more on the 'side' of NILP, and hence pro-labour. By far the greatest polarization was reflected by the 'pro-Britain/anti-Ireland' component. 'Corruption', 'social conservatism', 'freedom' and the constitution also reflected high polarization.

Overall, the analysis of manifesto references by domain was highly successful. It reflected the clear distinctions between 'overt' and 'technical' political/sectarian issues, and the increasing relevance of the latter in the shape of 'government' and 'freedom'. The dimensional analysis produced results which could easily be interpreted, which accorded with most of the received wisdom on Ulster's party system and which also allowed some non-obvious conclusions to be drawn. Notable among these were the lack of structure in references to social welfare, despite their frequency; the ambiguous relationship between references to democracy and to the constitution; and the importance of political/sectarian issues in discriminating between the parties, notwithstanding the way in which these were camouflaged in the manifestos. In addition, the first stage dimensional analysis enabled some ambiguities in the position of NILP to be clarified.

(iii) Second-stage factor analysis

A final organization and presentation of the data was achieved using a second-stage factor analysis. Factor scores for each manifesto were calculated for each of the eleven principal components discussed above, and these were used as input to a second-stage analysis. The results are presented in Table 8.4 and Figure 8.1. Various solutions to the factor

Michael Laver and Sydney Elliott

TABLE 8.4

SECOND STAGE FACTOR LOADINGS AND CORRELATIONS OF ORIGINAL VARIABLES WITH SECOND STAGE FACTORS

VARIABLES		
1 EXTERNAL RELATIONS		
1.1 PRO-BRITAIN/ANTI-IRELAND	.78	.02
101A RELATIONS WITH BRITAIN: POSITIVE	.88	-.05
102B RELATIONS WITH IRELAND: NEGATIVE	.73	-.15
101B RELATIONS WITH IRELAND: POSITIVE	-.36	-.42
2 FREEDOM AND DEMOCRACY		
2.1 FREEDOM AND DEMOCRACY	-.51	-.32
2.2 PRO-CONSTITUTION	.33	.09
202 DEMOCRACY	-.45	-.25
201 FREEDOM AND DOMESTIC HUMAN RIGHTS	-.51	-.47
204 CONSTITUTIONALISM: NEGATIVE	-.12	-.05
203 CONSTITUTIONALISM: POSITIVE	.39	.06
3 GOVERNMENT		
3.1 AUTHORITY NEGATIVE LOADING	-.61	-.15
3.2 CORRUPTION	.21	.29
305 GOVT. EFFECTIVENESS AND AUTHORITY	.64	.08
303 GOVT. EFFICIENCY	-.31	-.04
301 DECENTRALIZATION: POSITIVE	-.01	.05
304 GOVT. CORRUPTION	-.34	-.46
4 ECONOMY		
4.1 ECONOMIC MODERNIZATION	-.09	.47
4.2 REGULATION VS. MARKET FORCES	-.05	.41
410 PRODUCTIVITY	.05	.54
411 TECHNOLOGY AND INFRASTRUCTURE	-.06	.62
404 ECONOMIC PLANNING	-.24	.05
408 ECONOMIC GOALS	.06	.37
403 REGULATION OF CAPITALISM	-.26	.21
5 WELFARE AND QUALITY OF LIFE		
5.1 SOCIAL SERVICES VS. SOCIAL JUSTICE	.12	.77
504 SOCIAL SERVICES EXPANSION	-.09	.62
503 SOCIAL JUSTICE	-.34	-.61
506 EDUCATION	.02	.55
6 FABRIC OF SOCIETY		
601 SOCIAL CONSERVATISM	.74	-.30
606 NATIONAL EFFORT	.62	-.47
601 DEFENCE OF NATIONAL WAY	.82	-.18
605 LAW AND ORDER	.28	-.05
7 SOCIAL GROUPS		
7.1 MINORITIES	-.08	-.29
7.2 LABOUR	-.37	.03
706 NON-ECONOMIC DEMOGRAPHIC	.04	-.27
705 UNDERPRIVILEGED MINORITIES	-.22	-.32
701 LABOUR	-.38	.04

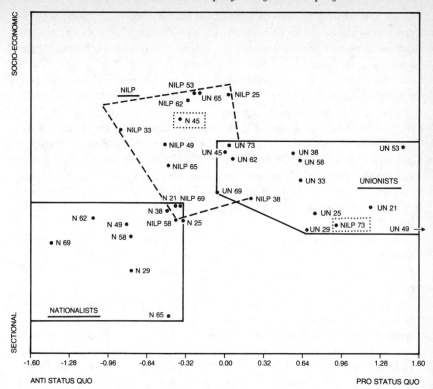

8.1 Two dimensional Northern Ireland party space

problem were investigated, but the most economical and interpretable result was that provided by a two factor orthogonal structure. As an aid to interpretation, Table 8.4 provides not only the loadings of the input components on these two factors, but also the correlations between the manifesto scores on these factors and the original coding categories used.

Both factors have a significant sectarian flavour. The difference between them is that while the first has high loadings on correlations only for political/sectarian categories, the second factor contrasts some political/ sectarian categories with those concerned with socio-economic policy. The first factor can be interpreted as 'pro status quo'. It relates the 'pro-Britain/ anti-Ireland' component to 'social conservatism' and 'government authority' and contrasts these with 'freedom and democracy'. Components in the economy and the welfare domains are ignored, although the correlations with individual variables show that social justice was misplaced in the welfare domain. The second factor relates the economic and welfare components and contrasts these mildly with 'freedom', 'social conservatism' and 'minorities'. While negative loadings of the first-stage components are not very high, the correlations with the original variables show that positive mentions of Ireland, 'Freedom', 'Corruption', 'Social Justice' and 'National Effort' contribute to this pattern. It makes sense, therefore to see this second factor as representing a 'socio-economic' *vs.* 'sectional' dimension, although it explains much less of the variance than the first.

Taking the two second-stage factor as 'pro *vs.* anti-status quo' and 'socio-economic *vs.* sectional interests', a spatial representation of the manifestos is made in Figure 8.1 (The 'socio-economic *vs.* sectional' dimension is weighted by its relative contribution to the total explained variance). From this it can be seen that, with the exception of one deviant case for each party, the parties occupy distinct areas in this 'policy space'. (The deviant cases were 1965 for the Unionists, 1975 for NILP and 1945 for the Nationalists).

As expected, the Unionists are in the pro-status quo area of the space, with socio-economic and sectional interests balancing each other out. This reflects high scores on the 'pro-Britain/anti-Ireland', 'Government Authority' and 'Social Conservatism' components, and low scores on 'Freedom and Democracy' and, to a lesser extent, Social Justice and Corruption. Unionist manifestos scored highly on both socio-economic and sectional interests, and these balance each other out. The Nationalists appear in the 'anti-status quo' area and 'pro-sectional interest' segment of the space. Hostile references to the regime and large proportions of sectional references are not balanced by large numbers of mentions of socio-economic policy matters. NILP appears as mildly 'anti-status quo' and definitely concerned with socio-economic rather than sectional interests. This two dimensional picture therefore seems to be an economical and plausible representation of the political reality of Northern Irish Party politics. We have a picture of the Unionist Party balancing the sectional interests to which it clearly appealed with the socio-economic policy which, as the permanent party of government, it was inevitably charged with making. In opposition to the Unionists we see two parties. NILP appears as less dramatically opposed to the status quo than the Nationalists. The two are distinguished by their expressed concern for socio-economic and sectional interests. Despite the apparently artificial exercise of taking the policies advanced by the Northern Ireland political parties at face value, the underlying structure of the messages they emit confirms most expectations of what the parties really stand for.

CHAPTER 9

SWEDEN AND DENMARK 1945–1982: ELECTION PROGRAMMES IN THE SCANDINAVIAN SETTING[1]

―――――― ～ ――――――

9.1 THE PARTY SYSTEMS

Here, as in Chapter 3, we analyse culturally related countries together – partly because the discussion can be presented more succinctly, but also because divergences stemming from different institutional structures (particularly from contrasting party systems) can be highlighted in an interesting way.

Sweden has a predominant party system overshadowed by the Social Democrats, who obtained 40–50 per cent of the votes from the 1930s, and governed from 1932–76, though occasionally in coalition. Their predominance was in part secured through the fragmentation of the opposition between the Conservatives – a fairly standard business-oriented group, strongest in the South; the Liberals – radical in European terms, with advanced libertarian and welfare positions; the Agrarians – traditionally non-conformist in religion, teetotaller in ideology and supportive of rural interests; and the Communists.

This five-party system emerged in Sweden from 1900–20 and has remained structurally unchanged from that date, in contrast to Denmark. However, relationships within and between the parties underwent substantial changes during the 1960s and 1970s. The Agrarian Party, responding to the decline of the rural population, changed its name to the Centre Party and very successfully extended its appeal to radical, free-thinking voters in the city on 'new' issues such as the environment. At the same time moves were made to commit the bourgeois parties to an electoral alliance against the Social Democrats, as it was obvious that no credible governmental alternative could emerge short of a coalition including all three. This encountered difficulties as the Agrarians had been in coalition with the Social Democrats in the 1950s and sympathized with them on many issues relating to the role of the state in society. The Liberal Party identified the Conservatives as their natural enemy on such questions as feminism. Moreover the 'bourgeois' parties were torn between two incompatible objectives: *jointly* to maximize the anti-Socialist vote and *individually* to minimize the loss of votes to other non-Socialist parties. The movement of votes between them has always been much greater than transfers to and from the Social Democrats. Thus formal party arrangements never became nationwide, and despite some cooperation between the three parties in Parliament they never issued any joint programme, statement or manifesto.

However in 1968 they did declare that they would form a coalition if they had a combined majority of seats in the now single-chamber Parliament. Under pressure from the media and some of their activists they actually formed a government in 1976. With considerable vicissitudes, the alliance endured to the beginning of the 1980s, when the Social Democrats again returned to power.

The chief difference between the Swedish and Danish party systems, from the 1920s to the 1960s, lay in the greater weakness of the Danish Social Democrats. In Denmark they took longer to build up support and oscillated around (and often just under) 40 per cent of the vote. Hence they were forced into coalition governments, or into governing from a minority position in the legislature. Since the other parties were individually much smaller, the Social Democrats nevertheless constituted the predominant party in the system. Natural allies were the Radical Liberals, on the left of European Liberalism: they were distinguished from the Agrarian Liberals, who were in the latter part of this period closer to the Conservatives as they sought to extend their appeal beyond their declining agrarian support. As in Sweden the Communists had split from the Social Democrats in the 1920s but had little support.

The system began to change in the 1960s with the irruption of the Socialist People's Party, a left radical group, which in 1966 gained 11 per cent of the vote, having already displaced the Communists in the legislature. This provided the Social Democrats with alternative support for their minority governments, at the price of radicalizing their policies, particularly in regard to welfare. The cost of financing old and new welfare schemes, opposition to NATO and hostility to the established parties formed the background to an extraordinary proliferation of new populist parties in the 1973 elections, spearheaded by the anti-tax Progressive Party, but including the Centre Democratic Party, the Christian People's Party, Single Tax Party, Left Socialists, and Communists.

With the leftward shift of the Social Democrats, the traditional bourgeois parties had drawn together and formed a coalition government in the late 1960s. However all the traditional parties formed implicit or explicit legislative voting coalitions during the 1970s. As the strength of the 'protest' parties declined (though they have never disappeared) rivalries between Social Democrats and the three old 'bourgeois' parties once again emerged, culminating in the 'four-leaf clover' government of 1982 which united Conservatives, Agrarian Liberals and two of the seventies protest parties (Centre Democrats and Christian People's Party) against the Social Democrats.

Four factors coincided to produce the explosion of new parties in Denmark and to prevent their emergence in Sweden:

1   The 5 per cent electoral threshold in Sweden.
2   The economic crisis in Western Europe in the 1970s caused a much more serious depression in Denmark, including an exceptionally high rate of unemployment. Sweden continued throughout the period to have one of the lowest unemployment rates in Europe.
3   The issue of European Community membership caused a deep conflict in Denmark which ran across established party lines. This may have triggered the fragmentation of the party system because it loosened traditional ties of party loyalty. The Swedish membership debate was rather low-key and the question was resolved once and for all in 1970 when the government declared that EC membership was incompatible with Swedish neutrality.
4   The fact that in Sweden the Labour Party had been in government continuously from 1932 to 1976. This meant that until 1976 there was an untried alternative to the government which could focus some discontentment at least among non-Socialist voters, while in Denmark with its many coalition governments all established parties were the target of protests.

9.2 PARTY DOCUMENTS AND THEIR PREPARATION

(i) Relevant elections

As with the other analyses our attention is focused here on the election programmes which give an authoritative indication of a party's policy position for the campaign. One peculiarity of the Swedish system has, however, affected the selection of these documents. Up to 1970 local elections also had a national importance and were fought by parties in the same way as parliamentary elections, because the County Councils and County Borough Councils formed the electorate for the indirectly elected First Chamber (abolished in 1970). As the government majority usually depended on seats in the First Chamber, all parties treated these elections in exactly the same way as national elections, publishing either an election manifesto or main election leaflet covering the whole range of party policy. A statistical comparison of local election documents with national, after both were coded, revealed no systematic differences between them in the way of space given to particular topics – even to local government! (Local party branches issued their own local literature on their records and candidates.) So both are amalgamated in the subsequent analysis. After 1970, parliamentary and local elections were held on the same day every three years, and party programmes cover both.

The ninety cases for Sweden therefore relate to the eighteen local and national elections held between 1946 and 1982. For Denmark cases derive from the sixteen national elections between 1945 and 1981 (a total of 136 programmes).

(ii) Types of party documents

Swedish and Danish parties issue four types of political documents. These are:

1. Party programme or programme of basic principles

This records the party's complete set of long-term policy goals and is prepared by one or more party committees and always adopted by the party congress. Since the late 1960s several parties in both countries have adopted elaborate consultation procedures where the local branches discuss and comment on the draft programme often, according to a detailed study plan, before the party congress meets. These documents remain valid over long periods. The Danish Social Democratic Party did not renew its programme from 1913 to 1960 and then again not until 1977, while the five Swedish parties have each produced three or four party programmes since 1945. Physically these programmes have expanded over the years from a few pages to pocket-sized books, often issued to all party members.

In Sweden the party programme is continuously updated and amended by the party congress, but in Denmark parties from time to time adopt working programmes (*arbejds program*), which translate the principles of party programmes into concrete policy measures. These working programmes are also a way of updating the programme of principle.

2. Policy programmes

Most parties issue policy programmes for a particular policy area, such as the arts, economy, family, health and welfare, education or housing. These single area programmes are more detailed than the main party programme, but like them set long-term targets and last a long time. In Denmark single issue programmes on the economy were produced by several parties during the 1970s. This type of programme is usually adopted by the party congress.

None of the different types of party programme is either composed or issued with specific elections in mind. Party programmes only effect elections to the extent that they influence the other documents described below.

3. Election manifestos

These are statements of general party policy for a particular election offering a selection of policies from the party programme determined by perceived electoral advantage. In contrast to the programmes which are written by and for party activists, the manifestos are written for a general audience. These documents are adopted through some form of internal democracy – usually either by a party congress or by the national executive committee.

In Sweden election manifestos were adopted by all parties in the 1940s and early 1950s and after 1968. Only the Centre Party and the Communists have issued manifestos for most elections since 1945.

Only after 1968 did manifestos become the main party vehicle for communicating with the electorate. Previously many manifestos were published in their entirety only in the party press and in some national and provincial newspapers. The Liberals, Socialists and Communists in particular seem not to have published their manifestos as separate leaflets for many of the early elections.

In Denmark the picture is more mixed. A party's election preparations are very much affected by how and when an election is called. In contrast to Sweden where all elections but one since 1945 have taken place on the fixed term dates predetermined by the Constitution, Danish elections – particularly since 1970 – have often been called unexpectedly and at short notice. This means that there is no fixed pattern for the type of policy statement issued by the different Danish parties for election campaigns. Sometimes a party will issue a manifesto or an election statement, sometimes it will issue the type of election literature discussed below and sometimes it will do both.

4. Election leaflets

These are issued by all parties in both countries for most elections. These are divided into:
— Specialized treatment of a party's policies in one area such as the

economy, welfare, the arts or sports; in Sweden also leaflets addressed to particular target groups, such as women, pensioners, young voters and white-collar workers – these being the four most popular target groups for special leaflets by most parties in most elections. This may be related to the fact that it is easy for Swedish parties to obtain excerpts from the population register which facilitates nationwide mailings to particular target groups.

— The main election leaflet or newspaper, several million copies of which may be printed and mailed to all households, or as many as the party can afford.

These election leaflets are prepared by or with advice from advertising specialists and usually approved by the party's central management committee or by the party executive.

These documents vary in size and style from party to party and over time. In Sweden the Labour Party issued a tabloid-sized 16–24 page newspaper for most elections between 1956 and 1968. This newspaper contained some pictures but was also densely packed with articles on each policy area and each branch of the social and education services, accompanied by interviews with ordinary citizens enjoying these services. The Conservatives on the other hand, produced glossy, short and punchy leaflets dealing with a limited number of policy points in a very popular fashion. In Denmark leaflets of all types have been produced by the parties including even duplicated or cyclostyled products from some of the smaller parties.

In Sweden the four main parties often distribute their main election leaflet through a central national mailing, while Danish parties usually rely on their branches for distribution, which of course means that distribution will vary according to the strength of the local party.

For both countries the documents used here are the party manifestos where one could be found, because this contains the party's basic set of electoral promises. For those years when a particular party issued no manifesto or none was found, the main election leaflet or newspaper was used. The actual documents selected for both countries are listed in Appendix A.

(iii) Selection of parties

Denmark presents a problem because the total number of parties which qualify for selection is very large; thirteen parties in all, though some have only existed since 1973, and two had declined before this time. We have nevertheless opted to include all thirteen in one analysis, since our use of factor analysis is deliberately one that abstracts over time. To check whether this distorted the analysis we did duplicate runs containing only the five major parties which have existed over the whole period. These, the Agrarian and Radical Liberals, the Conservatives, Communists and Social Democrats, represent the core fight between workers and bourgeois that has characterized post-war Danish parties. The results, and the party positions where they can be compared, are so similar that there appears to be no risk of distortion to counterbalance the information retained by using all parties in the analysis. Unlike the four country comparisons in Chapter 3, the information can also be presented more fully when two countries only are involved. Even the Independents and Liberal Centre are included because they have enjoyed blackmail or coalition potential at one time or another, though they have never reached 5 per cent of the vote.

(iv) Coding

The general coding scheme worked well for both countries with a few sub-categories added to catch special peculiarities (e.g. references to the Nordic countries were added as an extra sub-category to Foreign Relationships Positive; for details see Appendix B). Some hard problems of interpretation occurred particularly with statements made by the Social Democrats pointing out the need for a strong state, rich in public resources to provide services for the citizens, and praising the virtues of public as opposed to private consumption and the general benefits of a large public sector. These are not exactly the same thing as 'Strong Government' and have been variously coded as 'Government Efficiency', 'Social Justice' or 'Social Welfare' or 'Infrastructure' depending on the context.

The Swedish documents were coded exclusively by Holmstedt. Rather than coder reliability the main proccupation here was the danger of variations between the different types of document used – particularly national and local election manifestos. Extensive statistical comparisons were therefore made between these documents which revealed no systematic differences.

The Danish manifestos and their equivalents were collected by Schou and coded by two students, Jan Bo Andersen and Eva Roth, under her supervision. The standard coding scheme presented no particular difficulties in the Danish cases and was used without modification for the statistical analysis. Uncoded sentences totalled 24 per cent for Sweden and 33 per cent for Denmark – a high proportion which is however comparable to that for Italy (Chapter 16) and Germany (Chapter 14). The explanation for Denmark appears, as elsewhere, to lie in the special concerns of the new parties after 1973, and for Sweden in the peculiarly Scandinavian concerns noted above which did not always fit the broad categories. The presumptions of a saliency coding were however validated by the relatively limited references to other parties or their policies: on average 8.5 per cent for

TABLE 9.1

TEN CATEGORIES MOST OFTEN EMPHASIZED BY EACH SWEDISH PARTY OVER THE POSTWAR PERIOD

COMMUNISTS		$\bar{X}$
504	SOCIAL SERVICES	9.10
412	CONTROLLED ECONOMY	5.68
106	PEACE	5.57
403	REGULATION OF CAPITALISM	5.45
503	SOCIAL JUSTICE	4.31
202	DEMOCRACY	4.24
408	ECONOMIC GOALS	3.99
413	NATIONALIZATION	2.86
105	MILITARY NEGATIVE	2.65
102	FOREIGN SPECIAL	2.35

SOCIAL DEMOCRATS		$\bar{X}$
504	SOCIAL SERVICES	18.90
506	EDUCATION	6.39
408	ECONOMIC GOALS	5.80
503	SOCIAL JUSTICE	4.95
414	ECONOMIC ORTHODOXY	3.58
703	AGRICULTURE	3.51
403	REGULATION OF CAPITALISM	3.43
410	PRODUCTIVITY	2.42
501	ENVIRONMENT	2.27
606	NATIONAL EFFORT AND SOCIAL HARMONY	2.15

LIBERALS		$\bar{X}$
504	SOCIAL SERVICES	13.29
506	EDUCATION	5.71
201	FREEDOM	5.61
401	ENTERPRISE	5.19
414	ECONOMIC ORTHODOXY	4.90
107	INTERNATIONALISM	4.52
202	DEMOCRACY	3.89
402	INCENTIVES	3.75
706	SOCIAL GROUPS	3.16
408	ECONOMIC GOALS	2.80

CONSERVATIVES		$\bar{X}$
414	ECONOMIC ORTHODOXY	16.46
401	ENTERPRISE	10.86
201	FREEDOM	7.11
504	SOCIAL SERVICES	6.16
402	INCENTIVES	5.41
506	EDUCATION	4.66
202	DEMOCRACY	2.53
303	GOVERNMENT EFFICIENCY	2.38
603	TRADITIONAL MORALITY	2.11
408	ECONOMIC GOALS	2.02

CENTRE PARTY		$\bar{X}$
504	SOCIAL SERVICES	11.04
703	AGRICULTURE	10.86
402	INCENTIVES	6.57
5011	COUNTRYSIDE	5.78
506	EDUCATION	5.00
501	ENVIRONMENT	4.29
3011	LOCAL GOVERNMENT	4.11
414	ECONOMIC ORTHODOXY	3.96
401	ENTERPRISE	3.77
411	INFRASTRUCTURE	2.58
301	DECENTRALISATION	2.57

TABLE 9.2

TEN CATEGORIES MOST OFTEN EMPHASIZED BY EACH OF THE TRADITIONAL DANISH PARTIES OVER THE POSTWAR PERIOD

1301 SOCIAL DEMOCRATS (N=16)

	Code	Category	%
1.	503	SOCIAL JUSTICE	9.58
2.	408	SPECIAL ECONOMIC GOALS	6.75
3.	504	SOCIAL SERVICES (+)	6.11
4.	410	PRODUCTIVITY	5.81
5.	706	NON-ECONOMIC GROUPS	5.78
6.	506	EDUCATION EXPANSION (+)	2.85
7.	403	REGULATION OF CAPITALISM	1.90
8.	701	LABOUR GROUPS (+)	1.64
9.	202	DEMOCRACY	1.59
10.	412	CONTROLLED ECONOMY	1.56

1302 RADICAL LIBERALS (N=16)

	Code	Category	%
1.	410	PRODUCTIVITY	5.99
2.	503	SOCIAL JUSTICE	5.06
3.	108	MILITARY (-)	4.88
4.	606	NATIONAL EFFORT/HARMONY	4.69
5.	706	NON-ECONOMIC GROUPS	4.34
6.	408	SPECIAL ECONOMIC GOALS	3.23
7.	402	INCENTIVES	2.97
8.	107	INTERNATIONALISM (+)	2.41
9.	504	SOCIAL SERVICES (+)	2.31
10.	(403	REGULATION OF CAPITALISM	2.22)
	(506	EDUCATION EXPANSION	2.22)

1303 CONSERVATIVES (N=16)

	Code	Category	%
1.	414	ECONOMIC ORTHODOXY	12.77
2.	401	FREE ENTERPRISE	5.41
3.	410	PRODUCTIVITY	4.91
4.	402	INCENTIVES	3.82
5.	706	NON-ECONOMIC GROUPS	3.16
6.	201	FREEDOM HUMAN RIGHTS	2.96
7.	408	SPECIAL ECONOMIC GOALS	2.74
8.	503	SOCIAL JUSTICE	2.47
9.	104	MILITARY (+)	2.34
10.	303	GOVT. EFFICIENCY	2.09

1304 AGRARIAN LIBERALS (N=16)

	Code	Category	%
1.	414	ECONOMIC ORTHODOXY	8.79
2.	410	PRODUCTIVITY	4.77
3.	402	INCENTIVES	4.28
4.	401	FREE ENTERPRISE	3.86
5.	503	SOCIAL JUSTICE	3.44
6.	408	SPECIAL ECONOMIC GOALS	2.54
7.	506	EDUCATION EXPANSION (+)	2.25
8.	201	FREEDOM/HUMAN RIGHTS	1.83
9.	601	NATIONAL WAY OF LIFE (+)	1.61
10.	303	GOVT. EFFICIENCY	1.58

1305 COMMUNISTS (N=16)

	Code	Category	%
1.	701	LABOUR GROUPS (+)	6.70
2.	503	SOCIAL JUSTICE	5.16
3.	202	DEMOCRACY	4.95
4.	105	MILITARY (-)	4.80
5.	413	NATIONALIZATION	4.46
6.	706	NON-ECONOMIC GROUPS	4.42
7.	504	SOCIAL SERVICES (+)	4.11
8.	106	PEACE	2.93
9.	403	REGULATION OF CAPITALISM	2.88
10.	410	PRODUCTIVITY	2.84

Denmark and 12 per cent for Sweden. The last figure compares interestingly with the 43 per cent of such references identified by Isberg and his associates in their study of Swedish elections of the mid–1960s, which included all types of party documents and television transcripts of discussions between different party representatives (see Chapter 1). Where parties have direct control of the content of documents, they obviously restrict such references more.

9.3 COMPARISON OF PARTY EMPHASES

Unusually, we commence our content analysis of the documents with comparisons within each set of national parties, before commenting in the next section on the overall distribution of emphases in the two countries. This is because these inevitably lead into some assessment of national and party system differences, missing from the analysis of a single country. The peculiarity of having a relatively low number of categories available for the factor analysis (see Table 9.3) also directly affects the domain analyses. Hence we begin with individual parties.

Table 9.1 gives the ten leading categories for the Swedish parties and Table 9.2 reports the corresponding distribution for Danish parties included in our analysis. A major point, which also emerges from the overall analysis, is the extent to which economics and welfare dominate the agenda for almost all parties. The Swedish Social Democrats overwhelmingly emphasize the Social Services (which come top of the list also for Liberals and Communists). There is potential for conflict in the Swedish Conservative stress on Orthodoxy and Enterprise and the left wing's secondary emphasis on Regulation of Capitalism. The Centre Party is unique in its heavy stress on Agriculture (only emphasized by the Social Democrats among the other parties). In its mix of emphases it stands half way between the Left and Right.

These tendencies also appear for the 'traditional' Danish parties. The Social Democrats again place most emphasis on Welfare objectives, putting Regulation of Capitalism and support of Labour Groups well down the list. A Controlled Economy in fact comes last of their leading objectives. The Conservatives on the other hand have a fairly red-blooded commitment to Free Enterprise, as shown by their top four emphases. Social Justice comes well down and Welfare is not mentioned. The Agrarian Liberals resemble the Conservatives in support of the free market economy but put more stress on Welfare. The Radical Liberals on the other hand stress Productivity and Specific Economic Goals – outside the Left/Right conflict – and put more stress than their divided brethren on Welfare. The Communists combine appeals to Labour Groups, Social Justice and Democracy with opposition to the Military – a stress shared with the Radical Liberals who in this case are further to the Left (or New Left) than the usually governing Social Democrats.

The smaller new parties share some emphases of related larger parties intermixed with concerns of their own, of which the most novel is the Christian People's and Centre Democrats' stress on Traditional Morality. While Economic Orthodoxy otherwise scores high for the latter the former are almost as concerned about Welfare as the Social Democrats. Apart from Welfare the Socialist People's Party stresses opposition to the Military.

Left Socialists resemble the Social Democrats but, in contrast to the latter, stress nationalization and opposition to the military. The Independents and Justice Parties, like the Conservatives, stress Economic Orthodoxy and initiative, but share a greater concern with Social Justice – given an idiosyncratic twist by Independents' negative position on Social Services. This puts them closer to the Progressives. The opposition to government spending in this area is, of course, not surprising given the political developments of the 1970s outlined above.

The differing patterns of emphasis among Scandinavian parties and the extent to which they cross-cut conventional Left–Right dimensions offer an interesting basis for the overall country comparisons and factor analyses to which we now turn.

9.4 AN OVERALL FREQUENCY ANALYSIS OF CATEGORIES

An initial point to stress is the separate nature of the two country analyses reported here. Although discussed together they were performed separately. For example decisions about the exclusion of infrequently mentioned categories were made independently for Sweden and Denmark.

Table 9.3 gives the means and standard deviation for each of the coding categories across the combined set of parties covered for Sweden and Denmark. Our exclusion criteria are that a variable is omitted from the analysis if its over-time mean across all the parties in a country falls below 1 per cent or under 3 per cent for any one party. We have kept strictly to this rule given the complexity of analysing two very 'multi' multi-party systems. The consequence is that only 23 of the original variables qualify for inclusion in the Swedish case. As a result only two domains, economy and social welfare, require a first-stage factor analysis. This certainly speaks to the dominance of these two policy areas in modern Swedish politics, and perhaps, to a very high degree of consensus in some areas, notably foreign affairs and 'social fabric' which yield complex factor solutions elsewhere. An equally small number of variables qualify for Denmark, but this still requires four first order factor solutions, because the

TABLE 9.3

DENMARK AND SWEDEN

MEAN SCORES IN EACH CATEGORY FOR RELEVANT PARTY MANIFESTOS

VAR. NO.	CATEGORY	DENMARK MEAN	S.D.	SWEDEN MEAN	S.D.
101	FOREIGN SPECIAL RELATIONSHIPS (+)	1.25	2.02	.56	0.85
102	FOREIGN SPECIAL RELATIONSHIPS (-)	0.44	1.25	.17	0.70
103	DECOLONISATION	0.07	0.35	.36	1.66
104	MILITARY (+)	1.09	1.46	.68	1.30
105	MILITARY (-)	1.89	3.47	.75	1.96
106	PEACE	1.15	2.29	2.98	4.77
107	INTERNATIONALISM (+)	1.05	1.59	2.22	3.34
108	EUROPEAN COMMUNITY (+)	0.40	1.02	0.24	0.57
109	INTERNATIONALISM (-)	0.11	0.50	.03	0.15
110	EUROPEAN COMMUNITY (-)	0.85	2.25	.10	0.44
201	DOMESTIC FREEDOM AND HUMAN RIGHTS	2.44	3.18	3.24	4.00
202	DEMOCRACY	2.53	3.29	3.77	3.16
203	CONSTITUTIONALISM (+)	0.29	0.82	.12	0.38
204	CONSTITUTIONALISM (-)	0.18	1.50	.26	0.62
301	DECENTRALIZATION (+)	0.69	1.42	2.16	3.53
302	DECENTRALIZATION (-)	0.08	0.33	.09	0.27
303	GOVERNMENT EFFICIENCY	1.52	2.67	1.05	2.31
304	GOVERNMENT CORRUPTION	0.04	0.36	.04	0.27
305	GOVERNMENT EFFECTIVENESS AND AUTHORITY	0.30	1.21	0.00	0.00
401	FREE ENTERPRISE	2.80	4.50	4.08	6.76
402	INCENTIVES	1.92	3.39	3.42	3.84
403	REGULATION OF CAPITALISM	1.84	2.66	2.74	3.30
404	ECONOMIC PLANNING	0.45	1.59	0.61	1.22
405	CORPORATISM	0.63	1.43	0.19	0.58
406	PROTECTIONISM (+)	0.09	0.46	0.22	0.55
407	PROTECTIONISM (-)	1.20	1.26	.14	0.38
408	SPECIFIC ECONOMIC GOALS	2.86	5.37	3.24	3.15
409	NEO-KEYNESIAN DEMAND MANAGEMENT	0.16	0.49	0.60	1.33
410	PRODUCTIVITY	3.88	4.32	1.49	1.41
411	TECHNOLOGY AND INFRASTRUCTURE	0.67	1.46	1.21	1.81
412	CONTROLLED ECONOMY	1.27	2.24	1.41	2.86
413	NATIONALIZATION	1.15	2.90	0.67	2.12
414	ECONOMIC ORTHODOXY	4.98	6.49	5.77	8.33

Continued...

TABLE 9.3 continued

		MEAN	S.D.	MEAN	S.D.
501	ENVIRONMENTAL PROTECTION	0.62	1.35	3.65	5.03
502	ART, SPORT, LEISURE, MEDIA	0.43	0.97	1.08	2.21
503	SOCIAL JUSTICE	5.02	4.43	5.15	4.24
504	SOCIAL SERVICES (+)	2.73	3.24	12.16	8.89
505	SOCIAL SERVICES (-)	0.92	2.34	0.73	2.07
506	EDUCATION (+)	1.76	2.99	4.24	3.34
507	EDUCATION (-)	0.18	0.65	0.02	0.19
601	NATIONAL WAY OF LIFE (+)	0.68	1.93	0.27	1.00
602	NATIONAL WAY OF LIFE (-)	0.01	0.14	0.00	0.00
603	TRADITIONAL MORALITY (+)	1.96	5.26	1.87	2.63
604	TRADITIONAL MORALITY (-)	0.04	0.23	0.00	0.00
605	LAW AND ORDER	0.76	1.54	1.09	1.63
606	NATIONAL EFFORT/SOCIAL HARMONY	1.35	2.79	0.82	2.28
607	COMMUNALISM/PLURALISM (+)	0.04	0.32	0.94	1.28
608	COMMUNALISM/PLURALISM (-)	0.01	0.16	0.00	0.00
701	LABOUR GROUPS (+)	1.95	3.84	0.46	1.09
702	LABOUR GROUPS (-)	0.18	0.71	.18	0.88
703	FARMERS AND AGRICULTURE	0.87	1.48	3.74	7.19
704	OTHER ECONOMIC GROUPS	0.79	1.59	.17	1.11
705	UNDERPRIVILEGED MINORITIES	0.50	1.31	.26	0.64
706	NON-ECONOMIC DEMOGRAPHIC GROUPS	3.21	3.59	2.32	2.81

foreign affairs domain is clearly more complicated in a country which is a member of both NATO and the EEC; 'Social fabric' also seems an area on which less consensus exists.

Otherwise the profiles are similar – half of all the qualifying Danish categories are in economy and welfare, slightly more than half for Sweden. Of the top ten categories for each country, six are in common: Social Services, Social Justice, Free Enterprise, Democracy, and 'Freedom and Domestic Human Rights' (the sixth, Specific Economic Goals, is uninformative). These clearly indicate two hallmarks of the Scandinavian political systems – the simultaneous importance of consensus on the welfare state, and the importance of a Radical-Liberal centre in competitive party politics. This is hardly surprising and tends rather to confirm, a) what most people see as a Scandinavian mode of politics, and b) that Denmark, sometimes thought of as somewhat outside 'pure' Scandinavia, fits well into the model.

9.5 DOMAIN ANALYSES

Foreign policy is of low salience to the Swedes – somewhat predictably, only the variables covering references to 'Peace' and 'Internationalism' qualify for inclusion, and these are input directly to the second-stage as variables in their own right. In Denmark five foreign affairs variables –

TABLE 9.4

FIRST-STAGE FACTOR ANALYSIS OF ECONOMICS DOMAIN - SWEDEN

VARIABLE		FACTOR 1 'LEFT - RIGHT' LOADINGS	FACTOR 2 'ECONOMIC DEVELOPMENT' LOADINGS
401	FREE ENTERPRISE	-.576	-.219
402	INCENTIVES	-.245	.567
403	REGULATION OF CAPITALISM	.812	-.248
408	SPECIFIC ECONOMIC GOALS	.079	-.122
410	PRODUCTIVITY	.329	.339
411	TECHNOLOGY AND INFRASTRUCTURE	-.035	.461
412	CONTROLLED ECONOMY	.520	-.301
414	ECONOMIC ORTHODOXY	-.544	.007
FROM THE UNROTATED SOLUTIONS: EIGENVALUE		2.46	1.50
% OF VARIANCE		31%	18%

Foreign Special Relations (i.e. NATO), Military Expenditure both as an object of approval and disapprobation, and Peace and Internationalism, produce an easily interpreted two-dimensional solution. Two factors with very similar Eigenvalues together explain 63 per cent of the variance. The first is unipolar – Foreign Special Relations and Internationalism dominate (at .75 and .78 respectively), supported by Peace at .61. Clearly we have a form of 'peace through strength' dimension, with the added (Scandinavian) ingredient that an internationalist good citizenship element is combined with, rather than opposed to, this position. The second dimension brings out the way in which Denmark is far from being NATO's most wholehearted member – it is a very clear militarism *vs.* anti-militarism dimension, with positive orientations at .81 and 'Peace' (this time *not* through strength) at .55. There is, in other words, a pacifism dimension cross-cut with one on which the question is, more or less – if we must have military preoccupations, how much must they be oriented to external alliances and international duties?

Neither country requires an analysis for the next two domains, covering 'freedom and democracy' and 'government structure'. For the freedom domain, the same two variables, 'Domestic Freedom and Human Rights' and 'Democracy' both alone qualify for direct input to the second-stage factor analysis. In the other domain Denmark has very little interest. One variable only, 'Government Efficiency', qualifies. In Sweden this is the less important of two variables, the other being Decentralization.

Complexity and importance enter when we come to economic affairs, though the Swedish case is relatively simpler. The rotated factor structure for Sweden's economics domain is given in Table 9.4. There are three factors with Eigenvalues of 1.00 or more, but the third is single loaded by 'Specific Economic Goals' and is not considered further.

The first factor satisfactorily reproduces a Left/Right economic conflict, loaded mainly by Free Enterprise and Economic Orthodoxy at one end; and Regulation of Capitalism and Controlled Economy at the other. (As rotation makes relatively little difference it is fair to say that this is very much the dominant division in Swedish economic debate, being nearly as powerful as the other two dimensions together.)

The second factor seems to represent the sort of non-partisan economic effort or development dimension that is reported for many countries. It is unipolar in effect, characterized by 'Incentives', (which need not have a conservative or *laissez-faire* bias in all systems), Technology, and Productivity. Stress on the need for this sort of 'effort-growth' dimension is truly compatible with any position in the Left/Right dimension, as is, of course, required with orthogonal dimensions.

It is presumably the greater complexity of its party system, and the absence of the long-term Social Democrat hegemony that leads to the

TABLE 9.5

FIRST-STAGE ANALYSIS OF ECONOMICS DOMAIN – DENMARK

VARIABLES		FACTOR 1 'LIBERAL ECONOMICS' LOADINGS	FACTOR 2 'CONSERVATIVE ECONOMICS' LOADINGS	FACTOR 3 'SOCIALIST ECONOMICS' LOADINGS
401	FREE ENTERPRISE	.56	.42	-.21
402	INCENTIVES	-.11	.71	.10
403	REGULATION OF CAPITALISM	.69	-.21	.37
407	PROTECTIONISM - NEGATIVE	.83	.03	-.16
408	SPECIFIC ECONOMIC GOALS	-.01	-.11	.02
410	PRODUCTIVITY	.10	.10	-.08
412	CONTROLLED ECONOMY	-.18	.11	.80
413	NATIONALIZATION	.13	-.25	.72
414	ECONOMIC ORTHODOXY	.08	.80	-.11
EIGENVALUES FROM UNROTATED SOLUTION		1.82	1.52	1.13
% OF VARIANCE		20%	17%	13%

slightly curious results for the Danish case, reported in Table 9.5. It is not that the clusters of variables thrown up by the analyses are strange, novel, or uninterpretable. Indeed they are familiar and clear, representing what can easily be seen as distinctively Liberal, Conservative and Socialist positions. But instead of appearing as one bipolar dimension, or even a bipolar Conservative–Socialist factor cross-cut by a 'liberal economics' factor, they appear as three unipolar factors.

The first factor is referred to as 'Liberal Economics' because, while stressing free enterprise, it combines this with opposition to protectionism, a category virtually unused in the coding of most countries. In addition it seems that one of the two different political meanings for 'Regulation of Capitalism' – the more American sense of keeping the Capitalist machine running well by preventing, for example, monopolies or restrictive practices, emerges here, rather than the more socialist version that shows in Sweden. In this case Regulation of Capitalism loads along with the other to mark out the 'liberal' position.

The second factor is equally clearly a unipolar Conservative factor, loading on Incentives, Economic Orthodoxy, and (though to a lesser extent), once again on Free Enterprise. It may be thought odd that the two primary dimensions of economic party competition in Denmark should describe a space characterized by Liberal *vs.* Conservative approaches, but the data are clear. In any case the crucial importance of centre party politics in Denmark, and the absence for so long of a really powerful and legitimate Right may well explain this case. The third factor, coloured mainly by heavy loadings for Nationalization and Controlled Economy is equally clearly a Socialist position. It should be noted that Regulation of Capitalism in its more Swedish sense joins this group.

The result is an unusually good example of the way factor analysis can partition out separate substantive 'meanings' of a raw variable correlation. There are two other factors, but of little consequence – the three we have discussed account for just 50 per cent of the total variance. The only trouble with this analysis is that it presumes positions on each of the Liberal, Conservative, and Socialist dimensions can be taken up irrespective of where a party stands on the other two. We can at least be sure that the left–right simplicity of the Swedish case is not present in the competitive politics of Danish economic policy making.

We can turn immediately to the only other domain that requires a first-stage factor analysis in these two countries – Social Welfare.

In Denmark the four variables qualifying for entry are Social Justice, Social Services (pro- and anti-) and Education, forming a single factor with an Eigenvalue of 1.61, explaining 40 per cent of the variance. It is a straightforward unipolar emphasis factor, with loadings of .70, .81 and .45 and .51 respectively for the variables. High scores indicate a relatively high concern for the area. Low scores indicate both de-emphasis and – through the negative scores on service expansion – at least a muted opposition.

In Sweden five qualifying variables produce a more interesting two factor solution with Eigenvalues of 1.61 and 1.34 explaining a total of 59 per cent of the total variance. Of these, given a varimax rotation, the second is the rough equivalent to the Danish single factor. Like many other country solutions in this domain, it loads most heavily on Education which seems to function everywhere as a non-partisan 'goodie' – the loading is .81, supported by .42 for Social Service expansion and .35 for the catch-all 'Art, Sport, Leisure, Media' category. Thus we have a basic unipolar 'emphasis–de-emphasis in welfare and State service provision'.

The first factor picks up, in part, the sort of 'new issues welfarism' of other chapters, being mainly loaded by 'Environmental Protection' at .88. This is supported, however, by a loading of .42 for 'Social Justice'. This has an unusual track record in this book, not occurring as significant in many countries, and not necessarily appearing in predictable correlations when it does qualify. In both Scandinavian countries it is important, being part of the general welfare domain for Denmark. In Sweden its combination with environmentalism on a factor where Social Services and Education are more or less zero loaded comes closer to its nature elsewhere.

Sweden's social homogeneity means we require no first-stage analysis for the social fabric domain. Only two variables qualify. Traditional Morality indicates some continuing religious basis for Swedish political identification, and it combines with Law and Order. These two variables go directly as input to the second-stage analysis.

Denmark also has this Traditional Morality dimension to its politics, but these reflect some social discord because of the qualification of both 'National Way of Life' and 'National Effort/Social Harmony'. The latter tends to be a different way of expressing concern with social discipline, often not easily distinguished from the more straightforward 'Law and Order' variable, and in this sense may be the Danish equivalent to Sweden's slightly surprising stress on the issue.

In any case a first-stage analysis *is* required for Denmark, which produces two factors. Their total variance explained is high at 72 per cent. The first factor is loaded more or less equally by National Effort/Social Harmony at .78 and National Way of Life at .70. The factor appears to be a straightforward 'Danish Solidarity' dimension, and contrasts interestingly with the second. This is essentially a unipolar dimension loaded by Traditional Morality at .89, though there is a supporting loading on National Way of Life at .42. The traditional morality question in Denmark, covering traditional Scandinavian concerns such as temperance, and new ones such as pornography, is undoubtedly more important than in Sweden. But it is clear from our analysis that it is a separate orthogonal part of the secular 'social discipline through solidarity', given here by the first dimension and in Sweden by two single variables. The separation is understandable given the uniparty emphasis on the question by the Christian People's Party.

In neither country is the interconnection of pluralist group demands such as to produce complexity in the Social Groups domain. In both countries the new liberalism common to Scandinavian politics puts 'non-economic demographic groups', for example women, into the qualifying list. Not surprisingly, given the long-term hegemony of social democracy, 'Labour Groups' is the only other entry to qualify in Denmark. It may be more surprising that it is not Labour, but 'Farmers and Agriculture' that qualifies for Sweden. The reason is presumably that no one has even doubted the vital role of agriculture in Denmark, nor of Labour in Sweden. Typically the absolute inevitabilities of policy do not need mentioning by anyone. The original variables from this domain, in both countries, enter the second-stage analysis directly.

9.6 THE SECOND-STAGE FACTOR ANALYSIS

In the Swedish case we have twelve input variables for the second-stage factor analysis, the point of which is to further reduce the original mass of information to a simple, preferably two-dimensional, model of political competition. These are eight of the original coding category variables, and four first-stage factors, two from each of the economic and welfare domains.

In total it takes four factors with significant Eigenvalues to reproduce the correlations amongst these twelve variables satisfactorily, but only the first two are particularly important. These two have Eigenvalues of over 2.0, and account between them for 36 per cent of the variance – the next two have Eigenvalues below 1.5 and only account together for 20 per cent. The details of the factor solution are given, in a slightly unusual way, in Table 9.6. It is often useful to refer to correlations between higher order factor and the original variables that make up the first-stage factors used to derive them. The higher order factors are, after all, based ultimately on correlations between original variables, and meant purely as summaries of the original data. In this case we have used so few first order factors that we carry out the interpretation entirely in terms of the correlations between original variables and the second-stage factors. Table 9.6 therefore reports those correlations above .30 between the original variables qualifying for analysis and the second-stage factors.

Seventeen variables have correlations at this level with one or other of the first two factors. Most correlate strongly with only one of the two, showing that we have useful summary measures of an internal clustering of

TABLE 9.6

CORRELATIONS BETWEEN ORIGINAL VARIABLES AND SECOND-STAGE FACTORS – SWEDEN

ORIGINAL VARIABLE		FACTOR 1 CENTRE VS. LEFT CORRELATIONS	FACTOR 2 RIGHT VS. LEFT CORRELATIONS
106	PEACE	-.42	
	DEMOCRACY	-.32	
202	DECENTRALIZATION	.37	
402	INCENTIVES	.46	
403	REGULATION OF CAPITALISM	-.40	.65
411	TECHNOLOGY AND INFRASTRUCTURE	.41	
412	CONTROLLED ECONOMY	-.51	.46
504	SOCIAL SERVICES	.38	
506	EDUCATION	.76	
604	TRADITIONAL MORALITY	.50	-.38
703	AGRICULTURE AND FARMERS	.52	
201	DEMOCRATIC FREEDOM AND HUMAN RIGHTS		-.850
401	FREE ENTERPRISE		-.55
410	PRODUCTIVITY		.46
414	ECONOMIC ORTHODOXY		-.41
503	SOCIAL JUSTICE		.37

our original categories. The first factor (they are both bipolar) contrasts a Centre/Liberal orientation in Swedish politics with a highly radical one. The radical end is loaded, negatively, by Peace and Democracy, but also by two anti-capitalist measures, Regulation of Capitalism and Controlled Economy. The other end concentrates on what we can somewhat abruptly describe as 'bourgeois liberal values', at least in the Scandinavian context. Thus Education is the highest single loading, (and Social Services correlated significantly), along with a non-ideological set of economic variables like Technology and 'Incentives'. What gives it in a Swedish context a distinctively Liberal/Centrist aura is the inclusion of 'Decentralization'; a specifically non-conservative opposition to state socialism, the inclusion of an appeal to 'Traditional Morality' especially important given the continuing, if minor role of religion in centrist Scandinavian politics, and the overt appeal to the farming and agricultural lobby. This whole factor represents then, a centre-left dimension, as opposed to a left–right conflict, because the right would end up with ambiguous middle positions on such a dimension.

As the second dimension, judged by its correlations, is a fairly straight-forward conservative–socialist conflict, such a two dimensional model fits well with the politics of a country with a long-term but now weaker Social Democrat hegemony; and an opposition to this which is so far from an Anglo-American Conservatism, that the 'centre' is effectively in opposition to both wings.

The 'right-wingedness' of one pole, the negative one, of the second dimension is certainly clear – high correlations with 'Freedom and Domestic Human Rights' and Free Enterprise, combined with Economic Orthodoxy gives the image of the classic liberalism that no longer holds a 'centrist', but rather a 'right wing' position in European politics. These are backed up, by 'Traditional Morality', one of the few variables to correlate with both factors. The other pole is marked by the presence of the two 'left-wing' economic variables of the other dimension, along with a stress on Productivity, and the presence of 'Social Justice'.

In Sweden this clearly has a radical connotation. The two dimensions then give us a 'centre *vs.* left' and 'right *vs.* left' model. This is entirely suitable for the Swedish context, and it should be remembered that the ordering between first and second carries little substantive import, especially as they are rotated factors.

We need now to compare those results with the Danish case, to see the extent to which we have a single 'Scandinavian' model or two very similar political cultures. Though not dissimilar it is less easy to interpret. The two-factor model is slightly disappointing in explaining only 32 per cent of the variance (with the full five factors 62 per cent of variance is covered).

The leading factor is a fairly orthodox left–right contrast. In terms of

TABLE 9.7

CORRELATIONS BETWEEN ORIGINAL VARIABLES AND SECOND STAGE FACTORS - DENMARK

VARIABLES		FACTOR 1 "OLD LEFT-RIGHT" CORRELATIONS	FACTOR 2 "NEW LEFT-RIGHT" CORRELATIONS
101	FOREIGN SPECIAL RELATIONSHIPS		.34
104	MILITARY (POSITIVE)	-.39	
105	MILITARY (NEGATIVE)	.38	.41
106	PEACE		.50
107	INTERNATIONALISM		.48
202	DEMOCRACY	.57	
303	GOVERNMENT EFFICIENCY	-.39	
401	ENTERPRISE	-.40	-.34
402	INCENTIVES	-.49	
406	PROTECTIONISM (POSITIVE)		.52
413	NATIONALISM	.42	
414	ECONOMIC ORTHODOXY	-.62	-.39
503	SOCIAL JUSTICE		.45
504	SOCIAL SERVICES	.30	.59
506	EDUCATION		.46
701	LABOUR GROUPS	.68	
706	NON-ECONOMIC DEMOGRAPHIC GROUPS		.47
	ORIGINAL EIGENVALUES	2.42	1.39
	% VARIANCE EXPLAINED	20%	12%

loadings with the inputs from the first-stage, it is weighted mainly by opposition to Conservative economics, and support for Labour groups. To this predominantly economic policy character one needs to add two factors typical of a Scandinavian sense of left and right – a concern for increased democracy, and a pacifistic, pro-disarmament approach to peace.

A very similar interpretation arises if one looks instead at the pattern of correlations between the first of the second-stage factors and the original variables. Here support for Labour Groups, Democracy, Nationalization and decreasing Military expenditure correlate positively at various levels between .38 and .68, whilst stress on Economic Orthodoxy, the need for Incentive in the economy, Free Enterprise, and *increased* Military expenditure have negative correlations between −.39 and −.62. It should be remembered that attitudes to military expenditure do not solely reflect international politics perspectives – they are also vital aspects of macroeconomic policy, being the only form of public expenditure commonly supported by those in favour of the retrenchment implied by Economic Orthodoxy, and the favourite targets for expenditure cuts amongst parties committed to protecting Labour groups (especially those in the public sector) or other left-wing economic policies.

If the first dimension is left–right in a fairly simple way, it nonetheless leaves out one common ingredient of such a schism, that covering welfare policies. Denmark has, of course, as large and almost as consensual a welfare state as anywhere in Scandinavia. Yet, especially since the rise of the new parties, and the appearance of the bourgeois party governments, there *has* been discussion on this. The second dimension is overwhelmingly concerned with this opposition, which largely cross-cuts the economic/ foreign policy divisions of the first dimension.

By a long way the main second factor loading in the second-stage analysis is with the welfare dimension, at .54. Only one other of the first-stage constructed inputs begins to be significant, which is the other foreign policy factor – 'peace through internationalism', but at only .39 its importance is obscure. The six main correlations with original variables support this. Ranging between .44 and .59, they include Social Service Expansion, Protectionism, Educational Expansion, Social Justice, Non-Economic Demographic Groups, and Peace. This latter echoes the 'peace through internationalism' of the factor inputs, but does not obscure the primary nature of the factor. There is a psychological connection between this sort of 'welfare-rights' dimension and a general sense of obligation to good international citizenship to promote peace. Notably, just as welfare legislation is not theoretically connected to the left/right economic split, this form of 'peace' attitude is different from the ideologically more demanding stress on arms reduction as a peace strategy. One is tempted to say that both are left–right factors, but the second is an emotional 'soft'-left position, the former a harder-edged class-conflict radicalism.

Alternatively one might claim that in contrast to Sweden, there are two different oppositions to the same left-orientation, Centre *vs.* Left and Right *vs.* Left, Denmark has a standard Left *vs.* Right opposition and a form of non-partisan, or at least non-ideological, opposition to the right.

9.7 SPATIAL ANALYSIS OF PARTY POSITIONS

It only remains to discuss the spatial positioning of typical parties. These show the mean position of each party for the whole post-war period. The plotting of Danish parties (Figure 9.1) certainly confirms the way in which the dimensions highlight alternative versions of a right *vs.* left conflict. The Conservatives, and the Agrarian Liberal Party, occupy a similar position in the quadrant that is right-wing in both senses; mildly to the right on the 'old left' dimension and on the 'new left' dimension. The Radical Liberals are more left on this than the Communist Party, probably because of the admittance of Internationalism. The Social Democrats lie to the far left on that second dimension but far nearer the right on the 'old left' factor than do the Communists. This seems a convincing portrayal of the relationships of the major Danish parties.

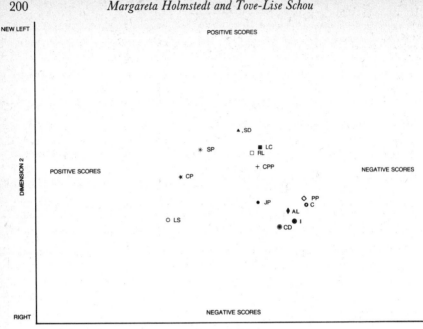

9.1 Mean position for each Danish party on first two second-stage factors

Most interesting is the positioning of the 'protest' parties, united only in a 'plague on both your houses' orientation to the 'old five' parties.

The Centre Democrats, an off-shoot from the Social Democrats, have moved rightwards on both dimensions. Whilst the Left Socialists are to the left of the Communists only on the orthodox, or 'old issues' left–right dimension, the Socialist People's Party is to the left of them only on the 'welfare and internationalism' or 'new left' spectrum. In general a convincing positioning emerges for all the protest parties, old or new, but it is in a space clearly dominated and defined by the 'old five'.

Turning to the same representation for Sweden we see that party cleavages in the higher order factors are again visually confirmed beyond doubt. The first dimension, which we identified as representing a centre *vs.* left cleavage does indeed maximally separate the Centre Party and the Communists.

The Liberals, the Conservatives, and the Social Democrats all have maintained average positions noted for ambiguous moderation on this dimension. In contrast, the second dimension opposes, at roughly equal positions, Communist, Social Democrat and Centre Party average positions with the Conservatives and, (a little less right–wing but still clearly in their camp) the Liberals. Both diagrams illustrate, (a) the different

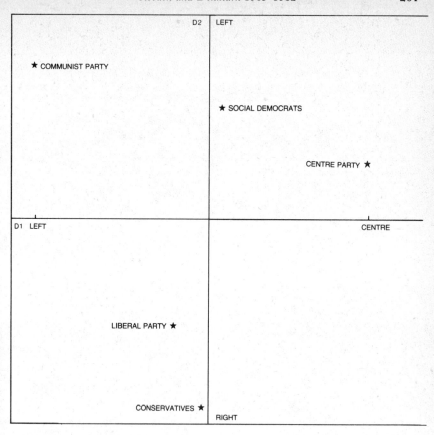

9.2 Swedish parties in two-dimensional space

meanings of 'left-wing' in Scandinavian politics, (b) the close connection between Conservative and 'Liberal' politics, given one of the meanings of 'Liberal', and (c) the distinct radicalism of centre parties, whether it is the *soi-disant* 'Centre' of Sweden or the 'Radical Liberals' of Denmark.

Though our interpretations have differed in detail, owing to the actual selection of parties, and the particular scorings of variables, both maps are essentially the same. Denmark and Sweden do indeed share a political culture, and one that is well manifested in this comparative data analysis. That the coding scheme, analytic technique and interpretative mechanisms should work on these two countries, as well as on Continental-European and Anglo-American data, testifies strongly to their overall comparative utility. With the confidence that this gives us in the validity of the representation, we can go on to the analysis of detailed party movements over the post-war period, to compare with those in the other countries.

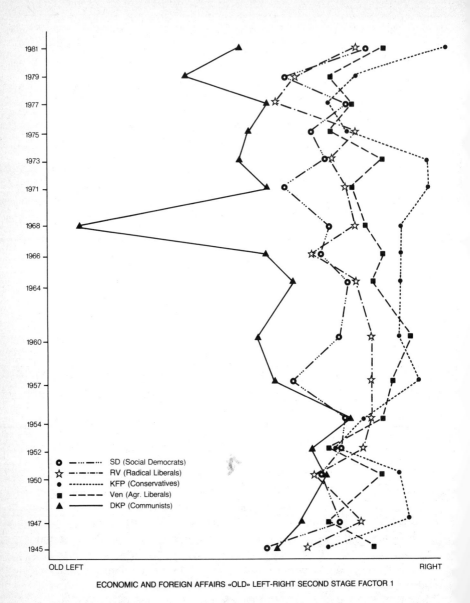

ECONOMIC AND FOREIGN AFFAIRS «OLD» LEFT-RIGHT SECOND STAGE FACTOR 1

9.3 Movement of five traditional Danish parties over time on the first dimension:
old left vs. right

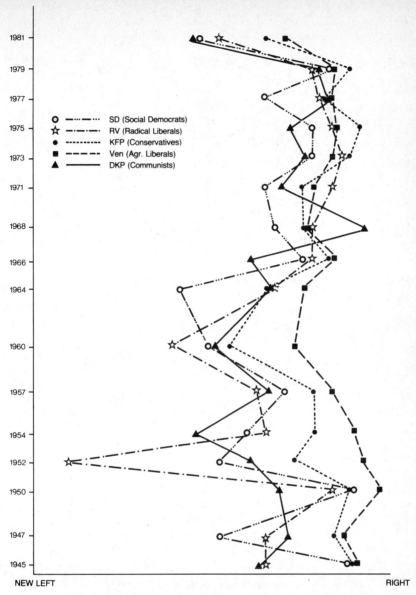

NEW LEFT   RIGHT

WELFARE AND INTERNATIONALISM NEW LEFT VS. RIGHT SECOND STAGE FACTOR 2

9.4 Movement of five traditional Danish parties over time on the second dimension: new left vs. right

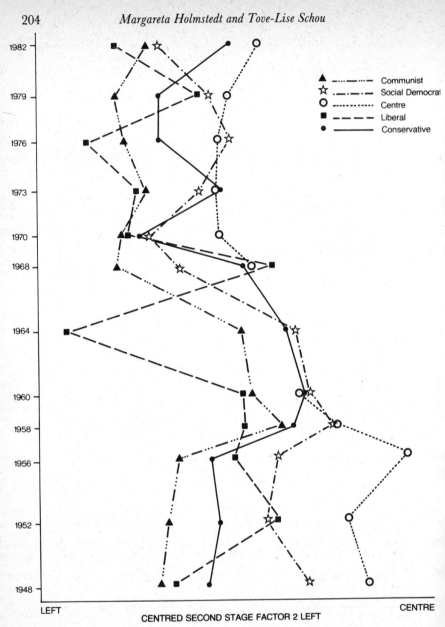

▲	·····----···	Communist
☆	·—·—·—·	Social Democrat
◯	·············	Centre
■	— — —	Liberal
●	—————	Conservative

LEFT

CENTRE

CENTRED SECOND STAGE FACTOR 2 LEFT

9.5 Movement of Swedish parties over time on the first dimension: centre vs. right

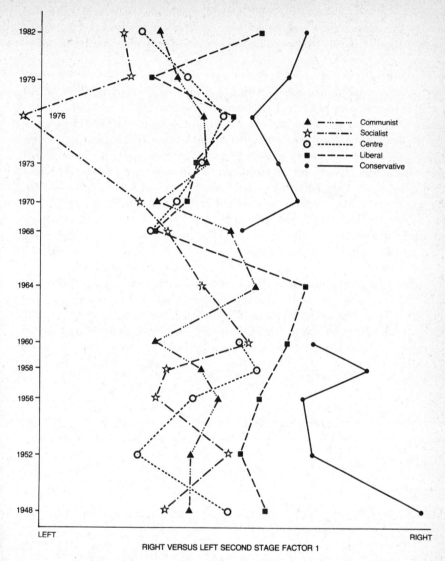

9.6 Movement of Swedish parties over time on the second dimension: left vs. right

Figure 9.3 shows movements of the traditional Danish parties on the first (Old Left *vs*. Right) dimension. While relationships between them have varied (Social Democrats and Conservatives particularly distancing themselves in 1971), the traditional governing parties seem about as close at the beginning of the 1980s as they were at the end of the war. The Communists are further away but on the second dimension of New Left *vs*. Right all parties are as close at the end as at the beginning. Parties have moved further apart in the early 1960s – possibly foreshadowing the change of coalition tactics by the Social Democrats. But they came closer even before the cataclysmic election of 1973.

Figure 9.5 shows corresponding movements of Swedish parties over time on their first dimension – which contrasts characteristically Centrist positions with those of the Left. With the exception of Liberal moves to the most left-wing positions in 1964, 1976 and 1982, this does contrast centre parties (particularly *the* Centre Party) with Social Democrats and Communists. The Conservatives occupied very median positions in the period leading up to their joint declaration of intent to govern with Liberals and Agrarians in 1968. Generally parties are closer, and somewhat more Left, at the end of the post-war period than at the beginning.

The Left–Right contrast places Social Democrats and Conservatives, not unnaturally, in contrast; with Communists in a rather surprising juxtaposition with Centrist parties in the middle of the dimension. The Social Democrats were most to the left in 1976, when they lost the election. Distances between parties in 1982 were comparable to those of 1948.

Again these plausible patterns support the validity of this type of analysis and provide valuable information on various aspects of party politics – particularly on prospects for coalition formation and policy agreements in Government, an area which we hope to investigate in our future research.

Notes

1 Research for the Danish part of this Chapter was supported by the Danish Social Science Research Council and the University of Copenhagen. Both contributions are gratefully acknowledged.

CHAPTER 10

THE NETHERLANDS 1946–1981

————— ∿ —————

10.1 INTRODUCTION[1]

The literature on Dutch party manifestos is sparse (Lipschits 1977, 1981; De Bruyn 1971). In this chapter we make a first attempt to compare them systematically, as distinct from analysing them impressionistically (De Bruyn 1971) or using them in an *ad hoc* manner – for example, to provide a basis for ordering the political parties of the Netherlands on a left–right dimension (Lipschits 1969; De Swaan 1973). Only one author has used methods similar to ours, contrasting the 1948 and 1963 election manifestos of the KVP, PvdA, VVD and ARP to see whether the parties have become more alike (Hoogerwerf 1963, 1964, 1965).

There are a number of reasons for this apparent lack of interest. In the first place it is difficult to make a distinction between election manifestos and other manifestos or platforms. Hoogerwerf argued; 'In the Netherlands a distinction is made between a party's election programme (listing among other things its objectives for a four-year parliamentary period), its constitution (containing the main principles of the party), its general political programme (its objectives for a period longer than four years), its provincial programme and its municipal programme' (Hoogerwerf 1964, p. 163). This may be so, but it is far from easy to distinguish clearly. All political parties have constitutions, and these are mentioned as such, but the line between election programmes and general political programmes has not always been clear. Moreover, some of the programmes are cited as 'urgency programmes'. In each case therefore one has to decide which programme has to be regarded as the election manifesto, and some of these decisions are inevitably rather arbitrary. A list of selected programmes is given in Appendix A.

The second reason is the large number of 'relevant' parties. Faced with the need to economize on time and effort we have opted for a simple criterion: parties were included only if they had taken part in at least one cabinet since 1945. These parties are:

ARP: Anti-Revolutionary Party (Protestant)
CHU: Christian-Historical Union (Protestant)
KVP: Catholic People's Party
PvdA: Labour Party
VVD: Liberal Party
D'66:   Democrats '66 (since 1966)
DS'70: Democratic Socialists '70 (since 1970)
PPR: Radical Party (since 1968)
CDA: Christian Democratic Appeal (since 1977: at first a federation, since 1980 a merger of KVP, ARP and CHU)[2].

The third reason is the ambiguous place of manifestos in Dutch politics. Political observers have not considered them to play a crucial role. Since the sixties, however, they *have* become more significant, since parties use them increasingly as a guide for their representatives. They also have a more prominent place in coalition formation, having become touch-stones for their success. Van Putten, (1971), may well be right in arguing that a systematic comparison of party manifestos could help 'rationalize' coalition-formation because the parties will have a better idea of what the others stand for.

10.2 THE BACKDROP: PECULIARITIES OF DUTCH POLITICS

The Netherlands has always been a country of political minorities. Up until the latter half of the nineteenth century politics was dominated by a latitudinarian bourgeois aristocracy. They founded a political tradition that gave rise to several liberal parties of which the present-day VVD is the heir presumptive. Against this dominant minority three disadvantaged minorities organized themselves at the end of the nineteenth century: orthodox Protestants, Catholics and Socialists. Each of these minorities created their own political parties, which for a long time featured prominently in contemporary Dutch politics: the Catholic KVP, the Socialist PvdA, and the Calvinist ARP. The latter split after a group of more conservative Protestants, most of them belonging to the Dutch Reformed Church, seceded to form the CHU.

The three emancipatory movements did not constitute a united front against the Liberals. Catholics and Protestants formed an uneasy alliance against the secular parties with strong anti-papal feelings lingering in the Protestant camp. On some issues Liberals and Socialists managed to cooperate, but mostly kept their distance. In order to 'protect' the members of these minorities from outside influences, i.e. each other, their leaders created not only the political parties, but a whole range of organizations covering almost every sphere of life. Thus the minorities became more or less separate subcultures, with their own cradle-to-grave infrastructure. This is what is meant by the Dutch word *verzuiling* (pillarization). The degree of pillarization was very high within the Catholic and Protestant subcultures, less well developed within the Socialist minority, and almost completely absent within the Liberal groups.

Pillarization never led to a complete isolation of the different groups within the population. Not only was it virtually impossible to prevent members meeting, but the leaders cooperated in administering the country. The resulting government by elite cartel managed to accommodate the various pillars by adhering to a number of 'rules of the game' of which the most important ones were the acceptance of the *autonomy* of the minorities, the *depoliticization* of most salient issues, *proportionality* in the electoral system , in appointments, subsidies, etc., and *secrecy* of decision-making. At the governmental level this resulted in coalitions of which the religious, centrist parties were almost permanent members.

The so-called 'politics of accommodation' was characteristic of Dutch politics for a long period and until the sixties was never seriously challenged from within the pillars themselves. In fact, members were quite apathetic, providing easy constituencies for their political leaders. Thus elections looked like censuses in which relative strength was once again established to provide a yardstick for the all-important rule of proportionality.

Although pillarization and elite cooperation survived a deliberate attempt at a 'breakthrough' after World War II, it ran into unexpected trouble in the late sixties. As in the rest of the Western world theological, sociological and moral changes had a huge impact. As a consequence the pillars began to crumble. Secularization, and the rapidly declining loyalty of religious voters to their respective parties ate away the strength of the KVP, ARP and CHU. In the 1981 elections these parties in combination polled a smaller percentage of the vote than the KVP gathered on its own in 1956. To stem the tide the three amalgamated in 1977, forming the CDA, and merged completely in October 1980. The Socialists were also affected by depillarization, but managed to recover by setting themselves up as champions of democratization and by rejuvenating the party. The Liberals, who never really embraced pillarization, remained relatively unscathed.

The result of all this was an increase in electoral volatility. This not only provided leeway for new political parties, such as D'66, PPR and DS'70, but also transformed elections into genuine struggles for the people's vote. Parties had to emphasize their distinctiveness in order to attract the growing proportion of floating voters – a process which led to increasing politicization and polarization. This process was accentuated by the influence of the new left movements in the late sixties and early seventies.

The new democratic mood created a need for parties to make clear to the voters what their plans and positions were, and under which conditions they would be willing to enter a government and with whom. Thus neo-democratic criticism of the elitist 'politics of accommodation' politicized even more an increasingly politicized situation.

The 'politics of accommodation' had not yet disappeared however, some parties, notably CDA and VVD, seemed to adhere – at least most of the time – to the old rules of the game. Other parties, especially the PvdA, preferred for a time a different set of rules, such as politicization, polarization, and majority rule. Thus both the PvdA and the VVD declared they would never enter a coalition government with the other – forcing the religious parties to choose between them. They moved from governments with the PvdA up to 1958 to governments with the VVD. Over the last 25 years the Socialists have been in government only three times. Moreover it has become increasingly difficult to form governments, with negotiations lasting up to 208 days!

The confusing political situation in the seventies has been aptly likened to a match between a soccer team and a rugby team. Both sides play ball, but they do so according to widely differing sets of rules. In the early eighties, however, contrasts between the parties have lessened: the traumatic experiences of government formation in 1972 and 1977 led Socialists to the recognition that they will need the other large parties in order to enter government again.

10.3 THE DRAFTING OF THE MANIFESTOS[3]

In the seventies and eighties, the initial drafting of the manifestos in almost all the parties was done by a programme committee, set up by the party executive. In the VVD, however, the party leader (i.e. the leader of the parliamentary party in the Second Chamber) drew up the first draft of the programme (until 1977). The PvdA has separate programme committees for various policy sectors; in 1977, for instance, six programme committees were involved in drafting the manifesto. Formerly, the ARP and CHU party leaders also played an important role in the drafting of manifestos, but this situation changed in the sixties.

The text prepared by the programme committee or party leader is first discussed by the party executive and then sent to the local party branches under the auspices of the party executive, except in D'66. This is organized on a strictly individualistic basis, which means that local branches do not play any role in amending the programme: every member receives his own copy of the draft and is allowed to propose amendments to the executive. These amendments are discussed during a special session of the Party Congress: local representatives may participate in discussions when they represent at least half of their local branch or can show 25 signatures of members of their branch.

In all other parties the local branches may propose as many amendments as they wish (for instance, more than 1,000 amendments were proposed to the relatively short programme of the PvdA in 1971). In the PPR this formal amending of the manifesto is proceeded by a consultation in which local branches give their opinions of the programme without any formal consequence.

The amendments of the local branches are sent to the next echelon in the party. This is a general procedure, except in the PPR and, of course, D'66. In the PPR the amendments are sent directly to the party executive.

In the three Christian parties (and now also in the CDA) and VVD these higher echelons (regionally organized and called *kringen* or *centrales*) accept or reject the amendments proposed by the local branches. The adopted amendments are sent to the party executive.

The local branches in CDA and VVD have the possibility of appeal against a decision of the *kringen* or *centrales* to the party executive. In some parties other groups may also propose amendments, such as the Young Catholics in the case of the KVP. 'Women in the VVD' had this opportunity in 1980. Individual members in D'66 and PPR may propose amendments during a session of the Party Congress, provided that they are supported by a certain number of other members.

The party executive (or the programme committee) gives its opinion on the amendments and sends them to the Party Congress. In D'66 the party executive does not play any role in the drafting of the programme. In the PPR and PvdA the amendments are categorized in three groups: 1. textual improvements (no discussion, only votes); 2. non-fundamental changes (short discussion and vote); 3. controversial amendments (extensive discussion and vote). In most parties the Party Congress determines the definite programme. Exceptions were KVP, ARP and CHU, where the Party Council, a smaller body which was the highest authority in the party when the Party Congress was not in session, had the same function as the congress in other parties. Finally, a small 'editing' committee polishes the manifesto into a readable text.

10.4 ELECTION MANIFESTOS IN DUTCH POLITICS

All local branches receive a copy of their party's manifesto. In some parties all party members are on the mailing list and many parties print the manifesto in part or *in toto* in the party magazine. Manifestos are further made available free, or at a low price. However, one has the impression that the role manifestos play in Dutch electioneering is a minor one. Under pillarization the parties had such faithful followers that campaigning was hardly necessary: most people voted for a particular party for other reasons than its programme.

The increasing importance of the election campaign due to depillarization and democratization may lead to a more prominent role for the manifestos, as well as to a greater need for parties to underline their own identity. This in turn may have stimulated the parties to write more into their election programme. The 1948 manifestos averaged 75 (quasi-) sentences, and the 1981 platforms 1,650. Because lengthy manifestos put voters off, the political parties print thousands of leaflets with popularized excerpts from the manifestos, sometimes confined to one topic intended for special target groups. In this respect the similarities to the Scandinavian countries are striking.

One crucial role manifestos play is that of the link between the party organization and its members on the one hand, and its representatives in Parliament on the other. Practically all parties require their parliamentary candidates to endorse the manifesto, and most require them to sign a written statement to formalize this endorsement. In the CDA and in one of its constituent parties, the ARP, and the PPR, candidates can withhold their endorsement for paragraphs in the manifesto. If these conscientious objections, or *gravamina* as they are called, are accepted by the party the candidate is allowed to deviate from the manifesto in Parliament on these particular points. In other parties, such as PvdA, a similar procedure exists, but is not formalized. In other parties (VVD, CHU, D'66), representatives are relatively unbound, although it is assumed that they will loyally execute the party programme. Only one party, the PPR, retains the right of 'recall' when MPs deviate from the manifesto without having made a prior *gravamen*.

The manifesto is clearly of great importance therefore in fixing the party's political position and anchoring party representatives to it. However, Dutch governments are always coalitions of various parties. This limits the role manifestos play, as the negotiated agreements which precede the formation of a coalition mean that no manifesto can be implemented in its entirety. As an indicator of the party's policy position at a time of general stock-taking the manifesto is unrivalled however, and it is this aspect we emphasize in the following analysis.

10.5 CENTRAL CONCERNS IN DUTCH MANIFESTOS

Of the domains distinguished in preceding chapters, Welfare and Economy are most frequently mentioned in Dutch manifestos. The

Welfare domain reaches the highest overall average, 24.1 per cent. This emphasis is repeated in the rank-order of the top ten variables from the basic coding, which is dominated by two variables from the domain, i.e. 'Social Services pro-Expansion' and 'Social Justice'. Furthermore 'Education pro-Expansion' ranks among the top variables in six elections, while 'Environmental Protection' has undoubtedly been one of the most important issues in the seventies. From 1971 onwards it ranked in the top ten categories and was the second most important issue, next to Social Services, in 1972 and 1977. The emphasis on Welfare is not surprising given that the Dutch welfare state is one of the most developed in the world.

The Economy domain was the most frequently mentioned from 1946 to 1971 (in the 20–30 per cent range), making it second most important for the whole post-war period. Relatively high proportions of the programmes have been taken up by economic categories, such as 'Enterprise', 'Incentives', 'Technology and Infrastructure' and 'Economic Orthodoxy'. In the fifties and early sixties – the period of seemingly everlasting economic growth – 'Enterprise' was seen as a keystone of the Dutch economy. In 1952, 1956 and 1959 this category received almost as much attention in the manifestos as 'Traditional Morality' and 'Social Services/Social Justice'. This and the emphasis on the other above mentioned categories illustrates the conservative economic views held by Dutch political parties in the period after the Second World War. Not surprisingly, a considerable shift in attention has taken place in the late seventies and 1981: the fight against inflation, high prices and unemployment led to relatively great emphasis on the category of 'Specific Economic Goals'.

The importance of pillarization is illustrated by the emphasis put on the Fabric of Society, at least in the forties and fifties. As a result of pillarization much attention was given to 'Traditional Morality' and 'Pluralism', especially among Calvinists and Catholics. In the immediate post-war period 'Traditional Morality' received more attention than any of the other categories. In 1946, 1948 and 1956 it was mentioned most often and in 1952 it belonged to the highest categories. But from 1959, 'Traditional Morality' received less and less attention. Depillarization and changing ideas on morality had the same impact on the categories 'Pluralism' and 'Corporatism', which makes this domain nowadays one of the least important ones.

In the immediate post-war period and in the sixties and seventies, categories from the domain of Freedom and Democracy were considerably emphasized. In the forties they were naturally linked to war experiences and pillarization. Freedom meant 'no more war' and democracy had to be read as 'no more dictatorship'. But freedom meant also freedom for one's own subcultural group to organize itself. In the sixties, however, other aspects became prominent. Freedom of speech, and more generally, freedom of expression were topics on which fierce discussions were held. In this period also the rather closed political system came under pressure. The increasing emphasis on democracy means greater possibilities of participation in politics, business and other aspects of social life.

Political parties have also given constant attention to Social Groups (10 per cent), although the subjects changed. In the forties and fifties farmers and other economic groups (especially retailers and shopkeepers) were emphasized. Then certain 'non-economic groups' came to the fore. In the Dutch case this emphasis is closely linked with the social welfare domain. It has been ranked in the 'top ten' since 1952 and takes third position overall. At first pensioners and disabled persons were the main groups, while later youth and women were most frequently mentioned.

Over the years External Relations has become slightly more important. None of its categories were mentioned very often in the forties and fifties (except for 'Foreign Special Relationships' during the fight over the independence of Indonesia, and to a lesser extent 'Decolonization' in the same period), but since the sixties 'Internationalism' (often in the form of aid to underdeveloped countries), 'Europe' and 'Peace' received increasingly more attention. The category of 'Internationalism' has ranked among the most important since 1963 and takes fifth position in the ranking over all post-war elections.

Finally, there is the least important domain, Government. Apparently this is and always has been a topic of minor concern to the Dutch political parties. Thus only 'Government Efficiency' received considerable attention in the elections of 1971 and 1972. Two of the new parties, D'66 and DS'70, were mainly responsible for this.

10.6 CODING

In all manifestos a number of sentences could not be coded, because they did not fit into one of the categories. The percentage of uncoded sentences varied from 5.5 per cent in 1952 to 15.7 per cent in 1959. Dutch manifestos usually tell the voters why theirs is the best party to choose, what good things it did in the past and what excellent things it will do in the future. Other parties are seldom mentioned, either in a positive or in a negative way. Important exceptions to this 'rule' are the manifestos of 1956 and 1959, when polarization between the VVD and PvdA increased drastically and the Liberals used a large part of their manifestos to tell the voters why they refused to join a cabinet with the Socialists.

Categories with less than 1 per cent of sentences overall and less than 3 per cent within any set of party manifestos have been eliminated from subsequent analyses according to our standard procedures. In general, parties make very few negative mentions of any issues, all 'negative' categories scoring less than 1 per cent. Apparently it is not done to

TABLE 10.1

TEN CATEGORIES MOST OFTEN EMPHASISED BY EACH DUTCH PARTY
(AVERAGE PERCENTAGES OVER ALL MANIFESTOS)

	ARP(8)ˣ	CHU(7)	KVP(8)	PvdA(10)	VVD(11)	D'66(4)	PPR(2)
1.	TRAD. MORALITY 7.8	TRAD. MORALITY 9.6	SOCIAL SERVICES 10.0	SOCIAL SERVICES 9.3	ENTERPRISE 10.8	SOCIAL SERVICES 9.4	SOCIAL JUSTICE 11.1
2.	SOCIAL SERVICES 6.6	SOCIAL SERVICES 5.8	TRAD. MORALITY 6.8	SOCIAL JUSTICE 7.6	SOCIAL JUSTICE 5.9	DEMOCRACY 9.2	INTERNATIONALISM 10.6
3.	PLURALISM 6.4	NON-ECON. GROUPS 4.8	ENTERPRISE 5.3	DEMOCRACY 6.1	ECON. ORTHODOXY 5.7	ENVIRONM.PROTECT. 7.8	SOCIAL SERVICES 9.8
4.	INCENTIVES 5.2	SOCIAL JUSTICE 4.5	SOCIAL JUSTICE 5.1	EDUCATION 5.2	SOCIAL SERVICES 4.3	SOCIAL JUSTICE 6.4	ENVIRONM.PROTECT 9.2
5.	ENTERPRISE 5.0	FARMERS 4.3	PLURALISM 4.3	NON ECON.GROUPS 4.5	NON ECON.GROUPS 3.9	INTERNATIONALISM 5.0	NON ECON.GROUPS 8.1
6.	TECHNOLOGY 4.6	FREEDOM 4.3	NON ECON.GROUPS 3.8	INTERNATIONALISM 4.2	EDUCATION 3.8	FREEDOM 4.9	DEMOCRACY 6.0
7.	SOCIAL JUSTICE 4.5	INCENTIVES 3.9	DEMOCRACY 3.7	TECHNOLOGY 4.1	FREEDOM 3.7	TECHNOLOGY 4.7	PEACE 4.6
8.	FARMERS 4.5	TECHNOLOGY 3.8	INTERNATIONALISM 3.5	RECREATION ETC. 3.9	RECREATION ETC. 3.6	NON-ECON.GROUPS 4.6	FREEDOM 3.8
9.	CORPORATISM 4.2	INTERNATIONALISM 3.2	EDUCATION 3.5	FREEDOM 3.8	INCENTIVES 3.5	EDUCATION 4.3	MILITARY NEG. 3.5
10.	NON-ECON.GROUPS 3.7	LAW AND ORDER 3.1	INCENTIVES 3.5	GEN.ECON.GOALS 3.3	INTERNATIONALISM 3.0	GOVT.EFFICIENCY 3.4	UNDERPRIV.MIN.GR. 3.0

ˣ BETWEEN BRACKETS : N

Continued...

215

TABLE 10.1 continued

	DS'70(3)	CDA(4)	PROGR. THREE(2)
1.	SOCIAL SERVICES 9.5	SOCIAL SERVICES 9.9	SOCIAL SERVICES 15.1
2.	GOVT. EFFICIENCY 8.8	INTERNATIONALISM 5.6	DEMOCRACY 8.4
3.	ENVIRONM. PROTECT. 7.3	ENVIRONM. PROTECT. 5.4	ENVIRONM. PROTECT. 7.9
4.	EDUCATION 7.1	DEMOCRACY 5.2	SOCIAL JUSTICE 7.2
5.	SOCIAL JUSTICE 4.9	SOCIAL JUSTICE 5.0	EDUCATION 5.7
6.	NON ECON. GROUPS 4.8	EDUCATION 4.5	INTERNATIONALISM 5.7
7.	RECREATION ETC 4.8	NON-ECON. GROUPS 4.4	TECHNOLOGY 5.2
8.	INTERNATIONALISM 4.7	RECREATION ETC. 3.8	GOVT. CONTROL 3.5
9.	TECHNOLOGY 4.3	TRAD. MORALITY 3.6	GOVT. EFFICIENCY 3.3
10.	ECON. ORTHODOXY 4.3	TECHNOLOGY 3.3	RECREATION ETC. 3.0

mention issues to which one is opposed – paralleling the other countries studied.

10.7 DIFFERENCES BETWEEN THE PARTIES

Table 10.1 contains the 1946–81 average for the top ten categories for each party. This table reveals differences of outlook among the parties in the post-war period, through the extent to which they deviate from the average manifesto and from each other. One should bear in mind, however, that some parties are much younger than others: consequently manifesto references may not only be a result of differences between parties, but also of differences in period. (We have however already stated the case for representing parties of different periods together in Chapters 2 and 9.)

Most parties agree on the importance of social welfare. Within all parties the categories 'Social Services', 'Social Justice', 'Non-economic Groups' and 'Education' have an important position: in six out of ten parties (or groups of parties) 'Social Services' ranks first, in ARP and CHU second, in PPR third and in the VVD manifestos fourth. 'Social Justice' receives slightly less attention, especially in the manifestos of the Christian parties

Among the 'old parties, the KVP and PvdA are most outspoken in their emphasis on social welfare issues; of course, the Socialists have close links with the working class and disadvantaged groups in society, and the KVP, which may be seen as a Catholic catch-all party, has to pay attention to all strata in society in order to keep the Catholic pillar together.

More divergences however can be found in the categories of 'Traditional Morality' and 'Pluralism'. 'Traditional Morality' used to be a major issue in all three religious parties, ARP, CHU, and KVP, and still is a relatively important issue in the manifestos of their successor, the CDA. This emphasis on Traditional Morality (especially on the importance of the family), Sunday rest (in earlier years) and anti-abortion is exactly the opposite of what occurs in the secular parties.

In the category of 'Pluralism' we find the same contrast except for the CHU. Unlike the ARP, which was the first party representing a pillar, the CHU was founded as a reaction against pillarization by more latitudinarian elements in the ARP. It was, therefore, originally opposed to pillarization and in the manifestos relatively little emphasis is put on 'Pluralism'. The amount of attention paid to 'Freedom' in CHU manifestos is further evidence of the distinction between this party and its religious partners. The idea of a corporatist structuring of society is closely linked with the concept of pluralism. In contrast the left secular parties emphasize Democracy and Freedom. This might be explained as their conviction that people should be free in moral issues and that politics should not interfere in problems of morality. The secular emphasis on 'Democracy' and

'Freedom' is also reflected in their attention to 'culture' (Art, Leisure, Recreation, and Media): PvdA and VVD mention 'culture' almost twice as frequently as the Christian parties.

The other central question is the economic one: to what extent should the government intervene in the economy? On the one side of this cleavage, the VVD strongly emphasizes 'Enterprise', 'Economic Orthodoxy' and 'Incentives'; whereas on the other side the left parties pay them little attention. More than the other parties, (though this does not appear in the table) the PvdA and the PPR stress the importance of 'Nationalism', 'Controlled Economy' and 'Economic Planning'.

As one would expect, the confessional parties take a position between Liberals and Socialists. In the structure of pillarization these parties include both employers and employees, both advocates of a passive economic role of government and of an active role, as well as farmers and the self-employed. It is therefore understandable that they avoid taking positions on any controversial economic issue.

The manifestos of the younger parties and party-groups reflect the importance of the new issues in the seventies. All put considerable emphasis on 'Environmental Protection' the social-welfare categories and 'Internationalism'. The new 'realistic' mood on government expenditure becomes visible in the attention paid to 'Government Efficiency'. Of course, DS'70 was known for its stress on retrenchment, but the manifestos of D'66 and 'the progressive three' put some emphasis on this point. 'Technology' and 'Education' are often mentioned by D'66, DS'70, CDA and the three progressive parties, whereas PPR manifestos pay much attention to 'Internationalism', 'Peace' and to the negative aspects of the military, reflecting the anti-militaristic mood in left-wing circles.

10.8 FACTOR ANALYSIS BY DOMAIN

The standard principal components analysis has been carried out within four domains: External Relations, Welfare, Social Fabric and Economy. The other domains did not qualify for this analysis since only one or two categories received enough attention for inclusion. From the Government domain only 'Decentralization' and 'Government Efficiency' received more than 1 per cent of mentions. The categories 'Freedom' and 'Democracy' qualified within the domain Freedom and Democracy, while 'Farmers' and 'Non-economic Groups' were the only Social Groups to qualify.

(i) External Relations

Two components were produced which had Eigenvalues greater than 1.0. They account for respectively 38.0 per cent and 21.7 per cent of the variance. The first factor loads heavily and positively on negative attitudes to the military (.71), 'Peace' (.80) and Internationalism Positive' (.87). It could well be described as 'Striving for a Peaceful World', since disarmament, peace and the need for international cooperation are the essential elements of this factor.

The second factor loads significantly and positively on positive attitudes to the military (.79) and the European Community (.79), and mildly negatively on negative attitudes to the military (−.39). It might be a hawkish position which puts much emphasis on a strong defence, but the positive valuation of the EEC is not a necessary addition to this position. Therefore it looks more like a positive attitude towards international obligations like NATO and the EEC.

(ii) Welfare

This domain also breaks up into two components with Eigenvalues greater than unity. The first accounts for 36.4 per cent of the variance and the second one for 21.8 per cent. It is surprising that two components emerge since at first sight all categories of this domain seem strongly linked to each other. The category 'Social Justice' causes the trouble. The first factor loads significantly and positively on 'Environmental Protection' (.75) 'Recreation, etc.' (.50) expansion of Social Services (.70) and of Education (.51), and this makes perfect sense.

Social Justice loads heavily on a second factor (at .93), on which 'Education' forms a negative pole (−.51). This makes this factor extremely difficult to interpret. It seems likely as in other cases like Northern Ireland that 'Social Justice' reflects attitudes other than those related to social welfare.

(iii) Social Fabric

Only three variables from the domain qualified for inclusion in this first-stage factor analysis. Quite understandably one factor loads strongly and positively on all of them. It is quite easy to explain why positive attitudes to 'Traditional Morality' (.85), to Law and Order (.57) and to Communalism (.86) are closely linked. All three categories are part of a conservative outlook on Dutch society – the neatly ordered life of earlier decades should be maintained. Consequently this factor has been labelled 'traditionalism'. It accounts for almost 60 per cent of the variance.

(iv) Economy

Eight out of fourteen categories of this domain qualified for the factor analysis. It is the only domain to produce three factors with Eigenvalues

TABLE 10.2

NETHERLANDS: FACTOR ANALYSIS BY DOMAIN: ECONOMY

VARIMAX ROTATED FACTOR MATRIX	FACTOR 1 CAPITALISM VS. CONTROLLED ECONOMY	FACTOR 2 NEW VS. OLD ECONOMIC ISSUES	FACTOR 3 REGULATION VS. ENTERPRISE
CATEGORIES			
401 FREE ENTERPRISE	0.71	0.27	-0.36
402 INCENTIVES	0.48	0.56	0.08
403 REGULATION OF CAPITALISM	-0.18	0.14	0.63
405 CORPORATISM	-0.13	0.73	-0.48
408 SPECIFIC ECONOMIC GOALS	-0.05	-0.73	-0.22
411 TECHNOLOGY AND INFRASTRUCTURE	-0.09	-0.05	0.81
412 CONTROLLED ECONOMY	-0.73	-0.03	0.09
414 ECONOMIC ORTHODOXY	0.86	-0.08	-0.07
FROM UNROTATED SOLUTION:			
EIGENVALUE	2.47	1.33	1.22
% OF VARIANCE	30.9	16.7	15.3

EXCLUDED CATEGORIES:

404 ECONOMIC PLANNING
406 PROTECTIONISM POSITIVE
407 PROTECTIONISM NEGATIVE
409 KEYNESIAN DEMAND MANAGEMENT
410 PRODUCTIVITY
413 NATIONALIZATION

TABLE 10.3

SECOND STAGE FACTOR ANALYSIS OF DUTCH PARTY MANIFESTOS
(RELATIONSHIPS WITH FIRST STAGE FACTORS AND ORIGINAL VARIABLES)

VARIMAX ROTATED FACTOR MATRIX	FACTOR 1 OLD LEFT-RIGHT	FACTOR 2 MODERNIZATION TRADITIONALISM	FACTOR 3 NEW LEFT-RIGHT
DOMAIN: EXTERNAL RELATIONS			
FACTOR 1.1 PEACEFUL WORLD	0.48	-0.46	0.54
FACTOR 1.2 PRO-TREATIES	0.03	0.02	-0.20
101 FOREIGN SPECIAL RELATIONSHIPS POS.	-0.41	0.27	0.12
104 MILITARY POSITIVE	-0.06	0.09	-0.39
105 MILITARY NEGATIVE	0.38	-0.39	0.50
106 PEACE	0.35	-0.52	0.53
107 INTERNATIONALISM POSITIVE	0.52	-0.44	0.43
108 EUROPEAN COMMUNITY POSITIVE	0.02	0.02	0.01
DOMAIN: FREEDOM AND DEMOCRACY			
201 FREEDOM AND HUMAN RIGHTS	0.08	0.05	0.06
202 DEMOCRACY	0.68	-0.09	0.09
DOMAIN: GOVERNMENT			
301 DECENTRALIZATION	-0.13	0.52	0.02
303 GOVERNMENT EFFICIENCY	0.20	-0.07	-0.49
DOMAIN: ECONOMY			
FACTOR 4.1 CAPITALISM VS. CONTROLLED ECONOMY	-0.46	-0.18	-0.30
FACTOR 4.2 NEW VS. OLD ECONOMIC ISSUES	-0.30	0.72	0.32
401 FREE ENTERPRISE	-0.52	0.14	-0.14
402 INCENTIVES	-0.60	0.26	0.09
403 REGULATION OF CAPITALISM	0.27	0.15	0.03
405 CORPORATISM	-0.42	0.76	0.17
408 SPECIFIC ECONOMIC GOALS	-0.06	-0.55	-0.37
411 TECHNOLOGY AND INFRASTRUCTURE	0.29	-0.06	-0.19
412 CONTROLLED ECONOMY	0.38	0.08	0.33
414 ECONOMIC ORTHODOXY	-0.37	-0.21	-0.29
DOMAIN: WELFARE			
FACTOR 5.1 SOCIAL WELFARE	0.85	-0.21	-0.19
FACTOR 5.2 SOCIAL JUSTICE	0.15	-0.00	0.74
501 ENVIRONMENTAL PROTECTIONISM	0.77	-0.18	-0.08
502 ART, SPORT, LEISURE, MEDIA	0.40	-0.19	-0.20
503 SOCIAL JUSTICE	0.20	-0.08	0.77
504 SOCIAL SERVICES EXPANSION POSITIVE	0.62	-0.05	-0.09
506 EDUCATION EXPANSION POSITIVE	0.51	-0.23	-0.55

Continued...

TABLE 10.3 continued

SECOND STAGE FACTOR ANALYSIS OF DUTCH PARTY MANIFESTOS
(CORRELATIONS WITH FIRST STAGE FACTORS AND ORIGINAL VARIABLES)

VARIMAX ROTATED FACTOR MATRIX	FACTOR 1 OLD LEFT-RIGHT	FACTOR 2 MOBILIZATION TRADITIONALISM	FACTOR 3 NEW LEFT-RIGHT
DOMAIN: SOCIAL FABRIC OF SOCIETY			
FACTOR 6.1 TRADITIONALISM	-0.59	0.52	0.01
603 TRADITIONAL MORALITY POSITIVE	-0.60	0.39	0.07
605 LAW AND ORDER	-0.20	0.38	-0.24
607 COMMUNALISM POSITIVE	-0.58	0.61	0.12
DOMAIN: SOCIAL GROUPS			
703 FARMERS AND AGRICULTURE	-0.61	0.19	-0.01
706 NON ECONOMIC GROUPS	-0.01	-0.53	0.09

greater than 1.0. They account respectively for 30.9 per cent, 16.7 per cent and 15.3 per cent of the variance.

The first factor is straightforward. It is the classic opposition between 'Economic Orthodoxy', 'Free Enterprise' and 'Incentives' on the one hand, and 'Controlled Economy' and to a lesser degree 'Regulation of Capitalism' on the other hand. This, of course, is a perfect left–right factor.

Interpretation of the second factor is more difficult, the categories 'Corporatism', 'Incentives' and to a lesser degree 'Enterprise' are opposed to the category of 'Specific Economic Goals'. It makes sense, however, if it is interpreted as a factor related to time. In the first years after the war attention was focused on 'Corporatism', 'Enterprise' and 'Incentives'. Gradually these issues lost relevance. The factor therefore makes sense as one of alternative foci of Dutch economic concerns over the post-war period.

The third factor could in interpreted in a similar way. On the one hand it loads heavily and positively on relatively new issues like 'Technology and Infrastructure' and 'Regulation of Capitalism' and negatively on such 'older' issues as 'Corporatism' and 'Enterprise'. However, it might be said that this factor again is a muted left–right one, opposing Regulation of Capitalism to Enterprise rather than outright control. This ambiguity is not too important, given that we do not use the factor in our second-stage analysis.

10.9 THE SECOND-STAGE FACTOR ANALYSIS

Table 10.3 shows the Varimax rotated solution of the second-stage factor analysis. It also contains the Pearson Correlation coefficients between the rotated factors and original categories. This has been done to make the interpretation of the solution easier.

The analysis produced three factors with Eigenvalues greater than unity, accounting for respectively 28.1 per cent, 17.0 per cent and 11.4 per cent of the variance. The first factor correlates positively conventional 'left-wing' emphases in the field of external relations (Military Negative, Peace, International cooperation), with Democracy, with 'left' economic topics (Controlled Economy, Regulation of Capitalism) and all welfare issues. It correlates negatively with classic liberal views on the economy, i.e. Free Enterprise, Incentives and Economic Orthodoxy. Furthermore, there is a strong negative correlation with three categories related to the religious dimension in Dutch politics, i.e. with Traditional Morality, Communalism, and Corporatism. The factor also correlates negatively with the category 'Farmers and Agriculture', which is a group traditionally supported by the Christian parties. In short, the factor can be regarded as the Left/Right-dimension in Dutch politics, where the right-wing pole groups classic liberal economic views along with religious views on morality and the organization of society.

Factor 2 shows a certain resemblance to the first factor. Again a strong correlation, although positive, is found with the Christian conservative categories, Traditional Morality, Communalism and Corporatism. Furthermore Decentralization is positively correlated with this factor; this is understandable as it reflects the 'pillarization' attitude – 'let things be organized by the groups in society'. Strong negative correlations exist with 'left' internationalist issues and the categories of Specific Economic Goals and Non-economic Groups. This might point to contrasts being due to differences in time: the religious, conservative issues received considerable attention in the immediate post-war period, whereas the 'left' internationalist issues, the fight against inflation, unemployment and high prices, and the emphasis on the rights of women and youth are clearly new issues in Dutch politics.

Factor 3 carries problems of interpretation. The factor loads positively on the left internationalist issues and, very heavily, on Social Justice. Besides, a positive correlation is found with the category 'Controlled Economy'. This would seem to be a left pole or, again, a left–right dimension. It is, however, quite difficult to identify the other pole; the factor shows negative correlations with Education Expansion, Specific Economic Goals, Government Efficiency and Military. In itself this does make sense as a right pole, although it is striking that right-wing economic positions do not show significantly strong correlations with this factor. It therefore might be interpreted as a left–right distinction, although *not* in the classic sense, but between the new parties – PPR, D'66, and the 'progressive three' on the one hand, and DS'70 on the other hand.

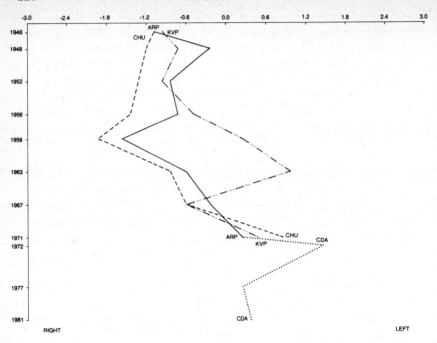

10.1a Party positions on first factor by election year (Christian parties)

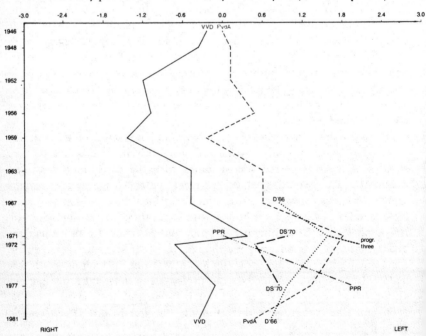

10.1b Party positions on first factor by election year (secular parties)

10.10 PARTY POSITIONS

Figures 10.1a, 10.1b, 10.2a and 10.2b show how parties have moved over the years on the two more important second-stage factors discerned in the previous section.

On the 'old Left–Right' dimension, parties appear to take the positions one would expect. Amongst the religious parties, ARP and CHU consistently take a (moderate) right-wing position, whereas KVP shows a strongly fluctuating picture (Figure 10.1a). At first, KVP joins ARP and CHU in a moderate right-wing position, which in 1959 and 1963 is reversed into a moderate left-wing stand. In these years, KVP even stands to the left of the Socialists. This might be caused by the fact that the coalition between KVP and PvdA broke up in 1958. The KVP then joined a coalition with ARP, CHU and VVD. To counteract these parties' right-wing stands, KVP had to move to the left. After the experience of renewed cooperation with the Socialists in the Cals/Vondeling cabinet in 1966, the KVP moved to the right again.

The successor to the three Christian parties, CDA, took a rather leftist position in 1972. This could be the reason for cooperation with the progressive parties in the 1973 Den Uyl government. In 1977 and 1981 the CDA again moved to the centre.

Overall, the Socialists have taken (moderate) left positions, their most right-wing stance being in 1959. The reason for this might be to promote another Christian-Labour coalition. From 1971 onwards it is clear that the party moved to the left, mainly under pressure from the New Left within the party. The traumatic cabinet formation of 1977 might well be the reason for the party's return to the centre.

As could be expected, the Liberals (VVD) have been on the right, with the sole exception of 1971 when all parties took a rather leftist stand. The party moved to the right again in 1972 and kept this position in 1977 and 1981.

The new progressive parties, D'66 and PPR, take a (moderate) left-wing position, whereas DS'70, a group of mostly old-fashioned Socialists who left the Labour Party in abhorrence of the methods and politics of the New Left, was more centrist.

In summary, parties generally behave as expected, although exceptional positions probably demand specific explanations. At first, parties seemed to be moderate on left–right issues. The emphasis on democratization at the end of the sixties caused all parties to move left. In 1972 polarization enlarged the distance between the left parties and the Liberals, but this diminished again in later years. In general one could say that the Christian parties take a centre position on this dimension which helps to explain why they always have been a necessary partner in government.

Figures 10.2a and 10.2b, show a more confusing picture although it can

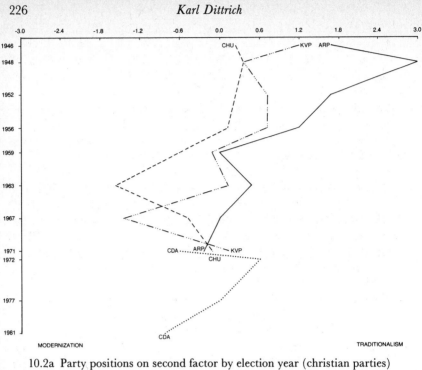

10.2a Party positions on second factor by election year (christian parties)

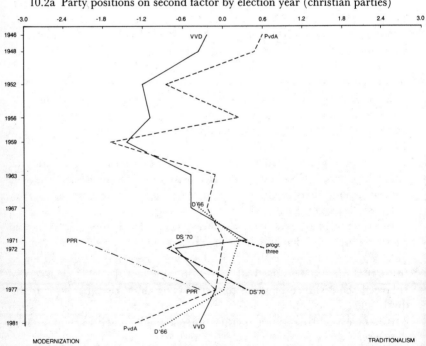

10.2b Party positions on second factor by election year (secular parties)

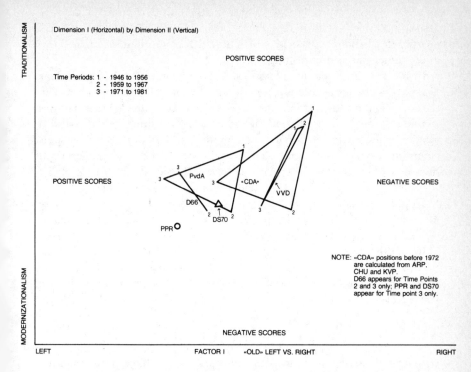

10.3 Spatial location of Dutch parties on the two leading dimensions

be interpreted quite sensibly. The Anti-Revolutionary Party has always been the most traditional party in Dutch politics. It is therefore not surprising that the party takes a rather extreme position up to 1956. After that the party seems relatively neutral on this dimension. The CHU always opposed pillarization and had a more tolerant view of what people were allowed to do. Consequently, among the Christian parties, this party takes the opposite stand from the ARP. The Catholics find themselves in most elections in a middle position. The (combined) CDA no longer deviates from the other major parties.

The Liberal party has always put a considerable emphasis on classic liberties. This makes this party's position on Factor 2 understandable. In the immediate post-war period the VVD was most outspoken in its 'anti-pillarization and anti-traditional values' attitude and put a premium on personal freedom. In later years these attitudes were more widely shared so do not appear as deviant.

The position of the Labour Party is ambiguous. Traditionally the party is a strong advocate of civil liberties, but at the same time the party was one of the pillars of Dutch society and, therefore, had to be in favour of some measures related to pillarization (especially the distribution of money among pillarized institutions). From 1963 onwards, the PvdA avoids an outspoken position in this field, which probably means that the importance of the dimension is diminishing.

In general, this is true for all parties. Although figures 10.2 makes it clear that parties change positions rather drastically, overall differences between parties have declined from the sixties. Consequently, Dutch politics nowadays could almost be characterized as a one-dimensional political system. This conclusion is reinforced by the fact that all three dimensions emerging from the analysis seem to relate to some kind of left–right division, whether this is a clash between classic liberal and socialist economic positions, or between 'modern' and traditional issues.

Figure 10.3 sums up the preceding discussion by presenting party movements on the first two factors simultaneously. It illustrates two major points. First there are tendencies to convergence between all the parties. However the effect of combining dimensions is also to demonstrate that the parties remain distinctive within their own clearly defined territories – as of course they would have to do if they did not wish to repudiate their own past record.

10.11 CONCLUSIONS

In part, this analysis confirms preconceptions that have been generally held about Dutch politics, in that some kind of left–right dimension has been assumed to exist along with a cross-cutting religious dimension. Our data show however that this has become less and less important. Even before the years of overt depillarization and deconfessionalization, the religious dimension had 'shrunk'. For this there might be two explanations. First, religious or traditionalist issues over the years lost importance in party electioneering. Parties did not compete with each other on these issues and to the voters it was crystal clear which parties stood for which positions. In the second place one might hypothesize that the importance of religion actually *did* diminish and that all parties – the religious ones along with the others – entered into competition with each other along the dominant left–right economic dimension. If this last hypothesis is true, it would mean that contemporary Dutch politics have to be seen as uni-dimensional.

A striking result is that Dutch parties show little difference on either of the two main dimensions. On the left–right, as well as on the traditionalist dimension, parties resemble each other very much, with few exceptions. This is partly explained by the inclusion only of (potential) government parties, but still it is astonishing that all parties show a tendency to move to the centre. Neither polarization nor the intensified struggle for votes seem to have driven them out to the wings. The need to build coalition governments pushes parties who actually want to enter government to adopt a rather moderate attitude in their manifestos.

Although the Dutch political system is so moderate, parties do sometimes change positions fairly sharply. Naturally internal developments might cause this, but there is also the possibility that coalition-experiences or expectations lead to parties taking a certain position for tactical reasons. It is therefore gratifying to know that further analysis of the manifestos will extend to agreements between parties during coalition-negotiations, (the declarations of policy and the Queen's speeches), which will shed new light on the process of cabinet formation. The data presented in this chapter therefore, are to be seen as the starting point for detailed analysis of this phenomenon.

Notes

1 I wish to thank Hans Daalder for his comments on an earlier version of this chapter and Rudy Andeweg for his cooperation at the beginning of this project: the first sections of the chapter still bear his mark.

2 The manifestos of DS'70 and PPR have *not* been coded for 1981, since these were no longer relevant parties; DS'70 lost all its seats. In the analysis are included common programmes of the three religious parties (KVP, ARP and CHU) for 1971 and 1972. Also included are common programmes of 'The progressive three' (PvdA, D'66 and PPR) for 1971 and 1972: in 1972 these parties did not have separate programmes. The 1952 manifesto of the CHU has not been coded since no copy has been found.

3 The information for the following two sections was obtained in interviews with: F.A. Bibo, director of the 'research bureau' of the KVP; J. Dirx, secretary of the programme committee of the PPR: J.G.H. Krajenbrink, secretary of the CDA; D. Kuiper, vice-chairman of the ARP; J. van Nieuwenhoven, assistant to the chairman of the PvdA; H. van Oorschot, Vice-Chairman of D'66; M.J. Tangel, assistant to the party executive of the VVD. I would like to thank them for their cooperation.

CHAPTER 11

BELGIUM 1946–1981

———— ∾ ————

11.1 POLITICAL PARTIES IN BELGIUM[1]

As with the Netherlands, Belgian politics were relatively straightforward until the mid-1960s. Following the introduction of universal male suffrage in 1919, the then two-party opposition between Catholics and Liberals gave way to a classic 'two-and-half' party system in which the Socialist Party replaced the Liberals as the Catholics' chief rival. With few exceptions, governments were coalitions between two of these three 'traditional' parties formed in response to their gains and losses at successive General Elections. Two major cleavages seemed to underpin this system – a 'left–right' socio-economic cleavage together with an older 'clerical/anti-clerical' division which had divided Catholics from Liberals ever since the foundation of the State in 1830. Both changed after the Schools Pact of 1958 and the so-called *Loi Unique* or economic austerity package introduced by the Eyskens (Christian–Social/Liberal) government in the wake of Congo Independence in the 1960s. The former was effectively a 'truce' between the three parties concerning the last major clerical/anti-clerical issue. The second threw into sharp relief the growing economic disparity between the country's two main language regions, Flanders and Wallonia. The sudden removal of the clerical/anti-clerical cleavage allowed what had hitherto been a submerged division to rise to the surface. This ran across all three traditional parties, and had rapid and profound effects upon the party system.

'Community' issues and associated sub-cleavages have progressively given rise first to new parties and then to forced divisions among the traditional parties – generally along language lines. The effects have been spectacular; whereas in 1958 only three parties presented themselves to the electorate with any certainty of winning seats, by 1978 that figure had risen to eleven.

230

Since 1962 Belgium has been divided into four linguistic areas, three in principle uni-lingual but with certain provisions for minorities, and one (Brussels) bilingual in the two 'national' languages, French and Flemish. Each of these four areas has now given birth to a non-traditional and more or less 'Federalist' party, though the German-speaking region is so small that it can be ignored. From the Flemish point of view 'Flanders' embraces the whole of the Flemish language region and (historically at least), Brussels. This means in practice that the Flemish federalist party the *Volksunie*, and the Flemish 'wings' of the traditional parties claim to represent the Flemish minority in the capital.

By contrast, the French-speaking 'Bruxellois' have traditionally felt themselves to be somewhat apart from the provincial Walloons (*Wallons*) of the French language region (*Wallonie*). Certainly, it is clear that Brussels is a very different place economically, socially and politically from the rest of French-speaking Belgium and the rise of distinct and somewhat different 'federalist' parties in Brussels and Wallonia respectively testifies to this. Nevertheless, language ties are strong and the two have maintained more or less close cooperation – particularly in Parliament where their members sit in a single group.

The French language has proved to be an even stronger unifying force among the traditional parties, which however, (apart from the Liberals between 1971 and 1979) have not found it necessary to organize separate parties for Brussels and Wallonia.

The Constitutional reforms of 1980 set up three new Councils with limited legislative power, which dealt principally with economic and planning matters in the Walloon region, cultural affairs, including education and personal social services, for the entire French-language Community, and a combination of all these functions for Flanders and the Flemish Community respectively, with each having an Executive responsible to it. In response to these developments the traditional parties (Christian-Socials, Socialists and Liberals) have divided into Flemish and French-speaking wings. The change may be more apparent than real however, as these wings continue to cooperate in Parliament and to share common services, thus constituting a close political family if not a strictly unified party in the traditional sense. These parties are briefly described below:

(i) The Christian-Social parties

The CVP and PSC, are simply the two linguistic 'wings' of the formerly united Christian-Social Party following the 1968 split over the Flemish demand that the French-speaking faculties of Louvain University in Flanders be moved to Wallonia. This division was so serious that the two 'wings' of the party fought the ensuing general election as distinct parties, each with its own manifesto. On the other hand, as the first of the traditional parties to split in this way, the CVP and the PSC have had time to work out a *modus vivendi* with each other.

The two parties are archetypal Christian Democrat in their philosophy, policies and electoral support. That is to say, they have a broad cross-class appeal based upon Christian values and a strong sense of 'social solidarity' in contradistinction to what they see as the class warfare approach of Socialism and the divisive nature of Liberal individualism. Necessarily, therefore, they cover a wide spectrum in terms of the socio-economic 'left–right' dimension but with a centre of gravity close to that of the political culture as a whole. The CVP is much the stronger partner and currently gathers about 45 per cent of the vote in the Flemish community. Until 1981, its French-speaking *alter ego*, the PSC, ran second to the Socialists in most of Wallonia with around 25 per cent of the vote there, and to the FDF in Brussels. Taken together, the two parties, with roughly 36 per cent of the national vote, are not only the strongest political 'family' in the country but also constitute the 'pivot' of the party system, making their presence indispensable for any conceivable governmental coalition. Since 1958 the CVP-PSC has dominated every Cabinet and, apart from a few months in 1973, every Belgian Prime Minister since that date has come from its ranks.

(ii) The Socialist parties

The SP and PS divided in 1978, the latter seeing electoral advantages in presenting a more radical 'Walloon' (and Brussels) image. So far, however, there is little evidence that this strategy has worked.

Socialists in Belgium have generally been characterized by a very pragmatic attitude. In the 1981 election the Francophone PS took a more 'radical' position while their Flemish colleagues stuck to their traditional stance.

Electorally, the PS is by far the strongest party in the older industrial areas of Wallonia with about 40 per cent of the region's popular vote while, until 1981, the SP ran second to the CVP in Flanders with around 20 per cent. In Brussels the two Socialist parties represent the third most significant political 'family', polling some 17 per cent of the vote. At the national level the Socialists remain the country's second largest grouping and frequently take part in government.

(iii) The Liberal 'family'

This now comprises the PVV and the PRL, and has had a chequered history. It abandoned anti-clericalism in 1961, moved rather markedly to the right, and adopted a new name, 'Party for Liberty and Progress', which its Flemish wing still retains. Following the party's failure to capitalize upon its extreme 'unitarist' policy during the 'Louvain election' of 1968, the Flemish PVV began to progressively 'distance' itself from the national party. Then, when threatened in its traditional 'fief' of Brussels by the meteoric rise of the FDF, the party in Brussels split into federalist and unitarist wings. After a long period of confusion, the Liberal 'family' finally settled into a *three-party* arrangement, one for Flanders, Wallonia and Brussels respectively, and this system survived until early 1979. Then, in anticipation of the European Elections, the Brussels party (which had become wholly Francophone) merged with its larger Walloon partner to form the PRL, thereby giving the Liberals the same simple two-party structure as the other 'traditional' camps.

(iv) The federalist parties

These do not form a 'family' in the same way as the Christians, Socialists and Liberals. Except for certain links between the FDF and the RW, there are no common structures and, in any event, the parties rarely share common outlooks on even non-'community' questions. They have generally all agreed upon the need for the reorganization of the Belgian State along federal lines but have differed violently regarding how this is to be done.

The oldest of the Federalist parties is the conservative Flemish *Volksunie* (VU). Founded in 1954, the party first entered Parliament in 1958 and reached a peak in 1971 with 21 Members of the Lower House and 18.8 per cent of the popular vote in Flanders – this coming largely from middle-class supporters of the CVP. The party supports a federal system based upon two states, Flanders and Wallonia, Brussels being jointly administered as a 'Federal Capital Territory'; restriction of that territory (and its associated bilingualism) to its present boundaries and the progressive elimination of the so-called 'facilities' for French-speakers in the capital's Flemish periphery. The *Rassemblement Wallon* (RW) originated in 1965 in dissident Socialist circles. The bulk of its electoral support comes from the heavily industrialized Sambre-Meuse valley, and it has thus always taken a left-oriented view. The RW made rapid electoral progress until 1971 taking 21.2 per cent of the Walloon vote in that year, but has slumped badly since.

The party made considerable efforts to modify its left-wing image during the years of its electoral success and to appeal to as wide a cross-section of voters as possible. However, following a short and unhappy experience in the first Tindemans government (1974–7), the 'reformist' and fundamentalist wings split, the former merging with the Walloon Liberals. The rump of the party has now apparently moved leftwards again.

The *Front Démocratique des Francophones* (FDF) emerged in opposition to the legislation of the early 1960s governing language choice in Brussels schools. Overwhelmingly middle-class in its leadership and in its electoral support, the FDF is a very different kind of party from the RW with which, however, it has maintained a close working relationship since 1965, particularly within their common Parliamentary group. Although not originally a Federalist party, the FDF subscribed *en bloc* to its Walloon partner's federalist policy in 1970. Today both parties stand for federalism *à trois* with Brussels as the third state on a footing of equality with the other two. The FDF (and the RW, for whom the issue is however of less direct relevance) is implacably opposed to the existing boundaries of Brussels, seeing them as an 'iron collar' (*carcan*) strangling the city's expansion. As befits its middle-class origins, the FDF is particularly concerned with education and environmental issues. Electorally, it has been the most successful of the three main Federalist parties having become the leading party in Brussels since 1971 when it took 39.6 per cent of the vote in the capital.

11.2 ELECTION PROGRAMMES IN THE BELGIAN CONTEXT

Belgian political parties invariably present well worked-out policy documents to the public at election times. These vary from two or three pages of duplicated typewriting to full colour glossy booklets of anything up to 100 pages, but all have in common the notion of being the authoritative statement of the paty's policy position at the time of the election in question. As such, a party's programme is accepted by all its candidates and constitutes the essential background to their own individual campaigns. Effectively, they are pledged not only to defend the programme in the campaign but also to seek the implementation of as much of it as possible in the event of their election.

In a country where no single party can realistically expect to obtain a majority of seats in Parliament and where, consequently, all governments must be coalitions, no party can expect to see the implementation of more than a part of its programme. In general, however, this seems to have little effect upon the nature of the documents themselves. Belgian party programmes cover much the same ground as those in other countries and in much the same depth.

Programmes are prepared according to procedures which vary for each party. While the traditional parties maintain elaborate procedures for consultation of, and approval by their constituency federations and/or membership at large, the newer parties have more streamlined and centralized procedures. So, at one extreme, the PS and SP Executives are supposed first to circulate a draft to constituencies for their comments and then to present a revised draft to a full Party Congress for debate and final adoption. At the other extreme, the RW's *bureau fédéral*, composed of the party's elected Officers and the Chairmen of each of the thirteen Parliamentary Constituencies in the region, draws up and adopts the party's election programmes entirely on its own authority. In practice, however, differences are not so extreme. Due to the increasing tendency of elections to be called with little warning, many of the older parties' procedures are being by-passed. Thus recently the PS and SP Executives have discussed and slightly amended draft programmes prepared for them by the parties' Research Department before presenting them to hastily summoned Party Congresses for rubber-stamping. Procedures in the other traditional parties are similar. Thus the influence of the professional Research Institutes is very significant and often decisive.

11.3 PREVIOUS RESEARCH

Although no work on the present scale has previously been carried out in Belgium, limited quantitative analyses of party programmes have been done, most notably by Guy Tegenbos (1974). On the basis of the electoral programmes published by nine parties for the Legislative Elections of 10 March 1974, Tegenbos counted 'programme points' classified in six previously defined 'sectors' (foreign, interior, cultural, social, economic and financial) and then into sub-sectors. Each party programme was then scored according to its stand on each particular issue, i.e. positive, negative, or indifferent.

With this information Tegenbos was able to calculate the degree to which any pair of parties agreed and/or disagreed with each other in terms of programme points both in general and for each policy sector in particular. The largest number any pair of parties had in common was the 479 shared by the PSC and the CVP. The lowest was between the Flemish Liberals, the PVV, and the Communist Party at 21. A count of opposing policies produced similar patterns of low (indeed, non-existent) disagreement between parties of the same 'family' and high disagreement between the Liberals and the Communists. The overwhelming impression was of a very low level of overall disagreement between the various parties and of the lack of clear-cut policy commitments.

Frognier and Delfosse (1974) also factor analysed the policy positions of the various Belgian parties at the time of the 1974 election employing the results of a newspaper survey of the various parties' positions. This produced two major factors which together accounted for some 75 per cent of the common variance in their indicators. In terms of the two-dimensional space these defined, they found a close identification of the three

Liberal parties with each other; a similarly close relationship between the three Federalist parties and another, less close relationship between the Socialist and Communist parties. Interestingly, however, there was a marked distance between the positions of the two wings of the Christian-Social Party, the PSC and CVP. Indeed the latter was as close to the Flemish Liberal position as it was to its Francophone *alter ego*. This last finding contrasts with that of Tegenbos which, for the same election, showed the PSC and CVP as having substantially more programme points in common with each other than did any other pair of parties. Hopefully our analysis, utilizing party programmes over the whole post-war period, may be able to resolve this point.

11.4 COLLECTION AND CODING OF DOCUMENTS

The identification of relevant documents is very simple in Belgium. In only one or two instances over the entire post-war period was there any doubt as to which document should be used for this purpose and in no instance did any programme prove untraceable. The great majority were supplied by the various political parties or by their associated Research Institutes. The latter, which are semi-independent organizations maintained by all significant parties in Belgium, are generally of a high standard and are acknowledged on all sides to play a significant role in the manifesto-drafting process. They are the obvious sources of past manifesto texts.

In some instances, actual copies of the party programmes distributed to the public were supplied. These are clearly the most useful since they allow layout and illustrations to be taken into account. In the majority of cases, however, there is only one archive copy so only a photocopy is available. In only one or two cases were post–1958 copies missing and in those cases the deficiencies were made up from the CEPESS reprint. CEPESS (*Centre d'Etudes Politiques, Economiques et Sociales/Centrum voor Politieke, Economische en Sociale Studies*) is the Research Institute associated with the PSC and CVP and occupies two floors of the parties' joint headquarters in Brussels. Since 1962 CEPESS has published a twice-monthly journal *Documents CEPESS/ CEPESS Documenten*, and the relevant issues have contained either the full texts or extensive summaries of all principal party programmes. Since 1974 these have appeared together in a special issue of the journal devoted solely to party programmes. These special issues also include the texts of the agreed coalition programme of the new government.

We had to refer to the party's own newspaper, *Le Peuple*, for the full texts of the Socialist Programmes for the years 1946, 1949, 1950 and 1954. A number of parties – particularly in recent years – have issued more than one document having some claim to be included in the analysis as an election programme. In some cases, this dilemma is easily solved as in 1971 when the Socialist Party published both an 'Electoral Programme' and an 'Electoral Platform'. Since both documents were published together, the decision was taken to treat them as a single document. Similarly, at each election since 1974, the French-speaking PSC has published its programme in the form of a series (of three or four) separate booklets each directed at a particular area of the country or dealing with a particular set of policies. It is clear that the various booklets are intended to be taken together so they, too, have been coded as single documents.

Those programmes published by each of the traditional parties prior to the 'split' appeared in two separate editions – one in each national language, and were otherwise supposed to be identical. Nevertheless, the use of a coding scheme based upon the full sentence would be bound to produce slightly differing scores according to the language version chosen. Such errors (which in any case are certain to be very small) are presumably reduced when the 'quasi-sentence' is the unit of analysis and, consequently, no attempt was made to try to control for them. Since each party's bifurcation the two versions of the programme have of course differed by content as well as by language.

All Flemish documents were coded by Hearl and the French documents by a Research Assistant. Eight of the latter were recoded by Hearl. Discrepancies, although not quantified, were few. The full list of the Election Programmes is given in Appendix A. Specific Belgian modifications to the general coding scheme are as follows:

(*i*) The specific issues of 'Overseas Aid' and 'Worker Participation or Control' in industry were separated out from the general categories 107 (Internationalism Positive) and 207 (Democracy) respectively. Both are frequently mentioned in the texts.

(*ii*) The typically Christian-Social concept of 'Social Harmony' was distinguished from 'National Effort' on the grounds that it appeals more to Christian morality than to patriotism. The particular ethnic and community divisions of Belgian society clearly necessitated the distinction between calls for Two or Three Regions in category 301 (Decentralization: positive) as this lies at the heart of the conflict between the two linguistic communities. Similarly, calls for 'Cultural Autonomy' (not at all the same thing as federalism in the Belgian context) had to be distinguished from more usual forms of Communalism. On the other hand, the distinction between the Church and State sectors of education, which had *a priori* been coded separately within Categories 607 and 608 (Communalism: positive and negative, respectively), had a very small take-up and has been eliminated.

(*iii*) Sub-category 7041 (Self-employed and small business, known as the 'Middle Classes' in Belgian political jargon) is of paramount importance in Belgium where all parties vie with one another for their support. It has accordingly been separately distinguished within category 704. Finally, category 706 (Non-Economic Demographic Groups) has separate sub-categories not only for the inhabitants of the country's four linguistic regions but also for Youth, Old People and Women – all target groups for parties' specific policy points and promises.

There is a problem regarding the status of the different manifestos issued by the various linguistic 'wings' of parties and/or by the separate 'regional' or 'community' parties into which the traditional parties have broken up. This problem was initially evaded by coding such documents separately. For the actual analysis, appropriate 'composite' programmes have been formed from the two original documents to represent the policy stance of each political family as a whole.

11.5 FREQUENCIES ANALYSIS

The attention parties have focused at each election on each of the seven principal domains has naturally varied over time with changing political conditions. External Relations received something like 5–8 per cent of mentions exceeding 10 per cent only once. Freedom and Democracy have received increasing attention since the 1960s as has the related domain of Government. This trend is clearly associated with the rise of the federalist parties over the same period. The percentage of manifesto mentions devoted to the Economy has also fluctuated and generally corresponded to the country's varying economic fortunes, and has increased significantly since the 1973 oil crisis. This domain also appears to be affected by the amount of attention given to Welfare; as the one grows so the other declines and *vice versa*. The Fabric of Society on the other hand, has shown a constant rate of around 8 per cent or so, while Social Groups has consistently been in the 20–25 per cent range making it on balance the single most important domain. This is not surprising given the fact that references to the inhabitants of Belgium's three principal language regions, Flemings, Walloons and the (French-speaking) *Bruxellois* were coded there. It is this, of course, which accounts for the domain's expansion during the early 1970s when federalist politics were at their height.

Finally, mention should be made of 'uncoded' references (never more than 18 per cent for any election year and around 11.0 per cent for most years). The programmes issued by the traditional parties in the immediate post-war years were often devoted to lengthy ideological analyses and/or historical explanations in addition to concrete political proposals. This tendency declined from 1946 and had virtually ceased by 1958. Another jump in uncodable statements is associated with the entry of the Federalist parties to the electoral scene, particularly that of the VU in 1961, and for similar reasons. As the new parties became better established there was a marked move in favour of specific policy proposals and the number of uncoded quasi-sentences diminishes accordingly.

TABLE 11.1

LEADING CATEGORIES MENTIONED IN BELGIAN PARTY PROGRAMMES

		ALL MANIFESTOS X̄	S.D	PSC-CVP (N=13) X̄	S.D	PSB-BSP (N=13) X̄	SD	LIBERALS (N=13) X̄	SD	VOLKSUNIE (N=8) X̄	SD	RASS.WALLON (N=5) X̄	SD	FDF (N=6) X̄	SD
504	SOCIAL SERVICES: POSITIVE	4.17	5.79	5.40	1.85	7.76	10.96	2.06	2.06	2.24	1.95	2.88	2.02	2.00	2.05
505	SOCIAL JUSTICE	4.13	3.99	4.60	3.47	6.35	6.41	2.72	2.01	3.32	2.21	3.76	4.05	2.71	1.43
411	TECHNOLOGY AND INFRASTRUCTURE	3.98	3.29	4.51	4.00	4.40	3.11	3.44	3.13	1.45	0.85	3.67	2.63	6.77	3.22
7041	"MIDDLE CLASSES"	3.49	2.98	3.66	1.74	2.75	4.33	5.82	2.22	2.33	2.07	2.14	1.34	2.39	1.65
401	FREE ENTERPRISE	3.28	5.34	2.33	2.73	0.61	0.89	10.26	7.25	1.64	2.56	0.42	0.74	0.53	0.76
3010	DECENTRALISATION (RESIDUAL)	2.98	2.92	1.84	0.70	1.90	2.11	1.59	1.17	4.78	3.79	6.91	4.15	5.46	2.73
703	FARMERS/AGRICULTURE	2.85	2.74	3.25	1.88	3.18	3.11	3.80	3.54	1.68	1.28	3.66	2.71	0.06	0.14
4081	FULL EMPLOYMENT	2.74	2.12	2.55	1.72	3.22	1.59	2.13	2.02	2.60	2.31	4.54	3.41	2.15	2.53
7067	WOMEN	2.63	2.74	2.10	1.51	3.37	3.29	2.48	3.74	1.09	1.65	3.00	3.34	4.22	1.38
506	EDUCATION: POSITIVE	2.61	2.44	3.54	2.28	3.53	3.27	2.24	2.17	1.79	1.41	1.24	1.83	1.67	2.01
7065	YOUTH	2.54	2.72	1.32	0.91	4.42	4.48	2.46	1.41	0.64	0.57	2.23	1.98	3.81	1.87
705	UNDERPRIVILEGED MINORITIES	2.49	2.21	2.72	2.14	3.18	1.71	3.24	3.13	0.98	1.05	1.69	1.96	1.54	1.09
2020	DEMOCRACY (RESIDUAL)	2.47	2.34	1.94	1.62	2.77	2.17	1.61	2.13	5.10	3.54	2.17	2.48	2.71	2.97
502	ART, SPORT, LEISURE, MEDIA	2.41	2.66	2.46	2.61	2.96	3.08	2.29	2.73	2.23	2.05	0.91	1.00	2.88	3.64
201	FREEDOM/HUMAN RIGHTS	2.37	2.41	2.12	1.62	2.06	1.69	2.99	3.96	1.92	1.70	2.31	1.99	2.91	2.49
303	GOVERNMENT EFFICIENCY	2.34	2.63	3.03	2.22	0.95	1.07	3.42	4.06	2.39	2.70	1.93	1.78	1.83	1.41
108	EUROPEAN COMMUNITY: POSITIVE	2.31	2.06	2.37	1.85	2.18	2.18	1.72	1.46	1.04	0.86	5.05	3.56	3.18	1.82
501	ENVIRONMENTAL PROTECTION	2.16	2.30	2.10	2.34	1.46	1.74	1.36	1.84	2.45	2.76	2.61	1.83	4.81	2.61
7061	FLEMINGS/FLANDERS	2.01	5.08	0.75	0.73	0.21	0.37	0.38	0.74	11.96	8.74	0.03	0.07	0.52	0.50
7066	OLD PEOPLE	1.99	2.17	1.19	1.08	3.70	3.29	1.83	1.25	0.97	1.08	1.33	1.21	2.30	2.66
7062	WALLOONS/WALLONIE	1.96	5.40	0.90	0.90	0.36	0.76	0.50	0.91	0.03	0.07	14.71	13.01	2.85	2.72
701	LABOUR GROUPS	1.84	2.17	1.39	1.09	4.17	2.78	1.69	2.17	0.45	0.46	0.86	0.39	0.79	0.66
403	REGULATION OF CAPITALISM	1.74	1.92	1.07	1.10	2.06	2.35	1.21	1.48	1.48	1.86	4.84	1.58	1.40	1.26
404	ECONOMIC PLANNING	1.67	1.77	2.26	1.26	2.79	1.96	0.21	0.40	2.06	2.61	1.48	1.04	0.78	1.03
402	INCENTIVES	1.61	1.77	2.31	1.62	0.72	1.11	2.14	2.35	1.78	2.21	0.95	0.68	1.18	1.03
414	ECONOMIC ORTHODOXY	1.59	2.49	0.89	1.13	0.54	0.69	4.43	4.43	0.96	1.12	1.14	1.66	0.44	1.08
7063	BRUXELLOIS/BRUSSELS	1.52	3.99	0.54	0.82	0.24	0.46	0.16	0.30	0.00	0.00	0.34	0.75	12.40	4.50
603	TRADITIONAL MORALITY: POS.	1.42	2.17	3.61	2.93	0.52	0.53	0.92	1.35	0.84	0.79	0.37	0.53	1.41	2.14
6061	SOCIAL HARMONY	1.28	2.15	1.82	3.28	0.42	0.81	2.16	2.95	0.90	1.18	1.65	1.27	0.29	0.47
410	PRODUCTIVITY	1.28	1.76	2.63	1.64	0.77	1.15	1.11	1.56	1.14	2.56	0.88	1.97	0.39	0.90
6072	CULTURAL AUTONOMY	1.28	1.82	1.15	1.04	0.69	1.38	0.05	0.13	2.68	2.10	1.74	2.91	3.26	2.16
608	COMMUNALISM: NEGATIVE	1.23	1.77	0.20	0.35	1.57	2.69	2.34	1.88	1.46	0.71	1.10	1.22	0.15	0.28
2021	WORKER PARTICIPATION	1.11	1.44	1.01	1.07	1.10	1.08	0.38	0.67	0.84	0.79	3.39	3.04	1.39	1.42
3013	THREE REGIONS	1.04	2.36	0.15	0.29	0.64	1.08	0.13	0.39	0.00	0.00	2.37	2.76	6.07	3.90
101	FOREIGN SPECIAL RELATIONS:POS.	1.01	1.74	1.54	2.03	0.39	0.72	1.57	2.67	0.80	0.87	0.19	0.40	0.92	1.27
305	GOVT. EFFECTIVENESS AND AUTHORITY	1.00	2.02	0.47	0.68	1.59	3.18	1.46	2.33	0.19	0.27	0.72	1.61	1.14	1.55
6070	COMMUNALISM (RESIDUAL): POS.	0.95	1.66	2.20	2.47	0.05	0.11	0.17	0.41	0.13	0.19	1.86	2.70	0.55	0.85
4080	SPEC. ECONOMIC GOALS (RESIDUAL)	0.94	1.73	0.47	0.73	1.93	2.86	1.24	1.64	0.26	0.07	0.69	1.13	0.54	0.69
1070	INTERNATIONALISM (RESIDUAL): POSITIVE	0.93	0.87	2.42	1.41	1.46	0.65	0.53	0.47	0.43	0.49	1.09	1.26	0.35	0.46
1071	OVERSEAS AID	0.91	0.99	1.10	1.09	0.76	0.79	0.58	0.68	0.99	1.29	0.66	0.77	1.60	1.38
104	MILITARY: POSITIVE	0.86	1.11	1.55	1.34	0.80	0.96	1.21	1.21	0.14	0.40	0.00	0.00	0.43	0.71
601	NATIONAL WAY OF LIFE: POS.	0.83	1.95	1.12	1.11	1.56	3.27	0.98	2.09	0.00	0.02	0.02	0.05	0.04	0.11
105	MILITARY: NEGATIVE	0.79	1.10	0.51	0.79	2.04	1.44	0.44	0.74	0.74	0.55	0.37	0.50	0.24	0.36
3012	TWO REGIONS	0.55	1.55	0.17	0.24	0.02	0.06	0.03	0.07	3.58	3.69	0.03	0.07	0.00	0.00
602	NATIONAL WAY OF LIFE: NEG.	0.36	1.64	0.31	1.05	0.02	0.02	0.00	0.00	2.01	4.01	0.16	0.37	0.00	0.00

Table 11.1 shows the mean scores in each of the leading categories and sub-categories for the entire 'national-level' data set, after the elimination of those which received less than 0.75 per cent overall (in place of 1.0 per cent in other analyses), or 2.0 per cent for any one party (in place of 3.0 per cent). This modification seems justified because two of the VU's most distinctive issues, positive emphases on Two Regions and negative on National Way of Life, would not otherwise have qualified for inclusion. Only one of the Christian-Social parties' top five categories is not one of the top five for Belgium as a whole; the exception consists of positive emphases on Traditional Morality: the single most specifically Christian category in the entire coding frame.

Both the Socialist and the Liberal 'family' has three of its top five issues in the national top five, being distinctive in these terms on two issues each, *viz.* Youth and Labour Groups for the Socialists and Farmers/Agriculture and Economic Orthodoxy for the Liberals. The federalist parties, by contrast, have only one (or none in the case of the RW) of their favourite issues in the national top five. As one might expect, however, they all make positive references to Decentralization. Equally expected is the stark contrast between the VU and the two Francophone Federalist parties on the issues of Two and Three Regions.

Thus, our coding scheme works well within the Belgian context. Not only are the parties typified by the issues we know them to be concerned with, but in several instances the ranking of issues also appears to correspond closely with the parties' known attitudes. So, for example, the close identity of concerns between the CVP–PSC and the SP–PS embracing Technology, Social Justice, Social Services, Education and Minorities (principally the Handicapped), clearly reflects these two parties' positions as the principal contenders for government office – contenders who must compete for the votes of the same or similar electors in the middle ground of politics. Nevertheless, the two parties' profiles, by illustrating their contrasting concerns for the Self-Employed (i.e. 'Middle Classes') and Labour Groups respectively, also reflect expected biases towards Conservatism and Socialism.

Among the three traditional parties the Liberals are easily the most right-wing in economic terms and this is very clearly demonstrated by their profile. On the other hand, the Liberal and Socialist (not to mention the Francophone federalist) high placing of Women among their top ten concerns reflects their long-standing anti-clerical tradition *vis à vis* the much more conservative moral position of the PSC–CVP, for whom the issue of women's rights scores fewer mentions than that of any other party except the similarly conservative VU.

Equally sensitive profiles emerge for the three Federalist parties. Firstly the extent to which each of them is still a single-issue party is demonstrated by the concentration each has on the interests of its own region. The VU and the RW rank Decentralization next in order of importance, while this issue is much less significant for the FDF. This, of course, reflects the reality that federalism is of much less direct interest to Brussels (indeed, to some extent it may even be inimical to the city's position as capital of the country). If, however, there *is* to be federalism then it is clearly in Brussels' interest that it be on the basis of Three Regions. This has long been the FDF's most basic demand and the one on which it parts company most violently with the VU for whom the conflicting policy of Two Regions is the main interest. Interestingly (and accurately), however, the details of Decentralization are of little significance to the RW since Wallonia is not a party to this particular dispute, and merely supports the Three Regions solution as a *quid pro quo* for the FDF's support for federalism in the first place.

Again, the profiles in Table 11.1 are sensitive to the fact that the RW is more to the left and the FDF more to the right; as an overwhelmingly middle-class urban party the FDF is concerned with such issues as the Environment and Freedom and Human Rights; and as a party from the industrial South, the RW is more interested in Full Employment and Worker Participation. Obviously, Farmers and Agriculture are of no interest to the FDF while Wallonia has an important agricultural industry and this difference is also reflected in the party profiles. The issue of 'Cultural Autonomy' (designed very largely to protect the interests of the two main language communities from interference by the other) is of crucial importance to the FDF, whereas the issue docs not figure at all among the RW's top ten; again, this exactly corresponds with the absence of threats to the French language in Wallonia.

The VU profile is also as expected – slightly conservative (e.g. concern with the Middle Classes), and lacking in enthusiasm for the National Way of Life. The accord between quantitative results and qualitative expectations confirms that the coding operation is successful and enables us to proceed with confidence to a factor analysis of the data.

11.6 FACTOR ANALYSIS BY DOMAIN

The standard analysis was carried out within each domain and the results are summarized below:

(i) Foreign relations

Two factors having Eigenvalues greater than unity were produced accounting for 26.2 per cent and 22.7 per cent respectively of the variance. After Varimax rotation, these factors are reasonably straightforward to interpret. The first of them opposes positive emphases on the European Community and on Overseas Aid to positive references to Foreign Special Relationships. Since the latter consists of mentions of African territories during the colonial period, the factor makes good sense as alternative foci of Belgian foreign policy over the post-war period; for the first fifteen years attention was focused on the Empire, and over the next twenty it shifted to the European Community and/or to Overseas Aid in general.

The second factor, which loads significantly and positively on all the remaining categories is clearly one of High/Low Concern with Foreign Affairs generally. Taken together, the two factors adequately summarize the foreign policy orientations of Belgian politics over the post-war period.

(ii) Freedom and democracy

The factor analysis of this domain only proved possible due to the fact that the standard Democracy category was sub-divided for the purposes of the Belgian domestic analysis into Worker Participation/Control and other references to Democracy. But for this, the failure of the two Constitutionalism categories to qualify would have meant that only two categories would have survived, making any kind of factoring superfluous. Under the circumstances, therefore, it is probably not surprising that the two principal components that are produced are, quite simply, 'Democracy' and 'Freedom', respectively, accounting for 44.8 per cent and 34.9 per cent of the variance within this domain.

(iii) Government

In this instance, it is the unrotated solution which gives the clearer picture and accordingly it is this solution which is described. Two factors are produced. The first, accounting for 27.9 per cent of the variance, straightforwardly opposes the three Decentralization categories to those two which can be said to be associated with the notion of a strong and effective central government. In other words, it is the 'Federalist–Unitarist' factor which we would, in any case, have expected to find. It is only plausible, therefore, that the second factor should then prove to be the opposition between alternative methods of Decentralization, *viz.* the Two, or Three, Regions solutions demanded by Flemish and Francophone interests respectively. This second factor accounts for 24.3 per cent of the variance.

(iv) Economy

This is the first domain to produce three factors with Eigenvalues greater than unity, due principally to the larger number of categories qualifying for inclusion. They are perfectly straightforward. The first is the classic opposition between Free Enterprise and Economic Orthodoxy on the one hand, and Regulation of Capitalism and Economic Planning on the other. It is the Right–Left factor and accounts for 23.4 per cent of the variance before rotation. The second, loading on Incentives, Productivity and Technology and Infrastructure is clearly one of overall economic performance. It has been labelled simply 'Productivity' and accounts for 17.6 per cent of the variance. The third factor is one of Economic Goals, including in particular Full Employment. In accordance with our standard procedures, however, the third factor will not be used in the second-stage analysis.

(v) Welfare

This domain breaks down into two components in a highly predictable manner, each of which accounts for about one-third of the variance. The first loads in excess of .90 on Social Justice and on positive references to Social Services Expansion; the other on the three remaining categories included in the analysis and can therefore be labelled 'Culture and Environment'.

(vi) Fabric of Society

Three dimensions are produced, the first loading significantly in only one direction, that is, positive references to Traditional Morality, Social Harmony and Communalism. The first two of these categories are at the heart of Catholic social teaching, while the third consists in practice of the demand for the Church and its associated ethical-cultural 'world' to be allowed the freedom to maintain and operate its own institutions independently of the state. In other words, the factor neatly encapsulates the core of the 'clerical' position in what has undoubtedly been Belgium's most important historical conflict, the clerical/anti-clerical opposition.

The second relates to a much more recent (and nowadays more salient) issue – that of Cultural Autonomy. It is perhaps significant that this issue – which is not to be confused with federalism *per se* (although it is closely related to it) is equally strongly opposed by positive references to the Defence of the National Way of Life. This suggests that the demand for Cultural Autonomy is seen as in some sense anti-patriotic *either* because it struck at the bilingual nature of the Belgian state in the early post-war years *or* (more likely), because it threatened the predominant position of the French language in that state.

The third factor is more difficult to identify. It opposes negative mentions of Defence of the National Way of Life: (a category associated almost exclusively with the VU) to negative references to Communalism.

This is composed of various anti-clerical attitudes more typically associated with the Socialist and Liberal Parties in particular and with French-speaking parts of the country in general. The three factors account for 28.9 per cent, 17.2 per cent and 16.6 per cent of the variance before rotation.

(vii) Social Groups

This is the only domain to produce four components, all quite easy to interpret and, taken together, a satisfactory summation of Belgian programmatic concerns in the area. The first factor is one of High/Low concern for the traditional welfare targets of Old People, the underprivileged, etc., the second one of High/Low concern for Bourgeois Groups and Women (a perfectly plausible combination in the Belgian context), and the third one of High/Low concern for the interests of the French-speaking Bruxellois. The fourth is bipolar and opposes the interests of Flemings and Walloons.

The four factors respectively account for 28.0 per cent, 16.5 per cent, 12.5 per cent and 10.2 per cent of the variance within the domain before rotation.

Table 11.2 summarizes the first-stage principal components analysis of the seven domains: eighteen first-stage factors were produced in all, fourteen of which (two from each domain) are used in the second-stage analysis.

11.7 SECOND-STAGE FACTOR ANALYSIS

Table 11.3 shows the Varimax rotated solution for the second-stage factor analysis, but as usual also contains the Pearson Correlation coefficients between the rotated second-stage factors and original categories and sub-categories.

Six factors having Eigenvalues greater than unity were produced. Factor 1 correlates positively with Worker Participation/Control, Regulation of Capitalism and Economic Planning, all associated with the 'Left'. On the negative side, the picture is clearer since virtually all the correlations stronger than −.30 are classic 'right-wing' ones such as Economic Orthodoxy and Free Enterprise. This first second-stage factor is therefore a 'Left–Right' dimension and would be unhesitatingly labelled as such were it not for the fact that it also appears to be bound up, on the 'Left' side, with the specifically Francophone federalist issues of Three Regions and Walloons/Wallonia. One explanation for this is the limited number of FDF-RW manifestos (i.e. six) in the analysis coupled with the RW's undoubted left-wing bias. Part of the distinctively Francophone dimension has been subsumed into what would otherwise have been a pure Left–Right one.

TABLE 11.2

SUMMARY OF FIRST STAGE FACTORS WITHIN EACH POLICY-DOMAIN

FACTOR	ROTATION	INTERPRETATION
F11	VARIMAX	EUROPEAN COMMUNITY VERSUS FOREIGN SPECIAL RELATIONSHIPS (NB. THE LATTER IS MOSTLY CONGO AND RUANDA/URUNDI)
F12	VARIMAX	FOREIGN AFFAIRS: HIGH CONCERN/LOW CONCERN
F21	VARIMAX	DEMOCRACY: HIGH CONCERN/LOW CONCERN
F22	VARIMAX	FREEDOM: HIGH CONCERN/LOW CONCERN
F31	UNROTATED	DECENTRALISATION VERSUS GOVT. AUTHORITY & EFFICIENCY
F32	UNROTATED	TWO REGIONS VERSUS THREE REGIONS
F41	VARIMAX	LEFT VERSUS RIGHT
F42	VARIMAX	PRODUCTIVITY: HIGH CONCERN/LOW CONCERN
F43	VARIMAX	ECONOMIC GOALS: HIGH CONCERN/LOW CONCERN
F51	VARIMAX	SOCIAL SERVICES & SOCIAL JUSTICE: HIGH/LOW CONCERN
F52	VARIMAX	CULTURE & ENVIRONMENT: HIGH/LOW CONCERN
F61	VARIMAX	CLERICALISM: HIGH CONCERN/LOW CONCERN
F62	VARIMAX	CULTURAL AUTONOMY: HIGH CONCERN/LOW CONCERN
F63	VARIMAX	NATIONAL WAY (NEG) VERSUS COMMUNALISM (NEG)
F71	VARIMAX	TRADITIONAL WELFARE TARGETS: HIGH/LOW CONCERN
F72	VARIMAX	BOURGEOIS GROUPS AND WOMEN: HIGH CONCERN/LOW CONCERN
F73	VARIMAX	BRUSSELS: HIGH CONCERN/LOW CONCERN
F74	VARIMAX	WALLOONS VERSUS FLEMINGS

Factor 2 is easy to interpret in the Belgian context. It opposes a clear and compact combination of Clerical and/or Socially Conservative issues to a broad mixture of Welfare and 'New Left' concerns. The factor has therefore been labelled 'Progressive *vs.* Conservative/Clerical'.

Factor 3 is the expected opposition between Government Effectiveness and Authority (loading on the positive end of the factor), and Flemish Federalism. It is only natural that Flemish nationalism, which has been an enduring feature of Belgian politics for many years, should have come to dominate the decentralist argument; especially since its Walloon equivalent has been 'absorbed' into the 'Left–Right' factor.

The three factors so far produced are, then, a manifestation of the classic three dimensions which Belgian political scientists and other observers have for so long identified and are respectively: socio-economic 'Left–Right', 'Clerical/Anti-Clerical', and 'Federalist–Unitarist'.

The three remaining factors present no problems. Factor 4 is over-

TABLE 11.3

SECOND-STAGE ANALYSIS FOR BELGIUM: VARIMAX ROTATED FACTOR MATRIX (AND CORRELATIONS WITH ORIGINAL VARIABLES)

	FACTOR 1 LEFT-RIGHT	FACTOR 2 PROGRESSIVE VS. CONSERVATIVE/CLERICAL	FACTOR 3 FEDERALIST UNITARIST	FACTOR 4 FREEDOM AND HUMAN RIGHTS	FACTOR 5 PRODUCTIVITY	FACTOR 6 SOCIAL SERVICES AN SOCIAL JUSTICE
DOMAIN ONE: EXTERNAL RELATIONS						
FACTOR 1.1 EC VERSUS FOREIGN SPECIAL RELS.	.54	.49	.05	.14	-.16	.30
FACTOR 1.2 FOREIGN POLICY: HIGH/LOW	.20	.14	.17	.59	.39	-.21
101 FOREIGN SPECIAL RELS. (I.E. MOSTLY CONGO): POS.	-.48	-.25	-.05	.13	.20	-.30
104 MILITARY: POSITIVE	-.05	-.12	.11	.42	.42	-.08
105 MILITARY: NEGATIVE	.07	.35	.18	.26	.08	-.23
1070 INTERNATIONALISM (RES.): POSITIVE	.12	.10	.12	.36	.30	-.31
1071 OVERSEAS AID: POSITIVE	.27	.45	-.03	.10	.16	.16
108 EUROPEAN COMMUNITY: POSITIVE	.42	.24	.05	.32	-.29	.36
DOMAIN TWO: FREEDOM AND DEMOCRACY						
FACTOR 2.1 DEMOCRACY: HIGH/LOW CONCERN	.62	.02	-.24	-.00	-.01	.04
FACTOR 2.2 FREEDOM: HIGH/LOW CONCERN	.08	-.00	-.03	-.85	.04	.04
201 FREEDOM AND HUMAN RIGHTS	.08	.06	-.00	-.82	.06	-.01
2020 DEMOCRACY (RESIDUAL)	.53	.05	-.26	-.21	-.06	.29
2021 WORKER PARTICIPATION/CONTROL	.58	-.09	-.11	.20	-.11	.39
DOMAIN THREE: GOVERNMENT						
FACTOR 3.1 DECENTRALISATION VS. GOVERNMENT AUTHORITY	.30	.09	-.70	-.11	.04	-.04
FACTOR 3.2 TWO REGIONS VS. THREE REGIONS	.06	.09	.81	.04	-.11	.07
3010 DECENTRALISATION (RESIDUAL)	.46	-.08	-.32	.00	-.19	.35
3012 TWO REGIONS	.04	-.06	-.74	-.07	-.04	.01
3013 THREE REGIONS	.36	-.02	.20	-.09	-.29	.29
303 GOVERNMENT EFFICIENCY	-.05	-.29	.21	.14	-.01	.32
DOMAIN FOUR: ECONOMICS						
FACTOR 4.1 LEFT VERSUS RIGHT	-.66	-.36	-.02	-.10	-.26	.28
FACTOR 4.2 PRODUCTIVITY: HIGH/LOW CONCERN	-.10	-.08	-.16	.07	.86	.10
401 FREE ENTERPRISE	-.47	-.31	.08	-.14	-.10	.13
402 INCENTIVES	-.20	-.05	-.11	-.17	.53	.17
403 REGULATION OF CAPITALISM	.42	.26	-.02	-.15	-.12	.12
404 ECONOMIC PLANNING	.37	.20	.02	.01	.42	-.26
4080 SPECIFIC ECONOMIC GOALS (RESIDUAL)	-.02	.29	.46	.16	-.13	-.10
4081 FULL EMPLOYMENT	.03	.08	.11	-.01	.20	.13
410 PRODUCTIVITY	-.19	-.21	-.08	.10	.74	-.12
411 TECHNOLOGY AND INFRASTRUCTURE	.02	.21	.13	.26	.42	.09
414 ECONOMIC ORTHODOXY AND EFFICIENCY	-.57	-.15	-.08	-.10	.13	.12
DOMAIN FIVE: WELFARE						
FACTOR 5.1 SOCIAL SERVICES/JUSTICE	.05	-.00	.09	.12	-.08	-.85
FACTOR 5.2 CULTURE AND ENVIRONMENT	.21	.76	-.00	-.17	.26	.05
501 ENVIRONMENTAL PROTECTION	.35	.48	-.14	-.28	.02	.32
502 ART, SPORT, LEISURE, MEDIA	.08	.66	.06	-.24	.16	.01
503 SOCIAL JUSTICE	-.07	-.04	-.10	.04	-.04	-.73
504 SOCIAL SERVICES EXPANSION: POSITIVE	.03	.05	-.04	.15	.00	-.76
506 EDUCATION EXPANSION: POSITIVE	-.10	.51	.08	-.02	.39	-.34
DOMAIN SIX: SOCIAL FABRIC						
FACTOR 6.1 CLERICALISM	.35	-.65	.29	-.14	.23	-.06
FACTOR 6.2 CULTURAL AUTONOMY	.47	-.18	-.46	.30	-.30	.21
601 NATIONAL WAY OF LIFE: POSITIVE	-.37	.12	.23	-.11	.25	-.23
602 NATIONAL WAY OF LIFE: NEGATIVE	-.07	-.19	-.26	.09	-.19	-.02
603 TRADITIONAL MORALITY: POSITIVE	.24	-.41	.20	-.13	.31	-.11
6061 SOCIAL HARMONY	.23	-.55	.32	-.15	.02	.05
6070 COMMUNALISM: POSITIVE	.23	-.58	.13	-.04	.21	-.15
6072 CULTURAL AUTONOMY	.46	-.03	-.40	.24	-.27	.26
608 COMMUNALISM: NEGATIVE	-.03	.02	-.16	.17	-.31	.09
DOMAIN SEVEN: SOCIAL GROUPS						
FACTOR 7.1 TRADITIONAL WELFARE TARGETS	.07	.69	.36	.18	-.19	-.19
FACTOR 7.2 BOURGEOIS GROUPS/WOMEN	-.52	-.05	.05	.06	.08	.17
701 LABOUR GROUPS	-.23	.26	.34	.17	-.09	-.17
703 FARMERS AND AGRICULTURE	-.44	.02	.01	.28	.12	-.12
7041 "MIDDLE CLASSES"	-.51	.01	.14	.10	-.02	.21
705 UNDERPRIVILEGED MINORITIES	-.17	.55	.14	.05	.13	-.16
7061 FLEMINGS AND FLANDERS	-.03	-.23	-.51	-.04	-.13	.05
7062 WALLOONS AND WALLONIE	.32	-.17	.03	-.01	-.11	.22
7063 BRUXELLOIS AND BRUSSELS	.24	.07	.13	-.10	-.13	.23
7065 YOUTH	-.03	.52	.32	.06	-.20	-.07
7066 OLD PEOPLE	.21	.53	.27	.08	-.23	-.12
7067 WOMEN	-.04	.45	.12	-.04	-.11	.11

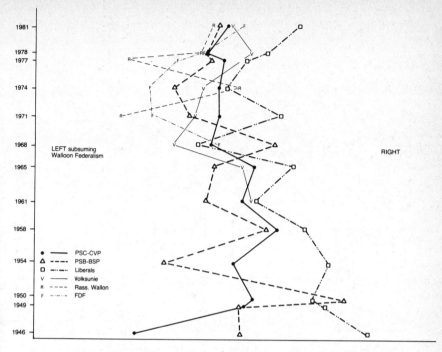

11.1 Movement of Belgian parties over time on the left-right dimension

whelmingly concerned with the issue of Freedom and Human Rights; Factor 5 with Productivity and Factor 6 with Social Services and Social Justice, all of course 'valence' issues which no political party is ever likely to oppose.

11.8 SPATIAL MOVEMENT OF BELGIAN PARTIES

We now turn to an examination of how each party has moved over time in terms of the first three second-stage factors. Post-war Belgian politics fall into two clearly differentiated periods – up to and including 1958; and from 1961 onwards. During the first period, it was the Left–Right and Clerical/ Anti-Clerical Dimensions that were most salient; after 1961 the latter was increasingly edged out by the Federalist–Unitarist Dimension. Results reflect this.

Not surprisingly Figure 11.1 shows that the Liberals have nearly always been the most 'right-wing' party in terms of Factor 1 and the Socialists the most 'Left'. The PSC–CVP, which began its post-war life with the very 'Labourist' programme reflected in the graph, almost immediately took up

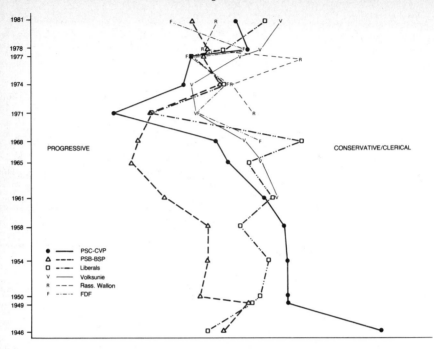

11.2 Movement of Belgian parties over time on the 'progressive vs. conservative'
general dimension

the centrist position with which it has subsequently been identified. Among
Federalist parties, the VU is virtually always to the Right of the other two
and the RW to the Left. The only exception is in 1974 when the latter was
seeking to modify its left-wing image. Perhaps the only thing which is
surprising about the patterns shown in Figure 11.1 is that the VU does not
appear as right-wing as popular opinion has always perceived it to be, and
this is confirmed by the fact that it does not appear with a sharply
'Conservative' profile in Figure 11.2. Indeed, until 1978 it was actually
outflanked by the RW, although this seems to have been due to the
moderation of its position in the years of greatest electoral advance. The
traditional party positions are however more clearly differentiated on a
dimension which was in the past most clearly associated with them and not
really with the federalists at all. At the end of the war it was still the
Liberals who were the most anti-clerical or 'progressive' but they soon
began to move towards the 'conservative' pole continuing to do so until
1969 after which year they moved sharply back again. In the meantime, the
PSC–CVP steadily abandoned its clerical position, until in 1971 it
appeared as the *least* conservative party in Belgium!

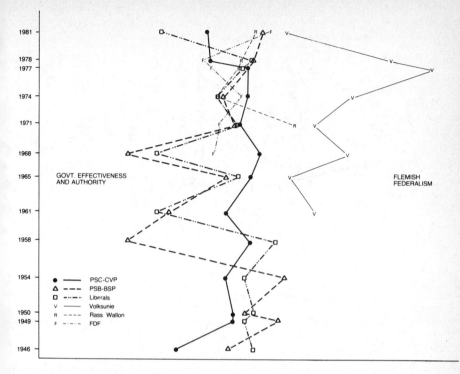

11.3 Movement of Belgian parties over time on the federalist-unitarist dimension

However, it is the relative placings of the three traditional parties at each of the first five post-war elections which matter in terms of this particular Dimension since it was then that it was at its most salient. The post-war revival of the old Catholic Party in its new guise as the PSC–CVP can clearly be seen as can the Liberal and Socialist Parties' shared commitment to anti-clericalism. Apart from a shift away from extreme anti-clericalism by the Liberals' over the ensuing twelve years, this pattern remained reasonably constant until after the conclusion of the Schools Pact following the 1958 election. Thereafter, the various paths traced by the different parties began to fluctuate wildly as the importance of the dimension diminishes. Nevertheless, a broad secular trend away from the clerical position is apparent for all parties, albeit attenuated for a time by the Liberals' attempt to attract the right wing PSC–CVP vote following their change of name in 1961.

The third second-stage factor, that associated with Flemish Federalism (Figure 11.3) also shows clear and generally explicable movements by the various parties, provided one bears in mind the complex nature of the

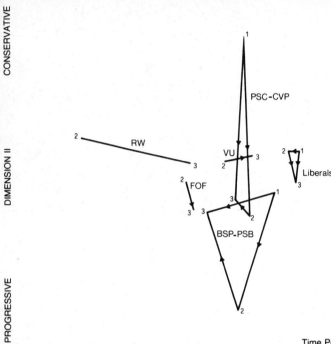

11.4 Spatial locations of Belgian parties on the two leading dimensions

so-called 'Community Cleavage' of which this factor is one manifestation. There are really two sub-cleavages involved, one opposing Federalist and Unitarist ideas about the organization of the Belgian State, and one opposing Flemish to Walloon and Brussels interests. The present analysis has probably not successfully disentangled these two despite the association between certain Francophone concerns and the left pole of Factor 1.

At first sight, for example, it seems that the VU became *more* federalist in the years following 1971 and less so in 1978 in spite of the fact that other evidence indicates the opposite. However, the RW simultaneously traced out a mirror image of the VU's path over the same period. It was precisely at the moment when the opposition between the two communities was at its sharpest that the two parties appear furthest apart on Factor 3. In other words the dimension is picking up the Flemish–Francophone conflict *as well as* the Federalist–Unitarist one but with a common pole in Flemish Federalism. Seen in this light, one would expect to find parties which are as *federalist* as the VU but not as Flemish to lie somewhere in the middle of the factor and parties which are anti-federalist (and hence not so Flemish) at the other extreme. If this explanation is accepted the pattern becomes readily interpretable.

The VU is at all times the most 'Flemish Federalist' party while the RW initially found itself in a similar position in 1971 before taking up an anti-Flemish although still federalist stance much closer to that of the FDF in subsequent years. It is clear that it is the least committed of the three Federalist parties to the concept. Insofar as the traditional parties are concerned the PSC–CVP has for most of the post-1961 period been the closest to the VU position – which is certainly plausible; while the Liberals and Socialists have been the most Unitarist in their attitudes. The quite extreme positions taken up by these parties in 1968 at the time of the 'Louvain election' is very striking as is the Liberals' reassertion of such a stance in 1981. Similarly, the Socialists' general drift toward the federalist position after 1974 accords well with recent political events culminating in the split between the party's two linguistic wings in 1978.

Putting the first two dimensions together we get a very neat picture in which each of the main parties occupies a very distinctive space, with little overlapping. The closeness of the VU to the Christian–Socials is confirmed. All parties were closer in the late 1970s than they were in the 1950s.

11.9 FACTOR ANALYSIS WITHIN THE LINGUISTIC COMMUNITIES

This latter point brings us, however, to the one important caveat which needs to be made about the entire analysis. It will be remembered that 'composite' manifestos had been computed for each of the three traditional political 'families' precisely in order to avoid certain problems associated with the division along linguistic lines in recent years. While this is reasonable, the procedure nonetheless has the effect of masking significant variations not only within the traditional political families but also between the linguistic communities themselves. Consequently two further analyses have been carried out and these are reported briefly below.

Firstly, the 'composite' programmes for those elections where a political 'family' had actually published two (or more) were disaggregated into their component parts and the analysis run again using precisely the same procedures and criteria as those employed in the principal analysis. The resultant second-stage factor solution was markedly different.

Six second-stage factors were produced of which the first three account for virtually half the total variance. The first factor loads on all those variables associated with Walloon and *Bruxellois* demands for Federalism with Three Regions and accounts for 16.0 per cent of the variance. The

second is the Flemish equivalent of the first, i.e. it is Federalism with Two
Regions and accounts for 15.7 per cent of the common variance. The
remaining factors were fairly easily interpretable; the third is Economic
Left–Right, the fourth Non-Economic Left–Right, the fifth is the equiv-
alent – albeit not so precisely defined – of the Conservative/Clerical–
Progressive dimension found earlier, and the sixth is the Freedom and
Human Rights factor which was also found in the principal analysis.

The major finding of this analysis therefore is that when the traditional
parties are not aggregated into families, the complex Federalist-Unitarist
dimension breaks up into two straightforward – and uncorrelated –
dimensions, one relevant to the Flemish Community, the other to the
Francophone.

The striking feature of movement on these is the very limited extent to
which each traditional political family has entered the Federalist half of the
dimension. Certainly there have been incursions but they appear to have
been 'one-offs' associated with particular events (such as the PSC's sudden
adoption of Francophone Federalism in 1968 at the time of the Louvain
election). But the overwhelming impression remains that, in fact, the
various wings of the traditional parties have not drifted very far apart from
one another even in terms of the very issues on which they might have been
expected to do so.

The fact that two simple although different Federalist–Unitarist factors
are produced by this analysis clearly indicates that an analysis carried out
at the level of the linguistic community itself would produce an even
simpler structure. Accordingly, the third and final analysis was conducted
for each of the two communities using only those programmes which had
been presented by the parties to the community concerned.

A simple and clear Federalist–Unitarist dimension was indeed produced
inside each community. In the Francophone case it was the first second-
stage factor, and accounted for 22.7 per cent of the variance; in the Flemish
case it was the second second-stage factor accounting for 14.6 per cent of
the variance. In each case, the most important remaining factor was a very
clear Left–Right one accounting for 22.7 per cent of the Flemish variance
and 15.2 per cent of the Francophone.

11.10 CONCLUSIONS

There is no doubt that the analysis of Belgian electoral programmes has
been very successful. Notwithstanding the many difficulties from the
increasingly complicated nature of the polity in the post-1961 period, as
well as early doubts about the reliability of some of the documentary
evidence (especially given the widespread belief in Belgium that party
programmes are not taken seriously by the parties), clear and interpretable

results have emerged. Furthermore, these results accord broadly with what other evidence would lead us to expect. The satisfying conclusion must be that they *are* valid and that we now have a rich and exciting data set with considerable potential for the further analysis of Belgian political history over the post-war period.

Note

1 I am deeply indebted to many people, both in Belgium and elsewhere, who helped in various ways with this research. In particular, without the extremely valuable and efficient assistance given by the following party Research Institute staff, the work could not have been undertaken at all: Mw M. Aerts of the Christian-Social Research Institute, CEPESS; Mr Oscar Debunne and Mw Y. Pauwels of the (Socialist) Emile Vandervelde Instituut; Messrs. J. De Meyer and J. Engels of the Liberal Paul Hymans Instituut; and Mw L. De Boel of the Volksunie. In addition, I was very grateful for the opportunity to meet and discuss the research with the Presidents of the CVP and FDF, Mr Leo Tindemans and Mme Antoinette Spaak, both of whom give me far more of their time and attention than I deserved.

Finally, of course, I owe a considerable debt to my friends and colleagues in the ECPR Research Group on Party Programmes and Manifestos. It has been a stimulating experience working with them.

CHAPTER 12

LUXEMBOURG 1945–1982
DIMENSIONS AND STRATEGIES

———— ⌒ ————

12.1 THE PARTY SYSTEM

Luxembourg is a small Grand Duchy of approximately 365,000 inhabitants situated between Belgium, Federal Germany and France. Its experience of competitive party politics goes back to the foundation of a 'Catholic Action Committee' to contest the 1848 elections in opposition to the then 'Liberal' hegemony in Parliament. The first socialist deputy was elected in 1896, while the country's first proper political party, the 'Social Democratic Party of Luxembourg', was founded in 1902. By 1914, the forerunners of today's three main parties, one Socialist, one Liberal, and one Christian-Democrat, were all fully organized. Since 1919 they have contested elections on the basis of universal suffrage, and have virtually monopolized Government. Of the others, only the Communists survived as a parliamentary party for the entire post-war period. However, they only participated in government once (the so-called 'Government of National Union' from 1946 to 1947). The Christian Social Party, CSV, led every post-war government until 1974; while the other two – the Socialists and Liberals – neatly alternated as the CSV's junior coalition partners in response to their varying fortunes at the polls.

As in Belgium, this deeply entrenched four-party system was rooted in a two-dimensional structure among the electorate which superimposed the newer socio-economic class cleavage upon the older clerical/anti–clerical one which had given birth to the original two-party system. Over the past twenty years, however, two important changes have taken place.

(*i*) The Socialist Party split in the late 1960s between its increasingly leftist-oriented, trade union dominated majority faction and its more moderate reformist leadership. The latter formed themselves into a new 'Social Democratic Party' with an apparently high degree of popular enthusiasm in 1970. In 1979 however they gained only 6.6 per cent of the vote and seemed a spent force. In early 1984 their remaining two deputies joined the CSV and shortly afterwards the party was formally dissolved.

(*ii*) There was also a slow shift in the relative policy positions of the Christian Democrats and the Liberals, similar to that experienced in West Germany. With the decline of church attendance, especially during the 1960s, the Liberals began to appreciate the dangers of being 'trapped' in a relatively right–wing position, with no coalition alternative to being junior partner to the Christian Democrats. While anti-clericalism was still a unifying force, there had at least been potential for an alternative Socialist–Liberal coalition from which the Christian-Social Party might be excluded. This threat ensured the Liberals an influence which their relatively weak electoral position could not. Once deconfessionalization began however, the Christian-Social Party lost substantial numbers of working-class voters to the Socialists, and a process of 'polarization' between the two big parties began to take place. In reaction to this the Liberals, under the guidance of a new, relatively young, progressive leadership, became more centrist as the two major parties moved to the left and right respectively. Whereas, even fifteen years ago, the Luxembourg party system resembled the old Belgian (or present-day Dutch) one, today it is essentially similar to that of West Germany, apart from the greater percentage vote for the Luxembourg Communists.

12.2 THE PARTIES TODAY

The Christian Social Party (*Chrëstlech Sozial Vollekspartei*, CSV), is the largest party. In spite of its transformation from a classic, centrist, main stream Christian Democratic Party akin to the Belgian, it remains conservative on traditional moral questions and continues to enjoy support from the great majority of practising Catholics. It is increasingly middle-class – committed to the market economy, to NATO, to the defence of Western values, to financial rectitude, and efficient and effective government. It is the strongest party in the rural East and North of the country but runs a poor second to the Socialists in the heavily industrialized South. Since the war its vote has varied between a high of just under 50 per cent in 1954 to a low of 30 per cent in 1974.[1])

The Luxembourg Socialist Workers Party (*Lëtzeburger Sozialistesch Arbechter Partei*, LSAP) overtook the Liberals electorally in 1919, and ran second to the CSV until 1979 (when it took only 20.4 per cent of the vote and dropped again into third place). The party has a strong Trade Union and working class base, from which it draws activists and MPs though there is no formal link with the Unions. It gains votes in all areas of the country although its main strength lies in the industrial areas, especially those of the South where the Grand Duchy's massive steel industry is concentrated. Here, however, the LSAP is in competition with the Communists who have also been traditionally strong in this region. The party is concerned mostly with wages, prices, pensions and welfare benefits, with housing and schools, and with the interests of labour groups generally.

The *Demokratesch Partei*, DP, or Democratic Party, is the post-war successor of the old Liberal Party, and inherited its anticlerical, rather right-wing image. As noted above it became more of a 'social-Liberal' party of the political centre during the late 1960s, and today more closely resembles its German and British cousins than the 'classic' stream of continental Liberalism. Electorally, this move was highly successful. Its parliamentary representation increased at three successive elections so that in 1979 it overtook the LSAP to become the second party in the *Châmber vun Députéirten*. It dominated the 1974–9 government, the first to exclude the CSV since 1926 and only the second to do so since before World War I. The DP vote seems to be firmly entrenched in the 'new' middle-class; among white-collar workers, executives, etc., especially in the new service industries which have been growing apace in recent years. Its greatest electoral strength is consequently in the better off suburbs and the commuter belt around Luxembourg City itself, although there is still a traditional following in the rural East and North constituencies.

The Communist Party of Luxembourg (*Kommunistesch Partei vu Lëtzeburg*, KPL) is a still largely unreconstructed pro-Soviet party with very deep roots in a section of the working-class population. It has been described as the most obscurantist in Western Europe. It has long had a strong local government base in parts of the South. Its vote has always been high for an industrialized Northern European country ranging from 5.0 per cent in 1979 to as much as 13 per cent in 1968, when it seems to have benefited from LSAP unpopularity.

12.3 THE ELECTORAL SYSTEM

Luxembourg possesses a unique and ingenious electoral system (described in Majerus 1976) which not only ensures party proportionality but also makes every successful candidate's seat dependent upon his or her personal vote rather than upon party preferment. This is achieved by a List system in which there is no preordained order of candidates, the necessary ordering being determined *after* the election solely according to the number of personal votes each candidate receives. Voters are not however compelled to cast personal votes (as they are in some other systems) having instead the opportunity to cast an unordered List vote. At most post-war elections a majority has opted for this course. This system makes elected *Députéirten* very conscious of particular constituency concerns and leads to a degree of 'clientelism' since they must continue to collect the vital personal votes upon which their seats depend.

12.4 DRAFTING PARTY PROGRAMMES

All political parties in Luxembourg present detailed party programmes at election times and circulate them widely. They fulfill three functions. Firstly, they give coherence to a party's election campaign – all its candidates being expected to support them. Secondly, they are intended as vote-catching devices containing what it is hoped are popular proposals. Finally, they provide some kind of anchor for a party's post-election activity whether in government (or coalition-making) or in opposition. They are significant elements in the Grand Duchy's political process. Partly due to the fact that Luxembourg Parliaments run for the whole of their statutory five year life, procedures for Programme drafting are lengthy and complex in all parties.

The 1979 LSAP Manifesto, for example, took two years to prepare. In 1977 the Party's National Executive appointed an *ad hoc* Programme Committee consisting of party officers, party officials and a number of *députéirten*, which over some half dozen or so meetings, drew up a first draft. This draft was first submitted to the National Executive for discussion and amendment and then to the party's branches and affiliated organizations throughout the country for their comments and proposed amendments on the basis of which the *ad hoc* Committee drew up a second draft. Again, the Party executive considered the draft and slightly amended it before submitting it to a specially convened Party Congress. The latter's decision is final and can by no means be taken for granted by the leadership whose advice is sometimes overruled (as in 1974, for example, when a proposal to introduce free public transport was adopted by the LSAP Congress).

Similar procedures are followed by the other major parties although, in the case of the DP at least, active involvement by the Congress is of relatively recent origin. However, in both the CSV and the DP it is the parties' policy 'working groups' (which more or less correspond to Parliamentary Committees) which drew up the initial proposals within their own spheres of competence. Consequently, the Programme Committees can be smaller since they have more of an editorial than a policy-initiation role than is the case in the LSAP.

It is perhaps less often the case in the CSV and the DP that the Party Congress defies the leadership – at any rate on important points. Rather, the delegates tend to spend much of their time and energy debating highly controversial but nonetheless peripheral issues while allowing complex matters of economic policy to go through 'on the nod'. (Indeed, it is an open secret that party leaderships are not always above deliberately including such issues precisely in order to divert the Congress' attention from the economic and fiscal parts of the programme. The DP leadership is alleged to have done this in 1979 when it proposed the granting of voting rights to foreign residents.)

12.5 CIRCULATION AND USE OF PROGRAMMES

Election Programmes are widely circulated. In 1979, for example, the LSAP had some 25,000 copies printed and the DP 30,000 while the CSV printed enough to be able to deliver one to every household in the country which implies a total print run of around 100,000. The documents are traditionally circulated to all party members, given to everyone who attends an election meeting (of which each party holds anything up to 200 or so) as well as to anyone who requests one. In addition, they usually appear in full in the party press. The documents are mostly well and attractively printed and contain quite specific policy pledges which the party in question is committed to implement so far as it can if it enters the subsequent Government. Consequently, following each election, Election Programmes become the guidelines for coalition negotiations and there is no doubt that programme contents are sometimes affected by coalition expectations. For example, in 1974 the LSAP clearly (although as it turned out wrongly) expected to be staying in opposition and so its demands were thought to be exaggerated. In 1979, the reverse occurred; the party expected to stay in Government and the Congress was consequently persuaded by the leadership not to insist on the 35 hour week which many delegates wanted to do. Similarly, the DP appears to have deliberately taken a line on the issue of state finance for 'private' (e.g. Catholic) schools which, while not being anathema to the CSV, could nonetheless be negotiated with the LSAP thereby keeping its coalition options open in 1979.

12.6 COLLECTING AND CODING THE DOCUMENTS

There are thus no problems in identifying documents to use in the analysis. However, none of the parties has any proper archiving system and consequently only those relating to the last two (or at most three) elections are available from them. But, Luxembourg does have a highly partisan national press. Three of the main parties, i.e. the LSAP, the DP and the KPL actually own daily newspapers while the CSV has regular inside pages under its own editorial control in the country's principal paper, the *Luxemburger Wort*, itself the property of the Catholic Church. Naturally enough, these newspapers print the full texts of the programmes of the party with which they are associated and all of them are fully archived both at the *Archives de l'Etat* and at the *Bibliothèque Nationale*.

Using these sources to supplement the few original copies obtained for recent elections from the various party Headquarters, full texts were obtained for 21 out of a potential 36 manifestos together with seven acceptable surrogates. The latter consist either of special editorials or articles in the newspaper in question designed to perform much the same function as the party programme and drawn from it or, in three cases, the full texts of the party leader's radio speech again clearly drawn from the party's programme. All but one of these surrogates are from the pre-1958 period. Finally, no Communist Programme was traced for 1974 although an approach to the KPL headquarters elicited a copy of a new *Grundsatzprogramm* adopted in 1973; it appears that it was this document upon which KPL ran the following year and it has been included in the analysis accordingly. No documents for the DP's predecessor, the *Groupement Patriotique et démocratique* were traced for the years 1945 and 1948 since the 'Groupement' was not organized as a political party being a purely parliamentary group at the time.

Virtually all the documents, including some with Luxembourgish titles, are in German, the only exceptions being two of the three radio speeches, which are in Luxembourgish (the third having been translated into German before publication). With these two exceptions, therefore, the entire set of programmes was coded by a German-speaking Research Assistant (Fenwick) while remaining texts were translated and coded by Hearl. No inter-coder reliability checks were conducted. A full list of the documents used in the analysis appears in Appendix A.

The standard coding frame worked well for Luxembourg after one or two additional sub-categories had been identified, all in the Social Groups domain. They were Railwaymen (who are a powerful force in Labour politics in Luxembourg), Viticulture and Wine Growers, the so-called 'Middle Classes' (i.e. essentially the Self-Employed), as well as Youth, Old People and Women. Each of these sub-categories scored more than 1.0 per cent of overall mentions and consequently qualified for inclusion in the standard analysis.

12.7 GENERAL ANALYSIS

Table 12.1 shows the mean scores and standard deviations for each category and sub-category rank-ordered by overall importance, for those which qualify for inclusion in the factor analysis. (The criteria are the standard ones used throughout this volume, 1.0 per cent overall or 3.0 per cent for any one party.) The Table also shows the means and standard deviations for each of the four principal parties.

First impressions are of a political system in which there is a fairly high degree of agreement between the three parties of government but clear differences between each of them and the Communist Party. The latter

TABLE 12.1

LUXEMBOURG: LEADING CATEGORIES ORDERED OVERALL AND FOR EACH PARTY

CATEGORY		ALL MANIFESTOS (N=33)		CSV (N=9)		LSAP (N=9)		DP (N=7)		KLP (N=8)	
		X̄	SD	X̄	SD	X̄	SD	X̄	SD	X̄	SD
503	SOCIAL JUSTICE	7.44	4.62	5.61	4.09	9.19	5.79	6.67	2.77	8.21	4.90
504	SOCIAL SERVICES EXPANSION: POSITIVE	7.11	5.39	7.30	4.41	9.54	5.44	8.98	5.76	2.52	3.64
506	EDUCATION EXPANSION: POSITIVE	4.67	5.46	5.40	3.91	7.42	7.78	4.02	4.40	1.34	3.10
7010	LABOUR GROUPS (RESIDUAL)	4.63	5.13	2.44	1.95	4.17	2.69	1.70	1.36	10.18	7.45
7040	OTHER ECONOMIC GROUPS (RESIDUAL)	4.40	5.67	3.75	4.63	4.23	6.61	7.32	7.81	2.76	2.84
105	MILITARY: NEGATIVE	4.18	7.33	0.25	0.48	5.69	8.41	0.75	0.90	9.91	9.58
7030	FARMERS/AGRICULTURE (RESIDUAL)	3.96	3.23	5.17	3.48	3.89	2.76	5.25	3.51	1.53	2.04
202	DEMOCRACY	3.76	3.26	2.88	2.09	5.68	3.81	4.26	2.29	2.16	3.68
404	ECONOMIC PLANNING	3.19	12.88	2.09	2.72	0.83	1.03	0.68	0.84	2.29	26.28
7041	"MIDDLE CLASSES" (I.E. SELF EMPLOYED)	3.17	3.10	3.03	2.19	2.58	2.02	5.08	5.35	2.32	2.06
603	TRADITIONAL MORALITY: POSITIVE	2.77	5.63	9.65	7.27	0.22	0.62	0.36	0.47	0.00	0.00
403	REGULATION OF CAPITALISM	2.73	4.17	1.35	1.28	3.24	3.53	0.95	0.97	5.27	7.03
502	ART, SPORT, LEISURE, MEDIA	2.56	3.02	4.15	3.26	2.06	3.06	3.72	2.97	0.32	0.78
201	FREEDOM/DOMESTIC HUMAN RIGHTS	2.29	3.61	1.26	0.91	3.30	4.93	4.42	4.68	0.43	0.86
411	TECHNOLOGY AND INFRASTRUCTURE	2.26	3.44	1.57	1.75	3.81	4.18	3.72	4.70	0.02	0.06
412	CONTROLLED ECONOMY	2.01	2.83	1.72	2.97	3.42	3.80	1.60	1.75	1.10	1.92
7061	YOUTH	2.01	3.47	4.37	5.86	1.26	1.33	1.14	1.19	0.94	1.62
601	NATIONAL WAY OF LIFE: POSITIVE	1.74	3.69	2.23	4.07	2.28	5.70	0.93	1.21	1.30	1.81
705	UNDERPRIVILEGED MINORITIES	1.61	1.79	2.28	2.01	1.53	1.43	0.61	0.61	1.82	2.38
101	FOREIGN SPECIAL RELATIONSHIPS: POSITIVE	1.53	1.74	2.14	1.72	0.68	0.71	1.73	1.81	1.67	2.36
408	SPEC. ECONOMIC GOALS (I.E. FULL EMPLOY.)	1.52	1.92	0.60	0.98	2.73	2.46	2.07	1.95	0.73	1.23
102	FOREIGN SPECIAL RELATIONSHIPS:NEGATIVE	1.45	2.93	0.77	1.98	0.28	0.62	0.78	1.54	4.10	4.65
501	ENVIRONMENTAL PROTECTION	1.42	2.42	2.06	2.12	1.27	2.51	2.39	3.54	0.02	0.06

Continued...

TABLE 12.1 Continued...

		X̄	SD	X̄	SD	X̄	SD	X̄	SD	X̄	SD
402	INCENTIVES	1.37	1.78	3.26	1.99	0.75	0.88	1.32	1.49	0.00	0.00
606	NATIONAL EFFORT/SOCIAL HARMONY	1.18	1.94	1.42	1.57	1.64	2.77	0.94	1.91	0.60	1.29
108	EUROPEAN COMMUNITY: POSITIVE	1.15	2.03	1.57	3.11	1.16	1.66	1.91	1.65	0.00	0.00
7011	RAILWAYMEN	1.15	2.10	1.29	1.75	1.08	2.21	0.89	1.19	1.30	3.11
304	GOVERNMENT CORRUPTION	1.12	4.35	0.06	0.12	0.00	0.00	1.60	3.39	3.17	8.27
414	ECONOMIC ORTHODOXY	1.10	1.48	1.11	1.14	0.59	1.27	1.09	1.04	1.67	2.24
106	PEACE	1.01	2.22	0.33	0.34	0.34	0.54	0.36	0.62	3.12	3.87
410	PRODUCTIVITY	1.01	1.65	0.53	0.64	2.19	2.65	1.08	0.99	0.15	0.42
7031	WINE GROWERS/VITICULTURE	1.00	1.77	1.84	2.71	0.64	1.33	1.45	1.33	0.00	0.00
110	EUROPEAN COMMUNITY: NEGATIVE	0.80	2.45	0.00	0.00	0.05	0.16	0.04	0.10	3.22	4.31

puts considerable emphasis upon a number of highly idiosyncratic issues such as, for example, Economic Planning, xenophobic attacks on Foreign Special Relations and the European Community, and on Peace, while the former share a common concern with such issues as Social Services Expansion, Social Justice, Education Expansion, Farmers and Agriculture and Other Economic Groups. Nevertheless, there are clear (and expected) inter-party differences between the three principal parties as well. The CSV's 'top ten' profile is dominated by positive remarks about Traditional Morality; the LSAP not only puts more emphasis than any other party on Social Services Expansion but is the only one of the three to have strong negative emphases on the Military and to emphasize Labour Groups among its 'top ten' (although, not unnaturally, it does share the last two with the KPL). The DP, for its part, lays particular stress upon the so-called 'Middle Classes' and upon Democracy, both issues associated with Liberal Parties elsewhere. Its very high placing of Social Services Expansion and Social Justice together with its marked lack of emphasis upon right-wing economic issues marks it out as a Liberal Party in the 'Social-Liberal' mould more akin to, say, its British and German equivalents than to its Dutch or Belgian ones.

12.8 FIRST-STAGE FACTOR ANALYSIS

The standard two-stage factor analysis applied generally throughout this volume used those categories and sub-categories which appear in Table 12.1. The domains of Freedom and Democracy and Government were not factored during the first-stage since only two and one categories respectively, qualified for inclusion. In these cases the original variables are input directly to the second stage.

Domain 1 (Foreign Relations) produced three first-stage factors accounting for 33.4 per cent, 24.8 per cent and 21.3 per cent of the common variance respectively. After rotation, all three appear as unipolar each loading overwhelmingly upon two categories. The first is opposition to Foreign Special Relationships in general (a loading of .93) and to the European Community in particular (.86). The second, loading almost equally on Military: Negative (.86) and Peace (.87), has been labelled after the latter. The third is the counterpart to the first, Foreign Relations: Positive (.87), while European Community Positive has a loading of .71.

Domain 4 (Economics) is not quite so straightforward, in that the expected Left–Right dimension does not emerge. (This is not an artefact of the exclusion of Free Enterprise. An additional analysis was carried out incorporating this variable and no significant changes emerged). Factor 4.1 is a matter of Employment (Special Economic Goals (.86) consisting overwhelmingly of this issue in practice) and of Productivity (.83). Factor 4.2, loading both on the typically right-wing Incentives (.71) *and* the left-wing Controlled Economy (.59), only makes sense as one associated with state intervention in the economy in the interest of Technology and Infrastructure (upon which it also loads heavily at .65) and it has been so labelled. Factor 4.3 opposes Regulation of Capitalism (.63) and Economic Orthodoxy (.60) to Economic Planning (−.71), a slightly odd result though this is perhaps regulation in its American sense rather than a Socialist one. It is the third factor in the domain, however, accounting for only 15.4 per cent of the variance, and not entering into the second-stage analysis. The other two factors account for 23.8 per cent and 16.9 per cent of the variance respectively.

Domain 5 (Welfare) gives a more satisfactory result. Two factors accounting for 44.2 per cent and 20.2 per cent of the variance are produced. The first of these is very clearly a 'Culture and Environment' factor in which Environmental Protection (.83), Art, Sport, Leisure and Media (.72) and Education Expansion (.76) load heavily while the other opposes Social Justice (−.75) to Social Service Expansion (.73), a not unexpected finding given that these are the only two categories left after controlling for Factor 5.1. Again however we encounter the opposition of aspirations for Social Justice to practical Social Services, which has appeared in other countries.

Domain 6 (Social Fabric), gives an even simpler result. This time only one factor explaining fully 54.6 per cent of the variance is produced, loading on all three categories in the analysis but particularly strongly on two of them – National Way of Life (.88) and National Effort/Social Harmony (.84). It has been labelled 'National Way of Life and Effort'. The fact that it also loads positively on Traditional Morality (.38) should not be surprising. It is, after all, a combination between the three categories factored here that is so distinctive about Christian Democratic values not only in Luxembourg but also in many other European countries.

In contrast to the simplicity of Domain 6, the first-stage analysis of Domain 7 (Social Groups) is more complex. Five factors are produced, three of which are unipolar and two bipolar. Since only ten categories went into the initial analysis, this solution can hardly be said to be parsimonious. Of the two factors which will be fed to the second-stage analysis, the first accounts for 26.3 per cent of the variance and loads on a package of categories that generally represent the more bourgeois elements in society. The second accounts for 17.6 per cent of the variance and opposes the interests of Old People (.84) and Railwaymen (.77) on the one hand to those of Youth (−.43) on the other.

12.9 SECOND-STAGE FACTOR ANALYSIS

In the second-stage analysis the nine first-stage factors and the three original categories were factor analysed using an unrotated solution which proved to be the more easily interpretable. This was because the Varimax

TABLE 12.2

LUXEMBOURG: SECOND-ORDER FACTOR ANALYSIS LOADINGS OF FIRST-ORDER FACTORS

UNROTATED FACTOR MATRIX

FIRST STAGE FACTORS		FACTOR 1 NEW ISSUES VS. ISOLATIONISM	FACTOR 2 DEMOCRACY, FREEDOM, SOCIAL JUSTICE	FACTOR 3 CONCERN FOR SOCIAL GROUPS AND POSITIVE FOREIGN RELATIONS	FACTOR 4 NATIONAL WAY OF LIFE	FACTOR 5 THE PEACE ISSUE
F1.1	FOREIGN RELATIONS: NEGATIVE	-.49	.08	.80	-.24	.23
F1.2	PEACE	-.56	-.07	.14	-.10	-.74
× 201	FREEDOM AND HUMAN RIGHTS	.12	.58	.25	-.06	.01
× 202	DEMOCRACY	.43	.59	.04	-.22	.08
× 304	GOVERNMENT CORRUPTION	-.28	-.24	.43	-.29	.34
F4.1	EMPLOYMENT AND PRODUCTIVITY	.10	.29	.07	.48	.04
F4.2	STAGE INTERVENTION	.73	-.38	.05	.05	-.09
F5.1	CULTURE AND ENVIRONMENT	.76	-.05	-.13	-.26	-.12
F5.2	SOCIAL SERVICES VERSUS SOCIAL JUSTICE	.18	-.50	-.09	.31	.15
F6.1	NATIONAL WAY OF LIFE	-.21	.19	-.01	.70	.07
F7.1	BOURGEOIS GROUPS	-.17	-.23	.20	-.00	.15
F7.2	OLD PEOPLE AND R'WAYMEN VERSUS YOUTH	-.31	.02	.45	-.17	.24
	EIGEN VALUES	2.46	1.84	1.64	1.48	1.05
	% OF VARIANCE	20.5%	15.3%	13.6%	12.4%	8.7%

× ORIGINAL VARIABLES DIRECTLY INPUT TO SECOND-STAGE ANALYSIS

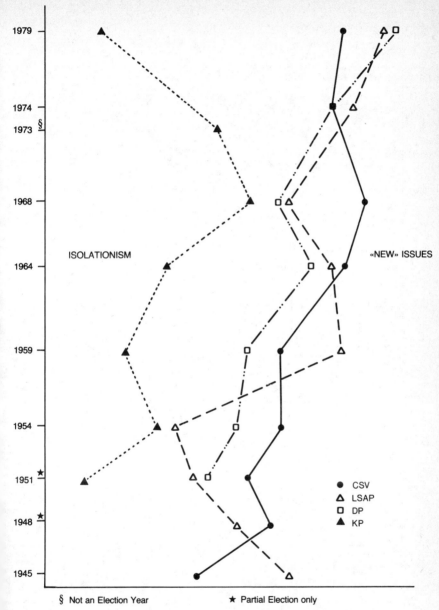

§ Not an Election Year   ★ Partial Election only

12.1 Second-stage factor 1 by election year: isolationism vs. new issues

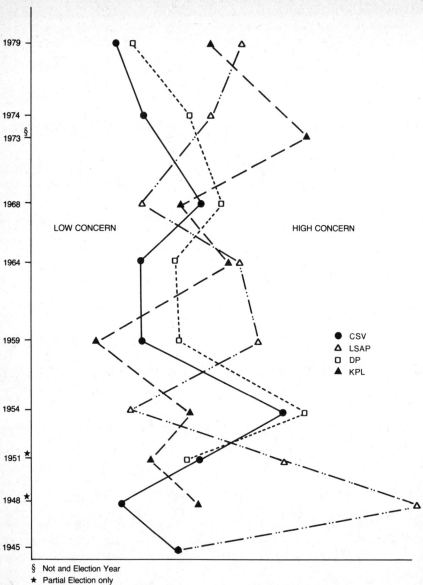

12.2 Second stage factor 2 by election year: social justice, democracy and freedom

rotated solution broke up the rather general first two factors into their component parts and consequently muddied the clear picture obtained without rotation.

Five second-stage factors were produced (see Table 12.2), the first accounting for 20.5 per cent of the variance and the second for 15.3 per cent.

Factor 1 appears to be an opposition between what might be termed 'new' concerns such as Technology, Environment, Culture, Decentralization, etc. on the one hand and the xenophobia distinctive of the Luxembourg Communist Party on the other. It has been labelled 'New Issues *vs.* Isolationism'. Factor 2 is essentially unipolar and is correlated with the original category of Social Justice, with Freedom and with Democracy. The effective absence of a negative end to this factor allows it to be labelled 'Social Justice, Democracy and Freedom: High Concern *vs.* Low Concern'.

Factor 3 correlates positively with a number of Social Groups, especially Railwayman and Women and negatively with Foreign Special Relations; Negative and Economic Planning. It accounts for 13.6 per cent of the variance. Factor 4 is a straightforward opposition between National Way of Life, National Effort and Productivity on the one hand and Peace on the other; it accounts for 12.4 per cent of the variance. Factor 5 accounts for a mere 8.7 per cent of the variance, is unipolar and concerned almost entirely with the Peace issue. In the case of the latter factors, different concerns are grouped because they 'belong' to the same party, such as concern for social groups and external xenophobia in the case of the Communist Party.

The interpretation of Factor 1 as being – at least in part – one of 'New' issues, is subsequently confirmed when factor scores on the first two dimensions are plotted against election years (see Figure 12.1 and 12.2). Insofar as the three parties of government are concerned there is a clear trend towards the new issue pole of the first factor over time.

The Communist Party on the other hand maintains a position which is simultaneously less 'New' than those of its rivals throughout the entire period while at the same time observing a similar trend until 1968 after which it appears to have reverted to its previous purist, and indeed isolationist, position. This particular graph clearly shows the KPL's position as an opposition of principle never once entering the arena of governmental politics. On the essentially 'valence' issue of Social Justice, Democracy and Freedom (Figure 12.2) which no party will ever oppose but which different parties will at different times emphasize, party positions interpenetrate much more. The two dimensional figure (Figure 12.3) shows even more clearly the interpretation of the parties of government, in contrast to the isolated position of the Communist Party.

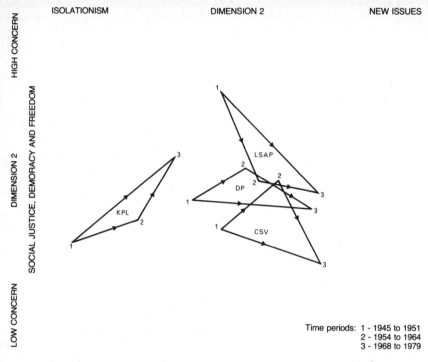

12.3 Spatial location of Luxembourg parties on the two leading dimensions: dimension 1 by dimension 2

What is interesting is the fact that nothing resembling a Left–Right dimension has emerged from the analysis. To check this finding a special analysis was made of the Economic domain, to the extent of constraining the number of factors that emerged to one. No convincing dimension of this type emerges, so it must be assumed – contrary to usual comment and discussion – that Luxembourg is not a country in which Left–Right political opposition plays much part – at any rate in election programmes.

12.10 CONCLUSIONS

The Luxembourg analysis supports a number of generalizations, each of them highly plausible even though they were not always predictable. Firstly, the most basic characteristics of the party system are confirmed. The three parties which share a governmental vocation show a high degree of consensus about the nature of the salient issues and those issues change systematically over time in much the same direction as they do in other developed countries. Secondly, there is a considerable gulf between these three parties on the one hand and the Communist Party on the other.

Thirdly, insofar as clear dimensions emerge from the analysis, these tend to be either 'valence' ones or conflicts about economic *management* as opposed to deep philosophical divisions of the Left *vs.* Right variety. This in turn leads to the conclusion that the clearly very robust oppositions that are such a distinguishing feature of Luxembourg politics are probably more a matter of personality than of political principle. Given the extremely small size of the country, by far the smallest considered in this volume, perhaps that is not so surprising after all.

Note

1 Owing to peculiarities of the electoral system it is not possible simply to add votes from the constituencies to get a nation-wide total, as Mackie and Rose (1974) do. Slightly differing estimates can be made through different methods. Percentages quoted in the text are the author's own.

CHAPTER 13

AUSTRIA 1949–1979[1]

──────── ⌒ ────────

13.1 POLITICAL PARTIES AND ELECTIONS SINCE 1945

Although contemporary Austrian politics seem remarkably peaceful, the predecessors of the three major parties were implacable opponents whose animosities caused the fall of the First Republic between 1934 and 1938. Their ideological *Lager* or 'camps' have influenced the thinking of present day parties. It is particularly appropriate therefore to study post-war party programmes to discover how and to what extent attitudes have come to resemble each other. It is also interesting to discover if the separation between parties remains the same in some areas while diminishing in others.

Of course the historical experience of civil war, collapse and external takeover itself affected the behaviour of parties in the post-war period. The formation of a Grand Coalition by the Socialists and the People's Party – so vital to political stability in Austria, and probably also to regaining independence – reflected the need to give at least two major political camps government responsibility.

The political parties that presently exist are the following (Pelinka 1981; Sully 1981):

1. The People's Party (*Österreichische Volkspartei*, ÖVP) is clearly the successor of the pre-war Christian-Social-Conservative camp. The Christian Socials as a party were moulded by political Catholicism (Diamont 1960) and – although the ÖVP claims to have made a new start in 1945 – its post-war development was again characterized by ties to Catholic associations.

2. The Socialist Party (*Sozialistische Partei Österreichs*, SPÖ), continues the tradition of the Social Democratic Party. Founded in 1889 the Social Democrats were the spokesmen of the great majority of the Austrian Labour movement. Even today the SPÖ has closer ties with Labour Unions than with other parties (Shell 1962).

3. The Freedom Party (*Freiheitliche Partei Österreichs*, FPÖ) evolved from the Association of Independents (*Verband der Unabhängigen*, VdU), founded in 1949. It

has its roots in the earlier German Nationalist movement and has so far not been able to decide whether to continue in this tradition or to develop along the lines of the Free Democratic Party of West Germany

4. The Communist Party of Austria (*Kommunistische Partei Österreichs*, KPÖ) could count on approximately 4 to 5 per cent of the valid votes during the first decade of the Second Republic. However, after the State Treaty was signed and especially after the Soviet invasion of Czechoslovakia in August 1968, its share of votes dropped below 1 per cent. For this reason it was not represented on the Austrian National Council during the 1960s and 1970s.

The electoral fortunes of these parties, and the different relationships existing between them, serve to distinguish the following phases in post-war political development:

1 1945 to 1955, the era of the 'Grand Coalition' from the allied occupation to the signing of the State Treaty;
2 1955 to 1966, the era of the late Grand Coalition and of its crises;
3 1966 to 1970, the era of an ÖVP majority government;
4 1970 to 1971, the experiment of a minority government by the SPÖ,
5 1971 to 1983, the era of a SPÖ majority government;
6 1983 to present, the first 'Small Coalition' formed by the SPÖ and FPÖ.

The parties included in the analysis are the ÖVP, SPÖ and VdU/FPÖ. The exclusion of the KPÖ is justified by its virtual disappearance in the late 1950s.

The Austrian party system is characterized by 'continuity' and 'concentration', which represent the essential difference between Austria and most other European countries (Pelinka 1981, p. 223). Continuity means that the development of the party system can be traced back, without interruption, for about a century. Concentration means the number of parties is small, because the electorate concentrates its votes to an unusual degree on a few parties. In an international comparison, the Austrian party system can be categorized as a two-and-a-half party system. Two parties dominate, one is clearly smaller, and there are no fourth parties to speak of. This happens in spite of a system of proportional representation which favours the growth of small parties, unlike the electoral procedures of the U.S., U.K. or even, to some extent, West Germany.

13.2 STRUCTURE AND INTENTIONS OF BASIC PROGRAMMES, ACTION PROGRAMMES AND ELECTION MANIFESTOS

The two major parties of the Second Austrian Republic have a long and continuous political tradition. But a closer look at their programmatic documents reveals that they have changed. Instead of clearly defined

programmatic statements based on dogmatic ideologies, the party platforms today are pluralistic in nature, sometimes to the point of ambiguity.
There is, however a technical difficulty to be dealt with in an analysis of
these changes which is also encountered in the cases of Scandinavia, the
Benelux countries, and West Germany. Several types of relevant documents are issued by the parties. In Austria for example the so-called 'Basic
Programmes' (*Grundsatzprogramme*) are only changed after substantial
theoretical debate and a special party convention, and may remain in force
for decades. They are not keyed to a particular party-leadership nor to a
particular election. Examples are the ÖVP 'Salzburg Programm' which
was unanimously accepted at the party conference in Salzburg in November 1972, the 'New programme' adopted by the SPÖ at a party conference
in May 1978 in Vienna; and the FPÖ 'Bad Ischler Programm' adopted in
1968 (Sully 1981, pp. 60–7; 88–96; 111–16).

In the Salzburg Programm the ÖVP described itself as a party of the
'progressive centre',[2] and of 'social integration',[3] uniting different groups.
Partnership and a peaceful resolution of conflict were preferred to the class
struggle. According to the Salzburg Programm (which replaced the 1965
'Klagenfurter Manifest') the concept of 'solidarism' still guides the party's
thinking; this means that the individual is reminded of his obligations to
society, and that in return the community guarantees him the chance of
self-development. Regarding religion the ÖVP, although it still upheld
Christian values, recognized the independence of the Church and of all
groups with an overtly religious purpose – both Protestant and Catholic.
Paralleling the willingness of the SPÖ to cooperate with Christians sharing
its beliefs, the ÖVP is willing to realize its aims with all who share its
fundamental principles. A new 'openness' is apparent in both parties in
contrast to the ideological rigidity of their predecessors.

In its new Basic Programme which superseded that of 1958, the SPÖ
cites freedom, equality, justice and solidarity as the guiding party principles. The programme however retains a reference to the need to create a
classless society, and discusses what it describes as the crisis and contra-
dictions of a capitalist system based on the profit motive. Basic Programmes in Austria still reflect historical and philosophical considerations.
For example the new SPÖ programme considers the struggle of the labour
movement to be divided into three historic phases. First, the fight for
political democracy and the Republic, followed by the establishment of the
welfare state, and an eventual third phase which will be characterized by
the achievement of full 'Social Democracy'.[4]

Fundamental changes have also taken place in the FPÖ. The revival of
the third, national-liberal camp in 1949 was accompanied by programmatic statements emphasizing cultural and racial links with the German *Volk*.
At the beginning of the 1960s the FPÖ decided to change its image and

portray itself as more 'liberal' and less 'nationalistic'. Thus work began on the formulation of a new Basic Programme, which was accepted at the 1968 Bad Ischl party conference. The programme opened with the words: 'We want a European federal state'.[5] Although the FPÖ now accepted the 'democratic republic of Austria'[6] it still insisted on the cultural community with the German *Volk*. Since the rest of the programme contained brief but rather platitudinous comments on freedom and democracy it cannot – unlike the ÖVP and SPÖ programmes – be considered a major contri- bution to the understanding of changes in the party system. This weakness was acknowledged, and during the early 1970s an FPÖ study group started work on a fresh draft programme.

There is also a second category of programmatic documents in the form of 'Action Programmes' (*Aktionsprogramme*). These do not contradict the respective Basic Programmes or Election Manifestos, but their emphasis is different. Austrian Action Programmes are very detailed policy statements worked out by experts for particular areas and addressed primarily to the decision makers rather than to the electorate.

Although no work on the scale of the present research had previously been carried out in Austria, a number of analyses of Basic Programmes have recently been done, most notably by Norbert Leser on the ÖVP Salzburg Programme and by Heinrich Schneider on the New Programme of the SPÖ. Both experts looked at the philosophical and theoretical foundations of the respective basic Programmes, compared the logical structure of the text and traced general changes in comparison with previous Basic Programmes (Leser, Schneider, 1979). A more detailed and comparative approach was taken by Albert Kadan and Anton Pelinka in their introduction and commentaries to the collection of Austrian Party Programmes edited by them in 1979 (Kadan and Pelinka, 1979). But again the volume contains only the Basic Programmes.

The closest to a content analysis was a study carried out by Helmut Ornauer (1974) who not only compared a number of election manifestos of Austrian parties but also tried to find out the extent to which the issues emphasized were taken up in the inaugural declarations of the new government. The analysis is however limited to the elections from 1956 to 1971 and only takes into account those manifestos which belonged to a party represented *in* government – all others being ignored.

The results of previous research can be summed up as follows: in their Basic Programmes the main parties show a growing tendency to converge. In foreign policy all emphasize the necessity to defend and safeguard neutrality. In domestic affairs the parties stress the importance of freedom, equality, democracy and social justice and recognize the need to create a humane society and to control economic growth in order to save the environment. Wider participation in the decision-making process in order to overcome the alienation of the individual in a bureaucratized society is also emphasized.

On the other hand parties still vary in the emphasis they place on state intervention, on the importance of the family as the nucleus of society or on codetermination and self-help in local communities. A survey dating from the mid–1970s (Fischer-Kowalski and Bucek, 1979, p. 210) showed that 42 per cent of the population found it increasingly difficult to detect major differences between the ÖVP and SPÖ. Although this leaves a majority still convinced that the two differ markedly, it is questionable whether most of the electorate are sufficiently well informed to judge. Only two-thirds of Austrians were aware that the SPÖ (the majority party in power) had drawn up a new programme in 1978, and only one-third had even a vague idea of its essential points.

Neither the Basic Programmes nor the Action Programmes have much of a general circulation. Election manifestos with their short and simple slogans are however widely distributed and more likely to influence the electorate. Furthermore, it is in these election manifestos that the true intentions of political parties in a cross-pressured situation between 'office-seeking' and 'ideological' motivations are revealed. In other words the type of document we are interested in analysing for this study is the *authoritative statement of party policy made for each specific election* in the post-war period, whatever its form. In this way we gain a realistic picture of the position of a particular party in the domestic political system, and can trace shifts in party positions over time.

13.3 COLLECTING AND CODING THE DOCUMENTS

The identification of relevant documents for analysis was not easy. In several instances it was a problem to decide which should be used, and in a few instances no programme of any kind could be traced.

The great majority of source documents were supplied by the various political parties themselves or by their associated research and training institutes – semi-independent organizations maintained by all parties in Austria, which undertake research and play a significant role, if not in the manifesto drafting process, at least in the training of party personnel and in supplying them with material.

In some instances of more recent elections in the 1960s and 1970s, we obtained actual copies of the party programmes distributed to the public. These were useful since they show layout and illustrations. In some cases however only photocopies were available. In several cases copies were missing but with one exception (FPÖ 1962) the deficiencies were made up by using reprints in party publications: party newspapers and party magazines, or brochures containing the annual reports of party officials.

Since 1945 the SPÖ has published such a magazine (*Der Vertrauensmann*) containing either the full texts or extensive summaries of all principal party programmes. We referred to this source for three early documents, the Socialist Programmes for 1949, 1953 and 1956. In a few other instances, when originals were no longer available, either reprints of the text or summaries in the Reports to the annual party conventions were used. This was the case with the Socialist Programmes for 1962 and 1970. The collection of the Austrian Party Programmes edited and annotated by Klaus Berchtold (1967) was an indispensable source for the early ÖVP and FPÖ documents.

A more serious difficulty arose from the existence of several types of documents with some claim to be election programmes. The relative success of the SPÖ in the elections of the 1970s was partly due to the image the party gained by presenting concrete alternatives to those of the Government on most important topics. These alternatives, worked out by experts in the form of detailed Action Programmes (some of them, for example the economic programme, were the size of a book) could not be included in the analysis because of their size. In this case the report of the party chairman Bruno Kreisky to the 1970 party convention was selected although the character of the text is exactly the opposite of the actual party programme. It is very short and the content naturally remains rather general.

Similar problems occurred with the other parties. The ÖVP manifesto for the 1956 election could not be traced and a short report by Secretary General Alfred Maleta *about* the manifesto reprinted in the ÖVP publication, *Österreichische Monatshefte* was substituted as an indirect reconstruction of the original content. In another case when, as in 1949, no ÖVP manifesto was available, another text (the 1945 *Programmatische Leitsätze der Österreichischen Volkspartei*) was used on the assumption that it was still representative of the party's position. Difficulties stem from the fact that the distinction between Basic Programmes, Action Programmes and Election Manifestos is not applicable to the case of the ÖVP and the FPÖ in the 1940s and 1950s. The documents used were intended as Basic Programmes, but being short and not as well structured as the Salzburg Programme they were directly used in the campaigns of 1953 and 1959. This is particularly true for the FPÖ. Until the Salzburger Bekenntnis of 1964 FPÖ documents are not, strictly speaking, election manifestos – as a matter of fact they do not correspond with the dates of the elections – but rather reflect the painful formation process of a party in search of its proper post-war role.

Whatever the problems in identifying relevant documents, Austrian parties do present more or less well worked-out policy documents to the public at election times. These vary from a dozen pages of duplicated typewriting (FPÖ 1975) to full colour glossy booklets of anything up to 60 or 70 pages (ÖVP 1970 and 1975) but all have in common the notion of being the authoritative statement of the party's policy position of the time of the election in question.

Programmes are prepared according to procedures which vary for each party and for each election. Basic Programmes go through elaborate procedures – consultation of and approval by their constituency feder-ations and membership at large are taken for granted. Election manifestos, however, are produced in a much more centralized fashion. So, at one extreme, Basic Programmes are supposed first to circulate as a draft to constituencies for their comments before a revised draft is presented to a full Party Congress for debate, amendments and finally for adoption. At the other extreme, election manifestos are often drawn up and adopted by the Party Chairman together with a few election experts among party executives and professional public relations men.

In practice, however, differences are not as extreme as these formal procedures imply. As there was a tendency during the coalition period to call for elections with little warning, formal procedures had to be by-passed even in cases where the document claimed the character of a Basic Programme. So for example discussion at the ÖVP Party Congress before the campaign of 1959 was replaced by a decision of an elected 'Political Committee' (*Politischer Ausschuss zu Grundsatzfragen*) and the decision on the party platform of the SPÖ for 1966 was made by the 'Party Council' (*Entschiessung des Parteirates vom 19. Januar 1966*).

The full list of Election Programmes obtained for the purpose of the present research is given in Appendix A. Because the coding had to be completed in 1982 the last documents included are those from the 1979 election.

In order that the standard coding scheme could be made to work for Austria a few specifications have to be made. Basically the interpretations made for the German case could be applied to Austria as well. However, there are the following few differences. Foreign Special Relationships Posi-tive means Neutrality and special relationships to the signatory powers of the Austrian State Treaty: France, Great Britain, USSR, the United States, and also to other neutral countries like Sweden and Switzerland. Military Positive, stands for a need for self-defence (*Selbstverteidigung*). Constitutiona-lism Positive, includes '*Neutralitätspolitik*' because Neutrality is a consti-tutional Amendment and not part of the State Treaty as often believed. In one case it was necessary to insert an additional sub-category into the coding scheme: Internationalism Negative (equals opposition to 'neutralism').

Coding was carried out by a German-speaking Research Assistant at the University of Essex under detailed supervision by Hearl, and in close consultation with Horner.

TABLE 13.1

LEADING EMPHASES OF AUSTRIAN ELECTION PROGRAMMES

CATEGORY		ALL MANIFESTOS (N=29)		ÖVP (N=10)		SPÖ (N=10)		FPÖ (N=9)	
		$\bar{x}$	SD	$\bar{x}$	SD	$\bar{x}$	SD	$\bar{x}$	SD
202	DEMOCRACY	9.16	6.61	6.79	3.56	7.56	4.52	13.56	9.03
503	SOCIAL JUSTICE	6.48	3.48	5.90	2.45	7.57	4.48	5.92	3.28
411	TECHNOLOGY AND INFRASTRUCTURE	6.36	5.59	4.70	5.29	11.09	4.85	2.95	2.66
504	SOCIAL SERVICES: POSITIVE	5.55	4.44	4.85	3.30	6.58	4.12	5.17	5.96
706	NON-ECONOMIC GROUPS	5.42	3.95	5.25	4.50	6.94	3.44	3.92	3.63
107	INTERNATIONALISM: POSITIVE	4.55	4.64	1.94	1.62	4.51	2.97	7.49	6.65
703	AGRICULTURE AND FARMERS	4.33	3.08	4.69	2.88	4.09	2.58	4.20	4.02
401	FREE ENTERPRISE	4.28	3.92	7.42	4.04	1.05	1.56	4.38	2.70
201	FREEDOM AND HUMAN RIGHTS	4.16	3.71	4.64	4.48	2.69	1.62	5.25	4.28
506	EDUCATION: POSITIVE	3.58	4.72	4.35	4.75	3.50	3.18	2.80	6.29
601	NATIONAL WAY OF LIFE: POSITIVE	3.27	4.67	2.85	4.46	2.94	3.41	4.10	6.29
410	PRODUCTIVITY	3.21	8.55	6.60	14.18	2.57	1.90	0.17	0.50
402	INCENTIVES	3.14	3.25	6.16	3.33	1.16	1.44	2.00	2.09
502	ART, SPORT, LEISURE, MEDIA	3.10	2.84	4.39	3.64	2.11	1.98	2.76	2.32
606	NATIONAL EFFORT/SOCIAL HARMONY	2.78	4.09	3.38	5.33	0.87	1.08	4.22	4.21
408	SPECIFIC ECONOMIC GOALS	2.64	2.92	3.13	3.24	3.37	3.47	1.29	1.21
414	ECONOMIC ORTHODOXY AND EFFICIENCY	2.62	3.17	4.07	4.22	1.58	2.60	2.19	1.86
203	CONSTITUTIONALISM: POSITIVE	2.28	2.64	2.83	3.24	1.19	1.41	2.89	2.84
404	ECONOMIC PLANNING	2.05	2.46	0.70	1.13	2.96	2.65	2.56	2.89
101	FOREIGN SPL. RELATIONSHIPS:POSITIVE	1.74	3.29	2.93	5.12	0.41	0.73	1.88	1.95
403	REGULATION OF CAPITALISM	1.55	3.35	0.16	0.51	3.25	5.25	1.19	1.34

Continued..

TABLE 13.1 Continued...

501	ENVIRONMENTAL PROTECTION	1.55	2.64	0.57	1.03	1.99	2.52	2.14	3.78
605	LAW AND ORDER	1.52	2.33	0.96	1.54	1.63	2.63	2.03	2.79
102	FOREIGN SPL. RELATIONSHIPS: NEGATIVE	1.49	2.71	0.49	0.50	2.98	3.76	0.96	2.29
701	LABOUR GROUPS: POSITIVE	1.48	1.82	0.93	1.09	1.99	1.69	1.53	2.52
303	GOVERNMENT EFFICIENCY	1.24	1.66	0.72	1.03	0.00	0.00	2.60	2.12
603	TRADITIONAL MORALITY: POSITIVE	1.03	1.66	0.97	1.93	0.64	1.28	1.53	1.78

13.4 FREQUENCIES ANALYSIS

Table 13.1 presents the full list of the 27 qualifying categories in order of their frequency of mentions across the entire 'national level' data set as well as within the parties. Categories which scored less than 1.0 per cent have been eliminated in accordance with the agreed procedure for the entire project and are no longer included in the analysis.

It is interesting that the single issue of most concern over the post-war period has been 'Democracy'. The fact that the standard deviation at 6.5 per cent is well below the mean score clearly shows that there has been little variation either between parties or over time on this issue. It is the No. 1 consensus issue as far as Austrian Manifestos are concerned. Obviously this is a reflection of the crisis of party government in the First Austrian Republic, culminating in the tragedy of the Civil War of 1934 and the *Anschluss* of 1938. Similarly, 'Social Justice' appears as a consensus issue having both a high mean and a low standard deviation. For what it is worth, the top few issues in the table have a strong Social Democratic flavour.

As far as other categories are concerned, Austrian parties emphasize international political and economic cooperation, strengthening international organizations and supporting the Third World (positive reference to Internationalism) whereas Military Security had to be excluded because of its extremely low score. And, compared to the high ranking domestic issues, the concern with Neutrality coded under positive references to Foreign Special Relationships is not remarkable. It seems Austrian parties worry more about Neutralism, otherwise negative references to Foreign Special Relationships would not have ranked so closely to positive references. More important – and indeed more interesting – are the individual party profiles.

One can see at a glance how far any one party is in broad agreement with the national consensus. The SPÖ, in fact, emphasizes precisely the same top five issues as does Austria as a whole – albeit not in the same order – indicating either that it is today a highly consensual *Volkspartei*, or that it effectively writes the political agenda, or both. The success of the SPÖ in elections over the last decade may follow from this. The ÖVP on the other hand, is in agreement with the other parties to the extent that it puts a high emphasis on Democracy and Social Justice but is distinctive in the importance it attributes to Free Enterprise, Productivity and Incentives. However it is rather a surprise that the self-styled *Volkspartei* has only two categories among the top five for Austria as a whole. The FPÖ, by contrast, has three favourite issues in the national top five. There is an unexpected contrast between the SPÖ and the ÖVP on Technology and Infrastructure. Most striking however is the fact that 'Democracy' is by far the leading category for the FPÖ. One explanation is that the FPÖ is trying hard to overcome the image of a reactionary party bound to an electorate still sympathetic to the (Nazi) past, and doubting the effectiveness of a democratic system. The same may be true for 'Internationalism'. After having defended the Germanic nature of Austria for so long the FPÖ now places great emphasis on the 'Europeanism' of the party, strongly advocating the participation of Austria in the EEC.

On the whole, results from Table 13.1 support earlier commentators' judgements. Not only are the various parties typified by the very issues we know them to be concerned with, but in many instances the ranking of issues appears to correspond closely with the parties' known attitudes to the various issues. So for example, the close identity of concerns between the ÖVP, the SPÖ and FPÖ embracing Social Justice, Social Services, Agriculture and Farmers, and Non-Economic Groups (categories ranking among the top ten with all three parties) clearly reflects the reality that Austrian parties are not all single-issue parties but contenders for the votes of the same broad constituency. Nevertheless, the contrasting concerns of the ÖVP and SPÖ for Education, Specific Economic Goals (i.e. full employment policy) and Regulation of Capitalism (ranking eighth, ninth and tenth with the SPÖ and FPÖ) indicate at least a relative bias towards the right and left of centre. On the other hand, the low placing of Traditional Morality certainly reflects the fact that the ÖVP has broken with the pre-war clerical tradition of the Christian Socials, who under all circumstances defended very conservative moral positions.

Again the profiles are sensitive to the fact that of the two major parties the Socialists are still more to the left and the ÖVP more to the right of centre, whereas the FPÖ, being a small middle-class party, is torn between two extremes. A liberal wing is credibly concerned with such issues as Social Justice and Social Services (third and fifth among the top ten) making the FPÖ a natural coalition partner after the SPÖ lost its absolute majority, but its right wing is definitely more reactionary than anything you can find in the ÖVP.

To sum up, therefore, the various party profiles based on election manifestos accord with political reality to a surprising degree, whereas in the so-called Basic Programmes the political parties are more inclined to cultivate the traditional camp mentality which fails to give a realistic picture of the office-seeking political parties in the political system of today. With a few exceptions – which can be explained – the picture given by our analysis is very close to what the experienced observer would look for *a priori*. The coding operation, with its underlying saliency assumptions, seems to have been a success, enabling us to undertake the factor analysis of the same data with a good conscience.

13.5 FACTOR ANALYSIS BY DOMAIN

The standard principal components analysis was only carried out within six domains, because after application of the exclusion criteria only one variable from the Government domain, namely 'Government Efficiency' was left. Factoring was not therefore carried out and the variable was directly input to the second-stage factor analysis. The other results are summarized below.

(i) Foreign Relations

Two components having Eigenvalues greater than unity account for 40.4 per cent and 34.5 per cent respectively of the variance. After Varimax rotation, these factors are reasonably straightforward to interpret. The first loads significantly on positive references to Internationalism: and negative references to Foreign Special Relationships. Since the latter consists to a large extent of mentions of the dangers of one-sided relations or of neutralism, whereas the first category means strengthening international organizations and international political and economic cooperation (including support of the Third World), the factor makes good sense as one of general high concern with Foreign Affairs. The second factor opposes positive references to Foreign Special Relationships to negative, i.e. Neutrality *vs*. Neutralism. Taken together, the two factors seem an adequate summary of the principal foreign policy orientations of Austrian parties over the post-war period.

(ii) Freedom and Democracy

Three original categories qualified for analysis within this domain. Two factors were produced which had Eigenvalues greater than 1.0, accounting respectively for 37.4 and 37.1 of the variance. It is surprising that two emerge, since at first sight all categories of this domain seem strongly linked to each other. The category 'Constitutionalism' causes unexpected trouble. The first factor loads strongly and positively on Constitutionalism and opposes Democracy. An interpretation could be that the rigid Rule of Law is an obstacle to more Democracy or *vice versa*: Democratization and Participation is considered to undermine the Rule of Law (*Rechtsstaat*).

(iii) Economy

This is the first domain to produce three factors with Eigenvalues greater than unity, due principally to the larger number of categories qualifying for inclusion. In both unrotated and rotated solutions, Factor 1 is clearly a

TABLE 13.2

FACTOR ANALYSIS BY DOMAIN: ECONOMY

A) UNROTATED FACTOR MATRIX

CATEGORIES		FACTOR 4.1 RIGHT-LEFT ENTERPRISE VS. INTERVENTIONISM	FACTOR 4.2 ECONOMIC STRATEGY	FACTOR 4.3
401	FREE ENTERPRISE	.81	.32	.25
402	INCENTIVES	.66	.47	.23
403	REGULATION OF CAPITALISM	-.56	.19	-.31
404	ECONOMIC PLANNING	-.59	.43	.43
408	SPECIFIC ECONOMIC GOALS	.30	.08	-.70
410	PRODUCTIVITY	.04	-.76	.11
411	TECHNOLOGY AND INFRASTRUCTURE	-.66	-.02	.39
414	ECONOMIC ORTHODOXY	.50	-.42	.38
	EIGEN VALUE	2.54	1.31	1.20
	% OF VARIANCE	31.7%	16.3%	15.0%

B) VARIMAX ROTATED FACTOR MATRIX

CATEGORIES		FACTOR 4.1 RIGHT-LEFT FREE ENTERPRISE VS. INTERVENTIONISM	FACTOR 4.2 ECONOMIC STRATEGY	FACTOR 4.3 PRODUCTIVITY VS. REGULATION AND PLANNING
401	FREE ENTERPRISE	.88	-.18	.14
402	INCENTIVES	.83	-.09	-.05
403	REGULATION OF CAPITALISM	-.44	.07	-.49
404	ECONOMIC PLANNING	-.05	.73	-.43
408	SPECIFIC ECONOMIC GOALS	-.01	-.74	-.22
410	PRODUCTIVITY	-.32	-.03	.70
411	TECHNOLOGY AND INFRASTRUCTURE	-.36	.67	-.09
414	ECONOMIC ORTHODOXY	.31	.00	.69
	FROM UNROTATED SOLUTION:			
	EIGEN VALUE	2.54	1.31	1.20
	% OF VARIANCE	31.7%	16.3%	15.0%

EXCLUDED FROM BOTH ANALYSES:-
406 PROTECTIONISM: POSITIVE
407 PROTECTIONISM: NEGATIVE
409 NEO-KEYNESIANISM
412 CONTROLLED ECONOMY
413 PUBLIC OWNERSHIP
405 CORPORATISM IS NOT APPLICABLE TO AUSTRIA

Right *vs.* Left dimension showing the classic opposition between Free Enterprise, Incentives, and Economic Orthodoxy (which have high positive loadings) on the one hand and Regulation of Capitalism and Economic Planning (which have high negative loadings) on the other. It is this Right/Left factor which accounts for 31.7 per cent of the variance before rotation. However, the meaning of the unrotated factors 4.2 and 4.3 is not clear until one looks at the rotated solution for these two factors.

The second factor loads on Economic Planning and Technology and Infrastructure *vs.* Specific Economic Goals (especially Full Employment and support of Farmers and Small Business) and obviously relates to Economic Strategy. The third factor from this domain is one of overall economic performance. It loads on Productivity, Economic Orthodoxy *vs.* Regulation of Capitalism and Economic Planning. It has been labelled 'Productivity *vs.* Regulation and Planning', and accounts for 15.0 per cent of the variance, but in accordance with standard procedures will not be used in the second-stage analysis.

(iv) Welfare

In this instance, it is the unrotated solution which gives the clearer picture. The domain breaks up into two components in a highly predictable manner. The first accounting for 34.0 per cent of the variance loads equally on Environmental Protection and positive references to Social Services. The second, Social Justice and positive references to Education accounts for 26.5 per cent of the variance. The two factors were respectively labelled 'Quality of Life' and 'Social Justice'.

(v) Social Fabric

Four variables from this domain qualified for inclusion. Two components were produced. The first, unipolar, factor is one of High Concern for Social Harmony and Traditional Morality. The second factor is bipolar and opposes positive references to National Way of Life: Positive to Law and Order. The factors 'Social Conservatism' and 'Social Integration' account for 34.8 and 30.6 per cent of the variance within the domain before rotation.

(vi) Social Groups

This is the only domain to produce just one component. Three categories qualified. Loading on Labour Groups, Farmers and Agriculture and Non-Economic Groups, the factor accounting for 42.6 per cent of the variance is simply one of High/Low Concern for 'Social Groups'.

Table 13.3 summarizes the first-stage principal components analysis of

TABLE 13.3

SUMMARY OF FIRST STAGE FACTORS

FACTOR	ROTATION	INTERPRETATION
F 1.1	VARIMAX	FOREIGN AFFAIRS: HIGH CONCERN/LOW CONCERN
F 1.2	VARIMAX	NEUTRALITY VERSUS NEUTRALISM
F 2.1	VARIMAX	DEMOCRACY VERSUS CONSTITUTIONALISM
F 2.2	VARIMAX	FREEDOM AND DEMOCRACY: HICH CONCERN/LOW CONCERN
ORIGINAL CATEGORY 303 GOVERNMENT EFFICIENCY		
F 4.1	UNROTATED	ECONOMIC: RIGHT-LEFT
F 4.2	VARIMAX	PLANNING AND INFRASTRUCTURE VERSUS SPECIFIC ECONOMIC GOALS
F 4.3	VARIMAX	PRODUCTIVITY VERSUS REGULATION AND PLANNING
F 5.1	UNROTATED	QUALITY OF LIFE: HIGH CONCERN/LOW CONCERN
F 5.2	UNROTATED	SOCIAL JUSTICE: HIGH CONCERN/LOW CONCERN
F 6.1	UNROTATED	SOCIAL CONSERVATISM: HIGH CONCERN/LOW CONCERN
F 6.2	UNROTATED	SOCIAL INTEGRATION: HIGH CONCERN/LOW CONCERN
F 7.1	UNROTATED	SOCIAL GROUPS: HIGH CONCERN/LOW CONCERN

the seven domains. Twelve first-stage factors were produced, eleven of which (not more than two from each domain in accordance with the standard procedure) will be used in the second-stage analysis.

13.6 SECOND-STAGE FACTOR ANALYSIS

Table 13.4 shows the Varimax rotated solution for the second-stage factor analysis. For an easier interpretation however, it also shows the Pearson Correlation coefficients between the rotated second-stage factors and the original categories and sub-categories where these are greater than 0.3 and were not input directly into the second-stage analysis. Five factors having Eigenvalues greater than unity were produced but of these five the first two are the most important.

Again it is clear which is the Socio-Economic Right–Left factor, because the first factor correlates positively with such categories as Free Enterprise, Incentives, and Support for Constitutionalism, all of which are issues associated with the 'right' in politics. On the negative side, the picture is also clear since virtually all the correlations stronger than 0.3 are classic 'left-wing' ones such as Regulation of Capitalism and Democracy. Even

TABLE 13.4

SECOND-STAGE FACTOR ANALYSIS: VARIMAX ROTATED FACTOR MATRIX
(AND CORRELATIONS r WITH ORIGINAL VARIABLES)

	FACTOR 1 SOCIO-ECONOMIC LEFT-RIGHT	FACTOR 2 NEW ISSUES VS. TRADITIONAL VALUES	FACTOR 3 INDIVIDUAL FREEDOM VS. ECONOMIC WELFARE	FACTOR 4 GOVERNMENT EFFECTIVENESS VS. SOCIAL SERVICES AND ENVIRONMENT	FACTOR 5 SOCIAL JUSTICE VS. SOCIAL HARMONY
DOMAIN 1: FOREIGN RELATIONS					
FACTOR 1.1 FOREIGN AFFAIRS	-.35	.57	.24	.07	.25
FACTOR 1.2 NEUTRALITY VS. NEUTRALISM	.54	.00	.52	.12	.03
101 FOREIGN SPL. RELATIONS: +	.55	.15	.52	.03	.08
102 FOREIGN SPL. RELATIONS: -	-.41	.60	-.11	-.15	.24
107 INTERNATIONALISM: +	-.24	.37	.39	.23	.19
DOMAIN 2: FREEDOM AND DEMOCRACY					
FACTOR 2.1 DEMOCRACY VS. CONSTITUTIONALISM	.76	-.06	.07	.17	.38
FACTOR 2.2 FREEDOM AND DEMOCRACY	.09	.35	.63	.34	-.42
201 FREEDOM AND HUMAN RIGHTS	.22	.35	.50	.42	-.32
202 DEMOCRACY	-.40	.22	.49	.08	-.54
203 CONSTITUTIONALISM: +	.70	-.02	.34	.23	.27
DOMAIN 3 GOVERNMENT					
303 GOVERNMENT EFFICIENCY	.06	-.21	.24	.72	.01

Continued...

TABLE 13.4 Continued...

	FACTOR 1	FACTOR 2	FACTOR 3	FACTOR 4	FACTOR 5
DOMAIN 4: ECONOMICS					
FACTOR 4.1 LEFT-RIGHT	.91	-.05	-.07	.02	-.33
FACTOR 4.2 PLANNING AND INFRASTRUCTURE VS. SPECIFIC ECONOMIC GOALS	.04	-.39	.06	.09	.14
401 FREE ENTERPRISE	.86	-.00	-.09	.02	-.25
402 INCENTIVES	.76	.02	-.26	-.12	-.38
403 REGULATION OF CAPITALISM	-.45	.18	-.07	.03	.11
404 ECONOMIC PLANNING	-.01	-.18	-.04	.19	.18
408 SPECIFIC ECONOMIC GOALS	.02	.18	-.31	-.32	.08
410 PRODUCTIVITY	-.20	-.04	-.11	-.02	.28
DOMAIN 5: WELFARE					
FACTOR 5.1 QUALITY OF LIFE	-.07	-.22	.04	-.41	-.05
FACTOR 5.2 SOCIAL JUSTICE	.00	-.01	-.06	.04	.52
501 ENVIRONMENTAL PROTECTION	-.13	-.41	.03	-.41	-.06
502 ART, SPORT, LEISURE, MEDIA	.05	-.34	-.11	.15	-.29
503 SOCIAL JUSTICE	.04	-.02	-.02	.14	.61
504 SOCIAL SERVICES: +	.01	-.26	-.01	-.52	-.21
506 EDUCATION: +	-.02	-.22	-.15	-.11	.20
DOMAIN 6: SOCIAL FABRIC					
FACTOR 6.1 SOCIAL CONSERVATISM	.07	.05	-.30	.44	-.44
FACTOR 6.2 SOCIAL INTEGRATION	.08	.86	.18	.18	.02
601 NATIONAL WAY OF LIFE: +	-.09	.75	.35	.12	-.15
603 TRADITIONAL MORALITY: +	.05	-.01	-.28	.37	-.47
605 LAW AND ORDER	-.22	-.71	.04	-.20	-.18
606 NATIONAL EFFORT/SOCIAL HARMONY	.10	.09	-.30	.54	-.36

Continued...

TABLE 13.4 Continued

	FACTOR 1	FACTOR 2	FACTOR 3	FACTOR 4	FACTOR 5
DOMAIN 7: SOCIAL GROUPS					
FACTOR 7.1	.02	-.05	-.70	.03	-.03
701 LABOUR GROUPS: +	-.19	-.01	-.54	.09	.09
703 FARMERS AND AGRICULTURE	.29	.01	-.66	.09	-.14
706 NON-ECONOMIC GROUPS	-.18	-.26	-.29	-.40	-.03

the category covering negative references to Foreign Special Relations makes sense in our context since the inclination to Neutralism is definitely greater with the Left than with the Right. This first second-stage factor is therefore 'Socio-economic Right–Left'.

Factor 2 is not as easy to interpret in the Austrian context. It opposes a broad mixture of such categories as Support for National Way of Life, Negative References to Special Relations, Support of Internationalism, and Freedom/Human Rights, to a compact combination of socially conservative issues. The factor has therefore been labelled New Issues and Internationalism *vs.* Social Conservatism and Traditional Values.

Factor 3 has Individual Freedom and Welfare loading amongst others on the positive end of the factor with positive references to Foreign Special Relations and Freedom/Human Rights, Democracy, Constitutionalism. The other pole is occupied by Farmers and Agriculture, Labour Groups and Specific Economic Goals. The two remaining factors present no problems of interpretation. Factor 4 is overwhelmingly concerned with Government Effectiveness and Authority opposed to Social Services and Environment. Factor 5 in turn opposes Social Justice to Social Harmony.

13.7 SPATIAL ANALYSIS OF PARTY MOVEMENT OVER TIME

As in the other analyses in this book, the scores which each party manifesto obtains on each dimension can be interpreted spatially, in a way which enables us to answer some of the questions posed at the beginning of this chapter about the relationships existing between the post-war parties, and whether they can be said to be moving closer to one another. Such an analysis also enables us to check our previous interpretations of the meaning of the factors.

Figure 13.1 shows that apart from the elections of 1959 and 1971, the ÖVP has been always the most 'right-wing'. Contrary to first expectations, however, the Socialists have not always been the most 'left-wing'. In 1956, in 1966 and 1975 the FPÖ proved to be left of the SPÖ. In general the two major parties appear in their expected places and take a clear stand on socio-economic issues. The position of the ÖVP in 1956, however is so far right as to make an explanation necessary. A closer look at historical developments reveals the reasons for this. Under Raab as Chancellor and Kamitz as Minister of Finance, the ÖVP in the 1950s followed the West German model of the 'social market economy' pretty closely. The famous *Raab-Kamitz Kurs* stood not just for a clear distrust of (unnecessary) state intervention in the economy but for just rewards to the most efficient and hardworking members of society. The programme betrays a more distinct *Abgrenzung* from the Socialists than was apparent in the late 1940s. But the

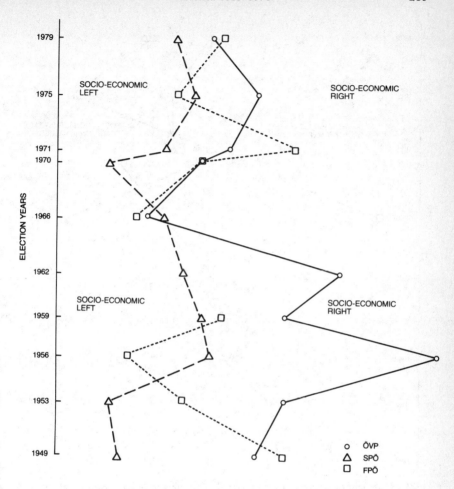

13.1 Movement of Austrian parties over time on the left-right dimension

explicit anti-Marxism of the ÖVP was not merely an economic phenomenon, it was also designed to attract votes from the German nationalist
camp.

Ever since the elections of 1970 the two major parties are not only much
closer to each other than in the 1940s and 1950s but for the last fifteen years
they have moved in tandem either to the right or to the left. This
demonstrates that the ÖVP and SPÖ are neither 'single-issue' parties nor
do they represent 'social classes'. They are rather 'catch-all' parties
(*Volksparteien*) responding with comparable means to comparable ends.

On the dimension New Issues and Internationalism *vs.* Social

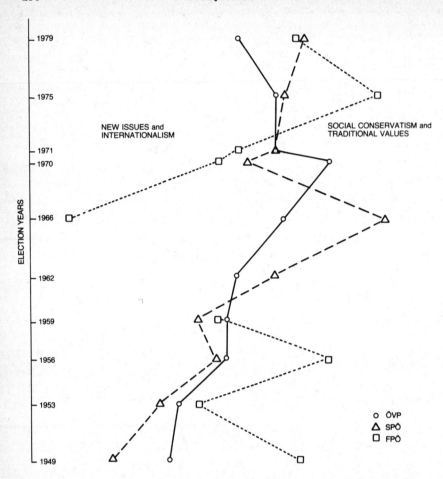

13.2 Movement of Austrian parties over time on new issues vs. traditional values
dimension

Conservatism and Traditional Values, a quite different picture emerges in
which the SPÖ in the immediate post-war years moved steadily towards
the Conservative space until 1966. In 1970 the Socialists moved back to the
New Issues position whereas the ÖVP has shown more sensitivity where
the second dimension is concerned. The overall trend is in the direction of
Social Conservatism and Traditional Values.

Dimension 2 makes sense as one of alternative foci of Austrian politics
over the post-war period. There is no doubt that in the 1940s and 1950s
attention was focused on developing something like a national identity, the
democratic consensus badly lacking in the First Republic, and a proper
place for Austria in international politics. Over the next twenty years

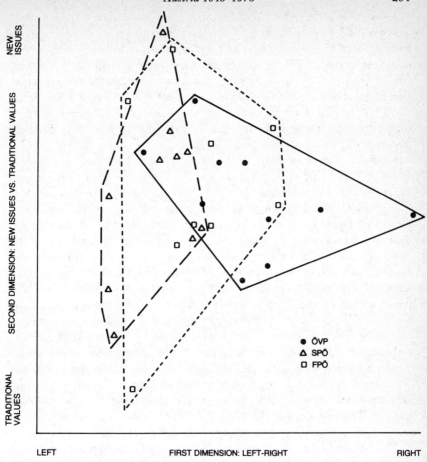

NEW ISSUES

SECOND DIMENSION: NEW ISSUES VS. TRADITIONAL VALUES

TRADITIONAL VALUES

● ÖVP
△ SPÖ
□ FPÖ

LEFT   FIRST DIMENSION: LEFT-RIGHT   RIGHT

13.3 First two second stage dimensions: territories occupied by each party in terms of these two factors taken together

however attention shifted to what might be called the 'quality of life'. Compared with the general trend it is again the FPÖ which shows the most ambiguous profile. It is torn between extremes so far as Dimension 2 is concerned. And the position in 1966 is still so far out of the mainstream that again we have to look for a plausible explanation in order not to raise doubts as to the reliability of the method.

In this regard, one has to recall that in the early 1960s, the party decided to change its image to a more 'liberal' one. This was a new development, and represented an attempt to break out of its 'ghetto' and make itself acceptable for governmental office. However the continuance of the Grand Coalition, even though tensions were apparent, reinforced its political

isolation. Thus the 1964 Salzburg party conference adopted a new programme which with the slogan 'freedom and progress' showed a great
awareness of liberal traditions and left positions. Under the influence of
the West German FDP great emphasis was also placed on the 'Europeanism' of the party. None of the other parties ever advocated the participation of Austria in the EEC as strongly as the FPÖ did in the 1960s. That
the FPÖ position is not accidental can also bee seen by looking at the first
dimension where the FPÖ in 1966 is again furthest to the left of all
Austrian parties.

Figure 13.3 puts positions on the first and second dimensions together,
showing that while each party occupies a distinctive area of the policy
space there is a considerable overlap. Post-war Austrian parties are definitely more consensual than those of many other countries, while not
altogether losing their ideological distinctiveness. The SPÖ shows a good
deal of continuity where Dimension 1 is concerned. Having had much
closer ties with the Labour Unions in the past, it still represents the
majority of workers. As a result the SPÖ manifestos do not vary much in
terms of the Socio-Economic factor. The situation is different when it
comes to Dimension 2 where the SPÖ covers much more space than the
ÖVP. Obviously it cannot deny its commitment to moral issues whereas it
shows the widest spectrum of positions along the line of the socio-economic
right–left factor. This is certainly not due to changes in overall policy
between 1956 and 1966 (the right/left extremes shown in Figure 13.3) but
is rather a reflection of the party's internal structure including strong
sub-organizations such as the Workers' and Employees' League (ÖAAB)
and the Business League (ÖWB). The ÖVP thus has no choice but to
adopt diverging if not contradictory views at the same time.

The FPÖ has the most ambiguous profile of all Austrian parties. Being
ashamed of the past it is more inclined than other parties to deny any ties
with its political predecessors than the other parties. As a result it oscil-
lates between extremes and there is no doubt that the office-seeking
motivation is strongest.

The dimensionality of Austrian politics has been the subject of academic
disputes. But on the basis of the territories occupied by each party in terms
of the two most important second-stage factors taken together (Figure
13.3), the small coalition between the SPÖ and FPÖ formed after the
elections in Spring 1983 seems to be absolutely logical. In making such a
statement one has to recognize a problem of method. The analysis is based
on programmatic documents showing *party intentions* and not necessarily
reflecting *real party policy*. In spite of these shortcomings (shared with other
studies done almost exclusively on the level of Basic Programmes) our
analysis of election manifestos gives a better indication of the actual
position of Austrian parties in the political system of today.

Notes

1 Derek Hearl of the University of Essex supervised the coding of the Austrian documents at the University of Essex. His comments on the method applied and his preliminary interpretation of the Austrian data set were most valuable to me. The coding work was financially supported by the 'Stiftungs-und-Förderungsgesellschaft' of the University of Salzburg. Both contributions are gratefully acknowledged.

2 *Das Salzburger Programm der Österreichischen Volkspartei*, ÖVP (ed.) Vienna 1972, p. 3 (No. 2.4).

3 *Ibid.*, p. 4 (No. 2.7).

4 *Das Neue Programm der SPÖ*, Dr Karl Renner Institut (ed.), Vienna 1978, p. 8.

5 *Das Programm der Freiheitlichen Partei Österreichs*, FPÖ (ed.), Vienna 1968 (No. 1).

6 *Ibid.*, (No. 1).

CHAPTER 14

ELECTION PROGRAMMES IN WEST GERMANY: 1949–1980, EXPLORATIONS IN THE NATURE OF POLITICAL CONTROVERSY[1]

———— ∿ ————

This study is concerned with the nature of political controversy in West Germany as reflected in the election programmes of political parties. What are the basic issue-dimensions? Where are the different political parties located within these? Do parties compete by direct policy confrontation or by emphasizing the importance of different issue-domains? These are the questions addressed in the analysis which carry over from the general theories discussed in Chapter 2, and which are particularly relevant regarding the development of party politics in post-war Germany.

14.1 THE INSTITUTIONAL FRAMEWORK

The Federal Republic was established in 1949. The three Western military governors ordered the setting up of a constitutional assembly by 1 September 1948. The leaders of the states were entrusted with the task of drafting a constitution. This work was completed by May 1949 and called the 'Basic Law' (*Grundgesetz*) rather than a 'Constitution' (*Verfassung*) to avoid the appearance of permanence and to underline the division of the country. For the same reason the Basic Law was only ratified by the state parliaments and not directly by the citizens.

There are three major national decision-making structures: the lower house of parliament (*Bundestag*), the upper house (*Bundesrat*), and the federal governmnent (*Bundesregierung*). The federal president (*Bundesprä-sident*), who is indirectly elected, serves primarily as the ceremonial Head of State and as a reserve power.

Among other functions, the *Bundestag* is in charge of legislation, the election and control of the federal government, headed by the Chancellor, the election of one half of the membership of the constitutional court (*Bundesverfassungsgericht*), and exercises some supervision over the state bureaucracy and the military. The *Bundesrat* can also initiate bills and must approve all legislation, although with different veto powers in different areas.

The executive authority is concentrated in the Chancellor's office. The Chancellor bears general responsibility for government policy. He nominates and dismisses cabinet ministers.

The members of the *Bundestag* are elected at least every four years. The election law is complicated. With the exception of the first general election in 1949, voters have had two votes: the first ballot (*Erststimme*) is cast in one of the 248 constituencies for a candidate who is elected by the relative majority of votes in the single-member constituency. The second vote (*Zweitstimme*) is decisive in establishing the overall distribution of the 496 seats in the *Bundestag*. This distribution is strictly proportional. From the number of seats so calculated the number of seats won directly by candidates in the constituencies is subtracted. The remaining seats are allocated to party lists of candidates, nominated at the state level. Only those parties which gain at least 5 per cent of the second votes or three seats directly in the constituencies are eligible for representation in parliament.

14.2 THE POLITICAL PARTIES

The Federal Republic has rightly been termed a 'party-state' (Grewe 1951). The role of the political parties in reconstruction after World War II has helped to reverse previous popular attitudes. Because they effectively translated policy into governmental programmes, and controlled governmental leaders, they lost their former image of ineffectiveness and unreliability. In addition, they were given a strong position by the Basic Law. Article 21 states: 'The political parties shall take part in forming the political will of the people. They may be freely established. Their internal organization must conform to democratic principles. They must publicly account for the source of their funds.' Rooted both in public attitudes and the constitution, political parties have increased their hold on government over the post-war period; they do indeed matter when it comes to any major decision (von Beyme 1981, 1983).

By law, political groupings have to meet certain requirements if they want to be officially recognized as a political party. They are obliged *inter alia*, to have a written programme agreed upon by a party convention. Since 1945 about 500 groupings have claimed recognition. Of these 48 have been permitted to take part in federal elections; 14 were able to win seats in the federal parliament. However, only four parties have been consistently represented in the Bundestag since 1949: the Christian Democratic Union (CDU), the Christian Social Union (CSU), the Social Democratic Party (SPD), and the Free Democratic Party (FDP) (Stoss 1983).

Here we analyse only three parties. Though formally independent, the

(Bavarian) CSU's federal election programmes do not differ significantly from those of the CDU, its larger sister party. Thus, instead of taking them separately, we shall concentrate on the CDU and generally speak of a three-party constellation in the post-war German party system. Together, these three groupings were able to win 62.1 per cent of the valid votes in the first federal election (1949). This went up very quickly and since 1961 has remained above 90 per cent. The new ecological party, the Greens, had by the end of our period (1980) not attained the national prominence which would justify its inclusion in our analysis, though its electoral successes of 1983 are to some extent foreshadowed by the emergence of new issues which also appear in the programmes of the established parties. (see Section 14.7).

Taking the major parties in order we will briefly review their leading institutional features and basic philosophy before describing the general form of competition between them which has had a strong effect on the development of their policy-orientations.

(i) Christian Democratic Union–Christian Social Union

This was one of the two major party groupings in the first Federal legislature of 1949, under the leadership of Konrad Adenauer, a Catholic Conservative from the Rhineland. The main ancestor of his party was the old *Zentrum* of the Imperial and Weimar days – representative particularly of Catholics. However the CDU must be regarded as a new attempt to unite practising Catholics and Protestants in a moderate Centrist party, mainly in reaction to their experience of Nazism. From the beginning its junior partner and representative in Bavaria was the Christian Social Union, a party with Bavarian nationalist leanings and a more conservative social and economic philosophy. From the outset the CDU/CSU opposed the 'almighty state'. Its *Ahlener Programm* of February 1947 favoured neither private nor state capitalism, but rather placed its emphasis on the policies of *Gemeinwirtschaft* which did not exclude the nationalization of big industries and co-determination in industry.

Events prompted a shift to a variant of the liberal market economy: a prime factor being the monetary reform (*Währungsreform*) of June 1948 which eliminated the controlled economy. Erhard's concept of a 'social market economy' (*soziale Marktwirtschaft*), based on private property but balanced by social regulations, proved to be successful and attractive to a large portion of the population. These developments are reflected in the Düsseldorf Guidelines (*Düsseldorfer Leitsätze*) of July 1949 on which the Union's campaign for the first federal election was largely based. This programmatic document, as well as a few others, already contained the major elements of CDU policy: adherence to christian values, democratic constitutionalism, liberal social order, social market economy, European unity, and reunification of Germany.

(ii) The Social Democratic Party

This had a more direct descent from the Imperial and Weimar party of the same name. Like its ancestor, it stood for a somewhat dogmatic form of democratic Marxism, based on the Heidelberg basic programme of 1925, and including nationalization of industrial corporations and banks as well as the division of large estates. It was however also strongly anti-Communist, and gradually modified its earlier ideological stance during the 1950s.

(iii) The Free Democratic Party

This too was the heir of earlier traditions, combining the post-war remnants of the old right-wing National Liberals and the left-wing Progressives. The preservation of individual freedom, the reunification of Germany, the rejection of Socialist planning and of clericalism, were among its primary political goals. The latter prevented an amalgamation with the CDU. With 11.9 per cent of the vote in 1949 it did however play a crucial role in giving the latter the opportunity to form a series of coalition governments up to 1966. Since 1949 in fact all but one (minor and short-lived) governments have been coalitions and the FDP has participated in almost all of them. Its decisions about coalition partners have been crucial in deciding which of the larger parties will provide the government, so it has played a big role in the political system despite its small size (often hovering just above the crucial 5 per cent of second votes).

14.3 THE DEVELOPMENT OF PARTY POLICIES IN THE POST-WAR PERIOD

The different relationships between the parties demarcate the following phases of post-war politics in the Federal Republic:

(i) 1949–1966

This period was dominated by CDU–FDP coalition governments, by the personalities of Adenauer and his Economics Minister Erhardt, and by an immensely successful post-war reconstruction of industry and society on the basis of free enterprise and the welfare state. During the period West Germany also became firmly integrated into the Western military alliance and into the European Community.

During this period the SPD passed from a sharply critical attitude to the new Social Market Economy. This transformation was exacerbated by the feeling between Adenauer and the old guard leader Ollenhauer, that no full-blooded Socialist alternative would ever be electorally acceptable or allowed to form a government coalition with the FDP. Changing leaders to the more programmatic and moderate Willy Brandt, it compromised with the social market economy in the Godesberg basic programme (1959) advocating 'As much competition as possible and as much planning as necessary.' Freedom, justice and solidarity were emphasized as the party's basic values: Marxist views were no longer prominent. Opposition to German participation in the Western Alliance and rearmament was dropped, and an effort was made to improve relations with the Catholic Church. From 1953 the SPD gained approximately 3 percentage points at each election until 1972.

Meanwhile the slight economic recession of the early 1960s, the visible hopelessness of any attempt at reunification with East Germany (signalled by the building of the 'Berlin Wall'), government scandals, and internal quarrels surrounding Erhardt's succession to the Chancellorship in 1963, all undermined the CDU position. Erhardt's attempt to develop a new programme centred round the 'Second Phase of the Social Market Economy' (*Formierte Gesellschaft*) was not accepted by the party. The economic recession undermined Erhardt's prestige, and the unwillingness of the FDP to balance the budget by raising taxes destroyed the coalition. The CDU/CSU entered a new coalition with the Social Democrats under Kiesinger (CDU) as Chancellor and Willy Brandt as Vice-Chancellor.

(ii) Grand Coalition 1966–1969

Although covering a short time period this was a turning-point in post-war politics for the following reasons:

1 It made the SPD respectable and showed it could actually form a government;
2 It gave the FDP motives for thinking of the SPD as an alternative coalition partner;
3 Left–wing student protest and growing right-wing extremism showed that political change was necessary and gave impetus to the moderate programme of reform advanced by the SPD. As a result an SPD–FDP coalition formed in 1969.

(iii) 1969–1982

This period saw successive coalitions of this type led by Brandt until 1974 and then by the new SPD leader Helmut Schmidt. In the first part of this

period governments initiated a new *Ostpolitik* involving détente, improvement of relations with the Eastern countries, especially East Germany, and
a programme of internal reforms – all well received. The treaties of
Moscow, Warsaw and the *Grundlagenvertrag* with the German Democratic
Republic (GDR) were signed during this term. A whole range of reform
programmes were started. The 'vote of no-confidence' (*Misstraungsvotum*)
which the CDU/CSU forced in April 1972 failed. New federal elections
were called and in November 1972 the SPD emerged as the strongest party
receiving 45.8 per cent of the vote. It soon became apparent, however, that
voter expectations of rapid improvement in East–West relations were
unrealistic and that there were definite economic and political limits to
reform. In 1974 Brandt resigned following the Guillaume spy scandal.
Helmut Schmidt's pragmatic middle-of-the-road political course was not
met with enthusiasm by the left. This is reflected in the highly controversial
programmatic discussion which followed. One important result was the
'Orientation-frame '85' (*Orientierungsrahmen '85*) which was accepted at the
Mannheim convention in November 1975. The effects of education and
science on social and economic development were given special attention.
However, many controversial issues were avoided, and political problems
became more complicated. The economy declined and the 'Ostpolitik' had
to adjust to a climate of deteriorating relations between the United States
and the Soviet Union. New political issues such as the negative effects of
economic growth and technological development emerged as important,
splitting the 'old' and the 'new' left. The Greens entered state parliaments
and internal tensions within the SPD grew. From the beginning of the
1980s the future of FDP–SPD collaboration was uncertain despite the
coalition's comfortable majority in parliament. In 1982 the FDP changed
alliances, initiating a new series of coalition governments with the
CDU–CSU. This fundamental change, whose long term consequences are
still uncertain, forms a natural end-point for our investigation.

   Our description of the period emphasizes the clash between SPD and
CDU policies rather than the part played by those of the FDP. In an
overall assessment this is correct, as despite its pivotal role the FDP has
had in effect to choose between the policies of the major parties rather than
imposing its own. More perhaps than its partners it tends to draw together
elements of opposing traditions: on the one hand liberals in an Anglo-
American sense, emphasizing welfare and freedom, and new issues such as
environmentalism and internationalism; and on the other hand liberals in
the Continental sense placing free enterprise and orthodox economics
above all. On the whole the latter dominated in the 1950s and 1980s,
whereas the reformers led the way in the late 1960s and 1970s. The
dominance of particular policy preferences both prompts, and reinforces
itself through, the choice of coalition partners.

The general developments outlined above form the general background against which specific programmes were prepared, and give point and content to the interpretations and analyses presented below. Before these, we have to consider more specifically the precise nature of the methods used to analyse the programmes and the type of data they produced.

14.4 SOURCES, DATA AND METHODS

As in Austria, the Netherlands and Scandinavia, German parties issue different types of programme for different purposes. They too have their Basic Programmes (referred to at various points in the preceding section) adopted by Party Congresses after long discussion and an intensive preparatory period, with widespread participation. (Like the other documents described below they pass between the Chairman, the Executive Committee, the Small Party Congress, the Main Committee, and sometimes special Congresses.) Such programmes are intended to give the party a basic orientation and philosophy for as much as a decade, and sometimes involve a radical reshaping of the party image – as with the crucial Godesburg Programme. While obviously central, such documents appear only at relatively long intervals and do not (and are not intended to) reflect election exigencies. The Basic Programmes are published by the party as booklets and circulate in millions.

To supplement them, the party issues Action Programmes. Like the Austrian, Swedish and Dutch, these are policies for specific purposes and areas – for example ecology. As each party maintains a Research Institute on the basis of state funds, these can provide input of high quality into such documents. They are somewhat less specialized than the Austrian and circulate to electors as well as to party activists – again in the shape of booklets published by the party.

As in the other countries, what interests us most are the election programmes (*Programme* or *Manifeste*). These consist of selections from the other documents, so in that sense they are closely related to them. However, the selection is obviously made with electoral purposes in mind.

Election programmes assess the importance of current political problems, specify the party's position on them, and inform the electorate about the course of action the party will pursue when elected. With a few exceptions all election programmes of the CDU, the SPD, and the FDP have been legitimized by party conventions. Thus, they represent the party's official point of view which is, of course, not only meant to unite the party internally, but – with the help of the mass media – to attract voters and win elections.

This analysis covers nine federal elections and logically there should thus be 27 election programmes or 'cases' for us to examine; however, in

1965 the FDP could not reach consensus on a common election programme and we are left therefore with 26 documents (see Appendix A).

Election programmes differ in size. The number of pages ranges from two (SPD 1949; FDP 1972; CDU 1961, 1965) to 116 (SPD 1965). On the average the SPD presented their case in 36 pages, the FDP in 21, and the CDU with only 15. Since the 1960s the trend among all three parties has been to longer and more elaborated election programmes. This finding reflects a general tendency documented in most chapters of this book.

The number of pages in an election programme is but a crude measure of size. The number of coding units forms a finer indicator but does not alter the picture.

The quasi-sentence is generally defined as the coding unit of the quantitative content analysis. The German study deviates for pragmatic reasons; most of the election programmes were rather long. Thus the paragraph, not the quasi-sentence was taken as the coding unit. This is not true for very short programmes; in these cases the quasi-sentence was used (SPD 1949; FDP 1972; CDU 1957, 1961, 1965). The decision to rely on the paragraph instead of the quasi-sentence does not cause much trouble, as far as the measurement of thematic emphasis is concerned. Paragraphs, like quasi-sentences, rarely deal with more than one theme or political problem. On the other hand, paragraphs differ more in size than do quasi-sentences. Thus, the proportions we report, which are based on the total number of paragraphs, may be subject to a size-bias.

The general coding scheme was designed to cover a wide range of programmatic statements in a number of different countries. Thus, it does not come as a surprise that some of the categories were not applicable to the German case and others showed very low use (15 categories did not reach an average of 1 per cent of the total number of coding units across all standardized party platforms). The reasons for lack of emphasis are in some cases very obvious. Decolonization, for example, was not one of Germany's concerns after World War II. In addition, the advertising nature of the party platforms does not easily lend itself to 'negative' policy positions. Others might have been misunderstood by the coders, like corporatism or Keynesian demand management. Following a general rule, these low-use categories were omitted from the further statistical analysis. Of the initial 54 categories 31 qualified for inclusion. Careful control of coding results suggested that another category be dropped and that two adjacent categories be collapsed. The specific German meaning of the remaining categories is discussed in Section 14.5 below.

The actual coding process is a notorious source of error. We have tested inter-coder reliability on a 3 per cent sample of the total number of coding units. Our test shows that inter-coder reliability is at the lower scale of tolerance: 100 out of 126 codes assigned matched. Scott's pi coefficient, which corrects for chance in the matches, reached .78. Coding was done by two social science graduate students.

A rather high proportion of coding units (an average of 24.6 per cent) could not be classified at all. This finding, however, is not too surprising. Most of these portions of text deal with very general assessments of the state of internal or external affairs or describe how other important actors (like the Soviet Union, the United States, etc.) judge and feel about them. Such evaluations are not of interest to us in this context. They range from 45.2 (CDU 1965) to 4.7 (CDU 1976). The other party programmes range more consistently around the overall average.

The data are statistically manipulated by factor analysis and discriminant analysis (Kim and Muller 1978; Klecka 1980). Factor analysis is used to identify underlying dimensions or themes within the seven broad issue domains which the classification scheme distinguishes on *a priori* grounds. This procedure should produce factors with high reliability and validity and is obviously preferable to factoring a larger but more heterogeneous set of variables. These factors are input to a second-order factor analysis to explore the overall structure of thematic concerns.

The factor analytic procedures do not take into account the underlying processes that generate the time series data which we are examining. In addition, the observations are probably not independent. One indicator of lack of independence is the trend in the mean (lack of stationarity). Although there is no really good solution for these problems we have controlled for the linear relationship between 'time' and the content variables. In some issue areas we do, indeed, find strong correlations between time and substantive issues (e.g. external relations and environmental protection). However, the factoring of the first-order partial correlations with time as the control variable, does not lead to interpretations which differ drastically from those guided by the factoring of the zero-order correlation matrices. Thus, for reasons of comparability with the other chapters in this book we have used the latter.

In the last section we use discriminant analysis, another multivariate technique designed to 'type' each party document as unequivocally as possible (described in detail in Chapter 18) to answer three questions; (1) is it possible to discriminate between the parties on the basis of the set of categories which are offered by the classification scheme; (2) how well do they discriminate, and (3) which are the most powerful discriminators?

14.5 FREQUENCY OF REFERENCES TO SPECIFIC ISSUES

The coding gave rise to the distributions reported in Table 14.1 for the three major parties separately and combined.

These cover leading issues for each party, in fact all the categories

TABLE 14.1

LIST OF QUALIFYING CATEGORIES FOR GERMANY AS A WHOLE AND
FOR EACH PARTY (TOP FIVE CATEGORIES FOR EACH PARTY HIGHLIGHTED)

	CATEGORY	ALL MANIFESTOS (N = 27)		SPD (N = 9)		FDP (N=9)		CDU (N = 9)	
		MEAN	SD	MEAN	SD	MEAN	SD	MEAN	SD
503	SOCIAL JUSTICE	5.53	2.72	5.57	3.02	6.02	2.83	4.99	2.51
411	TECHNOLOGY AND INFRASTRUCTURE	4.57	3.75	5.95	3.70	3.90	4.02	3.86	3.55
504	SOCIAL SERVICES (+)	4.11	2.63	5.61	3.09	3.03	2.62	3.70	1.42
201	FREEDOM AND DOMESTIC HUMAN RIGHTS	4.00	3.53	3.61	4.57	3.94	1.93	4.61	3.92
101	FOREIGN SPECIAL RELATIONSHIPS (+)	3.95	3.11	5.05	2.91	2.88	2.72	3.92	3.59
706	NON-ECONOMIC DEMOGRAPHIC GROUPS	3.22	3.72	2.76	2.76	3.56	5.25	3.33	3.06
703	FARMERS AND AGRICULTURE	2.94	2.95	2.55	2.92	3.47	3.52	2.80	2.61
414	ECONOMIC ORTHODOXY	2.91	2.86	2.01	1.89	1.91	1.87	4.80	3.68
108	EUROPEAN COMMUNITY	2.80	2.34	2.22	1.41	2.46	1.85	3.71	3.31
506	EDUCATION EXPANSION (+)	2.70	1.85	2.95	1.77	3.24	2.06	1.92	1.62
106	PEACE	2.68	2.47	3.01	2.99	1.36	0.97	3.66	2.61
403	REGULATION OF CAPITALISM	2.56	2.82	1.56	1.01	2.19	1.59	3.94	4.34
701	LABOUR GROUPS (+)	2.46	2.27	3.59	1.91	1.88	1.92	1.91	2.70
303	GOVERNMENT EFFICIENCY	2.44	2.68	2.68	2.87	1.76	1.03	2.86	3.65
606	NATIONAL EFFORT/SOCIAL HARMONY	2.35	2.74	1.94	3.22	1.55	1.34	3.55	3.11
408	SPECIFIC ECONOMIC GOALS	2.30	2.78	2.54	2.74	2.17	3.24	2.18	2.66
603	TRADITIONAL MORALITY (+)	2.15	1.84	1.59	1.12	2.27	2.30	2.60	1.97
202	DEMOCRACY	1.98	1.71	2.62	1.90	2.47	1.73	0.84	0.80
305	GOVT. EFFECTIVENESS AND AUTHORITY	1.77	2.78	2.77	3.32	1.94	3.25	0.59	0.91
104	MILITARY (+)	1.76	1.34	1.40	0.93	0.93	0.92	3.00	2.01
501	ENVIRONMENTAL PROTECTION	1.70	2.05	1.54	1.91	1.88	2.57	1.68	1.82
605	LAW AND ORDER	1.68	2.63	1.65	1.88	0.92	0.79	2.45	4.13
402	INCENTIVES	1.54	1.75	1.26	1.44	1.64	1.15	1.71	2.53
503	ART, SPORT, LEISURE, MEDIA	1.29	1.43	1.40	1.25	1.47	1.75	1.00	1.33
401	FREE ENTERPRISE	1.25	1.55	0.73	1.40	0.85	1.07	2.16	1.82

collecting enough references to be used in subsequent factor analyses under our rules (receiving 1 per cent overall and/or at least 3 per cent of references within any of the parties).

As mentioned above, negative references in such areas as Foreign Special Relationships, Military, Internationalism and the EC drop out entirely. Economic Planning, Corporatism, Protectionism, Keynesian Demand Management, Controlled Economy and Nationalization also fall from the Economic Domain, leaving only emphases on liberal economic policies combined with technological development. This is a consensus which inclines towards the conservative side, though it is worthwhile noting also the consensus on welfarism.

There is also a strong consensus on the emphases reported; on the whole and certainly on the top five categories, SPD concerns coincide with the general average. Social Justice and Social Services come first and third in the general distribution, Freedom and Domestic Human Rights fourth and Foreign Special Relationships fifth. SPD rankings are not quite the same, but almost. Social Justice is also the top concern of the other two parties, and Freedom and Rights occupy a high place – no doubt partly owing to German history, but also appearing in regard to economic initiative.

Where the CDU parts company is in its special commitment to Economic Orthodoxy – where for once there is a strong contrast with SPD and FDP emphases – and in its stress on Regulation of Capitalism. This is not unduly emphasized by, the SPD because in Germany regulation figures more as the characteristically liberal-conservative doctrine of social market economy (*sozialverpflichtete Marktwirtschaft*), than as a Socialist measure.

The major stresses on which the FDP distinguishes itself relate to special groups – Non-Economic and Agricultural. The CDU also puts a substantial emphasis on the former. Naturally the SPD emphasizes Labour Groups more – in fact they constitute its sixth leading category, leading over Peace where it shares an emphasis with the CDU but not with the FDP. The divergencies, however, are minor compared with other countries.

14.6 THE RELATIVE IMPORTANCE OF THEMATIC CONCERNS

These specific issues are grouped into seven broad themes: (1) External Relations, (2) Freedom and Democracy, (3) Government, (4) The Economy, (5) Welfare and the Quality of Life, (6) Fabric of Society, and (7) Social Groups, which varied substantially over time. The economy dominated CDU programmes until the end of the 1950s. The party talked about the concept of social market economy (1949), how well the concept worked (1953), and in what ways all social groups benefitted from the social market economy (1957). Throughout the 1960s and 1970s external relations received the highest attention. Military security, the NATO alliance, reunification of Germany as well as European questions were the prominent themes. In 1980 the Welfare State and how to pay for it became central.

The picture is quite different for the SPD. In 1949 the party stressed social groups and general problems of the democratic organization of society ('Freedom and Democracy'). Welfare issues were emphasized in 1953 and questions of the organization of the economy in 1957. In the 1961 election programme the SPD presented itself as a party ready to govern. In fact, the election programme was labelled 'Government Programme' (*Regierungsprogramm*). Thus, it does not come as a surprise that 'Government' ranked highest at this point in time. Another voluminous election programme was issued in 1965. It contained a comprehensive review of all policy areas with special emphasis on economic problems. From 1969 to 1980 Welfare and Quality of Life was dominant. The party advertised what it had done to improve and secure the 'net of social security' (*Netz der sozialen Sicherheit*) as well as other measures taken to guarantee 'social peace' (*sozialer Frieden*) in the country.

The FDP gave social group politics as well as economic problems the highest attention in the 1950s. From 1961 to 1980 Welfare and Quality of Life received top priority with the exception of 1972 when External Relations ('Ostpolitik' in particular) was stressed. In general the FDP pattern of thematic concerns is similar to that of the party's coalition partner. This may indicate a tendency to emphasize the FDP's own position within policy domains which are of high importance to the respective coalition government.

Over the whole period, three policy domains make up for almost half of the 'average' election programme's content: The Economy (16 per cent), Welfare and the Quality of Life (16 per cent), and External Relations (15 per cent). With some variation, the pattern holds true for all three parties under study. Most of the federal election campaigns have, indeed, focussed on these themes. Among the policy domains receiving less attention, the CDU election programmes show an above average interest in societal problems (Fabric of Society), the SPD places a relatively higher weight on the Government, while the FDP gives Freedom and Democracy more attention.

14.7 DIMENSIONS IN POLICY DOMAINS

As in the other chapters, we now proceed to analyse the internal structure of each of the seven broad policy domains or themes. A summary of the overall results is presented in Table 14.2 – we discuss these under separate sub-headings below.

TABLE 14.2

THE STRUCTURE OF POLICY DOMAINS: RESULTS OF FIRST ORDER FACTOR ANALYSES

CODE CATEGORIES AND POLICY DOMAINS		FACTOR 1	FACTOR 2	H^2
EXTERNAL RELATIONS				
106	PEACE	.785	-.365	.751
104	MILITARY POSITIVE	.785	.168	.645
101	FOREIGN SPECIAL RELATIONSHIPS POSITIVE	.527	.240	.336
108	INTERNATIONALISM, EEC POSITIVE AND PRO-EUROPEAN GENERAL	.361	.536	.419
107	INTERNATIONALISM, POSITIVE	.069	.630	.402
105	MILITARY, NEGATIVE	.058	-.741	.553
	PERCENT OF VARIANCE	29.1	22.7	51.8
FREEDOM AND DEMOCRACY				
203	CONSTITUTIONALISM, POSITIVE	.806		.650
201	FREEDOM AND DOMESTIC HUMAN RIGHTS	.607		.369
202	DEMOCRACY	.601		.362
	PERCENT OF VARIANCE	46.1		46.1
GOVERNMENT				
301	DECENTRALIZATION, POSITIVE	.689		.475
303	GOVERNMENT EFFICIENCY	.643		.413
305	GOVERNMENT EFFECTIVENESS AND AUTHORITY	-.629		.396
	PERCENT OF VARIANCE	42.9		42.9
ECONOMY				
403	REGULATION OF CAPITALISM	.825	.134	.699
404	ENTERPRISE	.762	.285	.662
414	ECONOMIC ORTHODOXY AND EFFICIENCY	.749	-.184	.595
402	INCENTIVES	.101	.802	.655
410	PRODUCTIVITY	.000	.848	.719
411	TECHNOLOGY AND INFRASTRUCTURE	-.051	-.500	.253
	PERCENT OF VARIANCE	34.9	24.9	59.8

Continued ...

TABLE 14.2 Continued

WELFARE AND QUALITY OF LIFE

501	ENVIRONMENTAL PROTECTION	.886	.061	.790
502	ART, SPORT, LEISURE AND MEDIA	.880	-.121	.790
506	EDUCATION, PRO-EXPANSION	.309	-.669	.544
503	SOCIAL JUSTICE			
504	SOCIAL SERVICES EXPANSION, POSITIVE	.202	.813	.702
	PERCENT OF VARIANCE	42.9	27.8	70.7

FABRIC OF SOCIETY

603	TRADITIONAL MORALITY, POSITIVE	.812	-.240	.718
607	COMMUNALISM, PLURALISM, PILLARIZATION, POSITIVE	-.240	.801	.699
605	LAW AND ORDER	-.315	-.733	.637
	PERCENT OF VARIANCE	36.4	31.5	67.9

SOCIAL GROUPS

701	LABOUR GROUPS, POSITIVE	.738	.544
703	AGRICULTURE AND FARMERS	.513	.263
706	NON-ECONOMIC DEMOGRAPHIC GROUPS	-.628	.395
	PERCENT OF VARIANCE	40.1	40.1

External Relations

Six categories qualify for inclusion in the factor analysis. In terms of frequency of mentions, 'Foreign Special Relationships Positive', is the theme which attracts most attention from all three parties under investigation. In the West German context this category is almost exclusively related to the German question: the issues coded here deal with reunification, the role of Berlin, the German Democratic Republic, and the 'Ost- und Deutschlandpolitik'.

'Internationalism: EEC positive and pro-European general' lumps together the initially different positions of the CDU on the one hand and the SPD and FDP on the other. While the former advocated the integration of the Europe of the Six, the latter favoured a cooperation with a wider range of Western nations, including Britain and the Scandinavian countries.

All election programmes talk about 'peace'. However, while peace is almost always linked with 'freedom' in the case of the CDU (*Frieden in Freiheit*), this value is more often associated with 'better understanding' (*Verständigungspolitik*) or 'renunciation of power' (*Gewaltverzicht*) in the SPD programmes.

'Internationalism Positive' addresses international political and economic cooperation, including aid to the Third World (*Entwicklungshilfe*) as well as general problems of world trade and of international organizations (UNO, UNESCO, etc.)

The categories 'Military, Positive' and 'Military, Negative' indicate problems of national security. The first contains the argument that proper security can be achieved by a strong Atlantic alliance (NATO) to which Germany should make a military contribution. Arms control, including nuclear weapons, a general and controlled disarmament are the key elements of the second category.

On the basis of these categories, factor analysis suggests a two-dimensional structure. We have labelled these dimensions 'military defence' and 'international cooperation'.

The question which underlies the first dimension may be phrased: how can one preserve peace and freedom for the Federal Republic? The answer stresses the importance of military strength at the one end of the 'military defence' axis, the other end is undefined. Thus, we speak of a 'high' and a 'low' concern with military defence regarding this dimension. In a more general sense the first factor deals with a strategy for survival in the light of a perceived threat from the East. On the average we find a higher concern with military defence in CDU programmes than in those of the SPD and FDP.

The second dimension offers alternative answers to the question of how to improve international relations. One stresses the importance of economic cooperation among the countries of the world, including Third World countries. The other answer focuses on arms control and disarmament as a means for creating better international relations. The FDP shows a greater preference for the economic approach; the SPD gives greater weight to arms control and disarmament; and the CDU takes a middle position.

Freedom and Democracy

'Freedom and Domestic Human Rights', covers both the individual freedom of self-expression and collective freedom, the freedom of the peoples.

'Democracy' elaborates on democratic participation and the need for a realization of the democratic principle in many spheres of life. This and other values of democratic government are frequently mentioned in connection with the West German Basic Law which is viewed as a major achievement on the road to democracy (Constitutionalism: Positive).

When submitted to factor analysis the three variables form a one-dimensional solution indicating that the organization of the polity should

follow the principles of freedom and democracy. The dimension emphasizes the degree to which the principles of freedom and democracy are
mentioned in the election programmes. Judged by their mean position on
this dimension the FDP ranks first and the CDU ranks last.

Government

Parties advertise their competence to govern. All parties within the Federal
Republic regard themselves highly in this respect and either point to a
successful record in the past or promise effective government in the future
('Government Effectiveness and Authority'). On the average, the proportion mentioning the party's competence to govern was almost five times
higher in SPD election programmes than in CDU election programmes.

An efficient bureaucracy constitutes another area of concern. A common
pledge made by all parties is that they will ensure a cost-conscious and
efficient administration which will serve the needs of the people ('Government Efficiency'). A third set of arguments relates to the specific problems
of federalism in Germany. Most of the discussion centres on policies which
involve federal, state and community action. All three parties under
investigation want to secure a smooth functioning of cooperation between
these different levels of government (Decentralization Positive).

Factor analysis yields a bipolar dimension which gives alternative
answers to the question of government. On the one hand, government is
linked with an efficient bureaucracy in a federal system (efficient federalism). On the other hand, a rather generalized competence to government
is also advertised (effective leadership).

The SPD scores high on efficient federalism, while the FDP advocates
effective leadership, and the CDU takes a position in between.

The Economy

Factor analysis shows two dimensions. The first opposes views about the
principles on which the economy should be organized. The second
dimension contrasts different means for the promotion of economic
productivity and full employment.

The following three variables define one pole of the first, goal-related
dimension:

- 'Regulation of Capitalism', where arguments stress the social
  elements of social market economy on the one hand and the
  commitment to guarantee competition by preventing cartel formation on the other.
- 'Enterprise'. Statements about the importance of entrepreneurship

and private capital formation define the core meaning of this category in the German context.

– 'Economic Orthodoxy and Efficiency'. Such goals as price stability, economic stability, growth and prosperity are aggregated under this label.

The position regarding the organizing principles of the economy can safely be labelled 'Social Market Economy'. The other pole of the dimension remains undefined. This is quite plausible because those categories which would indicate the opposite model of a '(Socialist) Planned Economy' had to be left out because of low use (Nationalization; Economic Planning; Controlled Economy). Thus, we shall speak of a 'high' and a 'low' concern with the theme of social market economy.

The second dimension provides answers on the means to be used to improve economic productivity and full employment. The variables 'Productivity' and 'Incentives' cluster on the one end of the dimension. Productivity is linked to full employment and the creation of jobs – both of which are regarded as consequences of the market mechanism. Incentives mainly refers to indirect (tax) measures which should help small business to function in a market economy. This position is thus related to the basic principles of the market economy model. The other end of the dimension is defined by only one variable: 'Technology'. According to this view, a growth of productivity and full employment can be achieved by sponsoring research and development as well as by the creation and improvement of an adequate infrastructure for the economy. The parties' location in this issue space confirm the expectation. On both dimensions the CDU most clearly represents social market economy positions. The SPD is closer to the 'undefined' pole of the 'social market economy' dimension and closer to the technocratic position on the 'productivity and full employment' dimension while the FDP's location is less clearly expressed.

Welfare and Quality of Life

Concerns for improvement of social security programmes such as social insurance schemes, public health or social assistance, are coded under 'Social Services Expansion, Positive'. This category in part overlaps with 'Social Justice'. Coders experienced difficulty in distinguishing the latter from the former. Statements about equal rights and equal opportunity as well as the need to support different social groups (the young, the old, consumers, etc.) are indeed closely related to social services in general. For this reason we shall interpret these two variables as indicators of a welfare state mentality which differ only slightly in content.

'Education: Pro-Expansion' covers statements about measures that should be taken to improve the education system including such diverse topics as vocational training and reform of the university system.

Two categories tap the quality of life theme: 'Art, Sport, Leisure and the Media' and 'Environmental Protection'.

Factor analysis reveals a clear two-dimensional structure. The first relates to the relative importance of this area. Only one end of the dimension is defined by the two variables which indicate these concerns. A counter position is not specified. On the average the FDP gives this issue the highest amount of attention, followed by the SPD while the CDU finishes last in this category.

The second dimension is related to social equality. The first answer suggests improvement of the welfare state, the second stresses the equal access to and the improvement of the educational system. It adds to the plausibility of this interpretation that the SPD is found to be the strongest supporter of the welfare state position, while the FDP is closer to the equal-access-to-education option.

Social Order

All election programmes concern themselves with aspects of the social order. Social order is mostly seen as precarious and readily disintegrating and thus needs to be reinforced. What is really at stake here is the issue of solidarity and who shall bring it about. All parties argue that Germans should try to get along with each other. They also note that citizens of the Federal Republic have an obligation to make a common effort to further the common cause and good (*Gemeinwohl*) because, after all, 'we' all share a homeland. ('National Effort, Social Harmony'.) According to the election programmes, attempts to undermine the *Gemeinschaft* will not be tolerated; crime, terrorism and political extremism will be countered by any party government through a strong police, an effective criminal law and an efficient court system ('Law and Order').

The two dimensions which emerge from factor analysis combine these four variables into a distinct pattern. The first dimension relates to the role of societal institutions such as the family and the churches. That they should be given an independent and important role seems to be indicated by the positively defined pole of that dimension. The opposite pole is undefined. Thus, we speak of 'high' and a 'low' concern on this dimension.

The second dimension presents a bipolar situation. One end is characterized by the quest for national effort and social harmony (*Gemeinschaft*); the other by the threat of coercion (law enforcement). Differences between the parties' average location are not very clearly expressed. FDP and CDU are closer to the appeal-for-harmony end of the dimension while the SPD is closer to the coercion end.

Social Groups

Political parties have social roots. When drumming up support they are likely to appeal to group interests. All parties promise something for the most important and well organized social groups, such as labour groups ('Labour Groups, Positive') or farmers ('Agriculture and Farmers'). They do, however, concern themselves with other non-economic social groups: the sick, the handicapped, the young, the old, refugees, war victims, former soldiers and victims of the Nazi regime ('Non-Economic Demographic Groups').

The three variables which qualified for inclusion in the factor analysis form one dimension (social group politics) which contrasts the economic interest groups on the one hand and the non-economic social groups on the other. As expected, economic interest groups did receive relatively more attention from the SPD. Both the CDU and the FDP had more to say about problems related to non-economic groups.

14.8 THE NATURE OF ISSUE-DIMENSIONS

The internal structure of each of the seven broad policy domains is revealed through factor analytic methodology. Thus, the wealth of details has been reduced to a limited number of underlying issue-dimensions. We have conceptualized an issue-dimension as representing two contrasting responses to a general political problem. However, the bipolar pattern which is implied by such a view was not observed for five out of a total of eleven factors which were empirically derived. By definition, unipolar issue-dimensions indicate that only one political position can be inferred from the available data. Although the 'counter-position' is empirically lacking, it has been interesting theoretically to speculate about what would have been a plausible alternative.

The contrast between bipolar dimensions and others resembles the distinction between position and valence issues (Stokes 1966), position issues being those on which the parties endorse opposed policies, while valence issues (like corruption) are those on which they can endorse only one alternative.

There is almost a balance of unipolar and bipolar issue-dimensions. A mix of these factor types is characteristic of all policy domains for which two-dimension issue structures were obtained: economy; welfare and the quality of life; external relations; fabric of society.

The unipolar factors indicate that military defence, freedom and democracy, social market economy, a high quality of life, and the protection of basic societal institutions are goal states which – at this level of abstraction – remain largely uncontested. Alternative positions appear on the

TABLE 14.3

DOMAINS, DIMENSIONS, POLICY POSITIONS AND CONCERNS:
AN INTERPRETATION OF THE FIRST ORDER FACTOR ANALYSES

DOMAINS	DIMENSIONS	POSITION 1/ HIGH CONCERN	POSITION 2/ LOW CONCERN
EXTERNAL RELATIONS	MILITARY DEFENCE	HIGH CONCERN WITH MILITARY DEFENCE	LOW CONCERN WITH MILITARY DEFENCE
	INTERNATIONAL RELATIONS	IMPROVE INTERNATIONAL RELATIONS BY ECONOMIC COOPERATION	IMPROVE INTERNATIONAL RELATIONS BY ARMS CONTROL
FREEDOM AND DEMOCRACY	CONSTITUTIONAL RIGHTS	HIGH CONCERN WITH FREEDOM, DEMOCRACY AND DOMESTIC HUMAN RIGHTS	LOW CONCERN WITH FREEDOM, DEMOCRACY AND DOMESTIC HUMAN HUMAN RIGHTS
GOVERNMENT	GOVERNMENT	GOVERNMENT VIA EFFICIENT FEDERALISM	GOVERNMENT VIA EFFECTIVE LEADERSHIP
ECONOMY	SOCIAL MARKET ECONOMY	HIGH CONCERN WITH SOCIAL MARKET ECONOMY	LOW CONCERN WITH SOCIAL MARKET ECONOMY
	PRODUCTIVITY AND FULL EMPLOYMENT	PROMOTE PRODUCTIVITY AND FULL EMPLOYMENT BY SUPPORTING THE MIDDLE CLASS (MITTELSTAND)	PROMOTE PRODUCTIVITY AND FULL EMPLOYMENT BY ADVANCING RESEARCH AND TECHNOLOGY
WELFARE AND QUALITY OF LIFE	QUALITY OF LIFE	HIGH CONCERN WITH QUALITY OF LIFE	LOW CONCERN WITH QUALITY OF LIFE
	SOCIAL EQUALITY	IMPROVE THE WELFARE STATE	SECURE EQUAL ACCESS TO EDUCATION
FABRIC OF SOCIETY	FAMILY AND CHURCHES	HIGH CONCERN WITH THE ROLE OF THE FAMILY AND THE CHURCHES	LOW CONCERN WITH THE ROLE OF THE FAMILY AND THE CHURCHES
FABRIC OF SOCIETY	NATIONAL SOLIDARITY	CREATE NATIONAL SOLIDARITY BY APPEALING TO GEMEINSCHAFT	CREATE NATIONAL SOLIDARITY BY ENFORCING THE LAW (RECHTSSTAAT)
SOCIAL GROUPS	SOCIAL GROUP POLITICS	SOLVE PROBLEMS OF ECONOMIC INTEREST GROUPS	SOLVE PROBLEMS OF NON-ECONOMIC SOCIAL GROUPS

TABLE 14.4

DOMAINS, DIMENSIONS, POLICY POSITIONS AND CONCERNS: THE LOCATION OF PARTIES

DOMAINS	DIMENSIONS	POSITION 1/ HIGH CONCERN	X̄	SD	X̄	SD	X̄	SD	POSITION 2/ LOW CONCERN
EXTERNAL RELATIONS	MILITARY DEFENCE	HIGH CONCERN	CDU .58	1.18	SPD .03	.76	FDP -.68	.59	LOW CONCERN
	INTERNATIONAL RELATIONS	ECONOMIC COOPERATION	FDP .16	1.13	CDU -.01	1.01	SDP -.13	.97	ARMS CONTROL
FREEDOM AND DEMOCRACY	CONSTITUTIONAL RIGHTS	HIGH CONCERN	FDP .25	.67	SPD .16	1.23	CDU -.39	.97	LOW CONCERN
GOVERNMENT	GOVERNMENT	EFFICIENT FEDERALISM	SPD .21	1.10	CDU -.05	.90	FDP -.18	1.07	EFFECTIVE LEADERSHIP
ECONOMY	SOCIAL MARKET ECONOMY	HIGH CONCERN	CDU .63	1.24	FDP -.30	.59	SPD -.37	.77	LOW CONCERN
	PRODUCTIVITY AND FULL EMPLOYMENT	SUPPORT THE MIDDLE CLASS	CDU .20	1.49	FDP -.00	.68	SPD -.19	.64	ADVANCE RESEARCH AND TECHNOLOGY
WELFARE AND QUALITY OF LIFE	QUALITY OF LIFE	HIGH CONCERN	FDP .15	1.28	SPD 1.28	.07	CDU -.21	.92	LOW CONCERN
	SOCIAL EQUALITY	WELFARE STATE	SPD .16	1.22	CDU .05	.54	FDP -.24	1.20	EQUAL ACCESS TO EDUCATION

Continued...

TABLE 14.4 Continued

		HIGH CONCERN	X̄	SD	X̄	SD	X̄	SD	LOW CONCERN
FABRIC OF SOCIETY	FAMILY AND CHURCHES	APPEAL TO GEMEINSCHAFT	FDP .36	1.23	CDU -.09	.98	SPD -.23	.80	ENFORCE THE LAW
	NATIONAL SOLIDARITY		FDP .03	.49	CDU .03	1.43	SPD -.06	.93	
SOCIAL GROUPS	SOCIAL GROUP POLITICS	ECONOMIC INTEREST GROUPS	SPD .30	.66	FDP -.12	1.23	CDU -.19	1.09	NON-ECONOMIC SOCIAL GROUPS

315

TABLE 14.5

THE STRUCTURE OF POLICY POSITIONS AND CONCERNS:
RESULT OF A SECOND ORDER FACTOR ANALYSIS

DIMENSIONS OF FIRST ORDER FACTOR ANALYSES	FACTOR 1	FACTOR 2	FACTOR 3	FACTOR 4	H^2
MILITARY DEFENCE	.150	.016	-.575	.329	.462
INTERNATIONAL RELATIONS	.780	-.072	.083	-.027	.622
CONSTITUTIONAL RIGHTS	-.172	-.316	.083	-.838	.840
GOVERNMENT	.167	.148	.457	-.023	.260
SOCIAL MARKET ECONOMY	-.292	.765	.023	.103	.682
PRODUCTIVITY AND FULL EMPLOYMENT	-.385	-.232	.723	.053	.729
QUALITY OF LIFE	.774	-.177	-.140	-.016	.651
SOCIAL EQUALITY	-.097	-.565	.156	.646	.771
FAMILY AND CHURCHES	.009	.080	.783	.142	.641
NATIONAL SOLIDARITY	-.831	-.156	.066	-.314	.818
SOCIAL GROUP POLITICS	.075	.829	.122	.079	.715
PERCENT OF VARIANCE	23.1	16.8	14.4	11.2	65.4

issue-dimensions of international relations, government, productivity and full employment, social group politics, social equality and national solidarity.

On average, the unipolar 'valence' issue-dimensions generate larger distances between the political parties than the bipolar 'position' issue-dimensions. This may be regarded as another indirect proof in support of the view that 'selective emphasis' rather than 'direct confrontation' is the characteristic mode of party competition.

Party locations along these dimensions form an interesting pattern. A 'left–right' emerges with respect to the economic and the social groups policy domains. The FDP scores high on such 'valence' issues-themes as constitutional rights, the quality of life, and the concern with the proper role of the family and the churches (Fabric of Society). The first two themes are not very much emphasized by the CDU while the latter does not meet a particular interest of the SPD. For the remaining bipolar issue-dimensions the SPD–FDP contrasts are more pronounced than either the SPD–CDU or the CDU–FDP differences.

14.9 THE GENERAL STRUCTURE OF THE ISSUE-SPACE

Second-order factor analysis reduces the eleven first-order factors to a four-dimensional issue-space. The emerging dimensions all cover pertinent

TABLE 14.6

POLICY POSITIONS AND CONCERNS: AN INTERPRET-
ATION OF THE SECOND ORDER FACTOR ANALYSIS

DIMENSIONS	POSITION 1/ HIGH CONCERN	POSITION 2/ LOW CONCERN
PRINCIPLES OF THE ORGANIZATION OF (WORLD) SOCIETY	INTERNATIONAL RELATIONS, IMPROVE QUALITY OF LIFE	PRESERVE NATIONAL SOLIDARITY
PRINCIPLES OF THE ORGANIZATION OF THE ECONOMY	HIGH CONCERN WITH SOCIAL MARKET ECONOMY	LOW CONCERN WITH SOCIAL MARKET ECONOMY
PRESERVATION AND SURVIVAL	PROTECT AND DEFINE THE ROLE OF SOCIAL INSTITUTIONS	PROTECT THE NATION STATE BY STRONG MILITARY DEFENSE
PRINCIPLES OF THE ORGANIZATION OF THE POLITY	SOCIAL JUSTICE AND SOCIAL EQUALITY	FREEDOM AND DEMOCRACY AS CONSTITUTIONAL RIGHTS

problems of any political system. The first dimension relates to the organization of (world) society. That national solidarity should be preserved and strengthened, to guarantee the survival and the functioning of society and the nation state is one possible response. The alternative stresses an international frame of reference and links the goal of the 'good' (world) society and international order to an improvement of the quality of life.

Organization of the economy characterizes the content of the second factor. A high concern with social market economy and social group politics falls at one end. The other is simply constituted by low concern for these.

Protection of important social institutions like the family and the churches on the one hand, and protection of the nation state by means of strong military defence forces, describe alternative responses to the general issue of preservation and survival

The fourth dimension contrasts different principles of the organization of the polity. Social justice and social equality are contrasted to constitutional rights like freedom and democracy.

The location of the parties on these overall issue-dimensions are difficult to evaluate. The average CDU position confirms expectations. It is pro-national solidarity, shows a high concern with social market economy and the protection of the nation state by strong military defence, and rates social justice and social equality high. These positions, however, are generally in opposition to those of the FDP while the SPD is characterized

TABLE 14.7

POLICY POSITIONS AND CONCERNS: THE LOCATION OF PARTIES ON SECOND-STAGE FACTORS

DIMENSIONS	POSITION 1/ HIGH CONCERN	$\bar{X}$	SD	$\bar{X}$	SD	$\bar{X}$	SD	POSITION 2/ LOW CONCERN
PRINCIPLES OF THE ORGANIZATION OF SOCIETY	INTERNATIONAL RELATIONS IMPROVE QUALITY OF LIFE	FDP .19	.80	SPD .08	.89	CDU -.25	1.29	PRESERVE NATIONAL SOLIDARITY
PRINCIPLES OF THE ORGANIZATION OF THE ECONOMY	HIGH CONCERN WITH SOCIAL MARKET ECONOMY	CDU .19	1.06	SPD -.06	.99	FDP -.15	1.05	LOW CONCERN WITH SOCIAL MARKET ECONOMY
PRESERVATION AND SURVIVAL	PROTECT AND DEFINE THE ROLE OF SOCIAL INSTITUTIONS	FDP .34	1.00	SPD -.10	.57	CDU -.20	1.33	PROTECT THE NATION STATE BY STRONG MILITARY DEFENCE
PRINCIPLES OF THE ORGANIZATION OF THE POLITY	SOCIAL JUSTICE AND SOCIAL EQUALITY	CDU .47	.85	SPD -.06	1.19	FDP -.46	.78	FREEDOM AND DEMOCRACY AS CONSTITUTIONAL RIGHTS

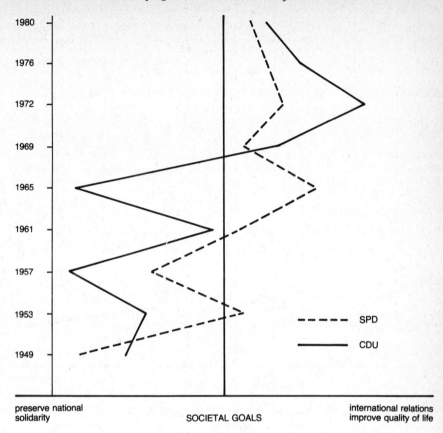

preserve national
solidarity
SOCIETAL GOALS
international relations
improve quality of life

14.1 From national solidarity to international relations and quality of life: the location of the SPD and CDU on the first dimension of the second order factor analysis

by a middle-of-the-road approach to all four dimensions. Whereas there might be reasons to explain and justify the outcome for the organization of the society, the polity and the issue of preservation, as far as the FDP and the SPD are concerned, the FDP's low concern with the social market economy poses a problem – though it may have wished here to emphasize policies not so closely associated with the CDU.

We can also look at party movements over time on the leading dimensions. Only two are actually illustrated (see Figures 14.1 and 14.2), but all seem to indicate both a 'government-opposition' effect and a 'Grand Coalition' effect. The latter is illustrated by the fact that in 1969 the SPD and CDU seem to have their smallest programmatic difference. About this

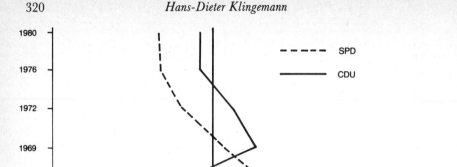

14.2 From conflict to consensus: changing concerns with social market economy and social equality, the location of the SPD and CDU on the second dimension of the second order factor analysis

point their time paths tend to cross each other, signalling changing emphasis on themes.

On 'national solidarity' *vs.* the 'better world themes', both major parties start with an emphasis on the former, then move towards the latter, with a slight reversal after 1972. While in government the CDU orientation was always more on the 'solidarity' end. In 1965 Erhard's idea of the *formierte Gesellschaft* shows up nicely. While in opposition the CDU probably tried to catch up on 'attractive' SPD themes. The whole pattern of government makes sense because 'national solidarity' was certainly at stake shortly after the war, and the theme crops up once more in the 1970s when unrest of different types posed the integration problem again.

The second dimension is defined by high and low concern (respectively) for the social market economy. The only time when positions were very different was 1949. After that the SPD in effect shifted towards acceptance

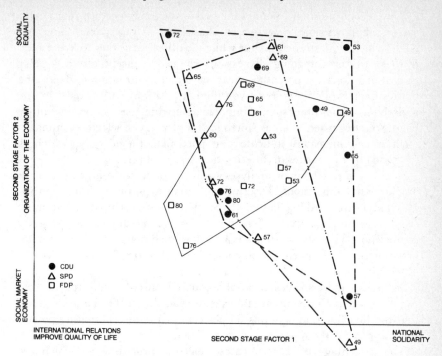

14.3 Positions of German parties on the two leading dimensions of the second stage analysis

– finally enunciated in the Godesberg basic programme (1959). While in government the SPD maintained this emphasis with some minor inconsistencies. But there was a great deal of consensus as we saw from Table 14.1 above, the SPD stressing the 'social' side more and the CDU the 'market' side.

14.10 THE NATURE OF GERMAN PARTY COMPETITION

Figure 14.3 puts the two dimensions together and is mainly interesting for the high degree of overlap between all parties. In a comparative perspective indeed, post-war German parties seem the most consensual of all.

What is the nature of competition as reflected in the election programmes? As we have already seen there is evidence for both 'direct confrontation' and 'selective emphasis'. Of course, the two modes are not mutually exclusive. Both can be pursued simultaneously on different issues; the real question is, which predominates? (Budge and Farlie 1983, 270).

'Direct confrontation' assumes that parties endorse specific proposals on each issue-dimension. 'Selective emphasis' means that parties advocate issues which work in their favour while the other parties try to avoid such themes. In the foregoing discussion we have conceptualized bipolar issue-dimensions as potential areas of direct confrontation. Here the parties have explicitly voiced two different positions with respect to one underlying issue-dimension. Unipolar issue-dimensions, on the other hand, were regarded as areas suited for the strategy of selective emphasis. Such issue-dimensions indicate one particular theme only, which is expressed by the parties in differing degrees of concern.

In the first-order factor analyses we have found five unipolar and six bipolar issue-dimensions. Discriminant analysis – the technique introduced and explained in Chapter 18 (Section 4) – can be used to determine the relative importance of these two types of issue-dimensions to party competition. Thus, we shall ask how well these dimensions 'discriminate' between the three parties, and which variables are the most powerful 'discriminators'.

In our case there are eleven variables but only three 'groups' (parties), so two discriminant functions are the most we can obtain. The analysis shows that the first function contains 80 per cent of the discriminating power; thus, it is by far the more important function.

The percentage of 'known cases' (election programmes) which are correctly classified is the most intuitive measure of predictive accuracy. In the present analysis 24 out of the 26 election programmes were correctly classified; thus, the classification based on the discriminating variables made 89 per cent fewer errors than would be expected by random assignment (tau).

To find out the relative importance of 'position' issue-dimensions and 'valence' issue-dimensions we look at the total structure coefficients, which are defined as simple bivariate correlations between the discriminant functions and the issue-dimension variables. These relations form a definite pattern. The first and most important function is almost exclusively related to the 'valence' issue-dimensions: military defence, social market economy, constitutional rights and quality of life. The second function, on the other hand, is defined to a large extent by 'position' issue-dimensions: social group politics, government, social equality and international politics. This finding strongly supports the 'selective emphasis' hypothesis advanced by Robertson (1976), and Budge and Farlie (1977, 1983). We shall return to a further (comparative) discriminant analysis in Chapter 18. Meanwhile, in its combination of historical description and quantification in an interpretation of German post-war politics, this analysis does point the way towards a more systematic cross-national analysis of party competition in Western democracies.

Note

1 I am indebted to Jürgen Falter, Dietrich Herzog, Jan-Bernd Lohmöller, Robert Philip Weber and the ECPR-Research Group on Party Manifestos for stimulating criticism and ideas. Achim Hubert converted the drafts into a readable manuscript, Lynn Jordal edited the text, Ute Klingemann and Jürgen Zimmermann provided indispensable assistance in the earlier phases of the project. Without their help this paper would never have been completed.

CHAPTER 15

FRANCE 1958–1981:
THE STRATEGY OF
JOINT GOVERNMENT PLATFORMS

———— ∿ ————

15.1 THE CHANGING PARTY SYSTEM

The French party system under the Fourth Republic was highly fragmented and polarized. The superimposition of several, largely independent, cleavages, produced a number of spiritual families (Communist,
Socialist, Centrist, Right) each represented by a distinct group in Parliament. Since none had enough seats to govern alone, parties could hope only
to participate in government coalitions. Typically, coalition formation was
initiated after the election, when Parliament convened to select a new
Prime Minister who would form a cabinet and present a government
programme. Since most participants kept their chances of joining the
winning coalition open until the last minute, there was little incentive for
them to have an agreed programme or indeed any programme at elections.
The organization of 'parties of notables' was virtually non-existent and
candidates would come forward in elections either on their own initiative
or under the sponsorship of local electoral committees.

Under the Fifth Republic, a new pattern of government formation
developed. Parties have been forced inexorably into one of two great
coalitions. This process of bipolarization was initiated by the emergence of
a coherent, lasting coalition of the Right, created to sustain the government's policy in Parliament. This was soon followed by a similar coalition
of the Left. Formal government programs are now issued at election time
with the support of coalitions of parties that can reasonably expect to have
a majority in the National Assembly. The party system has also become
less fragmented, thanks to the regrouping of the Centre parties.

This centripetal drive in the party system stems from the appearance at
the outset of the Fifth Republic of a dominant, voter-oriented, party. After
1962, the Gaullist Party successfully outgrew the traditional cleavages in
French society and became the dominant pole around which a stable

Centre-Right majority was built. The party system did not stabilize itself around one pole however. Other parties were soon forced to join, sometimes with, or against the Gaullists. Most influential in this process was the emergence of the Presidency as the main focus of power.

The dominance of the President in governmental and electoral affairs is now fully accepted. Political parties gain or lose politically as well as electorally from the outcome of presidential elections, and so give them a lot of attention. One explanation for bipolarization lies in the presidential ballot system. A candidate must win a majority of the vote cast at the first ballot in order to be elected, and failing that, a second ballot is organized between the two candidates best placed at the first ballot. The second ballot rule forces the parties to make alliances to maximize the chance that the least desirable candidate will be eliminated.

Presidential candidates have naturally sought the support of broad party coalitions in order to increase their chances of being elected. But to govern effectively, presidents also need the support of a coherent parliamentary majority, capable of sustaining governmental action between presidential elections. It is not surprising, then, that 'serious' contenders in presidential elections have sought to marshal the support of broad party coalitions that would provide them with the necessary political underpinning. In addition, three out of four presidential elections have been a second ballot duel between François Mitterand, the candidate of the Left and the winner of the 1981 presidential contest, and the candidate of the Centre-Right Majority – General de Gaulle in 1965 and Valéry Giscard d'Estaing in 1974 and 1981. The parliamentary elections that followed – 1967, 1978 and 1981 respectively – can be seen as continuations of these great presidential duels.

The centripetal pressures in French party politics thus extend to parliamentary elections. Since 1958, France has had a single-member constituency majority system with two ballots. To be elected at the first ballot, a candidate must obtain an absolute majority of the vote cast. To be included in the second ballot, he must win at least 12.5 per cent (10 per cent prior to 1976) of the registered electorate, and this high threshold eliminates many candidates. Isolated candidates, who do not enjoy a broad party base and nevertheless succeed in passing the line at the first ballot, lack the support of friendly allies at the second ballot, where most seats remain at stake. As a result, the struggle at the second ballot is one between the Right and the Left with little room for outsiders.

The three factors mentioned above – dominant party, presidentialism and electoral system – have thus provided a powerful incentive for parties of the same tendency to unite so as to maximize their potential for victory. On the other hand, one should not underestimate the centrifugal forces working in the parties. First, ideological divergences are still very much present, particularly within the Left. Second, the electoral system itself encourages competition between parties of the same tendency at the first ballot since the parties always have the possibility of regrouping at the second ballot. Finally, the time-lag that currently exists between parliamentary and presidential elections allows individual parties to align with the coalition partners of their choice in two successive elections – and these may not be the same.

15.2 SELECTION OF PARTIES AND MANIFESTO EQUIVALENTS

The criterion used for the selection of parties is the formation of a parliamentary group in the National Assembly (*Assemblée Nationale*). Article 19 of the Rules of Procedure requires that 30 members (about 6 per cent of total membership) sign-in to constitute a group. This eliminates a number of otherwise numerically 'relevant' parties which are too small to constitute a group. These were eliminated from the sample with one exception (Communist, 1958). Individual *députés* who do not belong to a group cannot compete for influential positions in the House. Hence small parties have an incentive to join a large group of similar ideology. Eventually, they will campaign in elections within the larger party. The criterion, although selective, therefore accurately reflects the process of gradual absorbtion of smaller parties by the coalitions of the Right or the Left. This gives us a total of 36 admissible parties (groups) over seven elections. The number of coded manifestos does not correspond to the number of admissible parties, however.

On four occasions more than one admissible party of the Centre-Right majority endorsed a joint government programme, or its equivalent, along with the principle of joint candidacies at the first ballot (1967, 1968, 1973, 1981). Each of these programmes was included only once in the sample.

All remaining parties campaigned on their own at the first ballot and a separate document was coded for each. The Common Programme of the Left (1973) was included in addition to the Communists' and Socialists' own platforms for that election.

To sum up, there are eight coded manifestos for the Centre-Right majority, nine coded manifestos for the parties of the Centre and fourteen plus one (i.e. fifteen) for the Left.

Party platforms for the three first elections of the Fifth Republic have been indexed in a single volume (Charlot 1970) and deposited at the *Fondation Nationale des Sciences Politiques* of Paris (and not always at the parties' headquarters). In later elections – and particularly from 1973 onwards – party programmes are available in the form of widely circulated books.

15.3 PREPARATION OF MANIFESTOS

(i) The ex-majority

Parties in the presidential majority are normally represented in the government. However, due to the time lag between presidential and parliamentary elections, there is the possibility that a party that had supported a presidential winner may campaign against the government in the next parliamentary election, thus increasing the risk that presidential and parliamentary majorities will not coincide.

To prevent this, Centre-Right government leaders have sought to lock all government coalition members into binding agreements in legislative elections. From 1967 onward the ex-majority governments have endorsed joint candidates in the first ballot on behalf of a common programme of government. The main objective of the coalition leadership being to remain in power, its programme has been identical to government action and programme preparation has fallen primarily upon the Prime Minister under the authority of the President who appoints him.

In 1967, Georges Pompidou set up the Action Committee for the Fifth Republic with the task of drawing a list of joint candidates of the majority and preparing a common manifesto on the basis of his own previous draft. Three tendencies were represented in the committee. The orthodox Gaullists – led by René Capitant – had a relatively small electoral following but they could claim General de Gaulle's support for amending Pompidou's manifesto draft – in particular with regard to the issue of participation. The Gaullist *inconditionnels*, the majority within the Majority, were represented by Jacques Chaban-Delmas. Chaban-Delmas and his friends gave full support to the Prime Minister. The last group in the sub-committee, that of the Independent Republicans, represented by Raymond Mondon, argued for a more European Policy and more economic freedom. The manifesto of the Majority was made public in February 1967. It was a compromise between the proposals of the orthodox Gaullists and those of the Government. Little of the Independent Republican party's proposals were retained in the manifesto. Giscard d'Estaing and his friends, however, managed to get 80 candidates endorsed by the Committee.

For the 1973 elections, the leaders of the three parties in the majority agreed, in a series of private meetings with the Prime Minister, Pierre Messmer, and a representative of President Pompidou, to endorse joint candidates under the label Union of Republicans for Progress. Messmer's programme was made public in a two hour speech at the Gaullist National Meeting held at Provins.

Similarly in 1978, it was Raymond Barre's responsibility to prepare the Blois programme which was finalized at a round table under the Chairmanship of the President of the Republic. The Gaullists had refused to endorse Barre's programme and conducted a separate electoral campaign with a programme of their own.

The 1981 parliamentary elections offer an interesting counter-example. It may be the exception that confirms the rule. In the light of François Mitterand's presidential success, Gaullist and Giscardien back-benchers rejected the defeated President's claim to arbitrate conflicts over Centre–Right candidacies. The powers of the ex-Prime Minister were also reduced to practically nothing and the task of endorsing joint candidates and establishing a joint platform was carried out entirely by party head-quarters.

(ii) The Left

The bipolar pressure which forced the parties of the Centre-Right to form a coalition has also been felt on the Left. The programmatic alliance of the Left emerged only after a preparatory phase of electoral cooperation between the Socialist Party (PS) and the Communist Party (PCF). Communists, Socialists and Left Radicals have only achieved withdrawal agreements for the second ballot (i.e. primaries), never going as far as joint candidates at the first ballot.

The parties of the Left are usually referred to as 'mass parties'. By contrast with other French parties – either parties of 'notables' which were essentially concerned with the nomination of candidates best able to win election, or parties of government which are set up above all to channel electoral support for the current ministerial team – the main objective of mass parties is the recruitment and mobilization of members, within a formalized system of membership located outside the parliamentary-governmental sphere on behalf of a doctrine. In mass parties, grass-root organizations, not electoral caucuses or governments, are the source of power and the basis of leadership.

Candidates in mass parties are nominated by the Federations with little interference from the party leadership. The Central Committee does not need to go beyond ratification of candidates nominated by the Federal Committees because the nomination of candidates is made on the basis of ability to best serve the interests of the party. The Central Committee of the party, once it has ratified the list of candidates presented to it by the Federations, publishes the electoral programme.

Mass parties depend heavily upon their doctrinal heritage as a guide for political action. All important decisions concerning the doctrine emanate from the Congress, which is composed of delegates elected by the Feder-ations in proportion to their size.

Electoral platform elaboration does not assume a high priority of mass party activities. The reason for this is simple. Mass parties, although they place emphasis on attracting votes, are not uniquely concerned with gaining office by means of electoral victory. A great deal of activity is devoted to mass mobilization and education. Electoral manifestos are only one means of mobilization, which must be preceded and prolonged by a variety of other activities such as demonstrations, strikes, party schools, party press, etc. Moreover, Party Congresses meet at regular intervals – every other year for the Socialist party, every three years for the Communist Party – which do not necessarily coincide with election years. As a result, the actual preparation of the electoral platform is entrusted to the legislative body of the party (Central Committee, *Comité directeur*) which must carry out the decisions of the members between two Congresses, often without ratification by the party membership.

This state of things has evolved somewhat in the past decade. Both the Communist and the Socialist parties have undergone a period of intense revision, spurred by the need to offer a credible programme of government as an effective alternative to Gaullism. The new emphasis on government programmes inevitably resulted in manifesto-related activities acquiring a high priority on party congress agendas.

The elaboration of the programme of the new *Parti Socialiste* (PS) in 1972 is a good illustration.

After the Epinay Congress which finalised the reunification of all Socialist forces, a number of *ad hoc* committees (*commissions spécialisées*) and working groups, composed of some 400, started to work on a new programme, under the auspices of a Special Committee for the programme (*Commission centrale du programme*), headed by Jean Pierre Chevènement, the leader of the Centre for Study, Research and Socialist Education (CERES). An initial detailed draft was reviewed by the Central Committee which then set the broad orientations to be followed by the various working groups.

The specialized committees forwarded their final draft in January 1972 to the Central Committee. The final draft was then sent to the Socialist Federations one month before the National Convention, for discussion and amendment. After eight months of intensive work, the programme, entitled *Changer la Vie*, was unanimously ratified by the delegates of the Federations, the members of the Central Committee and the parliamentary group gathered at the Suresnes National Convention.

The Communist Party also searched for a programme of government. An initial sketch, entitled *The Goals of the Party*, was published in 1959. This programme was to constitute the doctrinal basis for negotiation with the other parties of the Left with a view to forming a joint government. It is important because it constitutes the first effort by French Communists to formulate a model of government in alliance with other political forces.

The real breakthrough in Communist political strategy occurred in 1962, however, when the Party abandoned its anti-SFIO posture in order to seek alliance with the Socialist leadership. The new political line was solemnly ratified at the seventeenth Congress in 1964. In December 1968, the Central Committee, at its Champigny session, adopted a statement of principle to be enacted in a future programme of the united Left. The *Champigny Manifesto* was given much publicity and edited for mass circulation in 1969. In September 1971, the Central Committee adopted a more detailed version of the manifesto which was published under the title *Changer de Cap*.

The new Communist emphasis on a governmental programme coincided with a sudden acceleration of the frequency of Communist Congress meetings in the 1970s as well as the broadening of the ideological debate in this party. Traditionally the PCF Congress only meets every three years, whereas in the 1970s there were no less than six Congress or Congress-like meetings.

Observers have not failed to note the ritual atmosphere of the Communist Party Congress, where decisions are always unanimous. Ideological debates in the Communist Party are not as democratic as in the Socialist Party. The fundamental difference here is that the PS is constituted of various tendencies which are in competition for the final programme. By contrast, the debate in the PCF is still limited to the preparatory stage of the programme and to minor points of doctrine.

15.4 MANIFESTO FORMAT AND CIRCULATION

Party programmes of the 1960s were usually published by the parties themselves in the form of short leaflets. In the case of several parties the only available party document was a speech specimen included in the party's *vade-mecum* for its candidates. Party programmes were often reprinted in the party press which usually had a restricted circulation – except for the weekly *L'Humanité-Dimanche* (500,000).

By contrast, the 1970s witnessed an avalanche of party programmes in the form of widely available paperbacks – often cheap pocket-books – brought out by independent publishers. Thus, between 1969, when the Editions Sociales (the publisher of the PCF) published the *Champigny Manifesto*, and 1980, when the PS programme *Projet Socialiste* was published by Flammarion, various publishers printed well over twenty programmes on behalf of practically all existing political parties. Even the small Parti Social-Démocrate, a minor member of the UDF coalition, had its *Manifesto for a French Social Democracy* published by Albin Michel (4,000 copies printed). As might be expected, the larger the party following, the higher the number of copies printed. There are exceptions to this rule,

TABLE 15.1

SOME ELECTORAL PLATFORMS OF THE 70'S. FORMAT AND NUMBER OF PRINTED COPIES

EAR	TITLE	PUBLISHER	EDITIONS	PRINTS	POCKET-
969	MANIFESTE DU PARTI COMMUNISTE FRANCAIS: POUR UNE DEMOCRATIE AVANCEE, POUR UNE FRANCE SOCIALISTE.	EDITIONS SOCIALES	1	100,000	YES
970	CIEL ET TERRE: PROGRAMME RADICAL. M. ALBERT AND J.J. SERVAN-SCHREIBER.	DENOEL	2	202,000	YES
971	CHANGER DE CAP: PROGRAMME POUR UN GOUVERNEMENT DEMOCRATIQUE D'UNION POPULAIRE.	EDITIONS SOCIALES	2	1,100,000	YES
972	PROGRAMME COMMUN DE GOUVERNEMENT DU PARTI COMMUNISTE FRANCAIS ET DU PARTI SOCIALISTE.	EDITIONS SOCIALES	1	1,400,000	YES
973	LE PROJET REFORMATEUR: PROGRAMME DE GOUVERNEMENT DU MOUVEMENT REFORMATEUR.	ROBERT LAFFONT	4	47,000	
975	DEMOCRATIE FRANCAISE. VALERY GISCARD D'ESTAING.	FAYARD	2	2,000,000	YES
977	PROPOSITIONS POUR LA FRANCE: RASSEMBLEMENT POUR LA REPUBLIQUE.	STOCK	1	92,000	YES
978	PROGRAMME COMMUN DE GOUVERNEMENT ACTUALISE: PARTI COMMUNISTE FRANCAIS.	EDITIONS SOCIALES	1	1,500,000	YES

SOURCE: THE PUBLISHERS

however. For example, Servan-Schreiber's *Ciel et Terre*, which was published at the time the owner of the weekly *l'Express* made his dramatic entry into the political arena, had over 200,000 copies printed, among which 60,000 were in pocket-books. These figures hardly coincide with the small influence and following of Servan-Schreiber's *Parti Radical*. Some publishers prefer not to divulge the number of copies sold. However, on the basis of data furnished by those who did, a rough estimate would be about one half of the printed copies sold to the public. Some figures are given in Table 15.1

The change in manifesto format must be seen in the context of the bipolar pressure which forced the parties to squeeze into broad coalitions capable of enacting a governmental programme. This prompted coalition headquarters (or governments) to address the voters directly on behalf of joint programmes. The significance of this should not be over-estimated, however. First, the change in format, because it extended to all parties, large or small, reflected the persistence of a traditionally fragmented party system just as much as the bipolar trend. Second, the publication of party programmes in the form of widely available pocket-books is only *one* method of political marketing, and is by no means a necessary condition for an electoral coalition's success. The new format may be seen as a phenomenon limited to the 1970s, a political advertising innovation first introduced by the united Left to underscore its willingness to take over the government and focus the electorate's attention. The formula, once successfully demonstrated, was then imitated by other parties. The eventual collapse of the Union of the Left may well have removed the motivation for parties to keep advertising their programmes in book form.

Has the change in format generated an additional concern with policy programmes in the electorate? There is ample evidence to demonstrate that the Union of the Left and the Common Programme were a significant cue for the voters. For example a SOFRES 1977 poll reveals that 43 per cent Communist and 32 per cent Socialist sympathisers had read or glanced through the Common Programme, against 21 per cent Republican, and 17 per cent Gaullist sympathisers. This is at least 11 percentage points above the proportion of Centre Right voters who had read Giscard d'Estaing's *Démocratie Française* (6 per cent).[1]

15.5 MANIFESTO CONTENT ANALYSIS

The content analysis was performed in Paris in 1979.[2] Most documents were coded twice, by independent coders who showed a satisfactory correspondence in their judgements. The study – though not the first content analysis of party programmatic statements (Cotteret and Moreau, 1969; Cotteret, Moreau and Emeri, 1976; Prost 1974; Labbé 1977) is the only attempt to factor-analyse national party programmes over a series of recent elections.

The general coding frame worked well in the French case and specially created sub-categories turned out not to be necessary. As in the other country analyses, certain general categories were excluded because of low frequency of mention – less than 1 per cent overall and less than 3 per cent by any individual party.

The number of references left uncoded is limited – a range of 4–14 per cent with a mean of 7.4 per cent. There is only a limited number of references to other parties in the documents – from 1 per cent to 10 per cent in any one year, with a mean of 3.6 per cent. Party competition in France, as elsewhere, is a matter of emphasizing favourable points rather than of direct argument with rivals. This also appears from the average percentage of references over the post-war period which are given for each 'tendance' in Table 15.2. Although 'Social Justice' is ranked highly by all parties (including the populist Gaullists), substantially different patterns of

TABLE 15.2

TEN LEADING CATEGORIES FOR PARTISAN TENDENCY

Communist (N = 6)

1.	701	Labour Groups (+)	6.86
2.	504	Social Services (+)	5.44
3.	503	Social Justice	5.43
4.	202	Democracy	4.98
5.	706	Non-Economic Groups	4.48
6.	602	Nat'l Way of Life (-)	4.07
7.	106	Peace	3.94
8.	413	Nationalisation	3.80
9.	412	Controlled Economy	3.72
10.	403	Regn. of Capitalism	3.44

Socialist (N = 7)

202	Democracy	5.96
503	Social Justice	5.58
504	Social Services (+)	5.23
106	Peace	4.40
701	Labour Groups (+)	4.30
506	Education (+)	3.97
201	Freedom/Human Rights	3.39
412	Controlled Economy	3.34
706	Non-Economic Groups	3.18
403	Regn. of Capitalism	2.71

Moderate (N = 4)

1.	201	Freedom/Human Rights	5.44
2.	601	Nat'l Way of Life (+)	4.03
3.	202	Democracy	3.68
4.	408	Specific Economic Goals	3.88
5.	203	Constitutionalism (+)	3.45
6.	503	Social Justice	3.42
7.	401	Free Enterprise	3.05
8.	704	Other Economic Groups	3.02
9.	402	Incentives	3.00
10.		Farmers & Agriculture	2.90

Gaullist (N = 6)

503	Social Justice	5.00
305	Government Effectiveness	4.75
203	Constitutionalism (+)	4.62
201	Freedom/Human Rights	4.11
202	Democracy	3.93
109	National Sovereignty	3.76
601	Nat'l Way of Life (+)	3.66
410	Productivity	3.48
402	Incentives	3.10
506	Education (+)	3.05

Centre (N = 6)

706	Non-Economic Groups	8.35
108	European Community (+)	8.27
6071	Catholic Schools	6.66
301	Decentralisation (+)	5.51
414	Economic Orthodoxy	5.06
503	Social Justice	4.84
703	Farmers & Agriculture	4.59
411	Technology & Infrastr.	4.16
402	Incentives	4.14
(506	Education (+)	3.44)
(202	Democracy	3.44)

Top Ten For France as a Whole

503	Social Justice	4.96
202	Democracy	4.50
706	Non-Economic Groups	4.38
504	Social Services (+)	3.78
201	Freedom/Human Rights	3.61
506	Education (+)	3.20
703	Farmers & Agriculture	2.92
106	Peace	2.66
203	Constitutionalism (+)	2.62
(301	Decentralisation (+)	2.51)
(411	Technology & Infras.	2.51)

TABLE 15.3

FIRST-STAGE FACTOR ANALYSIS OF THE ECONOMY DOMAIN

VARIMAX ROTATED FACTOR MATRIX	FACTOR 1.1 CAPITALISM VS.	FACTOR 1.2 ECONOMIC
CODE CATEGORIES:	CONTROL	GOALS
402 INCENTIVES	.908	.054
413 NATIONALIZATION	-.823	-.121
412 CONTROLLED ECONOMY	-.729	-.328
403 REGULATION OF CAPITALISM	-.619	-.533
401 ENTERPRISE	.534	-.064
410 PRODUCTIVITY	.414	.063
414 ECONOMIC ORTHODOXY	.399	.658
408 ECONOMIC GOALS	.167	.875
411 TECHNOLOGY	.093	.268
404 ECONOMIC PLANNING	.092	.754
FROM UNROTATED SOLUTION:		
EIGENVALUE	4.30	1.57
PERCENT OF VARIANCE	43.1	15.7

emphasis appear on other topics, especially between Communists and Socialists on the one hand and Gaullists on the other.

Direct confrontation did take place in the 1970s partly as a result of bipolarization and the attempts at joint government programmes. In the 1973 elections, for example, the Gaullist majority sought to undermine the credibility of the Left in government, and a significant portion of Messmer's *Discours de Blois* was devoted to a critique of the Common Programme of the Left.

Direct confrontation of ideas between parties of the same tendency is usually muted (it would be counterproductive). However, the parties of the Left did exactly that in the 1978 election, when it had ended in a stalemate. Socialists, Communists and Left Radicals published their own respective programmes. Each included the modifications – mostly minor ones – that had been accepted by all negotiating parties, as well as their own proposals for revision which had been rejected by the other partners.

15.6 DOMAIN ANALYSES

The loadings of the original categories on each of the fourteen first order factors are reported below, along with the factor's respective contribution to variance within themes. The loadings reported may result from Varimax rotation while the percentage of variance explained is that resulting from the unrotated solution. We start with the economy which is a central domain.

TABLE 15.4

FIRST-STAGE FACTOR ANALYSIS OF THE WELFARE DOMAIN

PRINCIPAL FACTOR MATRIX

CODE CATEGORIES:	FACTOR 2.1 SOCIAL SERVICES	FACTOR 2.2 LEISURE
506 EDUCATION	.923	.088
504 SOCIAL SERVICES POSITIVE	.894	-.140
503 SOCIAL JUSTICE	-.417	-.584
502 SPORTS AND LEISURE	-.248	.810
FROM UNROTATED SOLUTION:		
EIGENVALUE	1.88	1.02
PERCENT OF VARIANCE	47.2	25.7

Economy

This domain includes the largest number of original categories even when four of them have been excluded from the analyses (Corporatism, Keynesian Demand Management, negative and positive references to Protectionism). Although a maximum of three factors was generated, the first factor is overwhelmingly important (it alone explains almost half the total variance). It taps a profound and lasting disagreement among the parties as to how the economy of the nation ought to be organized. The second factor is less polar than the first. Its principal component scores (Economic Goals and Planning) reveal a concern with the long-term economic development of France, the need to solve pressing economic problems, whatever the means. Note that economic planning (*planification indicative*) is a neutral symbol, a technique for economic development which is accepted from all angles of the political spectrum. The third factor, which is not reported in Table 15.3 emphasizes – not surprisingly – technology.

Welfare

This theme competes with the economy for overall importance. The analysis produced a maximum of two factors. The first accounts for some 47 per cent of the total variance. This is a non-polar factor. By contrast with the economy, the quasi-unidimensionality of the welfare theme results from a consensus among the parties over advocacy of social welfare. (But note the opposition between Social Justice and Social Services, also encountered in other countries). The wide acceptance of the welfare state by French parties is evidenced by the growing importance of the theme as well as the presence of three of its component symbols (Social Justice,

TABLE 15.5

FIRST-STAGE FACTOR ANALYSIS OF THE SOCIETY DOMAIN

PRINCIPAL FACTOR MATRIX	FACTOR 3.1 ANTI- VS.	FACTOR 3.2 PRO-SYSTEM
CODE CATEGORIES:	PRO-SYSTEM	
602 WAY OF LIFE NEGATIVE	.823	.334
607 COMMUNALISM POSITIVE	.664	.607
605 LAW AND ORDER	-.606	.419
601 WAY OF LIFE POSITIVE	-.508	.607
606 SOCIAL HARMONY	.476	-.244
FROM UNROTATED SOLUTION		
EIGENVALUE	1.97	1.08
PERCENT OF VARIANCE	39.4	21.7

Social Services and Education) among the five categories mentioned most often overall. The second factor opposes Social Justice to the new concerns encapsulated in the Arts, Sports, Leisure and Media.

Society

The analysis of the theme reveals most clearly the antagonistic attitudes of the Left and the Right with regard to the current fabric of society. The category 'negative references to National Way of Life' was used to code various references and word associations – such as transition to Socialism, popular struggle, crisis of capitalism, necessary profound changes in the social structures, and the like – which are found almost exclusively in Communist and Socialist parlance.

In this respect, it should be noted that there has been a reinforcement of Marxist rhetoric in recent manifestos of the parties of the Left. The Socialist and Communist parties 'retrieved' many ideas of May '68 which extended their respective traditional ideological heritage. Ideological continuity was also reinforced by the economic crisis of the mid–1970s. While the parties of the Centre-Right majority responded to it by emphasizing a more egalitarian policy within the current societal framework (Chaban-Delmas' concept of the 'new society'), the Left proposed a transformation of the framework itself. Thus, in response to the detailed proposals of the Centre-Right in 1972, the PS set out to 'change life' (the very title of the Socialist programme in 1973). The two main signatories of the Common Programme had also to focus on their mutual doctrinal heritage in order to achieve agreement. This produces the strong contrast between support for, and opposition to the existing framework evidenced by the first factor in Table 15.5. The second factor is unipolar and seems to express a somewhat blurred form of support for the system.

TABLE 15.6

FIRST-STAGE FACTOR ANALYSIS OF EXTERNAL RELATIONS DOMAIN

PRINCIPAL FACTOR MATRIX

CODE CATEGORIES:		FACTOR 4.1 PEACE	FACTOR 4.2 INTERNATION- ALISM
105	MILITARY NEGATIVE	.880	.254
103	DECOLONIZATION	.800	-.007
106	PEACE	.634	.292
110	EEC NEGATIVE	.543	-.469
101	SPECIAL RELATIONS POSITIVE	-.403	.003
108	EEC POSITIVE	-.403	.672
104	MILITARY POSITIVE	-.247	-.599
107	INTERNATIONALISM	-.083	.796
109	NATIONAL SOVEREIGNTY	-.058	-.725
	FROM UNROTATED SOLUTION:		
	EIGENVALUE	2.51	2.34
	PERCENT OF VARIANCE	27.9	26.0

External relations

There are nine categories in this theme, with the exclusion of negative references to Special Relations (essentially negative mentions of U.S. Foreign policy and the Atlantic Alliance, particularly by the Communists).

The two principal factors tap two sets of connected attitudes. One advocates Peace, Decolonization and a smaller defence budget, the other opposes Internationalism and Europeanism with the (essentially Gaullist) idea of National Sovereignty. A third factor was obtained with positive attitudes to the Military and to National Sovereignty highly loaded.

Groups

Only one category (Labour Groups Negative) was excluded while a sub-category 'Families' was created. The two factors that are generated by the analysis ('Middle Class' and 'Labour') are relatively unipolar and in opposition. The three highly loaded categories in the first factor (Families .91, Economic Groups, and Farmers .70) indicate a dimension of concern for conservative middle-class interests and values. The second factor, with emphasis on Labour (.86) and Minorities (.62), gives a definite leftist tilt to the dimension. The category Farmers is relatively highly loaded in both factors (.71 and .54). This indicates a general concern for an electoral clientele which has traditionally been subject to attention by all the parties.

Freedom and Democracy

This theme produced two dimensions: one is predominantly concerned with the constitutional problem (Constitutionalism Negative .87, Constitutionalism Positive −.76, Democracy .56). This was the main concern of the 1958 election but its importance diminished in subsequent elections as all the non-Gaullist parties came to accept the basic features of the new regime including presidential election by direct suffrage. As a result, the overall share of the theme Freedom and Democracy which was unusually high in 1958, decreased in the 1960s. The second factor is an unipolar one dominated by symbols of Freedom (.83) and Democracy (.53). This might come as a surprise to some readers who argue that freedom and democracy mean quite different things depending upon whether they are mentioned by Communists or Gaullists. This is entirely plausible, yet our coding strategy, in accordance with the general coding instructions, was to take the symbols mentioned at their face value, i.e. coding what the parties actually said, not what we thought they really meant. Not surprisingly, then, Democracy is the leading category, the only one which is mentioned by all the parties in all elections, closely followed by Freedom.

Government

Two categories were eliminated within this theme (Government Corruption and Decentralization Negative). Positive emphases on Decentralization were not exclusive to the Socialists. The Gaullist party has repeatedly advanced decentralizing proposals in its electoral manifestos. As expected, the two factors generated within the theme are antagonistic. The first taps a concern about government decentralization as opposed to government effectiveness (Decentralization .87, Efficiency .60, Effectiveness −.55). The second factor expresses the typical Gaullist posture of support for a disciplined majority in Parliament, supporting a powerful President, and a centralized administration of prefects to carry out governmental decisions without interference from local politicians. (Loadings are .70 for Government Efficiency and .75 for Government Effectiveness).

15.7 DIMENSIONS IN FRENCH PARTY COMPETITION

The 14 factor scores for each of the 31 party manifestos were used as input variables in the second-order analysis. Five factors were extracted from this final analysis, each interpretable in terms of the initial components (see Table 15.7).

TABLE 15.7

SECOND ORDER FACTOR ANALYSIS OF WITHIN-THEME FACTORS

PRINCIPAL FACTOR MATRIX

CODE CATEGORIES:	FACTOR 1 LEFT-RIGHT	FACTOR 2 LIBERALISM- POPULISM	FACTOR 3 FREEDOM- CONSTRAINTS
CAPITALISM VS. CONTROL	.856	-.186	-.004
ANTI- VS. PRO-SYSTEM	.776	.046	.180
ANTI-CONSTITUTIONALISM	-.722	-.030	.376
INTERNATIONALISM	-.708	.005	.040
GOVERNMENT EFFECTIVENESS	.558	.515	.243
LEISURE	-.496	-.310	.143
DECENTRALIZATION	.461	-.328	.169
FREEDOM	.381	-.220	.689
LABOUR AND MINORITIES	-.271	.624	.382
MIDDLE CLASSES	.214	.212	-.505
PRO-SYSTEM	-.194	-.204	-.143
SOCIAL SERVICES AND EDUCATION	.170	.169	-.208
PEACE	-.048	.873	-.048
ECONOMIC	.039	-.075	-.600

FROM UNROTATED SOLUTION:

EIGENVALUE	3.72	2.12	2.02
PERCENT OF VARIANCE	26.6	15.2	14.5

The first factor accounts for 26.6 per cent of the total variance. It is a polar factor contrasting clusters of first order factors which are, themselves, polar. Limiting our interpretation to the four principal loadings, it is clear that the two positively loaded variables reflect a coincidence between two dominant cleavages in French party competition. The first cleavage is the traditional economic cleavage over government intervention in the economy. The second cleavage opposes positive attitudes towards the dominant societal arrangements and negative attitudes. This dual cleavage is only one component of the dimension generated by the factor however. It is contrasted with a different set of opposed values and attitudes as reflected by the next pair of negatively loaded variables. This is also a dual partisan cleavage which concerns the constitutional issue and the French posture in foreign policy.

The dimension is therefore complex but eminently interpretable. It takes account of several cleavages each of which may separate parties allied on others. Thus, in particular, the posture of the Centre parties towards the issue of nationalism *vs.* internationalism is opposed to that of the Gaullist party, while these two political families agree on the economic-societal cleavage. *Vice versa*, the Communists who disagree most strongly with the Gaullists on domestic policy matters tend to agree with them on supporting a nationalistic posture in foreign policy.

TABLE 15.8

AVERAGE DISTANCES OVER TIME BETWEEN FRENCH PARTIES AND TENDENCIES
(OVER THE THREE DIMENSIONS OF THE SECOND STAGE FACTOR ANALYSIS)

ELECTIONS	ALL PARTIES	ACROSS TENDENCIES	WITHIN LEFT TENDENCY	WITHIN RIGHT TENDENCY
1958	1.35	1.56	1.73	.32
1962	1.28	1.46	.89	.96
1967	.90	.88	.59	1.41
1968	1.10	1.08	.66	1.53
1973	.81	1.01	.0	.29
1978	.92	.99	1.03	.54
1981	.86	.86	.80	.75
AVERAGE	1.03	1.20	.81	.84

Despite this caveat, the first dimension of French party competition appears to be a predominantly Left–Right dimension with economic, societal, institutional and foreign relations components.

The second factor accounts for 15.2 per cent of the total variance. Four variables are significantly weighted: Peace, Labour and Minorities, Government Effectiveness, and Decentralization, with the last negatively weighted.

The picture which emerges is reasonably clear. The dimension is one of support of nationalistic values, the working class and the poor, and government effectiveness, as opposed to emphasis on internationalism and European integration, the middle classes and government decentralization. The partisan cleavage thus uncovered cuts across the traditional Left–Right economic cleavage of the first factor. Specifically, the Communist and Gaullist philosophies and 'authoritarian' or populist styles are pitted together against the more liberal values of the Centre and the Socialists.

The third factor, which accounts for 14.5 per cent of the total variance, taps three first-order factors; Freedom as opposed to Economic Goals and Middle Classes. The dimension is one of emphasis on freedom as opposed to the constraints of economic goals (associated with support of Economic Orthodoxy) and the defence of middle-class private interests. The leftist tilt in this third factor is not surprising. The symbol of individual freedom is no longer the appendage of the Centre-Right in France. Finally, two lesser factors (not reported in Table 15.7) account for 9.2 and 8.7 per cent of the total variance respectively and tap positive attitudes toward leisure and national sovereignty.

15.8 SPATIAL POSITIONS OF THE PARTIES

The respective spatial positions of the three main parties (Communists, Socialists and Gaullist) are plotted in a two dimensional space (Figure 15.1), along with platforms of the Christian Democratic MRP and its heirs (CD in 1967, PDM in 1978 and Reform Movement in 1978).

The vertical dimension is the first second-order factor. A high score on this dimension indicates strong support of capitalism, the current fabric of society and national sovereignty (all reminiscent of right-wing values). The second dimension (horizontal axis) in the figure corresponds to the second factor and contrasts populistic-authoritarian values in foreign policy and government with more liberal views.

Note first that the parties have clearly defined 'territories' in the space. The Communist platforms are all situated in the lower right-hand quadrant, the Socialist platforms in the lower left-hand quadrant (with two exceptions) and the Gaullist and Centre platforms are all (with the exception of Christian Democrats in 1967) situated in the upper half of the Figure, with, rather predictably, Centre manifestos close to the origin. Note also that the Gaullist and Communist manifestos tend to cluster along the second (horizontal) dimension, while the Centre and Socialist manifestos are spread more evenly along the two dimensions.

Have the changes in the French party system been accompanied by an ideological rapprochement or distancing? This can be estimated through a set of simple measures. Four distances between party platforms have been derived and then compared across elections. One measures the distance between all four parties in the analysis (it therefore includes six measures), two measure the distance between the pairs of parties in each tendency (one measure each) and the last measures the average distance across tendencies (four measures). The distances were computed over the three first factors. However they gave mixed results. On the one hand, the average of the distance between all four party platforms has decreased over time therefore indicating some increase in overall consensus when all distances are taken into account. On the other hand, the average of the distance across tendencies has remained higher overall than the distance between all platforms, while the average of the distance between platforms of the same tendency has decreased significantly. In other words, the decrease in the total average party distance over the seven elections of the Fifth Republic is due rather more to the *rapprochement* between party platforms of the same tendency, than to one between party platforms across the major ideological divisions.

Changes over time on the two leading dimensions can also be displayed graphically (see Figures 15.2a and 15.2b). Looking at the array of parties

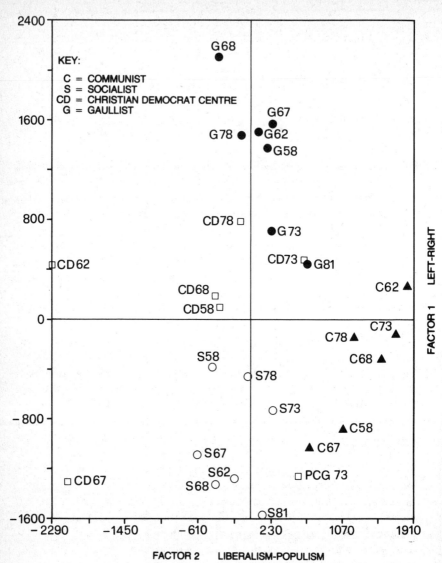

15.1 French electoral platforms, 1958–1981

on the separate dimensions brings out a point which is implied but not obvious in Figure 15.1, i.e. that the array does not coincide with the Left–Right order which is accepted by tradition and which places the Communist Party to the left of the Socialists. The explanation for the switch of parties observed here must be looked for in the components of the

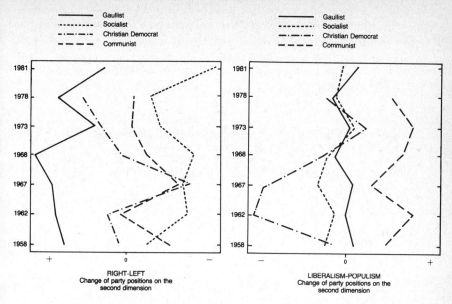

15.2 a and b Change in French party positions on the first and second of the second order dimensions over time

first second stage factor. This factor opposes two pairs of bipolar dimensions. One is the traditional economic-societal Left–Right dimension where the parties cluster in the following fashion:

Centre   Communists
Gaullists   Socialists

The other, which is a government decentralization and external relations dimension, orders the parties in different clusters:

Communists Centre
Gaullists   Socialists

The conjunction of these two party orderings, places Gaullist and Socialist platforms at opposite sides for the first dimension of French politics while the Communist Party and the Democratic Centre assume positions that are more central.

In this small but significant modification to conventional *a priori* ideas about ideologies and party relationships in France we find a justification and confirmation of the methods applied in this analysis. The results are sufficiently close to what we generally know about French politics to be plausible, while at the same time modifying and refining our knowledge. This result allows us to place the French findings within the comparative analysis with some confidence. Generally speaking our analysis has also confirmed that saliency rather than direct confrontation is the stuff of French party competition – as has appeared also in the other countries.

Notes

1 Sondage SOFRES (1977) in *l'Opinion français en 1977*, SOFRES, Paris, Presses de la FNSP, 1978, p. 284.
2 The coding work of Marie-Claire Lavabre of C.E.V.I.P.O.F. was supported by the Nuffield Foundation small grants scheme. Both contributions are gratefully acknowledged.

CHAPTER 16

ITALY 1946–1979:
PARTY PLATFORMS AND
ELECTORAL PROGRAMMES UNDER
THE REPUBLIC

———————— ～ ————————

16.1 INTRODUCTION

The 1983 legislative elections aggravated Italy's crisis of governability. The Christian Democrats who as the largest party had dominated successive post-war governments, suffered a startling decline in support. Yet, this was not sufficient to produce a major change within the political system. The parties that gained most from Christian Democrat decline were their traditional coalition partners, the small centre parties. This was sufficient to gain a Socialist the premiership, but not to turn a Socialist-led 'third force' into a credible alternative to Catholicism or Communism. Of the opposition forces, the Communists, long excluded from government (save on a marginal basis in 1978–9), managed to hold their levels of support constant. But they are no nearer than before to participation in government. The neo-fascists (Italian Social Movement) increased their vote drastically. However, they are so marginalized within the political system that this is nowhere near large enough to alter the balance of power. Thus, the centre-left coalition continues as the most likely pattern until the next elections. And the political system continues to face a stalemate.

The basic absence of change should not obscure the fact that party votes during the 1970s and 1980s have been more variable than in earlier years. Why? In the past votes were determined by *custom* or *clientelistic systems*. Certain regions, such as the North-East and the Centre have become closely identified with Catholic and Socialist/Communist support respectively. In the South, clientelism has been a more important determinant. The system of patronage has advantaged those parties that have held the reins of power, particularly the Christian Democrats.

These determinants no longer exert their previous influence. Problems of economic growth, particularly severe in the over-inflated public sector, have undermined the basis of clientelism. Quite simply, public favours

345

have become scarcer, and so too has reciprocal support. Second, many traditional loyalties appear to have broken down, owing to the socio-economic transformation since World War II. Migration, urbanization, and industrialization all took place on a massive scale during the 1950s and 1960s. As millions migrated to the cities and the northern industrial regions, traditional family and community ties were weakened. There has been a gradual strengthening of the Communist vote (until 1976), and fluctuations among some of the smaller parties of the centre. Observers also point to the effects of secularization on Italian political life. This process may partially explain the recent success of the centre lay parties. It may also explain changes in the basis of Christian Democratic support, and also its decline. The vote of *opinion* has almost certainly increased at the expense of *custom* (traditional loyalties) and *exchange* (clientelism).

As they have attempted to adjust to socio-economic and political change, parties have sought to redefine their identities. It is these which concern us here. Electoral programmes form an important part of the party image. An analysis over the post-war era should provide a much better understanding of the development of the Italian party system. It will identify the ideological framework within which party competition takes place, the ideological profiles of political parties, and the ways in which they have adjusted to changing socio-economic and political circumstances. This paper constitutes a preliminary investigation. Party manifestos from all the major parties have been included, but the investigation focuses mainly on Christian Democrats, Communist, Socialists, Liberals, and Republicans. As in the case of the other countries studied here, the core is formed by a spatial analysis of the emphases in the party programmes. These cannot be understood however without some appreciation of the part which parties play within the Italian political system.

16.2 PARTIES AND POLITICAL FAMILIES

Italy has a multi-party system, in which no single party has an absolute majority of seats or votes. On Sartori's criteria (Sartori 1976) it is an extreme case of a multi-party system. Twelve parties are currently represented in the national legislature, though the majority have no more than a handful of seats. The two parties that dominate are the Christian Democratic Party, which won 32.9 per cent of the vote in the 1983 elections; and the Communist Party, which won 29.9 per cent. The next largest parties are the Socialists, with 11.4 per cent of the vote, and the extreme right-wing Italian Social Movement, with 6.8 per cent. Of the remaining parties, only the Republicans (5.1 per cent) have more than 5 per cent of the vote.

A number of circumstances determine the proliferation of political parties. First, the electoral system, is rigidly proportional. There are fairly large constituencies and a national pool of seats for remaindered votes. Second, Italy, unified only just over a century ago, is marked by deep social and political cleavages. The main cleavages are those between working-class and bourgeois parties; and between clerical and lay parties. Though regional divisions are important, they do not emerge as central to the functioning of the national party system.

These underlying divisions give rise to different groupings of parties. Not all belong exclusively to one category. Indeed, there is a good deal of overlap. But, as an organizing principle, it is useful to distinguish parties in terms of the political families to which they belong. On this basis, the working-class or socialist 'family' consists of the Communist Party (PCI), the Socialist Party (PSI), the Social Democratic Party (PSDI), and the Proletarian Democrats (DP). The bourgeois 'family' consists of the Liberal Party (PLI), the Republican Party (PRI), and the Italian Social Movement–National Right (MSI–DN). The clerical 'family' consists of the Christian Democrats (DC); while the lay anti-clerical 'family' consists of the Radical Party (PR).

Beginning with the working-class 'family', the oldest party is the Socialist Party, founded in 1892. For many years, it was deeply divided between reformists and maximalists. In 1921, the maximalists finally left to form the Communist Party. Like other democratic parties, the Socialist Party was banned during the Fascist dictatorship. But, the party was active in the Resistance Movement, and emerged from the war with considerable prestige. In the Constituent Assembly elections of 1946, the Socialists reaffirmed their old position as the major party on the left with 20.7 per cent of the vote. Since then, until 1979, the party suffered steady decline, and the Communists have become the major representatives of the working class. The Socialist decline began, first, with the secession of reformist and pro-Western elements to form the Social Democratic Party in 1947. The Social Democrats gained 7.1 per cent of the vote in the 1948 elections. In that election, the left-wing elements that now controlled the Socialist Party formed an electoral pact with the Communists. By the 1950s, the party had begun to move slowly away from the Communists. This move was prompted partly by reactions to the Hungarian Uprising, and partly because Nenni (the PSI leader) wanted to bring the party more into the mainstream of the Italian political system. At all levels of the party it was a difficult move. The Socialists laid themselves open to the exception-ally well-organized competition of the Communists on the left. By 1963, however, the party had established itself as a new reforming partner for the Christian Democrats, and later, as the leading party among the group of lay centre parties in the Christian Democrat orbit.

The move to the centre also saw a rapprochement between the Socialists and the Social Democrats. In 1965, the two parties merged. But, by 1969, they had split again amidst growing social discontent throughout the country. The party's participation in government, meanwhile, had led in 1967 to the breakaway of its more left-wing elements to form the Italian Socialist Party of Proletarian Unity (PSIUP). This party fought two elections, gaining 4.4 per cent of the vote in 1968, and 1.9 per cent in 1972. Subsequently, it was absorbed into the Communist Party.

The advantage of government for the Socialist Party was that it gained access to patronage and a clientelistic vote. But, conversely, it suffered from involvement in the corruption and inefficiency of the system. Meanwhile it lost its working class vote to the Communists.

During the 1970s, the Socialists, in reaction to the growth of protest and the decline in their vote, were cautious about participating in Christian Democratic-led governments. By the late 1970s, however, the party had been revitalized under the right-wing leadership of Craxi. The Socialists are once again squarely in the so-called 'constitutional arc' of centre parties. They have also renewed collaboration with the Social Democrats, seeing themselves as leaders of a 'third force', an alternative to both Catholicism and Communism. The 1983 elections showed the limited success of this strategy. Gains were made, but not as much as the Socialists had hoped.

The Social Democrats, for their part, have remained a minor force in Italian politics, though they have participated in many governing coalitions. Their socialist links have become ever more tenuous. By 1979, their share of the vote had slipped to 3.8 per cent.

The Communist Party is now the dominant force within the socialist 'family'. The Communists' electoral and political fortunes were made during the post-war era. Much of the party's success stems from its organizational ability. After the Socialists had split in 1947, the Communists became the largest of the working-class parties. Their vote-share increased at every national election until 1979, going from 18.9 per cent in 1948 to 34.4 per cent in 1976. In 1979 and 1983, however support for the party fell, as it ceased to 'capture' protest.

From the 1960s onwards, it had stood virtually alone as the voice of opposition on the left, and the only credible alternative government. No longer aggregating merely working-class protest towards socialist goals, the Communist Party had best expressed growing dissatisfaction with the Christian Democrats. The latter, as leaders of the government, were seen to be totally ineffective in dealing with the economic crises, social unrest, and civil disobedience that characterized the 1970s. The Communists provided the only possibility of change.

With the regional government reform of the 1970s, it had also been able to establish important power bases at the regional, as well as at the local and provincial levels. This gave it the opportunity to project itself as modern and efficient, capable of dealing with social, economic and urban problems in a competent and honest manner, without resorting to the clientelistic and often corrupt practices of the Christian Democrats. Its increasing involvement with government and *de facto* acceptance of basic features of the existing system, did on the other hand render it less successful in aggregating the protest, which in the 1970s took other forms, often violent.

On the extreme left-wing fringes of the party system are a number of very small working-class parties which have fought elections periodically, like the Socialist Party of Proletarian Unity (PSIUP), mentioned earlier. The Democratic Party of Proletarian Unity for Communism, established by dissident Communists in 1974, fought elections in 1976 and 1979. The leftward shift of the Socialist Party after 1979 enabled the party to join forces with the Communists for the 1983 elections. Finally, Proletarian Democracy (DP) is a far left party with roots in the students' and workers' protests of the late 1960s.

At the other end of the scale are the bourgeois parties. These parties also constitute a divided 'family', but, in contrast to the Left, it is weak. The Liberal Party founded in 1848, is older than the unitary state. The Republican Party is slightly more recent. Despite having a long history, and having played a major role in Italian politics during the pre-fascist era, both parties have been of minor significance in post-war politics. The tasks of defending bourgeois interests and of integrating Italy into the Western alliance have been left to the Christian Democrats. However both parties have exercised a greater influence than their size would indicate.

The Liberal party emerged in the 1950s as the party most closely identified with the interests of industrial capital. However, Christian Democrat competition prevented it from making a major impact. Its main tremor of vitality came in 1963, when it doubled its share of the vote to 7 per cent. This success coincided with the 'opening to the left' by the Christian Democrats which involved the participation of the Socialists in government and a reformist social and economic programme. The Liberals gained the support of those opposing reform, but lost it when the government's lack of reforming ability became apparent.

The Republicans hold a pivotal position on the centre-left of the political spectrum between the Christian Democrats and the Socialists, and have served in many post-war coalitions. They were one of the prime movers in bringing the Socialists into the 1963 government. Later, they pressed for closer links with the Communists. Despite its enlightened image, the Republican Party has never succeeded in establishing a mass base, except in a few localized areas. Instead, the party has gained, and still retains, the character of a liberal, intellectual group. As dissatisfaction with the

Christian Democrats increased after the 1979 election, La Malfa became the first non-Christian Democrat to be given the opportunity to form an administration. He failed, but one year later in 1981, his successor as leader of the party, Spadolini, became Prime Minister. The relative success of this administration led to the Republicans enjoying their greatest electoral success in 1983.

On the extreme right of the political system is the Italian Social Movement–National Right, known as neo-fascists, a merger of Monarchists (PDIUM) and the Italian Social Movement (MSI). The Monarchists represented those nostalgic for the old regime, having a largely clientelistic base in the South, while the MSI represented the interests of those who had lost in the change from fascist government to democracy. The neo-fascists should not be underestimated. They attract considerable support among disaffected youth, and among the southern petite bourgeoisie. From the 1950s onward, they have increased their vote at times when the centre has exhibited minimal reformist tendencies.

Founded in the early post-war era, the Christian Democratic Party inherited the political traditions of the Popular Party, which in the interwar years had integrated the Catholic masses into the unitary state. The Christian Democrats are more broadly based than their predecessors. As early as 1946, they had succeeded in establishing themselves as the major political force in Italy with 35.4 per cent of the vote, and they have remained so ever since.

Several factors combined to consolidate their position. Fascism and Monarchy had crumbled thus creating a power vacuum. The situation was complicated by radical demands for social change being made by the left-wing parties that had been protagonists of the Resistance (Catholics had also played an important role). The old bourgeois parties had been discredited by allowing Mussolini to gain power. In addition, they had no organizational base. The only functioning political structure with sufficient domestic and foreign prestige to assert its authority was the Catholic Church. The Christian Democrats were thus able to build a bridgehead to government through the Church. Their success in 1946 was followed by an absolute majority in the 1948 elections. By this time, they had integrated many of the Southern notables into their ranks. In subsequent years, the party succeeded in establishing a symbiotic relationship between state, public administration, and the enormous public sector of the economy. This relationship, with all the patronage that it involved, allowed the Christian Democrats to move away from Church influence. The party, then, finally established its hegemony through mass clientelism.

Only in the last decade have successive economic, social, and civil crises, combined with the secularization of Italian society, undermined the traditional dominance of the Christian Democrats. Since 1976, the party has been closely challenged by the Communists.

The Christian Democratic Party is best described as centrist. Its support comes from all classes in society, as it attracts the Catholic working class, the bourgeoisie, and Southern clientelistic networks. It cannot simply be described as a conservative party. It has included important reforming elements and personalities, from de Gasperi to Moro.

The Radical Party is the only party that fits comfortably into the anti-clerical 'Family'. (Strong anti-clerical tendencies exist however in many other parties, ranging from the Communists to the Liberals.) It was founded in 1954 as a breakaway from the Liberals. The intention was to create a party representing the democratic (and civil libertarian) traditions of liberalism. For many years, the Radicals were virtually invisible. But, in the 1970s they re-emerged at the head of several important civil-libertarian (and anti-clerical) battles. These included the referendums on divorce and abortion. By 1979, the Radicals were enjoying considerable electoral success, partly resulting from the impetus of these battles. But they also succeeded in taking support away from the Communists and Socialists, who were increasingly being perceived as part of the political establishment, following their support for the government of national solidarity formed in 1978–9. In 1979 the Radicals became Italy's fifth largest party with 3.8 per cent of the vote. In recent years, however, the campaign of parliamentary obstructionism pursued by the Radicals has irritated electors. In addition, the Communists moved back into opposition. Thus, in the 1983 elections, the Radicals saw their vote fall considerably.

16.3 INTERPRETING THE ITALIAN POLITICAL SYSTEM

How do the parties interact, and what consequences do their interactions carry for the working of the system as a whole? Two well-known interpretations are those of Galli (1966) and Sartori (1972).

Galli argues that Italy has a two-party system, in so far as the Christian Democrats and the Communists obtain about 70 per cent of the popular vote. Yet, the system is imperfect since there is no alternance in government of the two major parties. The cause of this 'imperfection' stems from the fact that the Communists, and not a social democratic party, represent the working class, and the Christian Democrats, not a lay bourgeois party, represents the bourgeoisie. Both are outside the mainstream traditions of liberal democracy. The Communists are permanently excluded from government, while the Christian Democrats are obliged to govern for the foreseeable future. The public may be ready for change, given the socio-economic transformation that has taken place within the country, but the parties are not prepared to make concessions to one another. The result is a stalemate and a grossly inefficient political system. It is inefficient in the sense that demands are not effectively channelled through the system, or met by government actions.

There are a number of difficulties with Galli's argument. First, change and alternance is no guarantee of an efficient system. A more serious problem concerns Galli's overestimation of the role of political parties. Political cultures, and especially Catholicism and Socialism, are deeply embedded at all levels of Italian society. Politics affects everyday life (work and social life, for instance) to a much greater extent than in many other Western democracies. So it is not only party elites that are frozen. In fact our analysis of the party programmes shows that most political parties have, at various times, radically changed their ideological orientations. Such changes at the political level however have not always been rewarded with support from electors. Thus, far from the parties not wishing to change, it is often the parties' traditional supporters who have not wanted change. In 1963, for instance, the Christian Democrats lost bourgeois support when they tried to present a more reformist image. The same was true in 1972, and again in 1983. The Italian bourgeoisie has been loath to surrender its privileged position, rejecting the integration of the working class into the process of government.

Sartori's model of the Italian party system focusses on its extreme fragmentation and polarization. He defines the system as 'polarized pluralism' on the basis of several characteristics. First, there are two anti-system parties, the Communists on the left and the neo-fascists on the right. They constitute a bilateral opposition to the governing centre, threatening the legitimacy of the political system. Second, the exclusion of the two anti-system parties from government means that they never have to live up to their election promises. The result is an inflationary spiral, which adversely affects inter-party competition, and leads to irresponsible opposition. Third, the centre parties form a centre pole, which opposes the two extremes. The opposition parties thus have no inducement to become more centrist and moderate. Instead, centrifugal forces predominate, leading to a continual weakening of the centre. Finally, party competition takes place in terms of ideological arguments, encouraging dogmatism and doctrinaire ideologies.

How well do the characteristics of this pessimistic scenario describe the Italian political system? Take first the questions of polarization and centrifugal tendencies. Farneti showed that centripetal, and not centrifugal, tendencies best characterize the elite level (Farneti 1983). At the mass level, there is no doubt that the left is powerful, and the right is tenacious. But can it really be said, as Sartori claims, that they have grown over time? The answer depends largely on how one defines the anti-system extremes. There is actually a trend *away* from the Neo-Fascists, apart from 1972 and

1983. If one defines the left-wing extreme as being the Communist Party, then there has been an increase of polarization up until 1976. Yet surely fellow-travellers should be included alongside the Communists. These included the Socialists and the Social Democrats until 1948, and then the Socialists alone until 1963, when they joined the centre-left coalition. From then on, the Communists had only minor 'partners' on the left-wing pole. Given this definition of the left-wing, there has been a slight *decrease* in the left-wing vote over the post-war era. In fact, it is the centre pole that has experienced the greatest increase as formerly left-wing parties have changed position. The increase in the centre has been gained at the cost of decreased homogeneity. The picture that emerges is certainly not one of increasing polarization. While centripetal tendencies have not replaced centrifugal ones, the system is at least more accurately described as stable polarization.

The stabilization of polarization has consequences for other aspects of Sartori's model. Consider the inflationary spiral of party ideologies. Our analysis of party programmes shows that during the 1970s, the major political parties fought one another less and less on alternative visions of the world and in spatial terms could indeed be said to have moved closer together. The Communist Party, for instance, no longer promotes the dictatorship of the proletariat, the myth of the Soviet Union, the evil of the West, etc. It now projects images of the acceptance of pluralism, the possibility of compromise with the Christian Democrats, the need for austerity to solve Italy's economic problems, a flexible interpretation of democratic centralism, the renunciation of increased nationalization and the acceptance of Italy's position in the Atlantic Alliance. Interestingly, as the Communist Party gave up its old ideologies, and conformed to the notion of 'responsible' opposition, it enjoyed greater electoral success. This experience runs counter to Sartori's predictions.

Nevertheless the Communists can hardly be regarded as a normal, fully-integrated party in the mainstream Western tradition. To this extent the key place assigned by Sartori to his notion of the anti-system party has considerable validity. The Communists are however anti-system only in a very special sense, as there can be little doubt about their basic loyalty to the 1948 Constitution. It might be more appropriate in fact to call them a non-system party.

The ambiguous position of the Communist Party in politics stems from the ambiguous position of the working class, which it represents, within society. In most other Western countries, working-class leaders are involved in political decisions and participate in government, at least to some extent. This however occurs less in Italy than elsewhere. The labour/capital division has been dealt with by repression or fictitious inclusion, or a mix of the two. Because of fascism, no kind of co-operative economic management based on Keynesianism emerged. In the post-war era, the Cold War justified the 'convention of exclusion'.

As the Communist Party was the main representative of this alienated working class, it became the major channel of communication between government and the excluded sector – less of a sub-culture within the general political system than a completely different sub-system with its own separate legitimacy. It is in this sense that it is different from the other parties in Italy and from most other Western political parties. In turn, the inclusion of a very large but 'separate' party with potential destabilizing power, differentiates the Italian party system from most of the ones considered previously, with the possible exception of the French. It is against this background that our analysis of the ideological emphases and electoral strategies of the parties needs to be set.

16.4 THE SCOPE OF RESEARCH

All political parties in Italy publish an electoral programme prior to the elections. It is distinct from the party programmes published by some parties at their congresses, which are not necessarily held in election years. This study is confined to the electoral programmes.

The increasing importance that parties attach to these can be measured by the sheer weight of the documents. In their early post-war years, they consisted of little more than two sheets of paper in which a dozen general points might be stressed. By the late 1950s, however, they had become much more detailed. Further, increasing publicity came to surround the unveiling of the programmes. This unveiling often took place in a political speech by the party leader at the Adriano Theatre in Rome. The speeches were reported in detail in the national newspapers, and it was by this mechanism that the newspaper-reading public was informed of the party programmes. However, the standard form in which manifestos/programmes have long been published is in the newspapers of the respective political parties: *L'Unità* for the PCI; *Avanti!* for the PSI; *Il Popolo* for the DC, etc. The programmes appear as pull-out sections of these newspapers, which have however, very limited circulations. They are read mainly by the party faithful, which for some minor parties is a very small number. Thus, it cannot be said that party programmes circulate widely. Most information that the public receives comes second-hand. National newspapers give considerable space to discussion of the programmes of the major political parties, and particularly their positions on specific issues. The national television and radio network (RAI) also provides a forum (probably reaching a far greater proportion of the population than the national newspapers) in which party leaders discuss and are questioned on their electoral programmes. Educated opinion, at least, is well informed on party ideological positions.

The preparation of the electoral programmes is generally carried out by senior committees of the various political parties. In the past, the two major parties – the Christian Democrats and the Communists – have made much of the wide-scale participation of party members in the preparation of the manifestos. Spreafico notes that in the 1958 elections, the Communists published a preliminary draft of their programme in *L'Unità* and invited comments from readers, some of which appear to have been heeded. The Christian Democrats in the same election, had sent letters the year before to 12,000 party section leaders, inviting their suggestions for the party programme. The difficulty with organizing wide participation in recent years is that none of the last four elections has been held as scheduled. With a climate of political uncertainty in Italy, every election since 1968 has been held prematurely. Thus preparations have been hurried, and have remained in the hands of the party leadership. Even when there has been time for wide participation, the leaders have generally had the final say as to contents of the programme. In some cases, this function is performed by the national secretary of the party concerned.

Our initial intention was to analyse the programmes of all national parties represented in Parliament and fighting elections during the period 1946–79. Finding that the programmes of a number of parties were lost we modified the plan, focussing our analysis on the three major parties – Christian Democrats, Communists, and Socialists – which together receive between 75 and 85 per cent of the popular vote. We obtained complete sets of programmes for these parties over the nine elections. We have also analysed less fully the programmes of the Liberals and Republicans. The Liberal programmes cover the elections up until 1976. The Republican programmes cover the elections of 1946, 1948, 1968, 1972, and 1976. Finally, we included single programmes of the other national parties for the 1976 election. These were used in background analysis. In all, a total of 44 programmes were coded.

The coding scheme followed that of the manifestos research group. However, sixteen special sub-categories were added to take account of the Italian political context (see Appendix B). Coding was carried out by a native Italian speaker at the University of Turin. Selective cross checks, both at Turin and Essex proved that there was a very good fit between the modified coding scheme and the party statements.

16.5 RESEARCH RESULTS

Frequency analyses

Table 16.1 shows the mean scores over leading categories for all coded programmes, and the separate distribution inside each party. Of the 71

TABLE 16.1

TOP TEN CATEGORIES FOR EACH PARTY: ITALY

PCI (N=9)

			$\bar{x}$	SD
1	503	SOCIAL JUSTICE	6.86	2.86
2	701	LABOUR GROUPS	5.76	4.61
3	504	SOCIAL SERVICES +	4.18	3.38
4	106	PEACE/DISARMAMENT	4.13	2.32
5	202	DEMOCRACY	3.90	2.56
6	301	DECENTRALIZATION +	3.76	2.44
7	506	EDUCATIONS +	3.32	2.61
8	201	FREEDOM	2.98	3.80
9	413	NATIONALIZATION	2.40	2.33

PRI (N=5)

			$\bar{x}$	SD
1	202	DEMOCRACY	5.11	4.31
2	201	FREEDOM	4.64	7.13
3	303	INST. EFFICIENCY	3.90	4.82
4	30302	JUDICIAL REFORM	3.38	5.33
5	301	DECENTRALIZATION	3.20	4.90
6	404	ECONOMIC PLANNING	2.84	3.31
7	50301	AGRARIAN REFORM	2.28	3.05
8	503	SOCIAL JUSTICE	2.24	1.01
9	408	ECONOMIC GOALS	1.91	4.28
10		PRODUCTIVITY	1.79	2.45

DC (N=9)

			$\bar{x}$	SD
1	20101	UNION RIGHTS	5.28	11.89
2	503	SOCIAL JUSTICE	5.26	6.09
3	60301	CHRISTIAN VALUES	4.52	6.22
4	504	SOCIAL SERVICES +	4.15	2.55
5	408	ECONOMIC GOALS	3.59	3.88
6	301	DECENTRALIZATION	3.56	2.36
7	410	PRODUCTIVITY	3.50	4.71
8	411	TECHNOLOGY/INFRA.	3.42	3.74
9	603	TRADITIONAL MORALITY	3.41	3.01
10	202	DEMOCRACY	3.26	2.62

PSI (N=9)

			$\bar{x}$	SD
1	701	LABOUR GROUPS	4.59	2.95
2	506	EDUCATION +	4.26	2.27
3	503	SOCIAL JUSTICE	4.18	3.07
4	106	PEACE/DISARMAMENT	4.16	4.79
5	504	SOCIAL SERVICES +	3.64	3.21
6	410	PRODUCTIVITY	2.44	3.21
7	404	ECONOMIC PLANNING	2.28	3.37
8.	202	DEMOCRACY	2.24	2.90
9	30301	ADMINISTRATIVE REF	2.16	2.96

PLI (N=8)

			$\bar{x}$	SD
1	401	ENTERPRISE	8.00	3.52
2	201	FREEDOM	4.38	4.26
3	202	DEMOCRACY	3.45	3.33
4	414	ECON. ORTHODOXY	3.00	3.92
5	403	REGULATION OF CAPITALISM	3.00	4.70
6	108	EUROPEAN COMMUNITY	2.50	2.25
7	50304	HOME OWNERSHIP	2.44	5.78
8	503	SOCIAL JUSTICE	1.78	1.36
9	701	LABOUR	1.78	2.54
10	704	OTHER ECONOMIC GROUPS	1.59	2.95

ALL (N=40)

			$\bar{x}$	SD
1	503	SOCIAL JUSTICE	4.19	3.78
2	202	DEMOCRACY	3.30	2.93
3	701	LABOUR GROUPS POSITIVE	3.27	3.42
4	201	FREEDOM AND HUMAN RIGHTS	2.97	4.47
5	504	SOCIAL SERVICES	2.97	2.89
6	106	PEACE AND DISARMAMENT	2.64	6.12
7	301	DECENTRALIZATION POSITIVE	2.64	2.64
8		EDUCATION, POSITIVE	2.62	2.59
9		PRODUCTIVITY	2.17	3.10
10		ENTERPRISE	1.93	3.38

Italian categories, the most popular was Social Justice with 4.19 per cent of mentions. It was followed by Democracy (3.30), support for Labour Groups (3.27); Freedom and Human Rights (2.97); Social Services (2.97); Decentralization (2.64); Peace and Disarmament (2.64); Education (2.62); and then two variables from the economic domain – Productivity (2.17); and Enterprise (1.93). Thus all the domains, except that of social fabric, have variables mentioned in the 'top ten'.

The most popular categories are those which parties find difficult to criticize. Parties were noticeably reticent in professing negative values. Many of the negative categories, and indeed some of the others, achieved very low scores. Where a category scored less than 0.75 per cent overall or 2.0 per cent for a single party, it was eliminated from the subsequent factor analysis. Table 16.1 also shows the top ten categories for each of the five parties we analysed. The Communists and the Socialists emphasize substantially the same issues. Indeed, four of the top five issues are shared: Social Justice, support for Labour Groups, Social Services, and Peace and Disarmament. The Communist Party, however, shows a continuing commitment to traditional working-class issues such as Nationalization, while within the top categories for the Socialist Party, there are a number of new-style reformist issues: Productivity, Economic Planning, and Administrative Reform. This difference reflects the movement of the Socialists towards the centre from the 1960s onwards. Like the Communists and the Socialists, the Christian Democrats share many 'social justice' issues, but they also include strong support for Traditional Morality and Christian values. There are certainly no strongly identifiable right-wing goals. Instead, the party shows a general commitment towards economic modernization which is entirely in keeping with a party of government. The two bourgeois or liberal parties – the Republicans and the Liberals – reveal interesting profiles. The Republicans are shown accurately as the 'critical conscience' of the centre. They believe in political liberties, greater democracy and participation, and general reform of the state. They combine these values with a general commitment to economic modernization, but one which is based on a neo-corporatist model. The Liberals, on the other hand, lay much greater stress on the market economy.

On a related question which casts light on party similarities and contrasts, only a very small percentage of sentences in the manifestos brought in references to other parties. Again this confirms the general finding from previous chapters that parties are more prone to emphasize the areas of their own advantage than to disparage those of other parties or to attack rival proposals.

Factor analysis by domain

The standard factor analysis was carried out within the subject 'domains' described in previous chapters.

(i) Foreign Relations

Two factors emerged with Eigenvalues greater than unity. The first accounts for 43.1 per cent of the variance, the second for 36.4 per cent. Referring to the Varimax rotated solution, the first factor loads heavily on Peace and Disarmament (.76) and Internationalism (.83). There are no negative loadings. We can interpret this factor as reflecting levels of concern over international cooperation. The second factor has a slight negative loading on Peace and Disarmament, but has an extremely high positive loading on the European Community (.93). We can best interpret this factor as levels of concern over the EEC.

(ii) Freedom and Democracy

Again two factors emerge with Eigenvalues greater than unity, the first explaining 35.9 per cent of the variance, the second 27.7 per cent. The first factor is tricky to interpret. It has a heavy positive loading on two special Italian categories, Freedom of Union Association (.86) and Workers' Participation (.81). It has lighter negative loadings on Freedom and Human Rights (−.23), Democracy (−.48). The factor reflects concern over workers' rights, and the negative loadings, since they are low, should probably be discounted. The second factor has high positive loadings on Freedom and Human Rights (.84) and Constitutionalism (.86). It reflects the perennial concern of the Italian political parties with constitutional rights (referring to the 1948 Constitution).

(iii) Government

Two factors have Eigenvalues greater than unity, the first explaining 35.0 per cent of the variance and the second 25.2 per cent. The first loads positively on Institutional Efficiency (.89), and two special categories – State Reform (.77) and Judicial Reform (.56). The negative loadings are too small to be significant. The factor clearly reflects, then, levels of concern for institutional reform. This theme has certainly become of increasing importance in recent years, and has been taken up by the Socialists and Republicans in particular. The second factor is the first one to produce a contrast between differently oriented ends. It has a high positive loading on Decentralization (.77) and a high negative loading on

Government Effectiveness (−.77). It reflects the ongoing arguments within the Italian political system between those who believe in greater participation and decentralization, and those who believe in a strong and effective government authority.

(iv) Economy

Four factors having Eigenvalues greater than unity emerge in the Economy domain, explaining respectively, 24.3, 18.1, 14.6 and 12.7 per cent of the variance. The first has high positive loadings on Economic Goals (.82), Productivity (.84) and Technology and Infrastructure (.78). None of the other loadings is significant. It can be interpreted, then, as general concern with economic growth and modernization. The second factor produces a dichotomy. It has high positive loadings on Enterprise (.87) and Economic Orthodoxy (.84). The only other significant loading is a negative one on Nationalization (−.55). This factor represents the basic arguments over economic ideology in Italy: state intervention *vs.* the free market. The third and fourth factors represent alternative means for economic management, though they are not necessarily in opposition to one another. The third factor has high positive loadings on Economic Planning (.81), and Full Employment (.80). The fourth has high positive loadings on Regulation of Capitalism (.74) and Keynesian Demand Management (.80). None of the other loadings is significant.

(v) Welfare

Three factors emerge in this domain, explaining respectively 28.6, 26.5, and 21.2 per cent of the variance. The first has high positive loadings on support for Social Services (.84) and support for Education (.81). It reflects levels of concern with social services. The second factor loads positively and heavily on Social Justice (.75) and Agrarian Reform (with particular reference to the reform of the latifundia) (.84). This factor reflects a much greater concern with social justice and social equality, rather than the specific provision of social services. The third factor has a high positive loading on Home Ownership (.94). This issue is very popular in the Liberal Party and reflects more conservative notions of self-helping social justice. Because of its specific reference to home ownership, we have labelled it by that name.

(vi) Social Fabric

As only three categories were fed into the factor analysis, only one factor with an Eigenvalue greater than unity emerged in this domain. We have,

TABLE 16.2

SECOND STAGE FACTORS EMERGING FROM ANALYSIS OF ITALIAN PARTY MANIFESTOS
(UNROTATED SOLUTION)

UNROTATED FACTOR MATRIX (AND CORRELATIONS WITH ORIGINAL VARIABLES)	FACTOR 1 LEFT-RIGHT	FACTOR 2 TECHNOLOGY VS. SOCIAL HARMONY	FACTOR 3 REFORM AND MODERNIZATION	FACTOR 4	FACTOR 6
DOMAIN ONE: EXTERNAL RELATIONS					
FACTOR 1.1 INTERNATIONALISM (HIGH/LOW)	-.49	.50	-.27	-.14	.04
FACTOR 1.2 EEC (HIGH/LOW)	.13	.30	.11	-.50	.49
106 PEACE AND DISARMAMENT	.46	.17	-.16	.12	-.43
107 INTERNATIONALISM: POSITIVE	.35	-.15	.01	.66	-.17
108 EEC: POSITIVE	-.38	-.02	-.12	.53	-.05
DOAMIN TWO: FREEDOM AND DEMOCRACY					
FACTOR 2.1 WORKERS' RIGHTS (HIGH/LOW)	.47	.06	-.73	.06	.02
FACTOR 2.2 CONSTITUTIONAL RIGHTS (HIGH/LOW)	-.12	-.56	-.01	.34	.44
201 FREEDOM AND HUMAN RIGHTS	-.01	.26	-.41	-.04	.55
20101 FREEDOM OF UNION ASSOCIATION	.15	-.84	-.03	-.09	.24
202 DEMOCRACY	.20	.33	-.25	.12	-.07
20201 WORKERS' PARTICIPATION	.14	-.61	.16	-.09	.13
203 CONSTITUTIONALISM	.04	.81	-.16	-.15	.56
DOMAIN THREE: GOVERNMENT					
FACTOR 3.1 INSTITUTIONAL REFORM	.38	.36	.51	.56	-.04
FACTOR 3.2 DECENTRALIZATION VS. GOVERNMENT AUTHORITY	-.20	.38	-.32	.16	.58

Continued...

TABLE 16.2 Continued

	FACTOR 1	FACTOR 2	FACTOR 3	FACTOR 4	FACTOR 5
301 DECENTRALIZATION	.46	.15	-.13	.50	.04
303 INSTITUTIONAL EFFICIENCY	-.13	.02	.80	-.06	.10
30301 STATE REFORM	-.11	.01	.68	-.07	.15
30302 JUDICIAL REFORM	.03	.26	.47	.04	.17
305 GOVERNMENT EFFECTIVENESS	-.29	-.05	-.14	-.20	-.41
DOMAIN FOUR: ECONOMY					
FACTOR 4.1 ECONOMIC GROWTH (HIGH/LOW)	-.04	.48	.46	.28	-.17
FACTOR 4.2 LEFT VERSUS RIGHT	.59	-.09	.21	-.51	-.01
401 ENTERPRISE	-.72	.06	-.37	.11	-.06
403 REGULATION OF CAPITALISM	-.08	.04	-.14	.03	-.29
404 ECONOMIC PLANNING	-.04	.00	.59	-.22	.09
408 ECONOMIC GOALS	-.20	-.24	.35	.23	-.22
409 KEYNESIANISM	.08	.00	.16	.18	-.22
40901 FULL EMPLOYMENT	-.03	.00	.51	-.18	.11
410 PRODUCTIVITY	-.20	.06	.50	.01	-.13
411 TECHNOLOGY AND INFRASTRUCTURE	-.03	-.07	.51	.19	-.17
413 NATIONALIZATION	.47	.04	.04	-.14	-.20
414 ECONOMIC ORTHODOXY	-.64	.12	-.17	.07	.00
DOMAIN FIVE: WELFARE					
FACTOR 5.1 SOCIAL SERVICES (HIGH/LOW)	.20	.67	-.31	-.08	-.10
FACTOR 5.2 SOCIAL JUSTICE (HIGH/LOW)	.76	.20	-.16	.31	-.12
503 SOCIAL JUSTICE (HIGH/LOW)	.54	-.60	-.08	-.14	.10
50301 AGRARIAN REFORM (LATIFUNDIA)	.58	.08	-.26	-.17	-.13

Continued...

TABLE 16.2 Continued

	FACTOR 1	FACTOR 2	FACTOR 3	FACTOR 4	FACTOR 5
50304 HOME OWNERSHIP	-.39	-.02	-.16	.21	-.10
504 SOCIAL SERVICES: POSITIVE	.17	.33	.18	.15	-.23
506 EDUCATION : POSITIVE	.37	.35	.15	.43	-.36
DOMAIN SIX: SOCIAL FABRIC					
FACTOR 6.1 TRADITIONAL MORALITY	-.59	-.16	.44	-.29	.36
603 TRADITIONAL MORALITY: POSITIVE	.15	-.66	-.09	.29	.07
60301 CHRISTIAN VALUES	.08	-.80	-.10	.15	.19
604 TRADITIONAL MORALITY: NEGATIVE	-.08	.37	.21	-.07	.48
DOMAIN SEVEN: SOCIAL GROUPS					
FACTOR 7.1 NON-ECONOMIC GROUPS	.51	-.07	-.02	.48	.47
FACTOR 7.2 WORKING CLASS VS. MIDDLE CLASS	.15	.61	.30	-.11	.22
701 LABOUR GROUPS	.84	.09	-.31	-.34	-.35
703 FARMERS	.46	.01	.00	.20	-.28
704 OTHER ECONOMIC GROUPS	-.07	-.17	.17	.39	-.22
706 NON-ECONOMIC GROUPS	-.17	.31	.15	.20	.56
70601 WOMEN	.28	.24	.31	.10	.47
70602 YOUTH	.04	.16	.48	.37	-.13
70603 OLD PEOPLE	.09	.16	.02	-.22	.59

therefore, to present the unrotated solution since no rotation was possible. The one factor we have explains 58.3 per cent of the variance, and loads heavily on Traditional Morality (.96) and Christian Values (.86). There is a lower negative loading on opposition to Traditional Morality (−.43). Thus, this factor expresses the division in the Italian political system between proponents of Traditional Morality, such as the Christian Democrats, and its opponents, such as the Radicals.

(vii) Social Groups

Our final domain is social groups. Four factors emerged with Eigenvalues greater than unity, accounting for, respectively, 31.5, 19.8, 14.7, and 13.3 per cent of the variance. Since we have more than one factor, we can revert once again to the Varimax rotated solution. The first factor loads very heavily on Non-Economic Demographic Groups (.98) with no significant loadings on any other categories. It reflects simply levels of concern with such groups. The second factor produces a division between middle-class and working-class concerns. It has high positive loadings on Women (.58) and Youth (.83), both traditionally middle-class areas of emphasis. It has a high negative loading on Labour Groups (−.59). The third factor reflects social libertarian concerns, with high positive loadings on Women (.71), and Old People (.71), and a high negative loading on 'Other Economic Groups' (−.67). The last factor reflects concern with working people. It has high positive loadings on Labour Groups (.59) and Farmers (.90).

Second-stage factor analysis

The second-stage factor analysis produced five factors with Eigenvalues greater than unity. The unrotated solution gave the most useful interpretation. In Table 16.2 we set out the full unrotated solution, which is followed by our interpretation of the first three factors to be produced. The figures in the table relating first-order to second-order factors are factor loadings, since the first-order factors were input to the analysis to produce the second-stage factors. The figures relating original variables to the second-stage factors are simple product-moment correlations and are used to aid interpretation.

The first factor reveals the classic left–right dimension in Italian politics with high positive correlations on Nationalization, Social Justice, and Agrarian Reform. These correlations are opposed by low negative correlations on Enterprise and Economic Orthodoxy. In Figure 16.1 we produce a diagrammatic sketch of party movements over Factor 1 at the various elections. A number of points should be noted. First, there has been a long-term trend towards the centre, particularly noticeable on the part of

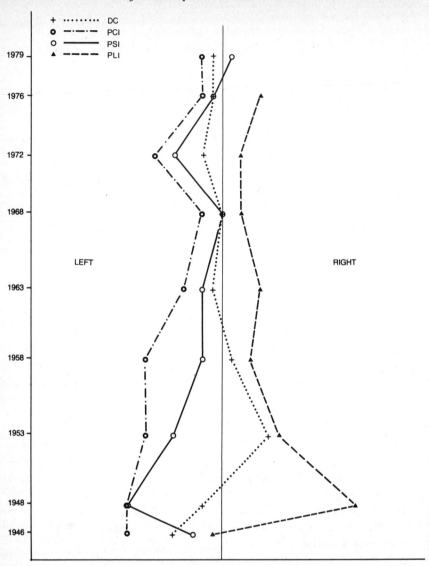

16.1 Movement of Italian parties on the left-right dimension: factor 1 by election year

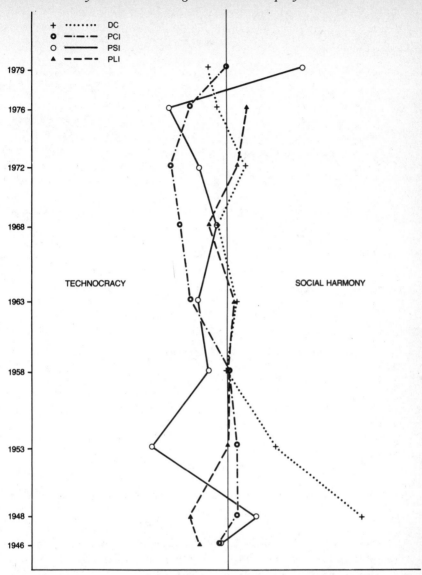

16.2 Movement of Italian parties on technocracy – social harmony dimension:
factor 2 by election year

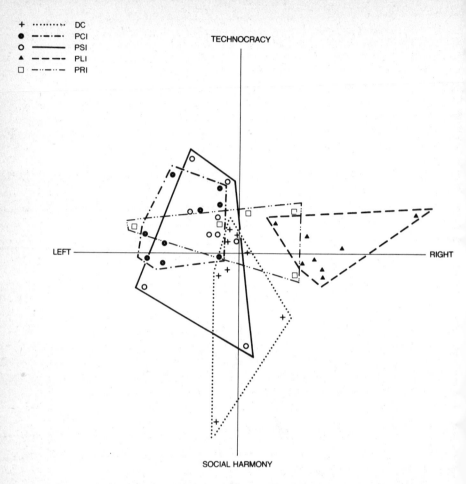

16.3 Plot of Italian parties on the two leading dimensions of the second-stage factor
analysis

the Communists and Socialists. In fact, by 1979, the Socialists stood to the
'right' of the Christian Democrats, coinciding with Craxi's taking over the
leadership of the party. Second, on the part of the Christian Democrats, it
is interesting to note the considerable rightward movement during the
early post-war period. Later, there was a steady movement leftwards,
which reached its peak in 1963 with the formation of the first centre-left
government. Since then, the Christian Democratic Party has quite clearly
remained a party of the centre. Third, in 1972, following the Hot Autumn,
there was a clear shift to the left by all three major parties as they tried to
respond to social protest. Fourth, in 1976, the election of the 'historic

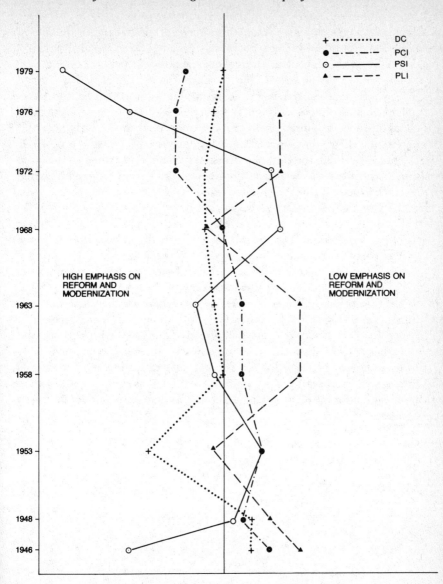

16.4 Plot of Italian parties on the reform and modernization dimension

compromise', all three major parties were very close on the left–right dimension. This closeness resulted from the substantial rightward shift of both the Communists and Socialists. Finally, the Liberal Party has remained on the right-wing throughout the post-war period.

The second factor reveals the 'social harmony' dimension in Italian politics. It also subsumes Catholicism. Figure 16.2 shows the party movements on this dimension. It is interesting to note the considerable change which the Christian Democrats underwent in the early post-war period. In effect, they were a Catholic Party in the first three post-war elections. By 1958, the Catholic stress on harmony was being emphasized much less. Both the Socialist and Communist Parties have emphasized 'social harmony' values to a limited extent. In 1979, however, the Socialists under Craxi gave great emphasis to traditional values.

Figure 16.3 shows the two-dimensional space occupied by the parties on the first two factors. The diagram fits well with the description of the Italian party system in the second section. Note the considerable overlap of the major parties, particularly of Christian Democrats and Communists.

Finally, the third factor provides a view of the 'reform and modernization' dimension in Italian politics. We have plotted the parties on this dimension in Figure 16.4. Interestingly, this dimension is the first one in which the Socialists take a more progressive line in recent elections than the other two major parties. Overall, however, there has been remarkably little difference between the Christian Democrats and the Communists during the post-war era – a finding which has quite revolutionary implications for the major interpretations of Italian party politics discussed above.

CHAPTER 17

JAPAN 1960–1980:
PARTY ELECTION PLEDGES[1]

———————— ∿ ————————

The purpose of this chapter is to shed new light on Japanese party politics by examining party pledges in general elections from 1960–80. First we locate our analysis in a broader substantive context. Then, on the basis of newspaper summaries of election pledges at general election times, we analyse how appeals are made to the general public by political parties, along the general lines followed elsewhere in the book.

17.1 THE PLACE OF PARTIES IN THE POLITICAL SYSTEM

Given the extensive changes produced by war and occupation in the 1940s, Japanese political practices display surprising continuity. Fundamental changes have taken place however within the context of existing institutions. Thus the 1947 constitution, which replaced that of 1889, declares that sovereignty lies with the people, not the Emperor, who remains however the symbol of Japan. The Diet, the Cabinet, and the Supreme Court, respectively, hold the highest legislative, executive and judicial powers. The Diet is composed of a House of Representatives (the main arena for legislation and politics) and a House of Councillors.

Parties also display some continuity. As institutions they evolved in opposition to the absolutist government of the pre-war era and until recently were weak in comparison to the state bureaucracy. Three factors shaped the new political parties after the war.

(i) In 1946, after all constraints on the formation of political parties had disappeared, political competition extended to left-wing parties including the Japanese Communist Party (JCP). For the first time, such parties briefly held office in coalition governments either headed by, or including Socialists.

(ii) Shortly before the first general election in August 1946, a large

number of politicians, businessmen, officials and other leaders were purged
by the occupation forces. Those who had been silenced for their anti-
government views took the most active part in reshaping party politics. In
addition, major reforms were carried out by political parties, business
corporations, trade unions, the military, parliament and the courts. Only
the bureaucracy was left substantially intact, as it was needed by the
occupation authorities for policy implementation, its wartime powers
being thus strengthened through the absence of countervailing forces. The
emergence of a predominant-party system in 1955 consolidated this
expanded role because the Liberal Democrats (LDP) could also rely on
bureaucratic support.

(iii) The 'Cold War' between the U.S. and the USSR led to the JCP
being directed towards a revolutionary and non-parliamentary role. This
led to its suppression by the occupation forces, rendering it negligible as a
political force from 1948 until a minor recovery in the 1960s.

Two major political rearrangements in 1955 (the unification of the
left-wing and the right-wing Socialist Parties and the merger of the Liberal
and the Democratic Parties into the Liberal-Democratic Party) considerably simplified the party system: the LDP occupied about 60 per cent of the
seats and the JSP about 35 per cent of the seats in the House of
Representatives.

A major trend from the mid-1950s until the late 1970s was a loss of votes
by the LDP and the JSP. This resulted from high economic growth and
massive urbanization which weakened the electoral influence of local elites
and trade unions, traditionally the major power bases of the LDP and the
JSP respectively. (The agricultural population shrank from 40 per cent in
the mid-1950s to 10 per cent in the mid–1980s.)

There was a concomitant growth in the size of the new urban population,
cut off from traditional political ties as a result of migration. Typically, this
section of the population organize their lives in the unfamiliar environment
without fully establishing a new social network. At first they abstain from
voting, but subsequently their grievances are tapped by urban-oriented
minor parties, such as the JCP, DSP, and the CGP. It is these parties which
have grown most conspicuously since the mid–1960s. It should be noted
however, that an equally large number of these voters have been attracted
to the LDP and the JSP, and that others continue to abstain. Around the
mid–1970s the LDP's electoral decline reached a point where its safe
majority was almost jeopardized. Political fluidity increased, splinter
parties broke away from the LDP and the JSP, and coalition schemes were
debated in each party in order to cope with this. Partial policy or electoral
campaigning agreements were concluded between some of the parties to
avoid intensifying competition among themselves over similar kinds of
voters. Each time the LDP encountered an internal crisis, some of the

middle-of-the-road and left-wing parties attempted to split it in order to team up with a secessionist group and form a government.

Shortly after, the LDP's nadir was reached amidst major scandals and eruptions of factional strife. A Conservative resurgence began in mid–1977, and since 1980 it has been clear that a new trend has set in. Several major factors contributed (Inoguchi 1983):

(i) Economic success – price stabilization being a major factor after the high economic growth, but also high inflation, of the 1970s.

(ii) Patronage again became important for the LDP's traditional clients in the stagflated world. Its major supporters (in agriculture, and small scale commerce and manufacturing respectively) have intensified their efforts to channel resources to the party in times of difficulty. LDP politicians on the other hand, felt the need to respond, which has once more strengthened ties with these groups.

(iii) One of the major criticisms directed against the Government in the 1960s and 1970s was that it gave little attention to social welfare and environmental issues. Vigorous legislation in the 1970s brought Japan up to the level of other industrialized countries in these fields by the mid–1970s.

(iv) Japan's increasing international prominence has also contributed to the Conservative resurgence, by feeding national self-esteem.

In addition to the Liberal Democrats, Socialists and Communists briefly dealt with above, the other parties covered in the analysis are:

Clean Government Party

The Clean Government Party, founded in 1964 with the full backing of its mother organization, the *Sokagakkai*. The *Sokagakkai* is a religious group which follows the beliefs of the thirteenth-century Buddhist monk, Nichiren, which they interpret in a very radical way. By putting forward candidates in the nationwide single district race for House of Councillors seats, the CGP and its predecessors were able to convert the *Sokagakkai*'s nationwide strength into parliamentary seats as early as the 1950s. Since the 1960s it has also been successful in winning House of Representatives elections. Its ideology is based on a brand of Buddhism tailored to the sentiments of its supporters with particular emphasis on moral rectitude and social reform. However, in 1980 the CGP concluded an agreement with the JSP 'toward a progressive coalition government' which left the *Sokagakkai* in some confusion. The CGP's funding is almost exclusively from its huge publication business and party membership fees. It lacks the LDP's links to business or the Socialist and Communist ties to trade unions.

Democratic Socialist Party

Right-wing factions of the JSP, disenchanted by the domination of 'doctrinaire' members, formed the DSP in 1959. The DSP's ideology is social democracy of a kind, with emphasis on 'within-system' reforms and a constant drive to share power. Its support comes from trade unions, intellectuals, an anti-*Sokagakkai* federation of the New Buddhist Group led by the *Rishokosseikai*, and a pro-South Korea association of Korean residents in Japan. Its supporters tend to work in the modernized sectors and are individualistic in their life style.

New Liberal Club

The New Liberal Club (NLC), was born in 1976 amidst turmoil in the LDP, which was plagued by the Lockheed scandal and related intra-party factional disputes. Disenchanted with the LDP's 'money politics' and factional strife, six members of the House of Representatives split from the LDP to form the NLC. In elections for the House of Representatives in 1976, they scored a major victory by winning 18 seats. However, in the House of Councillors election in the spring of 1977, they only succeeded in getting three members elected and subsequently faced splits – between those favouring coalition with the LDP versus those favouring a middle-of-the-road coalition with the CGP, the DSP, and the JSP. The only clear differences from the LDP are that the NLC does not propose to revise the Constitution; stresses cheap government and educational reforms; and has friendly ties with China. Its supporters in 1976 were predominantly urban.

United Socialist Democratic Party

The USDP emerged in 1976 out of the merger of a few groups of right-wing moderates which had split or withdrawn from the JSP in the preceding few years. The USDP ideology is socialism of a sort with emphasis on individual freedom, world peace, participatory democracy and ecology. Its supporters are predominantly urban. The bulk of its support comes from floating voters and non-voters disenchanted with the 'rigid' and 'doctrinaire' stance of the established left-wing parties, the JSP and the JCP, and from those who have been active in various citizens' movements like anti-pollution, anti-big business, and anti-war movements, consumer protests and local community reforms.

17.2 ELECTIONS

Elections took on a different meaning after 1955 when the conservatives merged to counteract the Socialist unification the same year. The Liberal

Democratic Party became a predominant party. occupying about two thirds of the seats in both Houses and denying opposition parties any chance of sharing or alternating power. Before that coalition governments had not been uncommon, with the JSP, for instance, heading or joining the Government twice in 1947–8.

The LDP obtained an absolute majority in the House of Representatives until 1976 and in the House of Councillors until 1967. Immediately after the election of 1976, the LDP managed to persuade some other elected members to enter the LDP and thus was able to retain its majority. From 1955–76 elections were routine because of the certainty with which the LDP was assured its governing status. Meanwhile, candidates of all parties were busy mobilizing support by satisfying material demands from local districts or from nationwide hierarchically organized, interest groups. The electoral system for the House of Representatives whereby three to five members are elected in the same district without party list reinforced this concentration on local activities.

On the national political scene, however, the opposition generally took 'purer' political stands on issues such as defence, economic growth, social welfare and the Constitution – 'purer' in the sense that they were not in a position to implement policy programmes in the foreseeable future and thus were free from the constraints which have to be faced in government. Thus, for instance, most opposition parties opposed the U.S.–Japan Security Treaty and the Self-Defence Force while not presenting concrete alternatives; and wanted to slow the economic growth rate while insisting on vast social welfare programmes. This had a strong appeal to those who felt that they were neglected or treated unfairly in various ways.

The LDP on the other hand, took its advantageous position for granted, and was assured of the powerful bureaucracy's help in drawing up and implementing political programmes without the necessity of appealing to voters. At least until 1972, the government budget was drafted almost completely by the Budget Bureau of the Finance Ministry and passed without amendment in the Diet. About 70–90 per cent of bills passed in the Diet were drafted by bureaucrats and a large number of them originated from the LDP's Policy Affairs Council (Iizaka et al., 1979). With these arrangements, the policy stands of political parties in elections have tended to be 'symbolic'. On the other hand, they are good indicators of where each party is located in the fairly simple multi-dimensional spectrum of Japanese politics under a predominant-party system.

17.3 PLATFORM AND MANIFESTO EQUIVALENTS

There is no established tradition in Japan of publishing specific documents before an election to clarify the party position on national issues. In this respect, Japanese political practice differs considerably from that of the UK for example. Hence it is not easy to determine what exactly should be taken as the equivalent to platforms and manifestos. There are basically three types of party documents: (1) basic party programmes which are adopted at the time of foundation or later when major political tenets are changed; (2) party documents issued, often annually, at party conventions, including (a) party policy lines; (b) party organizational activity lines; (c) party policy statements; (d) party resolutions; and (3) pre-election statements made by some parties and not by others, but not always by the same party at different times. This makes it impossible to choose equivalents across parties in the same time frame.

What are comparable and indeed standardized are newspaper summaries of parties' election pledges, reported in major newspapers, which can be neatly presented in tabular form. We have used the *Asahi Shimbun* summaries since 1960. Although there have been fifteen general elections between 1945 and 1980, we are forced for the time being to drop the first seven general elections held from 1945 to 1959 due to the lack of regular newspaper coverage. From 1960 however there has been a systematic procedure, in which about two weeks before election day, the *Asahi Shimbun* (as well as other major newspapers) asks for each party's policy stands on certain issues it deems important. Each party spells these out within the same limited space. The *Asahi Shimbun* does not edit the parties' responses and it prints them in tabular form. Thus, the newspaper summaries are a reliable, authoritative, and convenient source for party positions at election time. They also reach large numbers, as the circulation of the major national papers runs into millions.

Such newspaper reports are of course themselves a distillation of the official party documents, so a word about the preparation and adoption of these is necessary. Most documents and programmes are produced by core party members; presented for discussion and scrutiny; and then revised/ratified at party conventions or full scale committees. This applies whether the document constitutes a party platform, party policy line, party organizational activity line, party policy programme or party resolution. The precise procedure differs between parties, with those on the left being more open to general discussion and influenced by internal factional disputes. Thus control of the key committees and conventions becomes a major concern.

Tightly knit parties such as the JCP and the CGP are most secretive about the production process and leadership control is more evident. But there is still interaction between the elite and the masses. For example, long and intense discussions were held over the draft of the JCP's 1961 platform: twenty-nine times in the mini-platform committee and three times in the Central Committee during 1958–61 (Sato 1977, p. 90).

The LDP does not attach such importance to the details of programmes because of its long-taken-for-granted government status; heavy reliance on central bureaucracy for policy-making; pragmatic attitudes; and representatives and candidates' concern with local matters.

The drafting committee of the party action line for the 1980 convention (January, 1980) for example, consisted of ten members and met twice before it completed the draft. The Committee Chairman consulted with the Prime Minister, top party leaders, and some members of the Policy Affairs Committee – none of whom showed much interest and treated the draft with benign neglect. After completion, the draft was submitted to the Policy Affairs Committee for discussion and approval. There was no discussion, no questions were asked and it was unanimously approved (*Asahi Shimbun* 20 January 1980).

Such party documents do not have a wide circulation in themselves but percolate through to the public by means of their general influence on political debate, as in other countries – but more directly in Japan through the newspaper summaries, to the analysis of which we now turn.

17.4 MAJOR CONCERNS OF ELECTORAL POLITICS

(i) Coding

These reports consist of summary tables composed of quasi-sentences which are used in Japanese where one has only limited space. They are in effect a concatenation of key words and phrases in each policy area. Given the very lucid format, coding reliability does not pose a problem. The general coding worked very well with the addition of some sub-categories to accommodate Japanese peculiarities. The tables were entirely coded by Inoguchi within a few days and selectively recoded two weeks later with a satisfactory correspondence between decisions. The format does not allow any references to other parties.

For later analyses, categories which appeared only three times or less in any one of the party statements of any one of the years were excluded. This differs from the standard procedures, which (owing to the very concise format) would exclude more than half the categories.

(ii) Relative importance of domains

As in other analyses, categories were grouped into seven broad domains. A number of trends are readily discernible:

(1) External relations is one of the three major domains to which much attention has been paid for the last twenty years declining however from the 20–30 per cent level of the early 1960s to a 15–20 per cent level in the late 1970s and 1980.

(2) Economics has maintained a 20–30 per cent attention level. It has a

TABLE 17.1

MAJOR CATEGORIES IN ELECTION PLEDGES JAPAN 1960-1980

CATEGORY	TOTAL	LDP		JSP		CGP		JCP		DSP		NLC		USDP	
		X̄	SD	X̄	SD	X̄	SD	X̄	SD	X̄	SD	X̄	SD	X̄	SD
SOCIAL JUSTICE	174	3.50	2.24	4.75	2.86	4.00	2.14	5.14	3.36	2.79	1.79	4.33	3.09	4.50	4.50
SOCIAL SERVICES (PRO-EXPANSION)	147	3.00	2.83	4.75	2.86	4.00	2.07	3.14	1.64	3.75	1.92	3.33	0.47	5.00	0.00
REGULATION OF CAPITALISM	106	2.25	1.48	2.00	1.22	2.71	1.67	3.43	2.56	2.62	1.41	1.00	1.41	2.50	1.50
TECHNOLOGY AND INFRASTRUCTURE	100	2.37	1.80	2.50	1.50	2.57	1.59	1.86	1.36	2.50	1.00	1.67	0.47	2.50	1.50
PEACE	97	1.75	1.48	3.25	1.71	3.00	2.14	2.71	1.48	1.75	1.98	0.67	0.47	0.50	0.50
GOVERNMENT CORRUPTION	97	2.00	2.18	1.87	1.69	2.57	2.32	3.00	1.69	1.12	1.27	2.33	1.25	5.50	0.50
OTHER ECONOMIC GROUPS	97	1.25	1.30	1.75	2.22	0.71	0.70	1.43	1.18	1.37	1.22	0.67	0.47	1.00	1.00
FREEDOM AND DEMOCRACY	94	1.37	0.99	2.00	2.00	2.43	2.13	3.57	2.06	1.87	1.17	1.00	0.82	3.50	1.50
INCENTIVES	86	1.87	2.20	2.25	1.71	2.71	2.43	1.86	1.36	2.37	1.73	0.67	0.94	0.00	0.00
MILITARY (NEGATIVE)	78	0.38	0.48	2.62	1.11	2.14	1.12	4.14	1.25	0.75	0.83	0.33	0.47	1.50	0.50
FOREIGN SPECIAL RELATIONS (NEGATIVE)	63	0.00	0.00	1.87	0.78	2.00	1.07	4.14	1.36	0.63	0.70	0.00	0.00	0.00	0.00
NATIONAL EFFORT AND SOCIAL HARMONY	63	1.62	1.22	0.87	0.78	1.43	1.99	2.71	1.48	1.62	0.86	0.00	0.00	0.50	0.50
FOREIGN SPECIAL RELATIONS (POSITIVE)	44	2.37	0.86	0.62	0.70	0.43	0.49	0.00	0.00	1.37	0.70	1.00	0.82	1.50	0.50
MILITARY (POSITIVE)	34	1.75	0.66	0.00	0.00	0.29	0.45	0.29	0.29	1.12	0.78	1.67	0.47	1.00	1.00
GOVERNMENT EFFICIENCY	31	1.00	1.94	0.13	0.33	0.86	1.36	0.43	1.05	0.37	0.48	2.33	1.70	1.50	0.50

complementary relationship with the social welfare domain. That is to say, as the social welfare domain expands, the economic domain shrinks and *vice versa*. The sum of these two domains has been 40–60 per cent. By 1972 the social welfare domain was the dominant policy issue. But when the economy became one of the major concerns, as was the case in 1980, the proportion allocated to the social welfare domain contracted somewhat.

(3)   Freedom and Democracy has recorded a 5–15 per cent level of attention, gradually decreasing. It appears that in the 1980s this domain became less an area of contention between the government and the opposition than it was in the 1970s.

(4)   The Government domain has expanded from zero in 1960 to 20 per cent in 1980. It appears that with the revelation of major scandals and the corruption of major LDP leaders in the mid-1970s, issues in this domain provided a major arena for electoral confrontation.

(5)   The Social Fabric domain has decreased from a 8–9 per cent level in the early 1960s to 1–2 per cent in the late 1970s. Law and order issues particularly have lessened in importance.

(6)   The Social Group domain has also contracted, from a 11–12 per cent level in the early 1960s to a 0–3 per cent level in the late 1970s. As socially weaker groups (workers and farmers for example) began to benefit from high economic growth with some notable income-equalization effects, appeals to these social groups ceased to constitute major electoral issues.

(iii) Major categories by party

Most important of all the categories are those related to social welfare and the economy. Social Justice, expansion of Social Services, Regulation of Capitalism, Technology and Infrastructure are the top four categories for almost all parties. Following these are Peace, Government Corruption, Other Economic Groups, and Democracy. The importance of peace as an issue reflects the tenacity of pacifism – generated by the experiences of the 1940s. The high frequency of reference to Government Corruption indicates the extent to which the oppositions try to take advantage of the government scandals which intermittently come to public attention. The category of Other Economic Groups refers, in effect, to the underdeveloped regions. Where there are no sharp class, linguistic, religious and ethnic cleavages, one of the most meaningful sources of division is regional-developmental disparity. Democracy is one of the key political values since 1945.

Looking at these categories by party, a more differentiated picture emerges. The LDP's top five categories are Social Justice, expansion of

Social Services, Regulation of Capitalism, Technology and Infrastructure, and support for Foreign Special Relations. The last is most distinctively the LDP's since the opposition parties do not put much emphasis on it. Being a catch-all party, the LDP's electoral pledges deal with all major concerns.

The JSP puts special emphasis on Social Justice and Social Services and Peace; and makes negative references to the Military. The JSP, the largest opposition party, tries to channel popular feeling against the excesses of the high growth policy and the alliance with the U.S..

The CGP's five major categories are Social Justice, Social Services, Peace, Regulation of Capitalism and Incentives. Since the CGP portrays itself as a party for those treated unfavourably by society, this makes sense.

The JCP stresses Social Justice, Military and Special Foreign Relations (in a negative sense), Regulation of Capitalism, and Democracy, and criticizes the government for its failure to bring about justice and democracy – especially to regulate excesses of the capitalist economy. The JCP is also very critical of close ties with the U.S.

The DSP's top five categories are Social Services, Social Justice, Regulation of Capitalism, Technology and Infrastructure, and Incentives – roughly those favoured by the CGP, minus the external relations categories with anti-U.S. overtones.

The NLC favours Social Justice, Social Services, Government Corruption, Government Efficiency and support for the Military. The NLC is very similar to the LDP except for its strong emphasis on government corruption and efficiency. The NLC was of course made up of members who walked out of the LDP precisely on such issues.

The major categories of the USDP, a party for those disenchanted with the JSP and to a lesser extent with the JCP, are Government Corruption, Social Services, Social Justice, Decentralization, and Democracy. The USDP thus puts an emphasis on these categories which can be termed as mildly socialist, weakly ecologist, and moderate reformist.

17.5 FIRST-STAGE FACTOR ANALYSIS WITHIN DOMAINS

In order to discover the major cleavages inside each domain, we examine each category using factor analysis, as in other chapters (see Table 17.2).

(i) External Relations

As expected, the first component is either anti-U.S. or pro-U.S., with categories related to the Japan–U.S. security treaty, (e.g. negative references to the Military (.24) and to Foreign Special Relationships (.23)). The second component reflects the principle of being nice to everyone (both

China and the USSR load very positively – .28 and .25, and Internationalism stands at .31) *vs.* hard-to-hide Hostility, – the anti-U.S. and anti-Soviet categories coming up jointly and strongly on the latter side (−.18 and −.14). One half of the variance is explained by these dimensions.

(ii) Freedom and Democracy

The first component is that of freedom and democracy which constitute two of the cornerstones of the Constitution. The second is related to type of freedom, i.e. Civil Liberties *vs.* Political Freedom. These two dimensions explain 87 per cent of the variance.

(iii) Government

The first component is that of government efficiency with the categories of Government Corruption (.57) and Government Efficiency (.53) loading high. The second is that of Government Effectiveness, with the categories of Government Effectiveness and Authority (.66) and Decentralization (.58) being located separately from the other categories. These two dimensions explain 68 per cent of the variance.

(iv) Economy

The first component is that of maximalist *vs.* minimalist government intervention in the economy. Such categories as Incentives (0.29), Protectionism (positive) (0.27), Productivity (0.24), and Keynesian Demand Management (0.21) are loaded on the positive side of the first dimension, whereas on the negative side the categories of Economic Orthodoxy and Efficiency (−0.16) stand out. The second is that of capitalism *vs* socialism. Such categories as Economic Goals (0.23) are loaded heavily on the positive side, whereas such categories as Controlled Economy (−0.37), Incentives (−0.15) and Economic Planning (−0.11) are important on the negative side. These two dimensions explain 41.9 per cent of the variance.

(v) Welfare and Quality of Life

The first component is that of progressive *vs.* traditional conceptions of welfare. Such categories as Environmental Protection, (0.47) and Social Services (positive) (0.43) are outstanding on the positive side, whereas such categories as Education (pro-expansion) (−0.26) and Social Justice (−0.18) are loaded on the other side. The second is that of Social Justice (0.66) *vs.* Education (−.47). The second dimension is somewhat difficult to interpret with each category heavily loaded on either one of the extremes,

TABLE 17.2

MAJOR THEMES IN ELECTION PLEDGES 1960-1980

	LDP X̄	SD	JSP X̄	SD	CCP X̄	SD	JCP X̄	SD	DSP X̄	SD	NLC X̄	SD	USDP X̄	SD
EXTERNAL RELATIONS														
FACTOR 1.1 ANTI - PRO- U.S.	-1.06	0.20	0.81	2.11	0.51	3.76	1.02	2.38	-0.59	3.29	-0.92	0.81	-0.60	0.49
FACTOR 1.2 INTERNATIONAL-ISM VS. HOSTILITY	0.55	7.16	0.32	9.29	-0.10	1.50	-0.96	7.59	0.17	5.13	-0.23	0.50	-0.15	0.50
FREEDOM														
FACTOR 2.1 FREEDOM AND DEMOCRACY	-0.38	3.67	0.27	13.96	0.04	3.58	0.79	7.95	-0.20	3.76	-0.84	0.12	-0.37	0.50
FACTOR 2.2 CIVIL LIBERT-IES VS. POLITICAL FREEDOM	0.26	2.56	0.43	5.76	-0.13	3.67	-0.11	22.47	-0.29	1.31	0.18	0.47	-1.00	0.50
GOVERNMENT														
FACTOR 3.1 EFFICIENCY	0.04	12.48	-0.30	2.16	0.08	6.81	0.09	3.49	-0.54	2.29	0.57	2.49	2.02	0.49
FACTOR 3.2 EFFECTIVENESS	0.46	11.96	0.15	2.98	-0.41	0.85	-0.20	0.39	-0.38	0.08	-0.75	0.30	2.32	0.51
ECONOMY														
FACTOR 4.1 DEGREE OF INTERVENTION	-0.27	2.71	0.42	11.35	0.40	14.95	-0.06	3.00	-0.07	4.66	-0.45	0.05	-0.84	0.49
FACTOR 4.2 CAPITALISM VS. SOCIALISM	0.49	15.83	0.01	5.11	-0.20	7.76	-0.45	2.33	-0.04	5.71	-0.21	0.25	0.75	0.49
WELFARE														
FACTOR 5.1 CONCEPTIONS OF WELFARE	-0.11	15.06	-0.18	3.37	0.47	6.62	-0.17	3.67	0.02	9.91	-0.33	0.01	0.52	0.50
FACTOR 5.2 EDUCATION VS. SOCIAL JUSTICE	-0.19	1.80	0.22	8.31	0.35	3.74	0.32	14.55	-0.52	3.43	-0.21	3.50	-0.05	0.51
SOCIAL FABRICS														
FACTOR 6.1 CONSERVATISM	0.66	14.47	-0.02	8.39	-0.25	4.24	-0.12	0.80	0.15	7.09	-0.79	0.00	-0.68	0.49
FACTOR 6.2 POLITICAL VS. CIVIL CONSERVATISM	0.21	9.43	-0.49	2.93	0.14	9.86	0.96	5.95	0.10	2.93	-0.71	0.00	-0.40	0.50
SOCIAL GROUPS														
FACTOR 7.1 OCCUPATIONAL GROUPS	-0.33	3.50	0.49	9.48	-0.36	2.86	0.29	10.72	0.24	8.94	-0.49	0.32	-0.58	0.50
FACTOR 7.2 UNDERDEVELOPED AREAS	0.10	8.88	-0.30	1.16	0.68	13.98	-0.05	4.92	0.03	7.05	-0.61	0.00	-0.62	0.46

though it is a contrast we have encountered in other countries. These two dimensions explain roughly 62.8 per cent of the variance.

(vi) Social Fabric

The first component is that of traditional conservatism, with Law and Order (0.54) and Traditional Morality (0.48) distinguishing themselves from other categories. The second is that of political versus civil conservatism with National Effort and Social Harmony (0.90) loaded heavily on the positive side and Traditional Morality (−0.51) on the other side. These two dimensions explain 84 per cent of the variance.

(vii) Social Groups

The first component is that of occupational groups (Agriculture and Farmers 0.49, Labour 0.40), and the second is Others (0.37) – really referring to geographical groups and underdeveloped areas.

Table 17.2 presents mean factor scores by party of the domain analysis results just presented. It is a summary of how much parties differ on the major dimensions of each policy domain.

(i) External Relations

External relations (along with freedom and democracy) is a domain with large inter-party differences. The LDP–JCP distance on the first dimension of external relations attests to this. On the first dimension the standard deviation is very large for most opposition parties (especially the CGP and the DSP) which in substantive terms means that they have recently modified their anti-U.S. postures.

(ii) Freedom and Democracy

Inter-party differences are very large as exemplified by an LDP–JCP distance which is second only to that in the external relations domain. The large standard deviations for the JSP and the JCP on the first dimension (Freedom and Democracy) indicates changes of stance.

(iii) Government

The two smallest parties, the NLC and USDP, score high on the first dimension (government efficiency and anti-corruption). The JSP is somewhat closer to the LDP on the second dimension (government effectiveness and authority).

TABLE 17.3

TWO STAGE ANALYSIS OF ELECTION PLEDGES 1960–1980

DOMAIN TITLE	FACTOR 1	FACTOR 2
	LEFT <u>VS</u>. RIGHT OR MAXIMALIST VS. MINIMALIST IN TERMS OF OCCUPATION REFORMS	GROWTH <u>VS</u>. WELFARE OR MID-INDUSTRIAL <u>VS</u>. POST-INDUSTRIAL ORIENTATIONS

EXTERNAL RELATIONS

FACTOR 1.1 ANTI-PRO U.S.	0.59		0.12
FACTOR 1.2 INTERNATIONALISM <u>VS</u>. HOSTILITY	0.01		0.51
PEACE	0.61	FOREIGN SPECIAL RELATIONS (+)	-0.68
INTERNATIONALISM	0.43	FOREIGN SPECIAL RELATIONS (-)	-0.71
FOREIGN SPECIAL RELATIONS, CHINA (+)	0.52	MILITARY (+)	-0.60
FOREIGN SPECIAL RELATIONS, THIRD WORLD (+)	0.32	MILITARY (-)	0.75
		FOREIGN SPECIAL RELATIONS, ASIA	-0.30

FREEDOM

FACTOR 2.1 FRREDOM AND DEMOCRACY	0.63		0.30
FACTOR 2.2 CIVIL LIBERTIES <u>VS</u>. POLITICAL FREEDOM	0.06		0.44
FREEDOM AND DEMOCRACY	0.57	FREEDOM AND DEMOCRACY	0.31
CONSTITUTIONALISM (+)	0.55	DEMOCRACY	0.36
		CONSTITUTIONALISM (+)	0.30

GOVERNMENT

FACTOR 3.1 EFFICIENCY	-0.63		-0.38
FACTOR 3.2 EFFECTIVENESS	-0.01		-0.05
GOVERNMENT EFFICIENCY	-0.45	GOVERNMENT EFFICIENCY	-0.36
GOVERNMENT CORRUPTION	-0.65		

Continued...

TABLE 17.3 Continued

DOMAIN TITLE	FACTOR 1 LEFT-RIGHT, OR MAXIMA- LIST-MINIMALIST IN TERMS OF OCCUPATION REFORMS	FACTOR 2 GROWTH VS. WELFARE	
ECONOMY			
FACTOR 4.1 DEGREE OF INTERVENTION	0.78		0.36
FACTOR 4.2 CAPITALISM VS. SOCIALISM	−0.30		0.55
INCENTIVES	0.56	INCENTIVES	0.37
PROTECTION (+)	0.64	ECONOMIC GOALS	0.45
ECONOMIC GOALS	0.54	CONTROLLED ECONOMY	0.38
PRODUCTIVITY	0.83	NATIONALISM	0.35
		ECONOMIC ORTHODOXY AND EFFICIENCY	−0.44
WELFARE			
FACTOR 5.1 CONCEPTIONS OF WELFARE	−0.04		−0.06
FACTOR 2.1 EDUCATION VS. SOCIAL JUSTICE	0.38		−0.07
		ARTS, SPORTS AND LEISURE	0.31
FABRIC			
FACTOR 6.1 TRADITIONAL CONSERVATISM	0.34		0.64
FACTOR 6.2 POLITICAL VS. CIVIL CONSERVATISM	0.46		0.20
DEFENCE OF NATIONAL WAY OF LIFE	0.31	DEFENCE OF NATIONAL WAY OF LIFE	−0.43
TRADITIONAL MORALITY	0.64	TRAD. MORALITY	−0.30
LAW AND ORDER	0.68	LAW AND ORDER	0.38
NATIONAL EFFORT AND SOCIAL HARMONY	0.42		
GROUPS			
FACTOR 7.1 OCCUPATIONAL GROUPS	0.31		0.69
FACTOR 7.2 UNDER-DEVELOPED AREAS	0.59		0.02
LABOUR GROUPS	0.66		
AGRICULTURE AND FARMERS	0.51		
OTHER ECONOMIC GROUPS	0.57		

(iv) Economy

On the first dimension of maximalist *vs.* minimalist government intervention in the economy, the LDP and the traditional opposition parties do not differ very much. Only the two small splinter parties, the NLC and the USDP, stand out on this first dimension. On the second dimension of free market *vs.* planned economy, the LDP–JCP distance is large but not as large as that in the domains of external relations and freedom and democracy.

(v) Welfare

On the first dimension of progressive conceptions of welfare, the CGP and the USDP stand out. The former demonstrates a special concern for welfare, while the latter emphasizes the environment.

(vi) Social Fabric

The LDP and the two splinter parties are poles apart on the first dimension of political conservatism. Among the opposition parties only the DSP shows a somewhat high value on this dimension, indicating their fairly conservative outlook.

(vii) Social Groups

It is not surprising that the JSP and the JCP make more frequent reference to weaker social groups than other parties, and the CGP makes frequent, less class-conscious references to underdeveloped areas.

17.4 SECOND-STAGE FACTOR ANALYSIS

On the basis of the principal components pooled from each domain analysis, a second-stage factor analysis was performed. Only two major factors were Varimax rotated. The first factor was right *vs.* left and the second factor was growth *vs.* welfare orientation. On one side of the first dimension one finds such categories as Foreign Special Relationships, negative (anti-U.S.), Freedom and Domestic Human Rights, maximalist government intervention in the economy, political *vs* civil freedom, and underdeveloped areas. On the other side one finds such categories as Government Efficiency, free market *vs.* planned economy, and conservative *vs.* progressive orientations in welfare.

In order to see the meaning of this dimension more clearly, the correlation coefficients between factor scores and values of original

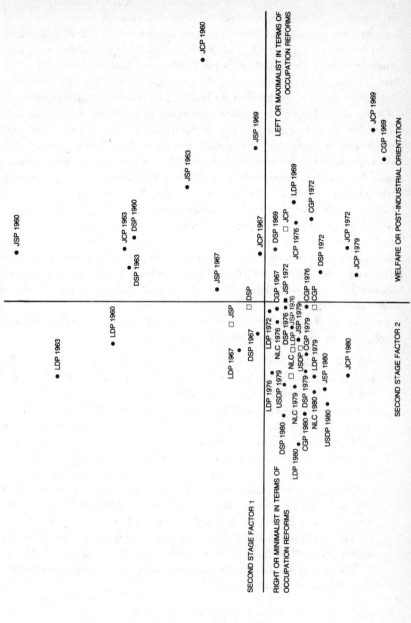

17.1 Location of parties at general elections 1960–1980

385

categories were examined. High positive values are observed for such categories as Peace, Freedom and Democracy, and Constitutionalism, Government, Incentives, support for Protectionism, Economic Groups, Productivity, Traditional Morality, Law and Order, National Effort and Social Harmony, Labour Groups, Agricultural Groups and Farmers, and Other Economic Groups. Except for Traditional Morality, and Law and Order, these categories represent the demands of the opposition parties, which tried to keep up the liberal-idealist themes of occupation reforms.

On the second dimension, prominent loadings are those of international-ism *vs.* hostility, free market, post-industrial concerns of social life, and occupational groups. As for original categories, the following are promi-nent and positively correlated:– Controlled Economy, Incentives, Nation-alization, National Effort and Social Harmony. Negative correlations exist with positive references to Special Foreign Relationships and to the Military, Government Efficiency, Economic Goals, Economic Orthodoxy and Efficiency, Defence of National Way of Life and Traditional Morality. This appears like a contrast between emphases on traditional concerns – national growth and related goals – and a concern with newer or at least less heavily economic issues. It could be interpreted as a development from industrial to post-industrial concerns, such as has been perceived by authors like Inglehart (1977).

Looking at the location of parties over time on the two-dimensional graph, we can see two major movements:

(1) All the parties have moved from left to right, or away from the occupation syndrome to post-Occupation reality. Not only have the smaller opposition parties, the DSP, the CGP, the NLC and the USDP, moved rightward, but also the JSP, the JCP and the LDP. Thus, the inter-party differences of 1980 are much less than those of 1960 on the left–right continuum.

(2) All the parties have gradually changed from a growth-first orienta-tion to a post-growth orientation. It is striking that the government and the opposition alike were located in growth-orientation spaces in the early 1960s despite the oft-commented disparity between the government's growth-first policy and the opposition's equity-first or welfare-first policy. In the 1970s all the parties put an emphasis on welfare-related policies. Nevertheless, the JSP, the JCP and the USDP put most. These movements reflect the shifts in substantive issue concerns already noted.

17.5 CONCLUSIONS

Our analysis has shown that election pledges are indeed good sources from which to identify the policy positions of the parties and major cleavages of electoral politics. The most important cleavages are left *vs.* right (or occupation syndrome *vs.* post-occupation realities) and growth *vs.* welfare orientation (or mid-industrial tasks and post-industrial concerns). More specifically, positions among the parties are most divergent in the domains of external relations, freedom and democracy, and social fabric, whereas their positions are most convergent on the economy, social welfare, and the quality of life. Party locations on the two dimensions demonstrate that inter-party differences have become less significant throughout the 1970s. Most parties are now far more right on the first dimension and are more welfare-oriented on the second dimension than they were in 1960 or 1970. The question of how these metamorphoses occurred will be the next priority for research in this area.

Note

1 Research for this chapter was supported by the Japanese Ministry of Education through a scientific research grant (1979–81) to the author.

CHAPTER 18

COMPARATIVE ANALYSES OF
POST-WAR ELECTION PROGRAMMES

———— ∾ ————

18.1 SUMMARY AND REVIEW OF THE COUNTRY
FINDINGS

(i) Coding

With the exception of Chapters 3 and 9 where we presented parallel but separate analyses of four 'Anglo-Saxon' democracies and two Scandinavian systems, each chapter has explored the dimensions and cleavages of party competition, within one country, independently, and in detail. Within the common coding frame of Appendix B, country investigators were free to introduce additional sub-categories to capture the idiosyncracies of their 'own' system. It is significant that many did not feel this need, or introduced no more than a few refinements and additions. It is also significant that most country-specific categories introduced at the outset of the coding, on the *a priori* assumption that they were necessary to accommodate idiosyncracies of the countries involved, were found to collect few references and had to be collapsed back into the general categories.

All this demonstrates that the general coding frame accommodated the major issues of party politics in a very diverse set of countries. It worked least well where it was least relevant, in the basically rural if developing society of Sri Lanka. This was not unexpected, but even here the results made broad sense.

In retrospect, other general coding categories might have been added. This is perhaps more obvious in the External Relations categories than elsewhere, as no direct reference is made to East–West relations nor to the leading alliances such as NATO (though references to foreign special relationships and military pick this up). However the country analyses showed no recurring need for extra categories of this kind. Indeed, no evidence emerged of the consistent absence of any necessary category throughout the specific analyses.

Of course additional sub-categories might also have functioned well – one cannot comment on hypothetical alternatives on the basis of how an existing categorization performed. It seems justifiable to argue however than any alternative set of categories must broadly resemble those we have. Given the general robustness of our findings it is also likely that they would emerge in much the same form under such a coding alternative.

The corollary of new categories is the 'stretching' of existing ones to encompass particular country meanings, or to accommodate references that might otherwise have been fitted by a new category. Such cases have been discussed explicitly and frankly in the country chapters. They exist, but not in exceptional numbers. The 'stretching' has been a logical development within the overall framework to fit the particular circumstances of a country. So it has not covertly smuggled in changes of meaning between categories bearing the same general name.

It is of course inevitable that any limited set of codes applied to so many countries, will encounter some difficulties. Nevertheless the difficulties here were sufficiently limited to show that the coding frame fitted well, and that the data generated through its application to election programmes is neither forced nor distorted. The frequencies obtained reflect real differences and similarities between parties and countries in the analyses. The genuinely comparable nature of the coding means that there is no technical impediment to the exploration of such differences and similarities through the creation of a unified comparative data set.

We use such a data base in the following analysis. Before we begin a statistical investigation, however, there are other findings from the individual chapters which need to be discussed and assessed.

(ii) Party competition as Selective Emphases

As the coding frame was essentially based on a saliency approach to party competition (Section 2.6), its validation through individual country analyses extends also to the underlying theory. It is true that as a result of initial doubts on the part of some members of the research group, explicit distinctions were made in limited areas between positive and negative references, e.g. to military, internationalism, social services, education, etc. It is striking however that negative and positive emphases seldom occur simultaneously – either one or the other is stressed within a party or indeed within a country as a whole. We thus have a detailed demonstration that direct confrontation is limited, even within specific areas.

In general confrontation occurs still less. A separate count was kept of

TABLE 18.1

THE TWO LEADING DIMENSIONS FROM THE SECOND-STAGE
FACTOR ANALYSIS OVER 20 POST-WAR DEMOCRACIES

COUNTRY	FIRST DIMENSION	SECOND DIMENSION
UNITED KINGDOM	LEFT VS. RIGHT	LIBERALISM VS. CLASS CONFLICT CONCERNS
NEW ZEALAND	LEFT VS. RIGHT	INTERNATIONALISM AND WELFARE VS. ISOLATIONISM
AUSTRALIA	LEFT VS. RIGHT	DISCIPLINE AND RESTRAINT VS. FREE PURSUIT OF GOALS
UNITED STATES	LEFT VS. RIGHT (IN A MODIFIED SENSE OF CONSERVATISM VS. INTERVENTIONIST LIBERALISM)	INTERVENTIONISM VS. NEW INTERVENTIONISM
CANADA	NEW LEFTISM	OLD LEFTISM
SRI LANKA	URBAN VS. RURAL	OLD LEFT VS. RIGHT
ISRAEL	NATIONALISM AND TECHNOLOGICAL PROGRESS	MODERNISATION VS. DEMOCRACY (ASSOCIATED WITH NEW ISSUES)
IRELAND	AUTHORITARIANISM AND ABILITY TO GOVERN	CAPITALIST ECONOMICS AND IRISH UNITY
NORTHERN IRELAND	PRO- ANTI-STATUS QUO	SOCIO-ECONOMIC CONCERNS VS. SECTIONALISM
SWEDEN	LEFT VS. CENTRE	LEFT VS. RIGHT
DENMARK	OLD LEFT VS. RIGHT	NEW LEFT VS. RIGHT
FINLAND[x]	SOCIALIST VS. CAPITALIST ORGANIZATION OF THE ECONOMY	CONTRAST BETWEEN GROUP NORMS AND INDIVIDUAL VALUES
NETHERLANDS	LEFT VS. RIGHT	NEW LEFT ISSUES VS. SOCIAL CONSERVATISM
BELGIUM	LEFT VS. RIGHT (BUT LEFT INCLUDES FRANCOPHONE ORIENTATIONS)	PROGRESSIVISM VS. CLERICAL CONSERVATISM
LUXEMBURG	NEW ISSUES VS. ISOLATIONSIM	SOCIAL JUSTICE AND FREEDOM
AUSTRIA	SOCIOECONOMIC LEFT VS. RIGHT	NEW ISSUES AND INTERNATIONALISM VS. SOCIAL CONSERVATISM
WEST GERMANY	ORGANIZATION OF (WORLD) SOCIETY	DEGREE OF CONCERN WITH THE SOCIAL MARKET ECONOMY
FRANCE	LEFT VS. RIGHT (ECONOMIC, SOCIAL AND FOREIGN AFFAIRS)	POPULISM VS. BOURGEOIS LIBERALISM

Continued...

TABLE 18.1 Continued...

COUNTRY	FIRST DIMENSION	SECOND DIMENSION
ITALY	LEFT VS. RIGHT	SOCIAL HARMONY (SUBSUMES CATHOLICISM)
JAPAN	LEFT VS. RIGHT	NEW ISSUES VS. CONCENTRATION ON ECONOMIC GROWTH.

x BASED ON BORG'S STUDY OF FINNISH ELECTION PROGRAMMES 1945-1966 (BORG, 1966), NOT ON A COUNTRY CHAPTER. THIS WAS A FIRST STAGE RATHER THAN A SECOND STAGE ANALYSIS, BASED ON PROGRAMMES TO THE MID-1960S, AND ON A SOMEWHAT DIFFERENT CATEGORIZATION FROM OURS, BUT SEEMS GENERALLY COMPATIBLE WITH OUR APPROACH.

each party's references to other parties. This confirmed the findings of the original British and American studies that the level of such references was on average less than 10 per cent of sentences in the election programme – and these are references to any aspect of the other parties, not simply to their policies. The Saliency Theory of Party Competition, which has important and immediately applicable consequences for our understanding of elections (see Budge and Farlie, 1983) and constitutes the basis of our approach to the data, is thus richly confirmed by the country analyses both in the details of coding and in the general results obtained from its use. It is also substantiated by the convincing results of the comparative analyses below. Parties compete by accentuating issues on which they have an undoubted advantage, rather than by putting forward contrasting policies on the same issues.

(iii) Comparability of the country analyses: leading dimensions of competition

In Chapter 2 we made an undertaking not to take the general comparability of data across countries for granted, but to ascertain first, through the results of the separate country studies, whether a real basis of comparison existed. In regard to the unforced, general applicability of the coding frame and its underlying theory, we have already decided that there is. The substantive results also show a quite unexpected degree of convergence between the independent country analyses. Obviously there are idiosyncracies and cases of non-comparability, particularly where countries have seemed idiosyncratic in the light of earlier, qualitative analyses – Ireland, Northern Ireland, Sri Lanka and Israel – to take the major examples. But what is remarkable is the limited range of leading dimensions which emerges, and their ready comparability across most countries.

This is dramatically shown in Table 18.1, which reports the interpretation of the two leading dimensions from the second-stage factor analysis, given by the country investigators themselves. What is most striking and dramatic is the emergence in most countries of a type of Left–Right confrontation – sometimes of two types of such confrontation in the shape of 'old left' and 'new left' issues.

This finding, which emerges spontaneously from independently-executed analyses of the country data, is a major – perhaps *the* major – finding of this volume. As such it requires a separate section (see 18.2 below) for its assessment and interpretation. From the point of view of the similarity between party appeals across countries and party systems, and the basis this offers for putting them together in a comparative analysis, the importance of the table lies in its resounding demonstration that the underlying cleavages, do indeed resemble each other very closely.

A comparative analysis therefore is not a matter of forcing essentially unlike systems into a common mould – of extracting mechanical averages from disparate data and coming up with unconvincing general interpretations. Such interpretations emerge spontaneously from the country data and offer authoritative support for their merger and for a genuinely comparative, cross national, analysis. This in turn answers some basic questions raised in Chapter 2 – for example, whether party ideology compares in importance with national distinctions or *vice versa*.

18.2 THE LEFT–RIGHT DIMENSION: INCIDENCE AND GENERAL INTERPRETATION

Obviously however, the major findings reported in Table 18.1 require further analysis and interpretation. The principal conclusion is the emergence of a central and clearly Left–Right cleavage in most of the countries under consideration – 15 out of 20, of which it is the first factor in 13 (or 14, if 'New Leftism' is counted in Canada).

With hindsight it is not surprising to find Left–Right divisions so generalized. Traditionally, most party conflict has been interpreted as an opposition of Left *vs.* Right, or as 'progress' *vs.* 'traditionalism' – especially common in newspaper and practical political discussions. This dimension has also been commonly assumed in political analyses – of which Down's assumption of a one-dimensional space of competition based on greater and lesser government intervention in the economy is best known (Downs 1957, pp. 100–30).

Nevertheless, subsequent empirical studies, usually based on surveys of electors' feelings of closeness to other parties, have complicated the picture – often showing other types of cleavage such as the clerical/anti-clerical – to be more important. (For a comprehensive review see Budge and Farlie

1977, Section 2.3.) It now seems that the generalizability and pre-dominance of the Left–Right cleavage has been resoundingly reconfirmed.

So it has, but with important qualifications which should be made before we discuss further implications:

(i) Our conclusions derive from analyses of material issued by the parties – that is, it reflects the way that parties ideally would like to organize competition between themselves. Parties do not have full control however. There is far from a full correspondence between manifesto emphases and election issues (Budge and Farlie, 1983, Table 6.4). Substantial numbers of electors may have preoccupations different from those which parties would ideally like to emphasize, and these may affect their votes.

Thus the space of party competition may well differ between parties and electors. In particular, the dominance of Left–Right concerns could be less among the latter. This in turn implies that our findings cannot be taken as an unqualified basis for the universal application of a uni-dimensional Downsian model of party competition. For that, parties and electors would have to be in the same space. Our study provides no direct evidence on electors' positions.

(ii) Even in terms of the prevalence of Left–Right conflict in party strategists' own conceptions, the findings have qualifications. The first of these relates to the restrictions on the parties considered in many analyses. There is a bias towards taking established, enduring and major parties. As new parties tend to base themselves on nationalism, environmentalism or popularism, their exclusion to some extent pushes the analysis towards an emphasis on long standing cleavages among which Left–Right divisions are inevitably prominent. This limitation should not be exaggerated however since studies like the Danish and Belgian, where there was the most dramatic destruction of the old party system, have included the new parties.

(iii) A more obvious point is that the factors extracted from the analysis are not associated with all variance in the original data – covering anything from 40–80 per cent. In other words they summarize general tendencies to which there are many exceptions. And these of course reflect the peculiari-ties and quirks in party systems which render them individual and unique.

(iv) In examining the general tendencies at work, we have focused in Table 18.1 on only a sub-sample. Most countries produced a four- or five-factor solution, with the amount of variance associated with less important factors in combination comparable to that associated with the first two. Moreover the second more idiosyncratic factor in Table 18.1 is often only marginally less important than the first.

(iv) There are five systems where a Left–Right dimension does not emerge clearly – the two Irelands, Luxembourg, West Germany and

Israel. Sri Lanka is also an ambiguous case, owing to the confused nature of the dimensions emerging from its party programmes.

An analysis of the exceptions and of the reasons for the absence of a Left–Right cleavage is instructive, and brings us back to a discussion of its substantive meaning in our investigation.

The case of Ireland (in both its parts) is perhaps most obvious. The dominance of nationalistic and nation-building concerns leaves little room for Left–Right cleavages – though the second, 'Fine Gael' dimension in the more settled Republic, does contain a hint of Left–Right issues with its stress on capitalist economics.

From this point of view Israel is similar – a recently founded state faced by external threats and the assimilation of extraneous elements, it would be odd if nation-building concerns did not predominate. In Sri Lanka the sharp urban–rural cleavages and communal conflicts typical of a developing society are more prominent than class or questions of economic control.

Luxembourg again is simply too small and too integrated economically with Benelux and the European Community to generate much conflict over internal economic management.

West Germany is the most surprising exception. Its large and powerful Social Democratic Party and the post-war confrontation with its equally large conservative rival has made some kind of Left–Right interpretation of its politics seem natural. But of course the confrontation has been muted by the Social Democrats' own acceptance of the social market economy since the late 1950s, their concentration on welfarism (a sure consensual issue anyway) and the overshadowing threat from the East. Both leading dimensions also reflect some of the concerns of the normal Left–Right confrontation, in the degree of emphasis on the social market economy and in the counterpositioning of national solidarity against international organization and quality of life.

The general conclusion is therefore that some form of Left–Right dimension dominates competition at the level of parties (so far as this can be generalized) where there is no overriding preoccupation with national identity or security. This statement is carefully phrased to accommodate both earlier qualifications on our findings, and the deviant cases.

What exactly *is* this Left–Right dimension? As we have seen from the detailed interpretations made in each country, it is a general label which seems plausible in the light of the particular loadings and connections with original categories which emerge from the individual analyses. However, since the term is so pervasive, there is a danger that it may have been used by different investigators to describe quite different clusters of variables.

But in our case it is clear that the clusters designated by the term are substantially similar, and that the meaning of 'Left–Right' is definite and reasonably constant throughout the analyses. Principally it refers to classic economic policy-conflicts – government regulation of the economy through direct controls or takeover (sometimes associated with Keynesian economic management) – as opposed to free enterprise, individual freedom, incentives, and economic orthodoxy. As noted in Chapter 3 the United States also reflects this contrast in a modified form, where 'regulation of capitalism' is about the most extreme form of interventionism imaginable and nationalization and direct controls are not mentionable.

Associated with the economic issues may be a contrast between liberal internationalism and nationalism/isolationism, as in France (Chapter 15), or between support for the Western alliance, on the one hand, and neutrality and pacifism on the other. There may also be elements of a conflict between traditional and progressive moral attitudes sometimes involving clerical issues. Only in Belgium does the dimension also seem to pick up elements of communal conflict, owing to the more advanced social attitudes of the Francophone population.

This characterization of the meaning of Left–Right – which emerges, it must again be stressed, directly from our data – fits well with conventional notions. These focus particularly on the contrast of economic philosophies, which is also central to our generalized dimension, but often associate with it progressivism *vs.* traditionalism, and power politics *vs.* pacificism abroad. The conventional characterization perhaps involves welfare more than our data-based one does – the absence of really sharp contrasts here is one of the surprises of the analysis. This may be due to the commitment of Christian Democratic parties as well as socialists to the welfare state. Some contrasts do emerge however, so that here too our findings do not diverge radically from conventional notions.

We have therefore a clear general picture of what a right- or left-wing position means for a party in issue-terms, which derives greater validity from its fit with earlier ideas. It is necessary however to stress one point in which it differs from these, as they are summed up particularly in Down's spatial model. That is, that positions on the dimension are defined by greater or lesser stress on issues – not by opposed policies on them. The implications of this are complex (Budge and Farlie, 1977 Chapters 5 and 7; 1978; 1982; 1983, Chapter 2) – but they certainly rule out a direct transfer of Downsian spatial reasoning into this dimension.

In Table 18.1 the second dimension often seems to reflect Left–Right contrasts in a modified form (Britain, New Zealand, the United States, Canada, Sweden, Denmark, Netherlands, Austria and possibly Japan). The most general way in which this comes up is in terms of a relative emphasis on 'New Left' issues, which shades into a contrast between new and traditional issues as in Japan. 'New Left' issues are defined as ones affecting the environment, the countryside, our extended category of Arts,

Sports, Leisure and Media, and the quality of life generally – as well as pacifism abroad. These contrast with 'Old Left' concerns such as Labour groups, Welfare, and economic control, and with 'Rightist' concerns with economic development, orthodoxy, efficiency, etc.

In its more general manifestation of new concerns *vs.* old concerns, this dimension can be identified with the hypothesized change of values between an industrial and a post-industrial society (Inglehart 1977). It is likely however that any study of changing societies over a 40 year period would identify issues which were more emphasized at the end of the period than at the beginning, and *vice versa*.

Certainly our coding categories were designed to be as 'timeless' as possible, in the sense of tapping recurrent concerns of politics rather than the specific issues which change between every election. While recurrent concerns will survive, they may nevertheless be emphasized more at some points in time than others, and it is this quite natural change which the 'New Issues' – and to some extent the New Left – dimensions pick up. Controlling for this effect by using as input to the factor analysis frequencies which are 'time-controlled' or 'de-trended' in some way, would eliminate or attenuate this dimension. The justification for such a procedure would be that we are interested in the underlying structure of party competition, not in transitory trends. On the other hand, temporal differences in emphasis can be regarded as a legitimate focus of the research. Parties do vary their interests and appeals to some extent, and such shifts are a natural object of study. In a first approach to the data it seems best to allow them to emerge, leaving the exploration of the 'timeless' structure to subsequent more sophisticated investigations.

It seems likely in any case that our major findings about the generalized Left–Right dimension would survive such a shift in focus. Of the other leading country dimensions in Table 18.1, most seem too situation-specific to be readily generalizable, as in Ireland. The absence of a general clerical/anti-clerical dimension is noticeable. It seems to be clearly discernable only in Italy and Belgium, though in the shape of 'social conservation' it also has a lingering influence in Austria and the Netherlands. Religious influences are hardly absent either from support or opposition to the status quo in Northern Ireland. Still, a religious dimension is strikingly absent from the majority of countries, considering that it has been identified as one of the most pervasive cleavages, along with class. (Lipset and Rokkan, 1967, pp. 1–39; Rose and Urwin, 1970). The same is true for urban-rural divisions, which appear only in Sri Lanka.

Two comments should be made on the underpresentation of other political divisions. The first is that the generalized Left–Right dimension itself captures elements of clericalism *vs.* anti-clericalism. This is hardly surprising where the main contenders are often a Christian party, repre-

TABLE 18.2

CONVERGENCE OR DIVERGENCE OF PARTIES ON A) LEFT-RIGHT DIMENSION
B) TWO LEADING DIMENSIONS OF SECOND STAGE FACTOR ANALYSIS

COUNTRY	LEFT-RIGHT DIMENSION	TWO LEADING DIMENSIONS
UNITED KINGDOM	D	LITTLE CHANGE
NEW ZEALAND	D	LITTLE CHANGE
AUSTRALIA	C	C
UNITED STATES	D	LITTLE CHANGE
CANADA	C	C
SRI LANKA	D	D
ISRAEL	-	LITTLE CHANGE
IRELAND	-	C
NORTHERN IRELAND	-	IRRELEVANT (TWO PARTIES CEASED TO EXIST)
SWEDEN		
DENMARK		
NETHERLANDS	C (IN 1970s)	C (IN 1970s)
BELGIUM	C	C (IN 1970s)
LUXEMBOURG	-	C (ALL PARTIES BUT COMMUNIST)
AUSTRIA	C	C
WEST GERMANY	-	C
FRANCE	LIMITED C	LIMITED C (WITHIN BUT NOT ACROSS TENDENCIES)
ITALY	C	C
JAPAN	C	C

C = CONVERGENCE   D = DIVERGENCE

senting the Centre-Right, and a traditionally anti-clerical Socialist or Communist party. The other point is the obvious one, that popular divisions – and the actual election issues themselves – are not identical with those which party strategists choose to stress. Urban rural and religious issues are found more frequently at the centre of election campaigns than these findings imply – though, certainly, in nothing like the same numbers as Left–Right issues (Budge and Farlie, 1983, Table 2.3).

18.3 CONVERGENCE OR DIVERGENCE OF PARTIES?

An important question raised in Chapter 2 was the extent to which parties could be said to be coming closer together or moving further apart over the post-war period. In a spatial sense such 'convergence' or 'divergence' has important consequences for the general level of consensus within party systems and for the consequences which these may have for their stability (Budge 1970; Sartori 1966, 1976).

Now we have identified leading dimensions of party competition (at least at the level of party strategists) we are also in a position to compare tendencies to convergence within them. This is particularly so because we can, for three-quarters of the countries, use the Left–Right dimension which they share, where movements give some indication of general tendencies at work among parties. We can also of course assess the nature of movements on the two leading dimensions in combination, for all countries.

Table 18.2 summarizes results from the spatial analysis of movements reported at the end of the individual country chapters. The question asked in each case is whether individual parties show tendencies to come together or move apart. This is obviously an approximate judgement which neglects the finer details of the country discussions, and assimilates larger change in some cases to much slighter change in others. There are also ambiguities in judging convergence in a temporal analysis such as the one the individual figures report. In particular, parties can be coming together in the last decade after having moved notably further apart in the 1960s (as in the Netherlands for example). Thus the overall state of convergence at the end of the 1970s may be no more than it was in the early 1950s.

Another complication is that, in multi-party systems, some parties may be moving together while others stay apart – as in Luxembourg, where the diehard Communists did not move towards the converging 'parties of government' – or in France, where agreement increased between parties of the same ideological *tendance*, but not across tendances.

These points are noted in the table as far as possible, though it is only a rough and approximate overall guide to the trends at work. Despite such qualifications, however, it emerges that there has been a strong movement to convergence in the 1970s in most party systems (with the important exceptions of neo-conservative Britain and the United States). While some parties did move apart in the 1960s, a majority have converged fairly consistently over the whole period.

However, movements are sufficiently mixed and varied over time to suggest that convergence is not a preordained or irreversible process. The situation may well change to one of divergence in the 1980s, under conditions of greater economic social, and international stress. All we can firmly say is that to the end of the 1970s parties were – overall and as a matter of empirical observation – converging.

Convergence owes its popularity in this type of analysis to Downs' prediction that – in a two-party system with the majority of electors clustered at one point – the parties move in terms of policy, to the position of the median elector in order to pick up as many votes as possible (Downs 1957, pp. 95–138). We should stress again that convergence based on a saliency theory and coding, carries a different significance from the direct confrontation between different policy positions on the same issues, postulated by Downs. Behind the spatial movements examined by us lie the parties' tendencies to emphasize the same or different issue areas. Agreement on what issues are important is a form of consensus with important consequences (Budge, 1970, pp. 59–80; 121–9). But it is not the same as agreement on specific policy preferences, though it may prefigure this or be associated with it.

In the most general terms, however, spatial movements on our dimensions are capable of acting as indicators of the overall level of consensus and indicate that it has increased among democratic parties up to this point.

We base this major finding on a collation of evidence from country chapters, rather than on statistical analyses of the comparative data set, because it is obviously most significant to examine party movement within the national context, and in relation to their main electoral rivals. The danger of a general analysis is that important individual movements are obscured through the creation of overall averages. It obviously matters much less, from the point of view of what we really mean by party convergence, whether the Australian Liberals are now closer to the Dutch Labour Party, than that they now are closer to the Australian Labor Party.

There are however other general questions raised in Chapter 2, for which a comparative statistical analysis is indispensable, provided it is not simply a mechanical averaging of disparate cases. The proven generalizability of the coding frame, however, and the similarity between substantive cleavages indicate that we did not ask the question as to whether nationality or ideology distinguishes parties more. That is, do parties 'belong' with their ideological counterparts in other countries, in some clear sense, or are country-specific characteristics so predominant that they defy any attempt at general classification? This is the question we will consider in the following section.

18.4 COMPARATIVE DISCRIMINANT ANALYSIS OF PARTY IDEOLOGICAL 'FAMILIES'

The country studies have shown that our analytic, conceptual, and methodological techniques are useful for analysing ideology within a

limited context. But the acid test lies in its ability to work outside national
or political-cultural contests. There are various ways one might demonstrate this capacity. One is the data-analytic technique known as multiple
discriminant analysis ('discrimination', for short). The aim of this technique is to maximize differences between selected groupings of cases (most
obviously parties). It essentially answers the question given the information we have about tendencies over a whole set of party (group)
documents; how far can we use this for unequivocal typing of individual
party programmes as belonging to that party? Like regression, discriminant analysis averages prediction variables in the best linear combination
to predict, (more properly to 'postdict'), the cases into the original target
variable categories (e.g. the party groups). This has already been applied
in the German case (Chapter 14, Section 10).

For us, the obvious procedure is to take groupings of parties, party
'families' as it were, and try to put a particular manifesto into a particular
party 'family'. If we can do this – if, say, a large number of manifestos
written by Christian Democrat parties across several countries, are accurately typed as Christian Democratic – we have shown that our coding
schemes pick out the essence of mainline party ideologies in a way that
transcends both the cultural and the national content.

We are in fact able to do more. As the linear combinations of predicting
variables, like a factor analytic solution but unlike a regression equation,
can be interpreted as measures of an underlying continuum, we can make
informed guesses as to what it is that makes parties alike. We can sketch
what makes Communists resemble other Communists, and different from
Liberals or other Centrists, and so on.

Even this does not exhaust the utility of the technique. Two further types
of information can be extracted. We can ask about ideological similarity –
which political party, from whatever country or election, said things that
were most like, for example, French Communist policy in 1968? If the
answer is the trivial one that they were most like themselves in the
precedent or subsequent election, fair enough. But this will not always be
so for all parties, and vital insights into the ways parties react to political
circumstances can be gained.

Finally for parties which we would not otherwise feel happy about
classifying, one can ask where they genuinely belong. The major U.S.
parties, for example, are not easily included in any simple typology of
parties that is centred on European, or even British Commonwealth, party
systems. But we can still intelligently ask whether the U.S. Democrats are,
on the whole, most like European Social Democrats or Conservatives. As
discriminant analysis bases its discriminant functions on known predicted
categories, the linear combination of the predicting variables can be used
in this way to fill in blanks. If no statistically reliable answer can be given

TABLE 18.3

CLASSIFICATIONS OF PARTY 'FAMILIES' ON A COMPARATIVE BASIS

EXTENDED CLASSIFICATION	RE-CLASSIFICATION FOR DISCRIMINANT ANALYSIS
COMMUNIST	COMMUNIST
LEFT SOCIALIST, SOCIALIST, RIGHT SOCIALIST	SOCIALIST
RADICAL LIBERAL, ECONOMIC LIBERAL, CENTRE-AGRARIAN	CENTRIST
CHRISTIAN DEMOCRAT, CONSERVATIVE, GAULLIST	CONSERVATIVE

from the sort of data reported in this book, this in itself would be revealing about the separateness of American political life.

There is a delicate balance to be drawn in such an analysis between bringing in an impossibly difficult discrimination problem, and putting too simple a question. Were we to throw all the more than 700 manifestos categorized into a highly refined multi-category typology, it is improbable that anything but the most trivial analytic results would emerge. On the other hand, little of general value would be discovered by merely asking whether, for example, our new data could distinguish between the extremes of the Left and the Right positions in a couple of countries. We have opted for a middle course.

One obvious source of difficulty in categorizing party stands is time, or historic period. It is simply unlikely that what party x had to say in 1945 will predict what it had to say in 1970, still less have a clear family resemblance to an ideological partner y in 1980. Consequently our first move towards simplification is to limit the time period under analysis. There is an easy way of doing this. As our French data set is restricted to the Fifth Republic, and French politics is sufficiently interesting and central to require inclusion, we have chosen a starting point to fit it. Rather than include the untypical birth pangs of the Fifth Republic, we have also chosen to include data only after De Gaulle's 'confirming' election of 1962.

The second problem is how detailed a classification of party families to use. We have opted for a broad typology with four categories. However we have built this up rather carefully, and with some precision, deliberately leaving a large number of parties unclassified. In fact the classification was a two-stage process. One investigator first fitted as many parties as he felt intellectually justifiable into a ten category typology. A second then collapsed this into a much simpler version. The version we use has only four categories. (1) Communist parties; (2) Socialist parties; (3) Centrist-

TABLE 18.4

PERCENTAGE OF CASES (INCLUDING ORIGINALLY UNCLASSIFIED CASES)
CORRECTLY CATEGORISED BY THE DISCRIMINANT FUNCTION

ACTUAL GROUP	NO. OF CASES		PREDICTED	GROUP		
		COMMUNIST	SOCIALIST	CENTRE	CONSER-VATIVE	
COMMUNIST	31	74%	26%	0%	0%	100%
SOCIALIST	129	5%	81%	6%	8%	100%
CENTRE	62	0%	15%	69%	16%	100%
CONSERVATIVE	101	0%	9%	9%	82%	100%

Liberal parties; (4) Conservative parties. The original classification is collapsed according to the scheme in Table 18.3.

All originally unclassified parties remained unclassified. Both typologies are in fact quite rigorous. For example, the Italian Communist Party, because of its history of moderation and 'Euro-Communism', is not set down either as Communist, or as anything else.

Taking only manifestos issued after 1962, we have 460 cases, of which 137 were unclassified as to party type. Of remaining 323 on which the main stages of the analysis are based, 10 per cent were classified as Communist, 40 per cent as Socialist, 19 per cent as Centrist and 31 per cent as Conservative. The analysis was carried out over the entire 19 countries, though some, the U.S. for example, had no 'classified' parties and only enter at the second stage where, on the basis of discriminant functions derived over already known classifications, they can be provisionally typed as belonging to one of the groups.

One can pass immediately to the best, if crudest, test of the application of this technique. How well can our data classify into this simple scheme? The results are given in Table 18.4.

As is immediately obvious, the data yield extremely good discriminant functions. On the strictest test, 78.3 per cent of the 323 known cases were classified correctly. A broader test would be to count a 'near miss' as reasonably correct – this would mean allowing Communist=Socialist, Socialist=either Communist or Centre, Centre=either Socialist or Conservative, and Conservative=Centre as 'correct' predictions. Given this, 304 cases (94 per cent) would be well predicted, leaving as serious errors only 19 cases. These, to be discussed shortly, are the 10 Socialist parties which would have been classified as Conservative, and 9 Conservative manifestos seen as Socialist.

Before discussing in detail the 'mistakes' and what happened to the 'unclassified' cases, we need to see how this classification was achieved, what linear combination of original variables was thrown up, and what interpretations we can give them. What, in simpler language, is the

TABLE 18.5

PARTY FAMILY AVERAGES ON THREE DISCRIMINANT FUNCTIONS

GROUP	FUNCTION 1	FUNCTION 2	FUNCTION 3
COMMUNIST	3.78	-1.22	-.54
SOCIALIST	0.14	-.87	.38
CENTRE	-1.1	.13	-1.31
CONSERVATIVE	-.68	1.41	.49

combination of electoral appeals that so satisfactorily differentiates between party families?

Discriminant analysis averages the input variables (in our case, the percentage mentions of a set of policy topics) into one or more linear combinations which best separate the groups; each such combination, a discriminant function, being uncorrelated with the others. While theoretically there are $N-1$ such combinations, (where $N=$the number of classification groups), they are extracted in decreasing importance as separators, and not all will necessarily be either important or statistically significant. In the present case three significant functions, the maximum for four groups, are derived, and all are statistically significant. They are chosen so that each makes the maximum contribution to differentiating between a particular pair of categories, regardless of the others. Thus if there is some combination of original variables that distinguishes between, say, Communism and Liberalism, with no particular relevance to the difference between Socialists and Conservatives, this will be derived. One thus has a truly multi-dimensional portrayal, with no preconceptions, that what distinguishes between the far left and far right should also distinguish the centre-left and centre-right. The results are empirical, not theoretically constrained, and are all the more useful as a result.

The nature of the discrimination we have is given by the summary in Table 18.5, which reports the group average positions on each of the three discriminant functions.

On the whole they are obvious contrasts – the first separates the left and right, though the greatest distance is, in fact between Communists and Liberals. The second produces a more stereotyped difference between Communists and Conservatives, with the Socialists close to the Communists but the Centre more or less neutral. On the third function, needed only for more refined classifications, the apparent absurdity of Communists and Centrists being close together but both far from a combination of Socialists and Conservatives shows how details of policy preference can confound traditional assumptions of ideological compatibility.

TABLE 18.6

LOADINGS OF ORIGINAL CATEGORIES ON ROTATED DISCRIMINANT FUNCTIONS

CATEGORY		FUNCTION 1 LEFT-WING ISOLATIONISM	FUNCTION 2 CAPITALIST TRADITIONALISM	FUNCTION 3 OLD VERSUS NEW CONCERNS
102	FOREIGN SPECIAL RELATIONS (NEGATIVE)	.671	-.062	-.084
413	NATIONALIZATION	.424	-.024	-.064
701	LABOUR GROUPS (POSITIVE)	.312	-.115	.218
403	REGULATION OF CAPITALISM	.279	.010	-.065
301	DECENTRALIZATION (POSITIVE)	-.259	-.200	-.235
110	E.E.C. (NEGATIVE)	.238	.142	.079
103	DECOLONIZATION	.210	.145	.120
305	GOVERNMENT EFFECTIVENESS AND AUTHORITY	-.199	-.004	.119
606	NATIONAL EFFORT, SOCIAL HARMONY	-.197	-.100	-.133
201	DOMESTIC FREEDOM AND HUMAN RIGHTS	-.195	.094	-.066
402	INCENTIVES	-.071	.477	.059
108	EEC (POSITIVE)	-.019	.395	-.031
401	FREE ENTERPRISE	.000	.362	-.026
603	TRADITIONAL MORALITY (POSITIVE)	.030	.310	.179
414	ECONOMIC ORTHODOXY	.050	.309	.020
303	GOVERNMENT EFFICIENCY	.051	.285	-.114
304	GOVERNMENT CORRUPTION	-.061	.267	-.050
604	TRADITIONAL MORALITY (NEGATIVE)	-.149	-.246	-.043
602	NATIONAL WAY OF LIFE (NEGATIVE)	.083	-.182	.081
607	COMMUNALISM/PLURALISM (POSITIVE)	.070	.170	.055
411	TECHNOLOGY	-.110	-.040	.534
501	ENVIRONMENTAL PROTECTION	-.005	-.001	-.472
502	ART, SPORT, LEISURE, MEDIA	.045	.233	.420
107	INTERNATIONALISM (POSITIVE)	-.263	-.047	-.317
106	PEACE	.107	-.034	.301
101	FOREIGN SPECIAL RELATIONS (POSITIVE)	-.071	.115	.262
504	SOCIAL SERVICES (POSITIVE)	.039	-.064	.241
704	"OTHER" ECONOMIC GROUPS	-.037	-.110	-.226
105	MILITARY (NEGATIVE)	.047	-.047	-.205
406	PROTECTIONISM (POSITIVE)	.002	-.126	.193

We still need to know the substantive meaning of these discriminating functions, the particular concatenation of our content analysis categories that catch the similarities and differences between the party families. As with factor analysis, the functions can be statistically rotated to facilitate interpretation. Table 18.6 gives the ten most highly loaded categories for each of the three rotated functions.

The first function, which distinguishes between Communist and Bourgeois parties, (especially 'Centrist' or 'Liberal' parties) is very simple, if somewhat more pragmatic than ideological in nature. The highest loaded variable, at .671, is the category for opposition to 'Foreign Special Relations'. As these are almost entirely references to relations with other Western capitalist countries, especially the United States and Britain, or to

Western economic and military alliances, above all to NATO, it is a very obvious discriminating variable. (The sixth most important variable backs this up being concerned with anti-EEC attitudes.) This version of Communist *vs.* Bourgeois foreign policy is further demonstrated by the heavy stress, more marked as our data are chosen from the latter part of the period, on Decolonization. For the rest, the obvious emphasis of Socialist economic policies with the appearance of Nationalization, and Regulation of Capitalism, and the strong negative loading for Decentralization, help to show why it is 'Liberal' parties that show the most marked opposition to Communism.

The second function is principally a 'united Left' *vs.* Conservative discrimination. Principally it collects together Conservative economic policies – Incentives, support for the EEC, Free Enterprise, Economic Orthodoxy, and the quasi-economic policy of Government Efficiency, often a synonym for cutting government expenditure. The presence of the Traditional Morality categories is inevitable given that we have included Christian Democrat parties, but this is an element in secular Conservatism as well.

The final discriminating function has the role of distinguishing between two unlikely pairings – Communism and Liberal/Centrist parties on the one hand, Socialists and Conservatives on the other. It is hardly surprising that it is not easily interpretable. The meaning basically comes from a contrast between 'new' and 'old' issues, which has appeared in many of the country chapters. Environmental Protection, Internationalism, Anti-militarism and a concern for non-traditional economic groups, describes the Communist/Centre pole. Stress on new technology, on positive orientations to 'Foreign Special Relations', to traditional forms of welfare are characteristic of the less idealistic Socialist, and welfare state Conservative, parties. To simplify matters for future reference we need labels – the first function can be described as 'Left wing isolationism', the second as 'Capitalist Traditionalism', and the third, the only really bipolar function, as 'Old *vs.* New Concerns'.

We shall be concerned mainly with the first two – they have in any case much the higher predictive value. (It is worth noting that all three are, statistically, highly significant. The third, weakest, function has a Chi Square of 102, with 52 degrees of freedom, yielding a zero probability of being an accidental data artifact.)

The next stage is to give some impression of how these functions, which yield an ideological map just as does factor analysis, portray spatial relationships between typical parties. Clearly it is impossible to represent many parties, and there is little point putting the predictive failures on a map that is meant to demonstrate the meaning of the technique when it works well. We have chosen, purely for heuristic purposes, 19 parties from

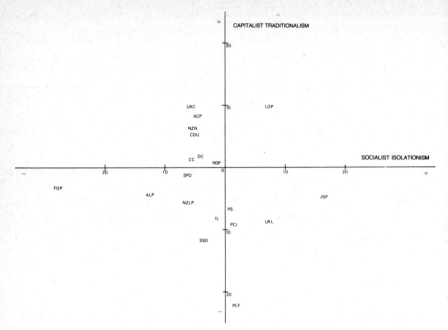

18.1 Comparative analysis: positions of 'typical' parties in the space of the first two discriminant functions

various countries, selected because readers will already have an intuitive idea of where they belong. Not all come from the same period in electoral history. However, when more than one party is chosen from a single country, they are all taken at the time of the same general election.

These party positions are plotted in Figure 18.1; the key to which parties they represent is given in Table 18.7. The diagram supports the immediate 'face validity' of the classification, but also demonstrates the dangers of too easily assuming that party families have no national idiosyncracies. Thus, taking the first (horizontal) dimension of 'socialist isolationism', the extreme contrst between the German FDP in 1972 and the Japanese Socialist Party in 1966 may seem curious. But of course all parties in Japan are highly isolationist at times (note the position of the Liberal Democratic Party). In addition, it is not just the Western integration of the FDP, but their robust defence of the free market that puts them where they are. The representation is, in fact, telling us that this is one of the few years the FDP is correctly predicted to be a Centrist/Liberal party. Left unclassified in our data, it usually takes on the colour of its coalition partner. The second, 'Capitalist Traditionalism' dimension causes fewer surprises, with a fine clutch of pure Conservative parties from Japan, Britain, Australia, New

TABLE 18.7

KEY TO PARTY POSITIONS IN FIGURE 18.1

DIAGRAM LABEL	COUNTRY	PARTY	YEAR
CDU	GERMANY	CHRISTIAN DEMOCRATIC UNION - CHRISTIAN SOCIAL UNION	1972
FDP	GERMANY	FREE DEMOCRATIC PARTY	1972
SPD	GERMANY	SOCIAL DEMOCRATIC PARTY	1972
PCF	FRANCE	FRENCH COMMUNIST PARTY	1967
PS	FRANCE	SOCIALIST PARTY	1967
PCI	ITALY	ITALIAN COMMUNIST PARTY	1963
DC	ITALY	CHRISTIAN DEMOCRATIC PARTY	1963
ACP	AUSTRALIA	LIBERAL PARTY	1975
ALP	AUSTRALIA	AUSTRALIAN LABOUR PARTY	1975
NDP	CANADA	NEW DEMOCRATIC PARTY	1980
CC	CANADA	CONSERVATIVE PARTY	1980
LDP	JAPAN	LIBERAL DEMOCRATIC PARTY	1966
JSP	JAPAN	JAPAN SOCIALIST PARTY	1966
IL	ISRAEL	LABOUR PARTY	1981
NZN	NEW ZEALAND	NEW ZEALAND NATIONALISTS	1963
NZLP	NEW ZEALAND	NEW ZEALAND LABOUR PARTY	1963
SSD	SWEDEN	SOCIAL DEMOCRATS	1964
UKC	BRITAIN	CONSERVATIVE	1966
UKL	BRITAIN	LABOUR	1966

Zealand and Germany at one end, opposed by the Western world's most intransigent orthodox Communist party, the French.

Obviously future and more detailed analyses will need to take account of different time periods and more countries. By itself Figure 18.1 shows how clearly there do exist, across time periods and national boundaries, real partisan families. It is particularly notable that the party family most obviously displayed is one of international conservatism, least often accepted as having an international identity.

In some ways one learns about as much about the structure of party ideologies, from looking at the mistaken classifications made by the technique, rather than to the successes. Eight Communist party manifestos, for example, were thought to be Socialist – as were nine Conservative (Christian Democrat parties). Why? Which parties were involved? Are the mistakes 'natural', confirming our intuitive uncertainties of classification? Or absurdities, manifest errors in technique or data collection?

Of the eight wrongly predicted Communist manifestos, one was the

Japanese, in 1963. The legitimacy of this party has been so doubtful, especially given its inheritance from American occupation, and the country's non-Communist Left has at times been so radical that such a 'mistake' is simply an example of statistics mirroring nature! The 'mistakes' in seeing Conservative and Christian Democrats as Socialists are much the same. The German CDU–CSU in 1965, the year before the famous Grand Coalition is indeed likely to have been curiously 'left' in its manifesto; the Italian Christian Democrats in 1979 were terrified of the left swallowing them, and in both 1964 and February 1974 the British Conservatives played (and lost) a 'moderation' card in elections. The remaining cases, two Australian manifestos for the Liberal Party in the mid–1960s and several Canadian Conservative programmes in the early 1970s, are very probably real failures in discrimination. Both systems in any case are well known for the vagueness and opportunism of their major parties.

One can also ask about the classifications made, on the basis of our evidence, for parties initially unclassified. It is one thing to admit that there are no obvious cues as to how one should group a party. It is quite another to deny that there may be systematic evidence, emerging from this sort of analysis, that would aid a useful classification.

One party where the obvious classification may not be accurate is the famously moderate and Gramscian Italian Communist Party. Put into the data set as unclassified, it was predicted as: Communist in 1963, Socialist in 1968 and 1972, Liberal/Centrist in 1976, and actually as Conservative in 1979. Of course this last entry is wrong (though Figures 16.1–16.4 certainly render such a mistake understandable) – but no-one could deny that the general trends in its ideological movement are entirely accurate.

This type of predictive mistake, arising from ideological change or inconsistency, is one thing. The other way our analysis goes wrong is less illuminating – it is a matter of coding categories failing to fit the political culture of a party system. Thus for the U.S., of the ten party positions for the two unclassified parties since the Presidential election of 1964, the record is bad. Twice, in 1968 and 1972, the Republicans (under Nixon it should be remembered) were classified as Socialist, the rest of the time being seen as Conservative. The Democrats were twice seen as Conservative – in 1968 and, alarmingly, under Carter in 1976. Although it has been shown in Chapter 3 that our coding scheme works well on the U.S. when treated in isolation, it fails to put these two parties in any intelligible location in a broader ideological context. This of course, may simply be another way of saying that American politics occupies a different universe from most Western party conflict.

On the whole therefore the three discriminating functions produce a comprehensible and valid characterization of world wide party competition. With these we have the ability to locate real cross-national party similarities that transcend, but are still congruent with, intuitive political wisdom.

18.5 A COMPARATIVE FACTOR ANALYSIS, USING THE INTEGRATED DATA SET

We return to our normal technique, factor analysis, to answer another, final, question about the comparative meaning of our findings. In the search for underlying dimensions of party ideology we have so far been looking for representations from within fields of political conflict, for spectra along which disagreeing parties can be arrayed. It is an open question, however, whether or not similar dimensions can be found inside ideological groupings, thus focusing disagreements which occur among parties of the same general persuasion. Along what main dimension do Socialist parties differentiate themselves for example? Is there an underlying structure to the arguments or policy stresses of Liberal/Centrist parties, such as would appear were several such parties, from different countries, to compete in some imaginary election? These questions, which basically relate to the creation of scales of Socialism, Conservatism and Centrism/ Liberalism, do however raise rather complex problems about the logic in terms of which we interpret our factor analyses.

A factor solution only arises because there are patterns of correlations between variables. But why do correlations occur between our variables, which represent relative emphases on particular policy categories in printed documents? The answer must be that political constraints, whether logical, psychological, empirical-budgetary, or ideological, force an emphasis on x to go with an emphasis on y, ignoring a and b. These constraints yield correlations inside particular contexts. Given the actualities of French politics one may be able to see why stressing the validity of the Fifth Republican Constitution requires one also to be in favour of French military independence and to endorse traditional morality, worry rather less about civil rights and totally ignore the charms of nationalization. But these are contextual. We have shown above, that the contextuality of correlations arising within inter-party competition is sufficiently low to allow valid international comparison and assimilation. These are however still embedded in the *ad hoc* situation of party competition. Suppose one strips this away and asks, instead, whether some of the constraints on relative emphases arise from the nature of the parties themselves? If this were so, a factor analysis of the clutch of Conservative parties should produce an intelligible factor, or scale, of Conservatism *per se*, rather than one arising from competition between Conservatives and others.

TABLE 18.8

FIRST (UNROTATED) FACTOR FOR "CONSERVATIVE ONLY" CROSS NATIONAL ANALYSIS

ORIGINAL CATEGORIES	FACTOR LOADINGS
104 MILITARY (POSITIVE)	-.375
107 INTERNATIONALISM (POSITIVE)	.363
301 DECENTRALISATION (POSITIVE)	.352
305 GOVERNMENT EFFECTIVENESS AND AUTHORITY	-.378
404 ECONOMIC PLANNING	.501
411 TECHNOLOGY AND INFRASTRUCTURE	.364
414 ECONOMIC ORTHODOXY	-.709
501 ENVIRONMENTAL PROTECTION	.433
502 ART, SPORT, LEISURE, MEDIA	.487
504 SOCIAL SERVICES (FOR EXPANSION)	.381
505 SOCIAL SERVICES (AGAINST EXPANSION)	-.314
506 EDUCATION (POSITIVE)	.358
606 NATIONAL EFFORT, - SOCIAL HARMONY	-.342
608 COMMUNALISM/PLURALISM (POSITIVE)	.422
UNDERPRIVILEGED MINORITIES	.459
NON-ECONOMIC GROUPS	.416

Briefly we now report on three such attempts to investigate the intra-party structure of electoral ideology. We take three of our previous four groups (there are not enough Communist parties for worthwhile investigation) and do one simple factor analysis in each case, across the whole set of coding categories. Naturally the results are messy – 54 variables do not yield neat factor solutions. But still they can yield, on each run, some sort of general first factor representing the best single linear combination of variables to account for as much as possible of the variance. If these first factors are essentially intelligible for each party family, we have reason to say we can locate, in a cross-national manner, the main stress of what Socialism, Liberal/Centrism, or Conservatism has been saying in the Western, democratic world.

We start with Conservatism – taken here, as before, to include European Christian Democracy, but still excluding a series of parties (in Ulster, the United States and elsewhere) which may really be Conservative, as well as awkward cases like the French Gaullists. The analysis yields, inevitably, a huge number of significant factors, 34 in all, collectively explaining 90 per cent of the variance. The first factor, with an Eigenvalue of 4.4, explains only 8.1 per cent itself, but is nonetheless the best summary measure that

TABLE 18.9

FIRST (UNROTATED) FACTOR FOR 'LIBERAL/CENTIRST ONLY' CROSS-NATIONAL ANALYSIS

ORIGINAL CATEGORIES		FACTOR LOADINGS
201	FREEDOM AND DOMESTIC HUMAN RIGHTS	.303
202	DEMOCRACY	.389
301	DECENTRALISATION (POSITIVE)	.408
305	GOVERNMENT EFFECTIVENESS AND AUTHORITY	−.356
403	REGULATION OF CAPITALISM	.329
410	PRODUCTIVITY	−.387
412	CONTROLLED ECONOMY	−.362
501	ENVIRONMENTAL PROTECTION	.441
502	ART, SPORT, LEISURE, MEDIA	.546
603	TRADITIONAL MORALITY (POSTIVE)	.375
605	LAW AND ORDER	.371
606	NATIONAL EFFORT – SOCIAL HARMONY	−.401
705	UNDERPRIVILEGED MINORITIES	.427
706	NON-ECONOMIC GROUPS	.561

can be derived. All parties from Ulster, Ireland, Israel and Sri Lanka are omitted, as are all the cases before 1962, and all that are not coded as Conservative or Christian Democrat in our original typology, leaving 176 cases altogether. Table 18.8 gives all loadings for the first factor above .300.

This turns out to be a very clear bipolar dimension of what might best be seen as 'new issues *vs.* old issues in Conservatism'. Low scores indicate a stress on military defence, on the need for effective and authoritative government, a high attachment to economic orthodoxy, an opposition to expansion of the welfare state, and a stress on social discipline. Opposed, at the other end of the dimension is a form of more gentle, socially aware Conservatism, which nonetheless does not commit itself to radical change or egalitarianism. Thus it stresses internationalism rather than military expenditure, decentralization rather than authority, extension rather than restriction of welfare, economic planning (which need not be directive) rather than economic orthodoxy, communalism, 'green' issues, and worries about minorities (though not about labour groups). As an example of a dimension of contrast *within* Conservatism, rather than between Conservatives and others, it could hardly be a better portrait of shifts in emphasis experienced internationally since the early 1960s. Other factors pick out different and further strands in conservatism. However, to demonstrate the way in which a set of correlations, derived by comparing emphases of parties from the same ideological group, produce a picture of the internal ideology, one factor is more than adequate.

The obvious next question is whether this dimension of Conservatism differs from one thrown up by other party families. Table 18.9 gives equivalent first factor loadings from the Liberal family over the same set of countries and within the same period. In this case the definition of Liberal is narrower than the Centre/Liberal group in the discriminant analysis – embracing both 'Radical' and 'Economic' Liberal parties, it covers only those associated with the Liberal International. Again 30 factors explain 91 per cent of the variance, with a first factor explaining 8 per cent and having an Eigenvalue of 4.3

Actually this first factor does not look massively different from the Conservatism scale. How indeed could it be, given that both derive from traditional 'bourgeois' party groupings? There are crucial differences – Liberals do, while Conservatives do not, incorporate traditional concerns for democracy and for civil liberties into their ideal. Distrust of strong governments (government effectiveness) and controlled economies, along with a concern for social discipline and effort, and for economic necessities like productivity, characterize what we shall call the 'hard' end of the Liberal spectrum. At the other end democracy/civil liberties (including decentralization) goes with a *laisser-faire* economic theory – the classic 'holding the ring' notion of Regulation of Capitalism. All the 'green' issues – environmentalism, art, sport, etc. (but not, let it be noted, traditional welfarism or educational-concern) – go at this end. The same emphases on groups (non-economic and underprivileged minorities) occur. The only surprises, perhaps, are the essentially 'un-soft' categories of 'Law and Order' and 'Traditional Morality', but these two fit the classic Liberal idea of maintaining the structure of society while interfering as little as possible. The dimension again represents what any theorist would see as degrees of orthodox Liberalism, on which parties could be arranged independently of contrasts with rivals of a contrasting ideological character. The similarities to our Conservatism dimension are inevitable, but the differences, especially in terms of economic theory and attitudes to the state, are equally striking.

In the same way we can hope to identify some of the central characteristics of Socialism, although in this case things are a little less clear. The basics of the analysis are very similar – 31 factors in all, explaining 88 per cent of the variance, and a first factor with an Eigenvalue of 3.999 explaining by itself 7.21 per cent of the variance.

Eleven variables, reported in Table 18.10, characterize this first dimension. It is clearly bipolar. The low or negative end would be filled by parties stressing alternatives to 'Foreign Special Relations', and the EEC, opposing military expenditure, favouring Nationalization, and heavily

TABLE 18.10

FIRST (UNROTATED) FACTOR FOR 'SOCIALIST ONLY' CROSS-NATIONAL ANALYSIS

ORIGINAL CATEGORIES	FACTOR LOADINGS
102 FOREIGN SPECIAL RELATIONS (NEGATIVE)	-.538
105 MILITARY EXPENDITURE (NEGATIVE)	-.716
110 EEC (NEGATIVE)	-.372
302 DECENTRALISATION (NEGATIVE)	.358
413 NATIONALISATION	-.291
502 ART, SPORT, LEISURE, MEDIA	.306
503 SOCIAL JUSTICE	-.595
607 COMMUNALISM / PLURALISM (POSITIVE)	.316
703 AGRICULTURE AND FARMERS	.558
706 NON-ECONOMIC GROUPS	.472

emphasizing the need for social justice. One can describe this as 'Old Socialism', the essence of familiar alternatives stressed by Labour and Socialist parties throughout the world.

In contrast, de-emphasis on these issues, and an emphasis on the positively loaded categories, would put a party at the high end of the spectrum. Here the stress is on the need to keep the state unitary, on 'new' issues like art, sport, leisure and media, concern with communalism, and for somewhat unlikely groups such as farmers and agricultural workers, and non-economic groups (typically women and sexual minorities, as well as traditional categories like 'the old').

This is a rag-bag collection, which does not cohere satisfactorily in contrast to the 'old Socialist' end. The lack of coherence may itself reflect reality however – the great difficulty Socialist parties have experienced in articulating anything positive to replace their previous concerns. Of course there are Socialist issues – the traditional welfare ones for example, and economic policy. But these will not show in such an analysis precisely because there is no disagreement amongst them in the Socialist camp, anymore than the values of private enterprise or incentives showed on the Conservative dimension or, one suspects, internationalism and peace appeared for Liberals.

Even given these reservations, there can be no doubt that we have uncovered certain fundamental bases of ideology inside the partisan groupings that transcend particular political cultures. As the comparative discriminant analysis demonstrated that we could also distinguish such groupings across national boundaries, the cross national utility and validity of our techniques seems assured. At the same time we have begun, with both analyses, to demonstrate the reliability of party 'families' as categories in comparative politics.

18.6 CONCLUSION AND FURTHER INVESTIGATIONS

In spite of the massive effort that has gone into producing both the comparative and country analyses of this book, they have to be regarded as in a sense preliminary given the great richness and potential of the data which this chapter particularly reveals. Even within the lines of comparative investigation pursued here, analysis can go further: more finely differentiated aspects of ideology can be distinguished, for example; and the less extended party families characterized. Other areas remain untouched: there is obvious scope for an explicit spatial representation of all or most parties on a cross-national basis, or for what generally happens if time is 'taken out' of our analyses. A more detailed, non-spatial investigation of the substantive connotation of the various ideologies and shifts within these also seems an urgent, and feasible, priority – at a country as well as at a general level.

It was of course obvious from the first glimpse of the collected documents that we were creating a basis for general scholarly activity which could never be entirely exploited by our own efforts. With time it has become even more clear that the richness and centrality of the data, and the many implications it has for different fields of research, render our own investigations selective rather than exhaustive. With a view to opening the way to other scholars we have made arrangements not only to deposit the whole cross-national set on open access at the various European Archives, but also to publish data and texts in micro-fiche. For those who are interested the sources of the various texts are also listed here in Appendix A (while Appendix B of course reports and justifies our coding frame).

While we are aware of the strict limits we have had to impose on ourselves to produce the report at all, we would nevertheless argue that it represents an essential preliminary to the further investigations that can be carried out. Details of the collection and political setting are obviously essential, but going beyond these to an exploration of internal structure and relationships is a first step that anyone approaching the data needs to take. The analyses reported here should therefore enable other investigators to go that much further and faster with their own concerns.

Even preliminary analyses are able to confront questions that have been discussed with much less of a solid evidential basis up to this point. Such are the problems of the major cleavages separating parties: the question of their convergence or divergence and of the 'inevitability' of one or the other; the nature and changes of party ideology. We hope to have provided answers which are reasonably conclusive for this level of analysis.

It is still true, however, that analyses of programmes in themselves cannot give *generally* conclusive answers even on these points, without reference to other materials (surveys, other election and governmental documents, direct observations) still less can they judge the external impact of programmes on government and electoral behaviour. The limited analysis undertaken in Chapter 1 for Britain and Canada illustrates this very well. For more extended analyses of 'impact' we need to collect or analyse supplementary data of the type indicated there.

The question of impact is important because it is central to the transmission of electoral opinion, through the parties, into government action – and hence to the normative theory of representative democracy. With the party programmes we have vital evidence on one aspect of this process – what the parties are committing themselves to, publicly, in a context unique to democracies (i.e. the competitive election). To explore the full meaning of such commitments we need to extend the investigation to the electoral and governmental level. This is the next priority for our Research Group, whose current lines of research form a bridge between the 'internal' analyses reported here and the other areas of political activity on which programmes have a potential bearing.

One of these – the impact of pledges and emphases on government action – has received preliminary investigation in Chapter 1 but is being extended, both in regard to the data collected and the comparative extent of the analysis.

In order to flesh out the empirical theory of representative democracy we need to investigate two other areas. First, the relationship between lines of division uncovered at programmatic level and lines of cleavage running through the respective electorates, needs to be explored. Perhaps an even more important, though related, question is how far movements at both levels correspond – how far is a convergence of programmes reflected in, or produced by shifts in the positions of the corresponding electorates? These are topics which have been investigated in some detail for Britain and the United States (Budge and Farlie, 1977, Chapter 11) but which now need to be followed up on a wider comparative basis.

Programmatic differences and similarities between parties in the shape of 'policy distances' within some kind of spatial framework, are also at the heart of another body of literature, concerned with government formation and coalition-building. The hypothesis that politicians' sole concern is securing office – with the concomitant hypothesis that only 'minimal winning coalitions' would form to secure and maximize the spoils (Riker 1962) – has tended to reverse itself over the last 20 years. The leading prediction now is, that ideologically continuous coalitions will form, however the full implications of this modification and its relationship to the office-seeking hypothesis have not been thought through systematically or exact trade-off functions determined. Nonetheless, the finding which shines through is that policy similarities are likely to have an important and in some cases determining influence on coalition formation.

Apart from theoretical confusion, the main obstacle hindering research on this point is the lack of any adequate measure of policy distance between parties. What has generally had to be assumed in previous research is some kind of Left–Right ordering based on intuition or even on joint participation in the coalitions which the ordering is supposed to predict! As our analysis has focused on this very question of the policy distances separating parties, and the cleavages constitute the spaces within which they are measured, its estimates are admirably adapted to test the proposition that the most ideologically contiguous coalitions form. Even more interestingly and perhaps in the long run more theoretically fruitful, the spaces reported here can be used to show how the process of coalition negotiation modified original party positions, which party cedes more in policy terms, and why. The major technical requirement is that government coalition pro-grammes be located in some way within the most appropriate party space, and distances measured on that basis.

All these lines of future research thus relate the internal characteristics of manifestos and their equivalents, to external phenomena which they can play an important role in explaining – to government action itself, to electoral reactions and shifts of opinion, and government and policy formation. All these will be dealt with in subsequent reports of our ECPR Group (Rallings et al. 1988); (Budge and Klingemann 1988); (Laver, Budge and Hearl (eds.) 1988).

Meanwhile, what we have here is an 'internal' analysis of the content of election programmes, with the nature of party divisions on policy, and of their shifts of ideological position. For the first time this analysis has been comprehensive, comparative, and exact. It has refined previous ideas – for example, by showing that a broad Left–Right division between democratic parties is surprisingly prevalent. But it is rarely the *only* division; moreover, it does not occur everywhere. The analysis has also established the validity of a 'saliency' theory of competition as opposed to an exclusively confront-ationist one, and demonstrated a general convergence of parties over the post-war period. There is evidence against taking this empirical tendency as irreversible or inevitable however. There has been no 'end of ideology' – it will probably always be with us, though tempered (as always) by practical considerations.

APPENDIX 'A'

SOURCES FOR THE
ELECTION PROGRAMMES
USED IN THE ANALYSIS

———————— ∿ ————————

The text here lists all source documents used in the analysis. Mostly the text is taken as the election programme for that year. Sometimes however the full manifesto or equivalent is reconstructed by combining two or more texts (usually newspaper reports) for that year. The procedure followed in each case is described in the appropriate country chapter. Countries are listed in the Appendix in alphabetical order.

AUSTRALIA

Australian Labor Party

1946	'Prime Minister announces Labour Policy'	SMH 3.9.46
1949	'Chifley gives Labour Policy'	SMH 15.11.49
1951	'Exchange Rate to be Maintained'	SMH 29.3.51
1954	'Evatt outlines Labour Policy'	SMH 7.5.54
1955	'Labour would increase Pensions ...'	SMH 10.11.55
1958	'Evatt Promises Wide Benefits ...'	SMH 16.10.58
1961	'Labour Plan on Housing'	SMH 17.11.61
1963	'Calwell Lists Main Poll Issues'	SMH 7.11.63
1966	'Conscription is the major issue at Poll'	AGE 11.11.66
1969	'Time for a Change, says Whitlam'	SMH 2.10.69
1972	'Whitlam: Labor's Policy for Australia.'	SMH 14.11.72
1974	'Labor Policy'	SMH 30.4.74
1975	'Whitlam pleads for another chance for Labor'	SMH 25.11.75
1977	'Labor Party Policy Speech 1977'	SMH 18.11.77
1980	'Hayden promises a more equal society'	SMH 2.10.80

Liberal Party

1946	'Menzies outlines Liberal Party's Policy'	SMH 21.8.46
1949	'Menzies gives Policy'	SMH 11.11.49

417

1951	'Menzies' Policy Speech'	SMH 4.4.51
1954	Joint Policy Speech; Federal Election 1954	Original
1955	Federal Election 1955; Joint Policy Speech	Original
1958	Federal Election 1958; Joint Policy Speech	Original
1961	''Good Government' Pledge by Menzies'	SMH 16.11.61
1963	'Menzies opens poll campaign'	SMH 13.11.63
1966	'Our greatest decade ahead'	AGE 9.11.66
1969	'Prime Minister's Policy Speech ...'	SMH 9.10.69
1972	'McMahon: Changing values ...'	SMH 15.11.72
1974	'Liberal Policy'	SMH 1.5.74
1975	'PM delivers Liberal Party policy speech'	SMH 28.11.75
1977	'Liberal Party Policy Speech 1977'	SMH 22.11.77
1980	'Plea by Fraser to nations:...'	SMH 1.10.80

National Country Party

1946	'Fadden for bigger tax cut'	SMH 4.9.46
1949	'Mr. Fadden gives details'	SMH 18.11.49
1951	'Woolgrowers told, "We saved you"'	SMH 5.4.51
1954	'Fadden hits at Labour'	SMH 11.5.54
1958	'McEwen tells of Government's achievements'	SMH 1.11.58
1961	'Pledge by McEwen to protect industries'	SMH 21.11.61
1963	'C.P. Policy announced by McEwen'	SMH 15.11.63
1966	'We will grow, prosper'	AGE 10.11.66
1969	'Farmers will get continued aid'	AGE 10.10.69
1972	'National body urged for development'	SMH 21.11.72
1974	'Poll is fight for democracy'	AGE 8.5.74
1975	'Rural discrimination to end'	SMH 27.11.75
1977	Protect your Future	Original
1980	Keeping Australia strong	Original

Democratic Labour Party*

1955*	'Bitter attack on Evatt by Joshua'	SMH 11.11.55
1958	Senator Cole's Policy Speech	Original
1961	'"New Concepts" needed for nations's problems'	SMH 9.11.61
1963	D.L.P. Policy Speech	Original
1966	For a safe and prosperous Australia	Original
1969	'Double defence spending – DLP'	AGE 14.10.69
1972	'DLP demands action on permissiveness'	SMH 13.11.72
1974	'Prescription for suicide'	SMH 29.4.74
1975	Federal Policy Speech	Original
1977	'The DLP policy in detail'	AGE 21.11.77

*Anti-Communist Labour Party in 1955

Australia Party

1969	'Bring home Diggers now – Turnbull'	AGE 1.10.69
1972	'Australia Party lays down its policy'	SMH 6.11.72
1974	'Barton's party puts inflation proposals'	SMH 29.4.74

Australian Democrats

1977	'Chipps, chat more of a party celebration'	SMH 21.11.77

Workers Party

1975	Workers Party Economic Policy (Advertisement)	SMH 29.11.75

KEY

SMH = *Sydney Morning Herald*
AGE = *The Age*

AUSTRIA

Österreichische Volkspartei

1949	Die programmatischen Leitsätze ÖVP, 1945	B 1967
1953	'Alles für Österreich', programmatische Grundsätze der ÖVP, 1952	Original
1956	'Schwerpunkte des Wahlkämpfes' and 'Von Wahl zu Wahl'	OMH 1956
1959	'Was wir wollen', Grundsatzprogramm der ÖVP, 1958	B 1967
1962	Wahlaufruf und Wahlprogramm der ÖVP	Original
1966	'Sicherheit für alle', Wahlprogramm 1966 der ÖVP	Original
1970	'Fortschritt und Sicherheit', das Arbeits programm der ÖVP	Original
1971	107 Vorschläge für Österreich	Original
1975	'Herausforderung 75', Wahlprogramm der ÖVP	Original
1979	'Für einen neuen Frühling in Österreich', Wahlprogramm 1979	Original

Sozialistische Partei Österreichs

1949	'An das österreichische Volk', Wahlaufruf 1949	DVM 1949
1953	'An das österreichische Volk', Wahlaufruf 1953	DVM 1953
1956	'An das österreichische Volk', Wahlaufruf 1956	DVM 1956
1959	'Geht mit der zeit! Geht mit der SPÖ!',	

Wahlaufruf 1959   DVM 1959
1962   SPÖ-Wahlparole: 'Österreich dienen!'   DVM 1963
1966   'Program für Österreich'   B 1967
1970   'Leistung, Aufsteig, Sicherheit für ein
       modernes Österreich', Wahlaufruf 1970   DVM 1970
1971   Für ein modernes Österreich und seine
       Menschen   Original
1975   Sicherheit und eine gute Zukunft für
       Österreich   Original
1979   Der österreichische Weg in die 80er Jahre   Original

Freiheitliche Partei Österreichs*

1949*   Das Programm des Verbändes der
        Unabhängigen, 1949   B 1966
1954*   Das 'Ausseer Programm' des Verbändes
        der Unabhängigen, 1954   B 1966
1956   Das Kurzprogramm der FPÖ, 1956   B 1966
1959   Richtlinien freiheitlicher Politik in
        Österreich   B 1966
1966   Das 'Salzburger Bekenntnis' der FPÖ, 1961   B 1966
1970   Formel 70   Original
1971   FPÖ-Schwerpunkte im neuen Nationalrat   Original
1975   Wahlplattform der FPÖ   Original
1979   Frei sein statt abhängig   Original

* Verband der Unabhängigen before 1956

KEY

B 1967 =   Klaus Berchtold (ed.),. *Österreichische Parteiprogramme 1868–1966*,
           Munich 1967.
DVM =   *Der Vertrauensmann* (Monthly Journal of the SPÖ).
OMH =   *Österreichische Monatsheft* (Monthly Journal of the ÖVP).

BELGIUM

Christian-Social 'Family'

1946   PSC–CVP Kerstprogramma (CEPESS reprint – extracts only)
1949   PSC–CVP Parti Social Chrétien – son Programme
1950   PSC–CVP 'Addenda' à la Brochure Parti Social-Chrétien 1949
1949   PSC–CVP CVP Programma 1954
1958   PSC–CVP Uw Beste Kans
1961   PSC–CVP Manifeste électorale du PSC
1965   PSC–CVP Platforme électorale du PSC – Contrat '65–'70

1968	CVP	De CVP doet het
1968	PSC	Feu vert
1971	PSC–CVP	Programme nationale du PSC 1971
1971	PSC	Programme d'Action régionale du PSC
1974	PSC–CVP	Programme électorale commun du PSC–CVP
1974	CVP	Programme d'Action régionale du CVP
1974	PSC	Programme d'Action régionale 'Wallonie-Bruxelles' du PSC
1974	PSC	La Région Wallonne
1974	PSC	Bruxelles
1977	PSC–CVP	Programme nationale du PSC 1977
1977	CVP	Meer dan ooit … Tindemans!
1977	PSC	Programme d'action régionale 'Wallonie-Bruxelles' du PSC
1977	PSC	Wallonie
1977	PSC	Bruxelles
1978	CVP	Er is een uitweg met de CVP
1978	PSC	Aller a l'essential pour rendre l'avenir possible
1981	CVP	Nu te nemen of te laten: een sterk nieuw beleid
1981	PSC	A la croisée des chemins
1981	PSC	Politiques spécifiques
1981	PSC	Programme pour la région wallonne et la Communauté française
1981	PSC	Bruxelles Oui, Séparatiste Non

Socialist 'Family'

1946	PSB–BSP	A tous les travailleurs!
1949	PSB–BSP	Programme du 4 ans
1950	PSB–BSP	Le parti socialiste belge s'addresse au pays
1954	PSB–BSP	La Plate-forme électorale du PSB
1958	PSB–BSP	Quatre années du Gouvernement de Gauche
1961	PSB–BSP	Plateforme électorale socialiste
1965	PSB–BSP	Programme pour les élections législatives du PSB
1971	PSB–BSP	Programme électorale du PSB
1974	PSB–BSP	Le programme socialiste pour une société progressiste
1977	PSB–BSP	Le programme du gouvernement du PSB
1978	BSP	Programma Vlaamse Socialisten: 17.12.78 Verkiezingen
1978	PS	Faire fâce – construire l'avenir
1981	SP	Verkiezingsprogramma
1981	PS	Le programme complet du parti socialiste

Liberal 'Family'

1946	PL–LP	Guide Pratique du conférencier libéral (extracts)
1949	PL–LP	Le parti libéral s'addresse au pays
1950	PL–LP	Le parti libéral s'addresse au pays
1954	PL–LP	Programme: Elections législatives 1951
1958	PL–LP	Programme du parti libéral

1961	Voilà pourquoi vous devez voter … 1	PL–LP
1965	Waarom PVV?	PLP–PVV
1968	Perspectives PLP	PLP–PVV
1971	Elections 1971: Programme nationale	PLP–PVV
1974	Het is Tijd!	PVV
1974	Plateforme électorale du PLP wallon	PLP
1974	Programme électorale du PLDP	PLDP
1977	Bekwaam, Zelfstandig, Verdraagzaam, Zeker	P.VPVV
1977	Plate-forme électorale	PRLW
1977	Programme du Parti libéral	PL
1978	U verdient écht beter	PVV
1978	Le programme du PRLW	PRLW
1978	Plate-forme électorale du Parti libéral	PL
1981	PVV – Nu of nooit	PVV
1981	PVV – nu of nooit – Persnota	PVV
1981	Projet pour le changement	PRL

Volksunie

1961	VU	De Politieke Toestand
1965	VU	Opgepast …
1968	VU	Een partij voor jonge dynamische mensen
1971	VU	Programma – Aktieplan
1974	VU	Aktieplan
1977	VU	In de politieke ontwikkeling van de voorbije kwaarteeuw …
1978	VU	Verkiezingsprogramma 17 december 1978
1981	VU	Werk en zekerheid in een Vlaamse staat

Rassemblement Wallon

1971	RW	Une force, une doctrine, une action
1974	RW	Bâtir la Wallonie, Assainir la politique
1977	RW	Être wallon
1978	RW	Wallon – maître chez toi
1981	RW	Programme du RW

Front démocratique des francophones bruxellois

1968	FDF	FDF 1968
1971	FDF	1971 FDF
1974	FDF	Programme FDF pour les élections du 10 mars 1974
1977	FDF	Bruxellois – maître chez toi
1978	FDF	La liberté d'etre Bruxellois
1981	FDF	FDF Bruxellois – Maître chez toi

Common Declarations/Programmes etc.

| 1974 | PL–FDF | Contrat de Programme de l'Alliance PL–FDF |
| 1978 | PSC–PS–FDF | Déclaration commune (des partis francophones de la majorité) |

CANADA

Liberal

1945   News release by the National Liberal Committee.
1949   'Resolutions adopted by the Third National Liberal Convention, Ottowa, 1948'.
1953   Collection of campaign speeches by party leader, published in *The Canadian Liberal*, Summer and Autumn, 1953.
1957   Campaign speeches by the leader taken from newspapers.
1958   *New Statements of Liberal Policy*, published by the National Liberal Federation
1962   *The Liberal Programme*, published by the National Liberal Federation.
1963   *The Policies of the Liberal Party*, published by the National Liberal Federation
1965   *Speakers' Notes*, published by the Liberal Party of Canada.
1968   As above
1972   Collection of campaign leaflets published by the Liberal Party of Canada and distributed by the Ottawa office.
1974   As above.
1979   As above.
1980   As above.

Progressive Conservative

1945   *Bracken's Charter for a Better Canada*, published and distributed by the Progressive Conservative Party.
1949   A letter stating policy signed by the leader of the Progressive Conservative Party and sent to newspapers.
1953   Campaign leaflets published and distributed by the Ottawa office of the Progressive Conservative Party.
1957   *A New National Policy*, published and distributed by the central office of the Progressive Conservative Party.
1958   Campaign speeches by the leader taken from newspapers.
1962   Taken from newspapers.
1963   Campaign leaflets published by the central office of the Progressive Conservative Party.
1965   *Policies for People*, published and distributed by the central office of the Progressive Conservative Party.
1968   Progressive Conservative Party Handbook, published and distributed by the Progressive Conservative Party.
1972   Campaign leaflets published by the central office of the Progressive Conservative Party.
1974   As above
1979   As above.
1980   As above.

CCF–NDP

1945   *Security with Victory*, published and distributed by the national office of the CCF

1949 *Security for All*, source as above.

1953 *Humanity First*, source as above.

1957 *Winnipeg Declaration of Principles of the Cooperative Commonwealth Federation*, source as above.

1958 Campaign leaflet published by the central office of the CCF.

1962 *The Federal Program of the New Democratic Party*, adopted by its founding convention and published and distributed by the central office of the party.

1963 Campaign leaflet published by the central office of the national party.

1965 Campaign leaflet published by the central office of the national party.

1968 *New Democratic Party Program*, source as above.

1972 *New Democratic Party Program*, source as above.

1974 *A Free and Generous Society . . .*, published and distributed by the central office of the NDP.

1979 *New Democratic Ideas for Working on Canada's Future*, source as above.

1980 *A Choice for Canadians: Policies of the New Democratic Party*, source as above.

Social Credit

1945 *The Social Credit Charter*, published and distributed by the Social Credit Association of Canada.

1949 Campaign leaflet published and distributed by the Alberta Social Credit League.

1953 Campaign speech by the leader published in newspapers.

1957 *It's Your Canada*, published and distributed by the National Social Credit Campaign Committee.

1958 Campaign leaflet published and distributed by the Social Credit Association of Canada.

1962 A Statement of Social Credit Objectives, Principles and Policies, source as above.

1963 Policy statement released by the National Social Credit Association of Canada.

1965 *Social Credit Candidate's Party Platform*, distributed by the Social Credit Party of Canada.

1968 *A Statement of Social Credit Objectives, Principles and Policies*, source as above.

DENMARK

Socialdemokratiet (Social Democrats)

1945 'Appel om Samling' (Appeal for Unity), delivered by the PM, Buhl. Published in *Folkets Stemme* (*The People's Voice*), Socialdemokratiets Valgavis 1945. Original.

1947 'Fremad paany' (Forward Again). Original.

1950 Socialdemokratiets valgmanifest (Social Democratic Election Manifesto). Published in *Valg-Orientering*, Det Konservative Folkeparti, 19.8.1950.

1953 April: 'Det sker nu i april' (It's happening now in April). Original

1953 Sept.: 'Familien Danmark går til valg' (The Danish Family Goes to the Polls). Original.

1957 'I bestemmer fremtiden' (You Decide the Future). Original

1960 Socialdemokratiets valgudtalelse 1960 (Social Democratic Election Statement). Original.

1964 Socialdemokratiets valgudtalelse (Social Democratic Election Statement), 'Aktuel politik', *Socialdemokratiske noter*, No. 6, 1964, 238–41.

1966 'På vej mod nye mål' (Towards New Goals). Original.

1968 'Valget gælder beskæftligelsen' (The Election is about Employment). Original.

1971 'Et godt parti fordi' (A Good Party Because ...). Original

1973 Valg'73 Socialdemokraterne (Election '73. the Social Democrats). Original

1975 Socialdemokraternes helhedsplan (Social Democrats' Overall Plan). Original.

1977 'Socialdemokratiet – et samlingspunkt i en splittet tid' (Social Democrats: a Meeting Point in Divided Times). Original.

1979 'For sammenhold og tro på framtiden'. (For Solidarity and Faith in the Future). Original.

1981 'Din hverdag er truet' (Your Everyday Life is Threatened). Original.

Det radikale Venstre (Radical Liberals)

1945 'Hvor står De Radikale?' (Where do the Radicals Stand?). Original.

1947 Det radikale Venstres Appel til Vælgerne, (The Appeal to the Electorate by the Radical Left). Published in 'Ugens Politik', The Radical Party.

1950 Det radikale Venstres valgmanifest (The Radical Liberal Election Manifesto). Published in *Valg-Orientering*, Det Konservative Folkeparti, 19.8.1950.

1953 April: Valget (The Election). Original.

1953 Sept.: De Radikales politiske udtalelse (The Radical Party Official Statement). Published by Arbejdernes Informations Central: Social demokratiet (the Workers' Information Centre: Social Democratic organization).

1957 'Valgets spørgsmål: Kamp eller samarbejde' (Election Questions: Conflict or Cooperation?). Original

1960 'Det radikale Venstre deltager ikke i overbud og løfter' (The Radical Party Will Not Make Promises it Cannot Keep). Original.

1964 Det radikale Venstres valgmanifest (The Radical Party Election Manifesto). Original.

1966 'Det radikale Venstre og fremtidens opgaver' (The Radical Party and the Tasks of the Future). Original.

1968 'Ingen patentmedicin kan genskabe sund økonomi' (Patent Medicine cannot Recreate a Healthy Economy).

1971 'De radikale vil forhindre, at dansk politik vælter til højre eller venstre' (The Radicals Will Keep Danish Politics from Extremes). Original.

1973 Det Radikale Venstres valgudtalelse (The Radical Party Election Statement). Original.

1975 Det radikale Venstres folketingsgruppe, valgudtalelse (The Radical Party Parliamentary Group, Official Election Statement). Original.

1977   'Valget gælder: et stabilt folkestyre med radikalt præg' (The Election: a
       Stable Democracy with a Radical Flavour). Original.
1979   Udtalelse fra Det Radikale Venstres landsmøde i Nyborg 15.–16. sept
       (Statement from the Radical Party Congress in Nyborg). Produced by party
       secretariat as the manifesto equivalent for the 1979 election, which was
       called on 28.9.79.
1981   'Ungdomsledighed bekæmpes' (The Fight Against Youth Unemploy-
       ment). Original.

Det konservative Folkeparti (The Conservatives)

1946   'Valget konservativt set' (The Election from a Conservative Viewpoint).
       Original.
1947   'Grib om Brændenælden' (Grip the Nettle). Original.
1950   Det konservative Folkepartis valgmanifest (The Conservative Party Elec-
       tion Manifesto). Published in *Valgorientiering*, Det konservative Folkeparti,
       19.8.50.
1953   April: 'Deres Lod i Vægtskaalen' (Your Weight on the Scales). Original
1953   Sept.: De Konservatives politiske udtalelse, Arbejdernes Informations
       Central: Social demokratiet (The Conservative Party Official Statement)
       published by the Workers' Information Centre.
1957   'Det bliver ikke bedre før vi faar en ny regering' (Things won't improve until
       we get a new government). Original.
1960   'En fremtid i frihed' (A Future in Freedom). Original.
1964   Det konservative Folkepartis valgmanifest (The Conservative Party Elec-
       tion Manifesto). 'Borgerlig ledelse mad tryghed, frihed, velstand eller
       socialistisk ledelse? (Bourgeois Leadership with Security, Freedom and
       Welfare or a Socialist Leadership?)'. Original.
1966   'Nu gælder det: retten til at eje' (Now is the time: the right of ownership).
       Original.
1968   'Tryghed og tillid (Security and Confidence)'. Det konservative Folkeparti's
       valgudtalelse, Folketingsvalget 23. januar 1968 (Conservative Party
       Election Manifesto for the parliamentary elections, 23.1.68.).
       Original.
1971   'De næste år (The Next Years)'. Original.
1973   'En ny regering – en ordentlig politik' (A New Government – a Decent
       Policy Lasts)'. Original.
1975   'Valget gælder fire år: Valg 75 (The Election Lasts Four Years: Election
       '75)'. Det konservative Folkepartis valgudtalelse (Conservative Party
       Election Manifesto).
1977   'Protestvalg igen eller positiv indsats? (Protest Election Again or a Positive
       Effort?)'. Published in *Vor Tid*, Det konservative Folkeparti, Februar 1977.
1979   'Sådan løser vi Danmarks problemer (This is the Way we Solve Denmark's
       Problems)'. Original
1981   'Sådan løser Danmark sine problemer' (This is the Way Denmark Solves its
       Problems). Original.

Venstre (The Liberal Party/Agrarian Liberals)

1945 'Venstre bygger Fremliden' (The Liberals Build the Future). Original.
1947 'Venstre blaeser til Samling!' (The Liberal Fanfare for Unity!). Original.
1950 Venstres valgmanifest (The Liberal Election Manifesto). Published in *Valgorientering*, Det konservative Folkepartie, 19.8.1950.
1953 April: Venstres valgopråb (The Liberal's Campaign Call). Original.
1953 Sept.: Venstres politiske udtalelse (Official Liberal Party Statement). Published by Arbejdernes Informations Central: Socialdemokratiet.
1957 Venstres valgudtalelse (Official Election Statement). Original.
1960 Venstres valgudtalelse (Official Election Statement). Original.
1964 'En ny regering. Venstre vil løse problemerne' (A New Government: the Liberals will Solve the Problems). Statement by Anders Andersen (leading candidate). Original.
1966 'Til vælgerne i Givekradsen. Program for Valgets hovedspørgsmaal: En ny regering' (To the Electorate in the Constituency of Give. The Main Themes of the Election: A New Government).
1968 Venstres valgprogram 1968 (Election Programme). Original.
1971 Valgudtalelse fra Venstres folketingsgruppe (Official Election Statement from the Liberal Parliamentary Group). Original.
1973 'En ny politik Venstre valg '73' (A New Policy for the '73 Election). Original.
1975 'Det første år – og de næste fire' (The First Year and the Four Next Years). Original.
1977 'Venstre '77. En liberal politik 8 Hovedpunkter' (Liberals '77 – A Liberal Policy: 8 Main Points). Original.
1979 Udtalelse fra Venstres Folketingsgruppe (Statement from the Liberal Parliamentary Group), 28.9.1979. Original
1981 'Gi' Danmark en chance' (Give Denmark a Chance). Original

Danmarks kommunistiske Parti (Danish Communist Party)

1945 'Folkets vilje – landets lov' (The Will of the People – the Law of the Land). Original.
1947 'Nøglen til Fremskridt for Folket og Danmark' (The Key to Progress for the People and for Denmark). Original.
1950 Kommunisternes valgmanifest (Communist Election Manifesto). Published in *Valgorientering*. Det konservative Folkeparti, 10.8.50.
1953 April: 'Valgmanifest fra Danmarks kommunistiske Parti 'For fred og frihed, for trygge levevilkår'' (Election Manifesto of the DKP, for Peace and Freedom, for Security). Published in the communist newspaper *Land og Folk*.
1953 Sept.: Kommunisternes politiske udtalelse (Official Communist Party Statement). Published by Arbejdernes Informations Central: Socialdemokratiet.
1957 'Det ku' bil' så godt ... men' (It Could Be Alright, But ...). Original.
1960 'Med kommunisterne for en ny politik' (With the Communists for a New Policy). Original.

1964 'Kommunister i folketinget' (Communists in Parliament). Original.

1966 'Sæt kommunister ind i folketinget' (Put Communists in Parliament). Original.

1968 'Det er samfundet, der skal laves om. Derfor må der kommunister til.' (Society Needs a Change: We need the Communists). Last page of a leaflet 'Den står vi ikke model til!' produced by Danmarks kommunistiske parti. Original.

1971 'Derfor Kommunister' (Therefore the Communists). Original.

1973 'Kommunisternes valgopråb: Fremad – ad nye veje' (Communist Party Campaign Call: Taking New Paths). Original.

1975 'For et godt og bedre nytår med en ny politik og med fremgang' (For a Good New Year With a New Policy and With Progress for the DKP). Original.

1977 DKPs Valgrundlag (Communist Party Election Programme. Original.

1979 DKPs Valgopråb (Communist Party Campaign Call). Original.

1981 'Sæt K folk i tinget Kommunister' (Put the Communists in Parliament). Original.

Retsforbundet (Justice Party/Single-Tax Party)

1945 'Økonomisk Frigørelse er Forundsætningen for personlig Frihed' (Economic Liberation is the Condition for Personal Freedom). Leaflet for a Copenhagen constituency. Original.

1947 'Ønsker De Frihed eller Tvang?' (Do You Want Freedom or Restriction?). Original.

1950 'Vejen frem', (The Road Ahead). The party election newspaper. Original.

1953 April: 'Lær Retsforbundet at Kende' (Get to Know the Justice Party). Original.

1953 Sept.: Retsforbundets politiske udtalelse (The Party's Political Statement). Published by Arbejdernes Informations Central: Social demokratiet.

1957 'Fremgang for Retsforbundet betyder Fremgang for hele det danske Folk' (Progress for the Justice Party Means Progress for the Danish People). Original.

1960 'Retsforbundets folketingsgruppe har idag følgende valgopråb' (The Parliamentary Group has Today Produced the Following Campaign Call). Original.

1964 Retsforbundets valgudtalelse (Official Justice Party Statement). Published in 'Aktuel politik', *Socialdemokratiske noter*, No. 6, 1964.

1966 Retsforbundets valgmanifest (Election Manifesto) Published in *Ret og Frihed*, Danmarks Retsforbund, November 1966.

1968 Valgopråb fra Danmarks Retsforbund (Justice Party Campaign Call). Original.

1973 'Det drejer sig om: Et selvstændigt Danmark, økonomisk frihed og social retfærdighed' (Dealing with: an Independent Denmark, Economic Freedom, and Social Justice). Original

1975 'Det drejer sig om: Valget den 9 januar er alene statsminister Hartlings beslutning' (Dealing with: the 9th of January election is the sole responsibility of PM Hartling). Original.

1977 Retsforbundets valgudtalelse 1977 (Official Party Statement). Original.
1979 Retsforbundets valgudtalelse 1979 (Official Party Statement). Original.
1981 'x E den 8. december' (Vote E on the 8th of December). Retsforbundet 1981. Original.

Socialistisk Folkeparti (Socialist People's Party)

1960 'SF Det ny parti i dansk politik' (SF, The New Party in Danish Politics). Original.
1964 SF's valgudtalelse (Official Party Statement). Published in 'Aktuel politik', *Socialdemokratiske noter*, No. 6, 1964.
1966 'Bal med de borgerlige?' (A Walz with the Bourgeoisie?). Original.
1968 'Spil ikke hasard med flertallet. SF sæt trumf på!' (Don't Gamble with the Majority. SF Plays the Trump!). Original
1971 Socialistisk Folkepartis valgprogram (SF Election Programme). Original.
1973 '. . . en stemme på SF er en *sikker* stemme' (A Vote for SF is a Secure Vote). Original.
1975 Valgmanifest for Socialistisk Folkeparti (Election Manifesto). Original.
1977 Socialistisk Folkeparti valgmanifest (Election Manifesto). Original.
1979 Socialistisk Folkeparti's valgmanifest (Election Manifesto). Approved by the party executive committee on 30.9.1979. Original.
1981 *SF Politik*. Election newspaper dealing with what SF stands for and is working towards; gives the essential points of the party programme. Original.

Centrum-demokraterne (Centre Democrats)

1973 'Med Erhard i midten: Centrumdemokraterne' (With Erhard in the Middle: Centre Democrats). Original.
1975 Centrum-Demokraternes valgoplæg (Centre Democrats Election Proposals Document). Original.
1977 'Politik – Så det er til at forstå' (Politics You Can Understand). Original.
1979 'Firkløver bringer lykke' MCVQ (A Four Leaf Clover Brings Luck). Original. 'Ny kurs – med nye folk' (A New Course with New People); Erhard Jacobsen formand for Centrum-Demokraterne' (Vote for Erhard as the CD Chairman); 'De kan stole pa CD' (You Can Trust the CD). Original.
1981 'Centrum Demokraterne x M ved valget 8. december' (The Centre Democrats; Vote for M in the 8 Dec. Election). Original.

Kristelig Folkeparti (Christian People's Party)

1971 '21. September KF's dag' (21 September is the KF's Day). Published in the party election newspaper *Ide – Politik*, Vol. 2, No. 5.
1973 'Valgets kerne-punkter' (The Crucial Issues at the Election). Original.
1975 '18 gode grunde til at stemme på Kristeligt Folkeparti' (18 Good Reasons for Voting for the KF). Original

1977 '18 gode grunde til at stemme på Kristeligt Folkeparti' (18 Good Reasons for Voting for the KF). Original.

1979 'Valget er et værdivalg' (The Election is an Election of Values). Original.

1981 'Nu må en ny regering til' (It's Time for a New Government). Published in the party election newspaper *Ide – Politik*, 20.11.1981. Original.

Venstresocialisterne (Left Socialists)

1968 Udtalelse fra Venstre-Socialisterne om Folketingsvalget den 23. januar 1968 (The Official Statement of the Left Socialists in the Parliamentary Election). Original.

1971 Venstresocialisterne (The Left Socialists). Original.

1973 VS: Program for Venstresocialisterne (VS Programme). Original.

1975 VS Venstresocialisternes valgavis. 'Hvad vil VS' (What Do the VS Want?). Vs election newspaper. Original.

1977 Valgudtalelse fra Venstresocialisterne (Election Statement). Original.

1979 Venstresocialisterne. Til pressen Valgets hovedsporgsmaal (The Main Questions of the Election: Answers for the Press). Original

1981 Venstresocialisternes valggrundlag (Campaign Statement). Original.

Fremskridtspartiet (Progress Party)

1973 Fremskridtspartiets valggrundlag (Progress Party Election Statement). Original.

1975 'De *er* jo enig med os i at: – afvikling af indkomstskatterne – begrænsning af papirvældet – sanering af lovgivngen – det vil vi i Fremskridtspartiet.' (The abolition of income tax, reduction of bureaucracy, reorganization of legislation – that's what the Progress Party wants). Original.

1977 'Den forældede skat' (The Outdated Tax). Published in the party periodical *Fremskridt*, 1977. Original.

1979 'Redningsplanen for Danmark' (The Safety Plan for Denmark). Original.

1981 'Fremskridtspartiet: Redningsplanen for Danmark' (Progress Party: The Safety Plan for Denmark). Original

De Uafhængige (Independent Party)

1953 Sept.: De uafhængiges politiske udtalelse (The Independents' Political Statement). Published by the Arbejdernes Informations Central: Socialdemocratiet.

1957 De uafhængige Valgavis 14. maj 1957 (Independents' Election Newspaper). Original.

1960 De uafhængiges valgprogram (Independents' Election Programme). Original.

1964 De uafhængiges valgudtalelse (Independents' Official Election Statement). Published in 'Aktuel Politik', *Social demokratiske noter* No. 6, 1964, pp. 269–71.

1966 De uafhængiges valgprogram 'Et borgerligt ord om politik x liste U' (The

Independents' Election programme, A Bourgeois Word About Politics –
Vote U), 22.11.1966. Original.

1968 'For Deres fremtids skyld ... luk op og læs' (For the sake of your future –
open and read). Original

Liberalt Centrum (Liberal Centre)

1966 Udkast til principprogram for Liberalt Centrum (Draft for a Programme of
Principles). Published in *Tidskrift for politisk orientering*, Liberalt Centrum,
October 1966.

1968 'Nu skal landet ledes fra stærkt centrum ... skab arbejdsglæde med L
Liberalt Centrum' (Now the Country needs to be led by a Strong Centre ...
Create the Joy of Working with the LC). Original.

FEDERAL GERMANY

Social Democratic Party (SPD)

1949 Richtlinien der Politik der SPD im Bundestag. Dürkheimer 16 Punkte.
Beschlossen in der Sitzung des Vorständes der SPD am 29./30. August 1949
Bad Dürkheim. Bestätigt von der Tagung führender Parteikorperschaften
am 6. September 1949 in Köln.

1953 Aktionsprogramm von 1952. Beschlossen auf dem Dortmunder Parteitag
am 28. September 1952.

1957 Ausarbeitung eines Grundsatzprogramms. Entschliessung, angenommen
auf dem Parteitag in München, 10.–14. Juli 1956.

1961 Das Regierungsprogramm der SPD. Bekanntgegeben auf dem ausserordentlichen Kongress in Bonn am 28. April 1961.

1965 'Tatsachen und Arguments. Erklärungen der SPD'. Regierungsmanns-
chaft. Verabschiedet auf der Arbeitssitzung der SPD. Regierungsmanns-
chaft in Bonn am 8. Januar 1965.

1969 Regierungsprogramm der Sozialdemokratischen Partei Deutschlands 1969.
SPD. 'Erfolg, Stabilität, Reform'. Beschlossen vom Ausserordentlichen
Parteitag der SPD am 17. April 1969 in Bad Godesberg.

1972 Wahlprogramm der SPD. Kundgebungen und Beschlüsse des Ausserordentlichen Parteitages in Dortmund, 12.–13. Oktober 1972.

1976 'SPD. Weiterarbeiten am Modell Deutschland'. Regierungsprogramm
1976–80. Kundgebungen und Beschlüsse des Ausserordentlichen Parteitages in Dortmund, 18.–19. Juni 1976.

1980 'Sicherheit für Deutschland'. Wahlprogramm 1980. Beschlossen von der
Sozialdemokratischen Partei Deutschland auf dem Wahlparteitag in Essen.
9./10. Juni 1980.

Free Democratic Party (FDP)

1949 Bremer Plattform 1949. Beschlüsse des 1. Bundesparteitages am 11. und 12.
Juni 1949 in Bremen.

1953 Wahlprogramm 1953. Beschlossen vom ausserordentlichen Bundesparteitag am 28. Juni 1953 in Lübeck.

1957 Aktionsprogramm 1957. Verkundet auf dem Wahlkongress am 5. Juni 1957
in Hamburg.

1961 Aufruf zur Bundestagswahl 1961. Beschlossen vom 12. Bundesparteitag
vom 23.–25. März 1961 in Frankfurt a.M.

1965 No election programme.

1969 'Praktische Politik für Deutschland. Das Konzept der FDP'. Verabschiedet
vom 20. Ordentlichen Bundesparteitag der Freien Demokratischen Partei
am 25. Juni 1969 in Nürnberg.

1972 'Vorfahrt fur Vernünft'. Wahlaufruf zur Bundestagswahl Verabschiedet
vom Bundesparteitag in Freiburg, 23.–25. Oktober 1972.

1976 Wahlprogramm. Verabschiedet vom Wahlkongress 1976 (a.o. Bundesparteitag) der FDP in Freiburg am 31. Mai 1976.

1980 'Unser Land soll auch morgen liberal sein'. Wahlprogramm der Freien
Demokratischen Partei für die Bundestagswahlen am 5. Oktober 1980.
Beschlossen vom a.o. Parteitag in Freiburg, am 7. Juni 1980.

Christian Democratic Party (CDU)

1949 'Düsseldorfer Leitsätze'. Verabschiedet von der Arbeitsgemeinschaft der
CDU/CSU in Frankfurt a.M., 15 July 1949.

1953 Hamburger Programm von 22. April 1953 für den zweiten deutschen
Bundestag. Verabschiedet vom 4. Bundesparteitag in Hamburg, 18.–22.
April 1953.

1957 'An das deutsche Volk'. Das Manifest der Christlich Demokratischen
Union, beschlossen vom 7. Parteitag in Hamburg.

1961 'Kölner Manifest'. Das Wahlprogramm der CDU zur Bundestagswahl
1961. Beschlossen vom 13. Bundesparteitag in Köln, 24.–27. April 1961.

1965 Düsseldorfer Erklärung der CDU. 31. März 1965. Beschlossen vom. 13.
Bundesparteitag in Düsseldorf, 28–31 March 1965.

1969 'Sicher in die 70er Jahre'. Kurt Georg Kiesinger, CDU. Verabschiedet vom
Wahlkongress der CDU in Essen, 8.7.1969.

1976 'Für die Freiheit die wir lieben. Für die Sicherheit die wir brauchen. Fur die
Zukunft die wir wollen'. Das Wahlprogramm der CDU und CSU 1976.

1980 Für Frieden und Freiheit in der Bundesrepublik Deutschland und in der
Welt. (Wahlprogramm der CDU und CSU für die Bundestagswahl 1980).
Verabschiedet auf dem 28 Bundesparteitag der CDU in Berlin, 18.–20. Mai
1980. Verabschiedet vom Parteiausschuss der CSU in Ingolstadt, 17. Mai
1980.

FRANCE

Parti Communiste Français

1958 *Que Proposent Les Communistes? Bulletin d'Information et de Propagande du Parti
Communiste Français*, 19, October 1958, pp. 16.

1962   *Vers l'Avenir*, Elections Législatives, Novembre 1962. Paris, Parti Communiste Français, 1962, pp. 16.

1967   *D'Aujourd'hui à Demain*, Programme du Parti Communiste Français, Elections Législatives de 1967, *l'Humanité-Dimanche*, 953, 7 November 1966, pp. 15.

1968   *Programme du Parti Communiste Français*, Eléctions Législatives de 1968, n.d.n 1., pp. 14.

1971   *Changer de Cap*, Programme pour un Gouvernement Démocratique d'Union Populaire, Paris, Editions Sociales, 1971, pp. 251.

1978   *Programme Commun de Gouvernement Actualisé*, Parti Communiste Français, Paris, Editions Sociales, 1978, pp. 191.

Socialist Tendency

1958   *Décision et Compte-Rendus*, 50ème Congrès National SFIO. Issy-les-Moulinaux, September 14, 1958. *Le Populaire de Paris* 15 September 1958.

1962   *Programme d'Action*, Elections Législatives, Novembre 1962, *Dossier du Candidat SFIO*, Paris, 1962, pp. 7.

1972   *Parti Socialiste: Changer la Vie*, Programme de Gouvernement du Parti Socialiste, Paris, Flammarion, 1972, pp. 249.

1978   *Programme Commun de Gouvernement de la Gauche*, propositions Socialistes pour l'Actualisation, Paris, Flammarion, 1978, pp. 128.

1981   Cent Dix Propositions pour la France, Manifeste du Parti Socialiste, Congrès Extraordinaire, Créteil, 24 January 1981, *Le Monde, Dossiers et Documents*, Les Elections Législatives de 1981, June 1981, pp. 67.

Centre Tendency

Christian

1958   *Fichier du Militant*, Elections Législatives, Novembre 1958. *Action Civique et Politique*, 11 October 1958, pp. 48

1962   *MRP. Dossier du Candidat*, Elections Législatives des 18 et 25 Novembre 1962. Paris, 1962, multigraph.

1967   Centre Démocrate, *Manifeste Electoral. Courrier des Démocrates*, 31, February 13, 1967, pp. 16.

1968   Candidate's Speech Specimen in *Dossier du Candidat Progrès et Démocratie Moderne*, Elections Législatives de 1968, Paris, pp. 6.

Radical

1958   *Documents Techniques Arguments et Ripostes*, Elections Législatives de 1958. *Note Générale d'Orientation*, Paris, Parti Radical et Radical Socialiste, 1958, pp. 5.

1962   *La France à l'Heure Européenne*, Manifeste du Rassemblement Démocratique Elections des 18 et 25 Novembre 1962. Paris.

Christian-Radical (Common Programme)

1972 *Le Projet Réformateur*, Jean Lecanuet et Jean Jacques Servan-Schreiber, Paris, Robert Laffont, 1972, pp. 31–80.

Moderate Technology

1958 *Fiches de Documentation CNIP*, Elections Législatives, Paris, Imp. Lange, 1958, pp. 82.

1962 *Fiches de Documentation CNIP*, Elections Législatives. Paris, Imp. Lange, 1962, pp. 68.

Gaullist Tendency

1958 *Dossier du Candidate UNR*, Elections Législatives, 1958. Paris, 1958.

1962 *Dossier du Candidat UNR*, Elections Législatives, 1962. Paris, 1962, pp. 32.

1967 Comité d'Action pour la Cinquième République, Manifeste: *Pour le Progrès, l'Indépendence et la Paix avec le Général de Gaulle*, 1967, pp. 6.

1968 *Manifeste de l'Union pour la Défense de la République*, Elections Législatives de Juin 1968, *La Nation*, 19 June 1968, pp. 2.

1973 *Programme de Provins*, Pierre Messmer, 7 Janvier 1973, *Le Démocrate*, January 1973.

1977 *Propositions pour la France*, présentées par Jerome Monod, Rassemblement pour le République, Paris, Stock, 1977, pp. 235.

Programmes Common to Parties from more than one Tendency

Communist and Socialist Tendencies

1972 *Programme Commun de Gouvernement* du Parti Communiste Français et du Parti Socialiste, Paris, Editions Sociales, 1972, pp. 192.

Socialist and Radical Tendencies

1967 *Une Politique des Réalités pour la République des Citoyens*, Manifeste de la FGDS. *Le Populaire de Paris*, 12298, 4 February 1967, pp. 17.

1968 *Programme de la FGDS*, Elections Législatives de 1968, *Dossier du Candidat FGDS*, Paris, 1968, pp. 13.

Moderate and Christian Tendencies

1978 *Le Programme de Blois*, Objectifs d'Action pour les Libertés et la Justice, présenté par Raymond Barre, Paris, Fayard, 1978, pp. 27–73.

Moderate and Gaullist Tendencies

1981 *Pacte pour l'Union de la Nouvelle Majorité*, déclaration commune, 15 mai 1981,

Le Monde, Dossiers et Documents, Les Elections Législatives de Juin 1981, pp. 15–16.

IRELAND

Fianna Fáil

1948 'Party Leaders on their Programmes, No. 1: Fianna Fáil'. *Irish Independent*, 23.1.1948.
1951 'To the Electors of West Galway'. Leaflet published by Fianna Fáil containing the 'Great National Reconstruction Programme'.
1954 'Radio Broadcast by An Tanaiste, Mr. Séan Lemass, on Tuesday, 11th May, 1954'. Dublin: Fianna Fáil, 1954, mimeo.
1957 'Campaign to Beat Crisis'. *Irish Press*, 16.2.1957.
1961 'Taoiseach Foresees Change in Population Trend'. *Irish Times*, 12.8.1961.
1965 'People Will Back Us All the Way Again: Taoiseach'. *Irish Press*, 17.3.1965.
1969 'Taoiseach Opens F.F. Election Campaign'. *Irish Times*, 28.5.1969.
1973 'Text of Taoiseach's Statement'. *Irish Times*, 6.2.1973.
1977 *Manifesto: Action Plan for National Reconstruction*. Dublin: Fianna Fáil, 1977.
1981 *Our Programme for the '80s*. Dublin: Fianna Fáil, 1981.

Fine Gael

1948 'Party Leaders on their Programmes, No. 3: Fine Gael'. *Irish Independent*, 26.1.1948.
1951 Election leaflet for Dun Laoghaire Rathdown Constituency.
1954 'Costello gives 13 Principles'. *Irish press*, 3.5.1954.
1957 'Taoiseach gives 16 Reasons for Supporting Fine Gael'. *Irish Times*, 1.3.1957.
1961 *What Fine Gael Stands For*. Dublin: Fine Gael, 1961.
1965 *Fine Gael Policy 1965: 'Towards a Just Society'*. Dublin: Fine Gael, 1965.
1969 *Winning Through to a Just Society*. Dublin: Fine Gael, 1969.
1973 'Statement of Intent'. Dublin: Fine Gael and the Labour Party, 1973, mimeo.
1977 *The National Coalition Government: Achievements. Programme for Progress*. Dublin: Fine Gael and the Labour Party, 1977.
1981 *A Better Future: Let the Country Win*. Dublin: Fine Gael, 1981.

The Labour Party

1948 'Party Leaders on their Programmes, No. 4: Labour'. *Irish Independent*, 27.1.1948.
1951 'Appendix I: General Election 1951 – Labour Party Manifesto. Labour's Way to Achieve Prosperity and Security' in *Administrative Council Report for 1950–51 and 1951–52*. Dublin: the Labour Party, 1952, pp. 52–4.
1954 'More for Social Services, Pensions'. *Irish Press*, 30.4.1954.
1957 'Appendix I: General Election 1957. Labour Party Election Programme', in *Administrative Council Report for 1956–57*. Dublin: the Labour Party, 1957, pp. 26–8.

1961 'More Planning is Labour Aim'. *Irish Times*, 13.8.196.
1965 'Labour Election Manifesto', *Irish Times*, 24.3.1965.
1969 'Appendix No. 1: 1969 General Election', in *Labour Party Annual Report 1969*. Dublin: the Labour Party, 1969, pp. 68–83.
1973 See Fine Gael.
1977 See Fine Gael.
1981 *Labour '81: Election Programme*. Dublin: The Labour Party, 1981.

IRELAND (NORTHERN)

Unionist Party

1921 'To the Loyalist Electors of Northern Ireland' BT 26.4.21
1925 'Premier's Election Manifesto' NW 16.3.25
1929 'Work together and win together. Lord Craigavon's Manifesto to the People of Ulster' NW 18.4.29
1933 'Lord Craigavon's Message to the Electors' NW 11.11.33
1938 'The Premier's Manifesto' NW 28.1.38
1945 'Plan for Prosperous Ulster' BN 30.5.45 and 'A Message to the People of Ulster' NW 30.5.45
1949 'A Message from the Prime Minister to the People of Northern Ireland' NW 25.1.49
1953 'Main Issue of the Election' BN 6.10.53
1958 'Ulster can reply to bullets by votes' BN 28.2.58 'Keep Ulster British says Manifesto' NW 28.2.58
1962 'Prosperity only if Constitution maintained' BN 12.5.62 and 'the Fundamental of Ulster's Prosperity' NW 12.5.62
1965 'Unionist Manifesto outlines 18 Points' BT 16.11.65
1969 'Election marks Crossroads for Northern Ireland' IT 15.2.69
1973 Peace, Order Good Government, Original

Nationalist Party

1921 'Partition means National Suicide' IN 7.5.21
1925 'Mr. Devlin's important Statement of Policy' IN 30.3.25
1929 'The National League's inspiring Manifesto' IN 18.4.29
1933 Document missing
1938 'Smash and Grab Election. Mr. Campbell on Government's Purblind and Stupid Administration' IN 25.1.38
1945 'Public Notice' and 'Election Address to the Electors: Falls Division' N 13.6.45
1949 'Anti-Partition Manifesto on Outstanding Issue in Irish Politics' IN 8.2.49
1953 Document missing
1958 'Unionist Conspiracy to keep Minority in subjection' IN 13.3.58
1962 'Nationalist Party state Policy' NW 17.5.62
1965 'Cooler Elections in North hailed by McAteer' II 20.11.65
1969 '15 Point Nationalist Manifesto' IN 20.2.69
1973 Document missing

Northern Ireland Labour Party

1921   Document missing
1925   'The Socialist Programme' NW 24.3.25
1929   Document missing
1933   'The Dock Contest: Alderman Midgeley's Promise to the Electors' BN 22.11.33
1938   'Labour attacks Government' IN 17.1.38
1945   Document missing
1949   Labour's Message to the Electors, Original
1953   'What Ulster Labour would do' BN 17.10.53 and Manifesto of the NILP, October 1953, Original
1958   Northern Ireland Labour Party Manifesto, Original
1962   Ulster Labour and the Sixties, Original
1965   Election Manifesto 1965: NILP, Original
1969   'Labour lists disparities with Britain'; IT 15.2.69
1973   Peace through Partnership, Original

KEY:

BN = *Belfast Newsletter*
BT = *Belfast Telegraph*
II = *Irish Independent*
IN = *Irish News*
IT = *Irish Times*
NW = *Northern Whig*

ISRAEL

Mapai (1949–61), Israel Labour Party (1965), Ma'arach (1969–81)

1949	'Mapai Stands for Peace'	PP 13.1.49
	'To All Members of Free Professions'	PP 23.1.49
1951	'Mapai's Past on Record: The Way Ahead'	JP 27.7.51
	'The Simple Truth'	JP 15.7.51
	'To the Masses'	JP 3.5.51
	'Appeal to Reason' (25 daily adverts.)	JP 29.6.51 –29.7.51 incl.
	'Responsibility'	JP 30.7.51
	'My Plan for the Future' (David Ben Gurion)	JP 27.7.51
1955	'The Index Stayed Put'	JP 24.6.55
	'Well is it the Truth?'	JP 1.7.55
	'Whose Hands are on the Wheel?'	JP 15.7.55
	'From the MAPAI Platform? The Mission of our Generation'	JP 25.7.55

'An Open Letter to the Voter'   JP 26.7.55

1959   'The MAPAI Platform, 1959'   JP 30.10.59
       'To the Citizens of Israel'   JP 3.11.59

1961   'The Pillars of State'   JP 30.6.61
       'Vote MAPAI'   JP 4.8.61
       'Tomorrow You Vote'   JP 14.8.61

1965   'For the '70s; Security and Peace'   JP 19.10.65
       'Towards the 1970s' (25 daily adverts)   JP 19.10.65–
                                                      31.10.65 incl.
       'Foreign Policy'   NO 8. 1965

1969   '1969 Election Propaganda'   Z pp. 159–62
       'In Conclusion'   JP 24.10.69

1973   '1973 Election Propaganda'   Z pp. 178–80
       'A Policy of Striving for Peace'   JP 30.12.73

1977   'The Tasks Ahead: Forward with Labour to
       Face the Future'   JPM 5.5.77

1981   'HaMa'arach ve haLikud: Ha hevdal hagadol'   Ma'ariv 29.5.81
       'Where we Stand'   JP 25.6.81
       'Israel now needs ...'   JP 17.4.81

Herut (1949–61), Gahal (1965, 1969), Likud (1973–81)

1949   'Historic Frontiers and Civic Freedom'   PP 10.1.49
1973   'Tenuat HaHerut Brings to Israel'   PP 21.1.49

1951   'Tenaut HaHerut'   JP 29.7.51

1955   'Economic Policy'   JP 8.7.55
       'What They Promised, What They did'   JP 15.7.55
       'If You Vote for Herut ...'   JP 22.7.55

1959   'It is Time for a Change'   JP 23.10.59

1961   'You Know Him'   JP 4.8.61
       'Citizens of Israel'   JP 11.8.61

1965   'A Constitution for Israel'   JP 20.8.65
       'Change of Administration'   JP 27.8.65
       'Work and Workers'   JP 8.9.65
       'Basic Economic Policy'   JP 14.9.65

'Housing for Young Couples'	JP 16.9.65
'National Health Insurance'	JP 20.9.65
'Principles of Foreign Policy'	JP 20.10.65
'Legislative Programme'	JP 21.10.65
'Air Pollution, Noise and Noxious Odours'	JP 22.10.65
'Legislation: An Ombudsman for Israel'	JP 25.10.65
'How to Reduce and Reform Income Tax'	JP 28.10.65

1969   'GAHAL's Record'   JPM 24.10.69
      'Any Plans to Re-divide the State of Israel'   JP 10.10.69

1973   'Foreign Policy and Defence.'   Z pp. 178–80
      'Today You will Determine Your and Your
      Country's Future'   JP 31.12.73
      'Do You Agree?'   JP 28.12.73
      'To All Citizens of Israel'   JP 26.12.73

1977   'The LIKUD Government: Its Platforms for
      Change and Leadership'   JP 13.5.77

1981   'Rosh Hamemshalah, M. Begin al'azrachi
      Israel'   *Ma'ariv* 28.6
      'Food for Thought'   JPM 19.6.81

Mafdal

1949   'Religious People Who Want a Modern State'   PP 24.1.49

1951   'Omen Mizrahi Women'   JP 13.7.51
      'Hapoel HaMizrahi'   JP 19.7.51
      'Quotation from the Economic Platform'   JP 27.7.51
      'Do You Agree ...' (5 daily adverts.)   JP 18.7.51–
      29.7.51 incl.

1955   Achievements of the National Religious Party   JP 1.7.55
      Achievements of the National Religious Party   JP 5.7.55
      'For Its Achievement Vote 'B''   JP 7.7.55
      'The National Religious Bloc was not Formed
      for the Election'   JP 21.7.55
      'Having Respect for Religion'   JP 22.7.55
      'How Shall We Educate Our Children?'   JP 22.7.55
      'To the Women of Israel'   JP 24.7.55
      'To Every Religious Jew'   JP 26.7.55
      'A Great Opportunity'   JP 26.7.55

1959   'Haifa Subway will not Operate on Sabbath'   JP 4.9.59
      'Who Will Protect Religious Values?'   JP 11.9.59

'Betar-Hapoel 0:2'   JP 25.9.59
'Towards a Turning Point in the New Year'   JP 2.20.59
'Our answer to the MAPAI Chief'   JP 9.10.59
'Haim Moshe Shapiro'   JP 30.10.59
'Today Only – Tomorrow is Too Late'   JP 3.11.59

1961 'What We Will Fight For in the Fifth Knesset' JP 4.8.61
      'Letter to the Voter'   JP 11.8.61
      'We Call Upon You to Vote'   JP 14.8.61

1965 'To Voters Who Cherish the Values of
      Traditional Judaism'   JP 31.10.65
      'What the National Religious Party Will try
      to Achieve'   JP 1.11.65

1969 'The Nation Pins its Hope on You'   JP 27.10.69
      'NRP Calls for More Settlement'   JP 15.9.69

1973 Speech by Social Welfare Minister Hazari and
      Rabbinical Statement on Foreign Policy,   Z pp. 181–83
      'Dear Voters'   JP 28.12.73

1977 'Dear Friend'   JP 15.4.77
      'You and I Have Met ...'   JP 17.5.77

1981 'Dear Citizen'   JP 29.6.81
      'Kol x 3' Ha'aretz (no date)
      'MAFDAL: Yeish rak achat' *Ma'ariv*   29.5.81
      'Kol kol leTehiya, kol neto lePares' *Ma'ariv* 28.6.81

KEY:

PP = *Palestine Post*
JP = *Jerusalem Post*
JPM = *Jerusalem Post Magazine*
Ha'aretz and *Ma'ariv* are Hebrew-language papers
Z = Zohar, D.N., *Political Parties in Israel*, Appendix.

ITALY

Democrazia Cristiana

1946 'Manifesto della Democrazia Cristiana: per il referendum istituzionale e per l'Assemblea Costituente', pp. 259–60, *Atti e Documenti della Democrazia Cristiana 1943–1967*, Cinque Lune, Rome, 1968. See also 'Messagio della Democrazia Cristiana agli Italiani' 31 May 1946, pp. 261–3 in DC *Atti e Documenti, op. cit.*

1948 'Appello della Democrazia Cristiana al paese, 4 March 1948: Salvare la libertà', pp. 377–8 in DC, *Atti e Documenti, op. cit.*

1953 'Appello della Direzione DC al paese per le elezioni politiche', 1 May 1953, p. 603 in DC, *Atti e Documenti, op. cit.* See also 'Consultà economico-sociale della Democrazia Cristiana' 1 May 1953, pp. 608–15 in DC, *Atti e Documenti, op. cit.*

1958 'Programma della Democrazia Cristiana per il quinquennio 1958–1963: per garantire al popolo italiano 'progresso senza avventura', 12 April 1958, pp. 928–937 in DC, *Atti e Documenti, op. cit.*

1963 'Programma elettorale della Democrazia Cristiana per la IV Legislatura', 28 March 1963, pp. 1473–1519 in DC, *Atti e Documenti, op. cit.*

1968 'Il programma della DC al servizio del paese', *Il Popolo*, pp. 4.

1972 'Gli impegni programmatici della Democrazia Cristiana', *Il Popolo*, 1 April 1972, pp. 2–3.

1976 'Il programma elettorale della DC' in 'Le promesse dei partiti', *Biblioteca della Libertà*, Anno XIII, September 1976, 61/62, pp. 85–127.

1979 'L'apello all'elettorato: la DC chiede maggiori consensi per un'Italia libera e stabile', *Il Popolo*, 12 May 1979, pp. 1–2.

1983 'Un programma per garantire lo sviluppo', *Il Popolo*, 5–6 June 1983, supplement pp. i–viii.

Partito Comunista Italiano

1946 'Il programma del PCI, *L'Unità*. 8 May 1946, p. 1.'

1948 'Il programma del Fronte Democratico Popolare'. See also 'Libertà e serenità, *L'Unità*, 20 February 1948, p. 1.

1953 'Per la pace, la libertà, il lavoro, la concordia sociale: il programma dei comunisti', *L'Unità*, 7 June 1953, p. 8 (published on the back page of the party newspaper on the day of the election). See also 'Il programma elettorale del partito comunista per un governo di pace e di riforme sociali, *L'Unità*, 17 April 1953, pp. 5–7 (Togliatti's speech to the PCI's Consiglio Nazionale, a few weeks prior to the election).

1958 'Il programma elettorale dei comunisti contro il totalitarianismo clericale e la minaccia di guerra atomica per una alternativa democratia di pace, di lavoro, di progresso', *L'Unità*.

1963 'Il programma elettorale del PCI', *L'Unità*, 3 March 1963, pp. 7–10.

1968 'E ora di cambiare, si puo cambiare: appello programma del PCI', *L'Unità*, 7 April 1968, pp. 9–10. See also 'E l'ora di cambiare', *L'Unità*, 24 March 1984, pp. 1, 12–13 (Longo's speech to the PCI's Consiglio Nazionale, setting out the party electoral programme).

1972 'Il programma dei comunisti: per un governo di svolta democratica' *L'Unità*, Special Issue, 20 March 1972.

1976 'Il programma elettorale del PCI' in 'Le promesse dei partita', *Biblioteca della Libertà*, Anno XIII, September 1976, 61/62, pp. 161–6.

1979 'Il programma dei comunisti per l'VIII Legislatura', *L'Unità*, 8 May 1979, Special Supplement, pp. 16.

1983 Not in analysis

Partito Socialista Italiano

1946 'Il programma del Partito Socialista per l'opera rinnovatrice della Costituente', *Sempre Avanti!*, 2 July 1946, p. 1. See also 'Si annuncia l'ora del socialismo', *Avanti!*, 1 May 1946, p. 1.

1948 No independent manifesto, see PCI manifesto for this year.

1953 There are several alternatives: (1) 'Gli eventi internazionali e interni convalidano la necessità per l'Italia dell'alternativa socialista', *Avanti!*, 8 April 1953, pp. 1, 4 (Nenni's speech to the Central Committee of the Socialist Party), (2) 'L'alternativa socialista garantisce al paese l'ordine democratico, il progresso sociale, la pace', *Avanti!*, pp. 1, 4–5 (Nenni's opening of the Socialists' electoral campaign at Teatro Lirico, Milan), (3) 'Il PSI agli elettori' *Avanti!*, 26 April 1953, p. 1; (4) 'L'alternativa socialista propone un programma concreto', *Avanti!*, 31 May 1953, p. 8.

1958 'Il programma elettorale del PSI, per una politica di alternativa democratica', *Avanti!*, 2 March 1958. Or 'Il PSI agli elettori', Rome, 1958.

1963 'Il programma del PSI', *Avanti!*, 23 March 1963, supplement of between pp. 12–13. Or PSI, *Elezioni politiche 28 aprile 1963. Il programma del PSI*, Rome, 1963.

1968 'Il programma socialista', *Avanti!*, 28 April 1968, pp. 6–7; 3 May 1968, p. 3; 5 May 1968, pp. 6–7; 12 May 1968, pp. 6–7; 17 May 1968, pp. 6–7; 17 May 1968, p. 3; 18 May 1968, p. 3; 19 May 1968, pp. 6–7. For an alternative version of the programme, see 'Nenni: abbiamo una politica giusta, chiediamo più forza per portarla avanti', *Avanti!*, 9 April 1968, pp. 1–3 (Nenni's speech opening the electoral campaign).

1972 'Il programma del PSI per le elezioni', *Avanti!*, Spring 1972.

1976 'Il programma elettorale del PSI', in 'Le promesse dei partiti', *Biblioteca della Libertà*, Anno XIII, September 1976, 61/62, pp. 299–314.

1979 'Il programma del PSI per le elezioni', *Avanti!*, Spring 1979.

1983 Sezione Propoganda della Direzione del PSI, *Rinnovare l'Italia, Governare Davvero, Il Programma Socialista per la Nona Legislatura*, Rome, pp. 78.

Partito Socialista Democratico Italiano

1948 L'Istituto di Studi del PSLI, 'Il nostro programma d'azione', *Critica Sociale*, 16 February 1948, pp. 83–6; 1 March 1948, pp. 101–11. See also for a short version of the programme for public consumption: 'Libertà e democrazia sono il presupposto del socialismo', *L'Umanità*, 7 March 1948, p. 1.

1953 'Programma politico del PSDI', *La Giustizia*.

1958 'Programma del Partito Socialista Democratico Italiano per le elezioni politiche del 1958 e la prossima legislatura', *La Giustizia*, No. 65, Anno 73 (new series), supplement, pp. 15.

1963 'L'azione dei socialisti democratici per il progresso generale del paese', *La Giustizia*, 12 February 1963, p. 1 (not the complete electoral programme which is untraceable, but the twelve instructions given by the party's central committee to the special commission which had the job of preparing the programme according to these policy instructions).

1968 See PSI for this year.

1972 'Il nostro programma: per il rafforzamento delle istituzioni democratiche, la crescità della società civile, e l'equilibrato sviluppo dell'economia nazionale', *L'Umanità*, 17–18 March 1972, pp. 5–11.

1976 'Il programma elettorale del PSDI' in 'Le promesse dei partiti', *Biblioteca della Libertà*, Anno XIII, September 1976, 61/62, pp. 267–98.

1979 'Programma del Partito Socialista Democratico Italiano', *L'Umanità*, 4 May 1979, pp. 3–5.

1983 PSDI, *Il PSDI agli Elettori: Indicazioni per un Programma di Governo 26–27 Giugno 1983*, Rome, 1983, pp. 30, supplement to *L'Umanità*, June 1983, No. 127.

Partito Liberale Italiano

1946 'La ricostruzione dello stato nel programme dell'Unione Democratica', *L'Opinione*, 11 April 1946, p. 1

1948 'Vota Blocco nazionale: i programmi concreti'

1953 'Villabruna apre a Torino la campagna elettorale', *Rinovamento Liberale*, Anno VI, No. 5 (speech by general secretary of the party at the Teatro Carignano, opening the electoral campaign).

1958 'Il Partito Liberale di fronte agli elettori: lineamenti di un programma', *Rinovamento Liberale*, Anno XI, No. 7, 15 April 1958, pp. 1, 3. See also PLI, *Programme Elettorale 1958*, Rome, 1958.

1963 Valerio Zanoni, 'Democrazia industriale', *Rinovamento Liberale*, Spring 1973.

1968 'Azione e programme liberale'.

1972 'Il PLI agli elettori'.

1976 'Il programma elettorale del PLI', in 'Le promesse dei partiti', *Biblioteca della Libertà*, Anno XIII, September 1976, 61/62, pp. 197–226.

1979 Partito Liberale Italiano, *Manifesto e Programma Elettorale del PLI*, Rome, 1983, cyclostated.

Partito Repubblicano Italiano

1946 'Il discorso dell'On. Giovanni Conti', *La Voce Repubblicana*, 7 May 1946, p. 1 (opening speech of electoral campaign at Liceo Visconti, Piazza Collegio Romano, Rome).

1948 Il Consiglio Nazionale del PRI, 'Il programma del Partito Repubblicano per le elezioni del diciotto aprile'.

1953 'L'ampio discorso di Reale a Roma', *La Voce Repubblicana*, 21 April 1953, pp. 1, 3 (opening speech of the electoral campaign).

1958 'Per uno stato moderno e democratico, una politica per la terza legislatura – il programma del PRI' *La Voce Repubblicana*, 9 May 1958, p. 3

1963 'Programma elettorale del PRI', *La Voce repubblicana*, 10 March 1963, pp. 16, special supplement.

1968 'La conferenza stampa di La Malfa a Tribuna Elettorale', *La Voce Repubblicana*, 9 May 1968, pp. 1, 2.

1972 'Il documento programmatico approvato dal Consiglio nazionale repubblicano', *la Voce Repubblicana*, 6 April 1972, pp. 1, 3.

1976 'Il programma elettorale del PRI' in 'Le promesse dei partiti', *Biblioteca della Libertà*, Anno XIII, September 1976, 61/62, pp. 249–65.
1979 'I Repubblicani verso gli anni ottanta. Il programma', *La Voce Repubblicana*, 20 May 1979, pp. 1, 2
1983 Direzione Nazionale del Partito Repubblicano, *30 Punti per una Legislatura: il Programma Repubblicano*, Piazza dei Capretari, Rome, 1983, pp. 95.

Movimento Sociale Italiano

1948 'Noi e gli altri', *La Rivolta Ideale*, 29 November 1948, p. 3 (the nearest approximation to an electoral programme, setting out the party's electoral aims).
1953 Movimento Sociale Italiano, *Programma per le Elezioni Politiche 1953*, Rome pp. 20.
1958 Movimento Sociale Italiano, *Lineamenti del Programma Elettorale del MSI*, Rome, 1958, p. 23.
1963 'La battaglia nazionale contro il centro-sinistra illustrata da Michelini alla 'tribuna Elettorale', *Il Secola d'italia*, 26 February 1963, pp. 1, 8.
1968 'Manifesto del Movimento Sociale', *Il Secolo d'Italia*, 7 May 1968, p. 3. See also 'Michelini una forza valida per una moderna politica nazionale e sociale', *Il Secolo d'Italia*, 11 May 1968, p. 1.
1972 'Impegni programmatici del MSI', in 'Le promesse dei partiti', *Biblioteca della Libertà*, Anno XIII, September 1976, 61/62, pp. 149–59.
1976 'Elezioni 1979: il programma del MSI–DN', *Il Secolo d'Italia*, 10 May 1979, pp. 5–7.
1983 Movimento Sociale Italiano–Destra Nazionale, *Il Messaggio degli Anni '80*, May 1983, Rome, pp. 45.

JAPAN

The source in every case is the *Asahi Shimbun*'s summary tables on each party's electoral pledges, which is normally published two weeks before election day. More precisely, they are:

'Parties pledge', *Asahi Shimbun*, 25.10.1960
'Parties demand', *Ibid.*, 24.10.1963
'Five parties pledge', *Ibid.*, 28.12.1967
'Five parties pledge', *Ibid.*, 7.12.1969
'Our parties' pledge', *Ibid.*, 19.11.1972
'Our parties' pledge', *Ibid.*, 15.11.1976
'Our parties' pledge', *Ibid.*, 18.8.1979
'Our parties' pledge', *Ibid.*, 3.6.1980

LUXEMBOURG
Chrëstlech Sozial Vollekspartei

1945 Das Programm der Christlich-Sozialen
      Volkspartei (Rechtspartei)   LW 13.10.1945

1948	Wahlprogramm der Christlich-Sozialen Volkspartei	LW 03.06.1948
1951	Wahlmanifest der Christlich-Sozialen Volkspartei	LW 26.05.1951
1954	Interview mit Staatsminister Bech and certain other articles	LW 7–29.5.1951
1959	Wahlmanifest der Christlich-Sozialen Volkspartei (CSV)	LW 22.1.1959
1964	Aktionsprogramm der Christlich-Sozialen Volkspartei	LW 2.6.1964
1968	Aus der CSV-Wahlprogramm (extracts)	LW 3–6.12.1968
1974	Wahlmanifest der Christlich-Sozialen Volkspartei 1974–1979	Original
1979	'Mat der CSV an d'80er Joren'	Original

Lëtzeburger Sozialistech Arbechter Partei

1945	Das Programm der Arbeiterpartei	TB 18.10.1945
1948	Various articles	TB 2–5.2.1948
1951	Wahlnummer	TB 30.5.1951
1954	'Für die Sozialistische Sicherheit!.'	TB 18.5.1954
1959	Wahlprogramm der Sozialistische Arbeiterpartei	TB
1964	Geh mit der Zeit, Geh mit den Sozialisten	TB
1968	'Fur ein modernes Luxembourg'	TB
1974	'Fortschritt und Verantwortung'	Original
1979	LSAP 1979 Programm	Original

Demokratesch Partei (Groupement Démocratique 1951–9)

1951	'Mir vum Groupement warden mat ro'heger Zo'versicht den Entsched vun de Wiéler of!'. (Speech by L. Dury on Radio Luxembourg)	LJ 2.6.1951
1954	'Ein letztes, ernstes Wort', (editorial)	LJ 29.5.1954
1959	Wahlnummer	LJ 21.1.1959
1964	Wahlprogramm der Demokratischen Partei	LJ 21–27.5.1964
1968	'Et huet ogelaut'!	Original
1974	DP Programmpunkte und Optionen	Original
1979	DP Wahlprogramm 79	Original

Kommunistesch Partei vu Lëtzeburg

1945	Document missing	
1948	'Das Programm des schaffenden Luxemburgs'	Z 4.6.1948
1951	'Fir e freit a glécklecht Lëtzeburg'! (Radio speech by Urbany)	Z 2.561954

1954	Wahlnummer	Z 6.5.1954
1959	Wahlnummer	Z No date
1964	'Richteg lenks stömmen'! (Radio speech	
	by Urbany)	Z 6.6.1964
1968	Sondernummer	Z No date
1974	Grundsatzprogramm, 1973	Original
1979	'Sechs Fragen zur Wirtschaftskris'	Z 2.6.1979

KEY

LW = *Luxemburger Wort*
TB = *Tageblatt*
LJ = *Lëtzburger Journal*
Z = *Zeitung vum Lëtzburger Vollek*

NETHERLANDS

ARP

1946	ARP	Program van actie voor de verkiezingen van 1946
1948	ARP	Program van actie voor de verkiezingen van 1948
1952	ARP	Program van actie voor de verkiezingen van 1952
1956	ARP	Program van actie 1956
1959	ARP	Program van actie 1959
1963	ARP	Program van actie 1963
1967	ARP	Program van actie k1967–1971
1971	ARP	Program van actie 1971–1975; see also joint manifesto CHU/KVP/ARP for this year, Gemeenschappelijk urgentieprogram 1971–1975
1972		Joint manifesto ARP/CHU/KVP for this year, Gemeenschappelijk manifest
1977	CDA	Verkiezingsprogramma 1977–1981
1981	CDA	Verkiezingsprogramma 1981–1985

CHU

1946	CHU	Urgentieprogramma 1945
1948	CHU	Urgentieprogramma 1946
1952		No document found
1956	CHU	Verkiezingsmanifest 1956
1959	CHU	Verkiezingsmanifest 1959
1963	CHU	Verkiezingsmanifest 1963
1967	CHU	Verkiezingsmanifest 1967
1971	CHU	Politiek werkprogram; see also joint manifesto CHU/KVP/ARP for this year, Gemeenschappelijk urgentieprogram 1971–1975
1972		Joint manifesto ARP/CHU/KVP for this year, Gemeenschappelijk manifest
1977	CDA	Verkiezingsprogram 1977–1981
1981	CDA	Verkiezingsprogramma 1981–1985

KVP

1946	KVP	Urgentieprogram
1948	KVP	Verkiezingsmanifest 1948
1952	KVP	Werkprogram (Verkiezingsprogramma 1952)
1956	KVP	Werkprogram (Verkiezingsprogramma 1956)
1959	KVP	Verkiezingsmanifest 1959
1963	KVP	Verkiezingsmanifest 1963
1967	KVP	Werkprogram 1967–1971
1971	KVP	Kernprogramma; see also joint manifesto CHU/KVP/ARP for this year, Gemeenschappelijk urgentieprogram 1971–75
1972		Joint manifesto ARP/CHU/KVP Gemeenschappelijk manifest
1977	CDA	Verkiezingsprogramm 1977–1981
1981	CDA	Verkiezingsprogramma 1981–1985

PPR

1971	PPR	Verkiezingsprogramma 1971; see also joint PvDA/D'66/PPR manifesto for this year, Hoofdlijnen van een regeringsprogram 1971–1975
1972		Joint PvDA/D'66/PPR manifesto for this year, Regeerakkoord van de progressieve drie
1977	PPR	Verkiezingsprogram 1977/81

PvdA

1946	PvdA	Urgentieprogram; Beknopt program
1948	PvdA	Urgentieprogram; Verkiezingsprogramma 1948
1952	PvdA	Verkiezingsprogramma 1952
1956	PvdA	Verkiezingsprogramma 1956
1959	PvdA	Verkiezingsprogramma 1959
1963	PvdA	Verkiezingsmanifest 1963
1967	PvdA	Verkiezingsprogram 1967
1971	PvdA	Verkiezingsprogramma 1971–1975; see also PvdA/D'66/PPR for this year, Hoofdlijnen van een regeringsprogram 1971–1975
1972		Joint manifesto PvdA/D'66/PPR for this year, Regeerakkoord van de progressive drie
1977	PvdA	Verkiezingsprogramma 1977
1981	PvdA	Verkiezingsprogramma 1981

VVD

1948	VVD	Urgentieprogramma
1952	VVD	Verkiezingsprogram 1952
1956	VVD	Verkiezingsmanifest 1956; Urgentieprogram
1963	VVD	Verkiezingsmanifest 1963; Urgentieprogram
1971	VVD	Verkiezingsprogramma 1971–1975
1972	VVD	Urgentieprogramma

1977   VVD   Verkiezingsprogramma 1977
1981   VVD   Verkiezingsprogramma 1981

D'66

1967   D'66   Verkiezingsprogramma Democraten '66
1971   D'66   Program; see also joint manifesto PvdA/D'66/PPR for this year, Hoofdlijnen van een regeringsprogram 1971–1975
1972   Joint PvdA/D'66/PPR joint manifesto for this year, Regeerakkoord van de progressieve drie
1977   D'66   Verkiezingsprogram 1977–1981
1981   D'66   Verkiezingsprogramma Democraten '66 1981–1985

DS'70

1971   DS'70   Verkiezingsprogram 1971
1972   DS'70   Verkiezingsprogram 1972
1977   DS'70   Verkiezingsprogram 1977

NEW ZEALAND

National Party

1946   Policy: General Election 1946   Original
1949   Policy: General Election 1949   Original
1951   'Capacity House Cheers Prime Minister'   NZH 14.8.1951
1954   A Record of Progress; General Election Policy   Original
1957   1957 General Election Policy   Original
1960   1960 General Election Policy   Original
1963   1963 General Election Policy   Original
1966   1966 General Election Policy   Original
1969   1969 General Election Policy   Original
1972   1972 General Election Policy   Original
1975   National Party Manifesto   Original
1978   1978 General Election Policy: 'We're Keeping Our Word'   Original
1981   This is Your Future: Politics for the Decade of the 80s   Original

Labour Party

1946   'Labour Party Policy'   NZH 30.10.1946
1949   'Labour Party's Election Manifesto'   NZH 2.11.1949
1951   'Labour Party Makes Promises'   NZH 18.8.1951
1954   'Policy of the Labour Party'   PRESS 20.12.1954
1957   N.Z. Labour Party Manifesto 1957   Original
1960   'Labour Party Stakes its Claim'.   NZH 1.11.60

1963	N.Z. Labour Party 1963 General Election Manifesto	Original
1966	1966 Election Manifesto	Original
1969	Labour's Election Policy 1969	Original
1972	Labour Party Manifesto 1972	Original
1975	The Labour Party Manifesto 1975	Original
1978	To Rebuild the Nation	Original
1981	'Getting New Zealand Working Again.'	Original

Social Credit League

1954'	'Social Credit's Four Policy Planks'	NZH 28.12.1954
1957	'Social Credit 'Keeping out of Bidding Contest''	NZH 8.11.1957
1960	'Tax Cuts, Help in Housing is Aim of Social Credit'	NZH 3.11.1960
1963	'Social Credit Manifesto'	NZH 7.11.1963
1966	'No Taxes on First £520'	NZH 3.11.1966
1969	'Social Credit offers Private School Aid'	NZH 6.11.1969
1972	General Policy	Original
1975	'The New Dimension'	Original
1978	'Bold New Policies'	Original
1981	'Social Credit Manifesto 1981'	Original

KEY: **NZH** = *New Zealand Herald*, Auckland.
PRESS = *The Press*, Christchurch.

SRI LANKA

United National Party

1947	Manifesto	Original
1952	Manifesto	Weerawardana 1952
1956	Manifesto	Weerawardana 1956
1960	Manifesto	CDN
1965	Manifesto	CDN
1970	Manifesto	CDN
1977	Manifesto	CDN

Sri Lanka Freedom Party

1952	Manifesto	Weerawardana 1952
1956	Manifesto	Weerawardana 1956
1960	Manifesto	CDN
1965	Manifesto	CDN
1970	Manifesto	CDN
1977	Manifesto	CDN

KEY:

Weerawardana 1952 = I.D.S. Weerwardana, 'The General Elections in Ceylon 1952', special supplement, *Ceylon Historical Journal*, II, 1–2 (1952).
Weerawardana 1956 = I.D.S. Weerawardana, *Ceylon General Election 1956*, (Colombo, 1960).

CDN = Ceylon Daily News, dates not available.

SWEDEN

Moderate Samlingspartiet (Conservatives)

1944 Election Manifesto, 'Hogerns Handlingsprogram' (Action Programme of the Right), pp. 4. P
1946 Election Manifesto, 'Valupprop – Till Sveriges Folk' (Election Appeal to the Swedish People). L
1948 Election Manifesto, 'Hogern sager i fran' (The Right Says No). P
1950 No document found
1952 Leaflets 'Hogern behovs nu' (The Right is Needed Now); and 'Det lonar sig' (It Pays). L
1954 'Vardagsdemokrati' (Everyday Democracy). L
1956 P
1958 Youth leaflet, 'Sa har vill Jarl Hjalmerson Lagga upp alspalet' (This is How Jarl Hjalmarson wants to Play the Game), pp. 2. P
 Leaflet, 'Detta ar allvarligt' (This is Serious). L
 Leaflet, 'Hogerpartiert att lita pa' (Trust the Right). L
 Leaflet, 'Allt jamkar sa fort numera' (Everything Goes So Quickly These Days). L
1960 Leaflet, 'Hogeralternativet – ett alternativ alltrantrapa' (The Right Alternative – an Alternative to Consider'). P.
 Leaflet, 'OMS? Nej!' (VAT? No!). P
 Leaflet, 'Att vilja sta pa egna ben' (To Want to Stand on One's Own Legs). P
1962 Magazine, 'Att idag ta var pa morgondagens mojligheter' (To Take Care of Tomorrow's Opportunities Today). L
1964 Leaflet, 'Konsten att fanga en miljon' (The Way to Make a Million). P
1966 No document found. L
1968 Magazine, 'Dags for sidbyte?' (Time to Change Sides?). P
1970 Election Manifesto, 'Samvarkan, rattvisa, ansvar' (Cooperation, Justice, Responsibility). P
1973 Election Manifesto. P
1976 Election Manifesto. P
1979 Election Manifesto, 'Framtid i Frihet' (Future in Freedom). P
1982 Election Manifesto, 'Framtid i Frihet' (Future in Freedom). P

Folkpartiet (Liberals)

1944 Election Manifesto. P
1946 Election Manifesto. L

1948   Election Manifesto, published in the press. P
1950   Election Manifesto, advertisement published in press. L
1952   Election Manifesto, advertisement published in press. P
1954   Election Manifesto, published in the press. L
1956   Election Manifesto, published in the press. P
1958   Election Manifesto, published in the press. P
1958   Election Manifesto, published in the press and as a duplicated news release. L
1960   Election Manifesto, 'Mojlighete mas artionde' (Decade of Opportunity) published in the press. P
1962   'For framtiden' (For the Future) leaflet. L
1964   Magazine for young voters, 'Liberal utmaning' (Liberal Challenge) no other document found. P
1966   Election Manifesto, duplicated press release. L
1968   'Din rost pa folkpartiet ger resultat' (Your Vote for the Liberal Party Gives Results). P
1970   E!ection Manifesto, duplicated press release. L, P
1973   Election Manifesto, duplicated press release. L, P
1976   Election Manifesto, 'Sociala Reformer utan Socialism' (Social Reforms without Socialism') published, L, P
1979   Election Manifesto, 'Ansvar och samforstand' (Responsibility and Mutual Understanding). L, P
1982   Election Manifesto, 'For frihet och rattvisa' (For Freedom and Justice). L, P

Bondeforbundet/Centerpartiet (Agrarian/Centre)

1944   No document found. P
1946   Election Manifesto, printed. L
1948   Election Manifesto, printed. P
1950   Election Manifesto, printed. L
1952   Election Manifesto, published in the press. P
1954   Election Manifesto, printed. L
1956   Election Manifesto, printed. P
1958   Election Manifesto, printed. P
1958   Election Manifesto, published in the press. L
1960   Election Manifesto, printed. L
1962   Election Manifesto, printed. L
1964   No document found. P
1966   Election Manifesto, printed. L
1968   Election Manifesto, 'Framtidspolitik i 40 punkter' (Politics for the Future in 40 Points). P
1970   Election Manifesto, 'Malet ar jamlikhet och decentralisering' (The Goal is Equality and Decentralization). L, P
1973   Election Manifesto, printed. L, P.
1976   Election Manifesto, printed. L, P
1979   Election Manifesto, printed. L, P
1982   Election Manifesto, printed. L, P

Socialdemokratiska Arbetarspartiet (Labour)

1944   Election Manifesto. P
1946   Election Manifesto, published in the press. L
1948   Election Manifesto, duplicated press release. P
1950   Election Manifesto, published in the press. L
1952   Election Manifesto, published in the press. P
1954   Election Manifesto, published in the press. L
1956   Election Manifesto, 'Fortsatt ekonomisk utjamning' (Continued Progress Towards Economic Equality), published in the press. P
1958   First of May Manifesto and Declaration. P
1958   Election newspaper. L
1960   First of May Manifesto and Declaration. P
1960   Election newspaper. P
1962   Election magazine, 'Battre och battre steg for steg', (Better and Better Step by Step). L
1962   First of May Manifesto and Declaration. L
1964   Election magazine, 'Ett handlingskraftigft samhalle', (A Society with the Strength to Act). P
1966   First of May Manifesto and Declaration. L
1968   Election Manifesto, press release 'Arbete, trygghet, utveckling', (Work, Safety, Development). P
1970   Election Manifesto, L, P
1976   Election Manifesto, published for the press. L, P
1979   Election Manifesto, published for the press. L, P
1982   Election Manifesto, 'Fred och arbete' (Peace and Work) L, P

Sveriges Kommunistiska Parti/Vänsterpartiet Kommunisterna (Communist)

1944   Election leaflet, 'Vad kommunisterna inte fick saga i radio', (What the Communists were not allowed to say on the radio). P
1946   Election Manifesto, published in the Communist daily newspaper. L
1948   Election Manifesto, published in the Communist daily newspaper. P
1950   Election Manifesto, 'For fred och hogre levnadsstandard' (For Peace and a Higher Standard of Living), published in the Communist daily newspaper. L
1952   Election Manifesto, published in the Communist daily newspaper. P
1954   Election Manifesto, published in the Communist daily newspaper. L
1956   Election Manifesto, 'Fram for arbetarseger i valet' (Victory for the Workers in the Election), published in the Communist daily newspaper. P
1958   Election Manifesto, 'For en fradsframjande och demokratisk politik' (For a Policy Promoting Peace and Democracy), published in the Communist daily newspaper. L
1958   Leaflet, 'Vad galler nyvalet' (What is the Interim Election About?). P
1958   Election newspaper. L
1960   Election Manifesto, published in the Communist daily newspaper. P
1962   Election Manifesto adopted by the Central Commitee, 'Vi har rad att ha det

battre' (We Can Afford Better), published in the Communist daily news-paper. L

1964   Article by the party leader on polling day, 'Socialistisk fornyelse' (Socialist Renewal), adopted by the Central Committee. P

1966   Election Manifesto adopted at a party conference, published in the Com-munist daily newspaper. L

1968   Election Manifesto adopted at a national party conference with the youth movement, 'For vänsterseger 1968' (Victory for the Left in 1968), published in the Communist daily newspaper. P

1970   Election Manifesto and statement on salaries, prices and taxation adopted by the party executive, L, P

1973   Election Manifesto adopted by the party executive, 'Med Vpk for vänster-seger' (With the Communists for a Victory for the Left), published in the Communist daily newspaper. L, P

1976   Election Manifesto, 'Arbetarpolitik och socialism for en battre framtid' (Workers' Politics and Socialism for a Better Future), published in the Communist daily newspaper.

1979   Election Manifesto adopted by the party executive, 'Radikal arbetarpolitik. vagen till socialism' (Radical Working-Class Politics. The Road to Social-ism). L, P.

1982   Election Manifesto adopted by the party executive, 'Fred, arbete, social rattvisa' (Peace, Work and Social Justice). P, L

KEY:

P = Parliamentary election
L = Local election

N.B.   Some election manifestos only have the title 'election manifesto'; *valmanifest.*

UNITED KINGDOM

The Conservative Party

1945   Conservative Manifesto 1945, (Churchill's declaration of policy to the electorate), pp. 113–23.

1950   Conservative Manifesto, 'This is the Road: the Conservative and Unionist Party's Policy', pp. 139–52.

1951   The Manifesto of the Conservative and Unionist Party, signed by Churchill, pp. 167–73.

1955   'United for Peace and Progress', The Conservative and Unionist Party's Policy, pp. 182–202; (starts with a 2-page personal statement by the then P.M., Anthony Eden).

1959   'The Next Five Years', The Conservative and Unionist Party's Policy, pp. 214–22.

1964   'Prosperity with a Purpose', Conservative and Unionist Party's Policy.

1966   'Action not Words: New Conservative Programme'.

1970 'A Better Tomorrow', with an introduction signed by Heath.
1950 'Firm Action for a Fair Britain' (Feb.)
1974 'Putting Britian First' (Oct.)
1979 The Conservative Manifesto 1979, *The Times Guide to the House of Commons*, May 1979.
1983 'The Challenge of Our Time', *The Times Guide to the House of Commons*, June 1983.

The Labour Party

1945 The Labour Manifesto, 'Let Us Face the Future: A Declaration of Labour Policy for the Consideration of the Nation'.
1950 The Labour Manifesto, 'Let Us Win Through Together: A Declaration of Labour Policy for the Consideration of the Nation'.
1951 The Labour Party Election Manifesto
1955 'Forward with Labour: Labour's Policy for the Consideration of the Nation'
1959 'Britain Belongs to You', The Labour Party Policy for the Consideration of the Nation
1964 'Let's Go With Labour for the New Britain'
1966 'Time for Decision'
1970 'Now Britain's Strong – Let's Make it Great to Live In'
1974 'Let us Work Together – Labour's Way Out of the Crisis' (Feb.)
1974 'Britain Will Win With Labour', with a forward by Wilson
1979 'The Labour Way is the Better Way', *The Times Guide to the House of Commons*, May 1979
1983 'The New Hope for Britain', *The Times Guide to the House of Commons*, June 1983

The Liberal Party

1945 Liberal Manifesto, '20-Point Manifesto of the Liberal Party'
1950 Liberal Manifesto, 'No Easy Way: Britain's Problems and the Liberal Answers'
1951 Liberal Manifesto, 'The Nation's Task'.
1955 'Crisis Unresolved'
1959 'People Count'
1964 'Think for Yourself – Vote Liberal'
1966 'For all the People: The Liberal Plan of 1966'
1970 'What a Life!'
1974 'Change the Face of Britain', introduction by Thorpe.
1974 'Why Britain Needs Liberal Government', introduction by Thorpe.
1979 'The Real Fight is for Britain', *The Times Guide to the House of Commons*, May 1979.
1983 'Working Together for Britain', Liberal/SPD Alliance Manifesto, introduction by Jenkins and Steel. Original. All manifestos up to 1974 taken from FWS Craig, *British General Election Manifestos 1900–1974*, London, Macmillan, 1974

UNITED STATES

Democratic Party

1948 Democratic Party Platform 1948
1952 Democratic Party Platform 1952
1956 Democratic Party Platform 1956
1960 Democratic Party Platform 1960
1964 Democratic Party Platform 1964
1968 Democratic Party Platform 1968
1972 Democratic Party Platform 1972. CQ Weekly Report Vol. XXX No 29, 15 July 1972
1976 Democratic Party Platform 1976. CQ Almanac Vol. XXXII 1976.
1980 Democratic Party Platform 1980. CQ Almanac 91-B-121B, 1980.

Republican Party

1948 Republican Party Platform 1948
1952 Republican Party Platform 1952
1956 Republican Party Platform 1956
1960 Republican Party Platform 1960
1964 Republican Party Platform 1964
1968 Republican Party Platform 1968
1972 Republican Party Platform 1972. CQ Weekly Report Vol. XXX, No. 35, 26 August 1972
1976 Republican Party Platform 1976. CQ Almanac Vol. XXXII, 1976.
1980 Republican Party Platform 1980. CQ Almanac 58B-84B, 1980

KEY:

CQ = Congressional Quarterly. All platforms up to 1968 taken from K. N. Porter and D. B. Johnson (eds.) *National Party Platforms 1840–1968*, Urbana, Ill., University of Illinois Press, 1970

APPENDIX B

BASIC RESEARCH DESIGN AND CODING FRAME

———————— ∾ ————————

Although we discuss methods of data collection and coding in broad outline in Chapter 2 (Section 5), we go into less detail there than for factor analysis (Chapter 2, Section 8). This is because collecting and coding decisions, though of fundamental importance, are even more technical; and closely tied to details of the overall coding frame. We therefore present our full description and justification here, in immediate juxtoposition to the frame itself, so that cross-reference is immediate and easy.

The Appendix therefore falls into three sections: a general account and justification of the decisions taken on quantification and classification of the election programmes – which refers also to certain aspects of the succeeding statistical analyses where data related decisions affected these (B1); a short account of operational procedures (B2); and the coding frame itself (B3). Some supplementary technical analyses will be reported in the associated microfiche publication.

B1 BASIC RESEARCH DESIGN

The research design for this book is the product of deliberation and experimentation over five years by a group of scholars. Although the basic outlines were fixed at the beginning of the project, the details are the product of a lengthy inductive process, and the result of technical problems which could not be identified ahead of time but had to be resolved as they occurred. Whilst this is true of most research projects in the social sciences, it was necessarily true of this one because of the need to achieve a very high degree of comparability in data collection and analysis over very different and often contrasting countries. The only two basic points to be fixed *ab initio* were that a specific form of content analysis would be used, and that relatively simple factor analysis would be undertaken as a data-reduction and reporting device. These two decisions stem from previous research experience with election programmes (Robertson 1976; Budge and Farlie, 1977). The purpose of this section is both to describe the details of the research design, and to explain why certain decisions were taken rather than others to solve technical problems.

456

(i) Content analysis

Content analysis has a long history in the social sciences, and our use is not particularly novel. The only thing requiring comment is our definition of the 'counting unit', the symbols used to constitute an observation. Particularly since the development of computer-aided content analysis, there has been a tendency to define specific words or precise phrases as the symbols to be searched for and counted in written material. Thus we might have looked for the number of occurrences of the word 'socialism' as an indicator of left wing economic policy, or the frequency of mention of the phrase 'public order' to indicate traditional conservative concerns with social strain. There are two reasons for not doing so. The first is that a cross-national study cannot rely on the identity of meaning of such simple lexical units, even given translation. Even between British and American English, the word 'socialism' varies intensely in connotation, whilst the French idea of 'ordre publique' has greatly different undertones from the common law conception of 'public order'.

Equally important, single words or predetermined phrases could not catch what we want, which is to measure the relative stress on certain ideas, policies, issues, and concerns. It is these, however expressed, that we need to catch. Consequently we adopted a natural unit, the sentence, as the counting unit. This involves not an automatic count, but a coding procedure. Each sentence is examined, and the coder then has to decide which of the long list of 54 concept-categories, *if any*, it expresses. This approach involves more risk of error than counting specified words, but allows for a much richer description of the content. Sentences that do not fit into one of the categories are treated as uncodeable. This latter count is reported in the analyses of different countries, and can often be indicative of important limitations in our analysis. Thus knowing that the manifestos of the plethora of 'new' parties in Denmark after 1973 sometimes had as much as 30 per cent of their sentences uncoded, whilst the traditional parties fit the comparative coding scheme well, is itself a useful fact. It helps demonstrate how little these parties, at least in their initial phases, fitted into the long-term structure of Danish party competition.

The coding scheme is given in detail below. It was developed from an earlier and much shorter scheme designed for the analysis of British party manifestos and later applied to U.S. platforms (Robertson 1976). Lengthy meetings of the experts who were to research the individual countries sought on this basis to create a list of categories that expressed (1) as closely as possible the most important issues and concerns in comparative politics that were common to at least several countries, and (2) in a way which had an internationally comparable meaning. Inside these relatively broad categories, special sub-categories could be used to catch more precise shades of meaning peculiar to a particular political system. The scope of the coding frame had to be very wide to cover issues adequately in so many countries, and hence many never were used fully in one country or another. Even where categories attract zero scores they are scores however – it is a fact that, let us say, anti-clericalism is never an issue in British politics, but can be important in countries as different as Belgium and Israel.

These categories were grouped into seven 'domains', common sets of categories covering broad areas of political debate; considerable attention is given to analysis within each domain. It is more likely that meaningful correlations will occur, and an important attitude structure will thus be revealed, amongst, say eight or ten aspects of foreign policy or as many as 14 different asepcts of economic policy, than across the whole 54 content – categories of international and domestic politics. Later the results of analyses within domains can be used in a second stage analysis to get such a macro view, but to start that way would be to lose too much information. We return to this point later.

These domains, the precise content of which are shown below, are deliberate *a priori* theoretical groupings of common issues. They contain varying numbers of primary categories. The number of such categories however is not a measure of their relative importance, but rather of the inherent complexity of the area of policy conflict they cover.

It can be argued that both the 54 initial categories, and the 7 domains, are often too detailed, and should have been collapsed together. In later work this may be done. One subsequent study, of Ireland, has indeed collapsed many of the more precise variables into broader ones, and derived a highly satisfactory description of Irish politics using far fewer than 54 categories, completely ignoring the domain analysis. However whilst it is always possible to reduce complexity by aggregating variables, one cannot make up for an initially over-aggregated coding scheme later, and our primary responsibility at this stage was to produce, with enormous labour, a general purpose data set, as rich and refined as possible, and with as precisely comparable a meaning for each variable in all countries as could be attained. This is what now follows below.

B2 OPERATIONAL PROCEDURES

As explained, the many election manifestos, party platforms, etc. were coded into a standard coding frame in as uniform a way as possible. The coding frame itself was elaborated at a face-to-face 'bargaining session' between the various national specialists early in the project. From the very beginning therefore everyone was clear about what the various themes and categories were intended to cover. The inevitable difficulties and problems associated with individual coding decisions were fully discussed by the national specialists at regular intervals and we are satisfied that the greatest possible standardization was achieved. A brief summary of procedures, problems and results is given in each country chapter.

In seven cases the documents, although collected by the national researcher, were sent to the University of Essex for coding and analysis. One of the editors (Hearl) personally supervised these operations employing a team of four assistants who referred all doubtful decisions to him. Over time, of course, these assistants became steadily more expert at the coding task. In the majority of cases, checks of one kind or another were performed, usually by the national researcher, on the accuracy and consistency of the coding; details of these checks are to be found in the individual chapters. In one case, Great Britain, Mik Laver arranged for the coding to be carried out by a very large team of students at Liverpool University in such a way as to allow extensive statistical checks on inter-coder reliability to be made.

The mutually agreed coding rules allowed for individual national circumstances by permitting the use of 'sub-categories'; in other words, each national researcher had full freedom to break down any of the standard categories in such a way as to be able to capture concerns particular to his/her country context subject only to the condition that this be done in such a way as to permit the re-aggregation of these sub-categories back to the standard ones for the purposes of comparative analysis. Some country contributors made extensive use of this facility while others used it either only to a limited extent or not at all. Again, details of this, where relevant, are to be found in the individual country chapters.

The standard categories were grouped into the seven 'themes' or 'domains' mentioned above each relating to a broad area of policy. The category numbers, which every contributor stuck to, reflect this for ease of reference. Thus categories in the External Relations domain are numbered in the 100 series, those in the Economics domain in the 400s and so on. The full coding frame, consisting of the standard categories grouped by domain, together with category 'specifications' is given below. It should be noted that the specifications are intended to be descriptive and illustrative of the types of issue covered by each category rather than exhaustive definitions.

B3 FULL STANDARD CODING FRAME

Domain 1 *External Relations*

101 *Foreign Special Relationships: Positive*

Favourable mentions of other countries where these are either specially dependent on or are specially involved with the relevant country. For example, former colonies; in the West German case, East Germany; in the Swedish case, the rest of Scandinavia; the need for cooperation with and aid to such countries; their importance to the economy and defence programmes of the relevant country.

102 *Foreign Special Relationships: Negative*

As 101, but negative.

103 *Decolonization*

Favourable mentions of decolonization, need for relevant country to leave colonies; greater self government, and independence; need to train natives for this; need to give special aid to make up for colonial past. This also includes negative references to Soviet Imperialism in Eastern Europe, especially in the United States.

104 *Military: Positive*

Need for strong military presence overseas, for re-armament and self-defence, need to keep to military treaty obligations, need to secure adequate manpower in military.

105 *Military: Negative*

As 104, but negative.

106 *Peace*

Declaration of belief in Peace and peaceful means of solving crises; need for international disarmament and desirability of relevant country joining in negotiations with hostile countries.

107 *Internationalism: Positive*

Support for UN, need for international cooperation, need for aid to developing countries, need for world planning of resources, need for international courts, support for any international aim or world state.

108 *European Community: Positive*

Favourable mentions of European Community in general; desirability of relevant country joining (or remaining a Member); desirability of expanding it and/or of increasing its competences; favourable mentions of Direct Election; pro-European Unity in general.

109 *Internationalism: Negative*

As 107, but negative

110 *Internationalism Negative EEC and Europe*

As 108, but negative.

Domain 2 *Freedom and Democracy*

201 *Freedom and Domestic Human Rights*

Favourable mentions of importance of personal freedom, civil rights; freedom of choice in education; freedom from bureaucratic control, freedom of speech; freedom from coercion in industrial and political sphere; individualism.

202 *Democracy*

Favourable mention of democracy as method or goal in national and other organizations; support for worker participation; for involvement of all citizens in decision making, as well as generalised support for symbols of democracy.

203 *Constitutionalism: Positive*

Support for specified aspects of a formal constitution, use of constitutionalism as an argument for policy as well as generalized approval for 'constitutional' way of doing things.

204 *Constitutionalism: Negative*

As 203, but negative.

Domain 3 *Government*

301 *Decentralization: Positive*

Support for devolution, regional administration of politics or economy, support for keeping up local and regional customs and symbols, deference to local expertise in planning, etc.

302 *Decentralization: Negative*

As 301, but negative.

303 *Government Efficiency*

Need for efficiency in government (e.g. merit system in civil service), economy in government, cutting down civil service; improving governmental procedures; general appeal to make process of government and administration cheaper and more effective.

304 *Government Corruption*

Need to eliminate corruption in government, and associated abuse, e.g. regulation of campaign expenses; need to check pandering to selfish interests.

305 *Government Effectiveness and Authority*

This includes references to government stability, especially in Italy.

Domain 4 *Economy*

401 *Enterprise*

Favourable mention of private property rights; personal enterprise and initiative; need for the economy of unhampered individual enterprises; favourable mention of free enterprise capitalism; superiority of individual enterprise over state, and over state buying or management systems.

402 *Incentives*

Need for financial and other incentives and for opportunities for the young, etc; encouragement to small businesses and one-man shops; need for wage and tax policies designed to induce enterprise; Home Ownership.

403 *Regulation of Capitalism*

Need for regulations designed to make private enterprise work better; actions against monopolies and trusts and in defence of consumer and small businessmen; anti-profiteering

404 *Economic Planning*

Favourable mention of central planning of consultative or indicative nature; need for this and for government department to create national plan; need to plan imports and exports.

405 *Corporatism* (Applicable to the Netherlands and Canada only)

Favourable mentions of the need for the involvement of employers and Trades Union organizations in overall economic planning and direction through the medium of 'tri-partite' bodies such as the SER in the Netherlands.

406 *Protectionism: Positive*

Favourable mention of extension or maintenance of tariffs, to protect internal markets; or other domestic economic protectionism.

407 *Protectionism: Negative*

As 406, but negative.

408 *Economic Goals*

General statements of intent to pursue any economic goals that are policy non-specific.

409 *Keynesian Demand Management*

Adjusting government expenditure to prevailing levels of employment and inflation.

410 *Productivity*

Need to encourage or facilitate greater production, need to take measures to aid this, appeal for greater production, and importance of productivity to the economy;

increase foreign trade; special aid to specific sectors of the economy; growth; active manpower policy; aid to agriculture, tourism and industry.

411 *Technology and Infrastructure*

Importance of modernizing industrial administration, importance of science and technological developments in industry; need for training and government sponsored research; need for overhaul of capital equipment, and methods of communications and transport (including Merchant Marine); development of Nuclear Energy.

412 *Controlled Economy*

General need for direct government control of economy; control over prices, wages, rents, etc. This covers *neither* Nationalization *nor* Indicative planning.

413 *Nationalization*

Government ownership and control, partial or complete, including government ownership of land.

414 *Economic Orthodoxy and Efficiency*

Need for traditional economic orthodoxy, e.g. balanced budget, retrenchment in crisis, low taxation, thrift and savings; support for traditional economic institutions such as the Stock Market and banking system; support for strong currency internationally.

Domain 5 *Welfare and Quality of Life*

501 *Environmental Protection*

Preservation of countryside, forests, etc; general preservation of natural resources against selfish interests; proper use of national parks; soil banks, etc.

502 *Art, Sport, Leisure, and Media*

Favourable mention of leisure activities, need to spend money on museums, art galleries, etc; need to encourage worthwhile leisure activities, and to provide cultural and leisure facilities: to encourage development of the media etc.

503 *Social Justice*

Need for fair treatment of all men; for special protection for exploited; fair treatment in tax system; need for equality of opportunity; need for fair distribution of resources and removal of class barriers; end of discrimination.

504 *Social Services Expansion: Positive*

Favourable mention of need to maintain or expand any basic service or welfare scheme; support for free basic social services such as public health, or housing. *This excludes education.*

505 *Social Services Expansion: Negative*

As 504, but negative.

506 *Education Pro-Expansion*

The need to expand and/or improve education provision at all levels. *But not* Technical training which is coded under 411.

507 *Education Anti-Expansion*

As 506, but negative.

Domain 6 *Fabric of Society*

601 *Defence of National Way of Life: Positive*

Favourable mentions of importance of defence against subversion, necessary suspension of some freedoms in order to defend this; support of national ideas, traditions and institutions.

602 *Defence of National Way of Life:Negative*

As 601, but negative.

603 *Traditional Morality: Positive*

Favourable mention of, e.g. prohibition, censorship, suppression of immorality and unseemly behaviour; maintenance and stability of family.

604 *Traditional Morality: Negative*

As 603, but negative.

605 *Law and Order*

Enforcement of all laws; actions against organized crime; putting down urban violence; support and resources for police; tougher attitudes in courts, etc.

606 *National Effort/Social Harmony*

Appeal for national effort and solidarity; need for nation to see itself as united; appeal for public spiritedness; decrying anti-social attitudes in a time of crisis; support for public interest; national interest; bipartisanship.

607 *Communalism, Pluralism, Pillarization*

Preservation of autonomy of religious, ethnic, linguistic heritages within the country. Preservation and/or expansion of schools with a specific religious orientation.

608

As 607, but negative.

Domain 7 *Social Groups*

701 *Labour Groups*

Favourable references to Labour, working class, unemployed, poor; support for Labour Unions, free collective bargaining, good treatment of manual and other employees.

702 *Labour Groups: Negative*

As 701, but negative.

703 *Agriculture and Farmers*

Support for agriculture; farmers; any policy aimed specifically at benefitting these.

704 *Other Economic Groups*

Favourable references to any Economically-defined group not covered by 701 or 703. For example, employers, self-employed, middle-class and professional groups in general.

705 *Underprivileged Minority Groups*

Favourable references to underprivileged minorities which are defined neither in economic nor in demographic terms, e.g. the handicapped, homosexuals, etc.

706 *Non-economic Demographic Groups*

Favourable mentions of, or need for, assistance to Women, Old People, Young People, linguistic groups and national minorities; special interest groups of all kinds.

Sub-categories used in country analyses

Austria	None	
Australia	4080	Specific Economic Goals except Full Employment
	4081	Full Employment
	6060	National Effort
	6061	Social Harmony
	7060	Non-Economic Groups except the following:
	7061	Youth
	7062	Old People
	7064	Aborigines
	7065	New Australians
Belgium	1070	Internationalism except Overseas Aid
	1071	Overseas Aid
	2020	Democracy except Worker Participation
	3010	Decentralization except Two or Three Regions
	3012	Two Regions
	3013	Three Regions
	4080	Specific Economic Goals except Full Employment
	4081	Full Employment
	6060	National Effort
	6061	Social Harmony
	6070	Communalism (+ve) except Cultural Autonomy
	6072	Cultural Autonomy
	7040	Other Economic Groups except 'Middle-Classes'
	7041	'Middle Classes'
	7060	Non-Economic Groups except the following:
	7061	Flemings and Flanders
	7062	Walloons and Wallonie
	7063	Bruxellois and Brussels
	7064	Youth
	7065	Old People
	7066	Women
Canada	None	
Denmark	None	
France	2020	Democracy except Worker Participation
	2021	Worker Participation
	6030	Traditional Morality (+ve) except Family
	6031	Family
Germany	None	
Ireland	None	
Israel	None	

Italy	10201	USSR and Eastern Europe, Negative
	20101	Union Rights
	20201	Workers' Participation
	20302	Regulating the Right to Work
	30301	Administrative and State Reform
	30302	Judicial, Legal and Police Reform
	40901	Support of Employment
	50301	Agrarian Reform (Latifundia)
	50304	Home Ownership
	50701	Private Schools
	60301	Christian Values
	60601	Popular Front
	60602	Alternative Normalization
	70601	Women
	70602	Youth
	70603	Old People
Japan	None	
Luxembourg	7010	Labour Groups except Railwaymen
	7011	Railwaymen
	7030	Farmers/Agriculture except Wine Growers
	7031	Wine-Growers/Viticulture
	7040	Other Economic Groups except 'Middle Classes'
	7041	'Middle Classes'
	7060	Non-Economic Groups except the following:
	7061	Youth
	7062	Old People
	7063	Women
Netherlands	None	
New Zealand	None	
Northern Ireland	101A	Great Britain/United Kingdom (+ve)
	101B	Ireland (+ve)
	102A	Great Britain/United Kingdom (−ve)
	102B	Ireland (−ve)
	410A	Technology in general
	410B	Productivity (Agriculture)
	410C	Productivity (Industry)
Sri Lanka	None	
Sweden	None	
Great Britain	None	
United States	None	

APPENDIX C

FACTOR ANALYTIC STRATEGIES
USED IN THE INVESTIGATION
OF ELECTION PROGRAMMES

———————— ~ ————————

There is no place in this book to describe or explain factor analysis in any detail, and it is improbable that anyone without at least a basic understanding of the technique will use our material. However all the studies in this work rely heavily on factor analysis in several ways, so it was thought useful to provide some notes on the detailed conventions we have adopted. The general considerations leading to the adoption of factor analysis for our research are briefly reviewed in Chapters 2 and 3 (Sections 2.8 and 3.4)

Because of the crucial need for comparability between the various country analyses, the Research Group spent a good deal of time at an early stage standardizing procedures, and deriving common solutions to the common problems faced. Consequently there is no reason to doubt the inter-comparability of the technical results in different chapters – though this does not, of course, extend to guaranteeing substantive comparability. Technical uniformity is further aided by the fact that, as the SPSS package of programmes is now almost universally available, it was possible to insist that the same programme should be used by all analysts. As a result we were able to operationalize our common decisions very precisely, to the point of specifying which options were to be selected on procedure cards inside the SPSS Factor Analysis program. In many cases the analyses were carried out entirely at the University of Essex by Hearl.

Factor analysis has two distinct, and not always maximally compatible uses, both of which are vital to the work described in this book. One purpose is data reduction, to summarise the complex data set of 54 primary frequency counts of political 'symbols'. Little comparative work could have been done had the data remained in this rich state. So a major concern has been the reduction of complexity, first inside each, and secondly across the (already simplified), domain structures into a very small number of over-arching dimensions. In the main, data has been treated so as to produce not more than 2 factors from each of seven domains covering the total of 54 variables. The resulting maximum of 14 factors have been employed as variables in their own right, and further subjected to factor analysis. At this second stage we have restricted our main comments to the two leading factors. Although this reductive technique involves much loss of information, this has usually been made up for by their greater simplicity of interpretation.

Such interpretation of variable correlations is, of course, the other major purpose of factor analysis. In all areas of quantitative social science one comes across sets of measures that turn out to be highly intercorrelated because they are all, in part, measures of a single underlying variable. It is clearly preferable to have one variable, mathematically derived from this clutch of interrelated partial measures. In this sense the process is again a data reduction technique. But if one aims to get good measures of the underlying communalities, one's principal focus will be on the clarity, the interpretability, of each of the factors derived, rather than simply keeping the number of derived factors as low as possible. These two aims are not, then, always compatible, and our stress has been on the whole towards data reduction rather than towards interpretability. We have extracted the minimum number of factors even if a larger number, perhaps given some rotation, would yield 'purer' factors, loaded only on a small number of variables.

The most important characteristic of our procedure has been its two-stage nature. Theoretically each country analysis could have taken all of the variables together and factored them, extracting a largish number of dimensions on which any combination of variables, no matter how different in substantive meaning, could have been associated together. There are two compelling reasons for not doing so. The first is substantive – we wished to be able to talk about the structure and interpreted meaning of policy conflict within broadly defined policy areas. Thus even if the highest correlation with stress on military expenditure was stress on Law and Order, or if economic orthodoxy always went hand in hand with a desire for social justice, our primary interest was with foreign affairs, economic policy and social welfare in themselves. Our first concern is with the nature of the dominant foreign policy dimension, rather than what empirical clustering of variables might define as an over-ordering factor of policy conflict. In any case we could not, normally, have used all the variables in a single stage. This is because, very simply, we usually have too many variables and too few cases. The number of variables is dependent only on our perceptions, our abilities to distinguish between shades of reference in political language. We have sought to maximize the cases, by studying all important parties in all post-war elections, and to minimize the variables as far as honesty and inter-cultural comparability would allow. Nonetheless in a typical case country there are around a dozen elections and three or four parties – the resulting matrix, with say 48 cases, and 54 variables, cannot, mathematically, be factor analysed.

The strategy we developed takes advantage of the existence of separate policy domains. Treating each one as a data set of its own, we have perfectly suitable material for factor analysis. Even the biggest domain, economic policy, has a maximum of 14 variables, and a data-poor country, like the USA, has nine elections and two parties. Therefore the data matrix, 18 cases by 14 variables, can sensibly be analysed.

The first stage, then, consists of taking the separate domains and producing a factor analysis inside each one. These factors, or rather the ensuing scores for each case on the new factors, given meaning by interpretation of the domain factor analysis, can be subjected to further manipulation, to yield a second stage factor analysis.

Two points immediately arise. How many factors are to be fed into the second stage, and what constraints should there be on them? Given the vital need for comparability between chapters, there was little real choice. We could not say that all significant factors from each domain should be used in the second stage. This approach, whether one meant by significance a statistical or a substantive test, would have produced a varying salien e of the different domains between countries. There had to be a fixed number – and this number had to be a small one. Not only was there a general purpose of data reduction, but the number of new variables submitted to the second stage had a ceiling. It had to be a number sufficiently small so that the resulting matrix was capable of factor analysis in a country with relatively few cases. As much of our emphasis anyway is on visual representation, and it is seldom the case that more than the first two factors in a domain interpret usefully, we settled on that number.

Two factor scores are derived from each domain where this is possible, giving a maximum input into the second stage of 14 variables. Apart from the inescapable fact that this procedure involves throwing away information where, for example, a domain yields several factors and there would be enough cases to analyse more than 14 second stage variables, there is another possible criticism. Taking two factors from each domain, regardless of how many more might be thrown up, means forcing an equal saliency on each policy area, regardless of its actual importance in the country. But this is a deliberate policy of ours to ensure cross-national comparability, not just an artefactual requirement of the process.

A second question relates to the nature of these first order factors. Normally where a two stage process is involved, an analyst will extract non-orthogonal factors – that is, the factors will be allowed to be correlated with each other. Indeed this is necessary in most research constructed on a two-stage basis – if the first order factors are not inter-correlated, it will not be possible to factor analyse them; factor analysis is, after all, a process of correlation decomposition. For two reasons we could not allow the extraction of correlated first order factors inside each domain. First, this would mitigate against data-reduction. Far more information is contained in two factors forced to be orthogonal, to measure statistically independent underlying variables than is captured by two correlated factors that represent partial measures of the same dimension. Secondly, we could not have produced inter chapter standardization, and hence comparability had we allowed non-orthogonal factor extraction. Orthogonal extraction is based on a mathematically unique solution to the variance decomposition problem, but there is no similarly unique, and therefore comparable, solution set if one extracts non-orthogonally. Nor was it necessary in our case. When it comes to second stage analysis it is indeed true that, as no factors from the same domain can be correlated, they cannot both load significantly onto the same higher order factors. There is nothing, however, to stop any pair of factors from different domains being correlated, and so we can perfectly sensibly restrict original correlation inside each domain and still analyse in two stages. There is a constraint on the solutions discovered in the second stage, but a rather useful one from the point of view of data reduction.

In the end the only 'states rights' decisions, questions left up to the separate authors, are the external ones in factor analysis of whether or not to use a rotation technique to provide greater interpretability of factors. As is well known differences between rotated and non-rotated solutions are usually very slim, but where an author prefers to rotate, he has done so. For those who wish to know, the SPSS default options of Principal Axis factoring with communality estimates in the main diagonal, followed by Varimax rotation where desired, have been employed throughout the analysis. (*SPSS Manual*, 2nd ed., Norman H. Nie, C. Hadlai Hull et al., McGraw Hill, 1975, p. 481). As no missing data exist, there are no analytic problems connected with this.

GENERAL BIBLIOGRAPHY

———— ◌ ————

Akita, G. 1967. *Foundations of Constitutional Government in Modern Japan, 1868–1900*. Cambridge, Mass.: Harvard University Press.

Allison, C. D. 1979, *Suburban Tokyo: A Comparative Study in Political and Social Change*. Berkeley, Calif.: University of California Press.

Allum, P. A. 1973. *Italy: Republic without Government?* London: Weidenfeld and Nicolson.

Arian, A. 1973. *The Choosing People: Voting Behaviour in Israel*. Cleveland, Ohio: Case Western Reserve University Press.

Axelrod, R. 1970. *Conflict of Interest*. Chicago: Markham.

Axelrod, R. 1972. 'Where the votes come from: an analysis of electoral coalition, 1952–1968'. *American Political Science Review*. Vol. LXVI, No. 1, 11–20.

Back, P. E., & Berglund, S. 1978. *Det Svenska Partivasendet*. Stockholm: AWE/Gebers.

Baerwald, H. H. 1974. *Japan's Parliament*. Oxford: Oxford University Press.

Banno, J. 1972. *The Establishment of the Meiji Constitutional System*. University of Tokyo Press.

Bara, J. 1974. *An Aggregate Ecological Analysis of Voting Behaviour in Four Commonwealth States*. London: University of London. Unpublished Ph.D thesis.

Barbelet, J. 1975. 'Tri-partism in Australia: The role of the Australian Country Party', *Politics*, Vol. 10, No. 1.

Barnes, S. 1977. *Representation in Italy*. Chicago: University of Chicago Press.

Barry, B. 1970. *Sociologists, Economists and Democracy*. London: Collier-Macmillan.

Beckman, G. M. & Kenji, O. 1969. *The Japanese Communist Party 1922–1945*. Stanford: Stanford University Press.

Benedikt, H. (ed.). 1954. *Geschichte der Republik Österreich*. München.

Benning, L. 1981. Quoted in *The Guardian* 1.11.1981

Berchtold, K. 1967. *Österreichische Parteiprogramme 1868–1966*. Vienna

Berger, G. M. 1976. *Parties out of Power*. Princeton: Princeton University Press.

Berglund, S., & Lindstrom, U. 1978. *The Scandinavian Party System*. Lund: Studentlitteratur.

Beyme, K. von. 1979. *Das Politische System der Bundesrepublik Deutschland*. Munich: Piper

Beyme, K. von. 1981. 'Do Parties Matter? – Der Einfluss der Parteien auf politische Entscheidungen', *Politische Vierteljahrschrift*, 22, 343–58.

Beyme, K. von. 1983. 'Theoretische Probleme der Parteienforschung', *Politische Vierteljahrschrift*, 24, 241–52.

Bille, L. *Danmark 1945–1980*. København.

Blaker, W. (ed.). 1975. *Japan at the Polls: The House of Councillors Election of 1974*. Washington: American Institute for Public Policy Research.

Borg, O. 1966. 'Basic Dimensions of Finnish Party Ideologies: A Factor Analytical Study', *Scandinavian Political Studies*, Vol. 1.

Buchhaas D. 1981. *Die Volkspartei: Programmatische Entwicklung der CDU 1950–1973*. Düsseldorf: Droste.

Budge, I. 1982. 'Issues in post-war British elections'. *Comparative Political Studies*.

Budge, I. 1983a. 'The need for a comparative theory of West European governments and an attempt to provide one'. *West European Politics*, 5.

Budge, I. & Farlie, D. 1976. *Voting and Party Competition*. London: Wiley.

Budge, I., I. Crewe and D. Farlie. 1976. *Party Identification and Beyond*. London, Wiley.

Budge, I., & Farlie, D. 1977. *Voting and Party Competition: A Theoretical Critique and Synthesis applied to Surveys from Ten Democracies*. London and New York: Wiley.

Budge, I., & Farlie, D. 1978. 'The utility of multi-dimensional spaces in explaining voting and party competition', *European Journal of Political Research*, 7.

Budge, I. 1982. 'Electoral Volatility: Issue Effects and Basic Change in 23 Post-War Democracies', *Electoral Studies*, 1, 147–68.

Budge, I., & Farlie, D. 1983. *Explaining and Predicting Elections: Issue Effects and Party Strategies in Twenty-Three Democracies*. George Allen and Unwin, London.

Budge, I. & Farlie, D. 1983. 'Party Competition – Selective Emphasis or Direct Confrontation: an alternative view with data'. In Hans Daalder and Peter Mair (eds.) *Western European Party Systems* London & Beverly Hills: Sage, 267–305.

Budge, I., Farlie, D. & Laver, M.J. 1983. 'What is a rational choice? Differing meanings within explanations of voting and party competition'. *Electoral Studies* 2 London: Allen & Unwin.

Burton, G., & Drewry, I. 1970. 'Survey of the Session 1969–70'. *Parliamentary Affairs* 23: 3. 1970.

Busteed, M. A. & Mason, H. 1970. 'Irish Labour in the 1969 Election', *Political Studies* 18: 3, 373–379.

Butler, D., Penniman, H. R. & Ranney, A. (eds.). *Democracy at the Polls: a Comparative Study of Competitive National Elections*. Washington: American Enterprise Institute for Public Policy Research.

Carrigan, D. O. 1968. *Canadian Party Platforms 1867–1968*. Toronto: Copp Clark.

Carty, R. K. 1981. *Party and Parish Pump: Electoral Politics in Ireland*. Ontario: Wilfrid Laurier Press.

Castles, F. G. 1978. *The Social Democratic Image of Society*. London: Routledge and Kegan Paul.

Catley, R. & MacFarlane, B. 1974. *From Tweedledum to Tweedledee*. Sydney.

Cerny, K. H. 1977a. *Germany at the Polls: The Bundestag Election 1976*. Washington: American Institute for Public Policy Research.

Cerny, K. H. 1977b. *Scandinavia at the Polls: Recent Political Trends in Denmark, Norway and Sweden*. Washington, American Enterprise Institute for Public Policy Research.

Chapman, R. M., Jackson, W. K. & Mitchell, A. V. 1962. *New Zealand Politics in Action*. Oxford: Oxford University Press.

Charlot, J. 1970. *Répertoire des Publications des Partis Politiques Français 1944–1967*. Paris.

Charlot, J. 1971. *The Gaullist Phenomenon*. New York.

Chubb, B. 1969. 'Ireland'. In Stanley Henig and John Pinder (eds.). *European Political Parties*. London: Allen & Unwin/PEP, 447–64.

Chubb, B. 1971. *The Government and Politics of Ireland*. London: Oxford University Press.

Chubb, B. 1974. *Cabinet Government in Ireland*. Dublin: Institute of Public Administration.

Chubb, B. 1979. 'Ireland'. In Stanley Henig (ed.). *Political Parties in the European Community*. London: Allen & Unwin/PSI, 118–34.

Clarkson, S. 1967. 'Democracy in the Liberal Party', in Thorburn, *op. cit.*

Cohan, A. S. 1982. 'Ireland: Coalitions Making a Virtue of Necessity'. In Eric C. Browne and John Dreijmanis (eds.). *Government Coalitions in Western Democracies*. New York: Longman, 260–82.

Cohan, A. S., McKinlay, R. D. & Mughan A. 1975. 'The Used Vote and Electoral Outcomes'. *British Journal of Political Science*, 5: 4, 363–83.

Cole, A. B. et al. 1966. *Socialist Parties in Postwar Japan*. New Haven, Conn.: Yale University Press.

Condradt, D. 1978. *The German Polity*. New York: Longman.

Cornish, B. 1968. *The New Republic*. Dublin; the Irish Labour Party.

Cotteret, J. M. & Moreau, R. 1969. *Le Vocabulaire du Général de Gaulle*. Paris: Colin.

Cotteret, J. M., Moreau, R. & Emeri, C. 1974. *Giscard d'Estaing, Mitterand; 54,774 mots pour convaincre*. Paris; Presses Universitaires Françaises.

Craig, F. W. S. 1975a. *British General Election Manifestos 1900–74* London: Macmillan.

Craig, F. W. S. 1975b. *The Most Gracious Speeches to Parliament 1900–74*. London: Macmillan.

Curtis, G. 1971. *Election Campaigning Japanese Style*. N.Y.: Columbia University Press..

Daalder, H. and P. Mair (eds.), 1983. *Western European Party Systems; Continuity and Change*. London, Sage.

Davies, A. F., 1971. *Australian Democracy*. Melbourne.

De Bruyn, L. P. J. 1971. *Partij kiezen: systematisch-vergelijkende analyse van de partij-programs voor de Tweede Kamerverkiezing 1971*. Alphen aan den Rijn.

DeWachter, w. 1967. *De Wetgevende Verkiezingen als Proces van Machtsverwerving in het Belgisch Politiek Bestel*. SWU, Antwerp.

Diamant, A. 1960. *Austrian Catholics and the First Republic*. Princeton, N.J. Princeton, University Press..

Di Palma, G. 1977. *Surviving without Governing: The Italian Parties in Parliament*. Berkeley, Calif., California University Press..

Downs, A. 1957. *An Economic Theory of Democracy*. New York: Harper and Row.

Drees, W. 1974. 'Kabinetsformaties en programs'. In J. A. Boeren (ed.), *Politiek, parlement, democratie: opstellen voor Prof. Mr. F. J. F. M. Duynstee.* Deventer, 1974, 81–7.

Duncan, G., Rallings, C. & Klingemann, H. D., (eds.) 1985. *Party Pledges and Government Performance.* London: Sage.

Duverger, M. 1974. *Political Parties.* London: Methuen, Third Edition.

Duus, P. 1968. *Party Rivalry and Political Change in Taisho Japan.* Cambridge, Mass.: Harvard University Press.

Edinger, L. J. 1968. *Politics in Germany.* Boston: Little Brown.

Elder, N., Thomas, A. H. & Arter, D. 1982. *The Consensual Democracies?* Oxford: Martin Robertson.

Ellwein, T. 1977. *Das Regierungssystem der Bundesrepublik Deutschland.* Opladen: Westdeutscher Verlag.

Emy, H. 1972. *The Politics of Australian Democracy.* Melbourne.

Engel, S., & Logan, M. 1980. 'Social Change and the Future of Australia'. In Evans, G. & Reeves, J. (eds.), *Labour Essays 1980.* Melbourne.

Farneti, P. 1983. *Il Sistema dei partiti in Italia 1946–1979.* Bologna: Il Mulino.

Fein, L. J. 1967. *Politics in Israel.* Boston, Mass.: Little, Brown & Co.

Fellner, F. 'The Genesis of the Austrian Republic'. In K. Steiner (ed.), 1981. *Modern Austria,* Palo Alto, Calif.

Finer, S. 1975. 'Manifesto Moonshine'. *New Society.* 13.11.1975.

Fiorina, M. P. 1981. *Retrospective Voting in American National Elections.* New Haven: Yale University Press.

Fischer-Kowelski, M. & I. Bucek (eds.) 1969. *Ungleichheit in Österreich.* Wien.

Flanagan, S. C. & Richardson, B. M. 1976. *Japanese Electoral Behavior: Social Cleavages, Social Networks and Partisanship.* Beverly Hills, Cal.: Sage.

Flechtheim, O. P. 1968. 'Parteiprogramme'. In Lenk, K., & Neumann, F. (eds.) *Theorie und Soziologie der politischen Parteien.* Neuweid, Luchterhand.

Flechtheim, O. P. (ed.) 1962–1971. *Dokument zur parteipolitischen Entwicklung in Deutschland seit 1945.* Vols. I–IX, Berlin: Wendler.

Flohr, H. 1968. *Parteiprogramme in der Demokratie,* Göttingen.

Frognier, A. P. & Delfosse, P. 1974. 'Le système des partis en Belgique'. *Res Publica.* Vol. XVI, 3–4, pp. 405–23.

Fukui, H. 1970. *Party in Power: The Japanese Liberal-Democrats and Policy Making.* Berkeley: University of California Press.

Fischer, H. 1981. 'Elections and Parliament'. In K. Steiner (ed.), *Modern Austria.* Palo Alto, Calif.

Gallagher, M. 1976. *Electoral Support for Irish Political Parties.* London & Beverley Hills: Sage.

Gallagher, M. 1981. 'Societal Change and Party Adaptation in the Republic of Ireland, 1960–1981.' *European Journal of Political Research,* 9: 3, 269–85.

Galli, G. 1966. *Il bipartismo imperfetto: Communisti e Democristiani in Italia.* Bologna: Il Mulino.

Galli, G. 1976. 'Le Promesse dei partiti'. *Biblioteca della Libertà,* Anno XIII, No. 61–2.

Garvin, T. 1974. 'Political Cleavages, Party Politics and Urbanisation in Ireland; the case of the periphery-dominated centre'. *European Journal of Political Research,* 2:4, 307–27.

Garvin, T. 1977a. 'Nationalist Elites, Irish Voters and Irish Political Development: a Comparative Perspective'. *Economic and Social Science Review*, 8:3, 161–86.

Garvin, T. 1977b. 'Belief Systems, Ideological Perspectives, and Political Activism; Some Dublin Evidence'. *Social Studies* 6:1, 39–56.

Garvin, T. 1978. 'The Destiny of Soldiers: Tradition and Modernity in the Politics of De Valera's Ireland'. *Political Studies*, 26:3, 328–47.

Garvin, T. 1981a. *The Evolution of Irish Nationalist Politics*. Dublin: Gill & Macmillan.

Garvin, T. 1981b. 'The Growth of Faction in the Fianna Fáil Party, 1966–1980'. *Parliamentary Affairs*, 34:1, 110–23.

Ginsberg, B., 1976. 'Elections and Public Policy'. *American Political Science Review*, Vol. 70, No. 1, pp. 41–9.

Gladdish, K. R. 1972. 'Two-party vs. multi-party: The Netherlands and Britain'. *Acta Politica*, VII, 342–61.

Grebing, B., 1966. *Geschichte der deutschen Arbeiterwegung*. Munich: Nymphenburger Verlagsanstalt.

Grewe, W. 1951. 'Parteienstaat – oder was sonst?' *Der Monat*, 3, 563–77.

Grønmo, S., 1975. 'Skillinjer i partipolitikken 1969–197', *Tidskrift for samfunnsforskning*, No. 2.

Grube, F. & Richter, G. (eds.) 1977. *Der SPD-Staat*. Munich: Piper.

Hackett, R. 1967. 'The Waffle Conflict in the NDP'. In Thornburn, *op. cit.*

Hammerich, K. 1977. *Kompromissernas Koalition – Person och Makspelet kring regeringen Fälldin*. Ystad: Raben and Sjogren.

Hancock, D. 1972. *The Policies of Postindustrial Change*. New York: Praeger.

Herman, V. 1974. 'What Governments Say and What Governments Do'. *Parliamentary Affairs* 27:1'

Henig, S. & Pinder, J. 1969. *European Political Parties*. London: Political and Economic Planning

Hiuchi, S. 1978. *Japanese Socialist Party*. Tokyo: Kyoikusha.

Hoogerwerf, A. 1963. 'Sociaal-Politieke strijdspunten: smeulend vuur'. *Sociologische Gids*. X, 249–63.

Hoogewerf, A. 1964. 'Latent socio-political issues in the Netherlands'. *Sociologica Neerlandica* II, 161–77.

Hoogewerf, A. 1965. *De Nederlandse Politieke Partijen en de Wereld van Morgen*. Elthetoi-brochure reeks, No. 17, May 1965.

Hori, Y. 1970. *Clean Government Party*. Tokyo: Kyoikusha.

Horowitz, D. & Lissak, M. 1978. *Origins of the Israeli Polity*. Chicago: University of Chicago Press.

Hotelling, H. 1929. 'Stability in competition'. *Economic Journal XXXIX*, 41–57.

Iizaka, Y. et al. 1979. *Tides Toward a Coalition Government* (*Rengo seiken eno Choryu*). Tokyo: Tokyo Keizai Shimpoza.

Ike, N. 1977. *A Theory of Japanese Democracy*. Boulder, Colorado: Westview Press.

Inglehart, R. 1977. *The Silent Revolution*. Princeton: Princeton University Press.

Inoguchi, T. 1979. 'Political surfing over economic waves: a simple model of the Japanese political-economic system in comparative perspective'. Paper delivered at the 11th World Congress of the International Political Science Association. Moscow, 12–18 August 1979.

Inoguchi, T. 1980. 'Economic conditions and mass support: Japan, 1960–1976'. In Paul Whitely, (ed.). *Models of Political Economy*. London: Sage.

Inoguchi, T. 1983. *Contemporary Japanese Political Economy*. Tokyo: Tokyo Keizai Shimpoza.

Isberg, M., Wettengren, A. & Wittrick, B., 1972. 'A Technique for Structural Content Analysis of Party Propaganda', *Scandinavian Political Studies*, Vol. 7, 83–106.

Isberg, M., Wettengren, A., Wibble, J. & Wittrock, B., 1974. Partierna infor valjarna. Svensk valpropaganda 1960–1966. Stockholm: Allmänna forlaget.

Juling, P. 1977. *Programmatische Entwicklung der FDP 1946–1969. Eine Einführung und Dokumente*. Meisenheim an Glan: Hain.

Kaack, H. 1971. *Geschichte und Struktur des deutschen Parteiensystems*. Opladen.

Kaack, H. & Kaack, U. (eds.) 1977. *Parteien-Jahrbuch 1973/1974*. Meisenheim an Glan: Hain.

Kaack, H. & Kaack, U. (eds.) 1978. *Parteien-Jahrbuch 1975*. Meisenheim an Glan: Hain.

Kaack, H. & Roth, R. (eds.) 1979. *Parteien-Jahrbuch 1976*. Meisenheim an Glan: Hain.

Kaack, H., 1979. *Die FDP. Grundriss und Materialen zu Geschichte, Struktur und Programmatik*. Meisenheim an Glan: Hain.

Kaack, H. & Roth, R. (eds.) 1980. *Handbuch des deutschen Parteiensystems*. Opladen: Leske.

Kaase, M. 1984. 'Personalized Proportional Representation, The Model of the West-German Electoral System'. In Lijphart, A. & Grofman, B. (eds.). *Choosing an Electoral System: Issues and Alternatives*. New York: Praeger.

Kadan, A. & Pelinka, A., 1979. *Die Grundsatzprogramme der Österreichischen Parteien*. Niederösterreichisches Pressehaus, St. Polten.

Kaplan, A. 1964. *The Conduct of Inquiry*. San Francisco: Chandler.

Kato, K. 1979. *Current State of Affairs in Education and Each Party's Education Policy*. Tokyo: Kyoikusha.

Kato, H. & Nakamura, H. 1980. 'A content analysis of campaign appeals in postwar national elections'. *Annals of Keio University's Institute of Journalism*. No. 15, 69–90.

Kavanagh, D. 1981. 'The Politics of Manifestos'. *Parliamentary Affairs*. 34:1, 7–27.

Kemp, D., 1978. *Society and Electoral Behaviour in Australia*. Queensland.

Kenny, K. J. 1972. *The Political System of the Irish Republic: two and a half parties in a developing nation*. Syracuse University: Ph.D. thesis.

Kim, J. & Muller, C., 1978. *Factor Analysis. Statistical Methods and Practical Issues*. Beverley Hills: Sage.

King, A. 1972. 'How the Conservatives Evolve Policies'. *New Society*, 20.7.1972.

Klecka, W. R. 1980. *Discriminant Analysis*. Beverley Hills: Sage.

Klingemann, H. D., 1983. 'Die Einstellunge zur SPD und CDU/CSU 1960–1980, Erste Explorationen in ein unbekanntes Land'. In Kaase, M. & Klingemann, H. D., (eds.), *Wählen und politisches System*. Opladen: Westdeutscher Verlag, 478–537.

Klingemann, H. D., Budge, I. & Robertson, D. (eds.) *Party Movement at Elite and Electoral Level*. London: Sage. Forthcoming

Kramer, G. 'A Dynamical Model of Political Equilibrium'. *Journal of Economic Theory*, 16, pp. 310–34.

Kremerdahl, H. 1975. 'Parteiprogramme in der parlamentarischen Demokratie der Bundesrepublik Deutschland'. In Hergt, S. (ed.) *Parteiprogramme*. Opladen: Hegen.

Kronwall, K. 1975. *Politisk Kommunikation i et Flerpartisystem*. Lund: Studentlitteratur.

Kuhnle, S. & Solheim, L. 1981. 'Party Programs and the Welfare State: Consensus and Conflict in Norway 1945–1977', *Skrifter*. No. 3, Oslo.

Kurokawa, K.& Kawanbe, H. 1979. *Economic and Financial Issues and Each Party's Policy*. Tokyo: Kyoikusha.

Labbé, D. 1977. *Le Discours Communiste*. Paris: Presses de la FNSP.

Lasswell, H. D., Leites N. and Associates, 1949. *Language of Politics*. New York: Stewart.

Lasswell, H., Lerner, D. & Pool, I. de Sola. *The Comparative Study of Symbols*, Hoover Institute Studies, Series C: Symbols No. 1. Stanford: Stanford University Press.

Laveau, G. 1981. 'The effect of twenty years of Gaullism on the parties of the left'. In W. G. Andrew and S. Hoffmann. (eds.). *The Impact of the Fifth Republic on France*. Albany: State University of New York Press.

Laver, M. J., Budge, I. & D. Hearl (eds.) Forthcoming

LDP 1979a *Japanese Political Parties*. Tokyo: LDP Public Relations Committee Publications Bureau.

LDP 1979b. *Japanese Political Culture*. Tokyo.

LDP 1979c. *Campaigning Strategy*.

Levine, S. 1979. *The New Zealand Political System*. Sydney and Auckland.

Levine, S. & Lodge, J. 1976. *The New Zealand General Election of 1975*. Wellington.

Linblad, I., Wahlback, K. & Wirklund, C. 1974. *Politik i Norden – En jamforande oversikt*. Stockholm: Aldus, Second Edition.

Lipschits, I. 1969. *Links en rechts in de politiek*. Meppel.

Lipschits, I. 1977. *Verkiezingsprogramma's*. The Hague.

Lipschits, I. 1981. *Verkiezingsprogramma's*. The Hague.

Lipset, S. M. and S. Rokkan. 1967. *Party Systems and Voter Alignments. Cross-national Perspectives*. New York. The Free Press.

Loewenthal, R. (ed.). 1979. *Demokratischer Sozialismus in der 80er Jahren*. Cologne; Europäische Verlagsanstalt.

Loewenthal, R. & Schwarz, H.-P. (eds.) 1974. *Die zweite Republik: 25 Jahre Bundesrepublik Deutschland. Eine Balanz*. Stuttgart: Seewald.

Lucas, N. 1974. *The Modern History of Israel*. London: Weidenfield & Nicolson.

Luykx, T. 1978. *Politieke Geschiedenis van België*. Vols. 1 and 2, Fourth Edition. Brussels; Elsevier.

Mackie, T. & Rose, R. 1982. *International Almanac of Electoral History*. Second Edition, London.

Maguire, M. 1985. 'Ireland'. In Peter Flora (ed.). *The Development of the Welfare State in Western Europe since 1945*. Berlin: Degruyter, forthcoming.

Mair, P. 1979. 'The autonomy of the political: the development of the Irish party system'. *Comparative Politics*, 11:4, 445–65.

Mair, P. 1982. 'Muffling the swing: STV and the Irish general election of 1981'. *West European Politics*. 5:1, 76–91.

Mair, P. 1983, 'The politics of the Fine Gael'. In A. Mogan (ed.) *Political Parties in Ireland*. Dublin: Turoe.

Mair, P. 1985. *The Irish Party System in the Post-War Period*. London: Frances Pinter.

Majerus, P. 1976. *The Institutions of the Grand Duchy of Luxembourg*. Ministry of State, Luxembourg.

Manning, M. 1972. *Irish Political Parties*. Dublin: Gill & Macmillan.

Manor, J. 1970. 'A New Political Order for Sri Lanka' *The World Today*, 370–86.

Manor, J. 1979. 'The Failure of Political Integration in Sri Lanka' (Ceylon). *The Journal of Commonwealth and Comparative Politics*. xvii, 21–46.

Masuda, J. 1979. *Tasks of Japanese Diplomacy and Each Party's Policy*. Tokyo: Kyoikusha.

Masumi, J. 1969. *The Political System of Contemporary Japan*. Tokyo: Iwanamishoten.

Masumi, J. 1969–1979. *A History Study on Japanese Political Parties*. Tokyo: University of Tokyo Press, 5 Vols.

Meisel, J. 1962. *The Canadian General Election of 1957*. Toronto: Toronto University Press.

Merkl, P. H. 1980. 'West Germany'. In Merkl, P. H. (ed.) *Western European Party Systems. Trends and Prospects*. New York: The Free Press.

Miller, S. 1972. *Die SPD vor und nach Godesberg*. Bonn: Verlag Neue Gesellschaft.

Mintzel, A. 1977. *Geschichte der CSU. Ein Überblick*. Opladen: Westdeutscher Verlag.

Mita, K. 1979. *Administrative Reform and Local Self-Government and Each Party's Policy*. Tokyo: Kyoikusha.

Mitani, T. 1967. *The Formation of the Japanese Party Politics*. Tokyo: University of Tokyo Press.

Mitchell, A. 1969. *Politics and People in New Zealand*. Christchurch.

Najita, T. 1967. *Hara Kei in the Politics of Compromise, 1905–1915*. Cambridge Mass.: Harvard University Press.

Nakamura, T. 1979. *The Economy and Politics of the Occupation Period*. Tokyo: University of Tokyo Press.

Namenwirth, J. Z. 1968. 'Value Issues and Themes in Political Rhetoric: A Factor Analysis of Detrended Value Indicators'. University of Connecticut, unpublished paper.

Namenwirth, J. Z.& Lasswell, H. 1970. *The Changing Language of American Values: A Computer Study of Selected Party Platforms*. Beverley Hills: Sage.

Namenwirth, J. Z. 1973. 'Wheels of Time and the Interdependence of Value Change in America'. *Journal of Interdisciplinary History* 3, 649–83.

Naar, W.-D., Scheer, H. & Spori, d. 1976. *SPD – Staatspartei oder Reformpartei*. Munich: Piper.

Obeyskere, G. 1977. 'Social Change and the Deities: Rise of the Katavagams Cult in Modern Sri Lanka.' *Man*. xii, 377–96.

O'Leary, C. 1979. *Irish Elections, 1918–1977*. Dublin: Gill & Macmillan.

Page, B. I. 1978. *Choices and Echoes in Presidential Elections: Rational Man and Electoral Democracy*. Chicago: University of Chicago Press.

Parlement en Kiezer (Dutch Parliamentary Yearbook), 1946–1978, The Hague.

Parsons, T., Bayles, R. & Shils, E. (eds.) 1953. *Working Papers in the Theory of Action* New York: The Free Press.

Passin, H. (ed.) 1978. *A Season of Voting: The Japanese Elections of 1976 and 1977.* Washington: American Institute for Public Policy Research.

Pelinka, A. 1981. 'Political Parties'. In K. Steiner (ed.), *Modern Austria.* Palo Alto, Calif.

Penniman, H. R. (ed.) 1975. *Britain at the Polls: the parliamentary elections of 1974.* Washington: American Enterprise Institute for Public Policy Research.

Penniman, H. R. (ed.) 1975. *France at the Polls: the presidential election of 1974.* Washington: American Enterprise Institute for Public Policy Research.

Penniman, H. R. (ed.) 1977. *Australia at the Polls: the national elections of 1975.* Washington: American Enterprise Institute for Public Policy Research.

Penniman, H. R. (ed.) 1977. *Italy at the Polls: the parliamentary elections of 1976.* Washington: American Enterprise Institute for Public Policy Research.

Penniman, H. R. (ed.) 1978. *The Australian National Elections of 1977.* Washington: American Enterprise Institute for Public Policy Research.

Penniman, H. R. (ed.) 1978. *Ireland at the Polls: The Dáil elections of 1977.* Washington: American Enterprise Institute for Public Policy Research.

Penniman, H. R. (ed.) 1978. *Israel at the Polls: The Knesset Elections of 1977.* Washington: American Enterprise Institute for Public Policy Research.

Penniman, H. R. (ed.) 1980. *New Zealand at the Polls: the general elections of 1978.* Washington: American Enterprise Institute for Public Policy Research.

Penniman, H. R. (ed.) 1980. *The French National Assembly Elections of 1978.* Washington: American Enterprise Institute for Public Policy Research.

Penniman, H. R. (ed.) 1981. *Britain at the Polls, 1979: a study of the general election.* Washington: American Enterprise Institute for Public Policy Research.

Penniman, H. R. (ed.) 1981. *Canada at the Polls, 1979 and 1980.* Washington, American Enterprise Institute for Public Policy Research.

Perlin, G. C. 1980. *The Tory Syndrome.* Montreal: McGill Queen & University Press.

Peterson, O. 1979. *Regeringsbilningen 1978.* Lund: Raben & Sjogren.

Pettersen, P. A. 1973. *Konfliktlinjer og partistrategie.* Oslo: Institute of Political Science, Ph.D.

Pinto-Duschinsky, S. 1981. 'Manifestos, speeches and the doctrine of the mandate'. In H. Penniman (ed.) *Britain at the Polls 1979.* Washington: AEI.

Pirker, T. 1965. *Die SPD nach Hitler. Die Geschichte der Sozialdemokratischen Partei Deutschlands 1945–1964.* Munich: Reutten.

Pomper, G. M. 1968. *Elections in America: Control and Influences in Democratic Politics.* New York: Dodd, Mead.

Pridham, G. 1977. *Christian Democracy in Western Germany.* London: Croom Helm.

Pridham, G. 1981. *The Nature of the Italian Party System.* London: Croom Helm.

Prost, A. 1974. *Vocabulaire des Proclamations électorales de 1881, 1885 et 1889.* Paris: PUF, 1974.

Rallings, C., I. Budge and D. Hearl (eds.). Election Pledges and Government Action (forthcoming).

Raschke, J. 1970. 'Parteien, Programme und 'Entideologisierung''. In *Aus Politik und Zeitgeschichte, Beilage zur Wochenzeitung das Parlament.*

Riker, W. H. 1962. *The Theory of Political Coalitions.* New Haven: Yale.

Robertson, D. 1976. *A Theory of Party Competition.* London & New York: Wiley.

Robinson, M. 1975. *Political Structure in a Changing Sinhalese Village.* Cambridge: Cambridge University Press.

Rose, R. 1974. *The Problem of Party Government.* London: Macmillan

Rose, R. 1980. *Do Parties make a Difference?* London: Macmillan.

Rose, R., McAllister, I. & Mair, P. 1978. *Is There A Concurring Majority About Northern Ireland?* University of Strathclyde. Glasgow: Centre for the Study of Public Policy.

Rose, R. & D. Urwin, 1970. 'Persistence and Change in Western European Party Systems since 1945', *Political Studies*, 18, pp. 287–319.

Rose, R. & D. Urwin, 1975. *Regional Differentiation and Political Unity in Western Nataions.* London, Sage Professional Papers.

Rovan, J. 1980. *Geschichte der deutschen Sozialdemokratie.* Frankfurt a.M.: Fischer.

Rowies, L. 1977. *Les Partis Politiques en Belgique.* CRISP: Bruxelles.

Rowley, K. 1973. 'The Political Economy of Australia since the War'. In Playford and Kirsner (eds.), *Australian Capitalism.* Melbourne.

Rumpf, E. & Hepburn, A. C. 1977. *Nationalism and Socialism in Twentieth Century Ireland.* Liverpool: Liverpool University Press.

Sainsbury, D. 1980. *Swedish Social Democratic Ideology and Electoral Politics 1944–1948.* Almqvist and Wiksell International, Stockholm.

Sainsbury, D. 1981. 'Theoretical Perspectives in Analyzing Ideological Change and Persistence: The Case of Swedish Social Democratic Party Ideology'. *Scandinavian Political Studies.* Vol. 4, (new series), pp. 273–94.

Sainsbury. D. 1983. 'Functional Hypotheses of Party Decline; The case of the Scandinavian Social Democratic Parties'. *Scandinavian Political Studies*, Vol. 6, (new series), No. 4.

Sartori, G. 1972. 'European Political Parties. The Case of Polarised Pluralism'. In La Palombara, J. Weiner, M. (eds.), *Political Parties and Political Development.* Princeton University Press, pp. 137–76

Sartori, G. 1976. *Parties and Party Systems: A Framework for Analysis.* Vol. I. Cambridge: Cambridge University Press.

Sartori, G. 1982. *Teoria dei partiti: Il caso italiano.* Milano: Sugarco.

Sato, H. 1977. *Nihon seito no Koryo (Platforms of Japanese Political Parties).* Tokyo: Minshushugi Kyokai.

Scalapino, R. A. & Junnosuke, M. 1962. *Modern Japanese Political Parties and Politics.* Berkeley: University of California Press.

Schattschneider, E. E. 1960. *The Semi-Sovereign People.* New York: Holt, Rinehart and Winston.

Schindler, P. 1983 'Zur Mandatsstärke der Koalitionsparteien und ihrem Anteil an Kabinettsmitglieder 1949–1982, *Zeitschrift für Parlamentsfragen.* 14. 26–7.

Schmitt, D. 1973. *The Irony of the Irish Democracy.* Lexington, Mass.: D. C. Heath.

Schoebohm, (ed.) 1981. *CDU-Programmatik. Grundlagen und Herausforderungen.* Munich: Olzog.

Schwan, G. 1982. *Sozialismus in der Demokratie?* Stuttgart: Kohlhammer.

Seifert, K. H. 1975. *Die politischer Parteien im Recht der Bundesrepublik Deutschland.* Cologne; Heymann.

Shell, K. 1962. *The Transformation of Austrian Socialism.* London.

Siune, K. 1975. 'Structure and Content of an Election Campaign on Danish Radio and Television'. *Scandinavian Political Studies,* Vol. 10, 130–55.

Siune, K. 1975. 'Valgudsendelser – platform eller vindue'. *Pressens Årborg.* Copenhagen: C. A. Reitzel, 114–120.

Siune, K. & Borre, O. 1975. 'Setting the Agenda for a Danish Election'. *Journal of Communication,* Vol. 25, 65–73.

Siune, K. 1976. 'Broadcast Election Campaigns in a Multiparty System.' Paper present at IPSA, Edinburgh.

Siune, K. 1978. *Kommunikationspolitik – programpolitik og konsekvensen for den politiske kommunikation.* 5. Nordisk kongress i statskundskab, Bergen.

Siune, K. 1979. 'EF-debatten 1972, et apropos til 1979. En analyse af programmer i radio og tv'. *Pressens Årbog.* Copenhagen: C. A. Reitzel.

Siune, K. 1981. 'Broadcasted Election Campaigns in a Multiparty System.' In Rosengren, K. E. (ed.) *Advances in Content Analysis.* Sage Annual Reviews of Communication Research, Vol. 9, Beverley Hills: Sage.

Siune, K. 1982. *Valgkampe i tv og radio. Politisk partiers anvendelse af tv og radio, herunder samspillet med journalisterne.* Aarhus: Politica.

Siune, K. 1982. 'Who Presented What?'. *Television in the European Parliamentary Elections of 1979. Final Report of a Cross-National Analysis.* London: International Institute of Communication, Tavistock House, pp. 306–31.

Sjöblom, G. 1968. *Party Strategies in a Multiparty System.* Lund; Studentlitteratur.

Smith, D. E. 1974. 'The Dialectic of Religion and Politics in Sri Lanka'. *Ceylon Journal of Historical and Social Studies,* IV, 111–18.

Spreafico, A. 1983. 'I Programmi'. In A. Spreafico & J. La Palombara (eds.), *Elezioni e comportamento politico in Italia.* Milano, Edizioni di Communità.

Sri Lanka Department of Census and Statistics 1974. *The Population of Sri Lanka.* Colombo.

Sri Lanka Department of Elections 1971. *Results of Parliamentary Elections in Ceylon 1947–1970.* Colombo.

Stein, M. B. 1973. *The Dynamics of Right Wing Protest.* Toronto: Toronto University Press.

Steiner, K. 1972. *Politics in Austria.* Boston.

Steiner, K. 1981. *Modern Austria.* Palo Alto, Calif.

Stoss, R. (ed.) 1983) *Parteien-Handbuch.* Opladen; Westdeutscher Verlag.

Stoss, R. 1983. 'Struktur und Entwicklung des Parteiensystems der Bundesrepublik: Eine Theorie'. In Stoess, R. (ed.) *Parteien-Handbuch.* Opladen: Westdeutscher Verlag.

Stokes, D. E. 1963. 'Spatial Models of Party Competition'. *American Political Science Review.* 57:2, 368–77.

Stokes, D. E. 1966. 'Some Dynamic Elements of Contests for the Presidency'. *American Political Science Review* 60, 19–28.

Sully, M. A. 1981. *Political Parties and Elections in Austria.* London.

Taylor, M. J. 1972. 'On the theory of government coalition formation'. *British Journal of Political Science,* 2, 361–72.

Tengenbos, G. 1974. 'Overeenkomst en Tegenstelling in de Verkiezingsplatformen'. *Res Publica,* Vol. XVI, 3–4, pp. 425–50

Thaysen, U. 1976. *Parlamentarisches Regierungsystem in der Bundesrepublik Deutschland*. Opladen: Leske.

Thomas J. C. 1975. *The Decline of Ideology in Western Political Parties: A Study of Changing Policy Orientations*. London: Sage.

Thomas, J. C. 1980. 'Ideological Trends in Western Political Parties'. In Merkl. P. H. (ed.) *Western European Party Systems. Trends and Prospects*. New York: The Free Press, 335–66.

Thornburn, H. 1967. *Party Politics in Canada*. Second Edition. Toronto: Prentice-Hall of Canada.

Torgovnik, E. 1972. 'Election Issues and Interfactional Conflict Resolution in Israel'. *Political Studies*. Vol. 20, I, 79–96.

Van Putten, J. 1971. 'Het vergelijken van verkiezingsprogramma's'. *Socialisme en Democratie*, XXVIII, pp. 27–35.

Vital, D. 1975. *The Origins of Zionism*. London: Oxford University Press.

Wandruszka, A. 1954. 'Österreichs Politische Structur'. In Benedikt, *Geschichte Österreichs*, München.

Watanuki, J. 1977. *Politics in Postwar Japanese Society*. Tokyo: University of Tokyo Press.

Watkins, A. 1981. 'Beware the Primrose Perils of the Pulpit'. *Observer*. 8.3.1981.

Wearing, J. 1981. *The L-Shaped Party*. Toronto: McGraw Hill.

Weber, R. P. 1982. 'The Long-Term Dynamics of Societal Problem-Solving: A Content Analysis of British Speeches from the Throne, 1689–1972, *European Journal of Political Research*, 10, 387–405.

Weber, R. P. 1984. 'Content analytic Cultural Indicators' in Melischek, G., Rosengren, K. E. & Strappers, J. (eds.), *Cultural Indicators: An International Symposium*. Vienna: Österreichische Akademie der Wissenschaften, 301–19.

Whitaker, R. 1977. *The Governing Party*. Toronto: University of Toronto Press.

White, J. W. 1970. *The Sokagakkai and Mass Society*. Stanford University Press.

Whyte, J. H. 1974. 'Ireland: Politics without social bases'. In Rose, R. (ed.). *Electoral Behaviour: a comparative handbook*. 618–51. New York: the Free Press.

Wildenmann, R. 1973. *Macht und Konsens als Problem der Innen-und Aussenpolitik*. Frankfurt a.M.: Athanaeum.

Winn, C. & McMenemy, J. 1976. *Political Parties in Canada*. Toronto: McGraw Hill Ryerson.

Witkon, A. 1970. 'Elections in Israel'. *Israel Law Review*, I, 42–52.

Woodward, C. A. 1969. *The Growth of a Party System in Ceylon*. Providence: University of Rhode Island Press.

Yoshihara, T. & Nishi, O. 1979. *Japanese Security and Each Party's Defense Policy*. Tokyo: Kyoikusha.

Young, W. 1969. *The Anatomy of a Party*. Toronto: Toronto University Press.

Zavos, S. 1981. *Crusade: Social Credit's Drive for Power*. Wellington.

Zelniker, S. & Kahan, M. 1976. 'Religion and Nascent Cleavages'. *Comparative Politics*, Vol. 9, 1, 21–48.

Zohar, D. N. 1974. *Political Parties in Israel: The Evolution of Israeli Democracy*. New York: Praeger.

INDEX

⌇

Abuhatzeira, Aharon, 116
Accommodation, politics of, *see* Pillarization
'Across-the-board' Appeals, 28
'Abstraction' (over time and ideological space), 35
Adenauer, Konrad, 296, 297, 298
Anglo-Saxon Democracies, 18, 37, 83, 388
'Anschluss' (Austria 1938), 279
Anticlericalism, 392, 395, 396, 457, *see also under individual countries*
Atlantic Alliance, *see* North Atlantic Treaty Organisation
Australasia, 16
Australia, 23, 37, Chap. 3 esp. 43–4, and 47–8
  Domain Analysis, *see* First-Stage Analysis
  Election Programmes: collection, 4; preparation, 47; sources, 417–19; types of document, 47–8
  Federalism, 43
  First Stage (ie. Domain) Analysis, 51–60; Foreign Relations, 51–4; Freedom and Democracy, 54; Government, 54; Economics, 56–7; Welfare, 57–8; Social Fabric, 58–9; Social Groups, 59–60
  Leading Categories, 50
  Left–Right Dimension, 64
  Minor Parties etc. omitted from Analysis, 49
  Parties: Australian Labor Party, 43, 68, 399; Country Party, *see* National Country Party; Democratic Labor Party, 43, 44; Liberal Party, 43, 68, 399, 406, 408; National Country Party, 42, 43, 49, 51, 68
  Party Movement over Time, 68
  Party System, 43
  Second-Stage Analysis, 60–72; First Factor, 64; Second Factor, 64–5

Austria, 18, 23, 37, 270–93, 395, 396
  Anschluss 1938, 279
  Civil War 1934, 279
  Coalitions, 270, 271, 291–292
  Consensus Issues, 290–291
  Domain Analysis, *see* First-Stage Analysis
  Elections and Electoral System, 271
  First Stage (ie. Domain) Analysis, 281–4; Foreign Relations, 281; Freedom and Democracy, 281; Government, 281; Economics, 281–283; Social Groups, 283–4
  Election Programmes; coding, 274, 280; collection, 274; circulation, 274; distribution, 274; leading categories, 279; missing documents, 275; preparation, 275; sources, 419–420; types of document, 272–3, 274, 275
  Left–Right Dimension, 283, 284
  Minor Parties etc. omitted from Analysis, 271
  Parties: Association of Independents (VdU), *see* Freedom Party; Communist Party (KPÖ), 271; Freedom Party (FPÖ), 270, 271, 272, 274, 275, 276, 279, 280, 288, 291, 292; People's Party (ÖVP), 270, 271, 272, 274, 275, 276, 279, 280, 288, 289, 290; Socialist Party (SPÖ), 270, 271, 272, 274, 275, 276, 279, 280, 288, 289, 290, 292
  Party Ideologies, 272
  Party Movement over Time, 288–92
  Party System, 270–71
  Second Stage Analysis, 284–8; First Factor, 284–8; Second Factor, 288; Third Factor, 288
  Sub-Categories, 276
Austrian Civil War, 279
Ayurvedic Physicians (Sri Lanka), 99

484

1